MW01617754

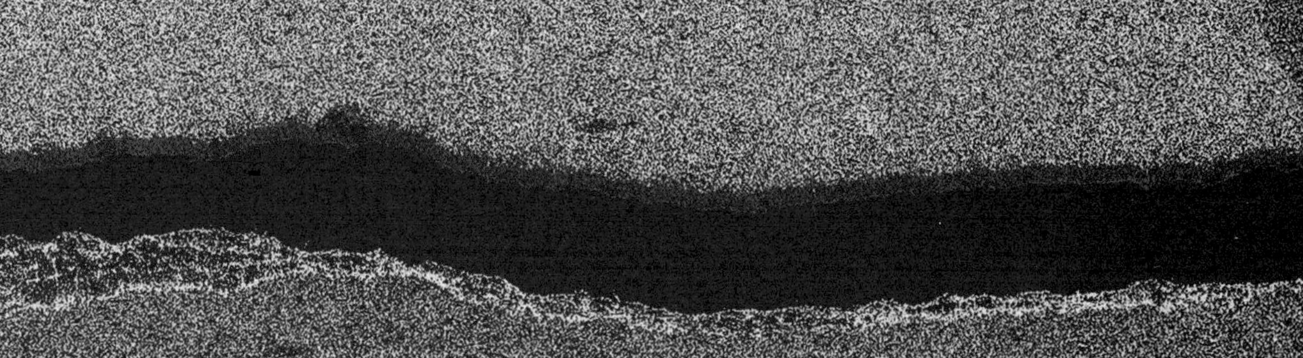

ANTON CORBIJN

U2 & i

SCHIRMER/MOSEL

february 1992
in berlin, establishing a relation with the car i painted for the 'one' video.
i clearly LOVE my own work!

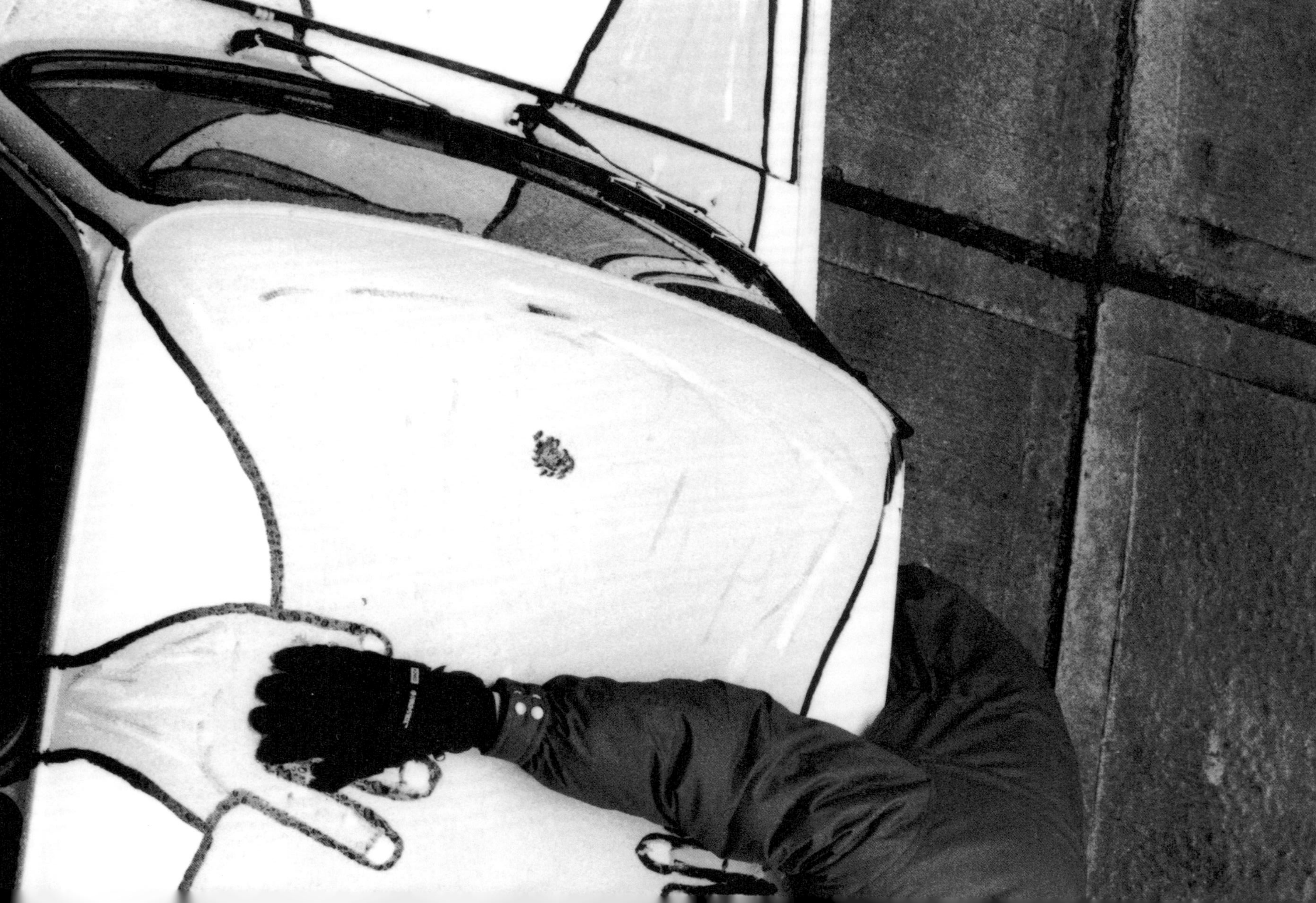

photo by aija quabert

december 1986

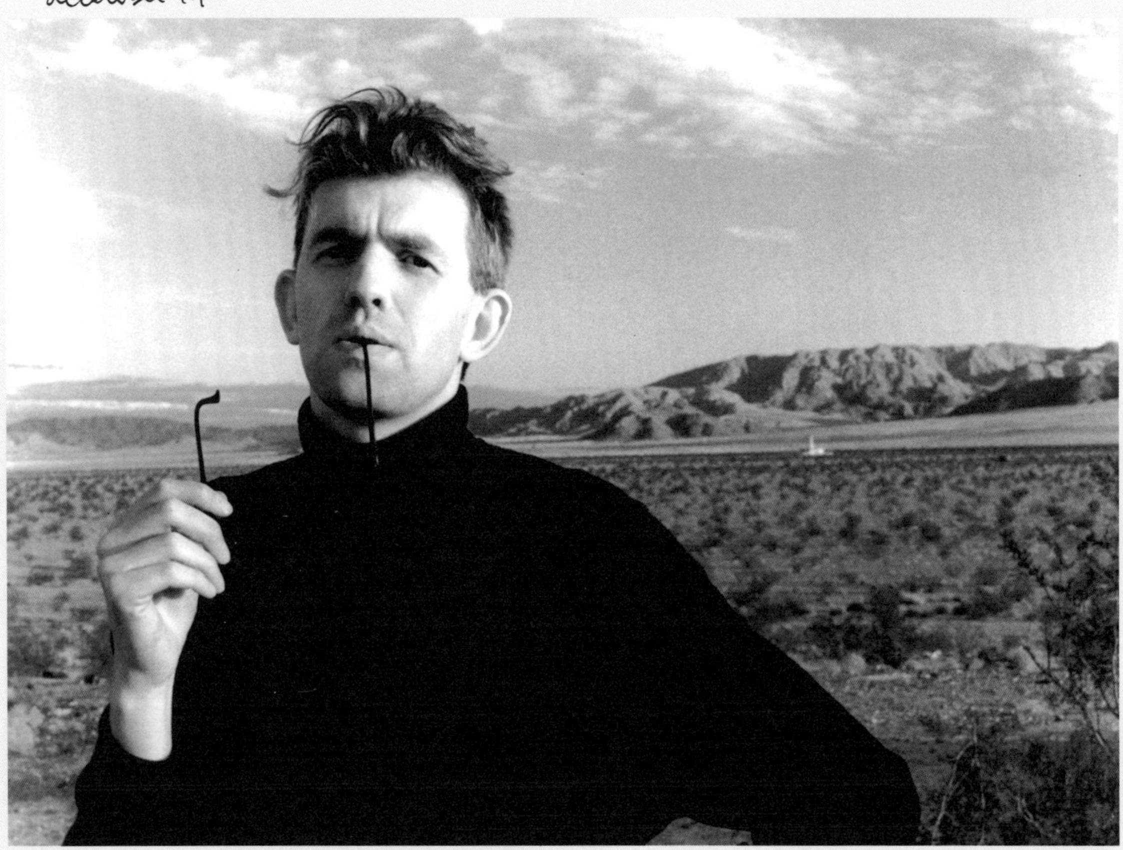

on the third day of the joshua tree shoot, i had clearly established a very serious relationship with the band, as this photo by the edge shows. trying to tell them how to pronounce "joshua tree".

IS IT 'i'?

ANTON CORBIJN

In 1982 when U2 asked me to photograph them for the next 22 years, my immediate reply was "I'm not sure if I have enough film". They had to laugh, although that was most probably about my accent. In fact, they laughed at a lot of what I said or suggested over the years, but fortunately I have managed to edit around this for the book. It would be too painful otherwise. For them, I think, as it would become obvious they don't take anything seriously. To cut a possibly long story short, I sat down with them after they offered me a drink in a New Orleans bar to discuss this pretty substantial proposal. I was doing some quick mathematics like there were four of them so it would take quite a bit of film indeed, they are probably catholic and want to have some family photos taken as well. And how would I get this bunch to look good as a whole without looking like a laughing stock, literally if I was to go by my experience so far. And then all of a sudden I got an idea. Some fast thinking on my part and unscrupulous borrowing of their first album title led me to suggest the following to them: I said "lads" (I got very easily into their kind of terminology), "lads, we should do a story of the band growing over 22 years from being a boy, to maturity. So you have the initial look of not knowing where you are but you are not fighting it, and after that you come into the early teenage years where you take yourself very serious, then you rebel and go wild and then you sort of accept who you are and bingo, you've arrived". I then went into the possibilities of their looks for all these periods and that really opened up a whole spectrum of many varying photo-opportunities. There were the non-matching outfits as they had on now, we could then evolve into black clothes for the more serious look and after that put on anything colorful that previous generations had thrown away and finally get into clothing that actually would cost some money and would fit. All these looks could go with various shades, headgear and props of course. We could throw in the odd cactus or some weird car. After another round of drinks they all agreed they not only would give it a go but also create the music to match these looks, which was a great idea from their end. Looking back, and to be fair to them, I have to say they more or less stuck to it. There has been the sudden odd call to wanting to look cool, but mostly I didn't have to put up much of a fight at all. I have also tried this approach with a few other people but it never worked as well since most bands want to have meetings and discuss stuff, which is not really how I want to run the show. If we had to do this all over again, the one thing I would change is the name. Why bother with two syllables when you can do with just one? 'i' would have done it for me.

austin, february 1982

a reluctant model, posing for bono i assume. it was early days yet.

From B to A and back again.

BONO: Do you like people who stare?
ANTON: I see, you're going straight for the kill. Well, I don't really like people who stare at me, no, not at all.
B: Would you look away or would you stare them back?
A: Depending on my mood but generally I look away. But then I feel I don't put myself in a position where people would stare at me, unlike yourself.
B: So even though you're interested in ze famous you don't want to be famouz yourself?
A: Well this is a misconception that I am interested in fame. Maybe I was initially but I am much more interested in artists, good artists, my aim in a sense is to meet most good artists and spend half an hour with them and have a sort of...
B: Dialogue.
A: Yes, dialogue and the photograph as a proof of meeting them, but that is it, it's ...
B: You're a fan! (laughs)
A: ... it's very, very basic. It is lovely to get into people's mindsets for a little while and I think that's more and more what I'm interested in, I find the whole celebrity thing less and less interesting. I'm not chasing Britney Spears or any of these people.
B: You chased my arse around a few tables.
A: Yeah but then you're good ...
B: I don't run very fast.
A: No, that is where I win.
B: Those big long legs running after me. Do you have any memory of staring at objects, you know as a young boy. What I'm, let me try and rephrase that ...
A: I feel I'm observing, not staring so there's a difference, it is a more active thing than staring.
B: Okay, observation; do you think concentrated observation could ever be described as staring? (Laughs) Did you ever change the way you perceived an object?
Staring at it or observing it, I mean as a young boy do you remember, was it people, was it objects ...? What made you keep your gaze on it for that long? People?
A: I'm not sure what it is called but I love seeing people walking.
B: Walking?
A: People all walk different; I like the difference of movements in people. I like to see how people drink a cup of coffee, very simple things. I think I was a daydreamer when I was young, an absolute daydreamer, I couldn't concentrate very well. I think I'm kind of a romantic at heart. It's all negative things in my book actually, but I made the best out of it by stumbling into photography. I don't think daydreaming is that positive and I appreciate much more someone like you, who's active.
B: I think you have been snapping moments out of dreams, making them and freezing them and creating them. Whatever started off in your imagination, it ends up on a page.
A: Yes, I think you could say that's been an investment, but it's my character and I'm now trying to switch it to a positive experience.
B: Right I see, well you know my father; his advice to me, it wasn't spoken more than suggested was; don't dream. To dream is to be disappointed. So that of course has made me into a megalomaniac, but you're right I don't like dreaming I like doing and I feel like the 60s was the age of imagination and then, even in advertising you can see this, in the 90s you had Nike's 'just do it' and I'm more the kind of person that just does it. I feel that if I have an idea I have a responsibility to execute it. I'm not sure, is it good for you?
A: Depends on the idea.
B: Your father was a preacher, a minister in the Protestant church. What was it exactly?
A: Dutch Reformed.
B: I find you very, coming from a confused half Protestant and half Catholic Irishman, very Protestant in terms of your work ethic. You know, you get up early in the morning and you work till late at night. Do you think that comes from your father? What is your mother like?
A: They're both quite religious. My mother also studied

county clare, ireland, july 1984

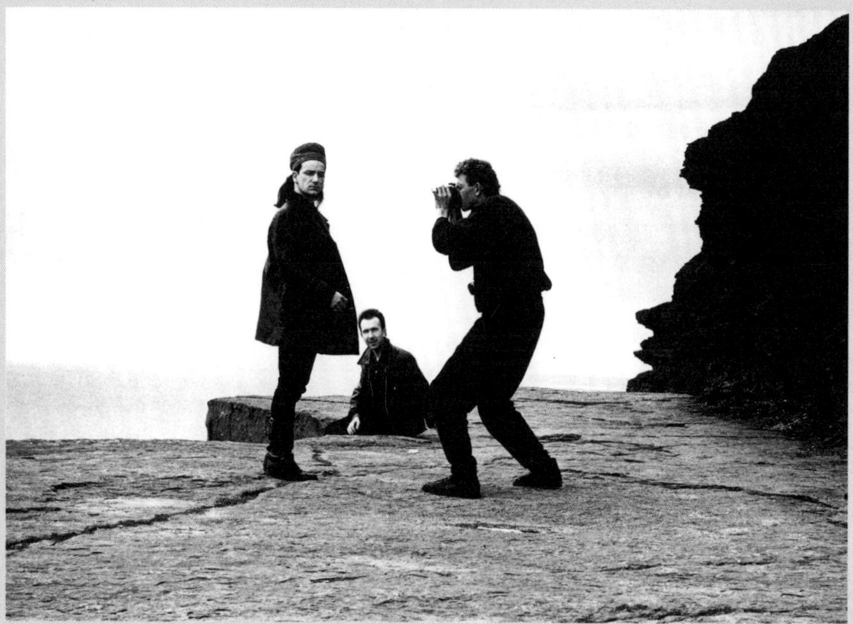

it was probably steve averill who took this photo of me trying to take a photo of bono at the cliffs of moher as part of the unforgettable fire shoot. i worked with minimal equipment in those days, just 2 35-mm camera's, one of which must have been picked up by steve for this shot. no assitant in those days.

theology. You once described this as death by cupcakes or teacakes or something ...

B: Yeah ... cupcake.

A: You know that whole thing where you always think of somebody who's ill or dying, helping somebody or visiting somebody, but don't do what you want to do yourself. A sense of duty was very much there and not very pro-active in the end – it is more a reaction to things that happen.

B: Do you think that pleasure was important to them?

A: I hope so, but I never experienced it with them.

B: Because your photographs can be very stoic and very iconic in the religious sense and you really get the sense of pleasures of the eye; like you feel that the eye that has taken these photographs has taken a lot of pleasure and the images I think that you're often attracted to, even though sometimes they can be severe, I think they can also be quite exotic and filled with sort of guilty feelings of fun and danger and things like that, as well as weighty thoughts. I think you have a great sense of fun yourself and that's in the photographs. So in that sense do you think that was probably just a reaction coming from a very ascetic background?

A: Probably, I respond very well to dark humour and maybe also to what you call the guilty pleasure. Secretly doing things and ...

B: Yeah, that's one of the things I think that you have to point out, looking over all these years of work as I have so many times: you do get, although you're such an honest and open person, you do get the sense in some of the work of guilty pleasure. So you haven't quite shaken off the ...

A: No, and I am not sure I ever will in the end. I think when I was young my pictures looked quite mature but now, I tend to make them look sometimes too young. I could easily try to compensate, but you get lighter as a character, well part of you gets lighter when you get older.

B: Yeah, I think that's true.

A: Because when I look at my old work I'd say, that's heavy.

B: Yes it's harder to be earnest the older you get and yet it's important not to let go of it completely.

A: Indeed. I think it's also the fact that you have a narrow focus when you're young; at least I had as a teenager. I would just look at the picture and nothing else was of interest to me, only the photograph and that meant so much to me. Now things like enjoyment come into your life and get an importance that wasn't there previously. Photography has saved me from shyness and being an unsociable person. And although I still have the feeling I come across kind of awkward in person, I do feel a big change in me these last few years. Also in the sense of where to focus on; more what the pictures actually say than who is on the photograph.

B: Well I think I know the answer to this question, but for a shy guy you're pretty funky on your feet and we've done some pretty fancy footwork together on the dance floor. And I think your friends would find you a much more elegant man than you find yourself, elegant in the sense that you put people at ease and you keep an eye out for them not only professionally but personally and I think that I've always felt a sort of light force and a kind of love of life from you as a person that used not to be reflected in the photographs.

A: Mm-m.

B: In fact there was an almost sort of gothic side to your photographs in the 80s, kind of religious and I think now your photographs are starting to look more like you.

A: Is that a good thing? (both laughing) ... Yeah okay, I think, you know I compare always, well not always, but we've worked together for so long I sometimes compare us a little bit.

B: Both tall!

A: ... and attractive to women! Let it be on the record. But you know, I think we've talked about this before with the videos. You like to present what you do as a very big thing whatever you put your energy into, you're happy to throw it out into the world as big as you can, but I think I'm almost the opposite. I go out and do my thing and ...

B: (laughing) Yeah, I am small man syndrome, you're tall man syndrome.

A: You think that's it? I think that's really fascinating to me and I think that has to do also a lot with your character; You are much more out there in the world, you're a tough guy and I think that comes across in that sense. I'm not a very tough guy and I'm very protective of my little things. The things I make I consider so much to be mine that in the past it hurt me when people cropped my pictures. In a sense I felt that in a lot of work I did, making photographs was a sign of friendship. Maybe it was a search for friendship, me going out with my camera and that's why in the past I sometimes felt hurt when 'my bands' worked with other people, I was so vulnerable, because to me it was like, it was actually my friends. I looked at it as a social thing almost.

B: Yeah well ...

A: ... very, very odd, you know, it took years of therapy to get rid of this crap.

B: Intimacy is a word you could not use here and I think you can see that as I was looking through the photos you showed me last night, twenty-two years of work with our band, there is some odd intimacy about taking somebody's photograph and we don't really like to have our photographs taken and ...

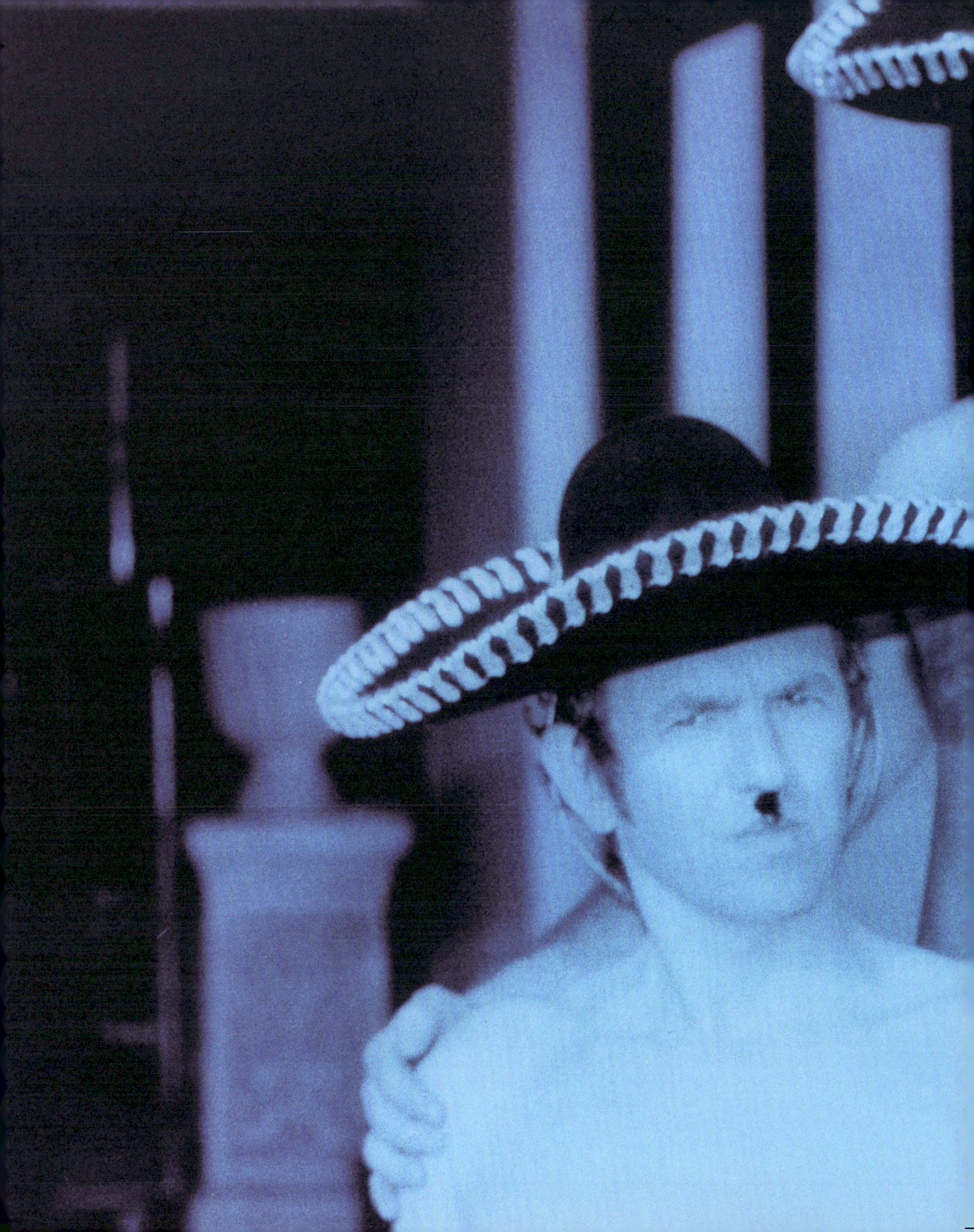

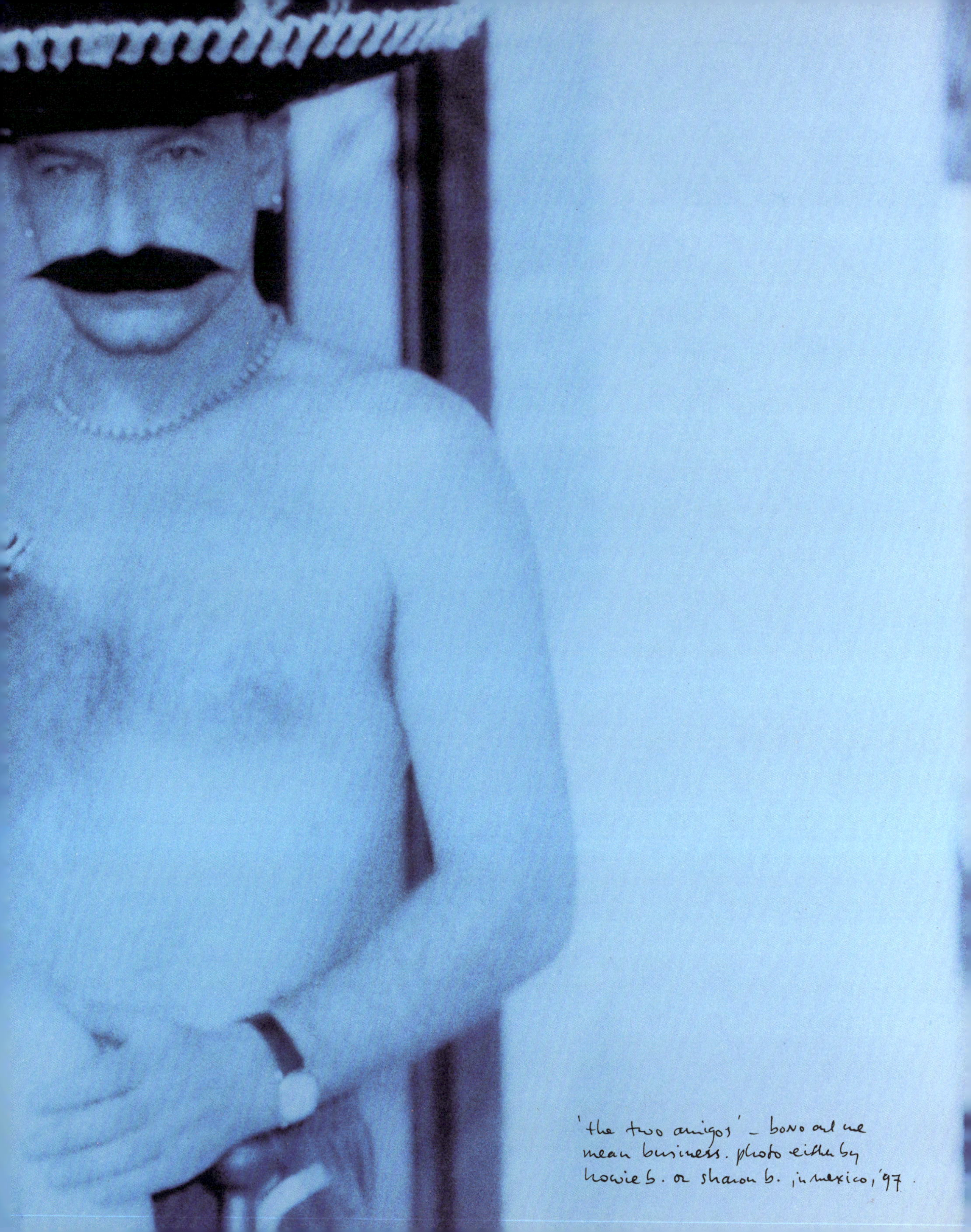

'the two amigos' – bono and me mean business. photo either by howie b. or sharon b., in mexico, '97.

A: You mean as humans or as U2?
B: No, I mean as a band we don't really like having them taken and we don't have many relationships with other photographers for that reason. So maybe it's not completely irrational what you're feeling, maybe it is pretty intimate. And the other thing, just going back to what you said there about your work and thinking I work in a grand scale and you work in a more small scale, I want to get this song on the radio, I want to get the show on the road, you're printing your book and get the book into lots of book shops, which is the equivalent of me being on the radio and then you have your exhibitions, which have done incredibly well now particularly in Europe and that's equivalent of putting the show on the road. I don't think there is too much difference, but what I will say is that I think photography falls maybe between two ages; the age of manufacturing, the digital future, the age of industry and the age of arts and crafts. So there is something of making a chair about a photograph or painting a picture. You're in the darkroom, it's homemade and yet they're printed up in the media. In fact, they drive our culture's insatiable appetite for images and in a way they created celebrity culture more than television did. But photography is somewhere in between those two, and I think you probably, as a person, err more on the side of the painter than you do of the scientist or a technician.
A: I know what you mean, I have no relations with other photographers, but I do with some painters. I feel alien to the profession in a sense.
B: So what's the most important piece of equipment then, to your mind?
A: It's the attitude.
B: Good, so ...
A: I have some questions regarding the work we've done rather than the broader aspect of photography. I remember in Groningen when you looked at the pictures you said that it showed going from innocence to experience; was there a particular period in those photos where you enjoyed looking at yourself?
B: Well I was very taken aback by the scale of the exhibition I saw in Groningen and I'm a little bewildered by the different phases of the band, which were now all under one roof and it made me very proud and it made me scratch my head, what were we thinking then, what we were thinking there. The room full of Bonos was a bit much in ways that weren't all obvious, okay it's hard to look at yourself full stop, but to be surrounded and stared back at by yourself over twenty-two years was something I won't forget. There was one photograph in particular that I couldn't put out of my mind for weeks and weeks and weeks and in fact it followed me around and informed a lot of the work that we just done on 'How to dismantle an atomic bomb'. I looked at the photograph and I saw what I might describe as my first face and there was still a lot of boyishness there, I was twenty-one I suppose, eyes that could drink the world but weren't in a way that interested in the world. It was just something very open about the face and I felt a sense of loss, not about age or lines, I prefer faces as they get older, but it was about innocence. There was something very powerful in the eyes and then a journalist came up to me and said, 'with all your experience what would you say to that young man'? And I immediately replied, 'I'd tell him you're right'. Don't second-guess yourself because you don't understand the power of not knowing. You don't understand the power of naivety when you're that age, so you try to rid yourself of your innocence and you try to become an experienced man of the world and you lose a lot along the way I think. The whole sort of emotional arc of the new album is about innocence and experience:

The more you feel the less you know
The less you find out as you grow
I knew much more then than I did now
Neon heart day-glow eyes
A city lit by fireflies
They were advertising in the skies
For people like us
And I miss you when you're not around
I missed you when you're not around
I'm getting ready to leave the ground

A: That is a face you can't get back.
B: No, you can't unfortunately unknow something, which is the thing about physics' material, that once they figure out how to split the atom, the toothpaste is out of the tube.
A: So this was the shot of you in a helicopter?
B: Shot in a helicopter just about to take off.
A: Is it fear of flying in your eyes?
B: Yes. (Laughs) The funny thing is I have a fear of heights, but not when the music is on, that's why I used to climb all over the rigging, but if somebody stopped the music they'd have had to send the fire brigade to get me down ... been up the moon.
A: Looking through my photographs of U2 I found a photo of you in Torhout/Werchter from '83 and you were walking on a ledge between the pit and the audience.
B: I never liked performers that had a comfortable distance with their audience, you know 'I'm here, you're there and I'm happy about that'. I was always trying to

attack in some way the distance whether it was diving into the crowd or with ZOO TV trying new ways of communicating, but I was never happy with the distance.
A: When I look at the twenty-two years that we worked together and the highs and lows I wonder what you think made it possible for us to stick together for that long a period of time? It wasn't always easy with me because I fucked up a couple of times and some periods were better than others. What made us go this far?
B: You're cheap. (laughs)
A: I was to start with but I will change that now. (laughs)
B: No you're not, you're, no, no. I have a history in my life and I think the band are like this too, a little less so but, as you know, I'm a very loyal if unreliable friend. I'm still very close with my very first friends, my childhood friends, 'the band' are my teenage friends and there's lots of other people I've met since then but I live in fear of short-term relationships and I often think that I'm never going to see people again. I suppose as a kid, I was fourteen, one day your mother never comes home again and so I've become very good at maintaining relationships and it's very important to me, long-term relationships. The other reason is a professional one. I find photography very difficult because the best work usually comes from experimenting ... you should try and find a side of yourself, to discover a side of yourself. It seems to me that art is about discovering beauty in unexpected places, it's an attempt to identify yourself. If you knew who you were you wouldn't become an artist. So I think what we have in our relationship is that we both are quite experimental. You are trying to bring us out of ourselves and we've tried some really far fetched plots and ...
A: Sure yeah.
B: ... and I love them all because they are revealing. You know it was Oscar Wilde who said; 'The mask reveals the man'. You can see people dressing up at Halloween or at costume balls and a whole other side of people comes out. So I think that you're very good at two things: letting us be completely who we are and challenging us to be somebody whom we're not, yet.
A: Yeah, Yeah
B: I used to say this to some people who asked me about your work; I used to say Anton doesn't photograph who you are, he photographs who you might be and in that sense you've had a lot of faith in us and what we could become and you gave us confidence at a time when we were very gauche and very awkward, and to believe in ourselves as artists and to believe that we could figure our visual side out, because that was very undeveloped early on. We had the musical and spiritual side of the band developed on but you really did give us confidence to take risks and to believe that we could look good as a band together. When I look in the mirror I just see a kind of mad head and I don't feel like a rock star, I don't think I look like one. I'm more like a boxer or a builder's labourer in my physical self than I am a pop star. But you liked the fact that we weren't effete in that very British rock sense of young, skinny men, could die any minute type of thing. There was something else going on with us and you kind of found a language for us I think.
A: I can see that initially being the case but then of course you've grown very much as a visual artist yourself too over the years.
B: Though there are exceptions, it's very difficult to find people who are as good as you. Not just to blow your trumpet for a minute, though I want to ... (laughs) ...
A: That is what the book is about Bono. Don't be shy now in the moment of truth. (laughing)
B: (screams) Blow my trumpet says the Dutchman.
A: I know Paul (McGuinness) has not always agreed with your choice of photographer.
B: I think Paul will love this book because his occasional criticism would be that the humour of the band wasn't coming through, but just in the 80s in particular. You see you weren't photographing the band, you were photographing our music and he was saying; 'you're going to look like the band too stupid to enjoy being at No. 1, you look so severe and so down' and he thought we were playing into stereotype, you know earnest young men, faces like, rock faces, rather than faces of rock stars.
A: I think he has a point, specially relating to the late 80s. I remember we were in LA in '88, you and I were sitting in a car and I was my usually depressed self at the time and very insecure about photography. You told me I should enjoy myself and it had a big impact on me. The 'Rattle and Hum' period was not a good time photography-wise for me. Just after The Joshua Tree I was very confused.
B: You hit a peak there.
A: Yes, but I managed fortunately to change my photography and it was great to see that you developed also a lot after that, musically you came to Achtung Baby.
B: And you experimented with colour. You were finding a sort of electrical charge from the colours. I think of those violets and turquoises that you got interested in almost magentas and yellows and you hit a word, just before we then hit it with Achtung Baby and it's a simple word, it's 'vivid'. These were luminous times.
A: Are there any challenges left for you visually? When you look at the book you see we go to the absurd from the most earnest, basic visuals, both in colour and in black and white.

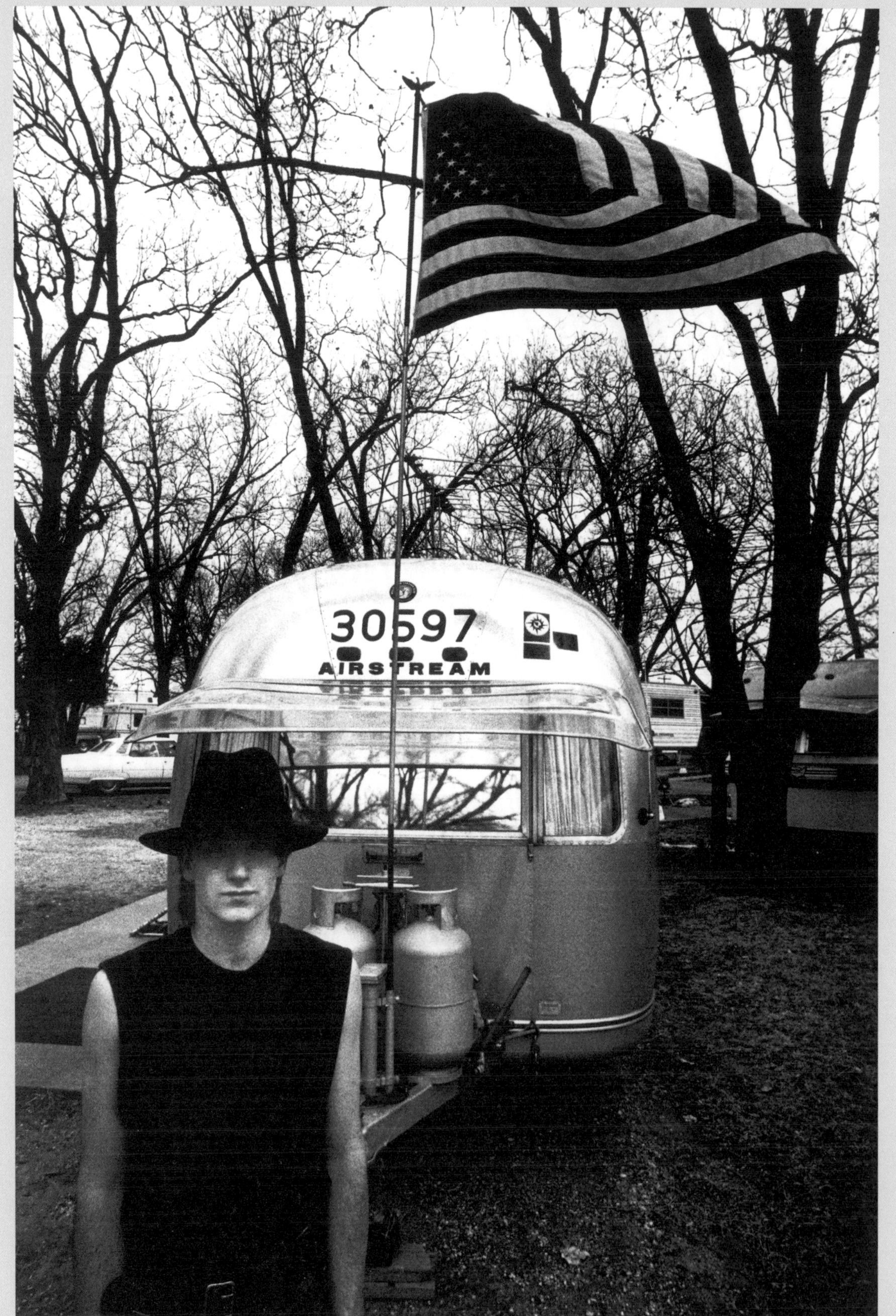

bono modeling for me in austin – i guess i was really into straight lines at the time.

B: These two albums, 'all the things' and 'how to dismantle' are of the same mould really and they're about the limitations of a rock band, but you know I like to dress up as a clown, so I think we have visually some challenges ahead.
A: But do you think that we ever accomplished visually what you had in mind?
B: Yeah, we really did. One of my favourite photo sessions was probably POP in Miami, the band looks best in that period for me. The period I am the proudest of is the ZOO TV (Achtung Baby) period because I really think we became a monster to feed a monster. The monster was the media and we became media darlings and as well as media pests. The reversing of what people thought we were. The faces in the crowd when we first came out on ZOO TV of disbelief, the people with their mouths open, 'what has happened to our band'. As Bruce Springsteen said to me once; 'when you've been at this a few years it's hard to surprise people', but we pulled that off, whether we can ever do it again, I don't know. I always liked the theatre of the absurd. Going back to the old Lipton village days of our sort of performance art period, when we were teenagers coming out of punk rock, and putting on little one-act plays in Grafton Street in Dublin with drills and with step ladders and just that sort of dada stuff. There is a part of me that is a sort of showman in the old sense of that word, in the show business: Roll up! Roll up! There is another side of me which is more shaman than showman, that kind of transfiguration where you go to a rock show and suddenly you're just in another place and that's important to me as well. And then there's a part of me that just likes you know rock and roll, which is just being in a band, with my mates and kicking out the jams. They're sort of the three strands that I think run through U2 for me.
A: I want to come back to what we talked about earlier, where I said that you think big and I don't and you said it wasn't that different in its outcome, but I guess the difference is that you think big at the conception of the ideas and I don't.
B: Yeah you're painting the raindrops, I paint the sky.
A: This relates specifically to the making of videos though for me.
B: The thing about being in a rock band is you get to be very intimate with people who don't know you and the most private thoughts are broadcast on these giant PA systems, radio stations, physical CD players, but don't you think you do the same. You do have intimacies with a person in terms of you take their photograph; it may be a small thing, but then they're published in the loudest possible way.
A: No, I think that; this is not a criticisms, this is how you think. I'm too inward thinking in general and I couldn't do it any other way, it is not in my character and the great thing is that my photos in the end are so personal. The photography is then so much about you, the photographer, and initially I didn't realise that.
B: Yeah, I know it's a very strong mood and I think in the end that's probably all we have to hold onto; that thought, that sound, that colour, that frame, that guitar sound, that high note, that out of focusness ...
A: I don't want to be defined by that please!
B: That can be no one else. I think if people can recognise you when you're not there, in a piece of work, you've already hit something.
A: That's partly because you and U2 have always been very stimulating to me, about taking risks and about experimenting with stuff and I've been able to develop for a big part thanks to U2.
B: Well the feeling is mutual and I think the debt is bigger at our end. As I said, you gave us a visual language and it's a language of your European eye on America, from the desert to the sort of other American-ness that we found occasionally in those rag 'n' bone shop pictures, which we even bumped into again recently in the sort of tangled metal of the shipyards there in Lisbon. I think we've disappeared into each other nicely in this book.

France, August 20th 2004

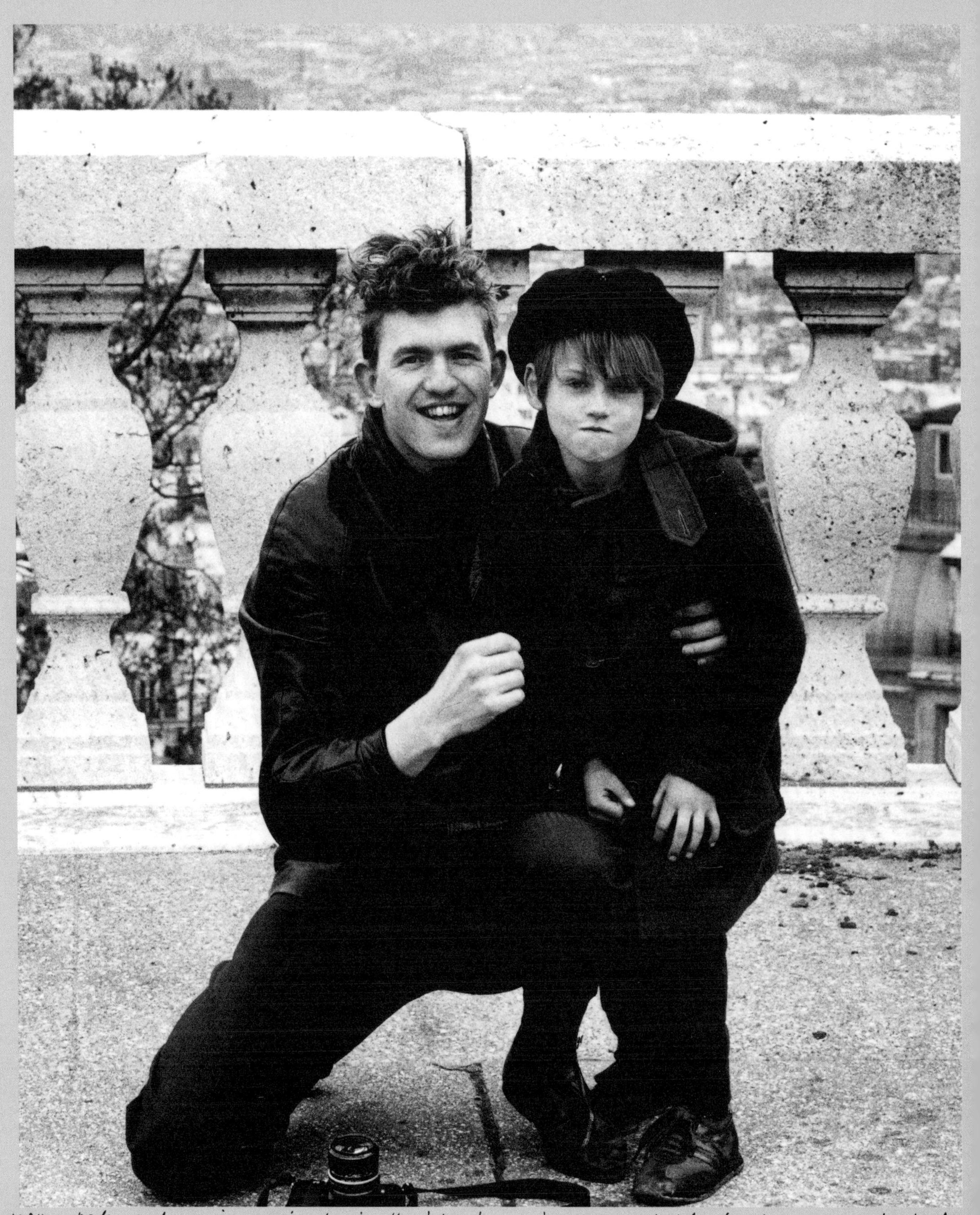

1984 – peter and me in paris during the 'two hearts beat as one' videoshoot. not sure who took the pho

About Anton & U2

HELENA CHRISTENSEN

I am sitting in my pink bedroom, about fourteen years old. Walls covered in posters of bands; the Cure, Cult, OMD, Killing Joke, Depeche Mode, Jesus and Mary Chain ... and of course U2.

Supposed to be doing my homework, but I'm just rocking away with my dad next to me, tapping his feet to the beat of New Years day... October... Pride... Partygirl – all the songs that carried me through my youth.

That is how I remember it; Bono's mesmerizing voice, Edge's insisting guitar, Larry's steady drums and Adam's pumping bass... they were the soundtrack to my teenage years, so full of hope, angst, love, confusion, strength.

Presently they continue to be the soundtrack to my life. I stare at the photographs of them and even though the years have gone by, the music has changed and the setting and tone are different, it is still the same intensity that they're staring back at me with. They are so utterly present in those shots, it feels as if they are right there with me, their eyes so piercing the photograph becomes 3-dimensional.

I have never before experienced such an emotional reaction to music. The melodies manifested themselves onto my soul, into my veins and gave me the feeling they would be with me for the rest of my life.

Just like the photographs; all those haunting images of penetrating eyes, stark landscapes, crashing lights. There is an honest intensity, a twisted reality, like something stirring under the surface. It leaves you with the feeling of having been drawn into the sphere – sucked in by the magnetism existing between them. There is a whole song going on in each image.

Anton shows them with such clarity and immediacy that they never feel like strangers; they are the four boys in the photographs and Anton is right there with them!

new york, feb. '03

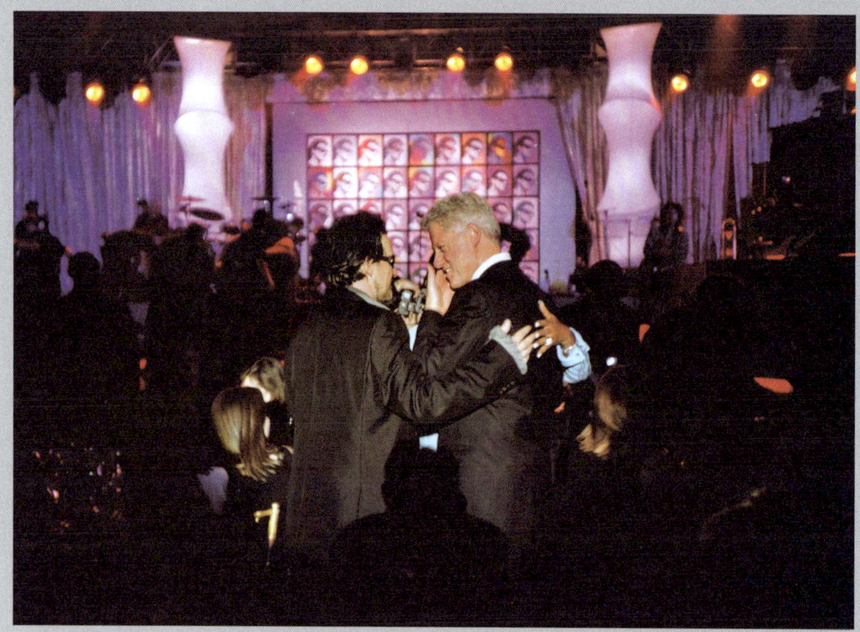

bono with clinton at the musicare person of the year award show in new york.

"Make joyful noise before the Lord," said the Psalmist. Bono has done just that, not only in good songs but in good deeds. The music of U2 has moved millions of people around the world.

But I am particularly grateful to Bono for the leadership he gave for debt relief to the poorest nations in the world, for greater support in the battle against AIDS, and for his work with me in continuing efforts in Africa.

In America he has shown an astonishing ability to reach across party and ideological lines to rally support for his causes. He has formed common ground where others have failed.

He is a continuing inspiration in these difficult times. He may well have done more good than any other private citizen in the world.

For Bono, "in the name of love" is more than a lyric; it is a way of life.

miami, april/may 1996

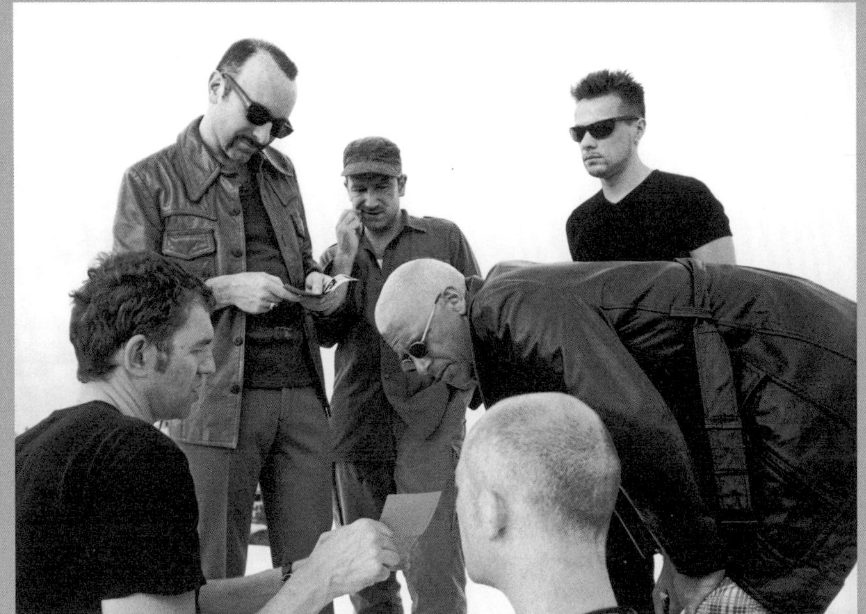

enthousiastic reception of my latest polaroid during the POP shoot. this is stylist Fintan F. photo by anja grabert

Anton Corbijn and U2

WILLIAM GIBSON

Being photographed by anyone other than a very close friend or a member of my immediate family has generally been somewhat less than enjoyable for me.

Indeed, under certain extreme conditions (heavy corporate multi-shooter gangbangs in Tokyo, for instance) it reveals itself as not only painful but potentially lethal – a process whereby orgones are almost visibly sucked from the haplessly cornered victim in a technologically-assisted species of charisma-vampirism – convincing me that those apocryphal tribesmen, instinctively convinced that each click of the shutter steals another layer of the soul, were and are entirely correct.

This is not the case, with Anton Corbijn. It was so peculiarly not the case, with Anton Corbijn, that the memory is of some special moment of absurdist grace: two ridiculously tall men, engaged in something profoundly non-vampiric, but which involved a camera, within sight of the green lung of St. Stephen's Green, Dublin.

I had met him, it being Dublin, through U2, his relationship with them having been both long and symbiotically fruitful.

I had gone there for a conversation, to be recorded for a magazine, and Anton had photographed us as we sat and drank and talked. Having met Bono and Edge previously, I was able to judge how much a part of their immediate culture this Dutch photographer was, a citizen not of Ireland but of U2's Dublin.

The only equipment I saw him use, aside from his camera, was a single string of cheap Christmas mini-lights, bunched back into a dark corner, behind us, to provide a faint hint of mysterious texture in the eventual black-and-white print.

Otherwise, he simply seemed to be not very urgently looking for something, in that room off their studios – say a cap he'd misplaced. Not a very valuable cap, but one he liked, and wouldn't willingly abandon. There was an ease to what he was doing that had nothing at all to with inattention.

He was looking for the images of U2 which he knew, from long experience, he would find. Wonderful images, the result at once of his own talent, theirs, and of that ease and warmth, that sense of family, they all moved within.

And that is how the images in this book came to be: The very tall Dutchman looking through bits of German or Japanese glass at these Irishmen, these inhabitants of a right-now future of their own imagining, and something happening: The cap found, yet again: Saved: The mini-lights glinting at the edge of one inky black bulb of Bono-shade, just when the shutter winked: Because Anton Corbijn was there, looking.

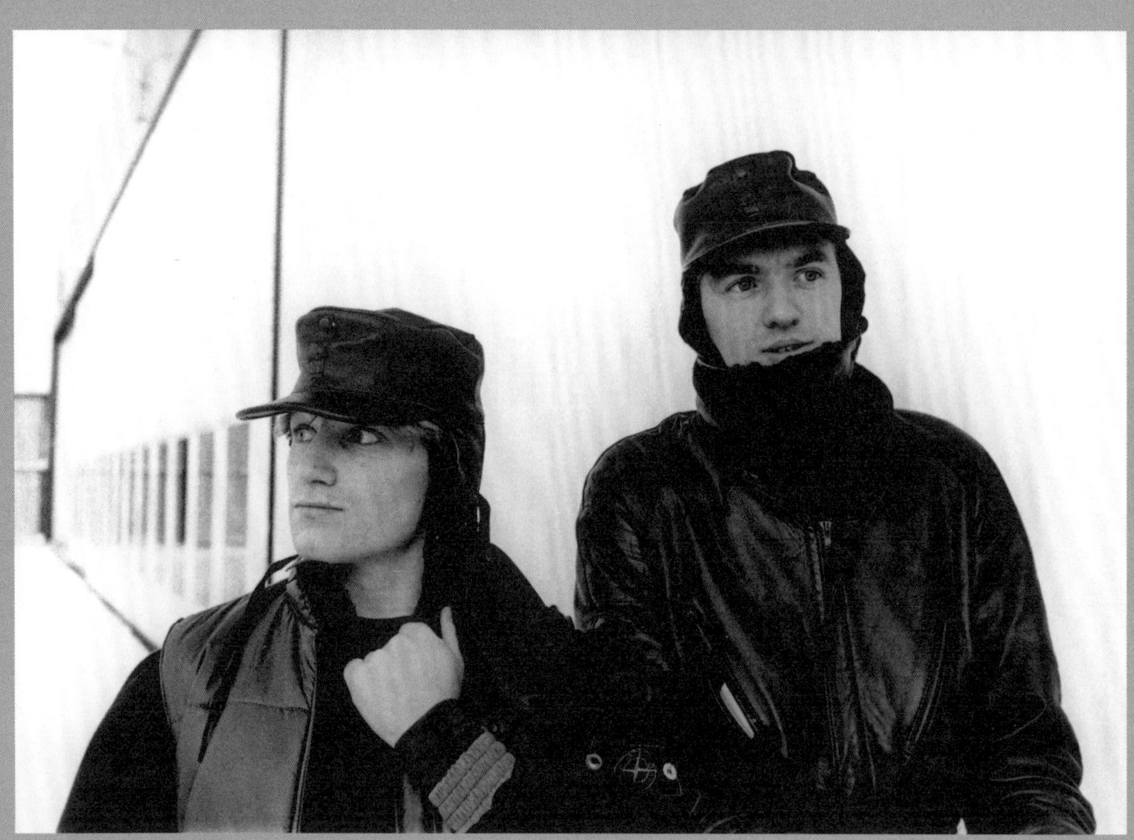

we tried everything, including dressing similarly, but somehow they can still tell us apart. I've given up now, but the photo above was in the innocent days of 1982. photo by edge.

I first met Bono, Larry, The Edge and Adam in 1979, when not many people would have known they were U2. They were just four naïve Irish boys excited about the idea of being in a rock group. I was about 22, and they were three or four years younger. Punk rock music had just happened, in the way these things happen, and so the four teenage boys, having already grabbed their positions in their new group, so that there was, as there often should be, a singer, a bassist, a guitarist and a drummer, were as likely to think of themselves as Joy Division as The Who. Their dreams were about The Ramones as much as they were about T.Rex.

Their hair was fairly short, in the UK punk way, and their music was fairly fast, as if they'd found it in a garage. They were as fired up by the thought of the Sex Pistols as they were in long distant awe of the Beatles. Actually, to be honest, they were just as driven by a highly enthusiastic, slightly dotty Scottish punk-pop band called the Skids as they were by the Rolling Stones or David Bowie. The manic, amateurish, occasionally delightful Skids encouraged Bono and his mates to feel they could definitely have a go at being a group, at playing gigs, even making a record.

The thought of being as out there, as beyond Dublin, as across the universe, as Lennon or Led Zeppelin was the dreamiest of fantasies. It's like, when you start to paint, you don't immediately think, I will be Picasso, I will be Pollock. That comes a little later, if it comes at all. In the beginning, U2 just wanted to get some paint on the canvas, just for the sheer glamorous thrill of it. They would be a group, because they could be a group. It might not go much further. It might go nowhere.

The Skids showed U2 that, first of all, you must find the canvas. It's actually not as easy as it seems. The canvas is blank. So blank it's intimidating. The next thing is to gleefully splash some paint on the canvas, to make it seem something like a picture. If it seems a little messy, pretend that it's abstract. Make it seem that you know what you're doing. Once the Irish got that paint on the canvas, as flamboyantly as their Scottish mentors The Skids, but somehow with more life, and feeling, and depth, there was just a hint that they could actually head out into a world and get, say, Joy Division in their sights. A hint that they could become a group called U2 that made proper records that could get played on a radio show somewhere near, you never know, The Clash, or at least Generation X. It might go further. It might go somewhere. It went somewhere for the Skids, all the way to London.

I first saw U2 play a show in a pub that was five minutes walk from where I lived in West Hampstead, North West London. The venue was so close to my flat I could leave a freshly made cup of tea in the kitchen and if I didn't like the group that was playing, I could make it back home and the drink would still be warm. I'd actually gone to the West Hampstead Moonlight to review an up-and-coming group called the Soul Boys. In hindsight, here was an example of a group, a gang of eager young boys who had grabbed their positions, their instruments, their moment, who really didn't know where the canvas was. It's quite possible that, even though they dreamt of being Roxy Music, or Talking Heads, they didn't actually know there was a canvas. For this group, it went no further. It went nowhere.

U2, looking so young they might have been fifth formers on some class project, were actually supporting the Soul Boys. U2 were so low in the world of pop they were all but invisible. This could have been it. Their moment. Their day in the dirty sun of London, on the far flung outskirts of the scene. One shot. Blank. Then back to Dublin, to everyday jobs, to a future contemplating what might have been. A collapse of the dream, but at least they gave it a go, at least they had that much in them.

When they burst onto the stage, and they did burst, because ultimately they were destined to burst out of their skin, there were about six or seven people in the pub basement watching the four boys bang and bounce around the stage as if they actually had something to say. The basement was roughly the size of my little flat. They might as well have been playing in my flat, just outside the kitchen. The kitchen would have been their dressing room. I could have made Adam a cup of tea.

It's a strange thing when you watch a new group who clearly want to make it play in a small club watched by a handful of people who aren't sure they're in the right place. There is certainly embarrassment in the air, for everyone concerned. The group might be a disaster, and they might well know it, and you are there to witness the disaster. There is nowhere to hide, for the group or their tiny audience. Now and then, you catch each others' eye, and there were a few times when me and Bono were almost staring at each other, if only for a split second, wondering whether this whole thing was working, this whole thing that inside the full flow of a young group trying to play world shattering rock and roll in a small dingy club on an unlovely Wednesday night is everything to do with life, and what's the point of it. He was dominating the stage, as if he was already Jagger, or Bolan, or Bono, and I was standing as casually as I could on the empty dance floor wondering if he was who he clearly claimed he was. (Adam gave me a cool, appraising look, as if to say, two sugars please.)

I had certain experience in this kind of thing, not least because around the time of punk there were lots of new groups prepared to brave the empty night air on the way to hoped for success. I had also seen Joy Division, the group U2 dearly wanted to emulate, because their rock and roll was so industrial and holy, play in front of a handful of people. I had seen Joy Division play in front of an audience that was so small, their singer Ian Curtis took it upon himself to leave the stage and dance where the audience would have been if there had been an audience.

It didn't matter that there were only five people watching Joy Division, because they acted as if there were thousands. They were concentrating so much on filling the canvas with some kind of original masterpiece. They were in effect playing for themselves, seeing how far they could go inside their own imaginations. Funnily enough, I'd also seen the Skids play in front of a tiny audience, and the thing with the Skids, these Scottish idiots who thought they could be grand and sensational, they just loved to show off. They bust through the potential embarrassment of playing in front of hardly anyone at all, and just had a blast. U2 were somewhere between the introspective urgency of Joy Division, playing something timeless with fantastic self-belief, and the extravagant, adolescent Skids, mucking about with rock and roll glory as if no one would notice they were making such a mess of the canvas it was almost laughable.

It's why I immediately liked U2, I think. Instinctively, I sensed they were half on the verge of being magnificent, and half on the verge of being exhibitionist fools. The foolish part of them was as striking as the magnificent part. The foolish part, their willingness to go for it from the word go, was ultimately what made the magnificent part of them work. Without being as foolish and as loveable as the Skids, they would never have reached the stage where they understood that they could be magnificent. It was the show off part of them I instantly fell for. There were barely more people watching them than there were in the group, but they still put on a show. They were serious, and they were playful. They were going somewhere, and they knew it. They would never be this low, this invisible, again. In fact, they were so confident that night, so inside the idea of being the U2 we would recognise playing the stadiums of the world, so sure that they would not always be this awkward, gawky, young and sweet, there was a sense that the super group was ready and waiting inside them. The baby group they were at the West Hampstead Moonlight, taking their first breath, screaming as they came into existence, nerves exploding, wet with bloody newness, alive with possibility, is inside them now that they are a super group. They've never lost that sense that the world is out there waiting for them to win over, and take advantage of, and change. They are no-where, and they have to get somewhere. On their very best songs, it's as though they are feeling the exhilaration of breathing for the very first time. They can take with them into their music a sudden perpetual sense of the astonishment of existence. Writing songs has always been their way of making sense of the Universe.

They never got so close to my kitchen again. I went over to Ireland to interview them, and they made me a cup of tea in their kitchen. I spent a few days driving around Ireland, watching them play to audiences that were growing by the day, hearing the group grow by the minute. They would start a show as overexcited as The Skids, flapping like teenagers all over the idea that they were a proper pop group, and end it closer to the faithful intensity of Joy Division, lost in the freshly available grandeur of themselves. Their music was moving out of the patched up neighbourhood garage on the edge of town and into a vast, spectacular church at the centre of the city.

I remember one morning we all gathered in the lobby of a small hotel in what I now can only remember as being the middle of Ireland. Firm and ancient green surrounded us and centuries of toil and tall stories felt pressed into the air. U2 had performed late the night before, at a ballroom called The Garden Of Eden, in a small sleepy town called Tullermeny that you feel only appears out of the Irish mist every thirty years. It was hard work to get up early ready to travel in our convoy of cars to the next town, the next venue, which I don't think was called The Tree Of Knowledge.

I suppose this primitive cavalcade touring the country roads and lonely hills of Ireland was the beginning of an epic, myth-making journey that was to eventually take U2 around the world in more ways than one. A journey that would see them pause occasionally to take stock, to seize the moment, to change clothes, to polish their dreams, to lose their minds, to play tricks with the light, to play with fruit, to win people over, to collect awards, to stand around in airports and have their photograph taken.

They went around the world so many times in so many ways that they ended up spinning through fame and fortune. They spun so fast and fantastically they were launched into the very heart of the church of Elvis. It's not known where this actually is, but it is certainly beyond Dublin, and it is definitely beyond reason. And it was way beyond our thoughts as we gathered for breakfast one morning in a hotel that was in a way built on the foundations of reason.

I have always remembered that morning. I don't remember much of what happened during the other days I shared some brief moments with U2 at the very beginning of their exploration of celebrity space and rock and roll heaven. I know I didn't appreciate how privileged I was to get this glimpse into the beginnings of what became authentic rock history. I remember that morning because as Bono and I were moving deeper into the serious four day rock interview that we were conducting as if I was Mailer and he was Lennon, a well turned out middle-aged couple overheard our impassioned conversation about life, love and the whole damned world, and picked up on something that Bono had said. I'm not sure what he said, but I imagine it was the kind of thing a singer in a rock band who really fancies himself as a singer in a rock band might say about how he was going to change the world, once he got there.

The couple managed very quickly to give the conversation what can only be described as a religious dimension. Jesus, and God, arrived, glowing with rude health. The middle-aged couple were very much God's people. I have some bizarre memory of them explaining to Bono and me how they'd seen a vision of Jesus just a few miles down the road, in a barn. I was not having any of this, mainly because this kind of talk makes me nervous, and also because I was alarmed to note that there seemed to be some attempt to claim Jesus as Irish. Bono, though, remained serene in the face of what I considered to be slightly demented. Bono was as happy to enter into speculative conversation with these gentle Jesus freaks as he was to play pretend rock God in a conversation with a visiting journalist. The primitive version of a U2 entourage were keen to get on their way, but Bono gave them his undivided attention, as if he had all the time in the world.

As Bono and the couple talked, I fell into a sneering silence. For me, any religious feeling I might have had as a young child had crumbled to dust as a teenager. Eventually, we were ready to leave. Bono and I sat in the back of one of the cars as we travelled to the next town on the itinerary. He had obviously been captivated by what the Jesus seekers had been talking about. I remember saying to him as the car left the hotel car park that they seemed to be talking rubbish, and the idea of seeing Jesus in an Irish country barn was plain daft.

Bono was annoyed with me. He put me in my place. He said, you should never be so dismissive to people however alien or cranky their position appears. As far as Bono was concerned, it wasn't so much what they were saying, or what they said they were seeing. It wasn't how they were talking. It was why they were talking. It was what they were looking for. It was the fact that they were searching for meaning, and he wasn't irritated or embarrassed by how they articulated that. He was tolerant enough, in fact mature enough, to see beyond the fact that the words they used to describe their spiritual quest seemed to involve banal clichés regarding God, and Jesus, and the light.

Bono was now ready to carry on with the rock and roll chat. I wasn't so ready. As the car spiralled deeper into the timeless Irish interior, I got the worst carsickness I've ever had in my life. We had just been talking to two people who seemed to have found the gates to heaven. Now I felt like I'd smashed into the gates of hell.

Perhaps I had felt the wrath of Bono, a man I was beginning to realise had levels of mental strength that could easily enter the supernatural. He was so angry with my patronising tone regarding the couple at the hotel that he had cursed me with an abominable nausea. Here was a man who was something more than just a singer in a rock-'n'roll band.

After a few hours of sheer torment as I tried to maintain the Mailer questioning while my insides turned inside out, and Bono just rehearsed all the grand, sweeping lines of reasoning and reckoning he would utilise as the international pop star he was becoming by the hour, I started to feel better. The relief when I eventually recovered was sensational. After feeling so dreadful, I now felt so happy. I put this down to Bono as well. He had forgiven me. He had driven me into the depths of despair. He had then lifted me higher and higher.

Boy, Bono could talk. Throughout the four days, he talked for himself, for the group, and, there was just a hint, although it would have been absurd to say it at the time, for all of mankind. I never interviewed the group again. I reviewed them occasionally, and for their first releases, caught up in the fever of having been involved with a successful group before they were famous, gave them good reviews. After a few years, the very thing that I'd enjoyed about Bono as an apprentice pop star, this tendency to talk and talk about the big things in life, this missionary zeal to make the world a better place through song, love and sensibility, started to annoy me.

The talkative Bono was a good thing when he was shouting for attention, and fighting for space. It struck me as a bad thing once U2 were a going concern. By the end of the 80s, it seemed he was talking too much, and the bossy Jesus thing was a little disconcerting. It seemed to contradict the experimental drive that had emerged out of the light and dark of Joy Division, the fire and rhythm of The Clash, the friction and focus of Public Image Ltd, the strangeness and sensuality of Eno. I happened to mention this a couple of times in print, putting emphasis on the fact that Bono talked too much for his own good and was the decadent king of those self-obsessed rock superstars driven by some kind of Messiah complex.

I thought that U2's determination to resist exiling their Christianity just because they were a rock and roll band had compromised their overall dynamic, giving them an earnestness and a straightness that undermined the tantalising wildness that had once made them seem so special. U2's unshakable commitment to the word of the Lord could make their infatuation with the epic and the spellbinding seem too specific and literal. There was too much electioneering, too much preaching, too much launching themselves way over the top.

I wasn't paying enough attention. I was thinking too narrowly, and I wasn't keeping up to date with Bono, The Edge, Larry and Adam and the way they were dealing with being what they had become. They had turned into the kind of monstrous commercial rock band that can seem cold and distant and irrelevant, exactly the phenomenon they'd reacted against when they formed. They were so gigantic it wasn't possible to be as intimate, sophisticated and aggressive as they wanted, and they responded to that by sometimes being rampant fabulists at odds with their commercial size, sometimes by being as obedient and traditional as is expected from the super-sized. Their faith, based around their very personal idea of Christianity, kept them intact amidst all the pressure, and they weren't afraid to acknowledge that through their work. The fact that some of their songs had a definite hymn-like quality was ultimately not something to underestimate. U2 had found this way to incorporate Catholic grandness and Protestant intensity into their music, and this didn't dilute it as a pop experience. It actually enriched it. The best pop songs are hymns, as much as they are magic spells, or mating calls, or commercial jingles, or items of fashion, or adventures in time, or ways of relieving the tedium of existence.

They also knew enough about pop culture to have fun with the idea of being so famous and so classic. They were sort of ingenious entertainment academics constantly inventing ways to play around with being what they were. They were explorers always entering new territory, always having to adjust to a new set of circumstances, always having to grow into something else, something new, while being exactly what they'd always been. U2 have not really changed as everything around them, musically, commercially, scientifically, emotionally, has changed beyond recognition. They still make their music, according to their own sense of time and place, and they still want to say things that carry weight, even as the idea of faith gets trashed by the escapist antics of the modern world. They've not changed, but they're always ahead of the game.

In fact, they have just got better and better at being U2, even when they seem to be getting it wrong. They have always travelled forwards, even if it seemed they had broken down, or crashed, or swerved off the road, or taken the wrong turning. They're always on the road, even when they've paused for a while, even when they've stopped for a minute to be photographed. Bono, up front, the speaker, the cheerleader, the big mouth busybody, because that was the role he was allocated back when they were like kid Skids, has become the only kind of post punk 21st century superstar there could possibly be in the way he mixes blunt Irishness, internationalism, art, music, diplomacy, philosophy, politics, fame and rock and roll. He's the only real example of such a superstar, and everything he did and does continues to make him perfectly qualified for such a role. He's gone and made the world a stage. He illuminates it with his sly, passionate intelligence, and leaps about it as if this is a way to transform himself from sinner to saint.

Bono's scholarly, provocative appreciation of the way

an entertainer can become political, how the singer of love songs can also have a serious message, how popular culture has taken over the world, how Elvis and God are the same thing in different clothes inside a different Las Vegas, how life is all we've got, has led to him becoming one of the most intriguing activists on the planet. He believes in things, and he wants to tell everybody he can all that he feels. That's something that can really get on people's nerves. It breaks all the rules. The rock star is just meant to operate inside the borders of entertainment. Bono is actually trying to break outside into the corrupt reality of the world, and do something about it. Who does he think he is?

The truth is, he's always been like that, even when only a handful of people were listening, and there's never been a point where he thought he should stop being a persistent, nagging, protesting, eroticised blabbermouth just because he now has a huge international audience. In a way, he's still at the beginning of whatever journey he's on, one I thought had begun on the side roads inside green and mysterious Ireland and that had ended as soon as he'd become a star, one that he could only take as a part of U2, as one of the boys. U2 have proved more than most that rock music has this tremendous transcendental power, and Bono as their mouthpiece, the role he adopted because he spoke the loudest, wants to take rock's revolutionary ideas and progressive values as far as possible out into the real world. With basic, belligerent rock'n'roll audacity he is prepared to battle with corporate entrenchment and governmental inflexibility: to prove that inventive thinking can subvert oppressive capitalist convention.

If Elvis watched over the 50s, 60s and 70s, both as pioneer and has-been, as someone who knew what he was doing and someone who didn't, as hero and zombie, as icon and victim, as redneck and seer, U2 have watched over the 80s, 90s and 00s. They've done this as group in control and group out of control, as artists and businessmen, as theorists and models, from the vinyl age to the virtual age. They've been fashionable and unfashionable, cool and uncool, babyish and Godlike, rootsy and futuristic, corny and radical, indulgent and selfless, foolish and magnificent, auto-tuned and iTuned. They know enough about music, image and celebrity to be able to roll out their Sun period and their Army years and their Hollywood movies and the vanity and the eccentricity and their comeback bravado and their God fearing singing and their soul-searching storytelling and their Las Vegas operatics all at the same time, inside the myth and naturalness of being U2. They know that what they can do as living legends can actually affect the grain of modern thinking, both frivolously, and profoundly, and they take their role seriously however scornful and dismissive the reaction.

Thinking back to the late 70s, when U2 first pounced into my life, on the way to conquering the world, I remember liking them because they had the galvanising cheek of the Skids, the chaotic idealism of the Clash, the violent romanticism of Joy Division. For me, this was right on the money. They were part Pistols, part Beatles, part pop, part rock, part punk, although it wasn't obvious that they could make this make sense beyond the fannish few.

Back then, we hoped that punk, as a force for change, might have a major impact on the world, and you could say that because of Bono and U2, it has. They were not a punk rock group, but they would not have happened without punk rock, and they wouldn't have had such a fierce independent spirit, and such a desire to merge revolutionary hard rock power with the troubling abstractions of faith. They would not have been so intellectually restless, so existentially curious, as intrigued by the avant-garde edge as much as the consoling pop centre. They would not have been so idiosyncratically political.

I think of those that have died or cried off, that have withered or not weathered well, Curtis, Strummer, Rotten, and Bono has taken on their energy, and taken it out into the world, taken what was realistic about their mystique and manner and planted it in the middle of this mass communication that is U2. That's when I realise what an extraordinary thing it is that Bono and U2 have done. They've done the thing that punk set out to do, in their own way, even if it meant sometimes doing things that made them seem square, or needy, or just plain mad. It's not just a punk thing, though, or an Elvis thing – there's Dylan and Springsteen in there as well, Pink Floyd and Leonard Cohen, Phil Spector and Kraftwerk, perhaps even Johnny Otis and Burt Bacharach, Johnny Rivers and Mohammed Ali, Yeats and Godard, and what about Sinatra and Garcia? All of this, and more, more knowledge about combining intelligence with show business, poetry with melody, sermons with rhythm, image with imagination, all of it filtered through the presence, or absence, of what Bono has always been happy to call God – even if that meant some people felt it was creepy, or old-fashioned, or just plain goofy. Bono could have dropped the direct and indirect references to God, talked about something vaguely cosmic in the way most rock stars do. But to use God as an embellishing part of the idea of U2 is actually more dangerous than not using Him. It's the kind of thing that Bono gets turned on by – punching into people's levels of comfort, attacking moral and ethical complacency, ignoring the apparent political and style correctness of the

august / september 2002 photo by guja

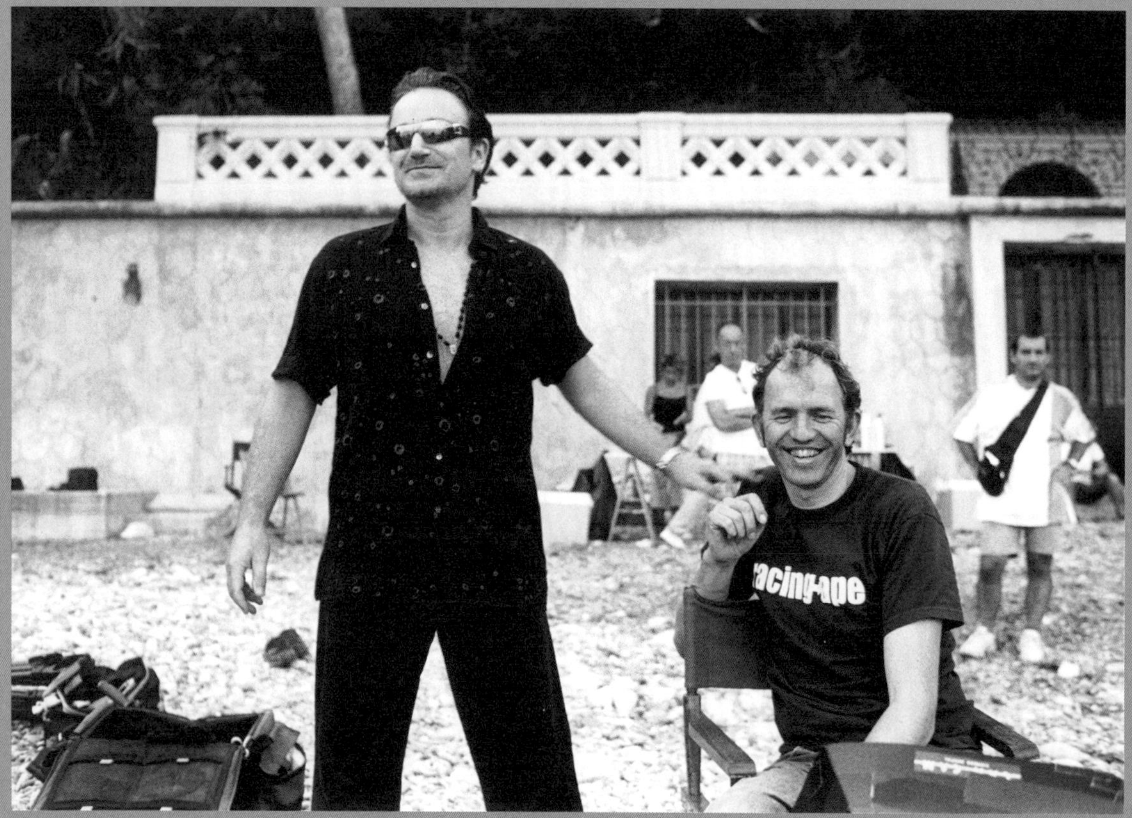

on the beach doing the 'electrical storm' video in the south of france.

times, fighting to dig up meaning when most people prefer to cover it up.

For Bono, God is what there is because we are alive, God is what there is because we have an imagination, God is what we must be scared of because He is a direct reflection of humanity, God is another way of saying love, which is another word rubbed bare of meaning over centuries of use and abuse. God is the beginning of a journey that takes you wherever you end up going. God might even be there at the end.

U2 supply a subtle, flashy soundtrack to this idea of God as emotion, as consciousness, as intelligence, to this idea of love as something the word cannot begin to articulate. This soundtrack has managed to positively exploit these ideas about God and love as vital energies that should always have contemporary relevance outside the way they are packaged, priced and sold at any given time. It has done so in a way that means we don't think of U2 as a Christian group simplistically clinging to a Biblical interpretation of life's mysteries. We think of them in the way that we think of The Beatles, The Who, The Rolling Stones, Led Zeppelin, or the Velvet Underground, Joy Division and Nirvana. We think of them as their own church, drawing us through a ravishing complication of noise and pleasure and originality into a state of mind where we can start to understand just what it is to be alive at this tumultuous point in history.

I saw Bono recently, sat in a restaurant. It was lunch time in the middle of the week. It could even have been 25 years to the day that I saw him sing at the West Hampstead Moonlight. I thought of everything that has happened to Bono and U2 in those time-twisting years, all the way from Dublin, which is just round the back of Memphis. I thought of another strictly mischievous dream washed rock star who wore bandit shades all of the time, for protection, for glory, to see for miles – Mott the Hoople's Ian Hunter. Like Hunter said, it's a mighty long way down rock and roll. You've got to stay young and you can never grow old, you climb up mountains and you fall down holes.

Sometimes you stay young by dying, other times you stay young by living.

Bono was on his own, waiting for someone. Perhaps he was waiting for no one. He'd found some time for himself, a rare thing now that the world is beginning to expect things from him that go beyond just singing songs and adopting poses. Even those people that don't rate him much expect things from him, even if it's just failure. Everybody wants something from someone as famous as Bono.

Considering he now mixes with Presidents and Popes, with Dylans and Jaggers, and he travels around the world as much an ambassador as a pop star, as much spiritual leader as MTV showman, elected by millions for his perception and power, he appeared quite ordinary, or at least he had camouflaged himself as an ordinary person. I guess he was off duty, but really there were too many people looking his way for him to be completely off duty. Even those who weren't looking at him directly were looking at him really.

He was still Bono, which is all he ever wanted to be, before he fully thought through the consequences. I thought, should I say hello, and ask him about something I've often wondered about – whether those people in the Irish hotel, the night after the Garden of Eden, reactivated his interest in religion, or whether he was so fascinated in what they were saying because he had held onto his interest in God even as he had fallen for Elvis, and The Who, and Joey Ramone. That might have just been me as the self-obsessed rock journalist wanting to feel I was at the centre of something significant. Bono probably didn't even remember the story about Jesus in the barn. I thought, perhaps I could see if he wanted a cup of tea.

He read a newspaper. He scanned the headlines in the way that headlines now scan him. He looked up occasionally, somehow sliding off the fact that he was the centre of attention. I caught his eye a couple of times, and for a split second I thought we were looking right at each other, as if we were working out if this whole thing was still working, this thing of doing good in the face of being so rich, so loudmouthed, so sensitive, so defiant. I bet actually he was looking right through me. It's one of his powers.

I was looking at Bono, who was acting just like he was Bono. He was clearly who he claimed to be. He would be Bono tomorrow; he would be Bono for as long as it takes. I was looking at Bono, and he was looking into the future. He had things on his mind, the kind of things you have on your mind when you are Bono, and you're on a ride, and people are listening to you, and you're determined to get it right, and you stop just to check you're still where you should be, and you're not totally on your own, or completely lost in the fury of your fame. Sometimes you stop just to have your photograph taken. Even then, you can sometimes still be moving.

Bono sat on his own at the centre of a world he can call his own. Perhaps he was waiting for the rest of U2 to arrive.

Perhaps he was waiting for Anton.

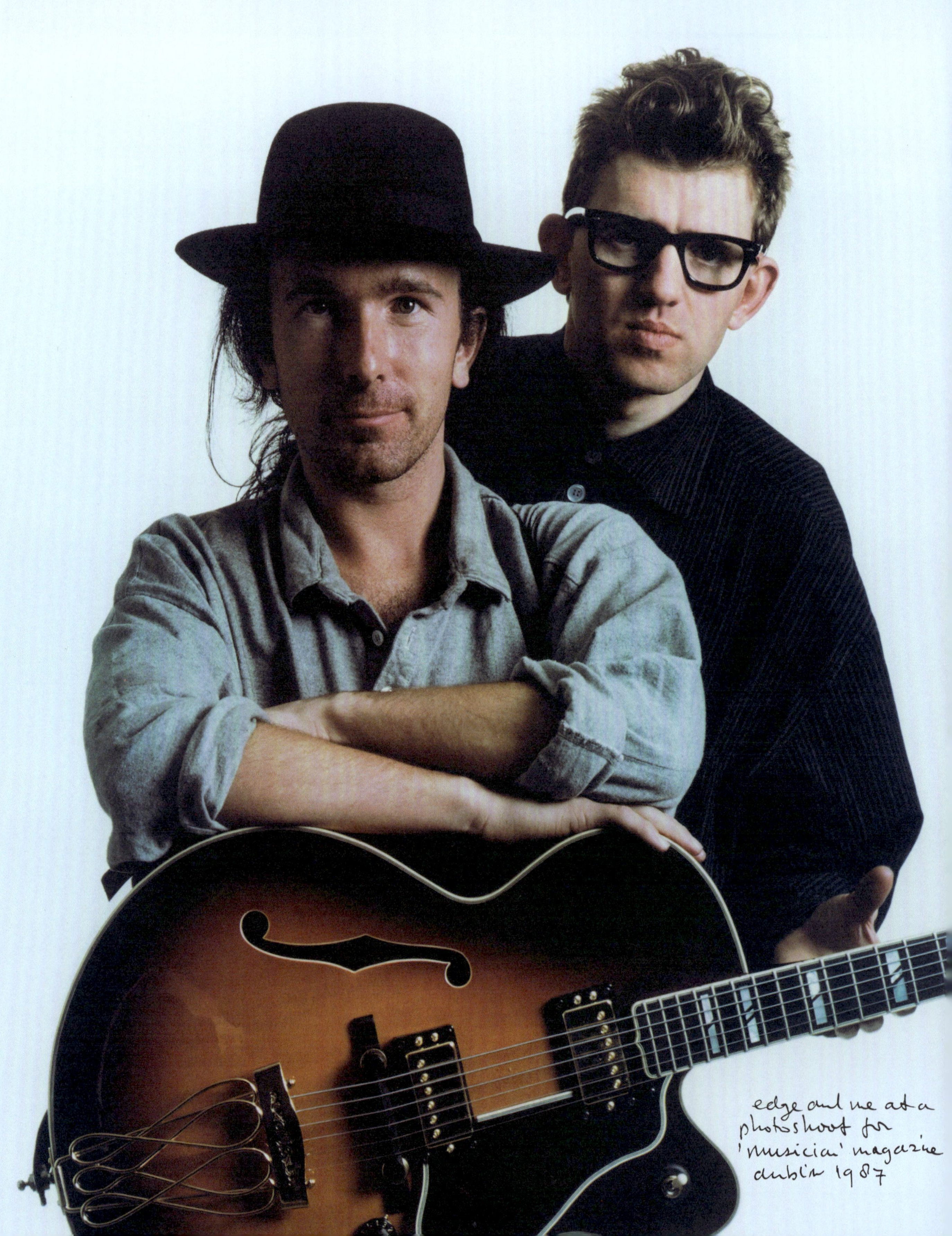

edge and me at a photoshoot for 'musician' magazine dublin 1987

Bono wearing my specs looks like the egghead intellectual he has inside him. Sadly, wearing Bono's fly shades doesn't reveal my inner rockstar.

Photographs can be cruel.

I was once photographed by Anton wearing a giant papier-mâché Bono head. That didn't make me look like a rockstar either and fortunately that picture isn't in this book.

Photographers can be kind.

U2 and Anton Corbijn deserve each other. They're strange in the same way.

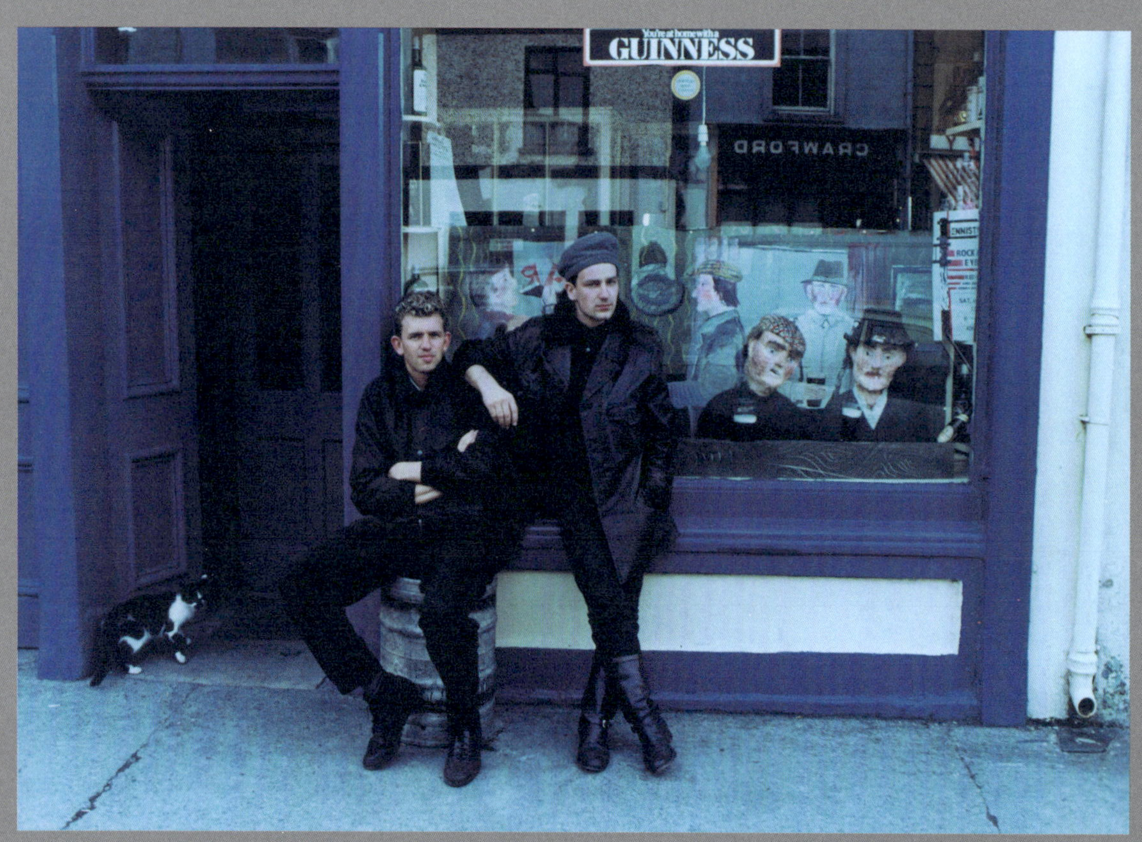

look what the cat brought in – relaxing during the 'unforgettable fire' shoot, somewhere in the west of ireland – photo by steve averill.

There is a photograph

MICHAEL STIPE

There is a photograph that was sent to me once, a postcard for a gallery opening. It is on my refrigerator, next to the warhol polaroid, the muhammad ali signed baseball card of his most famous fight; the revolving gallery of nephew and goddaughter drawings held up by magnets, a thom yorke-sketched 'do not disturb' sign from a dressing room door, a picture of my hero and fellow georgian, martin luther king, jr., a note from my favorite hotel. The photograph postcard for a gallery opening is a picture of bono, the singer of u2, taken by anton corbijn, the photographer. I believe it has been there for almost 10 years, longer than any of the other things mentioned above, and I have never once felt the need to take it off. In fact I tried once, returning home after many months away, in a vain attempt at clutter-free-ness which just didn't suit me. But it stayed put.

I don't think anton or his gallerist expected that postcard to weather the test of time on my refrigerator, but it has. Im not sure that bono even realizes that its there. Im pretty sure that neither anton, bono, edge, larry, nor adam have any idea of the enormous impact that they have had on me, in my life, challenging and prompting me either in person or through their work. It is a rich gift to offer to anyone, the ability to inspire, and for me that gift has not gone unnoticed.

The thing about Anton

The thing about anton is that he's really tall. He comes from a strange place and he loves music. He has a sense of humor that could knock over large ships on the ocean. He has a love of people that is palpable and a serious eye. He has taken pictures that to me redefine beauty. His eye is acute and revelatory. His subject matter is never mundane or accidental. If it appears to be you need to look closer, because there is something there you havent considered yet. There is a marriage between anton corbijn and the gentlemen of u2, a marriage that I often find myself jealous of. There is a connection between his eye and their collective brain, between their complete lack of fear and his brain. It is a stunning dance to watch, with a soundtrack to match. The word iconic is maybe overused in a culture where we celebrate the very act of being celebrated. But I will say this; when it comes to the work of these 5 men, and the connect between them, iconic is the word that, to me, feels most accurate.

tokyo, dec. 1993

photobyuija

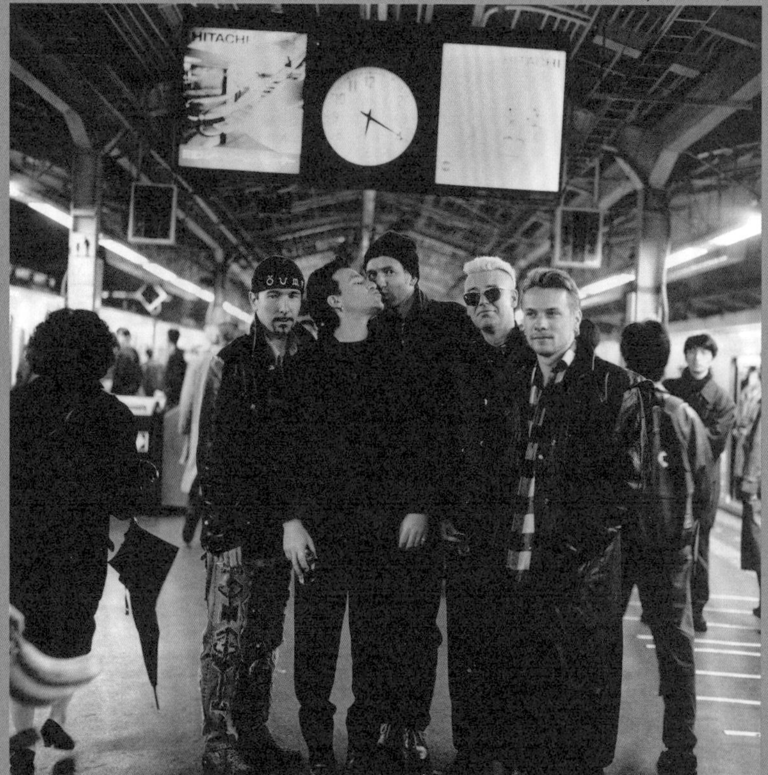

kiss and tell – the usual story with the usual suspects on a train platform in tokyo.

The invisible band member

WIM WENDERS

There are people on this planet
who can't exactly be keen any more to be photographed.
Bono, Edge, Adam and Larry must belong to that tribe.
"Overexposed, commercialized, handle me with care",
as The Traveling Wilburys sang,
and they knew what they were talking about.

I have worked with U2
and I have had them in front of my camera.
So I know intimately
how each of them in his own particular way protects
himself, shields himself against the lens and acts for it
at the same time.
"Celebrity" is a dangerous sword that cuts both ways.
And I can't help seeing that dilemma in many a
photograph taken of the band.
And certainly 99.99% of the people equipped with
cameras
will just see that when they take pictures of the lads:
"Celebrity!"
"Rock'n'Roll!"

Not so the Dutchman,
the fifth band member who plays a silent instrument.
"And behind the lens, Ladies and Gentlemen:
Anton Corbijn!"
His view is a brotherly view,
he is not impressed by sex, drugs and Rock'n'Roll,
fame or fortune.
He couldn't care less about celebrity, that's for sure.
He sees and shows us what he saw:
four young men whose path he understood
and whom he liked a lot.
And what these pictures also show:
They trusted his gaze and liked him a lot as well.
You don't put your heart in just anybody's hands.
When you're a Rock'n'Roll star,
you don't just stand behind your father
and let him hold or play your instrument
with somebody taking THAT picture
whom you do not trust blindly.

Anton saw U2 grow up for more than twenty years,
from being incredibly young and tender-faced sons
themselves to being fathers,
of a whole new generation of musicians and bands
who all tried to sound like them.
Anton went through lots of hairstyles and wardrobe
changes with them.
(You might just study the evolution of eye-wear in these
pictures!)
Anyway: You see these four age and get wiser
(well, I know Bono will find that debatable)
and you see the eye that watched them grow
gain experience as well.

But you also see a constant
that never changed over all these years.
The honesty,
fragility,
humanity
and emotional strength
that marked both the unique careers of this band
and of their photographer par excellence.

THE PHOTOGRAPHS 1982 - 2004

NEW ORLEANS

1982 february

in the early 80's i was the main photographer for the english musicpaper the New Musical Express, the NME, and it was them who asked me to shoot U2 in New Orleans for a coverstory. On the plane over from London i was listening to a cassette of 'october', the album they just released. I wasn't too impressed on first hearing. This might sound a little arrogant now, but i was making trips like this frequently for the NME so it didn't feel as special as it might sound now. the main reason for me to do this trip was that i'd never been to new orleans and wanted to check it out. I was to meet the band on a boat as it was their concert location for that evening. You have to start somewhere and we started at the top, with the President'. This photo of larry and bono i took shortly after meeting them there, prior to stepping on board.

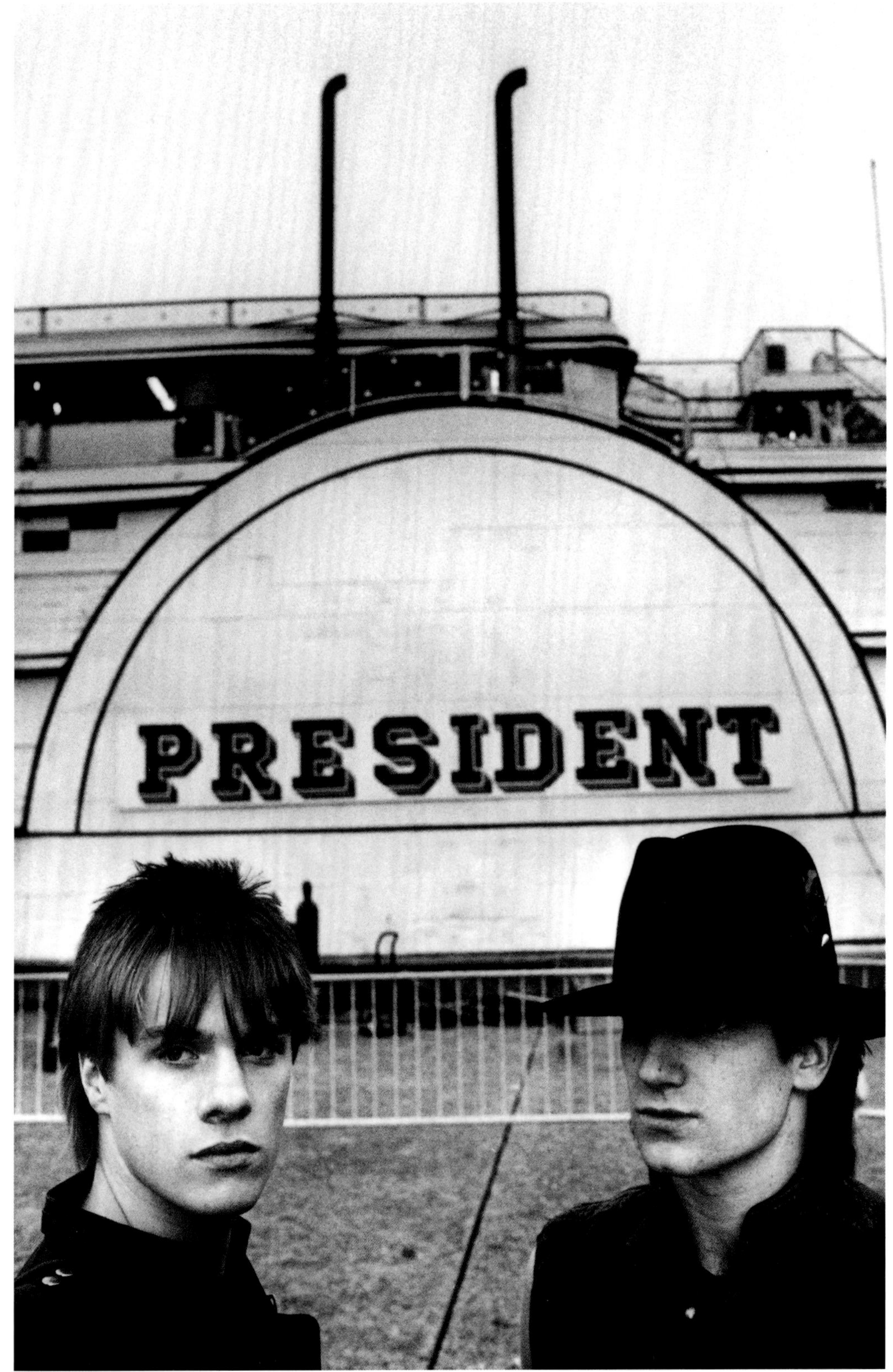
PRESIDENT

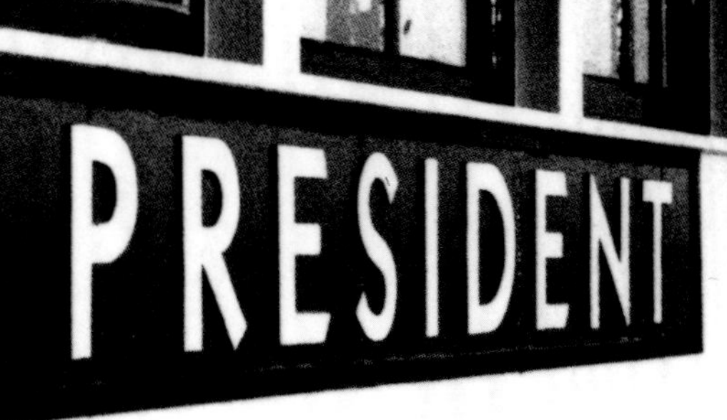
PRESIDENT

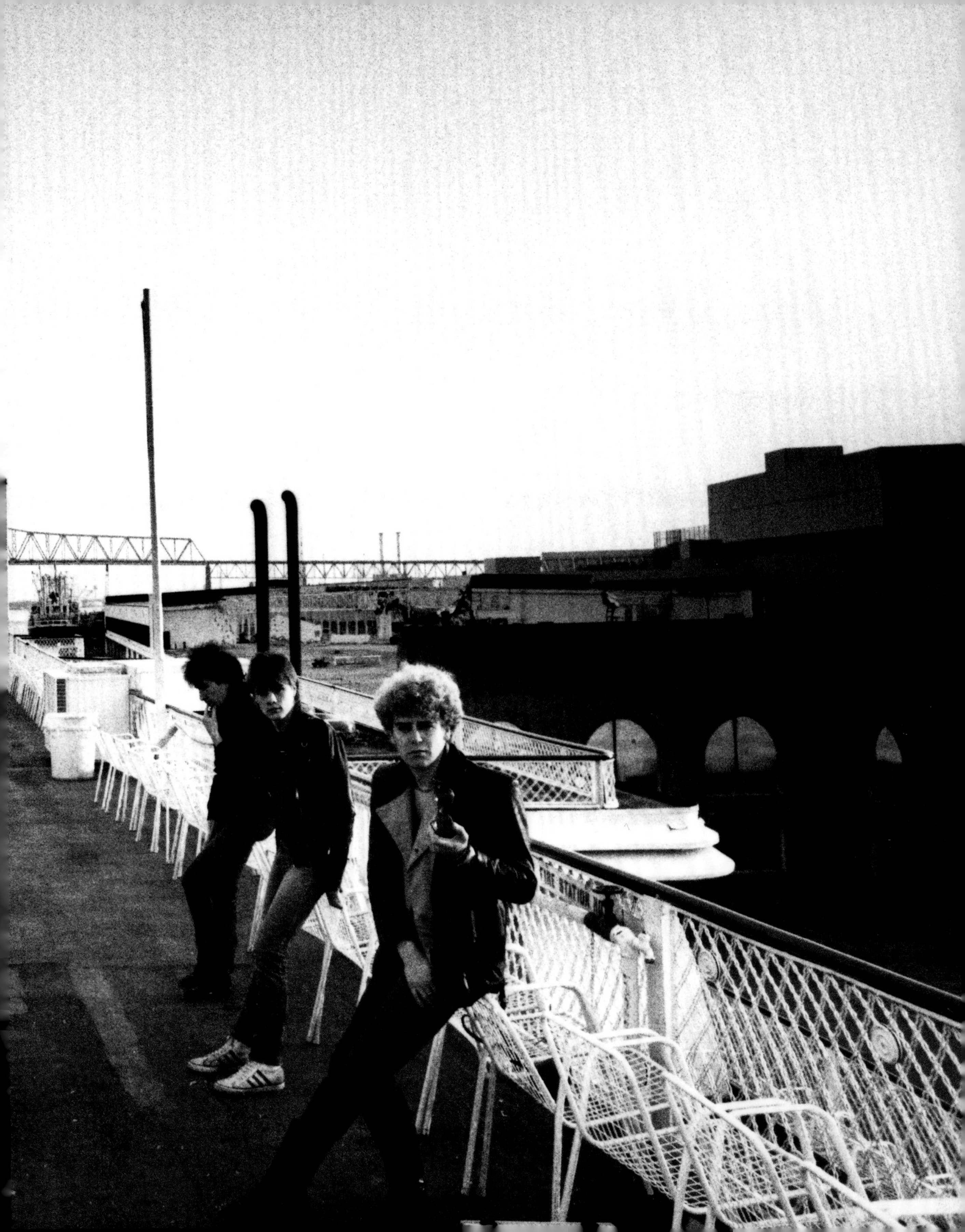
FIRE STATION

in some of these photographs the band look serious, a little miserable maybe. looking at it now i think that had a lot to do with my simple way of shooting – the amateur rule: shoot with the sun behind you. The band wasn't miserable, they had the sun straight in their eyes!

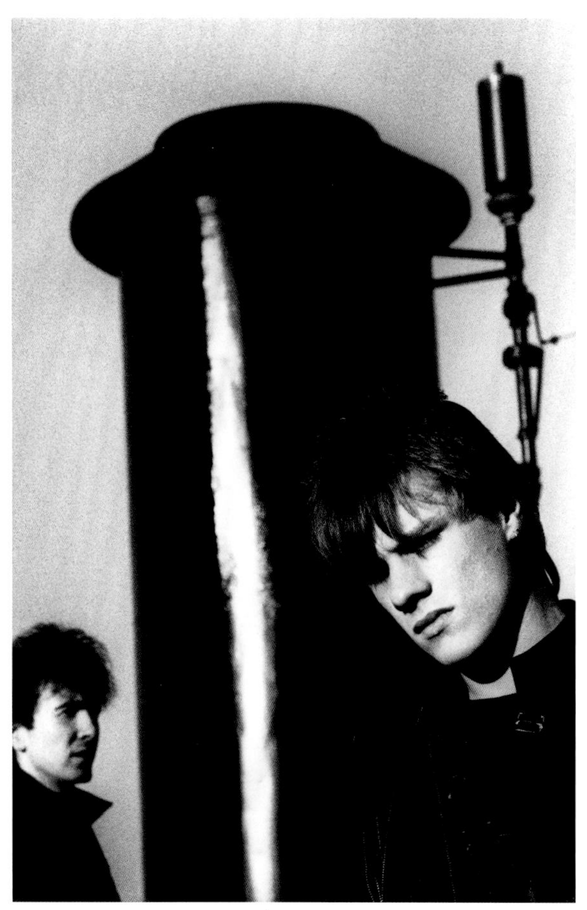

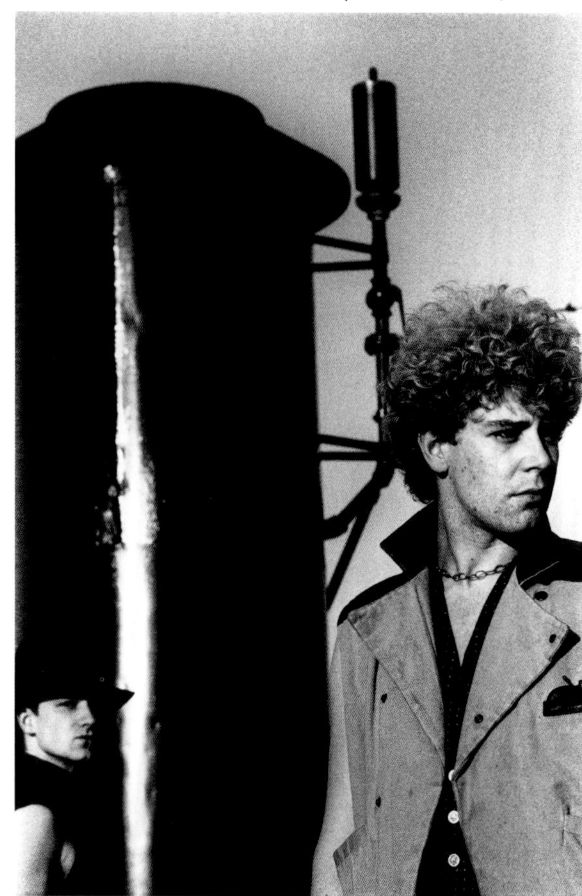

in the evening U2 would play on this boat and i thought i'll politely show my face for a few songs and leave and check the town out. little did i realise that the boat actually took off once the show started and i had to stay for the whole show on the s.s. president floating on the mississippi. if i'd be more poetically inclined, i'd say i never got of their boat.

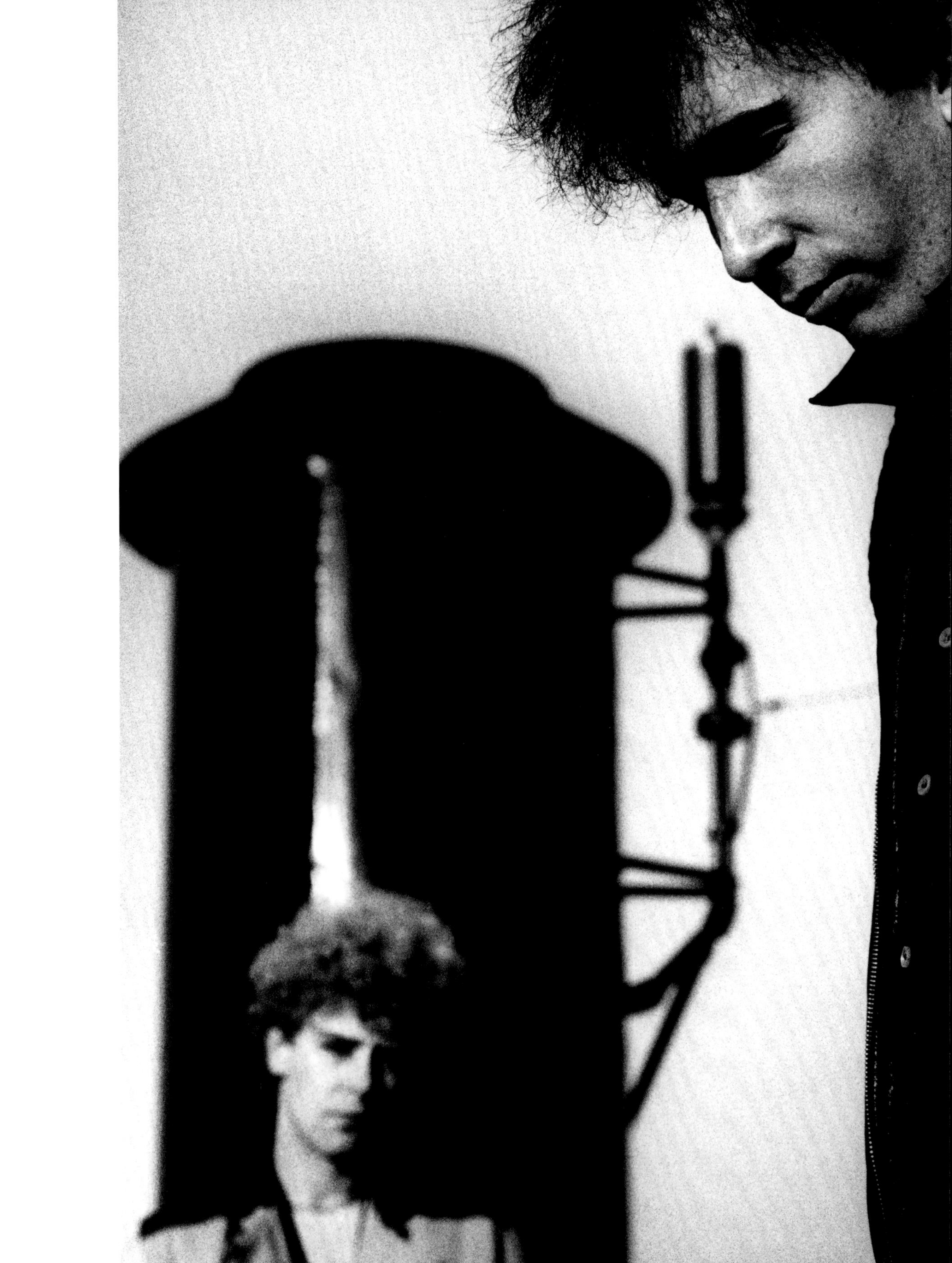

AUSTIN

february
1982

i know it is obvious but it might not be for everybody - i just introduce the models only once: ADAM

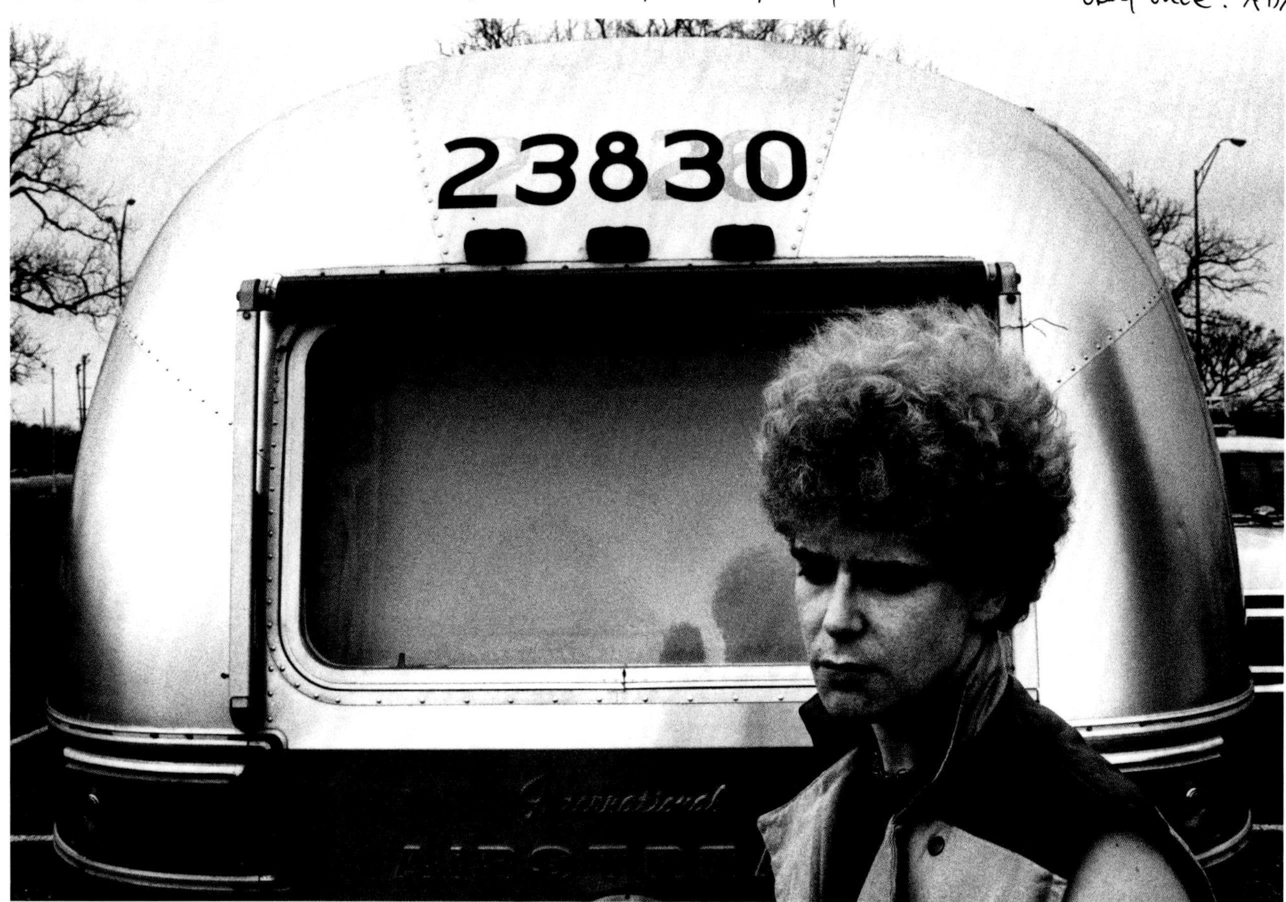

we drove in a minibus from New orleans to austin in texas where their next show was. in austin i saw this trailer park with those amazing looking airstreamers and i have to admit i am prone to all things americana - all those TV series you grow up with have an enormous influence on your likes and dislikes. we just had to use these for some photographs.

EDGE

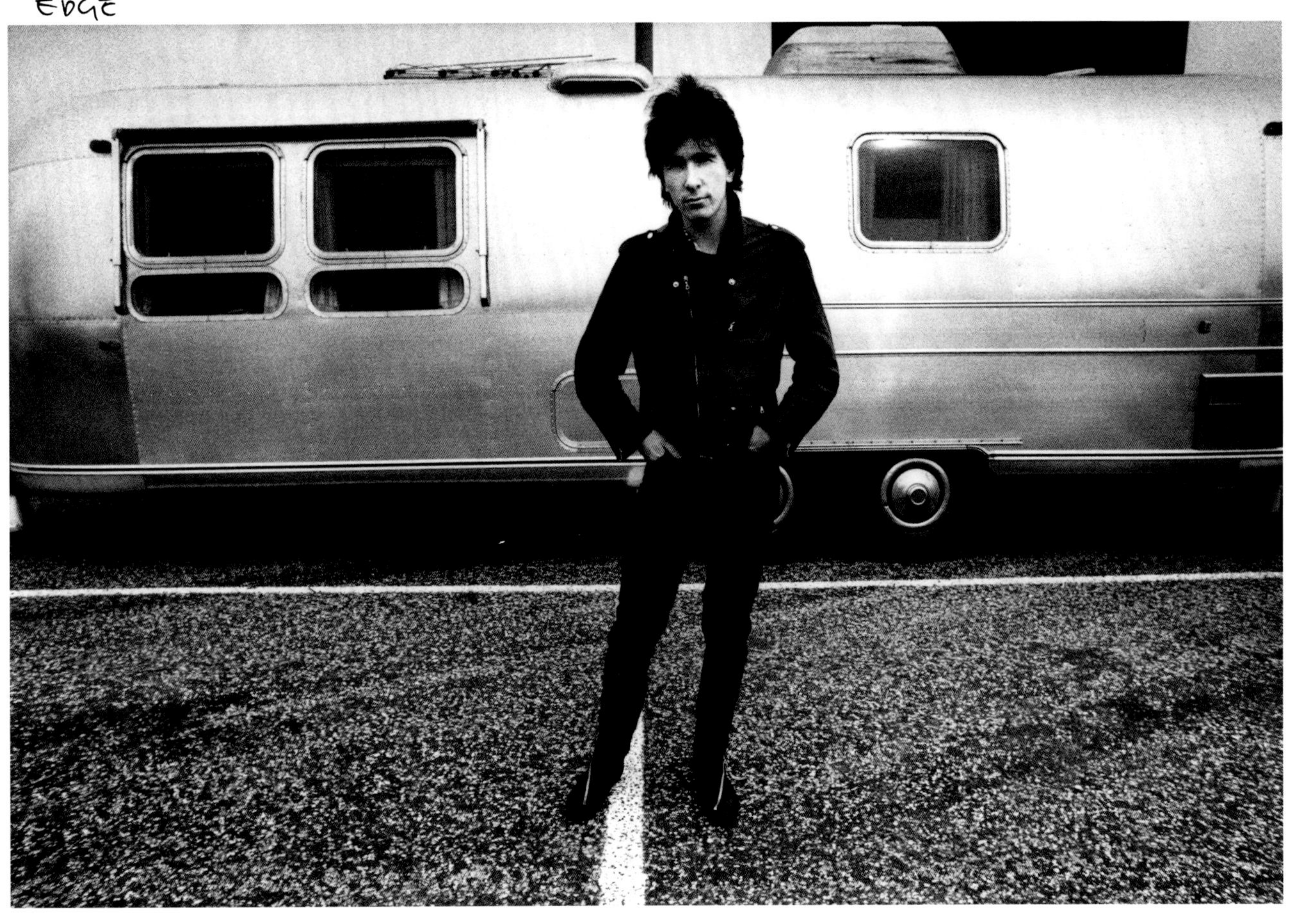

i remember that i liked edge's shoes so much that i bought the same ones when i returned to london. they were ankle height and had zips.

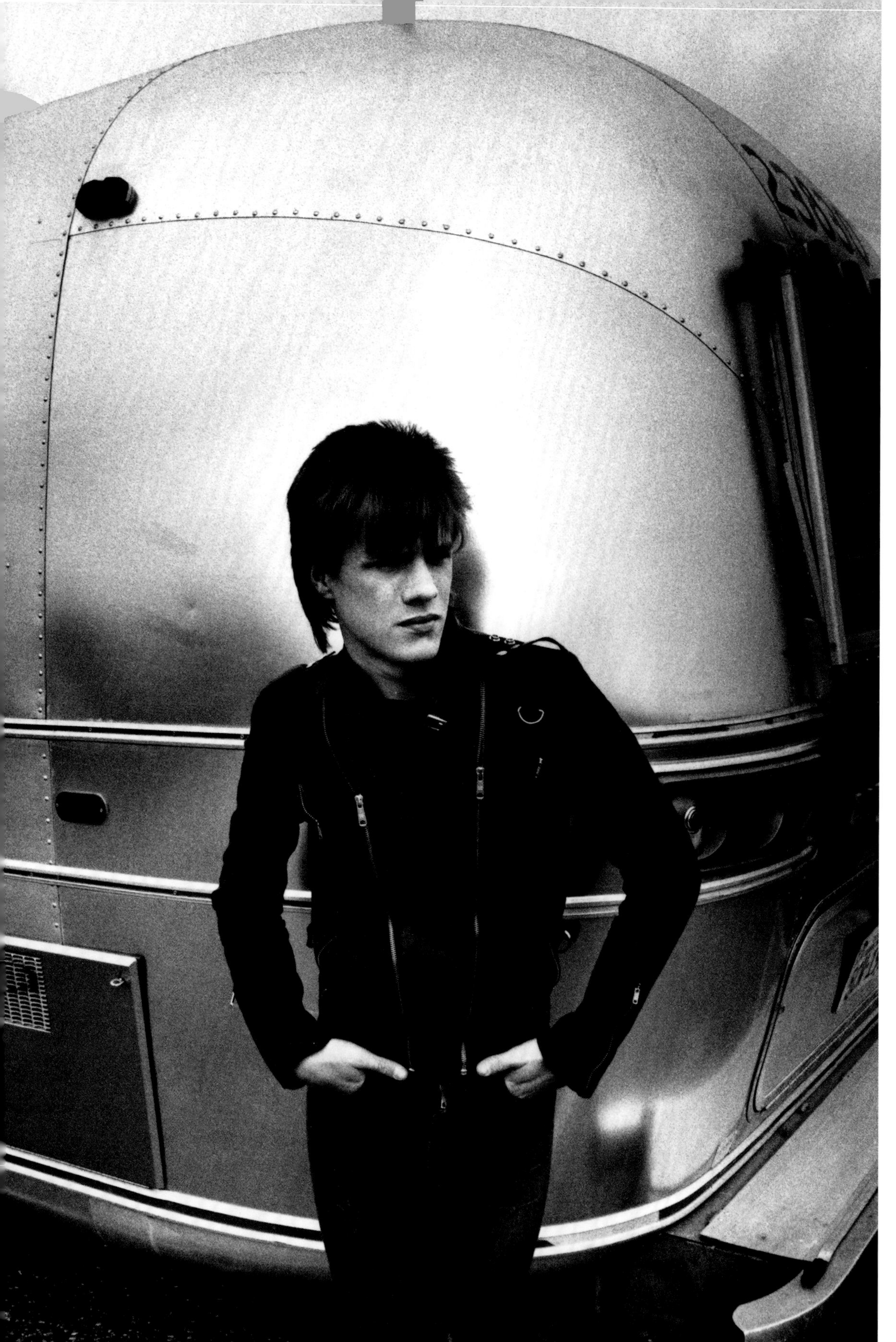

LARRY

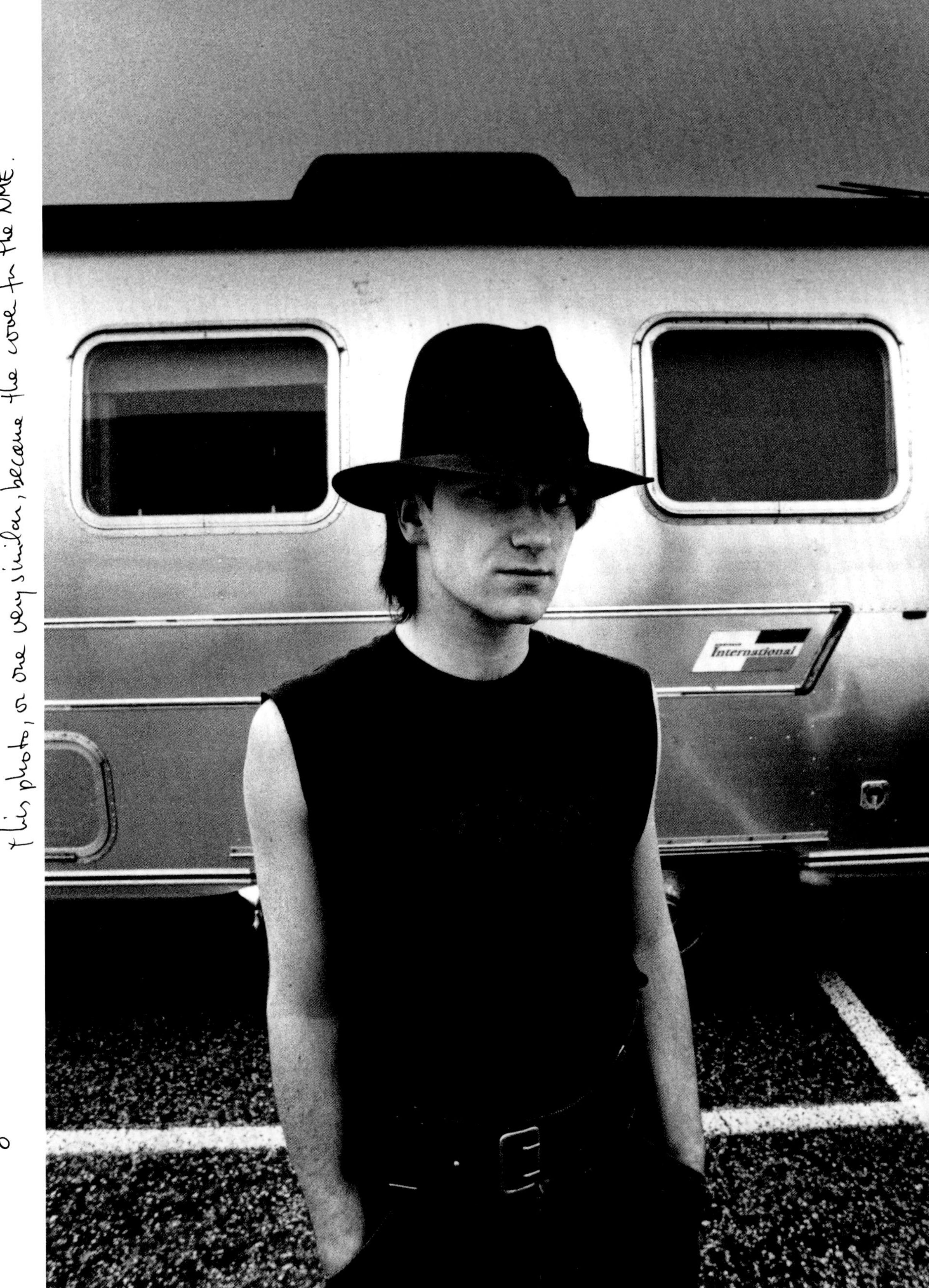

this photo, or one very similar, became the cover for the NME.

bono

COPENHAGEN

1982 december

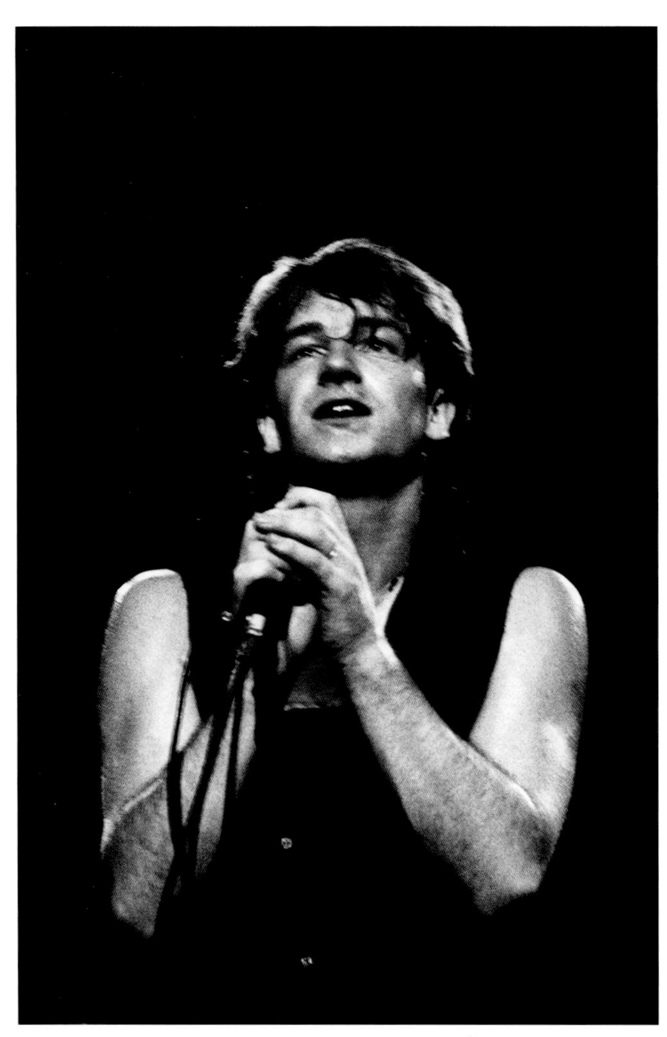

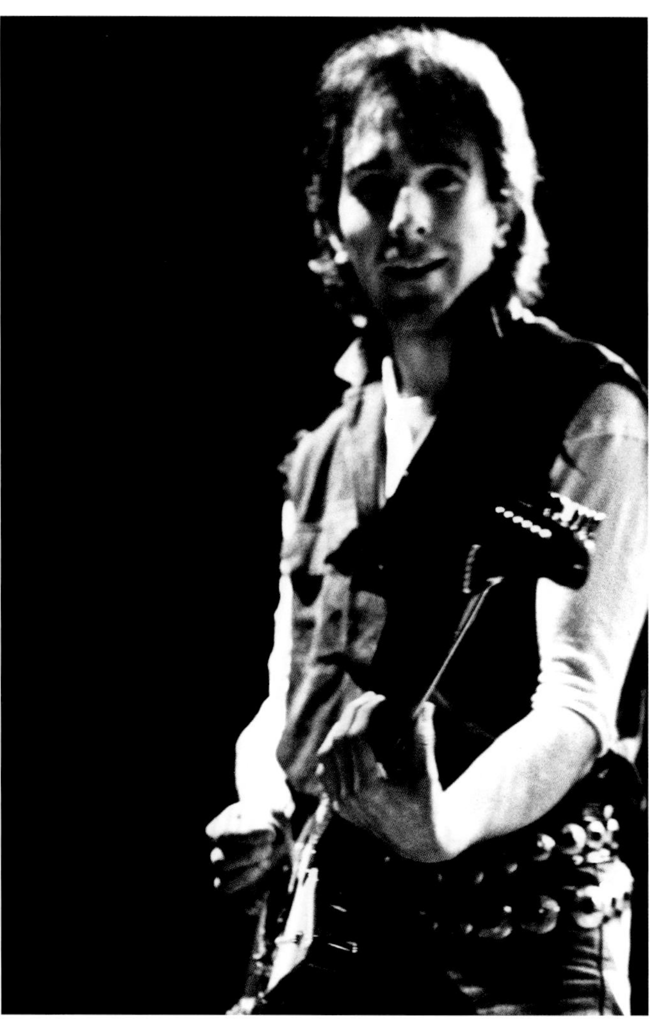

u2 had asked me to take some photos for their new album - it was a reaction to their liking my new orleans/austin photographs and i was very pleased. i flew to copenhagen and saw one of their 'pre-war' concerts that night before we headed off to sweden to shoot for the album.

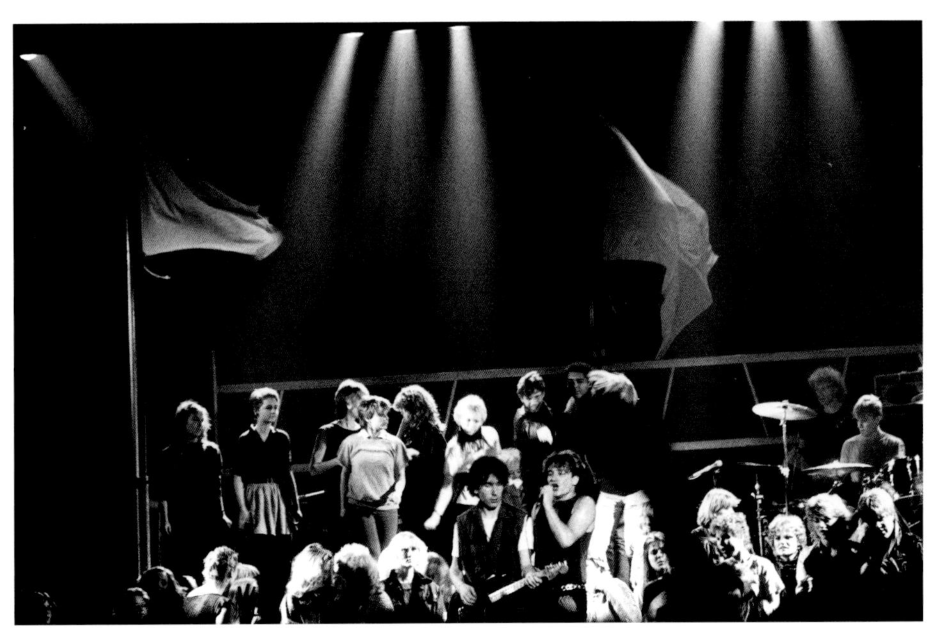

they had a stage with white flags and invited people from the audience to join them on stage. mostly girls by the look of it. a friend of theirs who lived in copenhagen, played electric violin for one or two songs that night. forgot his name.

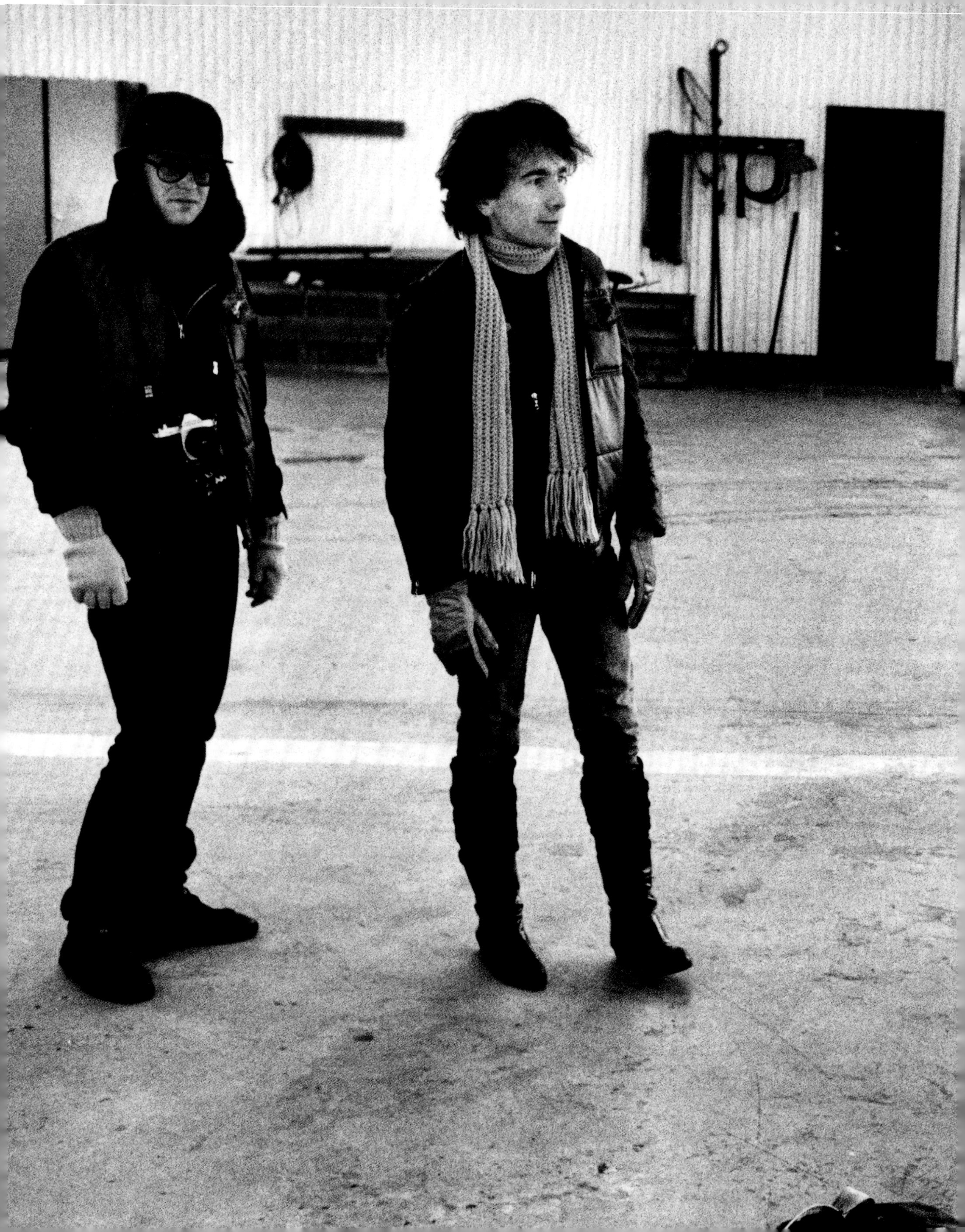

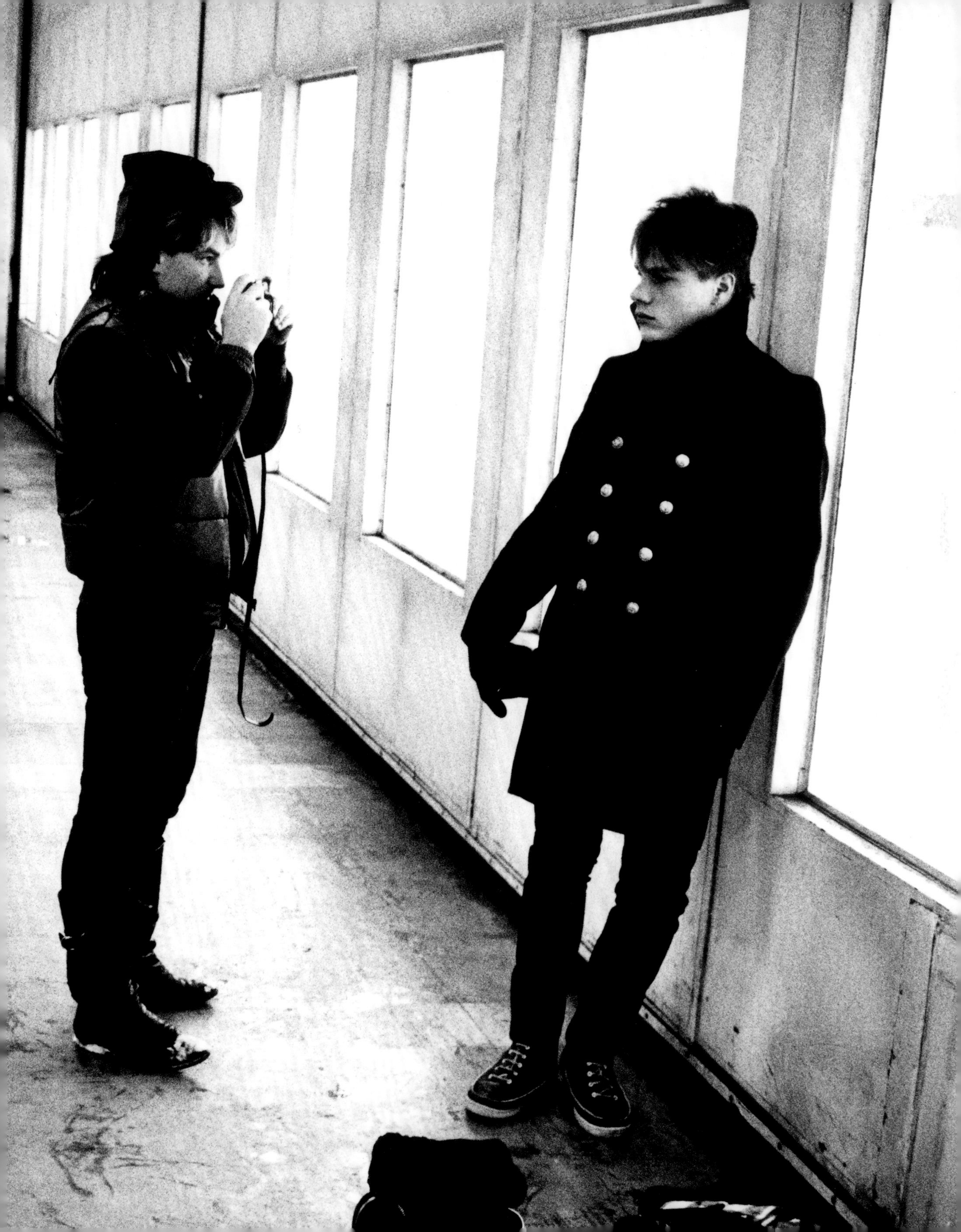

SWEDEN

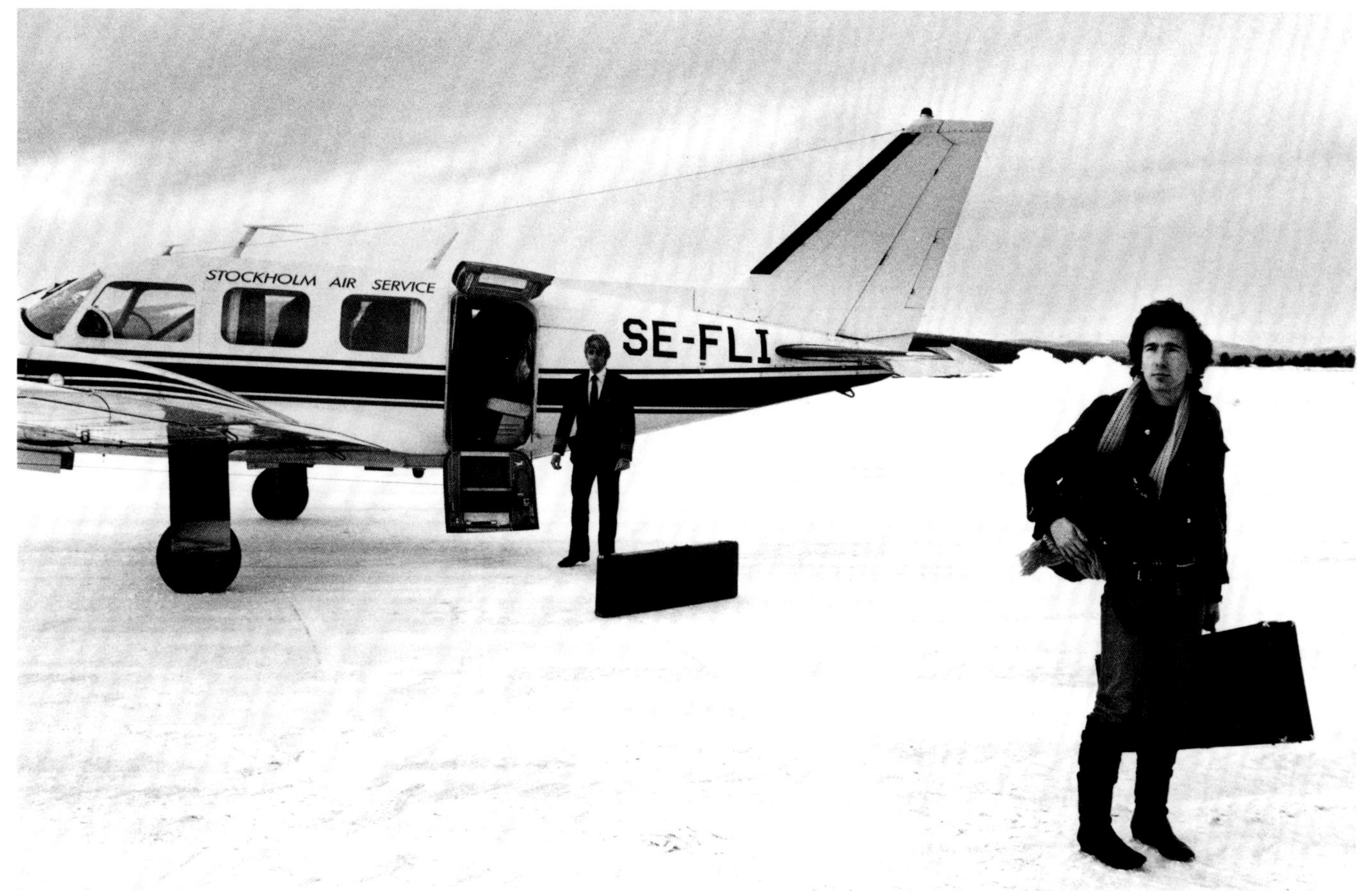

we flew from stockholm to another airport north of stockholm and (can't remember the name of airport.) from there we were to go by helicopter to the location of the videoshoot for 'new year's day'. on the previous spread you see the band waiting, killing time before getting into the helicopter.

december 1982

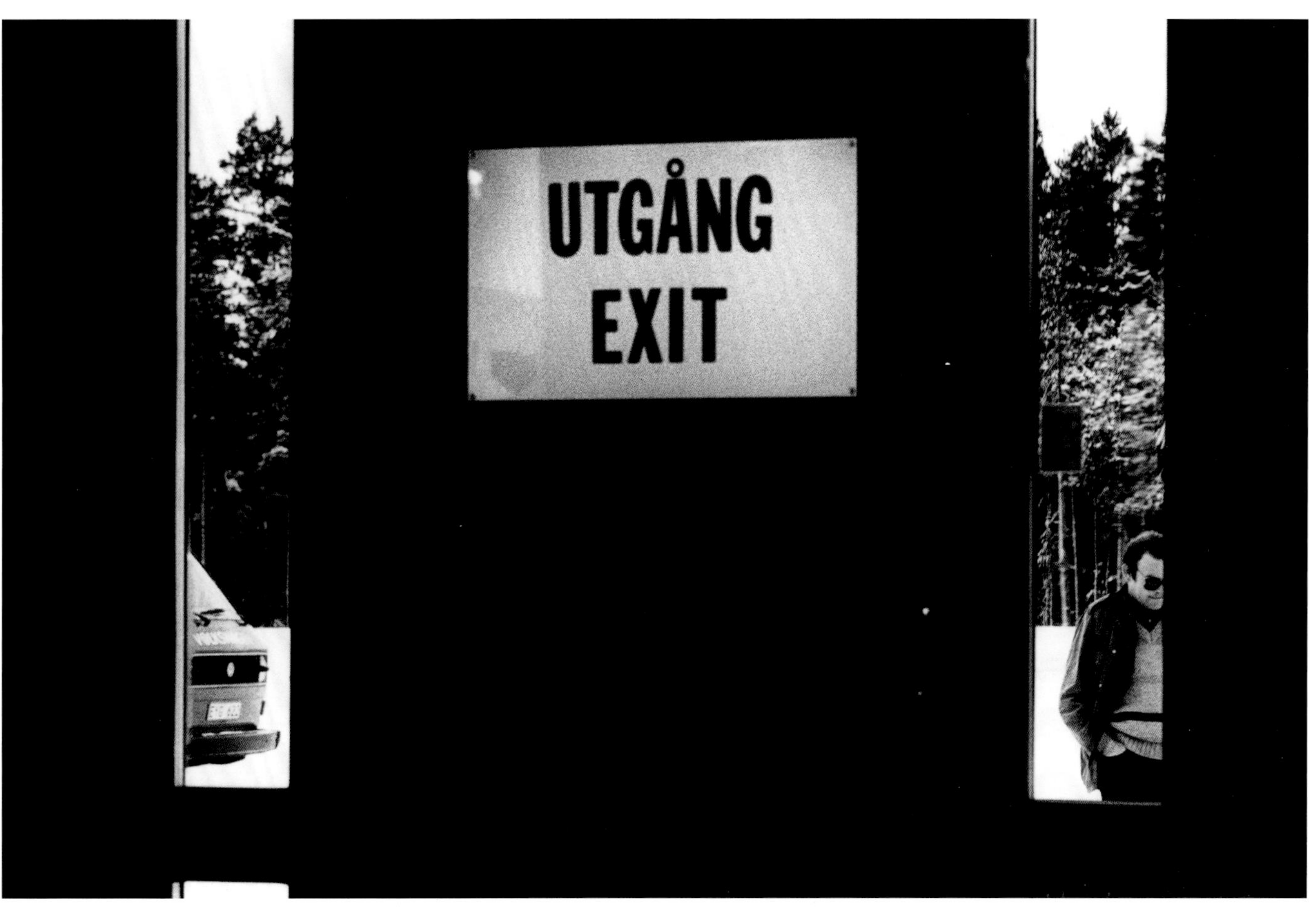

as the helicopter only a handful of people, paul mcguinness and myself had to stay behind and await its return to fly us also the video shoot. the helicopter didn't come back for hours though as the video director decided to use it for some aerial shots. paul was livid having to wait without knowing what was going on, this is pre-mobile phones, and is seen here pacing up and down outside the airport building.

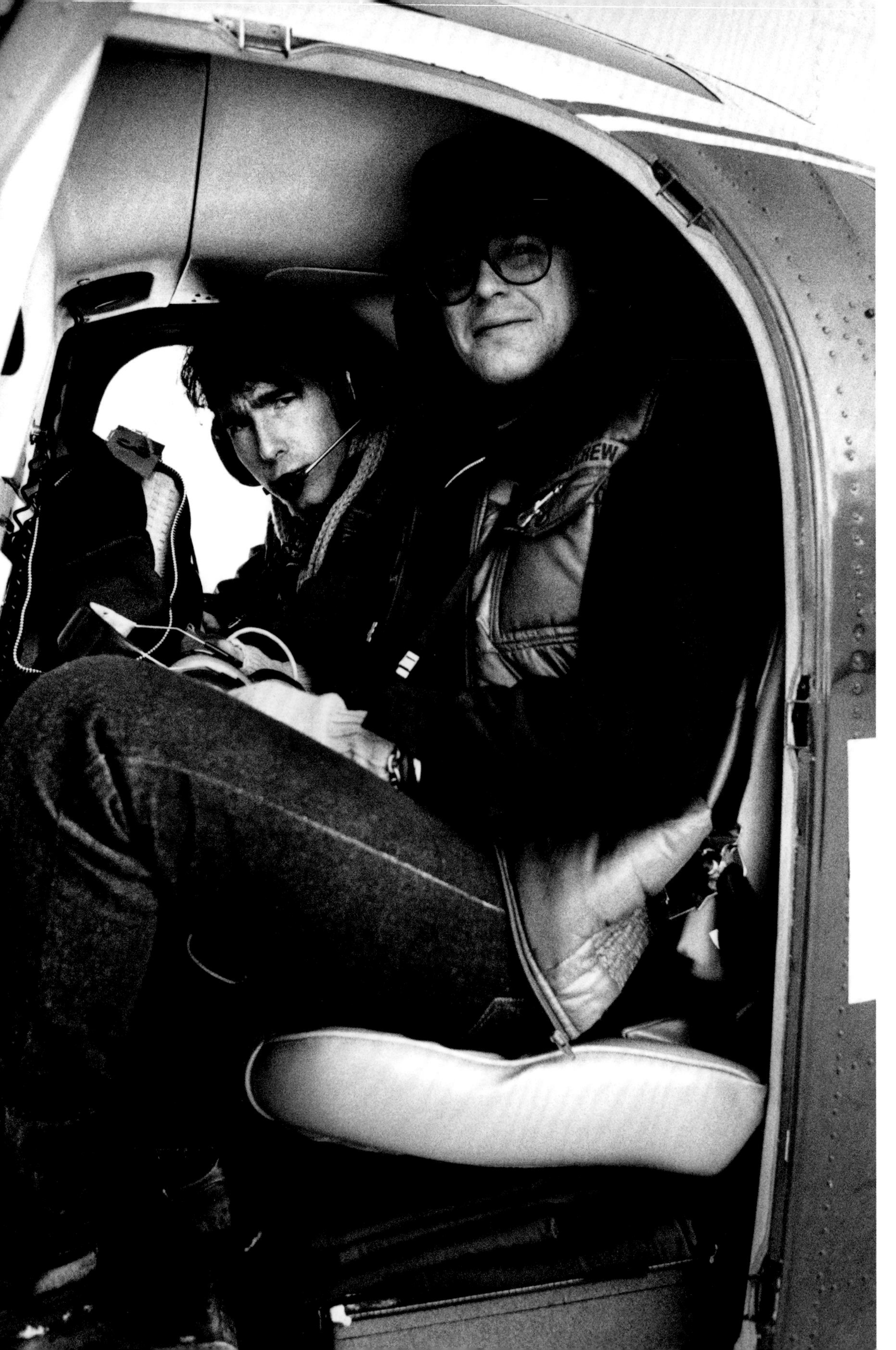

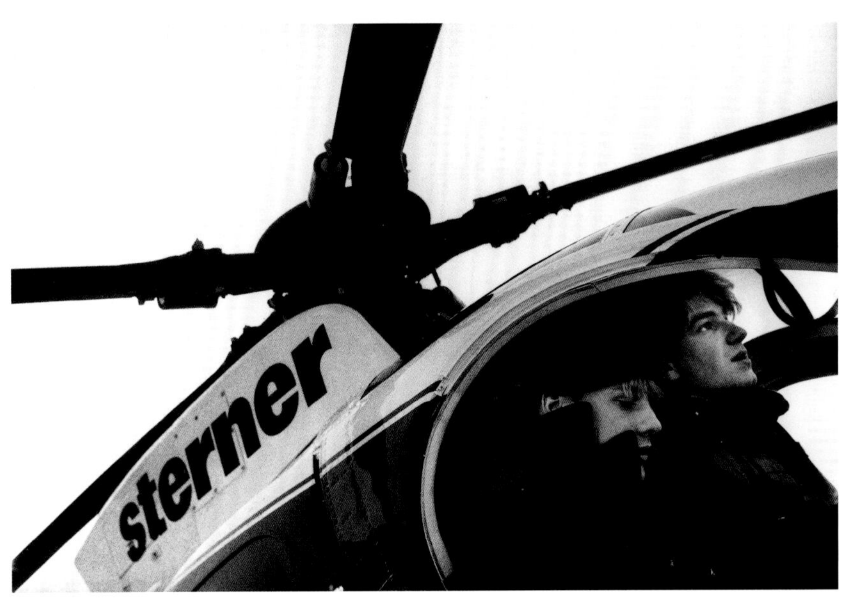

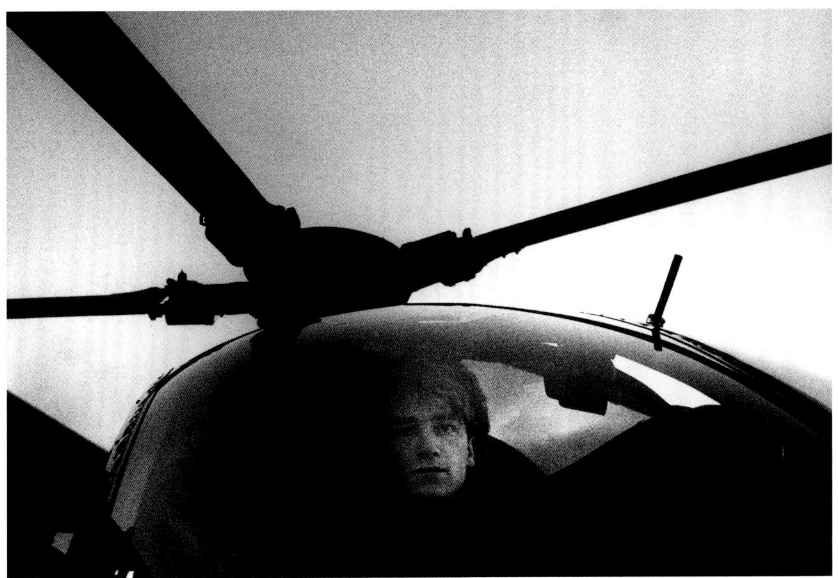

this is the photo that bono refers to in the interview.

this photo was after much discussion used as the gatefold (inner) photo for the war album. thanks to steve averill, the designer, who argued my case.

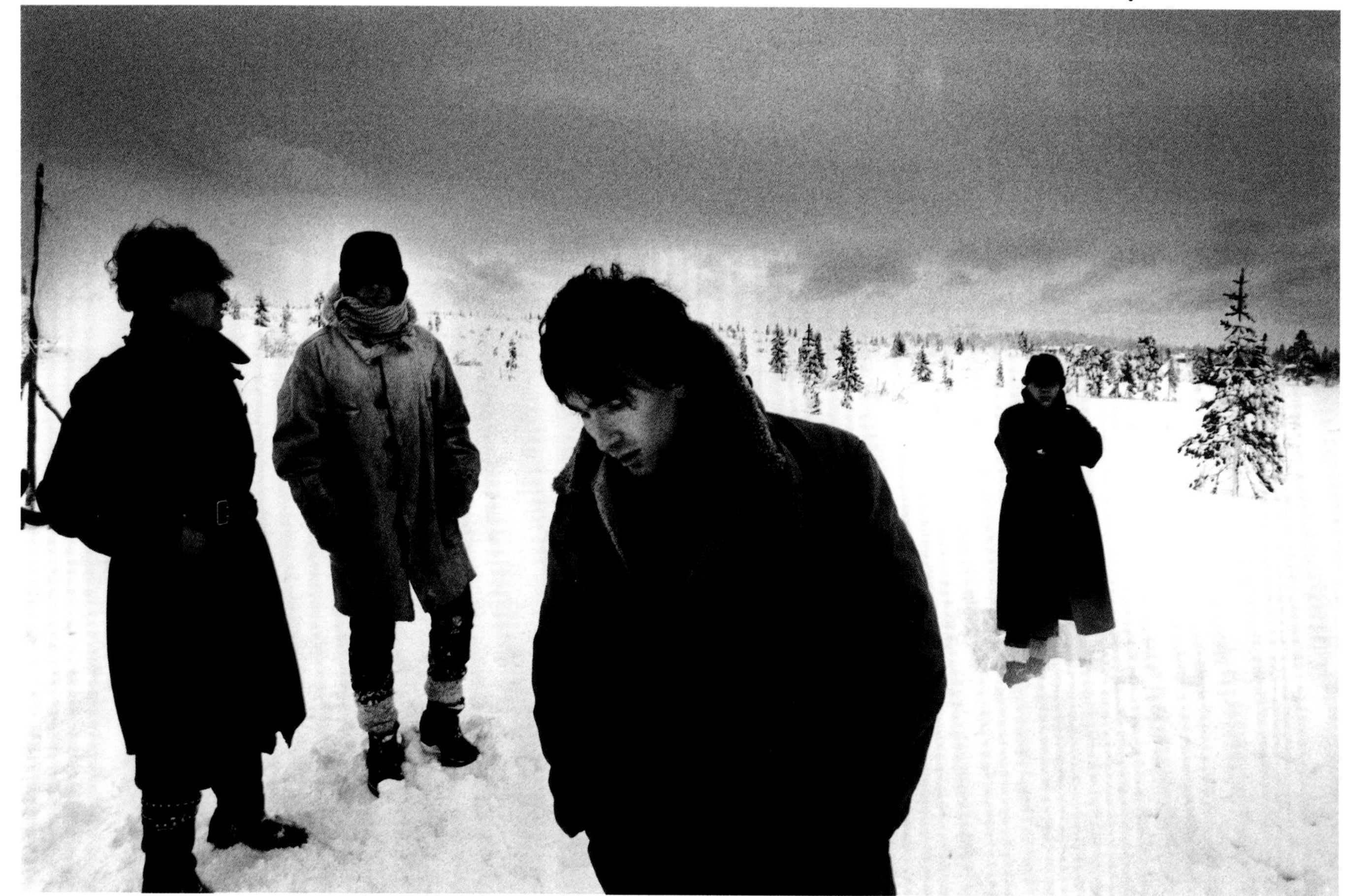

when the helicopter finally picked us up and dropped paul and me at the videoplace, i had to run to where the action was in order to get any photos at all as daylight is sparse in scandinavia in the winter. before my fingers froze i managed to take a few photos of them playing the song and a few posed photos. i was happy it was brief as i am not cut out for the cold.

in the evening, well 4pm onwards, the videoshoot moved to another location where
the band played the song around a campfire. i couldn't get close enough
to this fire.

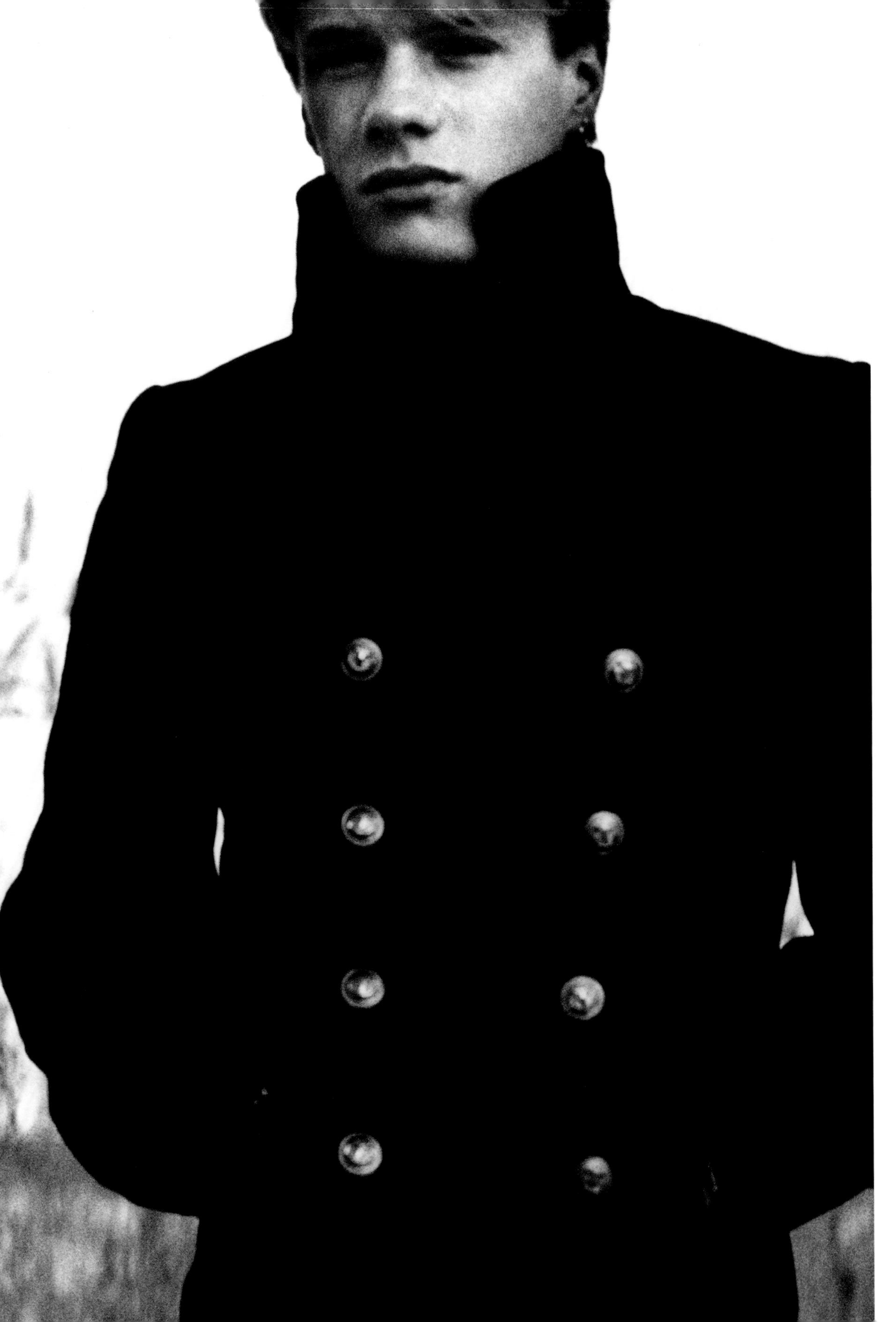

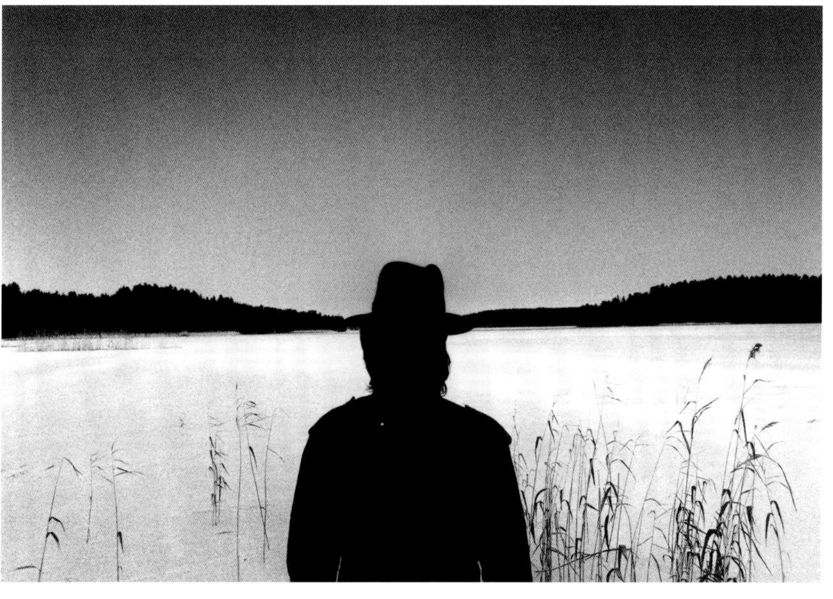

s we ended up
ith little time
n photographs
ing the video-
oot, we took
hour the next
ay to shoot
bit more,
omewhere near
tockholm. it
was a beautiful,
unny day and
used the graphics of the frozen lake to blend in with bono facing the lake.
on the left is larry at the same location.

IRELAND feb. 1983

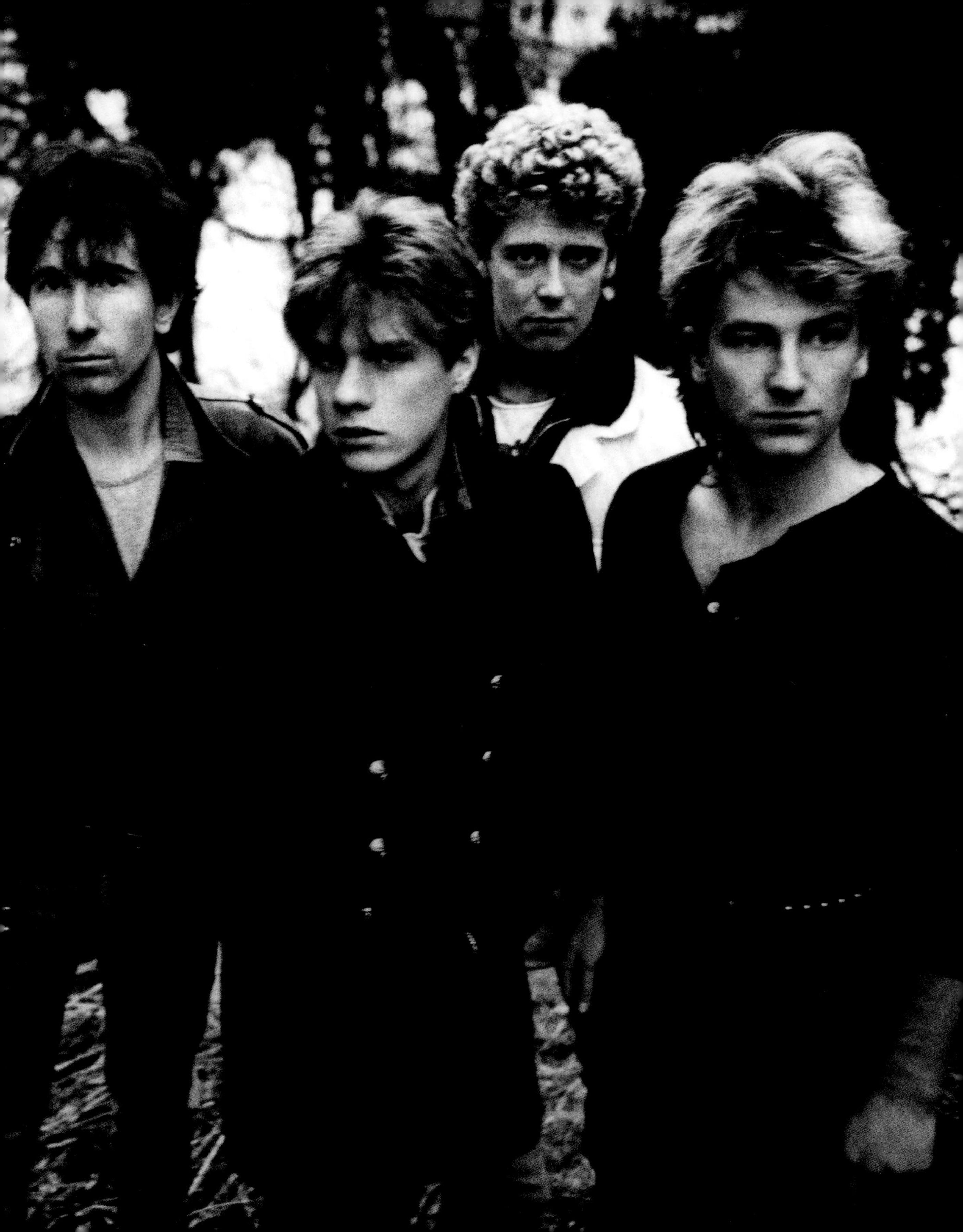

i think it was Valentine's day that

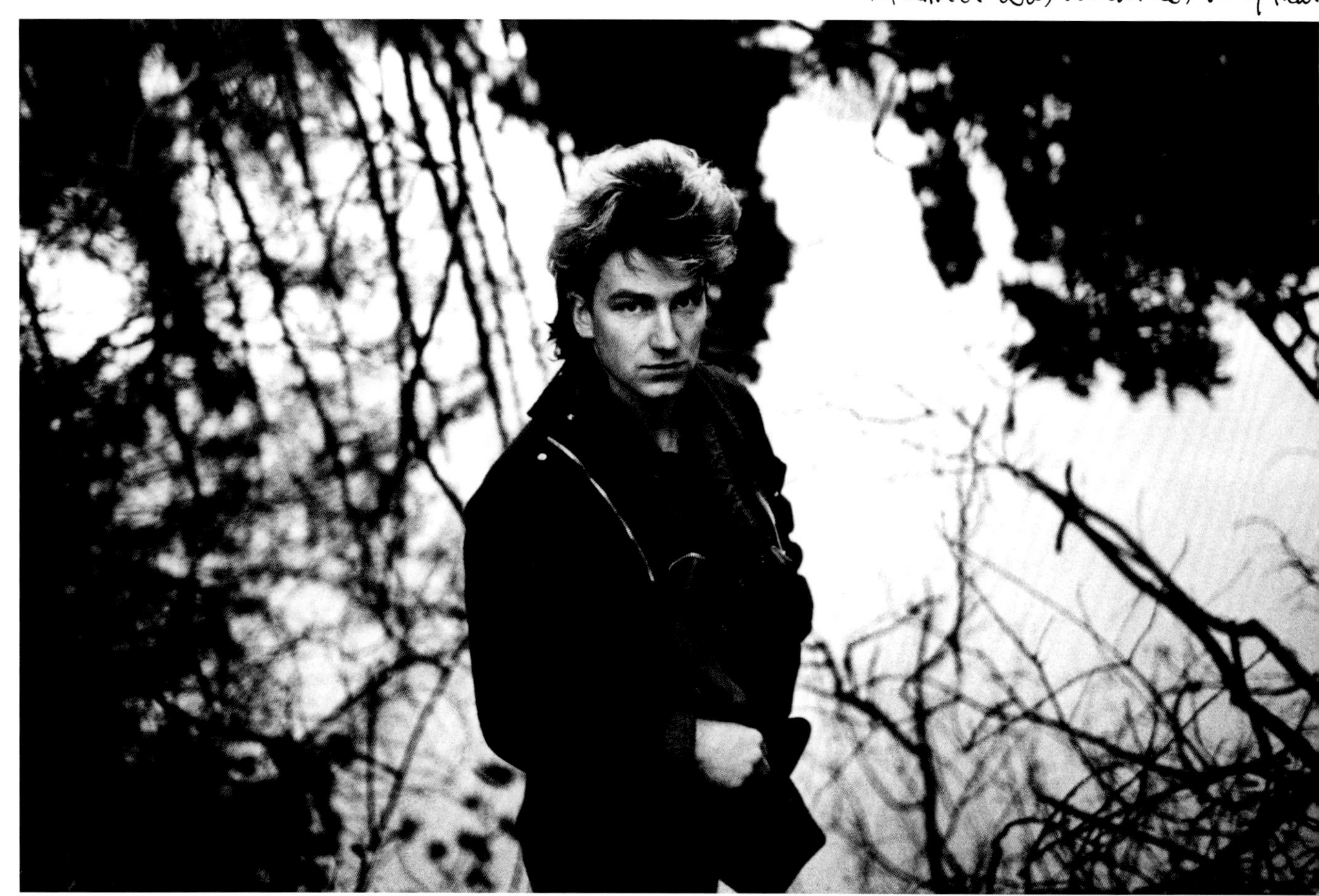

once again this was a shoot for the NME, and again for the cover. I had seen the cover for WAR by that time and wanted to do some photos of Peter Rowan (the 'boy') who was featured on the album cover and the band as i had never seen them together on a photo. we went to Peter's family to ask permission and once given we drove out into the countryside looking for a suitable location. we stumbled upon this amazing, fairy tale lake pond and took most of the photos there. the light was really beautifull and the feeling at the place a little eerie

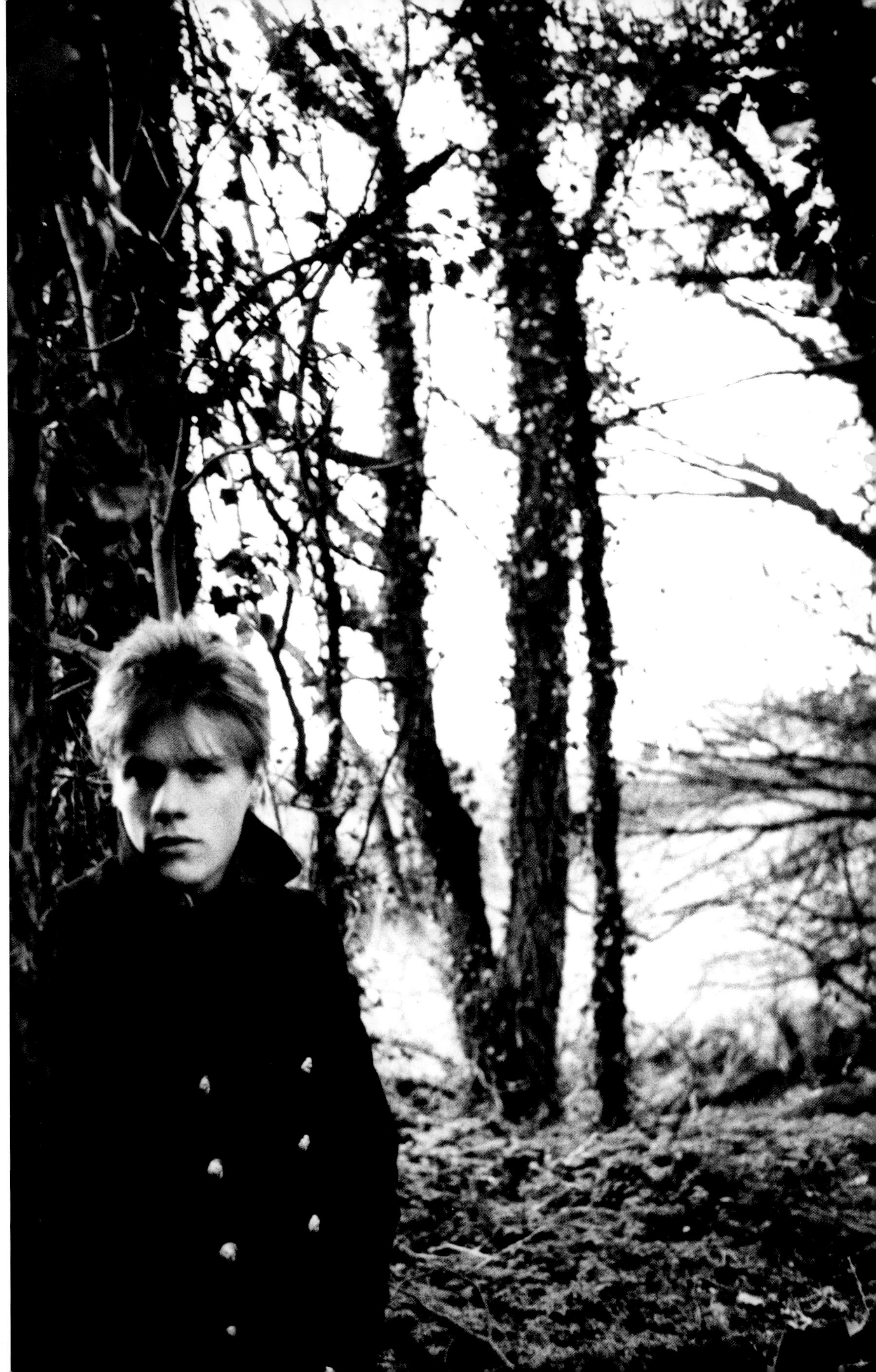

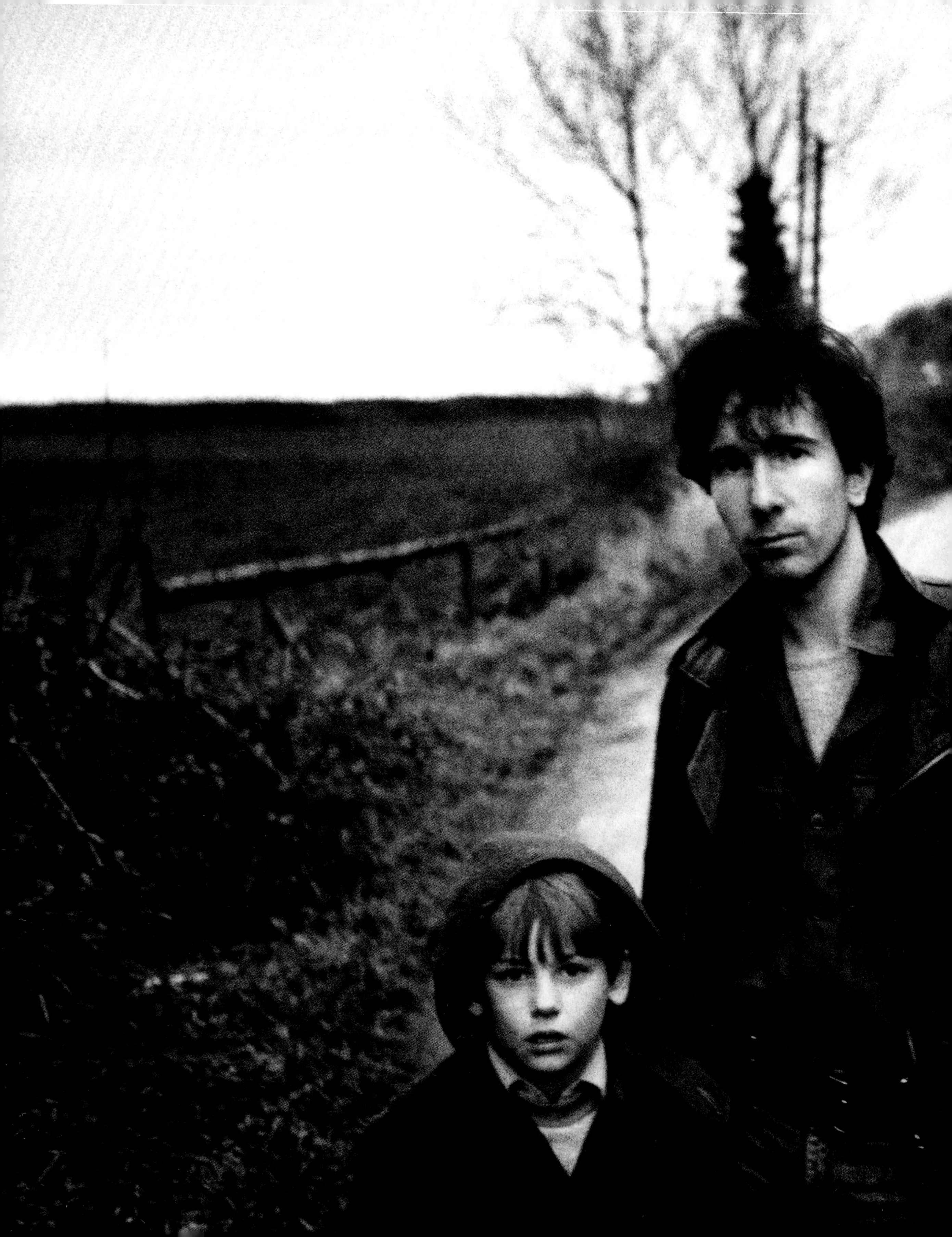

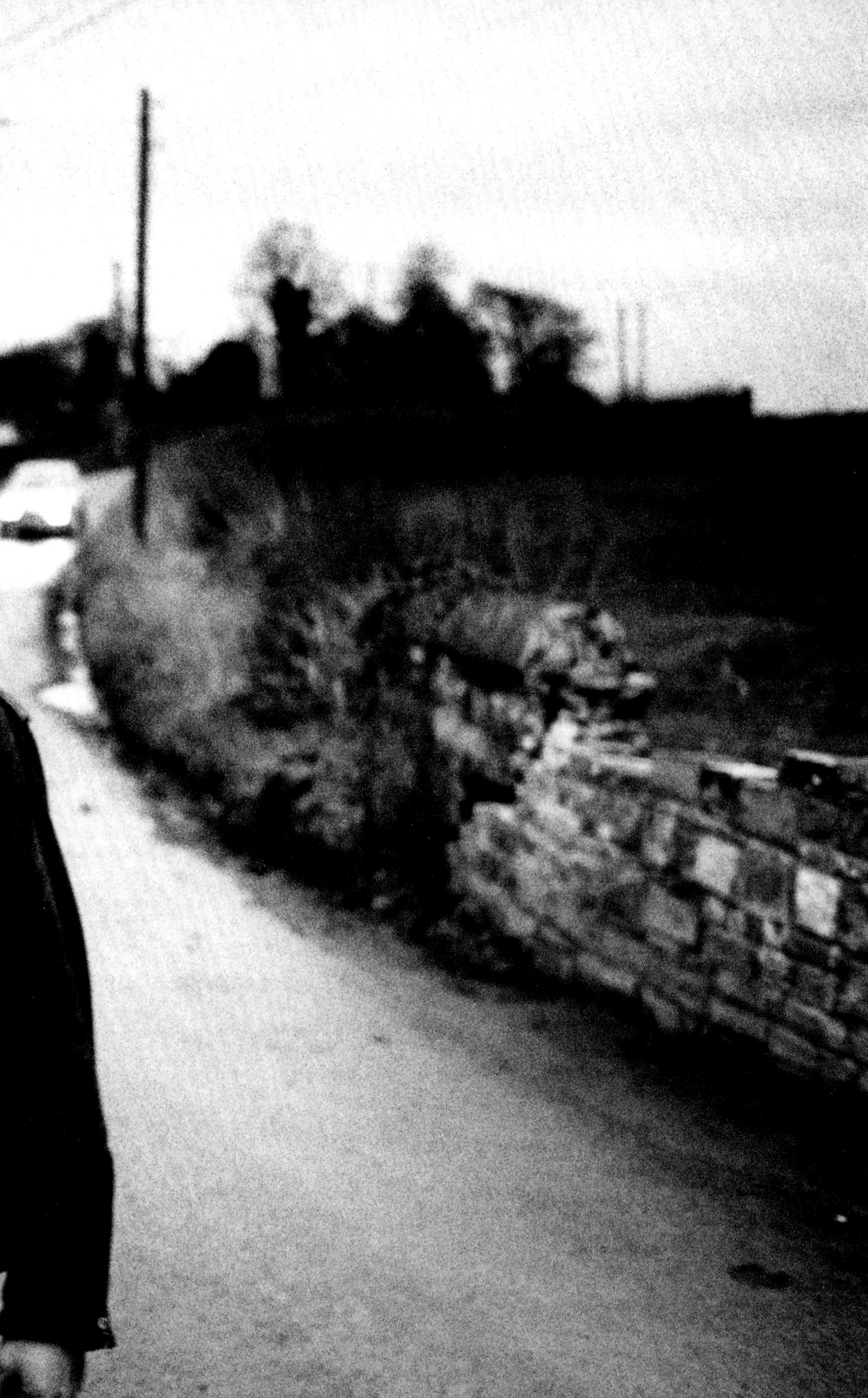

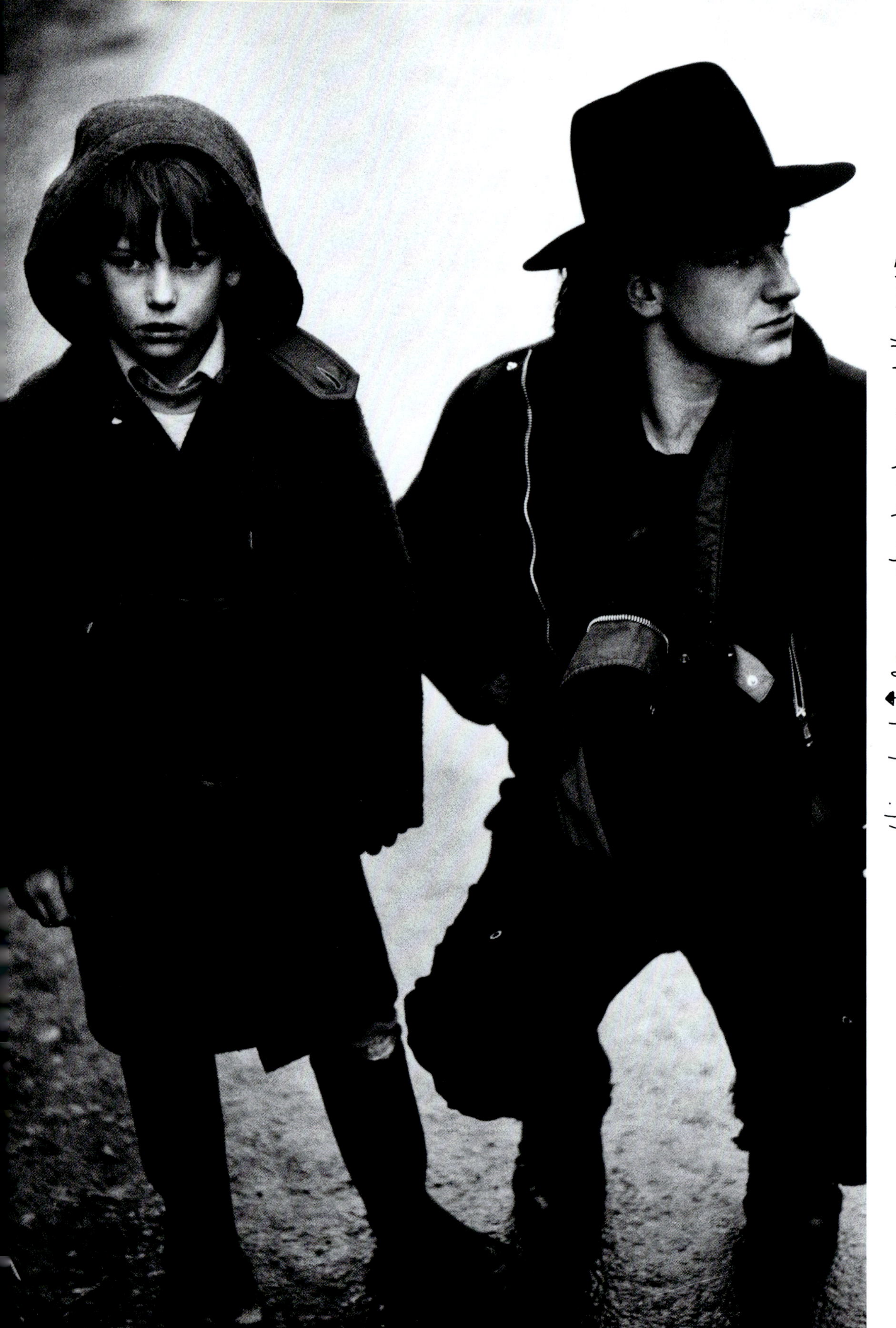

this photo ↑ became the front cover of the NME

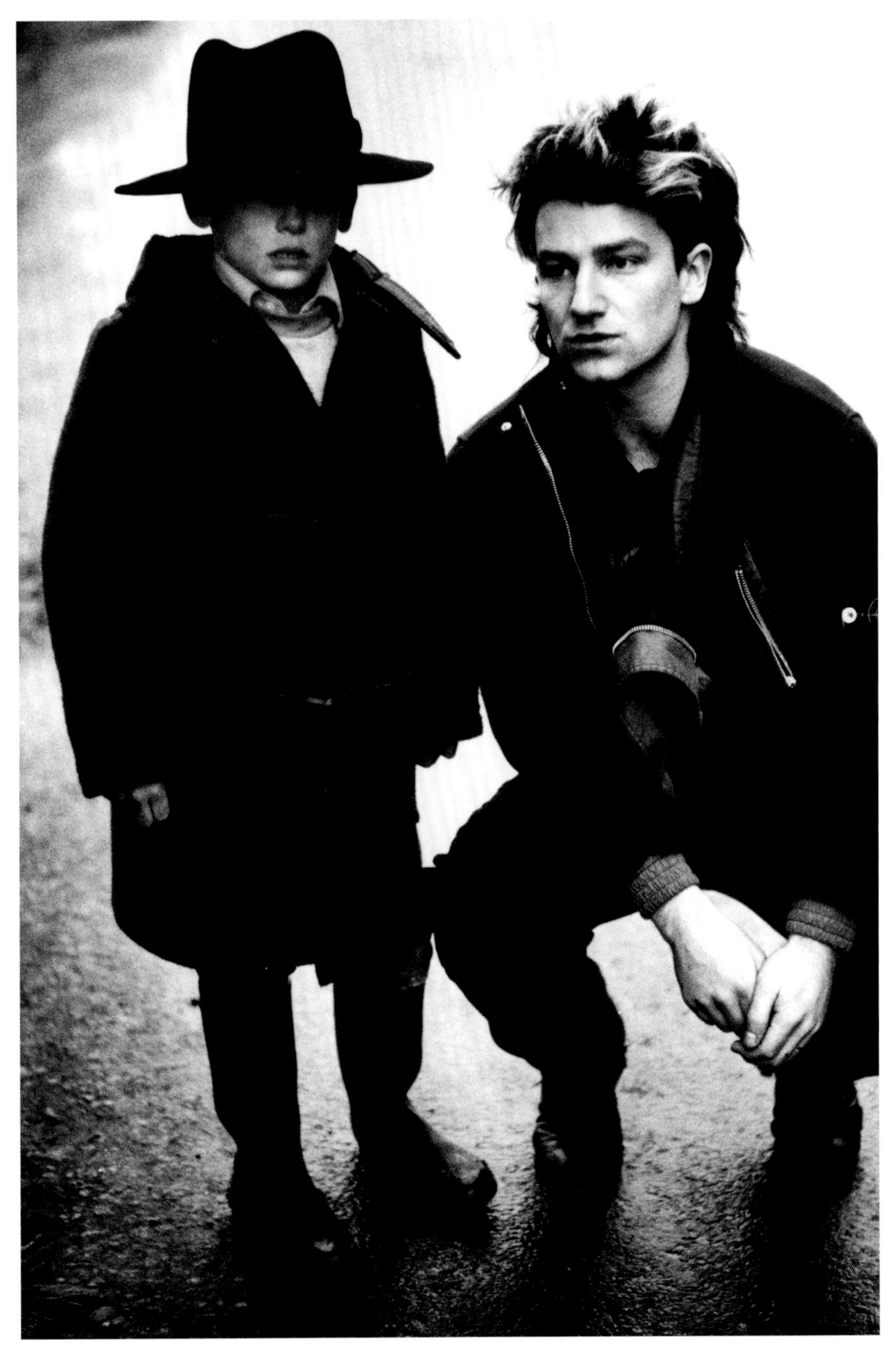

Peter wearing Bono's hat – this was the start of a habit of exchanging accessories for photographs; we will see more of this in future shoots.

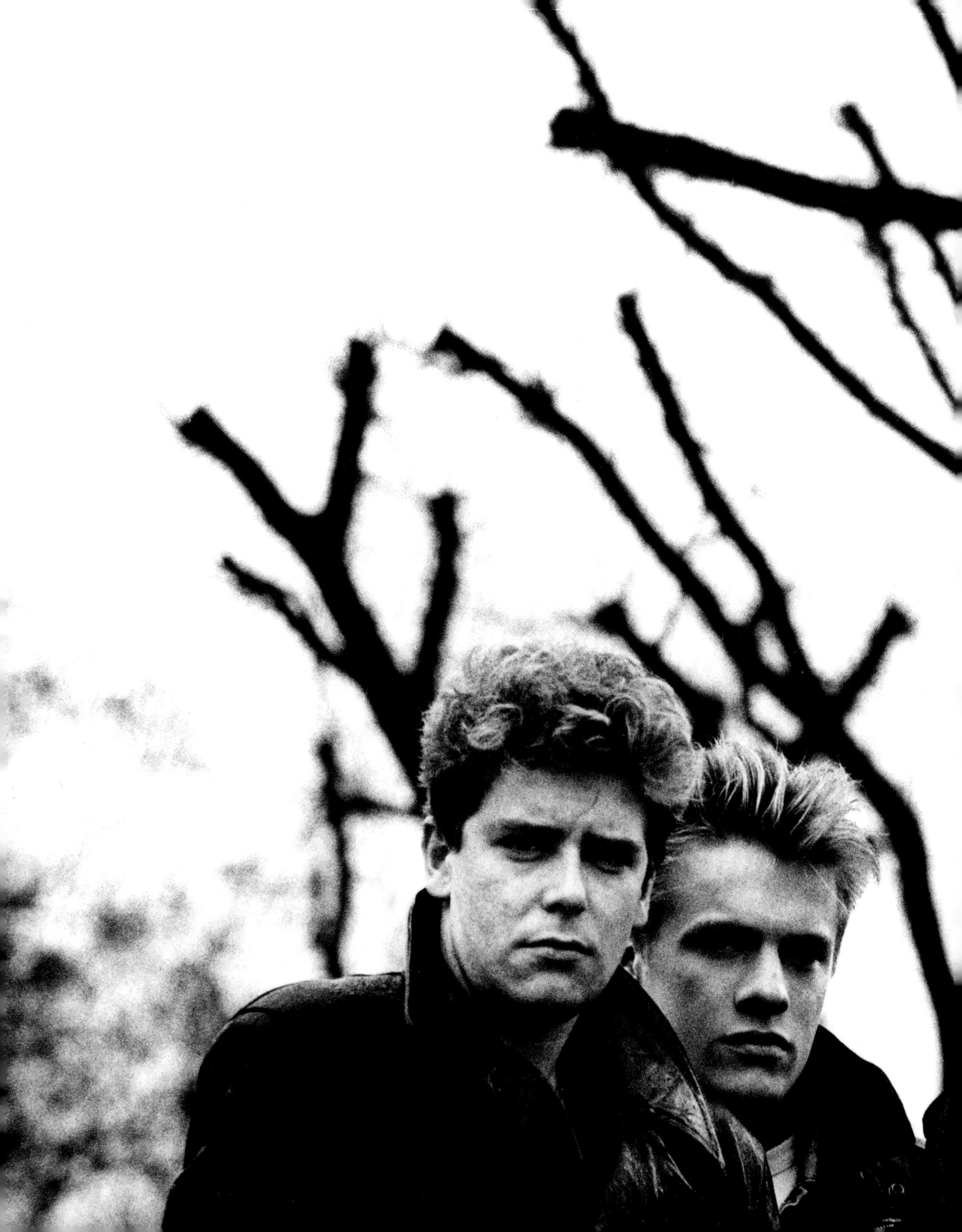

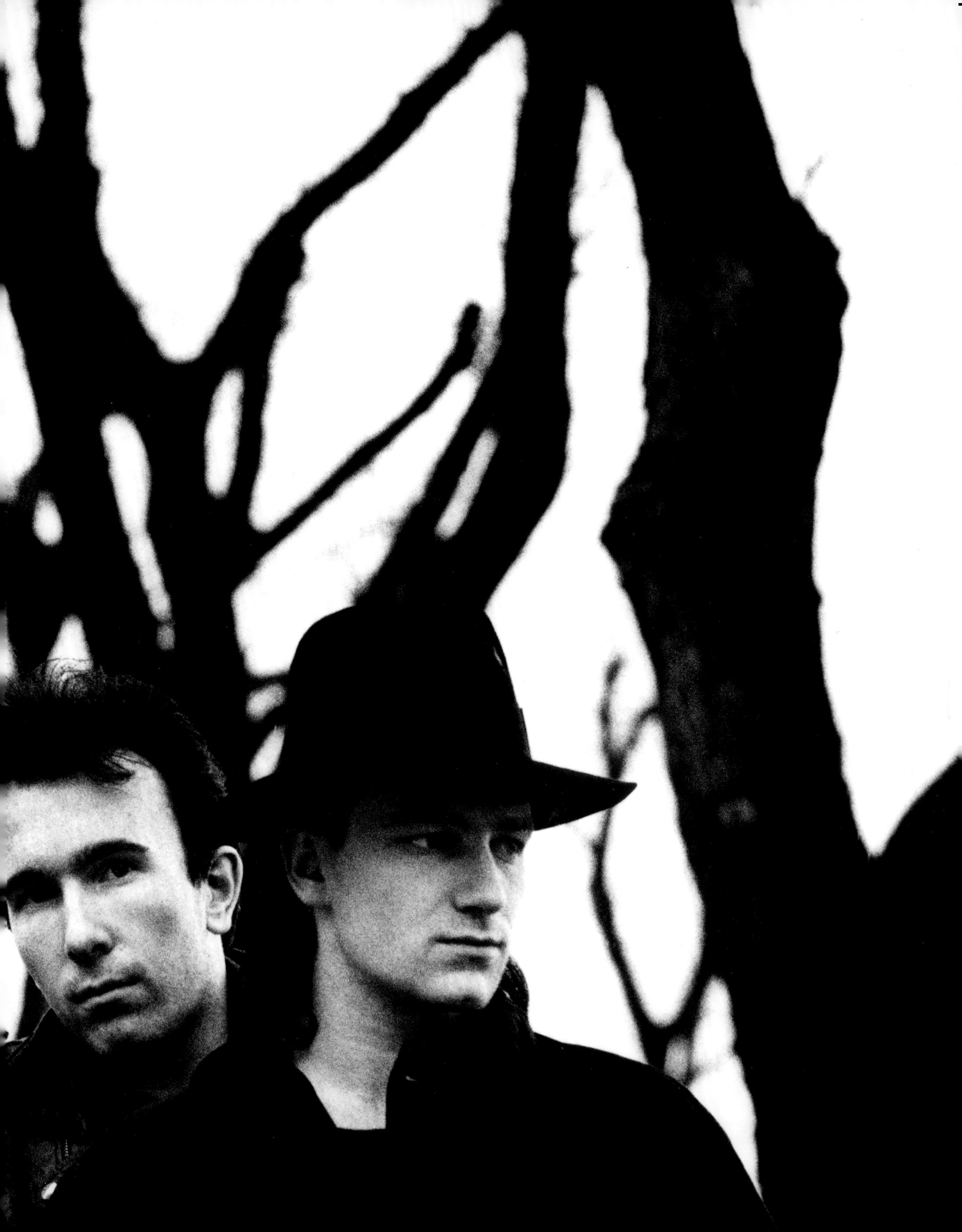

PARIS
1983 march

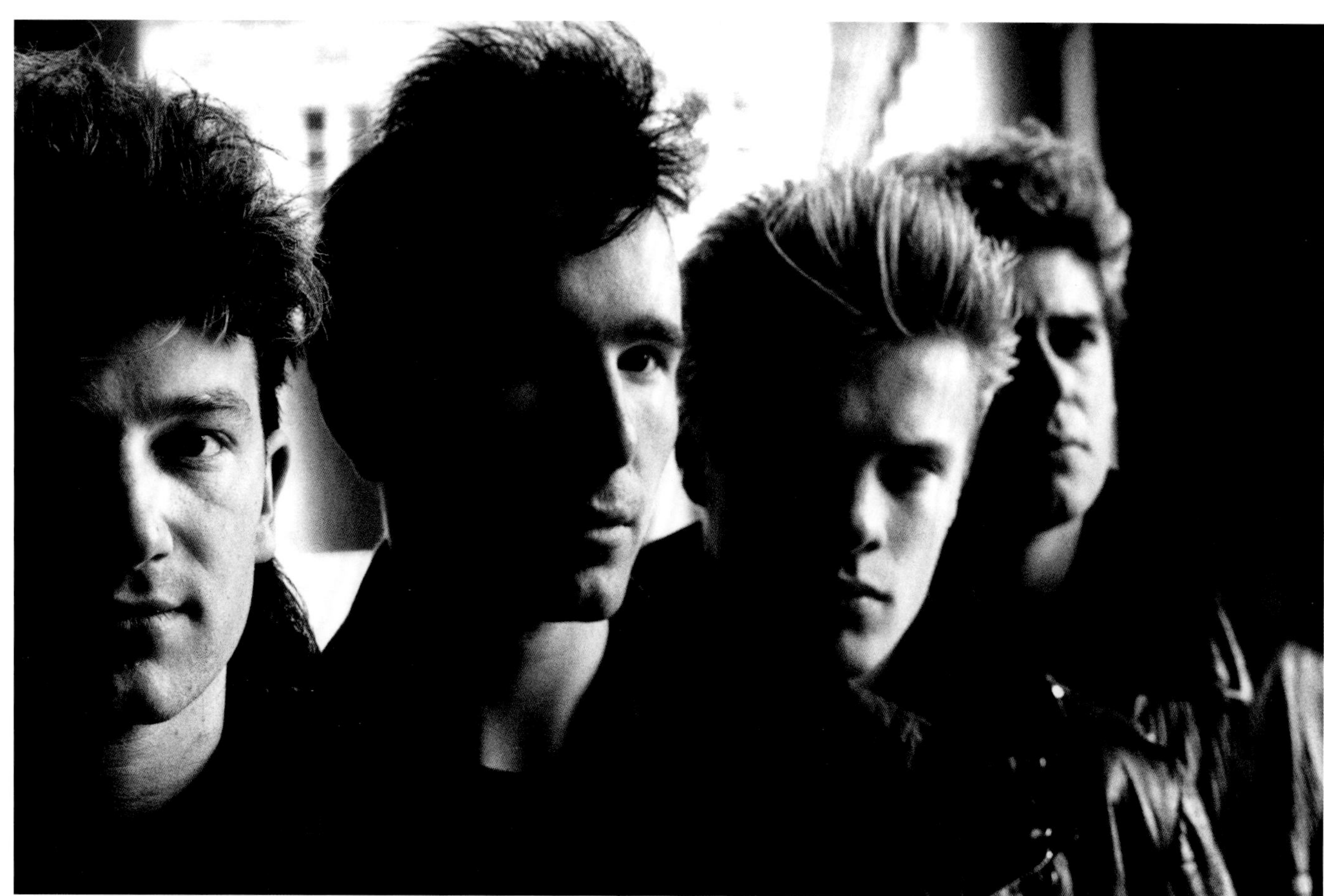

Paris in the rain – we are standing underneath something, some gallery ceiling, doing some photos quite quickly. i had parked my car very badly in a sideroad and when i got back to it there were at least a dozen parisien drivers ready to have a go at whoever was blocking the whole street. i ran and drove off. je m'excuse!

the photo overleaf was taken near the sacre coeur and a similar photo was used for the cover of 'pride' and made into a backdrop for the stage of the subsequent tour.

this is the back of the Notre Dame

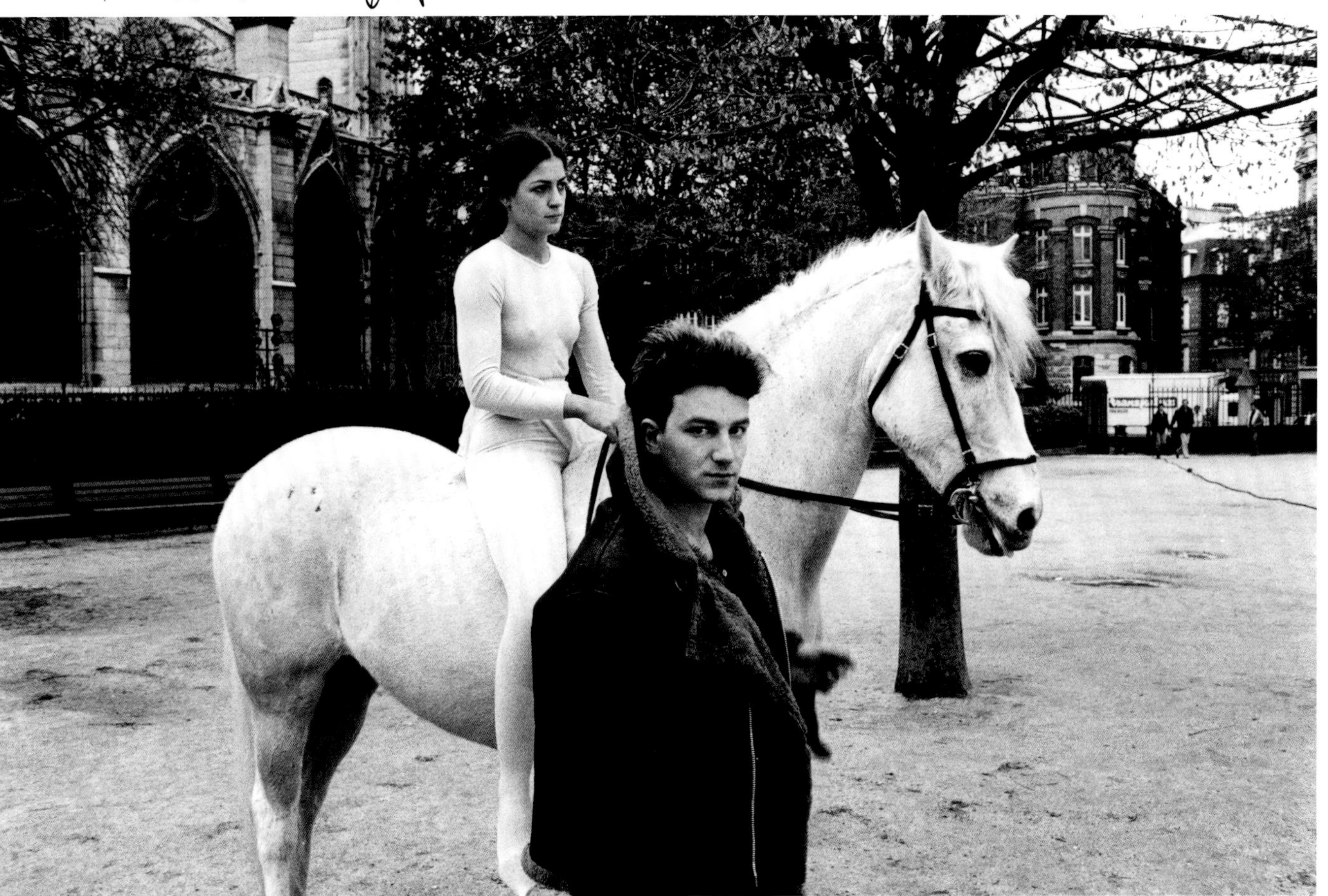

we were in paris for the video making of 'two hearts beat as one' and most of it was filmed around the sacre coeur. i had suggested to make a video of 2 people having sex but it wasn't taken up. the girl and the horse are 'extras' in the video.

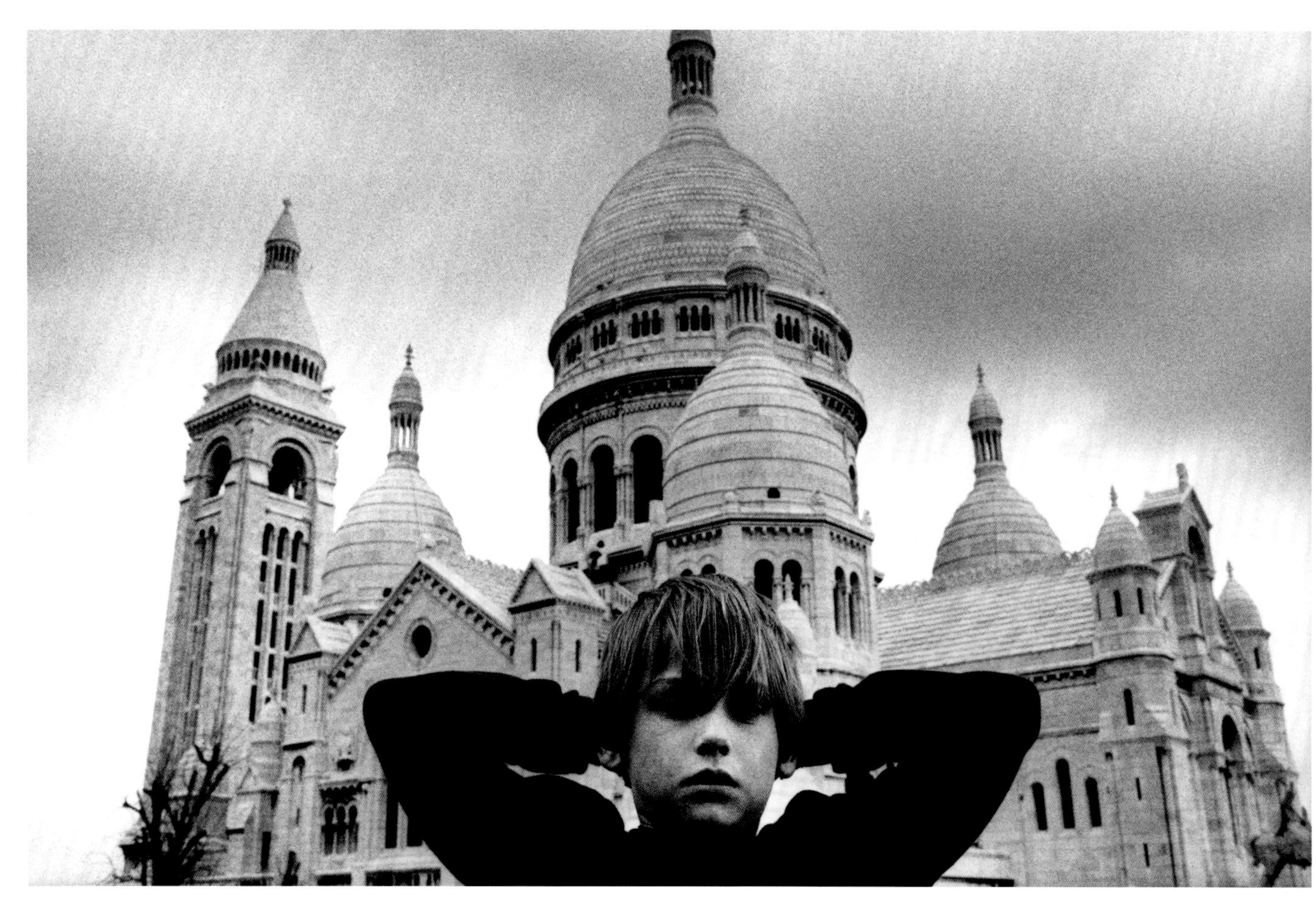

i was trying to copy the pose peter had for the WAR cover with the same coeur behind him. he had (and probably still has) such a great and strong facial expression.

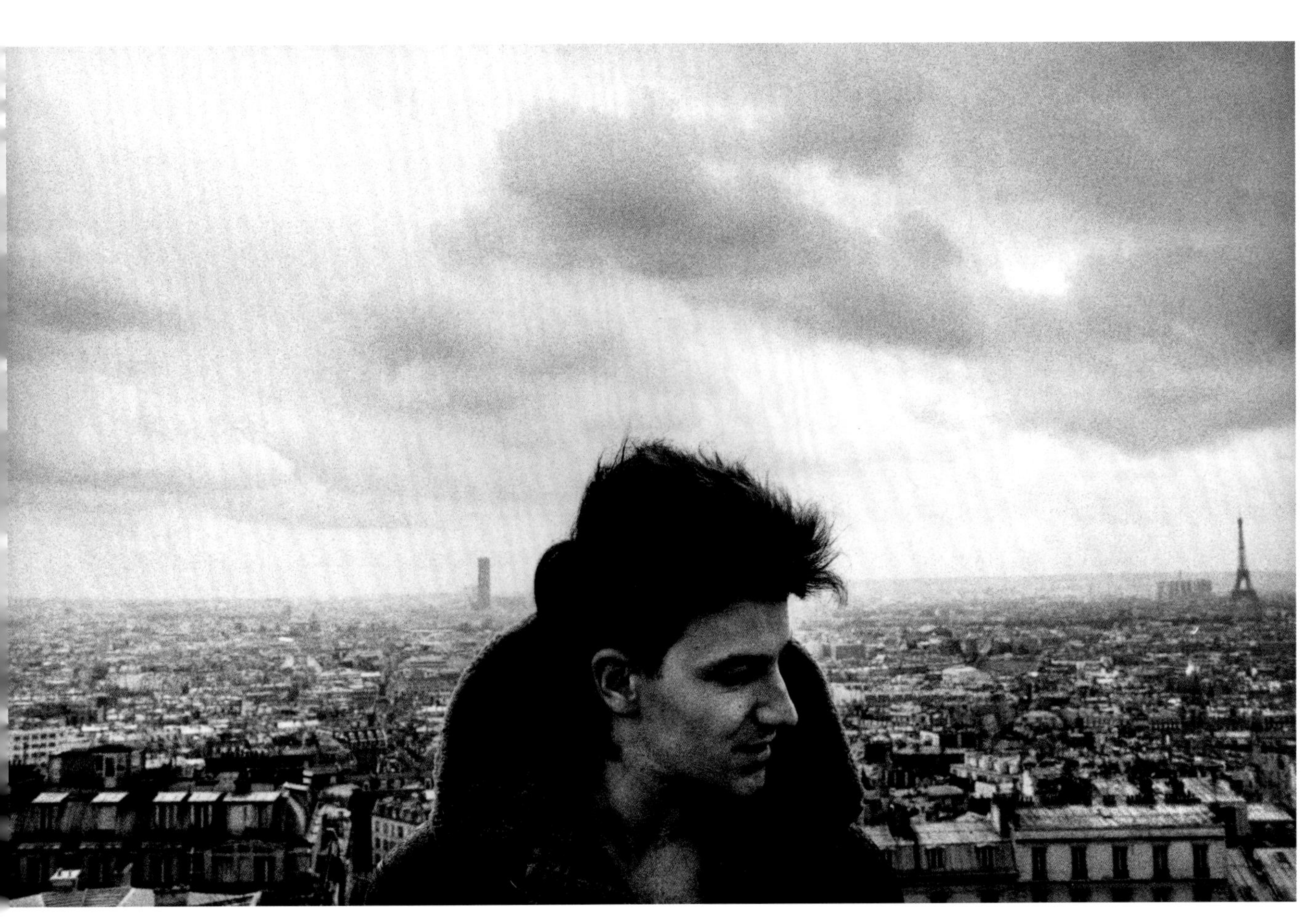

this, for a long time, was one of my favorite photos of Bono.

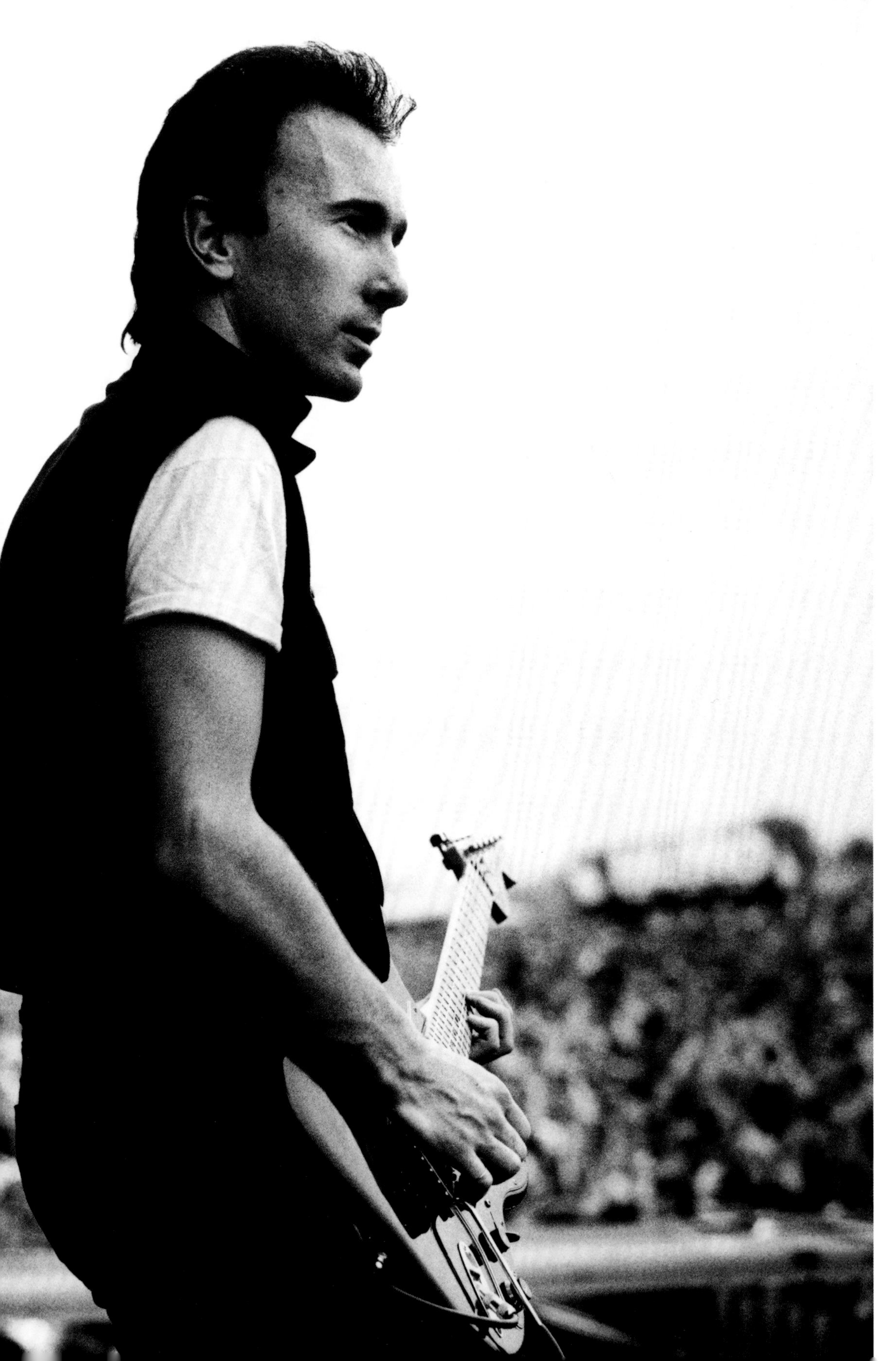

BELGIUM
1983
july

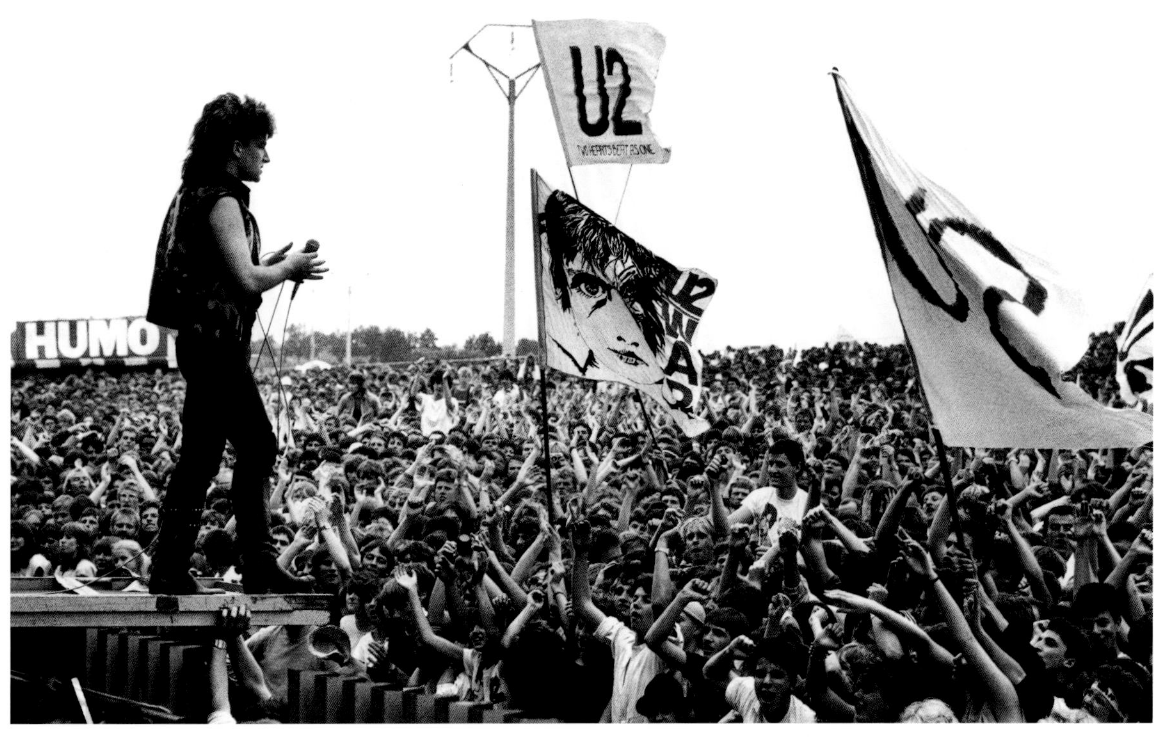

U2 played a couple of festivals in europe in the summer of 1983 and these photos were taken at one of the 2 festivaldays they played in belgium. i can't recall if this was at torhout or at werchter, 2 places in belgium that both have the same festival, a day apart. the use of the white flag at U2 shows some took hold overhere.

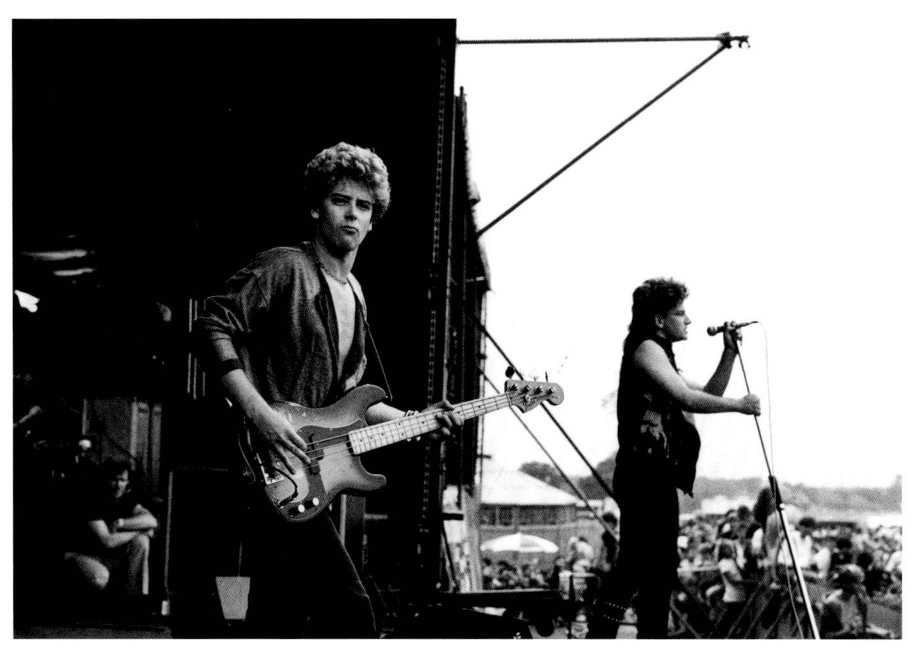

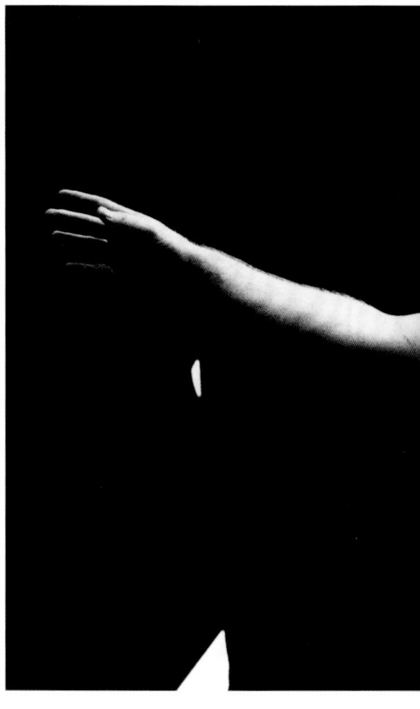

as i have never considered myself much of a concert-photographer, although i have a large archive of it since that was what i started with in the early 70's, you won't find too many 'live' photos in this book. i use them more to accentuate changes of their concert-concepts and/or stage-designs.

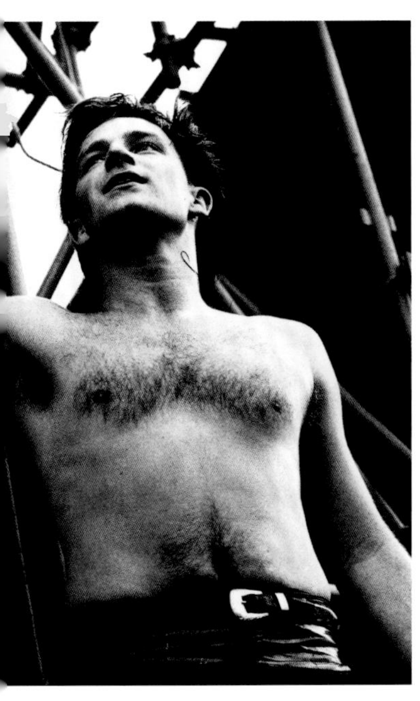

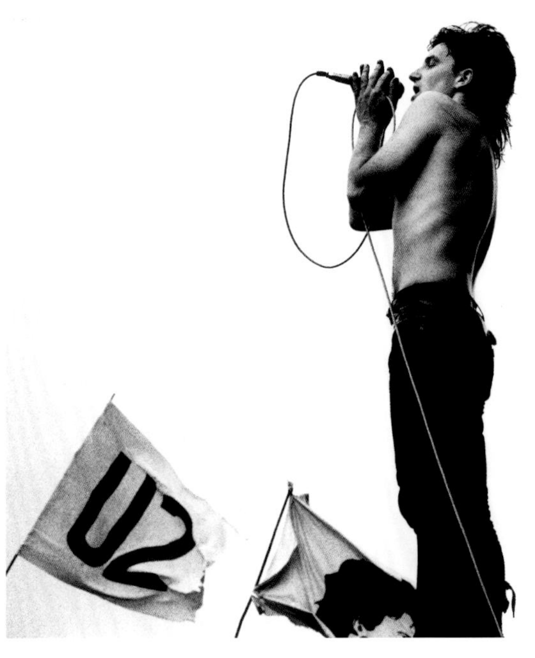
U2

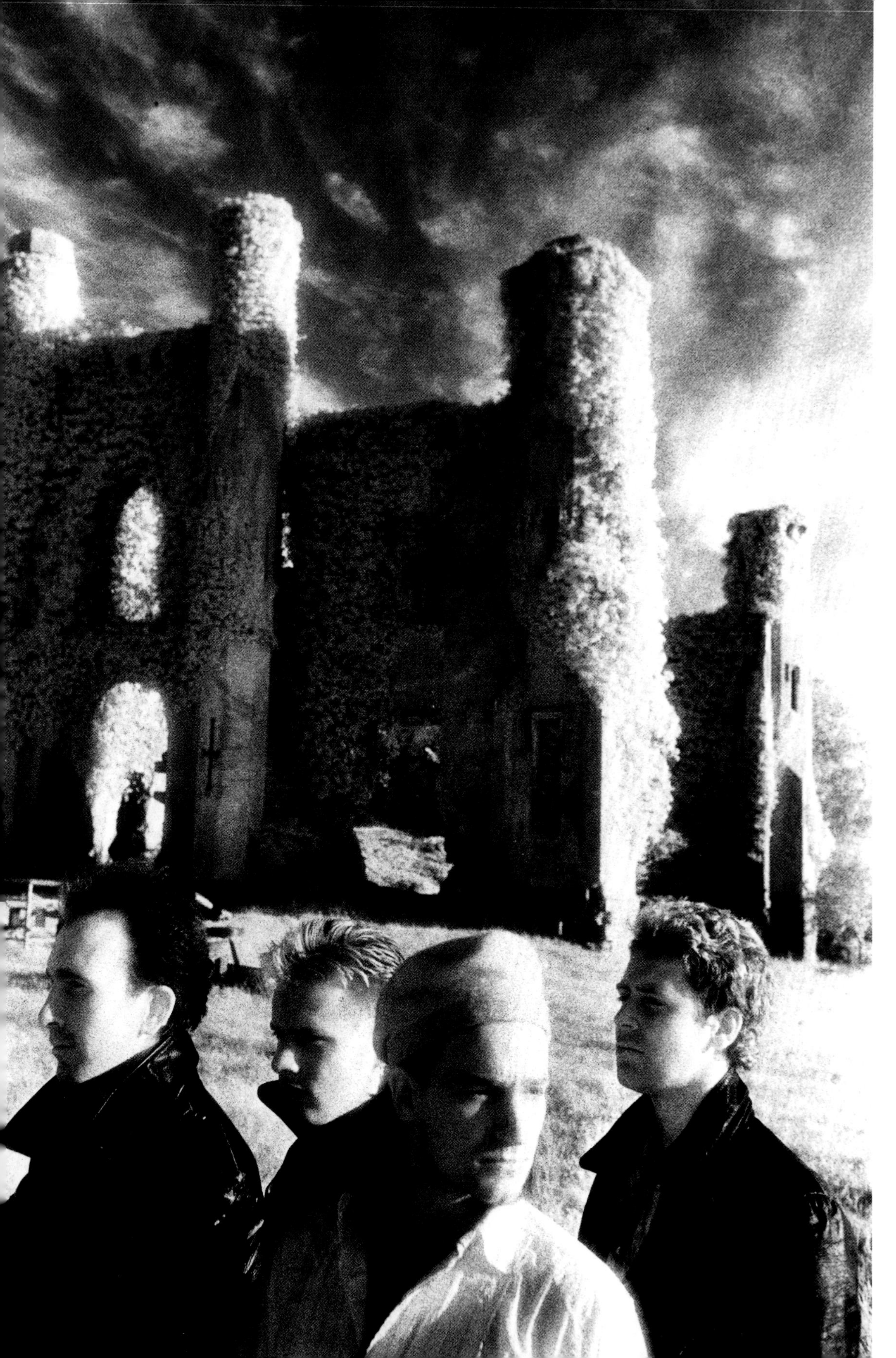

IRELAND 1984

august

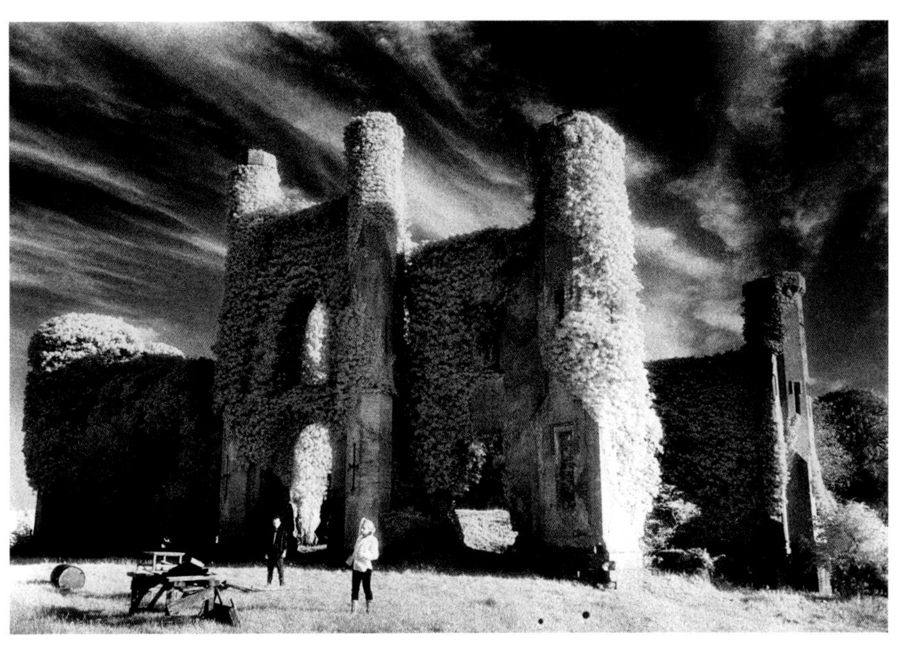

this photo of bono and edge in front of moydrum castle is the cover of the Unforgettable Fire album. Designer Steve Averill had the idea of shooting ruins of castles in infrared for this project and so we traveled to a couple of ruins and took photographs, mostly in infrared, which gave it a kind of haunted look.

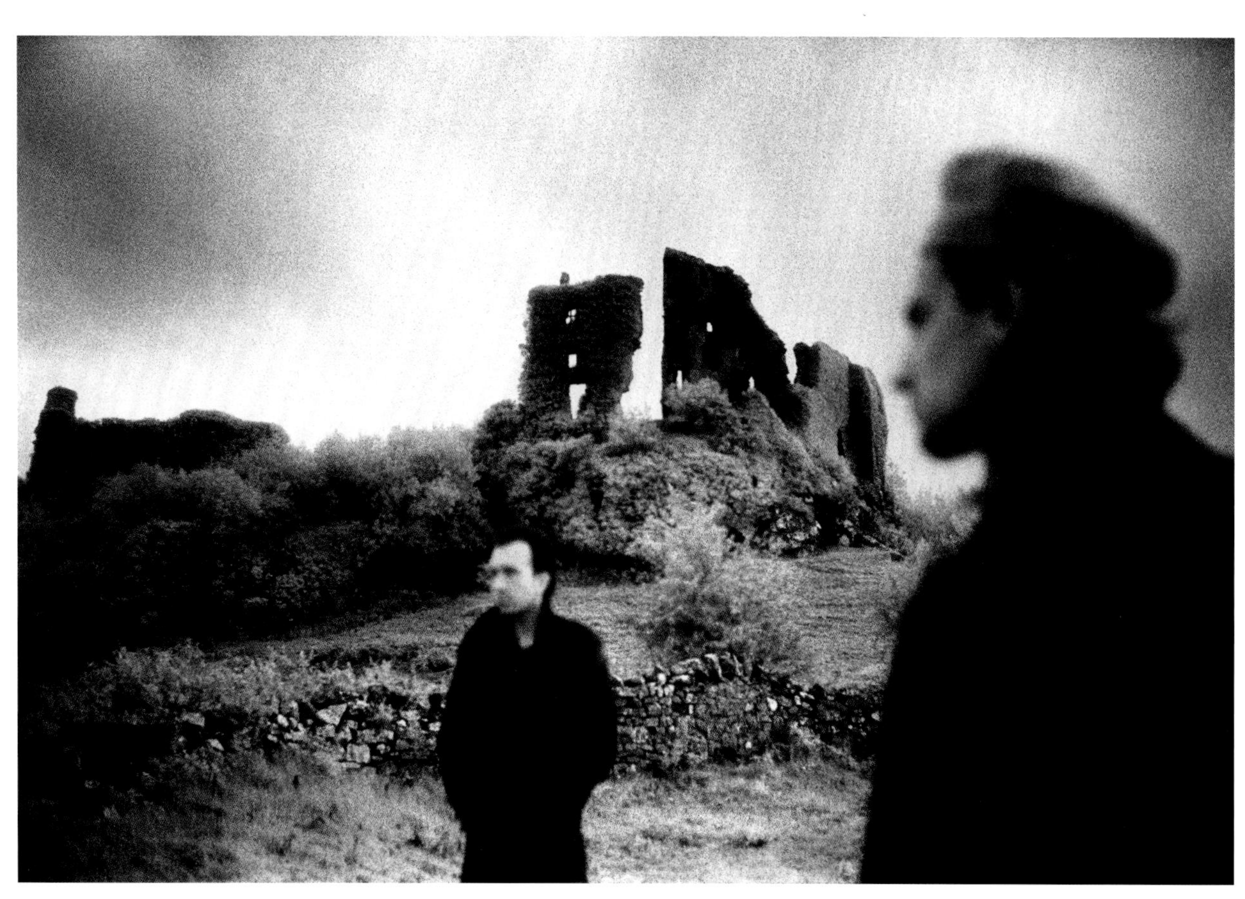

another day, another ruin. again i used infrared film for this to get this explosive, ghostlike atmosphere. we traveled for a couple of days as a very small team. i worked without assistant, don't think i ever had one up till that point. i developed and printed my own photographs and film, and when i was tired the prints generally got darker and the most frequent complaint about my work would in eventually be that it was unprintably dark.

these two photos or very similar ones were used as vinyl labels for the album. not sure if they surfaced on the cd version (i don't have one)

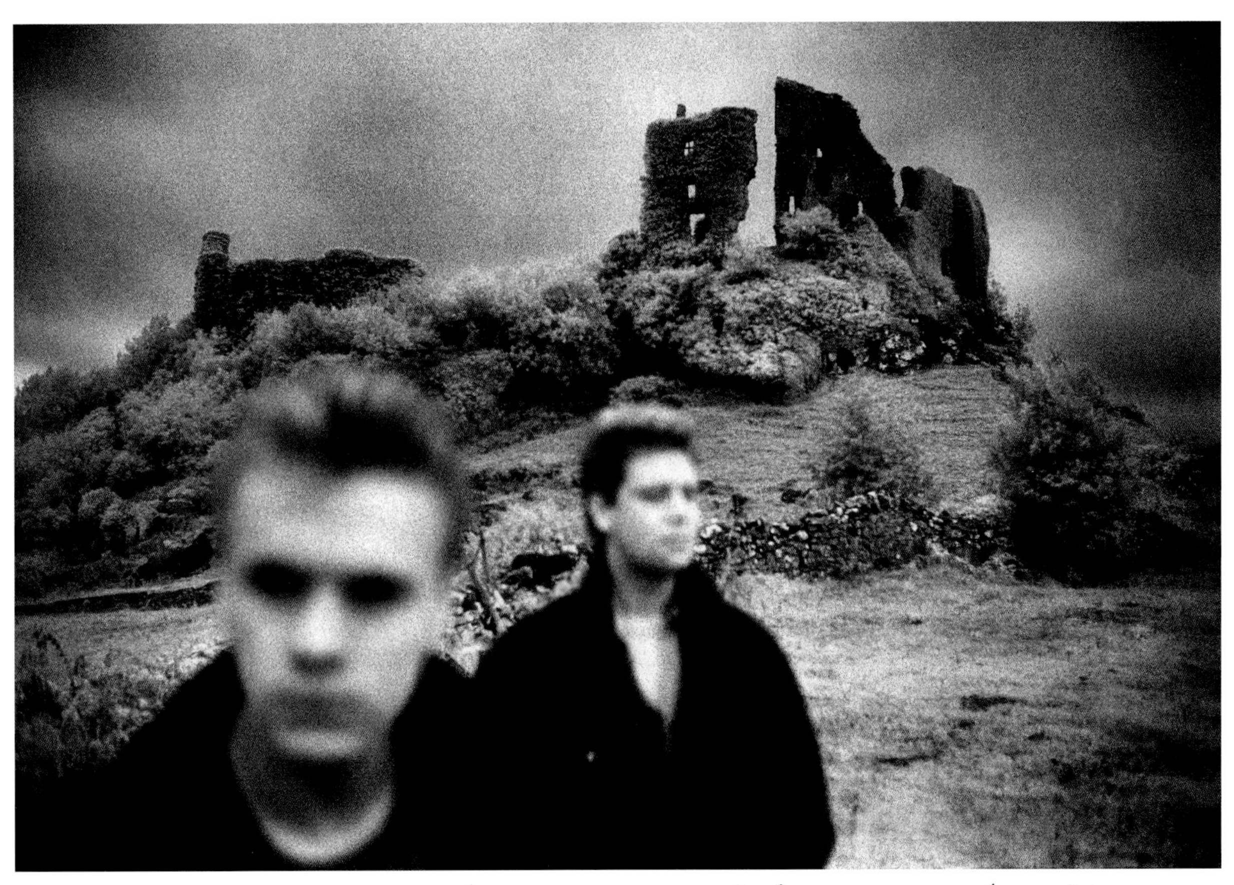

i can only imagine what the complaints were when they saw these infrared ~~prints~~ photographs at the newspapers. although focussing infrared film is different from any normal film, the out-of-focusness of the bandmembers is on purpose. it is a method that i have infrequently used but apparently enough to justify me being the butt of many an out-of-focus joke by U2 and others. Gentlemen, please, it has a purpose! honest.

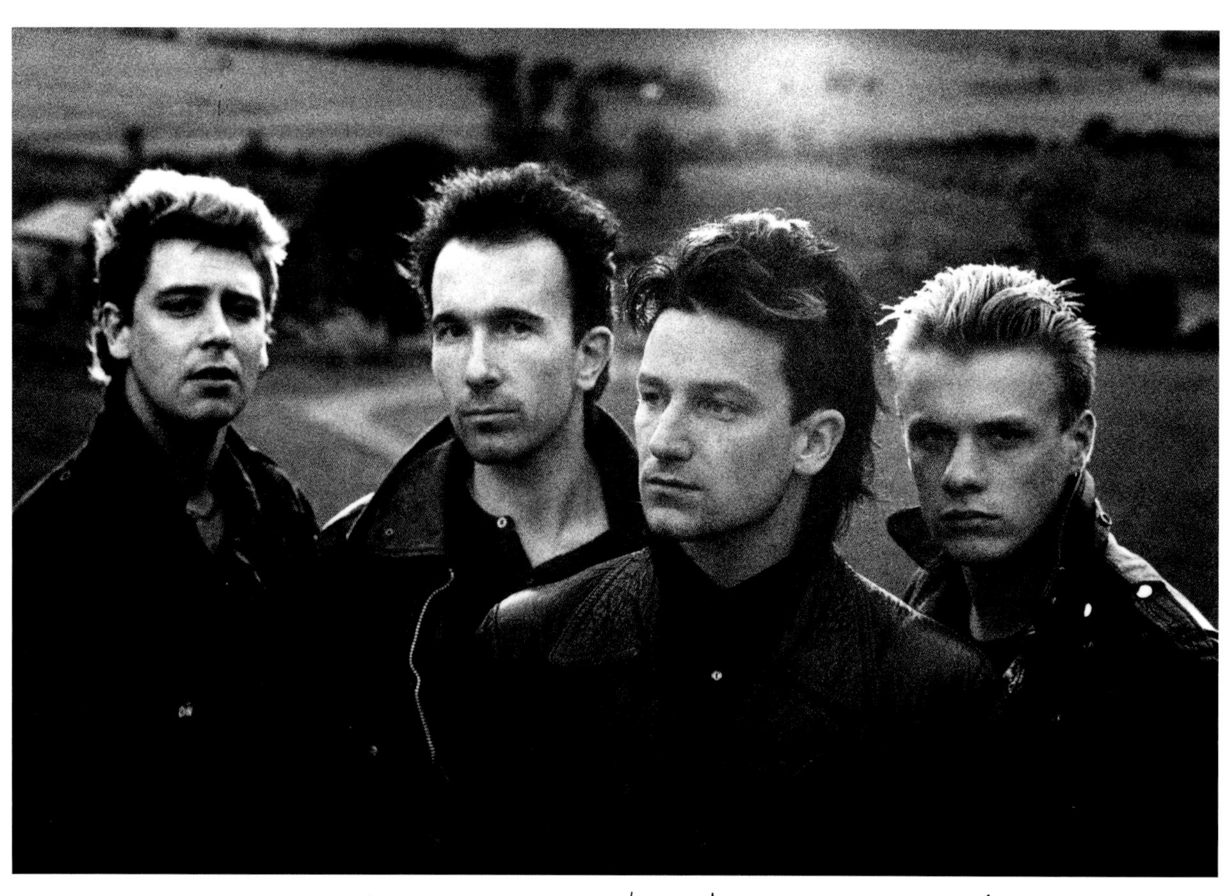

a groupshot taken during this trip but not sure where exactly.

the edge showing why he's called the edge.

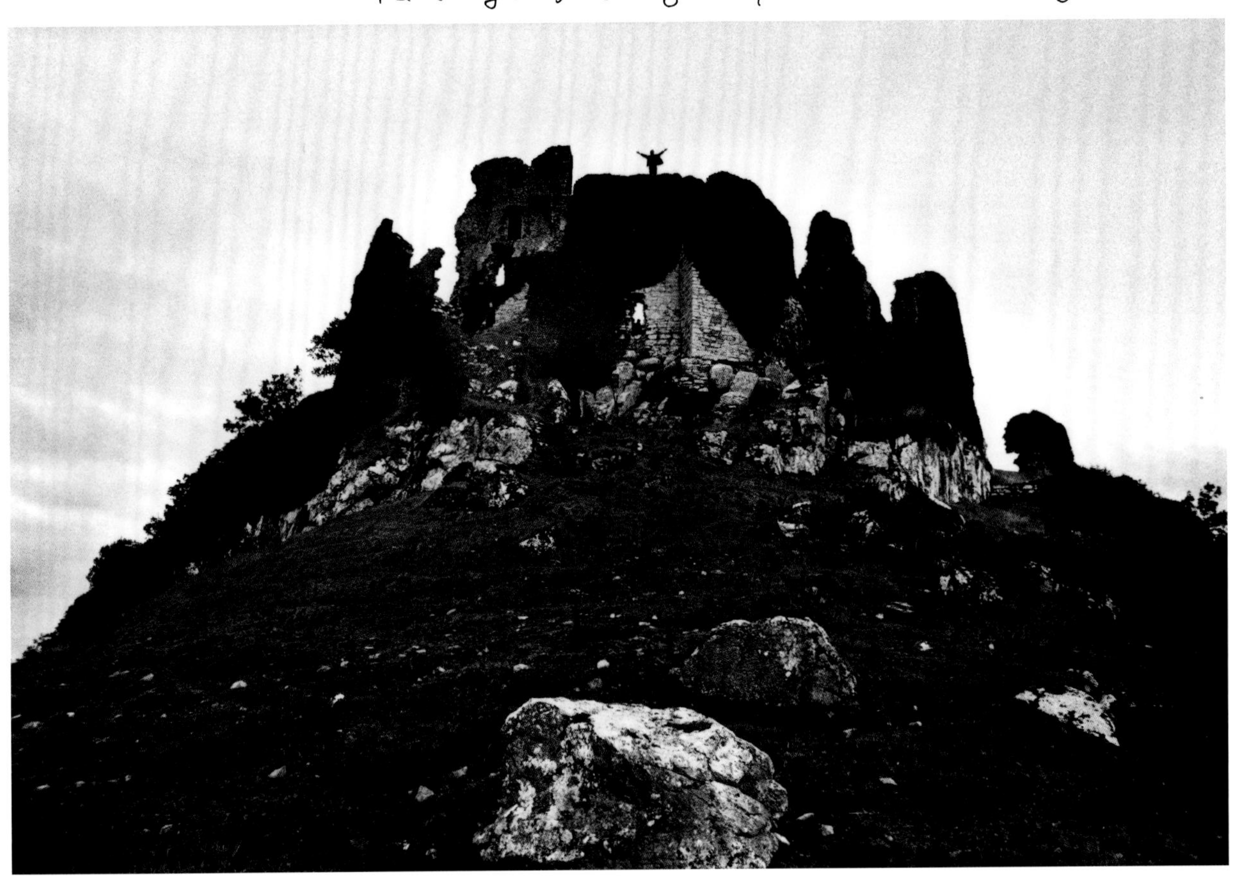

the spread overleaf shows bono at the cliffs of moher, a famous location in Ireland's western part.

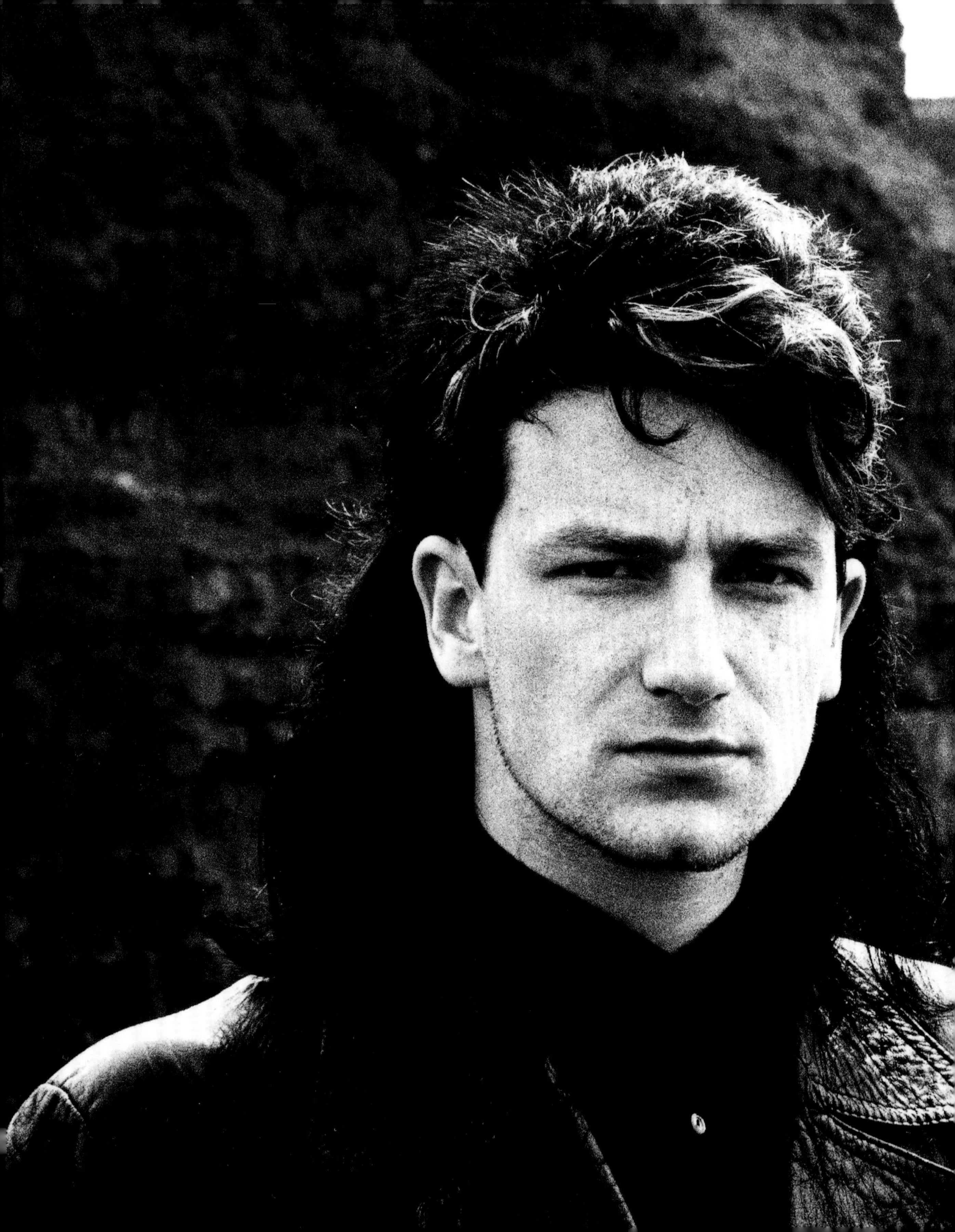

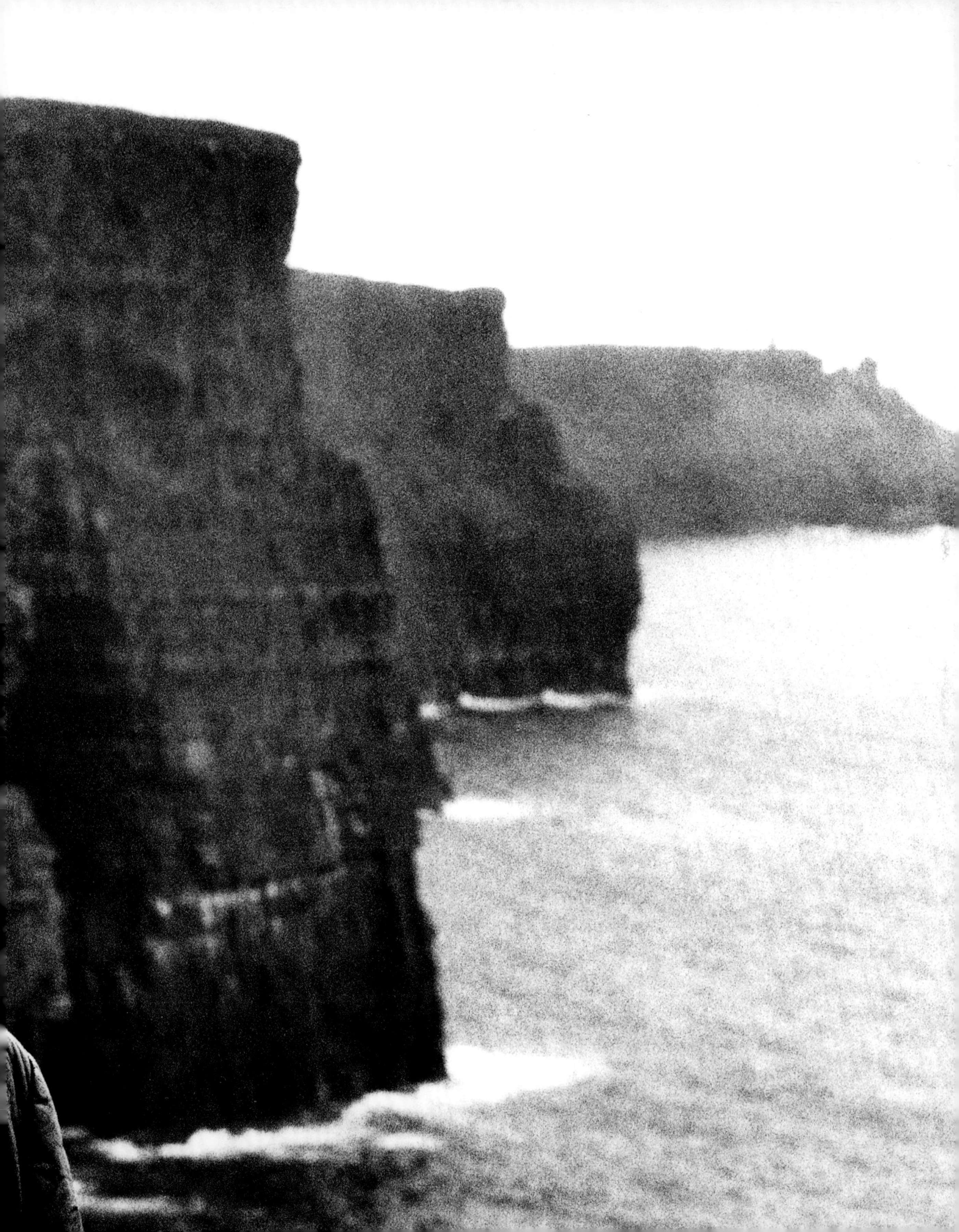

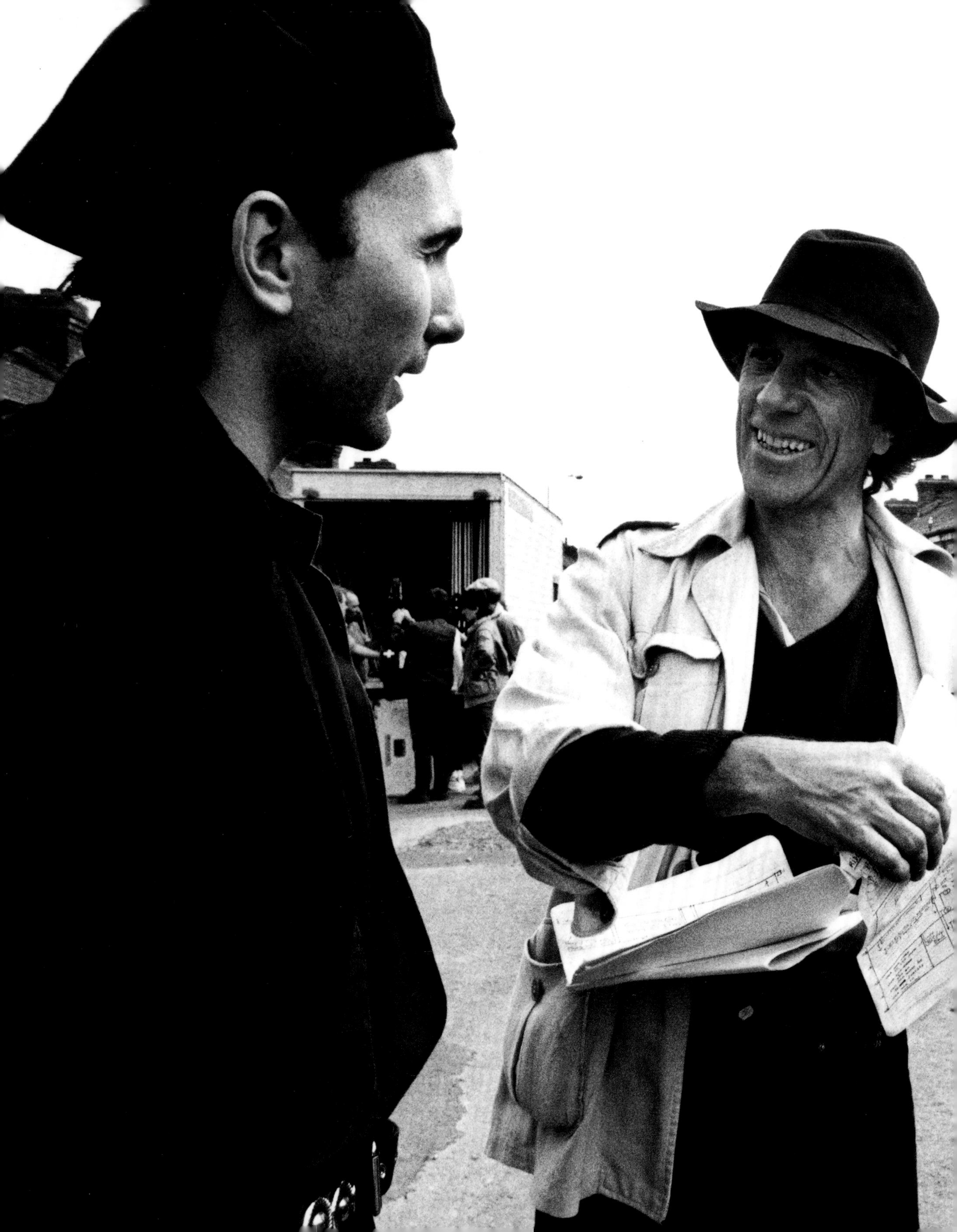

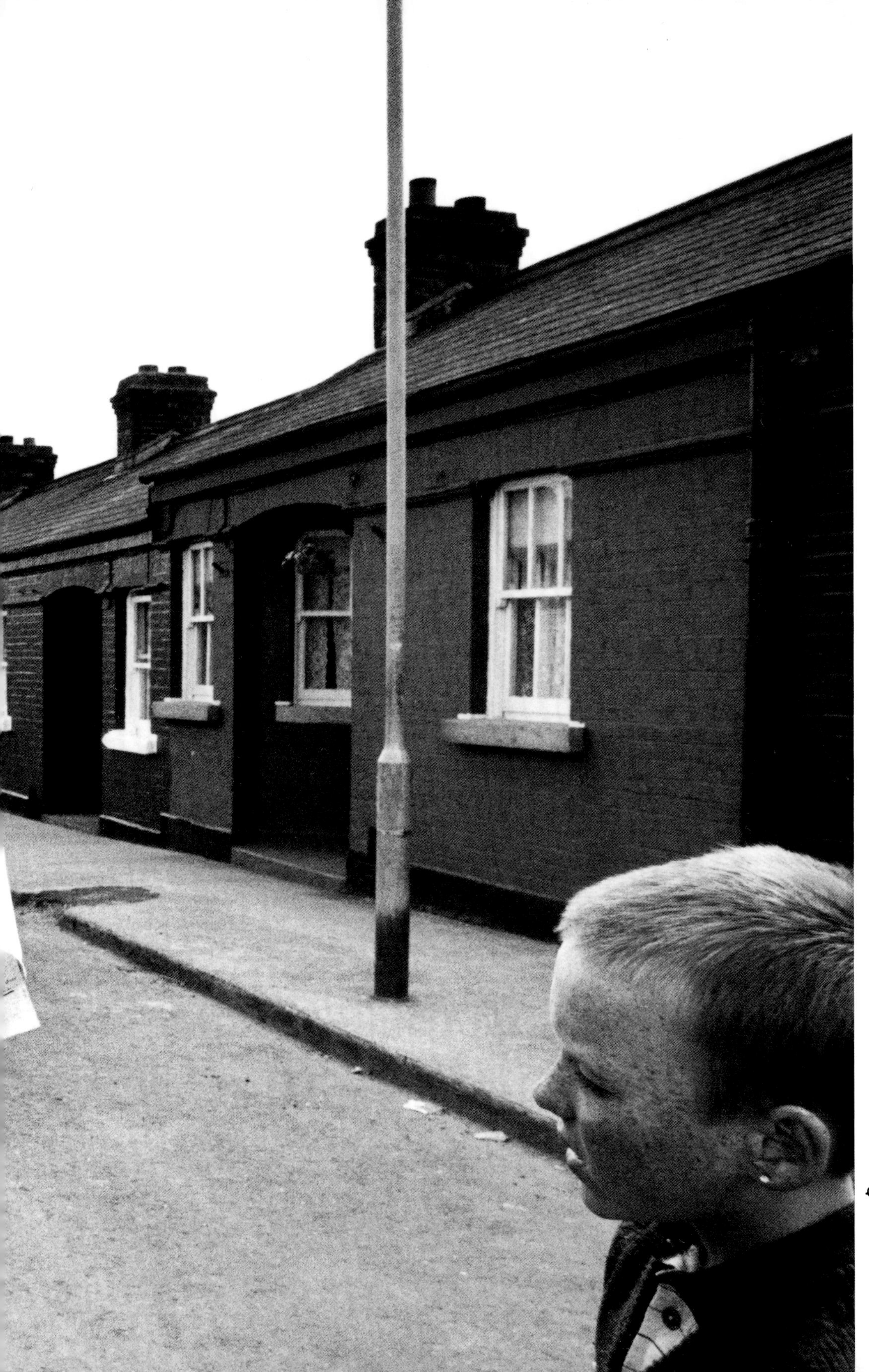

DUBLIN 1984 august i think

edge with director donald cammell and a local talent on the right.

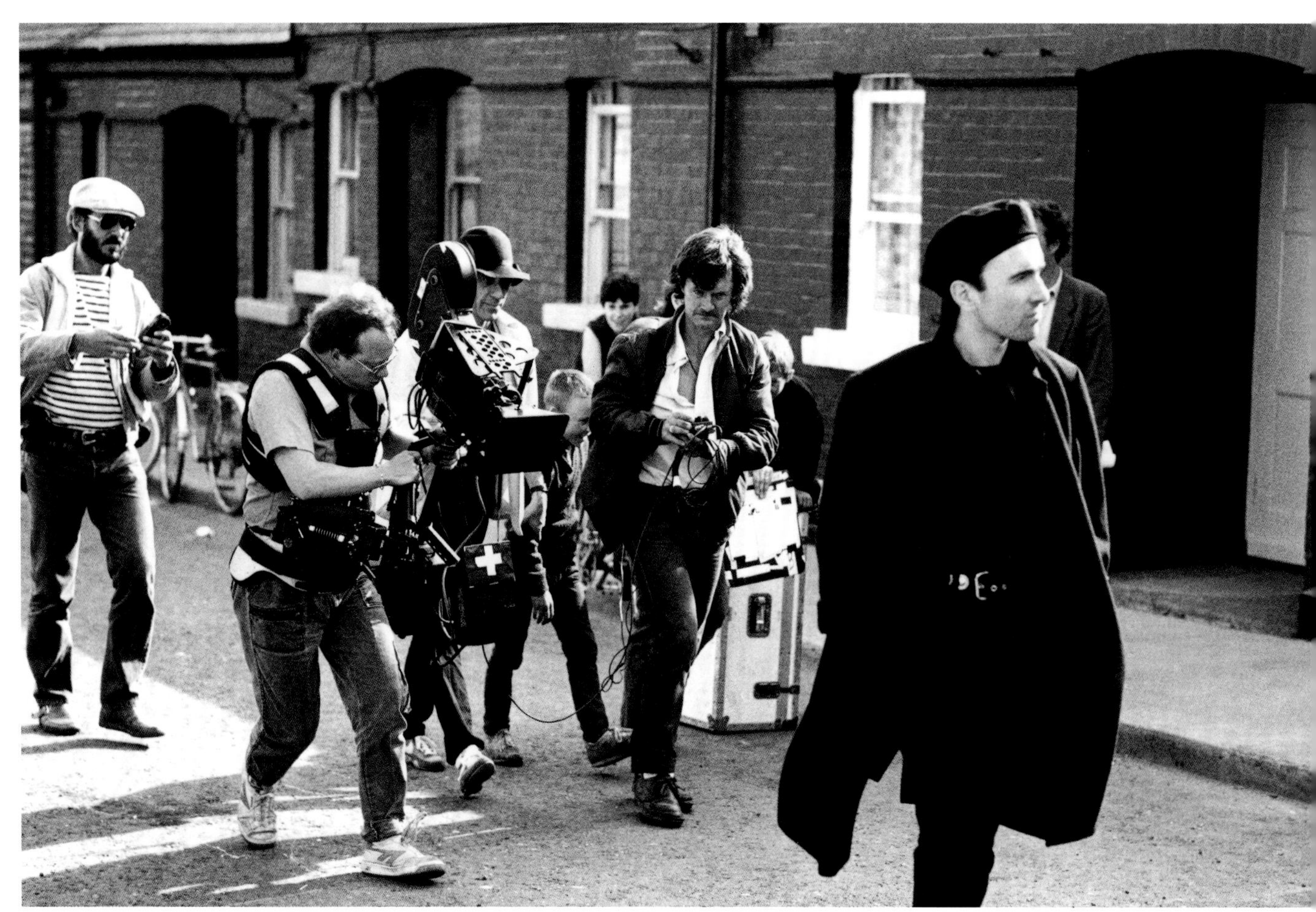

Donald cammell (great director, he made a great film 'The white of the eye' and co-directed cult movie 'Performance' in the 60's) came over to dublin with what looked in my eyes then, a very large and professional crew to make a video for 'pride'. all was filmd in dublin and part of it is edge walkig past the small houses near the liffe.

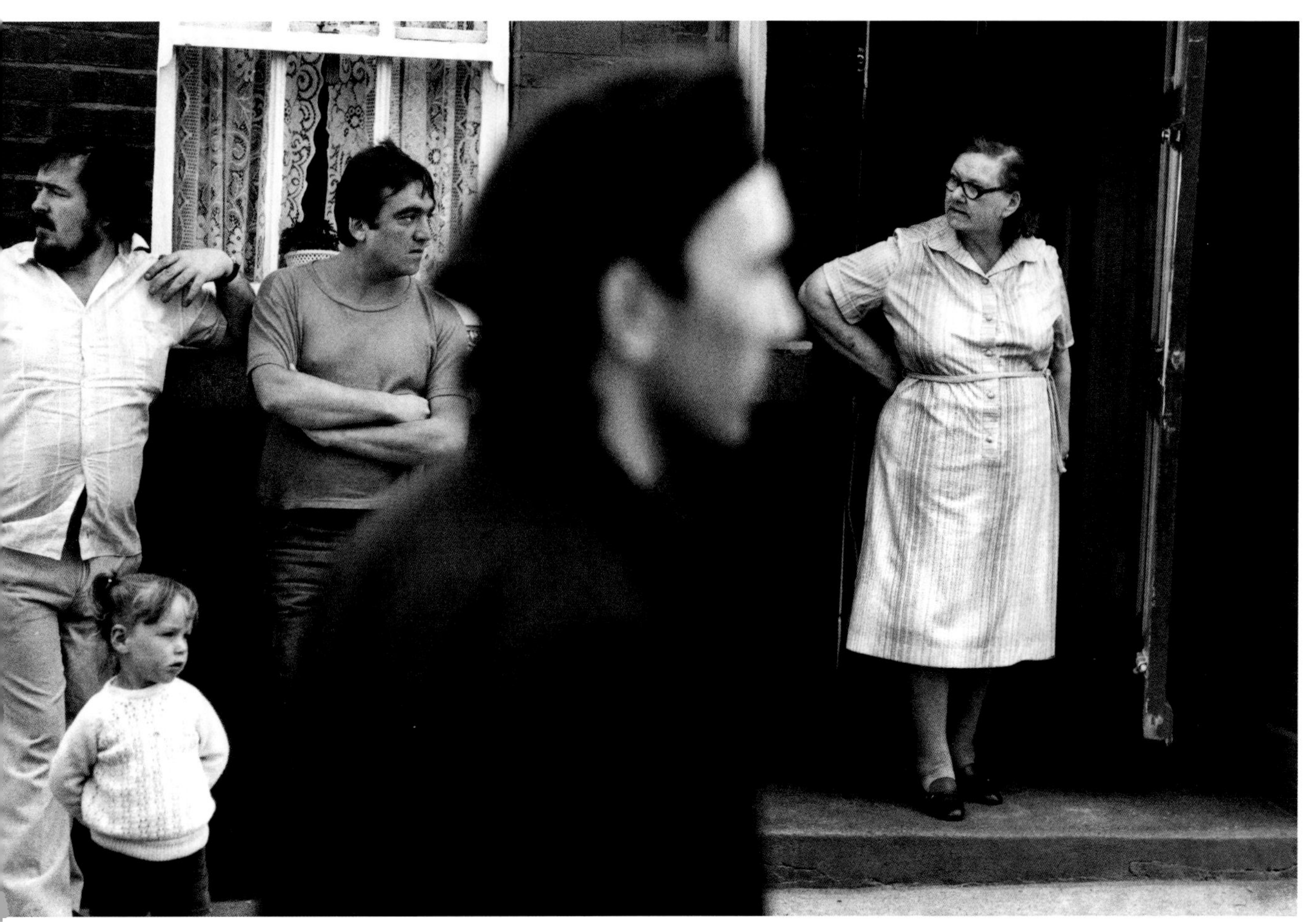

edge with real people, not extras.

HOUNSLOW

august 1984

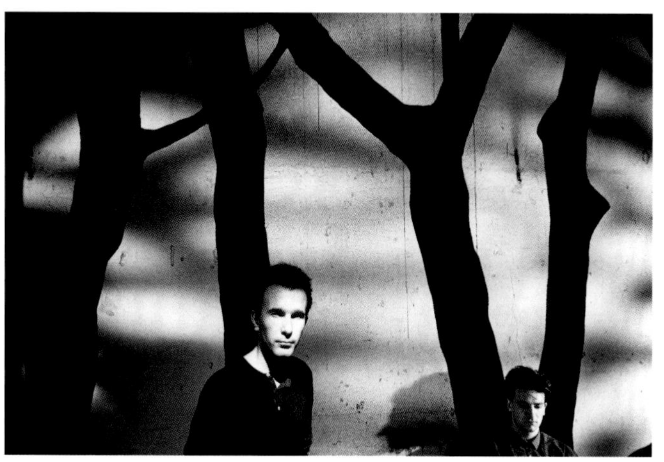

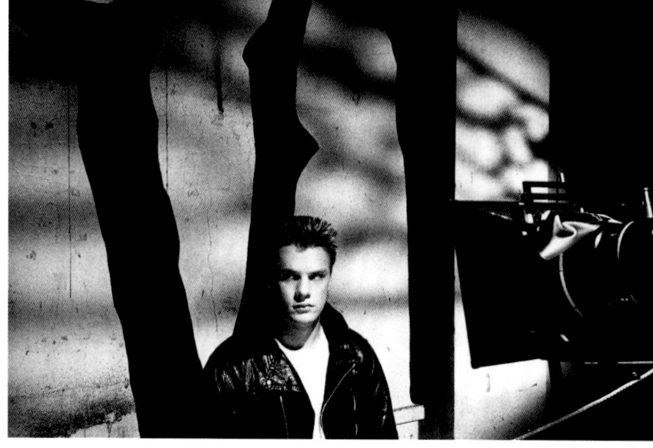

after u2 had expressed some reservations about the video for 'pride' by donald cammell, i had offered to make an alternative video for the song. i wish i hadn't! it wa my first year of making videos and the inexperience showed. the video is best forgotten and only a few people have ever seen a glimpse of it. it is a 'one take only' video, a shot of the band standing in front of a painted wall (trying to link it with the pl of the trees in paris 1983 which was the single-cover for 'pride') - they are badly lit an looking solemn, in total contrast to the vibe of the song. as a result it took another eight years before i was asked to do another video for them.

the video was shot in some basement near Heathrow as the band were due to fly off to australia that day.

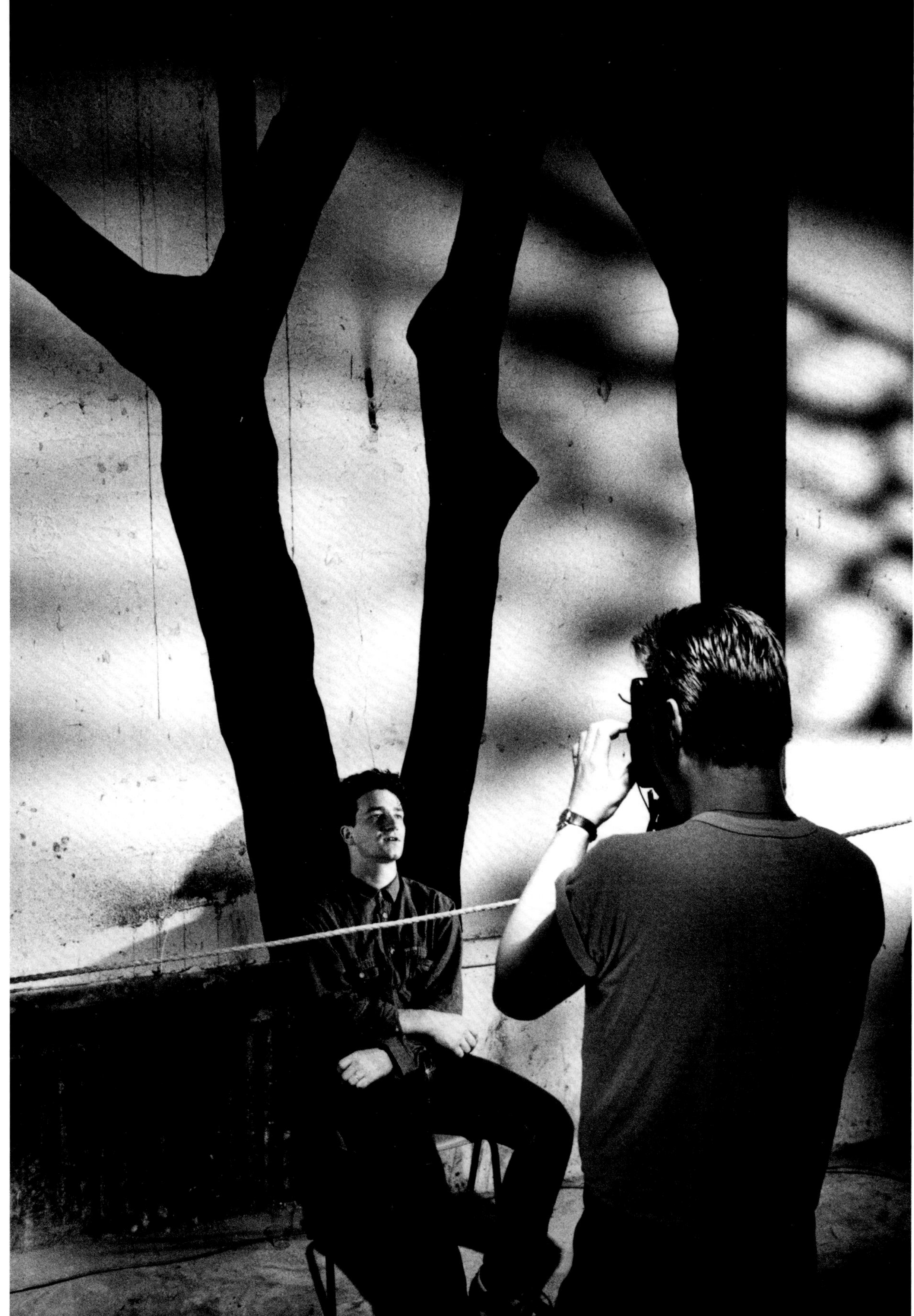

larry taking a photo of bono

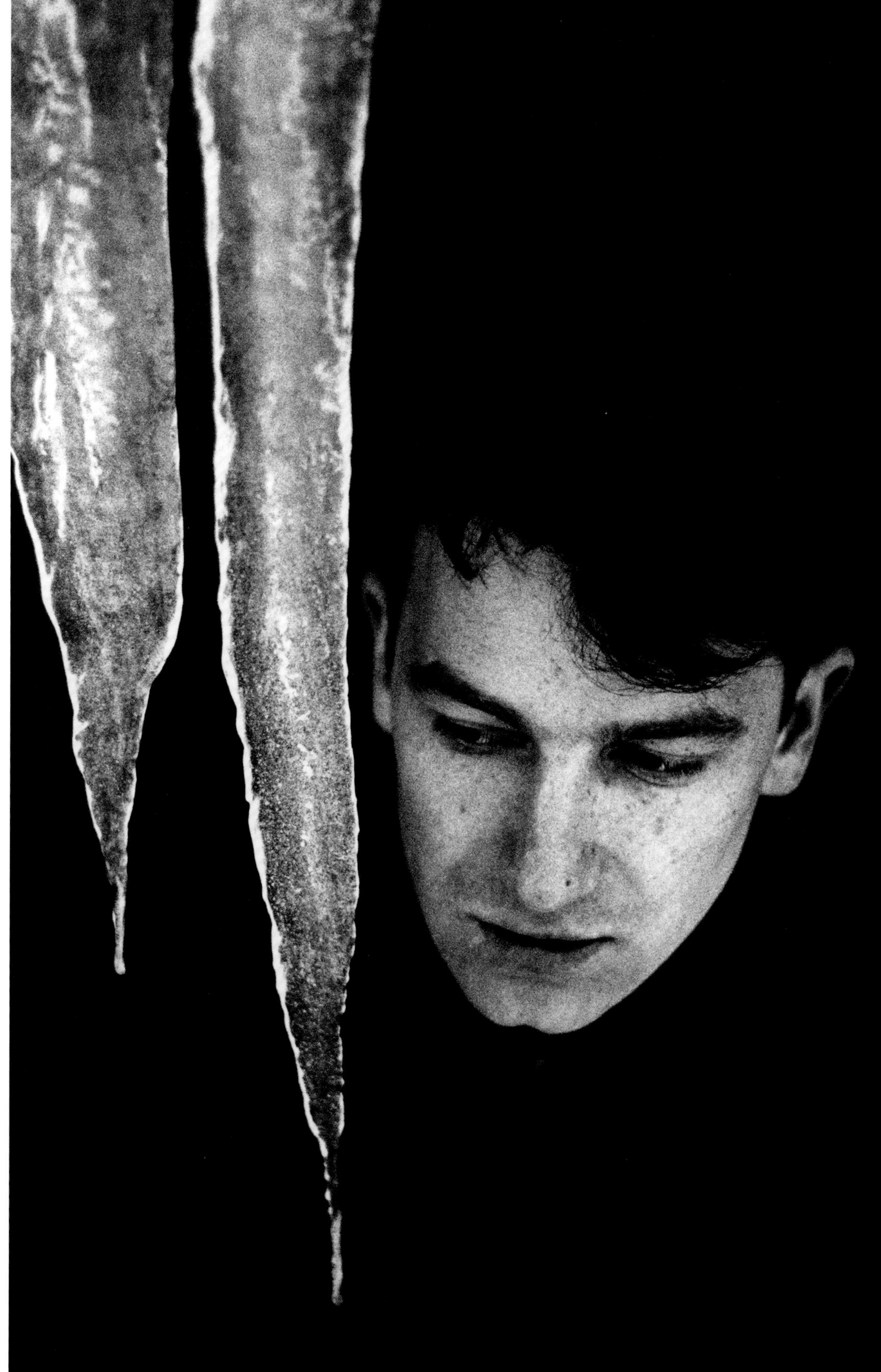

sweden 1985

january

another videoshoot in the winter in sweden. this time for the 'unforgettable fire' single. it was really cold and i had just been ill and in hospital for a long time so the cold hit me harder than usual. i recall shooting without any feeling at all in my fingers and just slamming my whole hand onto the part of the camera where the button is in order to get photos. this was the coldest shoot we ever did though so i guess it wasn't just me who was affected.

Brrrrrrrrrrrrr

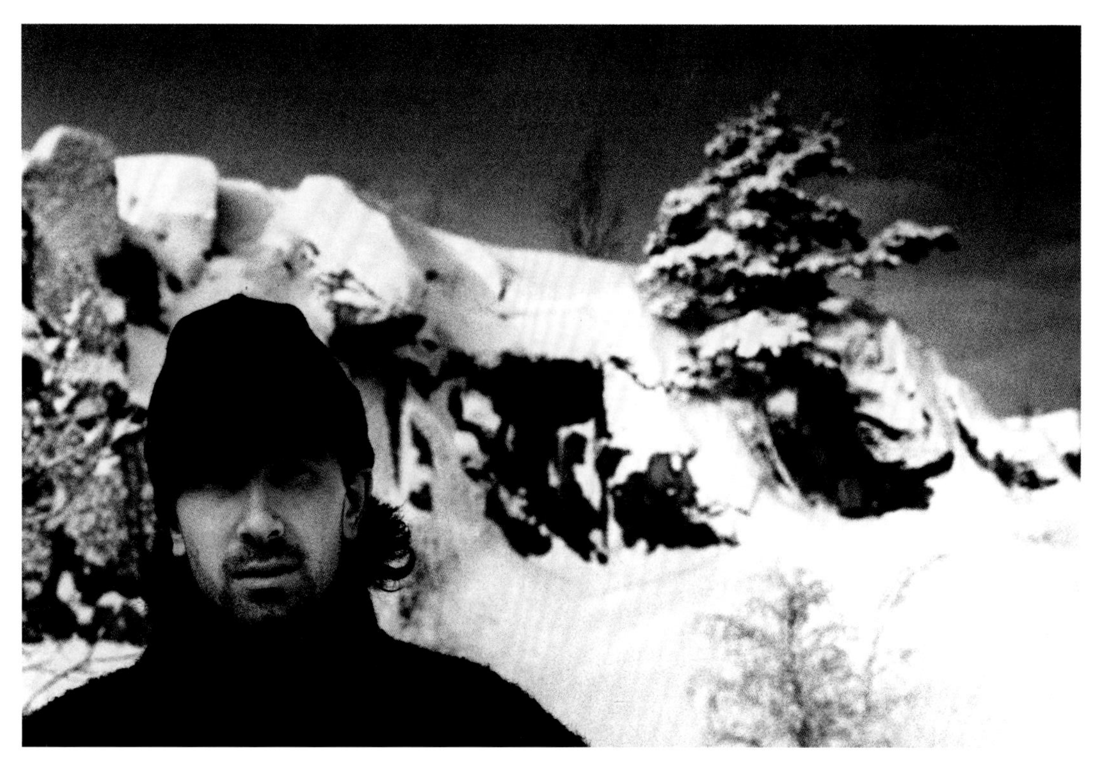

on location for the video – edge above and
adam and larry on the
right →

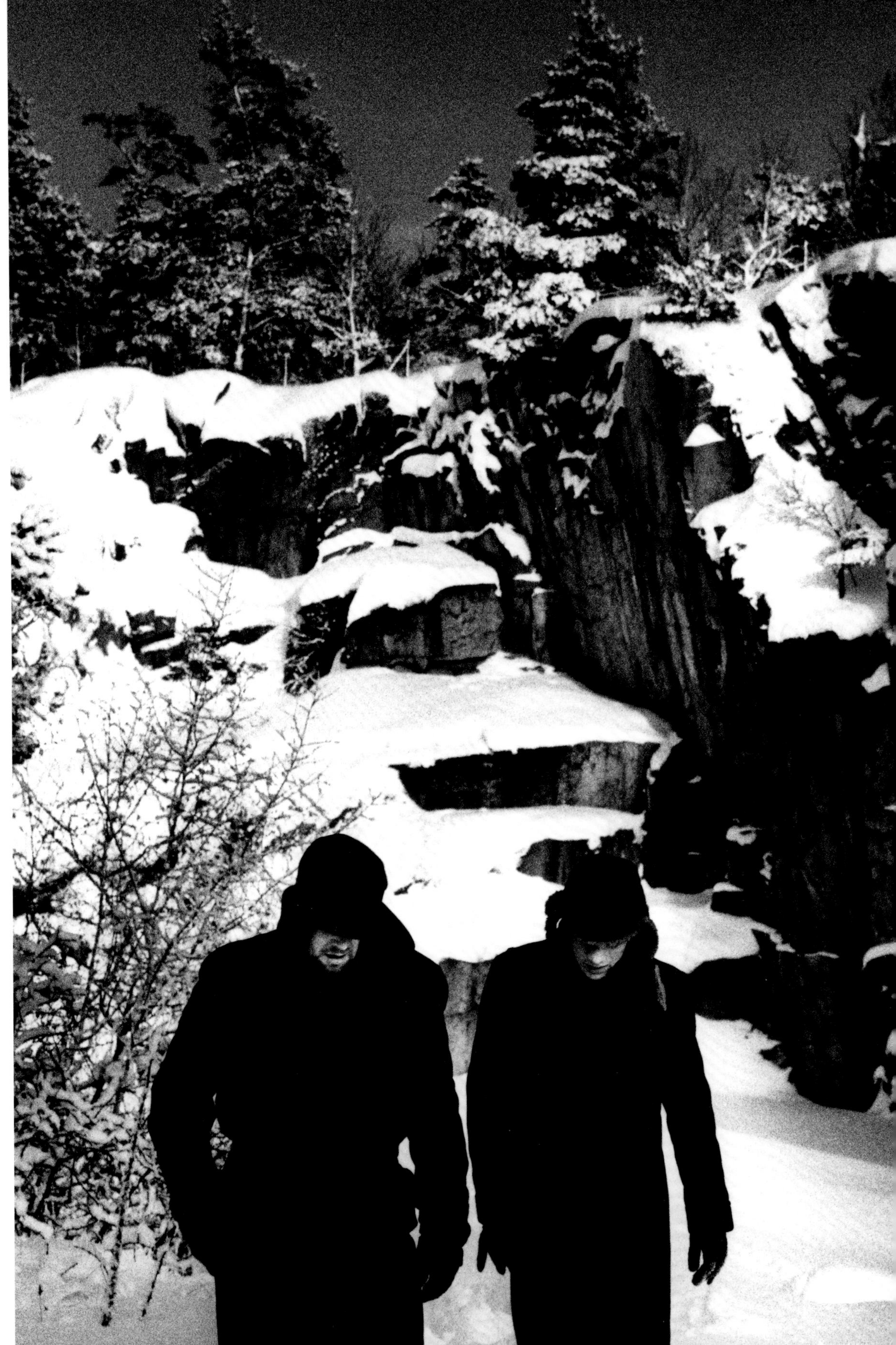

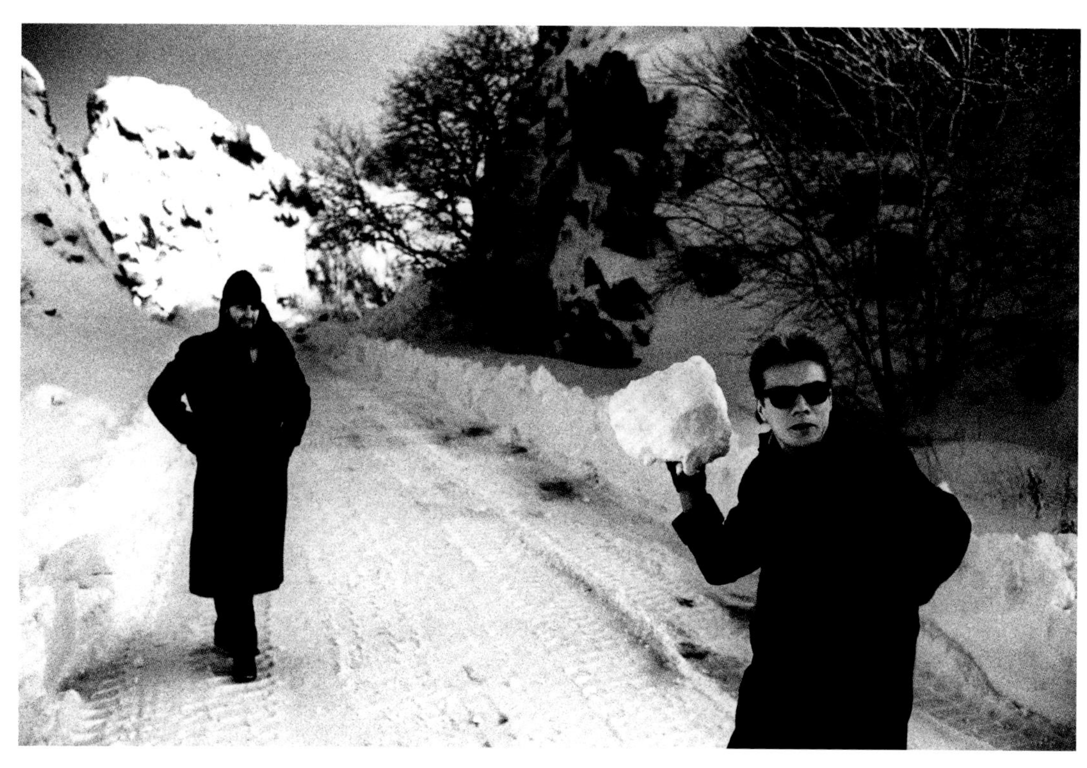

lunch break i guess.

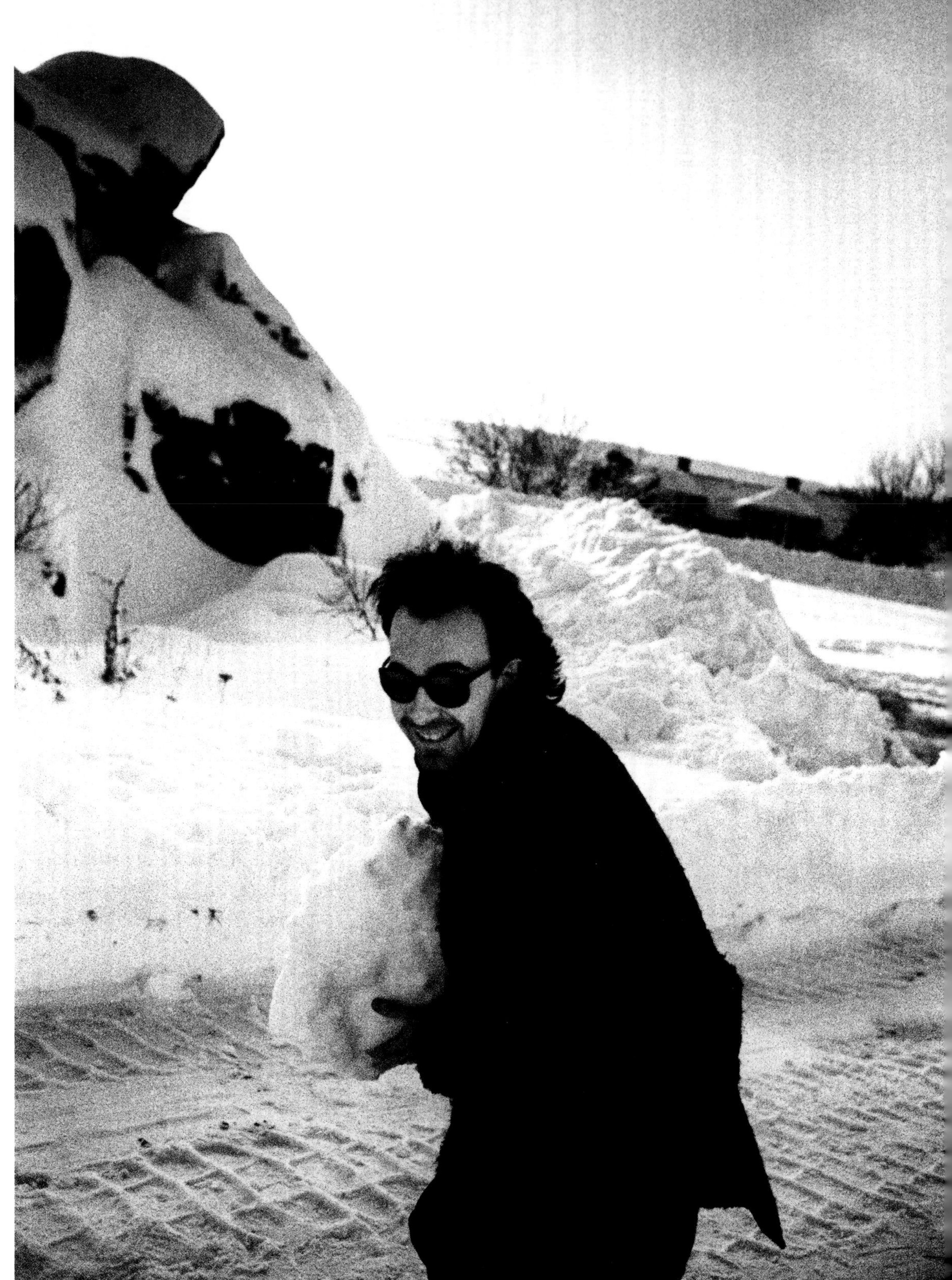

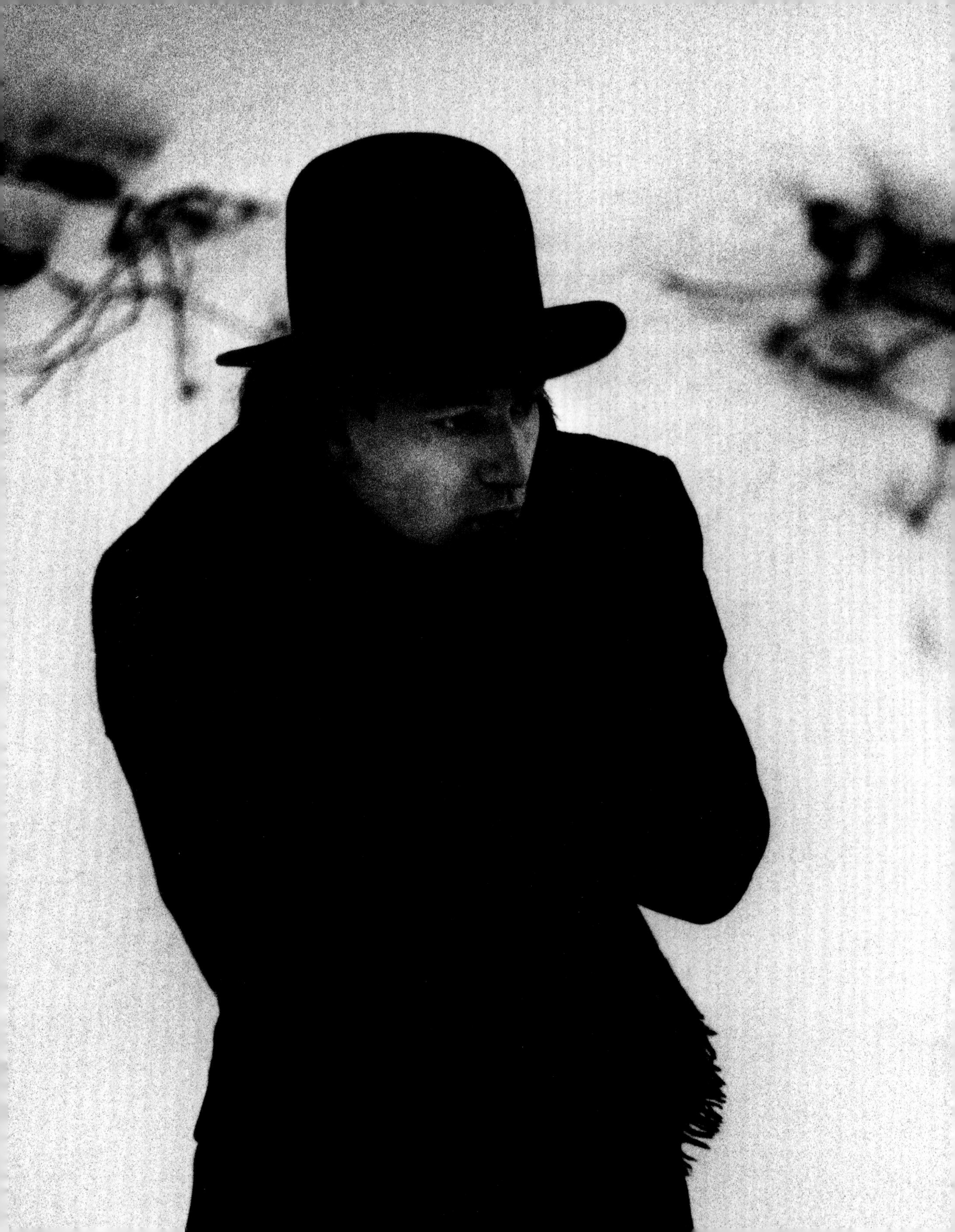

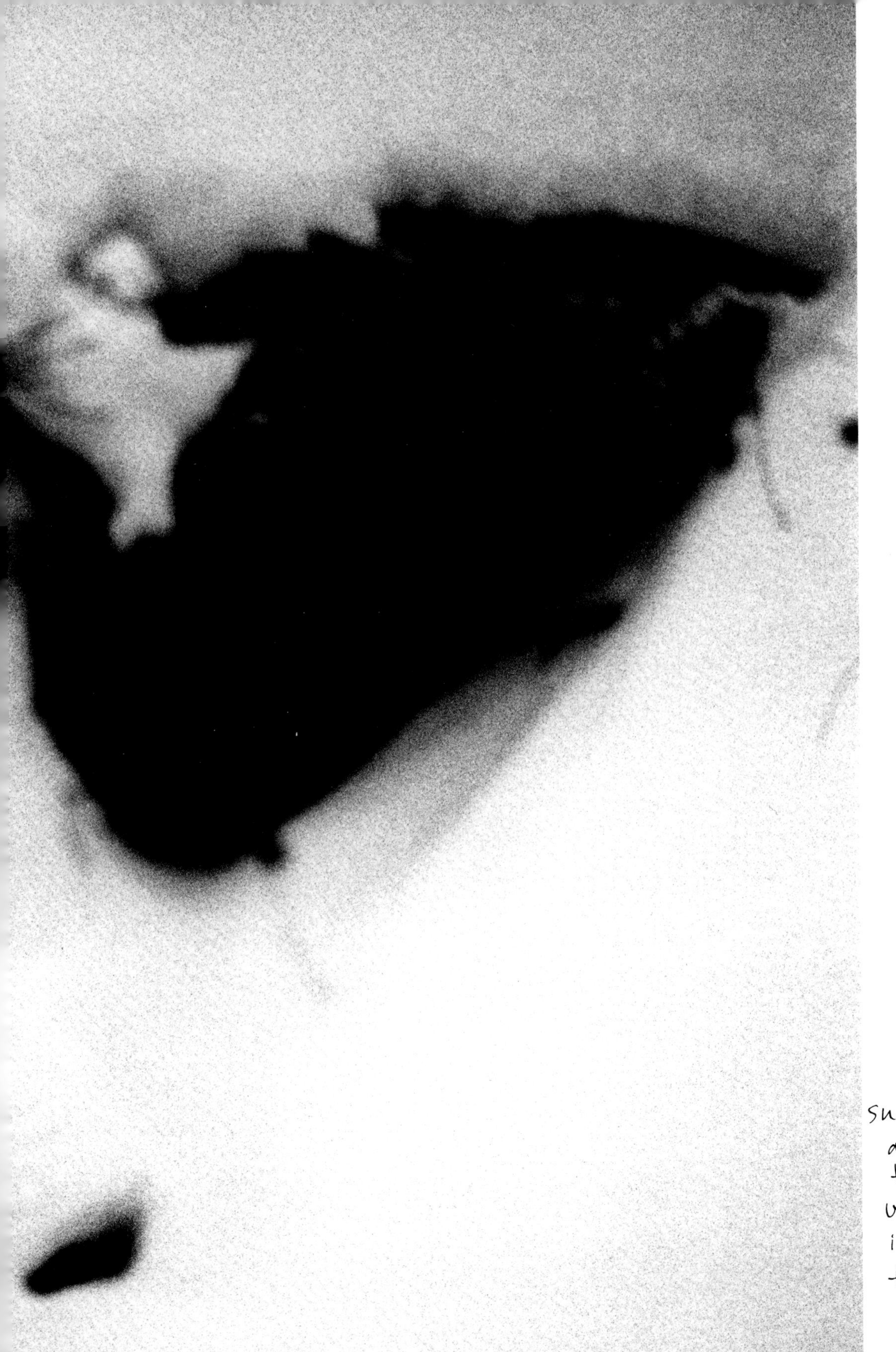

Snow landscapes and snow on the ground – all very beautiful in black & white, throwing great shapes.

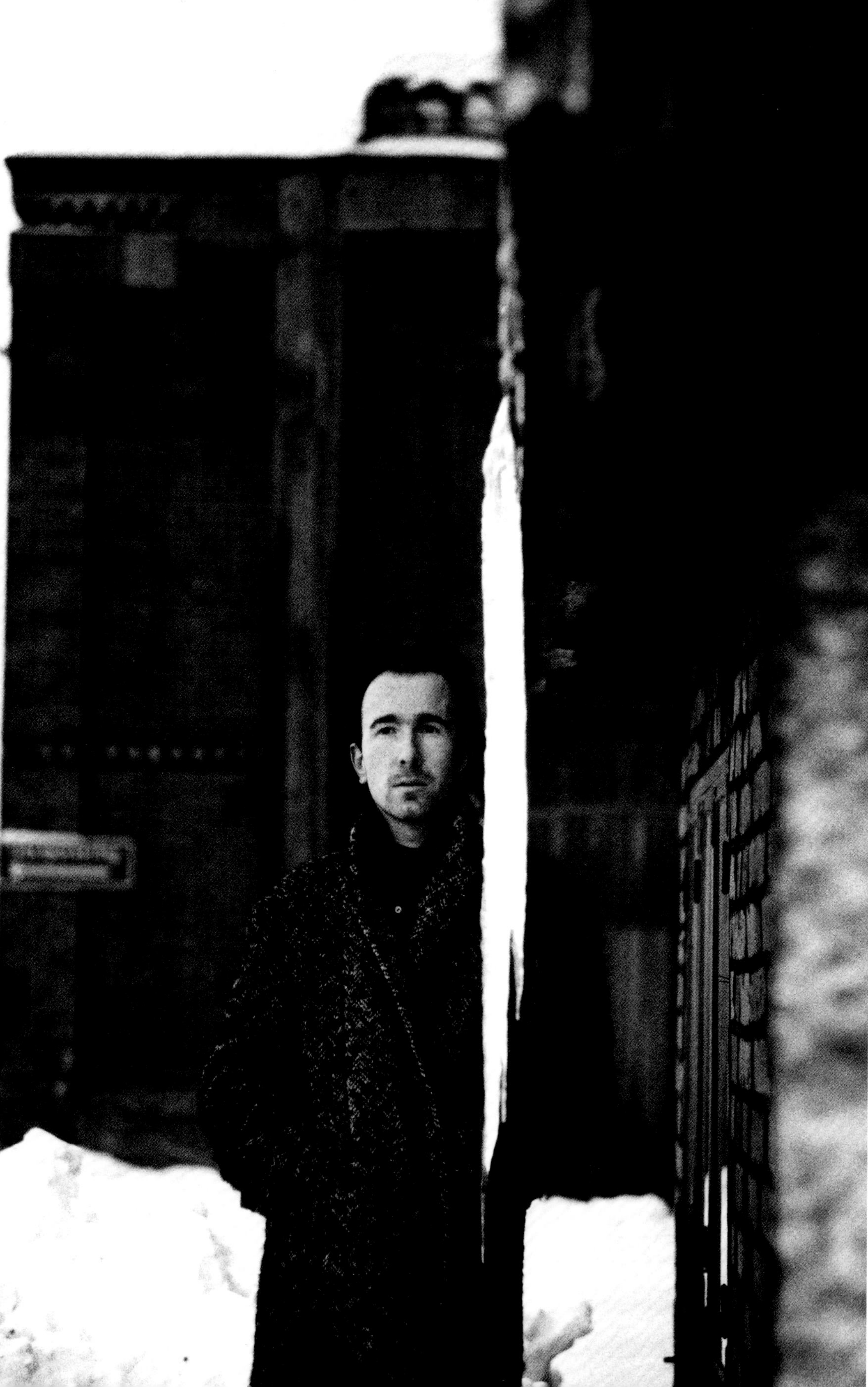

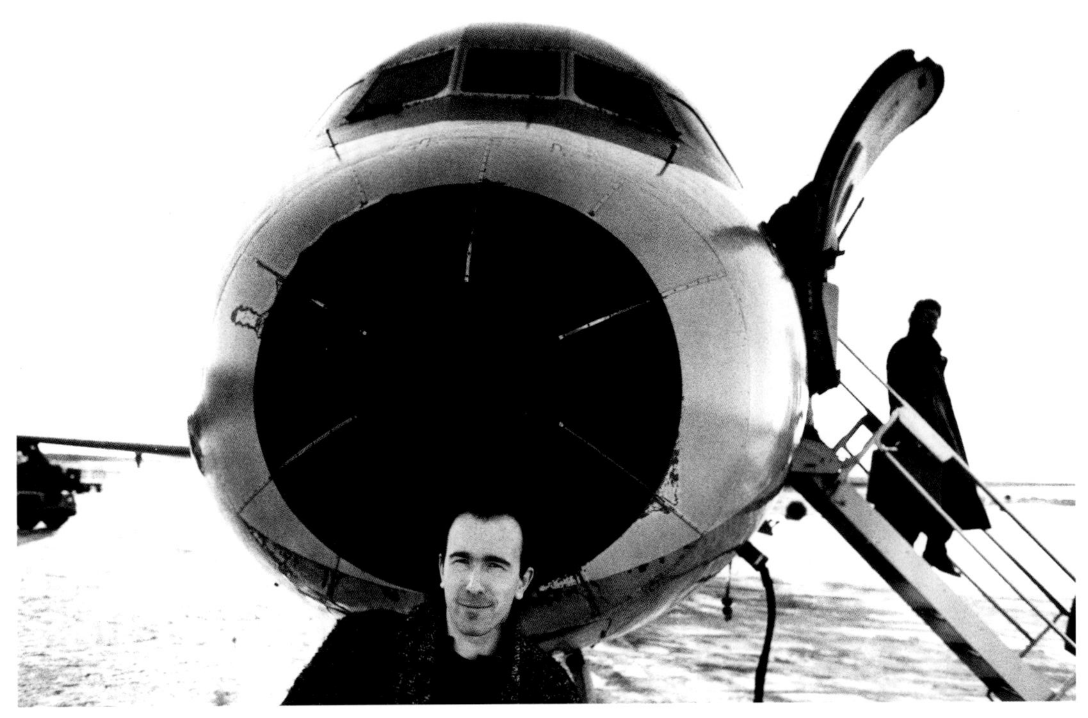

i must have so many photos of edge standing next or in front of airplanes - he really takes to them.

PHILADELPHIA 1985 march

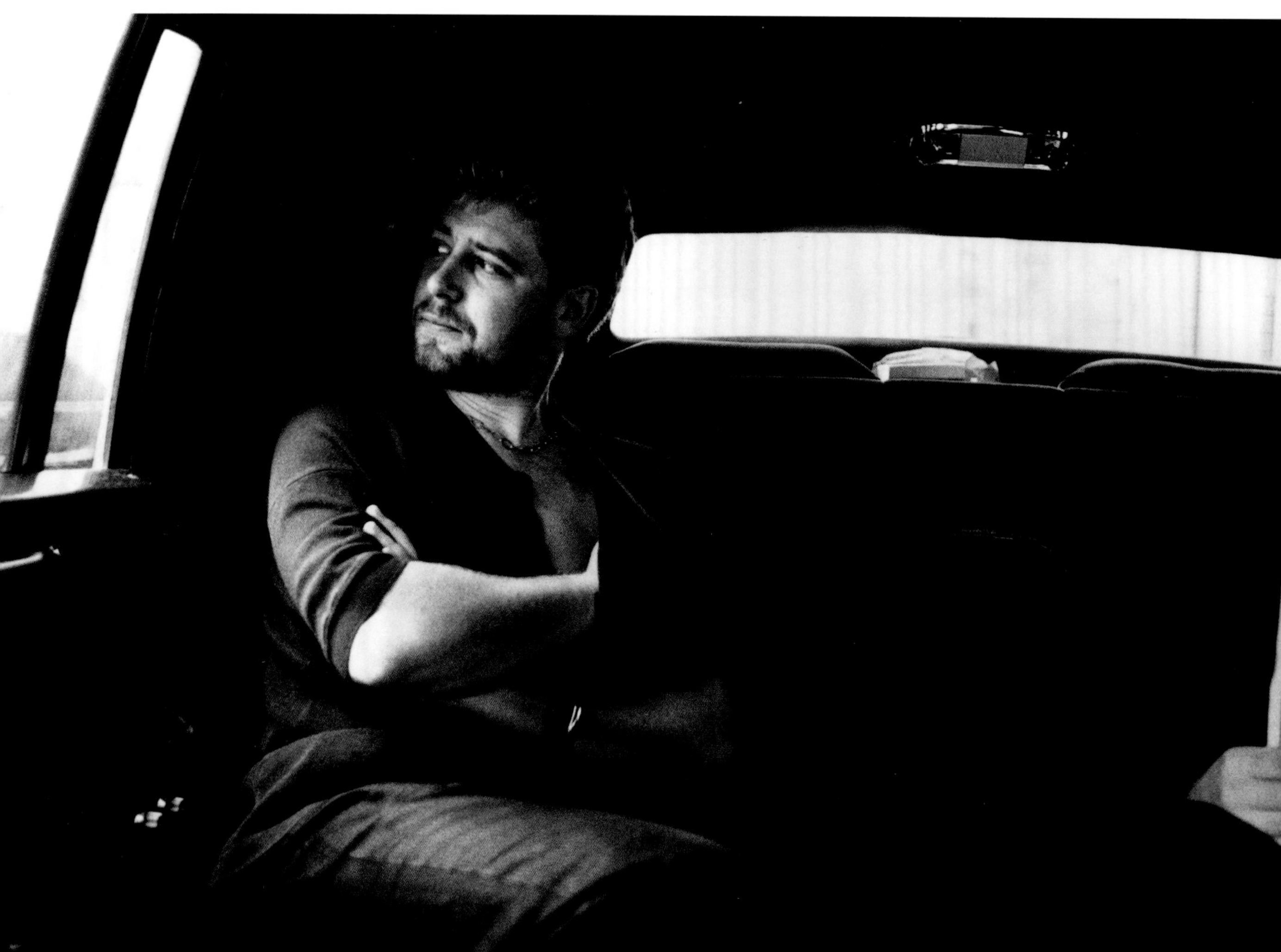

on a trip to shoot another frontcover for the NME in Philadelphia. i saw a concert the night before and did a shoot in daytime the next day. for some reason, bono was very distant that day and you can tell in the photos. i also did some portrait photograph later in the hotelroom with him which are not included but there is one (well-known) photo of him without top which is very intense.

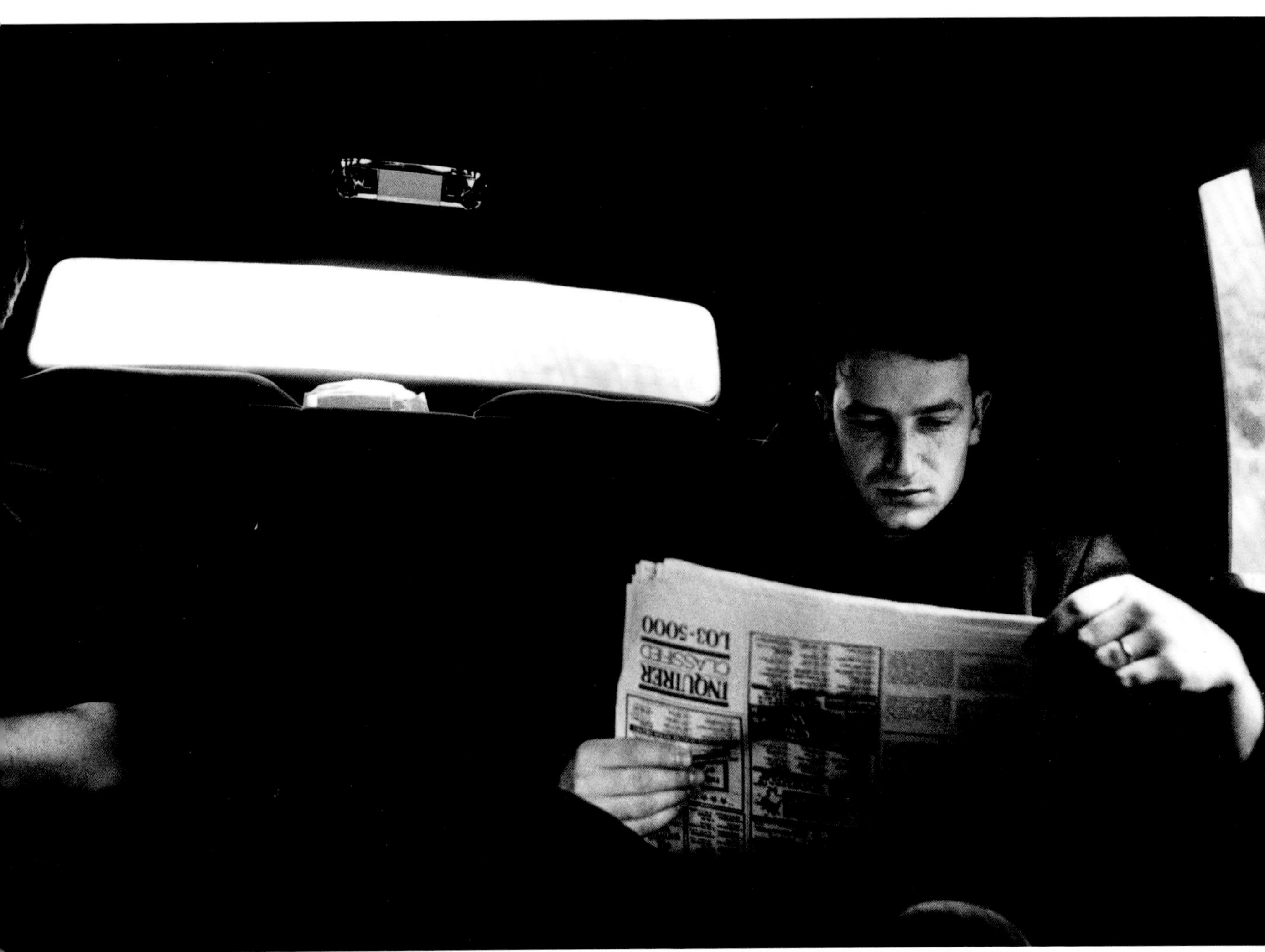

these photos show adam and bono on the way to the photo-location that i had found.

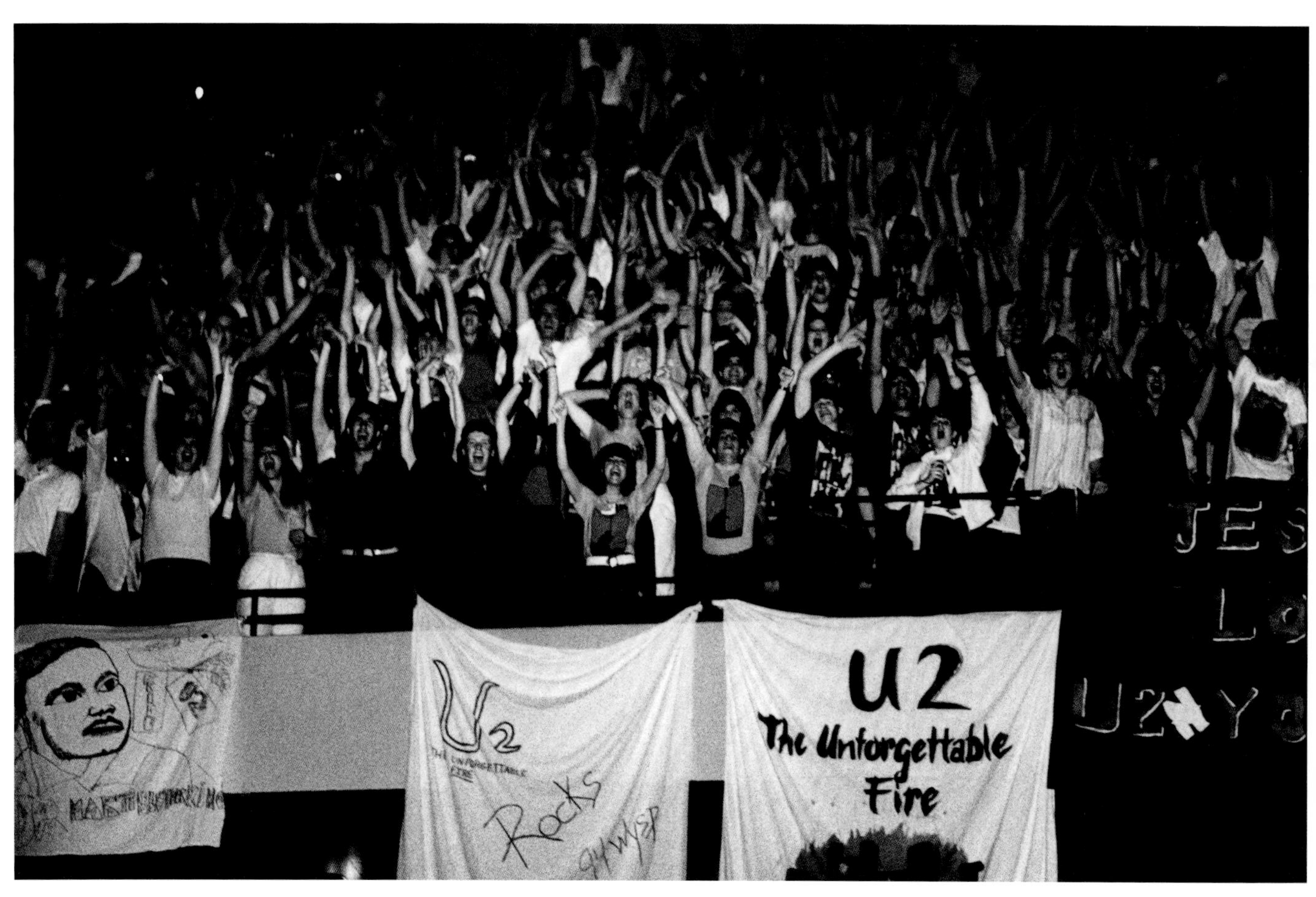
U2
The Unforgettable
Fire
U2
Rocks
94 WYSP

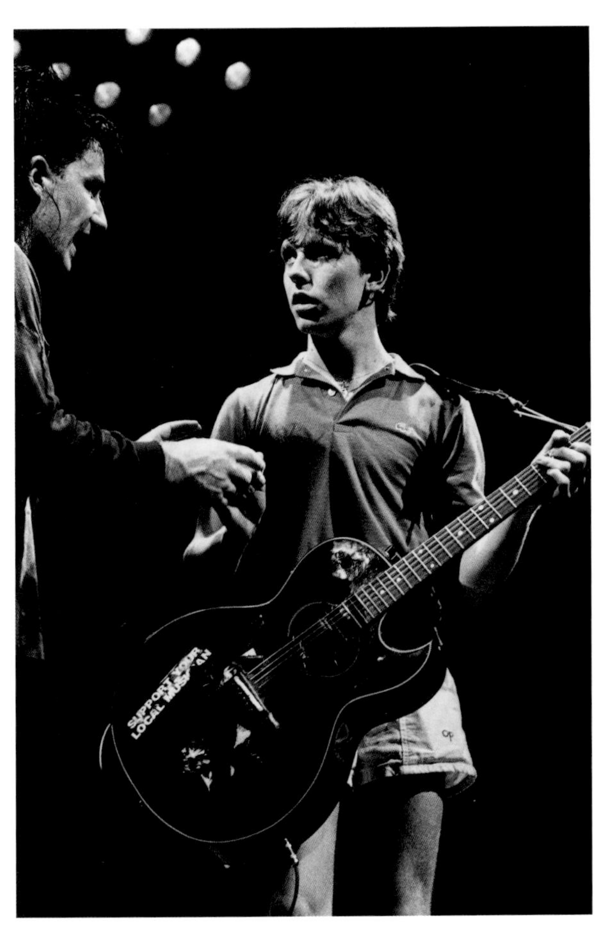

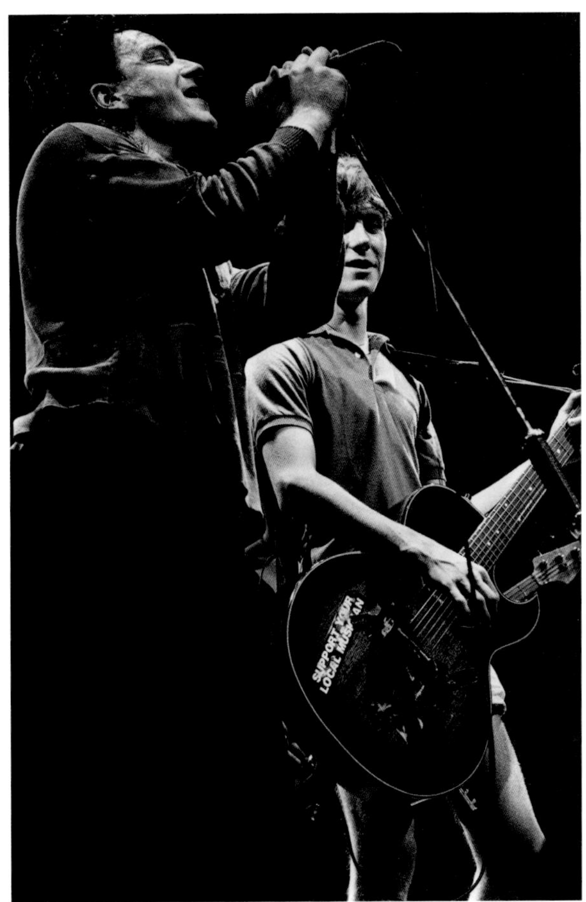

a feature of the U2 shows at the time was to get a young local musician to come on stage and play a song with them. above is the lucky kid from philadelphia.

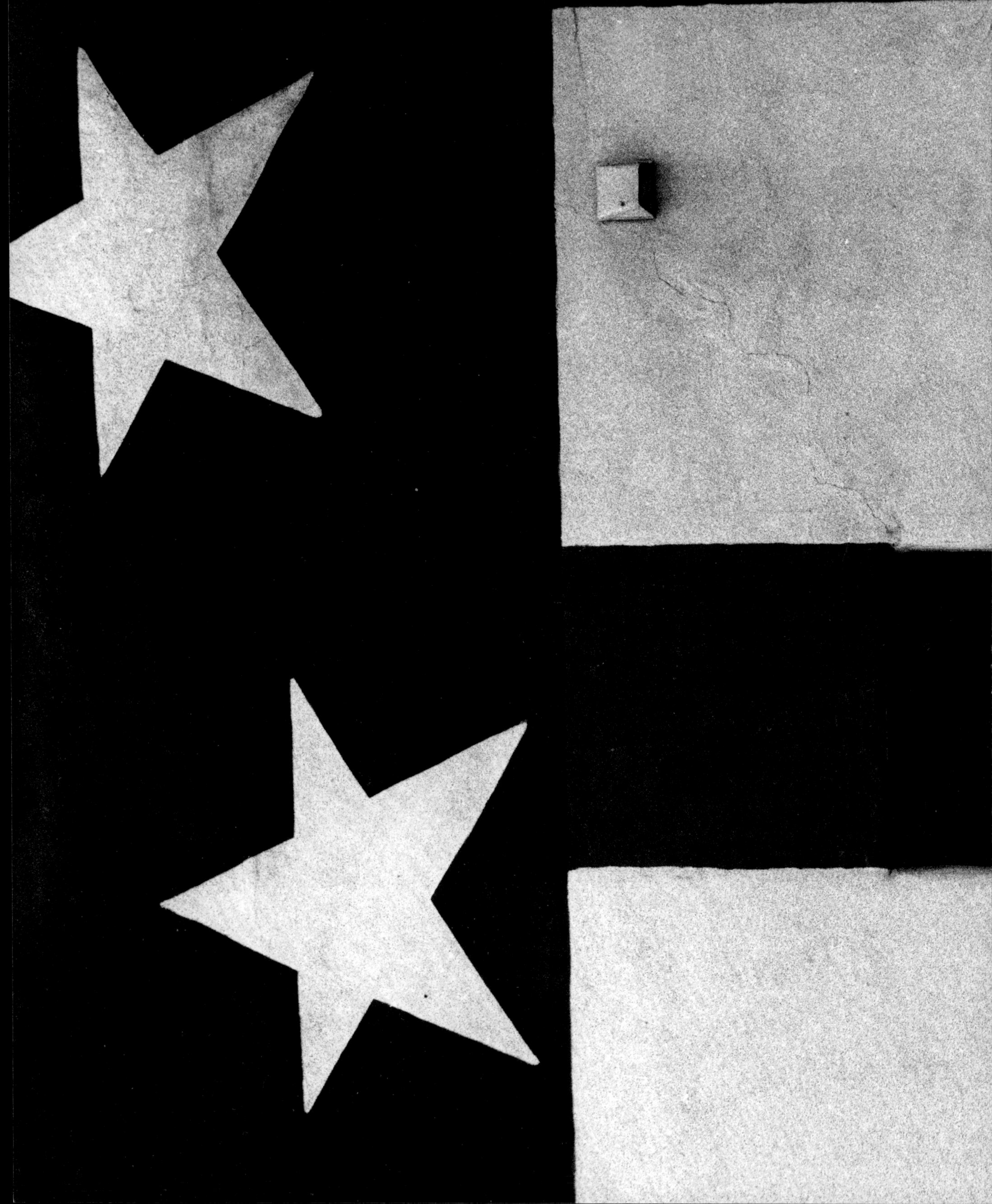

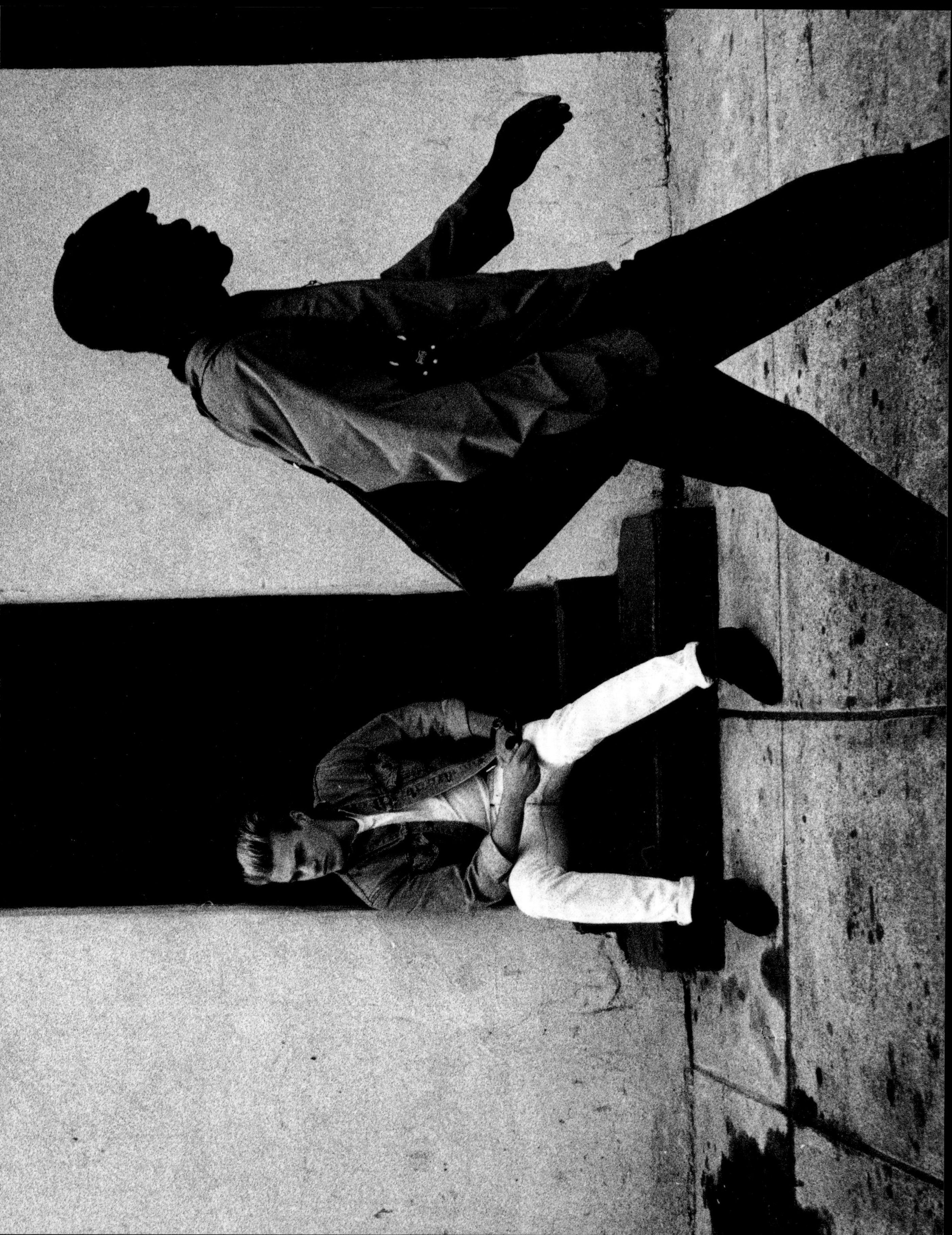

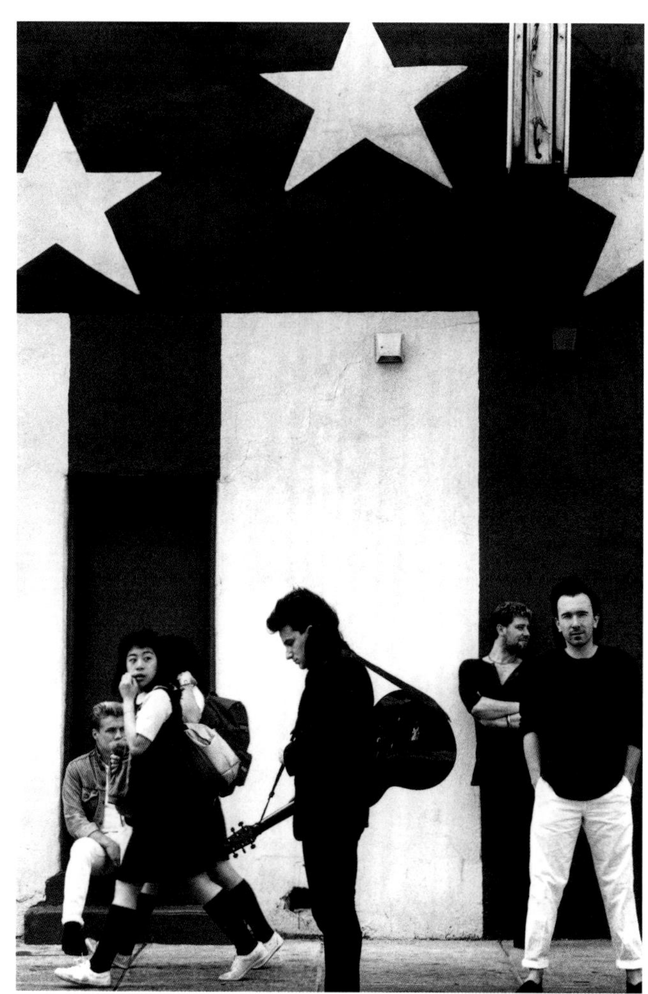

i had found this building that was painted like an america flag, stars and stripes. it seemed a good spot to take some photographs to show U2 were on tour in the States. i particularly enjoyed taking photos when pedestrians just walked thru the frame – i was standing across the road so no-one realised photos were being taken.

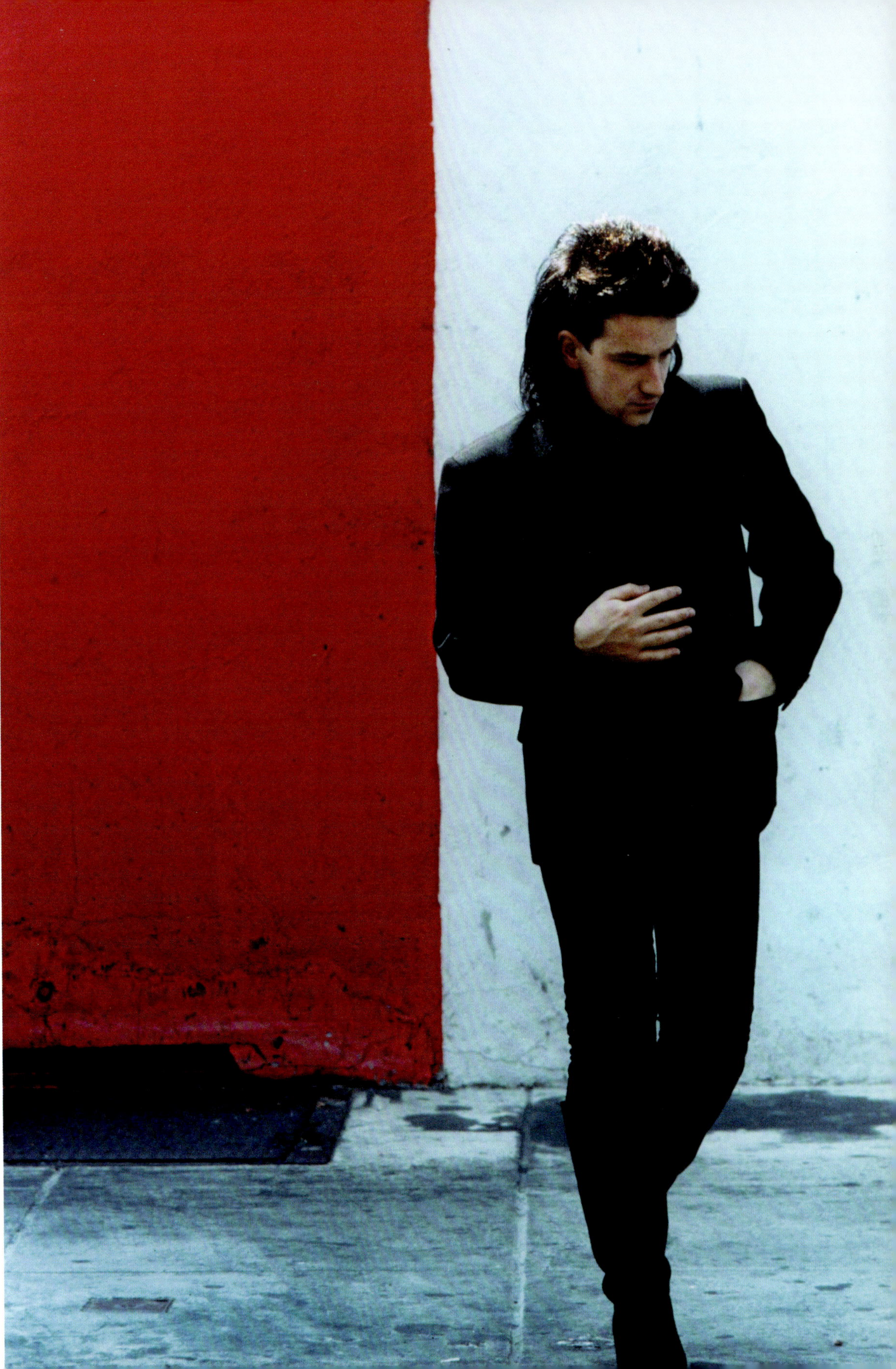

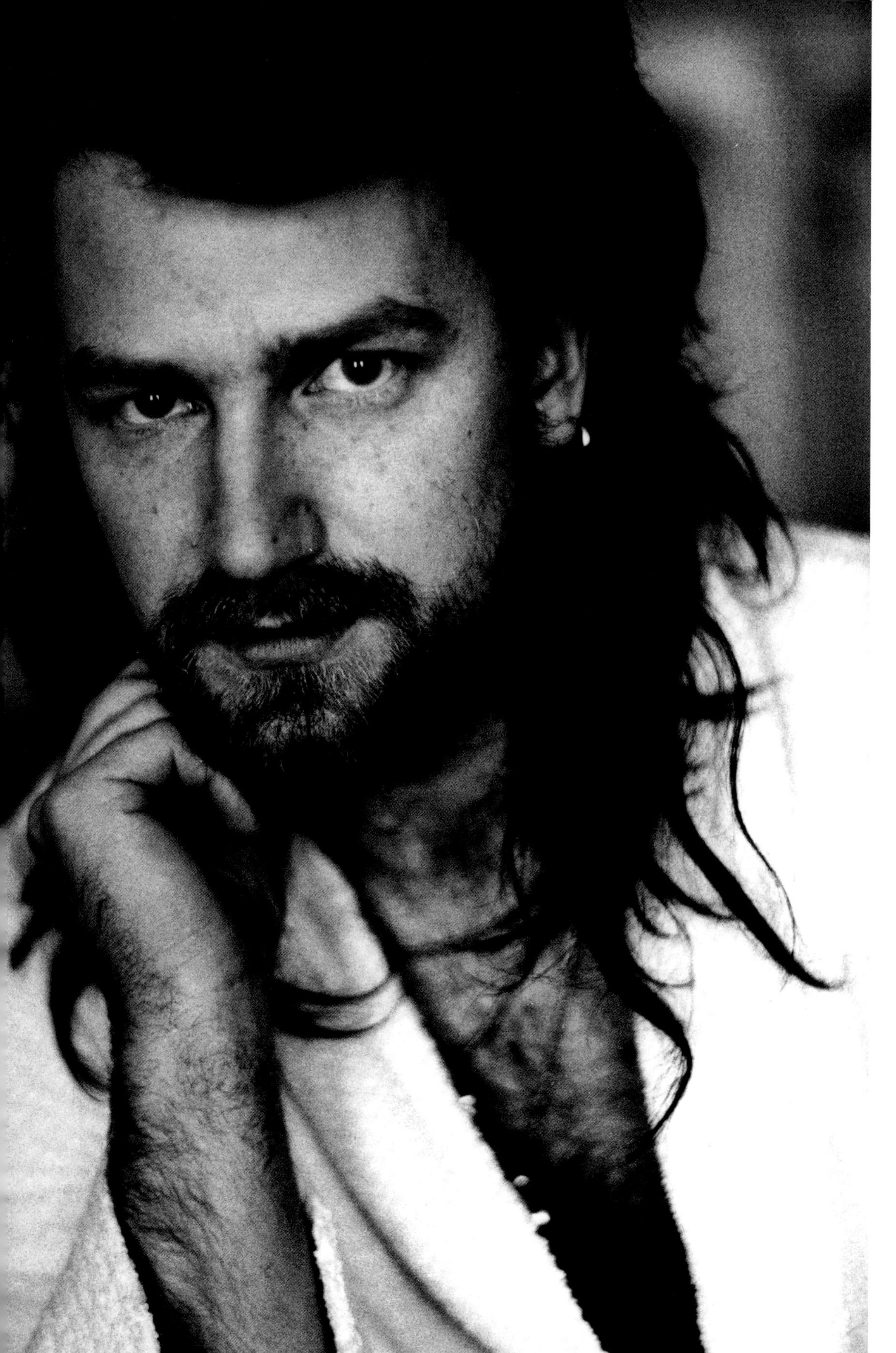

londo
1986
march

bono just
came back
from afri
and was
staying a
few nights
in london
where i
visited hi
in his ho
room. ~~en~~
~~his bath~~

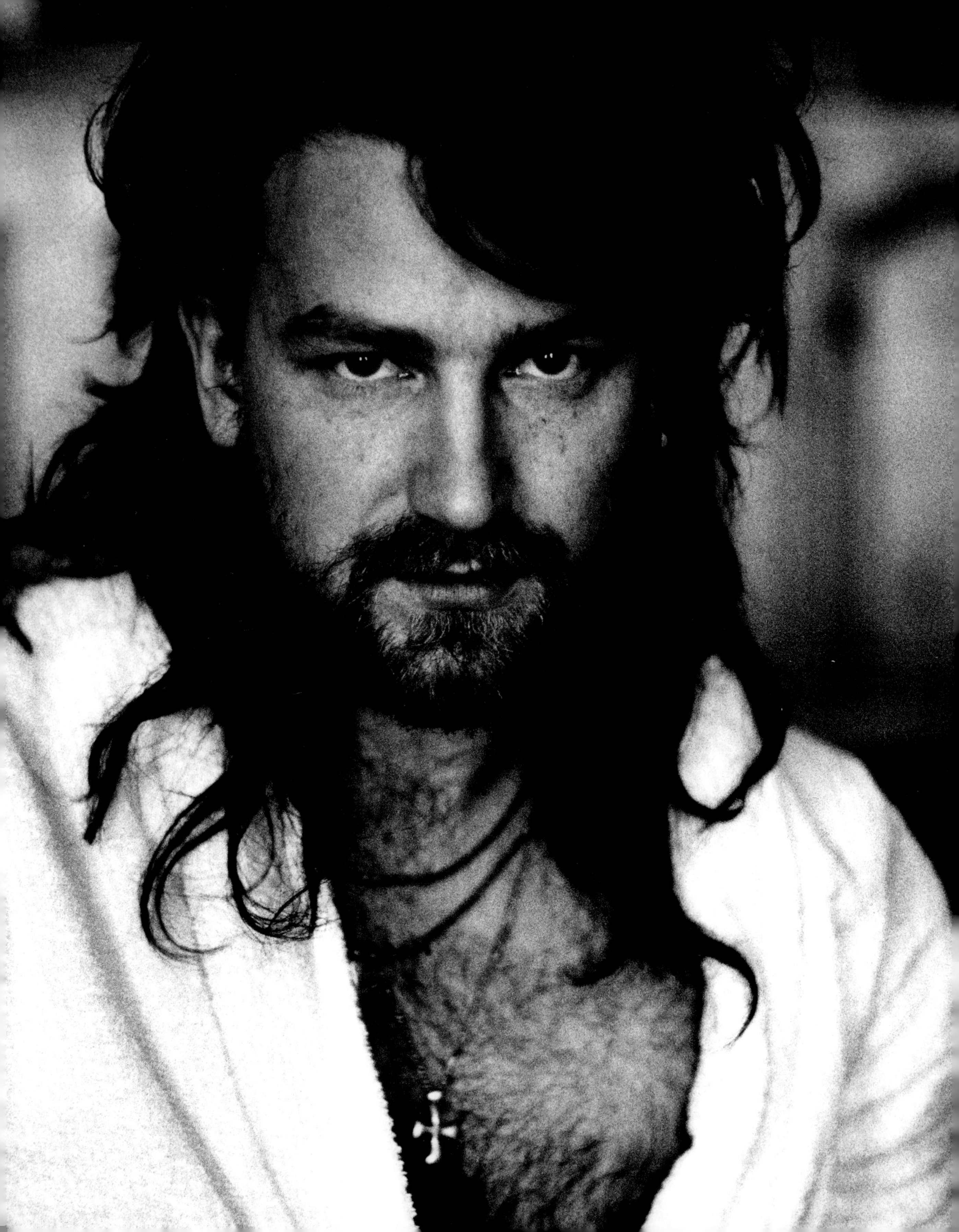

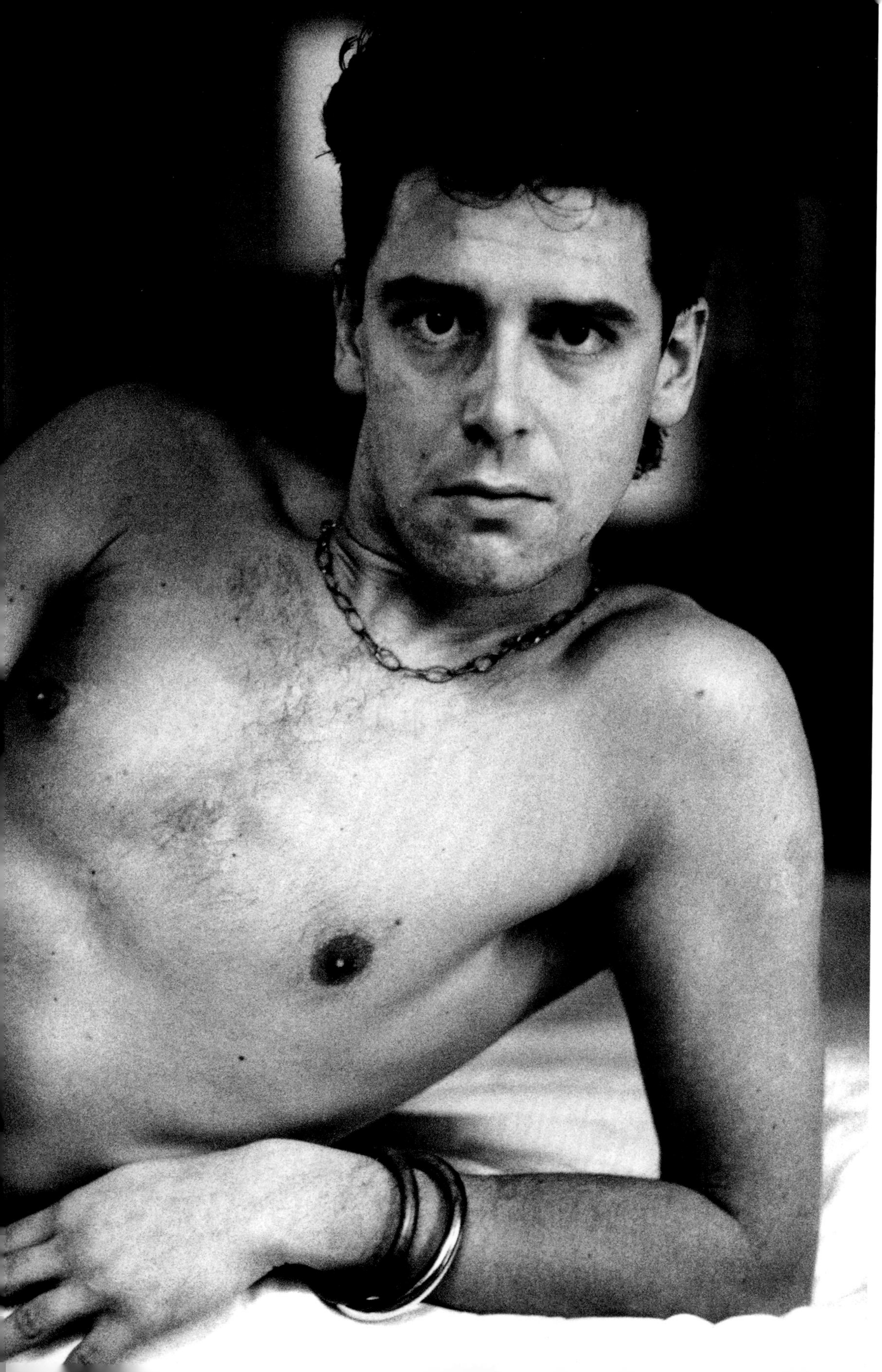

LONDON 1986 august?

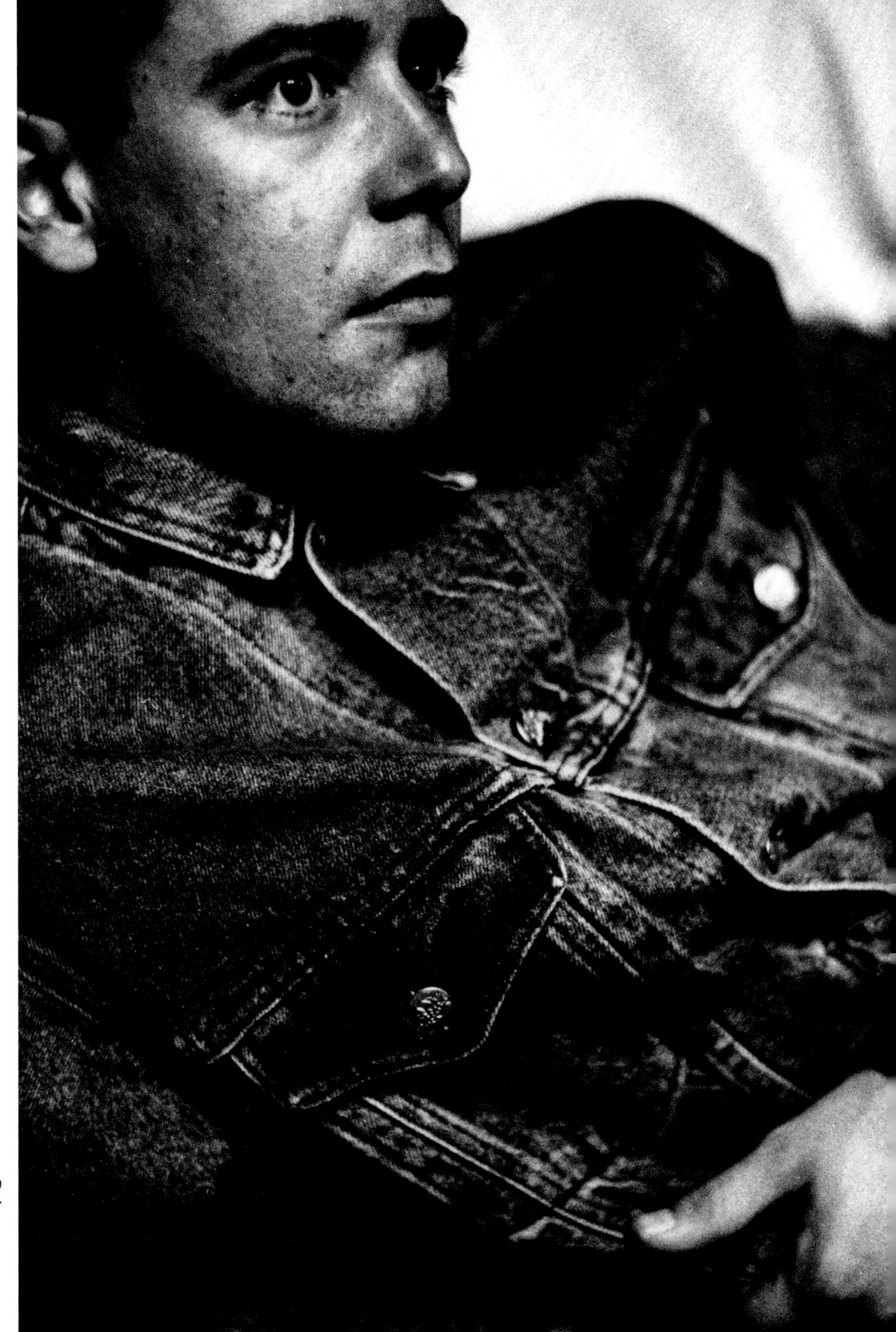

exploring
adam,
in a london
hotelroom.
is it of
interest to
know that
photographed
dam more
often naked
than i have
any other man?

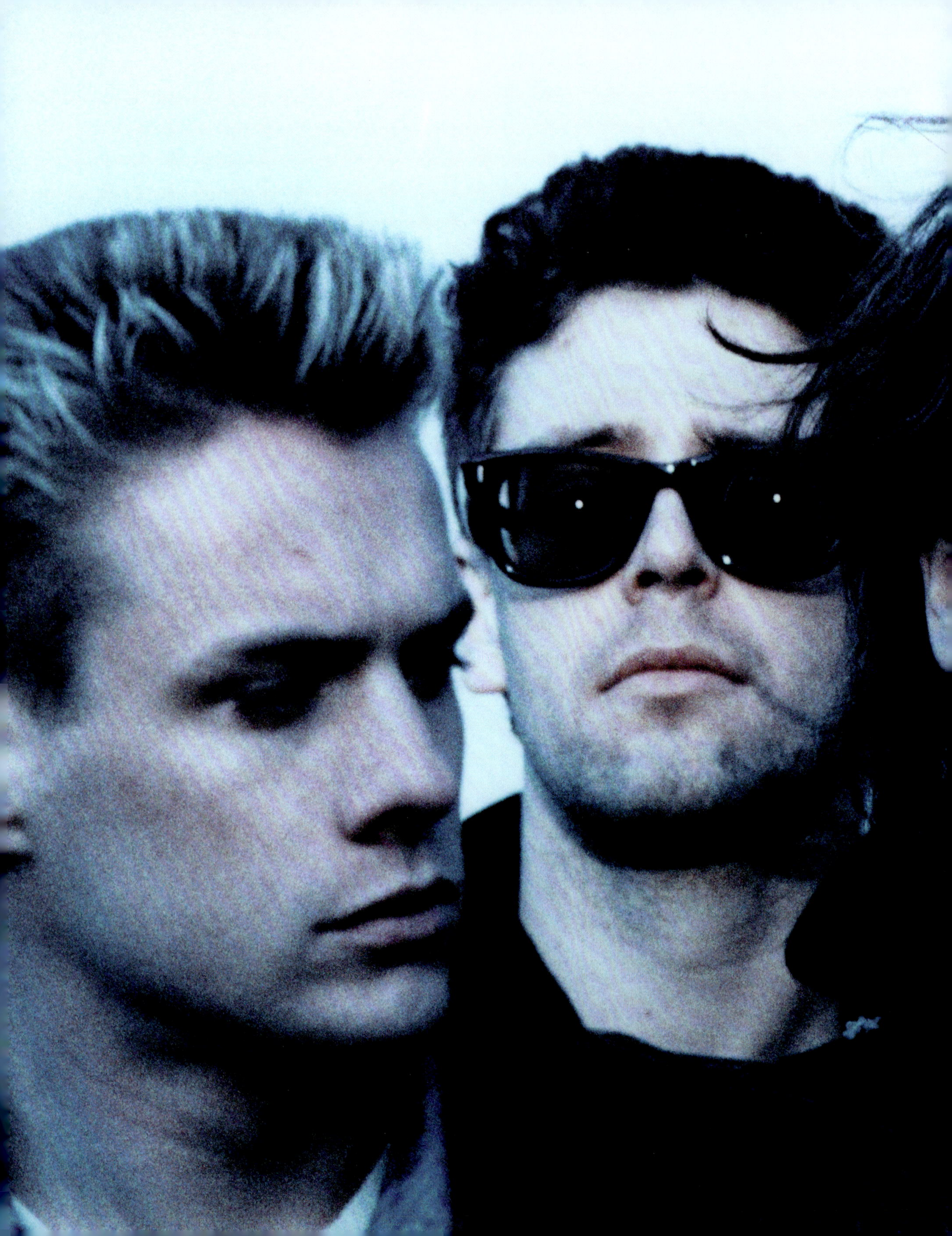

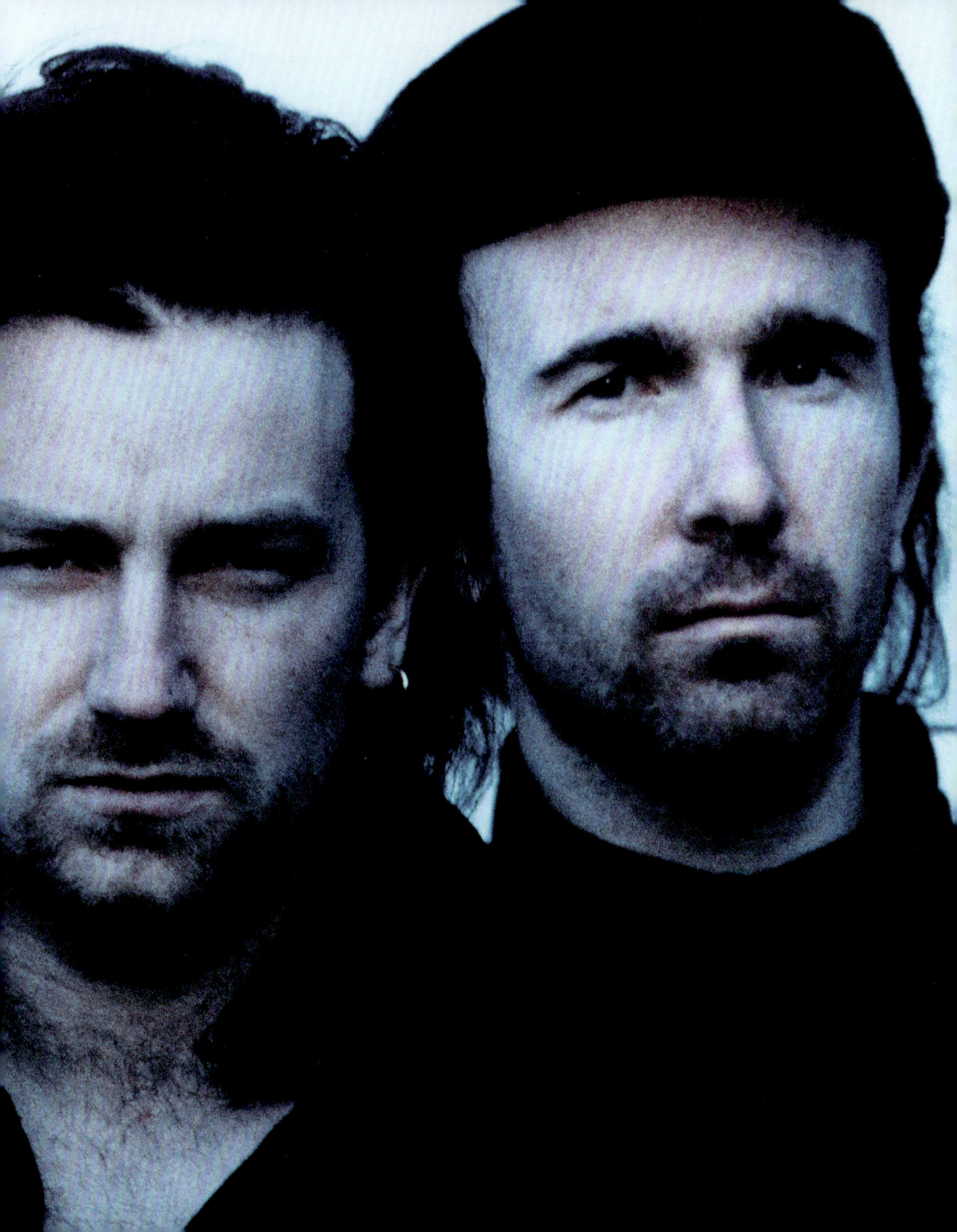

DUBLIN 1986 march

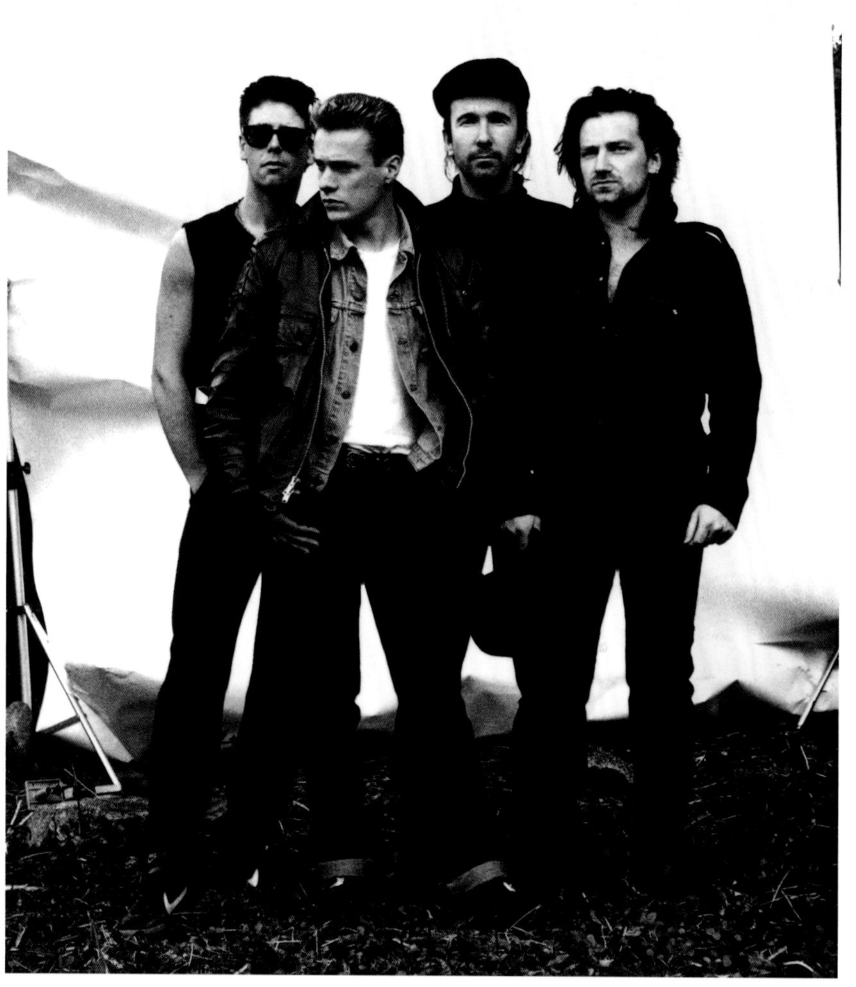

this is a
photo after
we got rid
of the
damaged
backdrop.
Bono looks
pretty
intense
because his
focus is on
making the
album and
that ~~goes~~
causes always
incredible
ups and downs
in his mood.

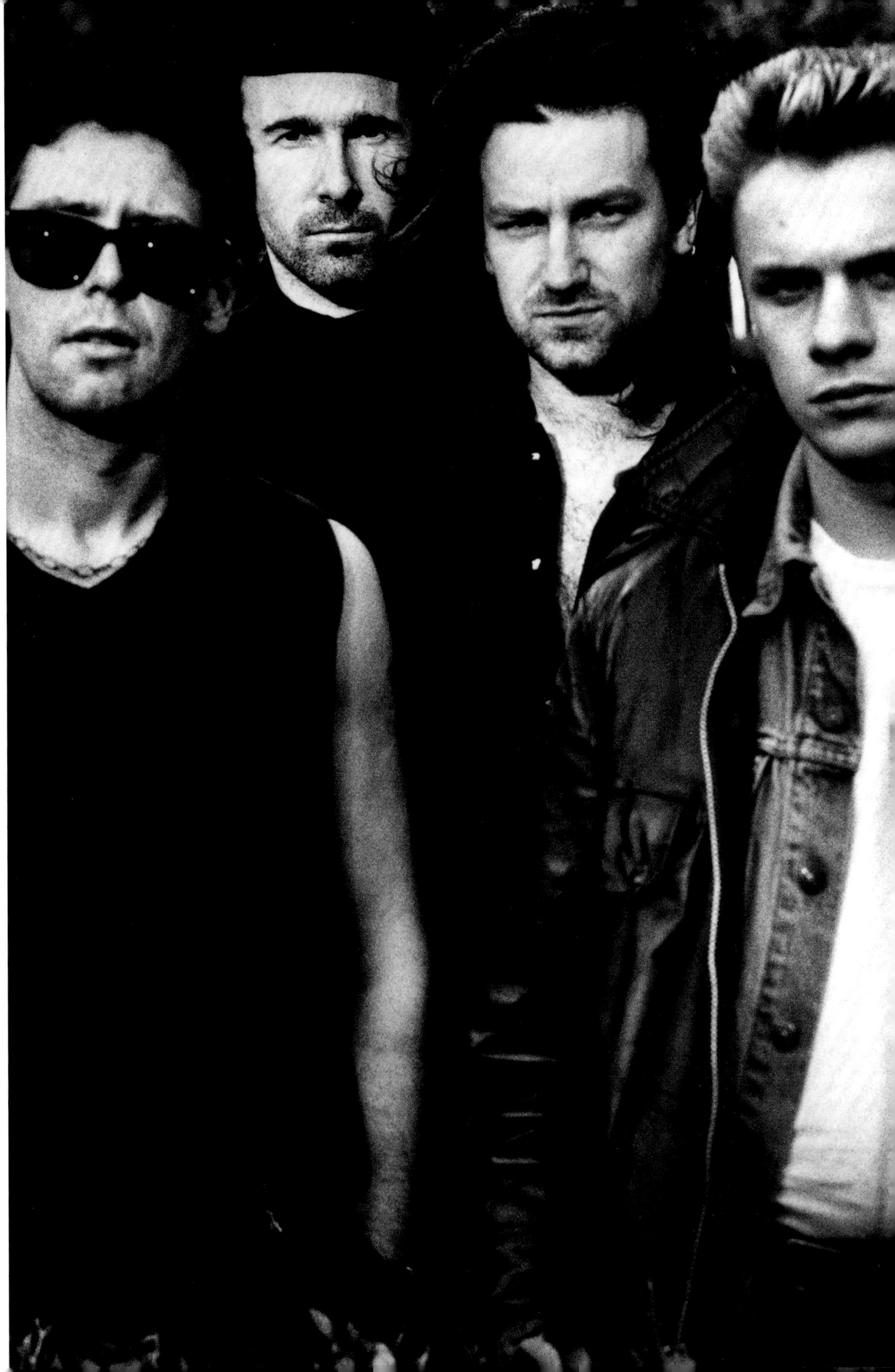

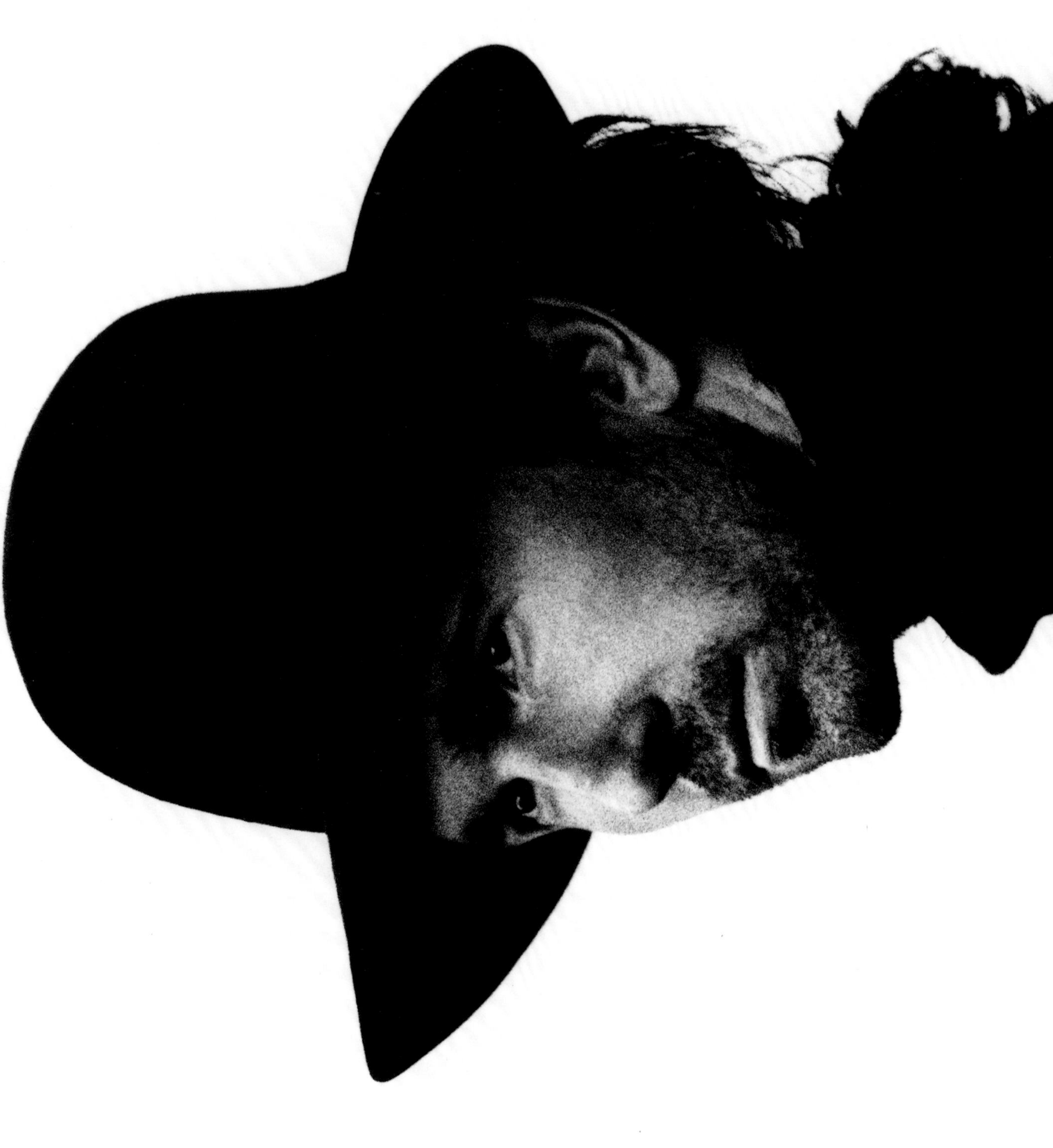

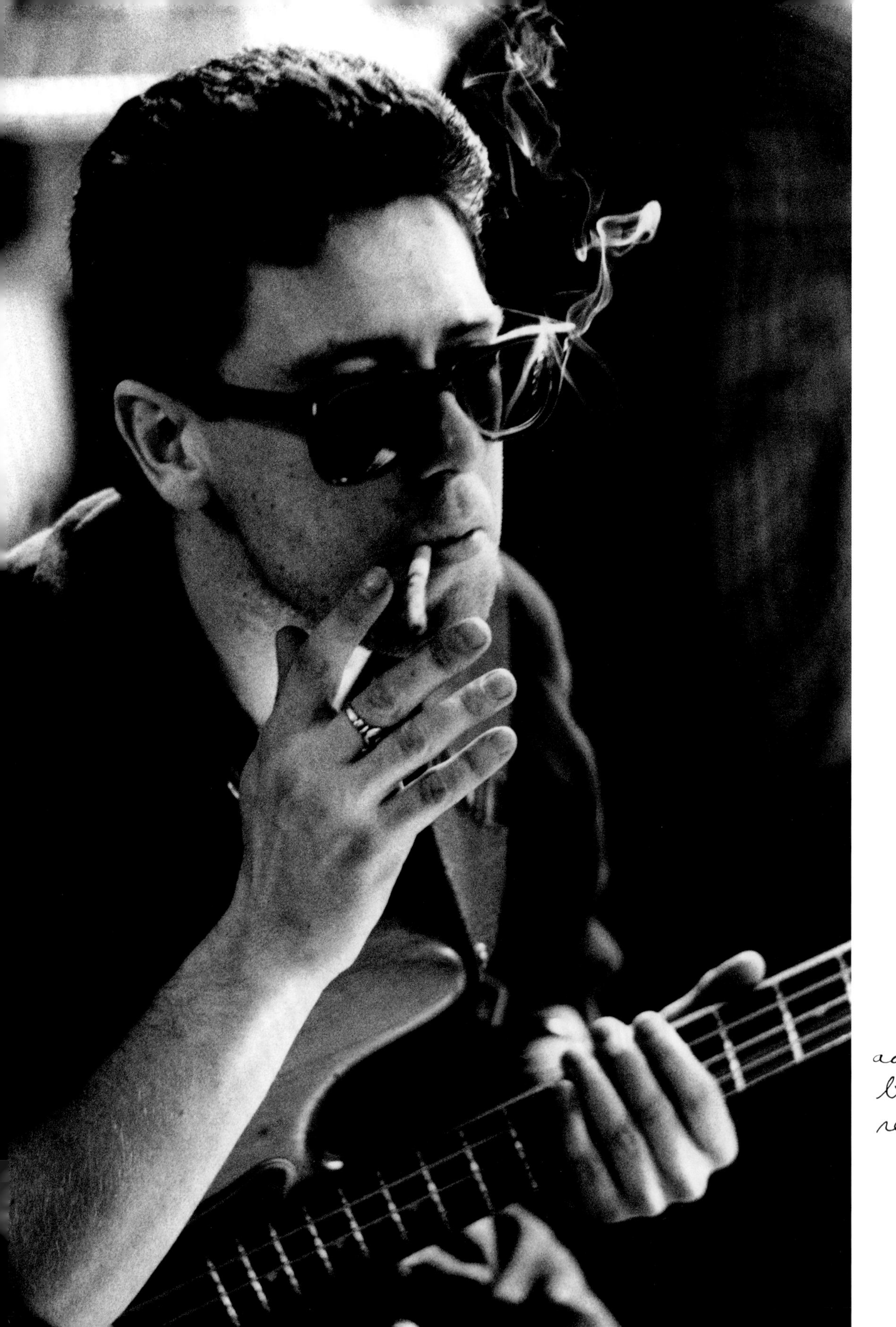

adam taking a
break during
rehearsals.

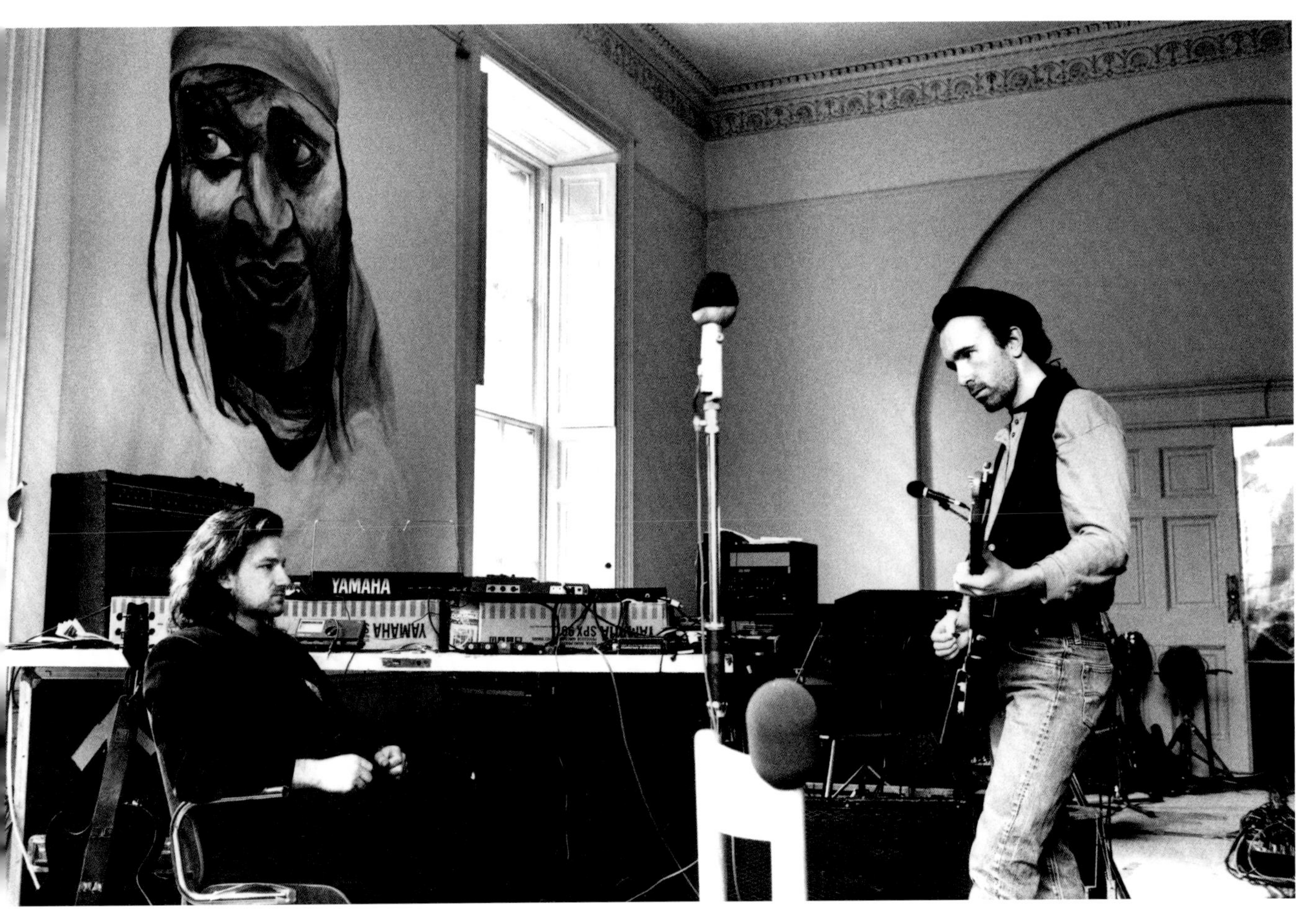

the house where they rehearsed and recorded the joshuatree was subsequently bought by adam.

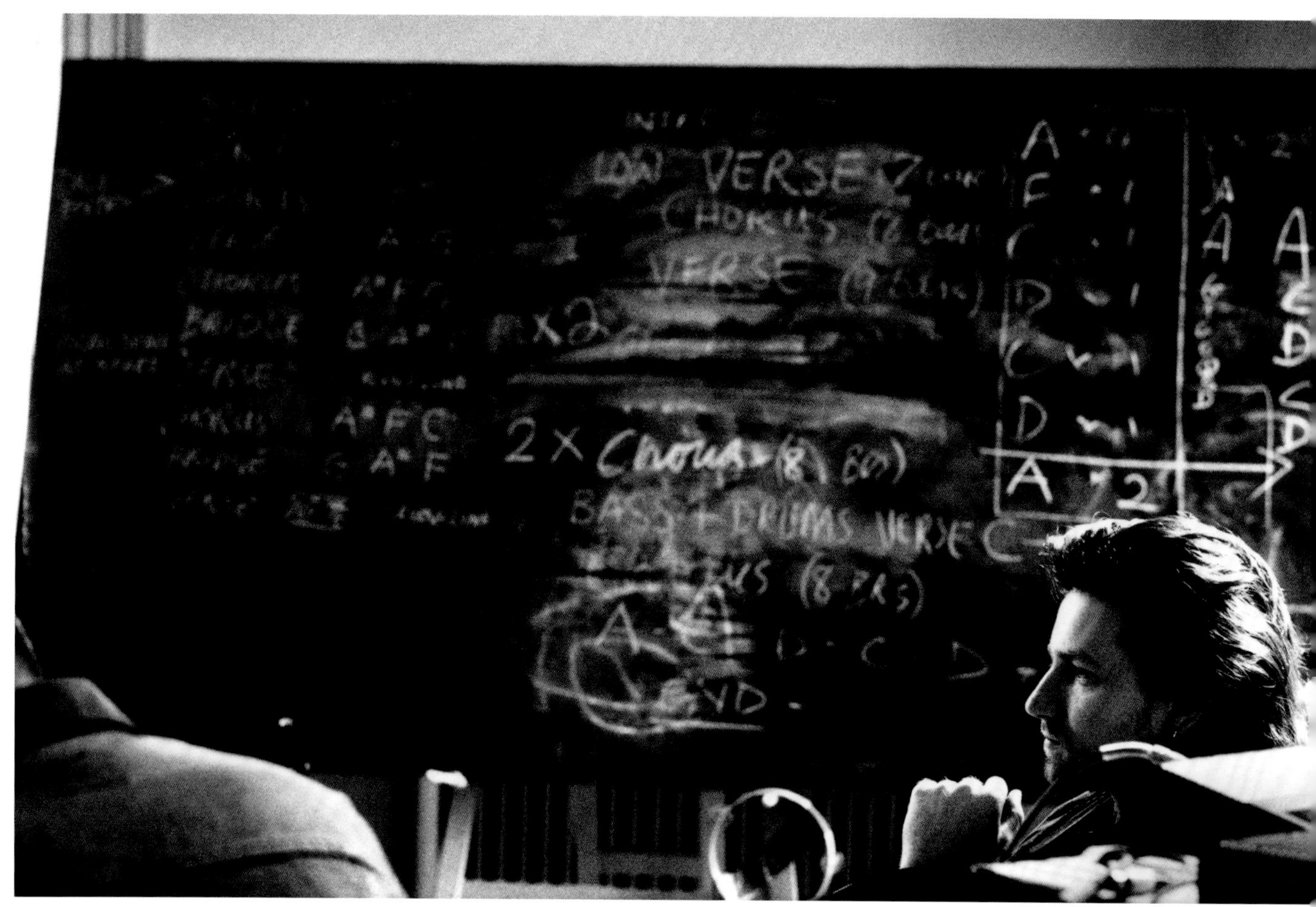

2 photos of bono, both showing him pretty intense. it is easy to read his mood unlike with the others who from the outside generally ~~are~~ look very controlled but can be boiling on the inside.

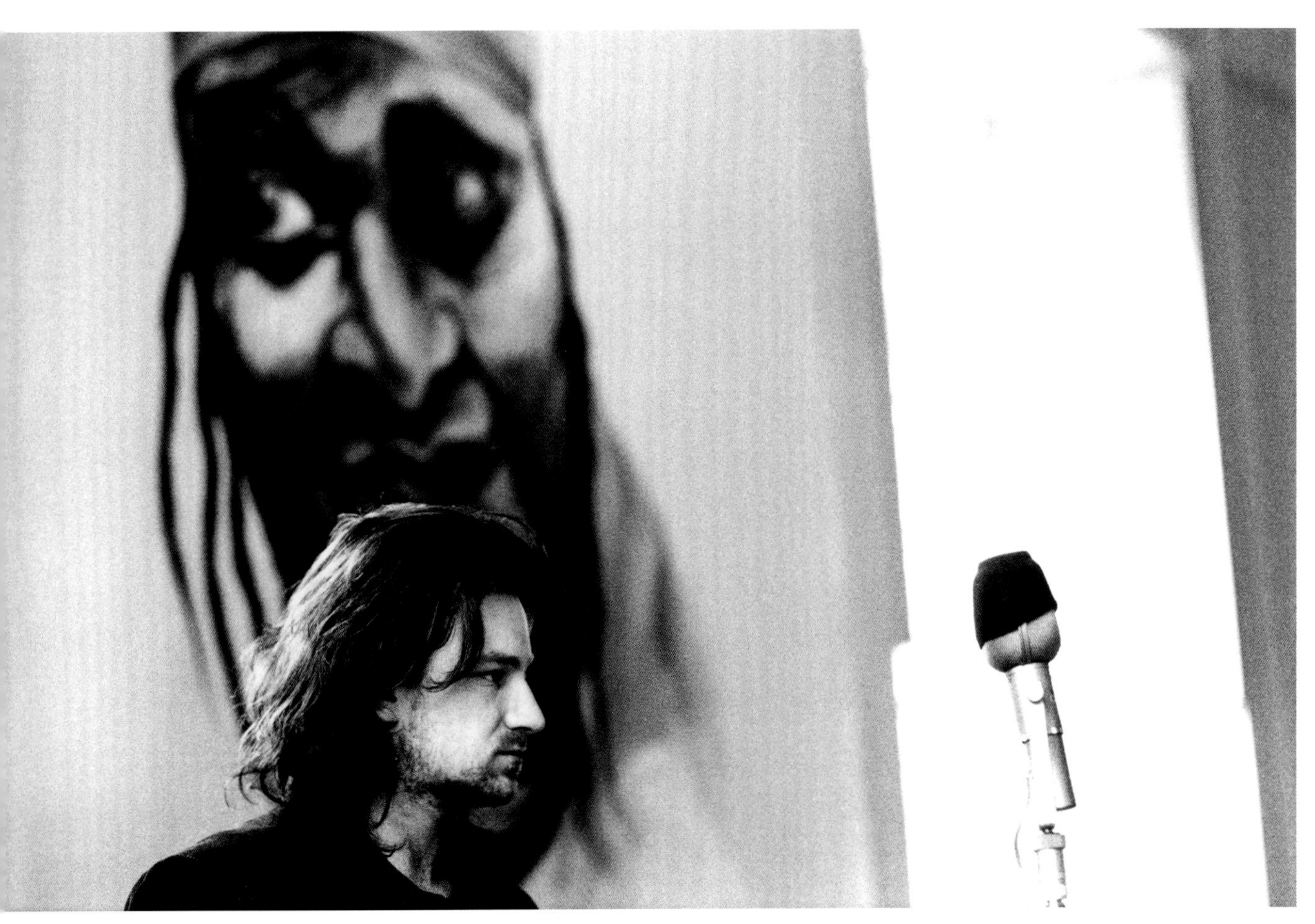

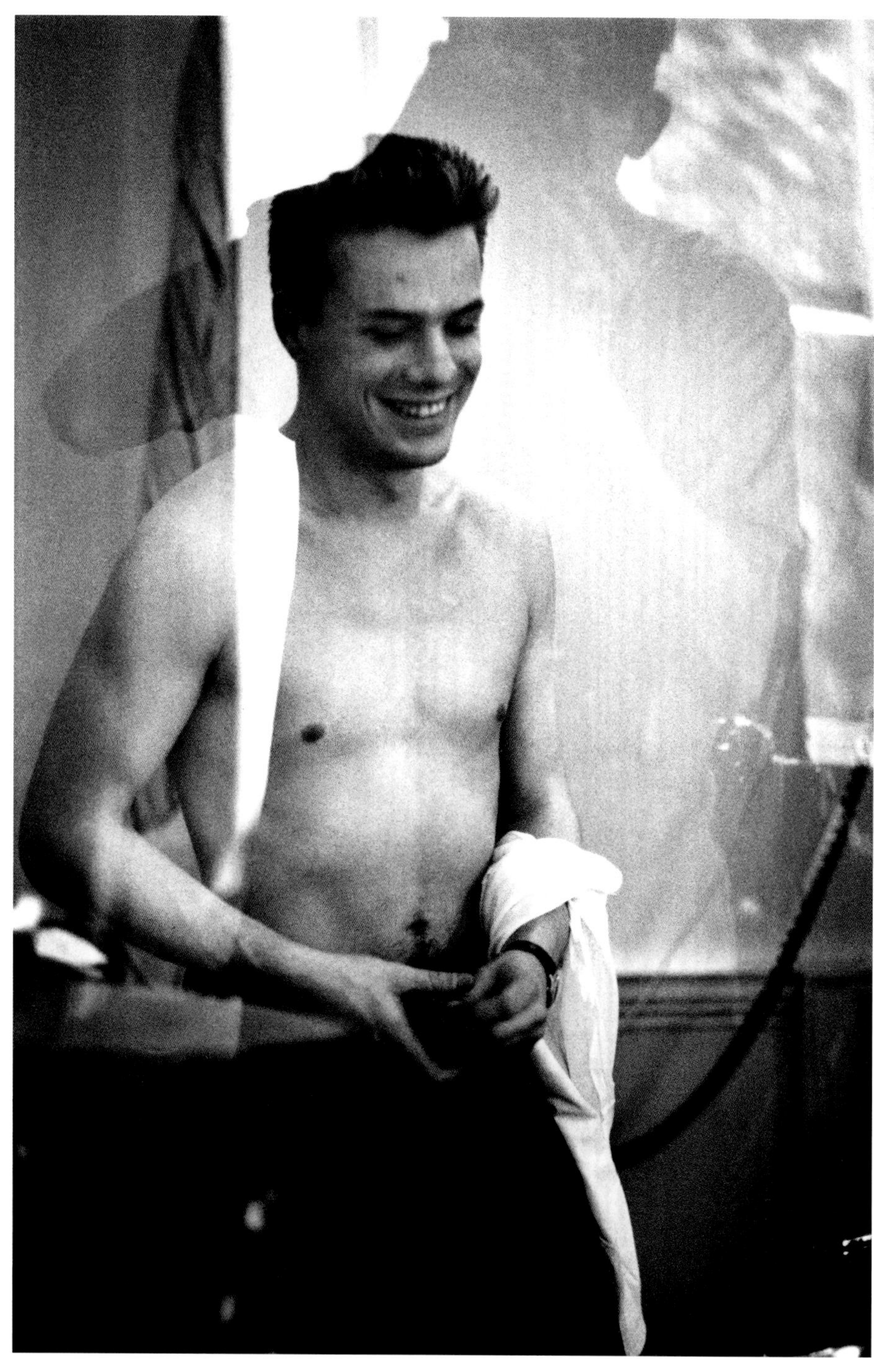

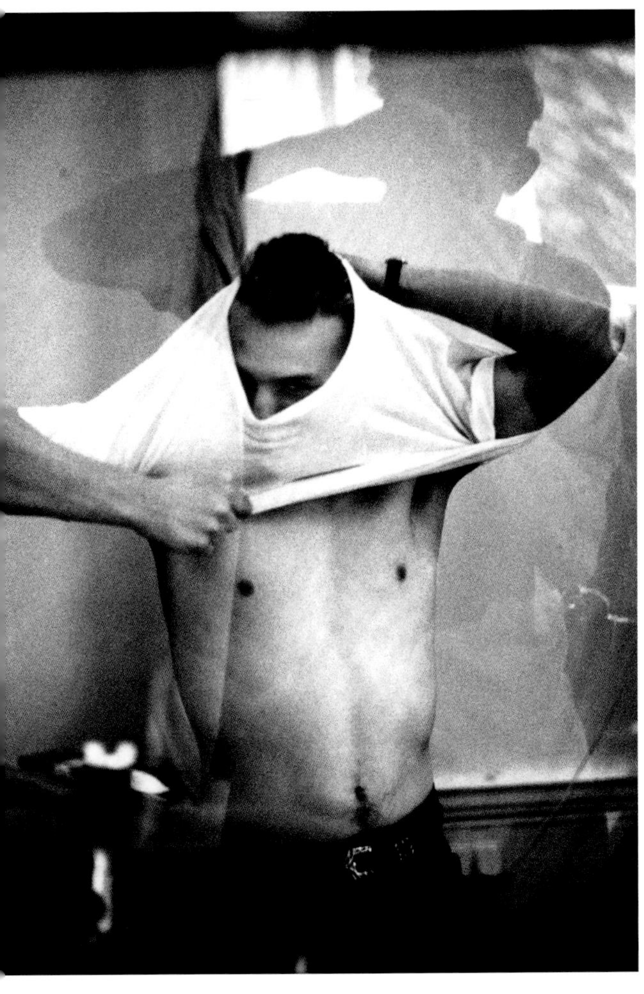

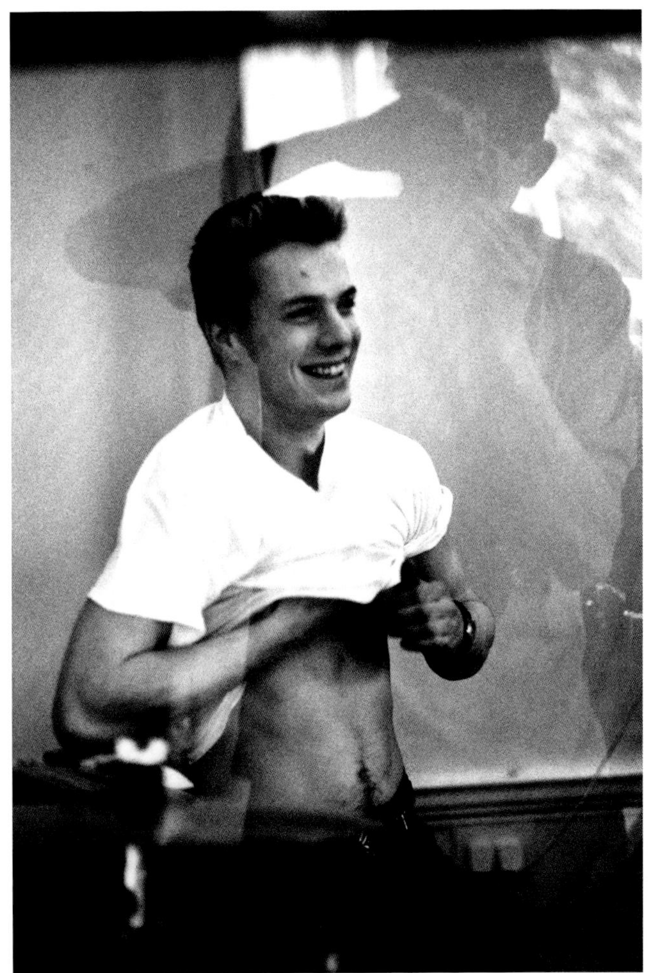

one for the ladies: larry changing into a white t-shirt with my reflection hanging over him.

the house is outside dublin, in the country-side, and had some animals strolling around as this photo shows: bono and a donkey (R.)

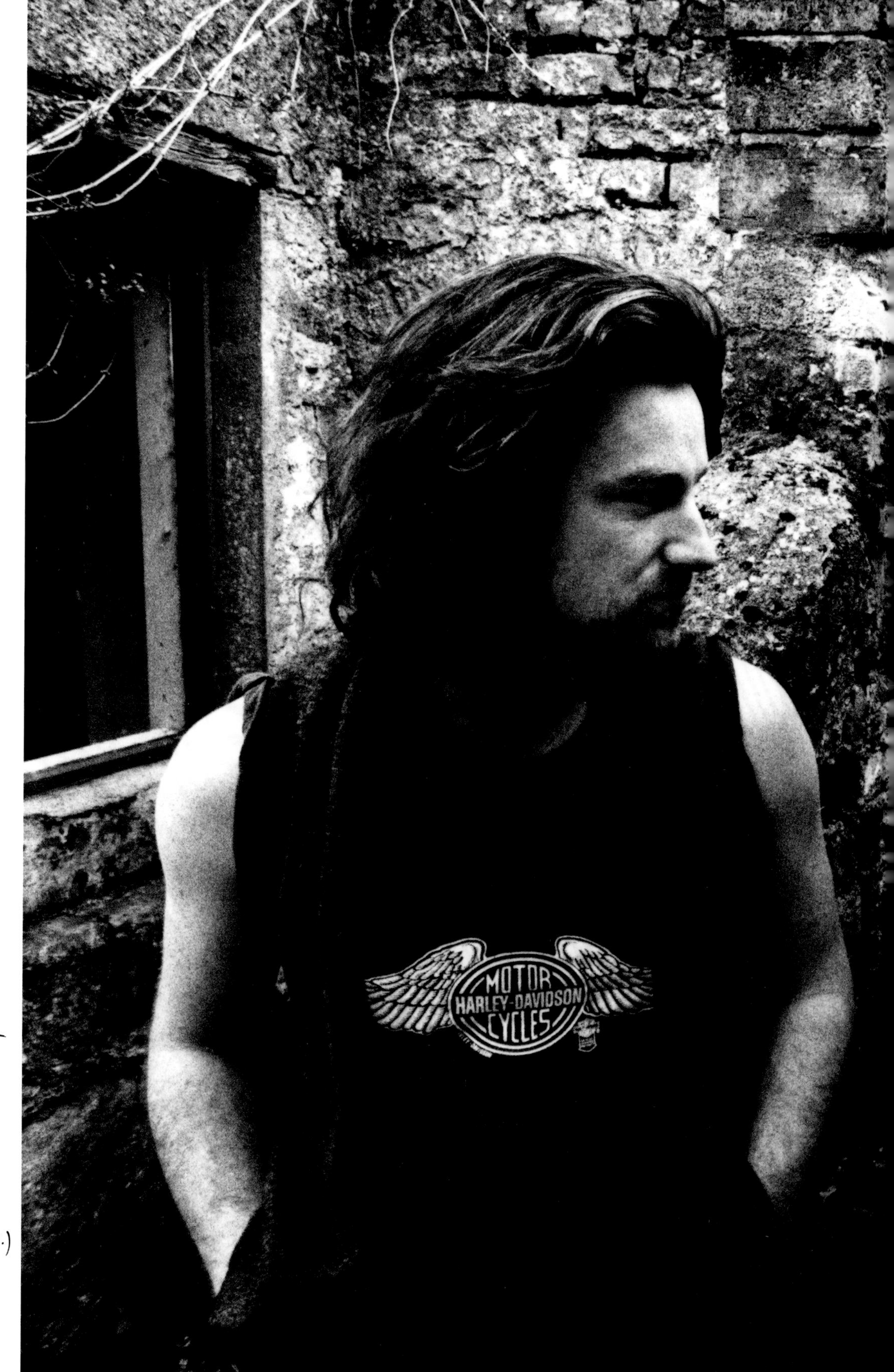

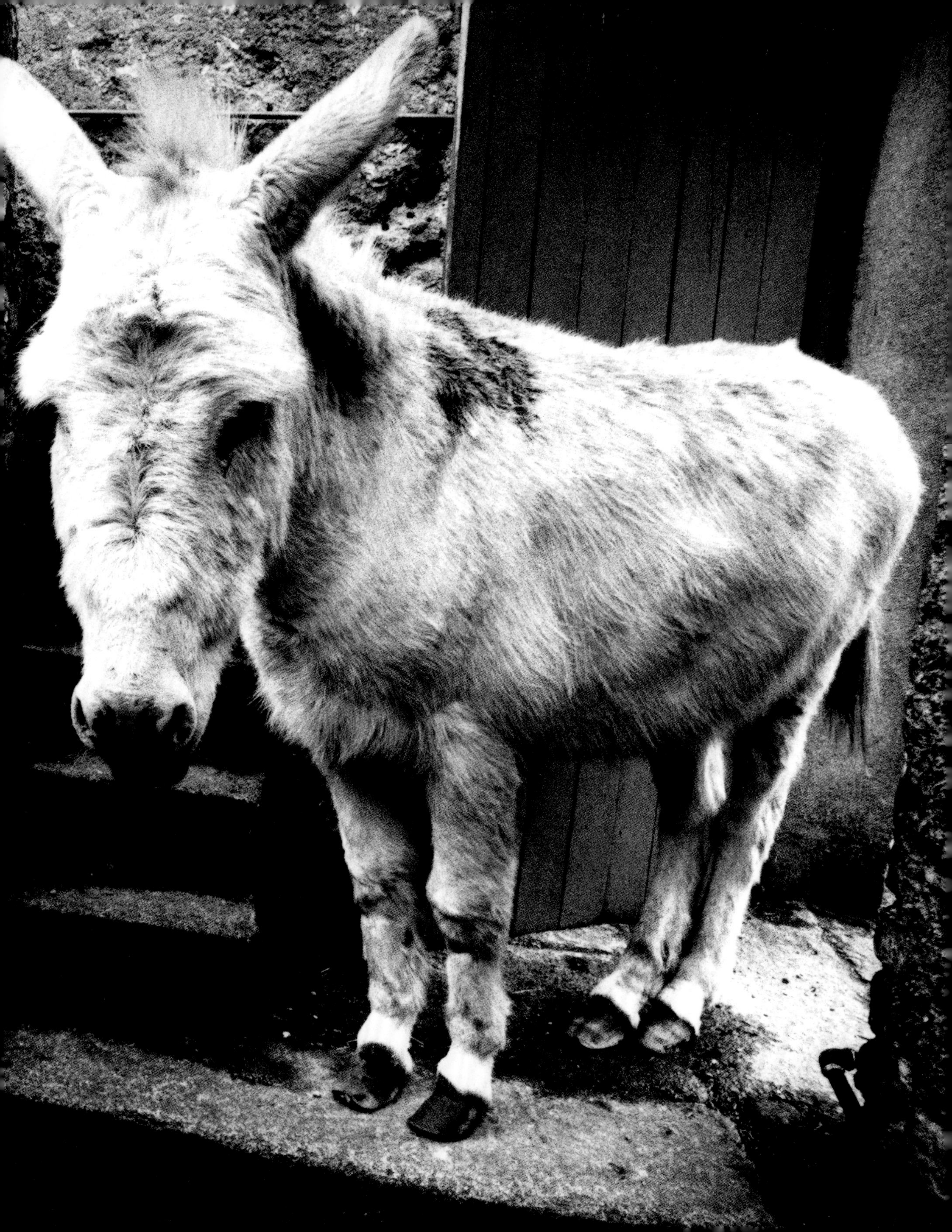

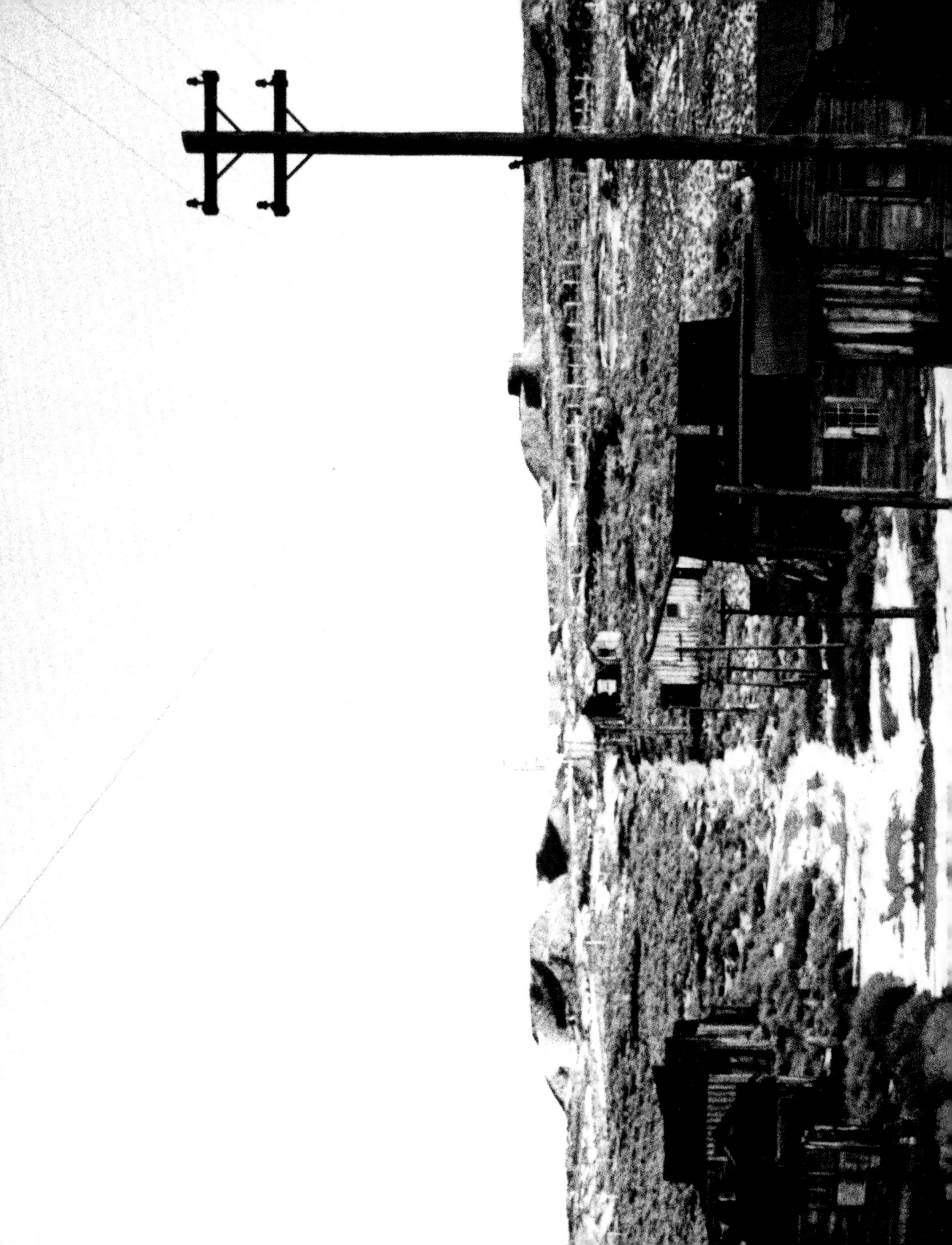

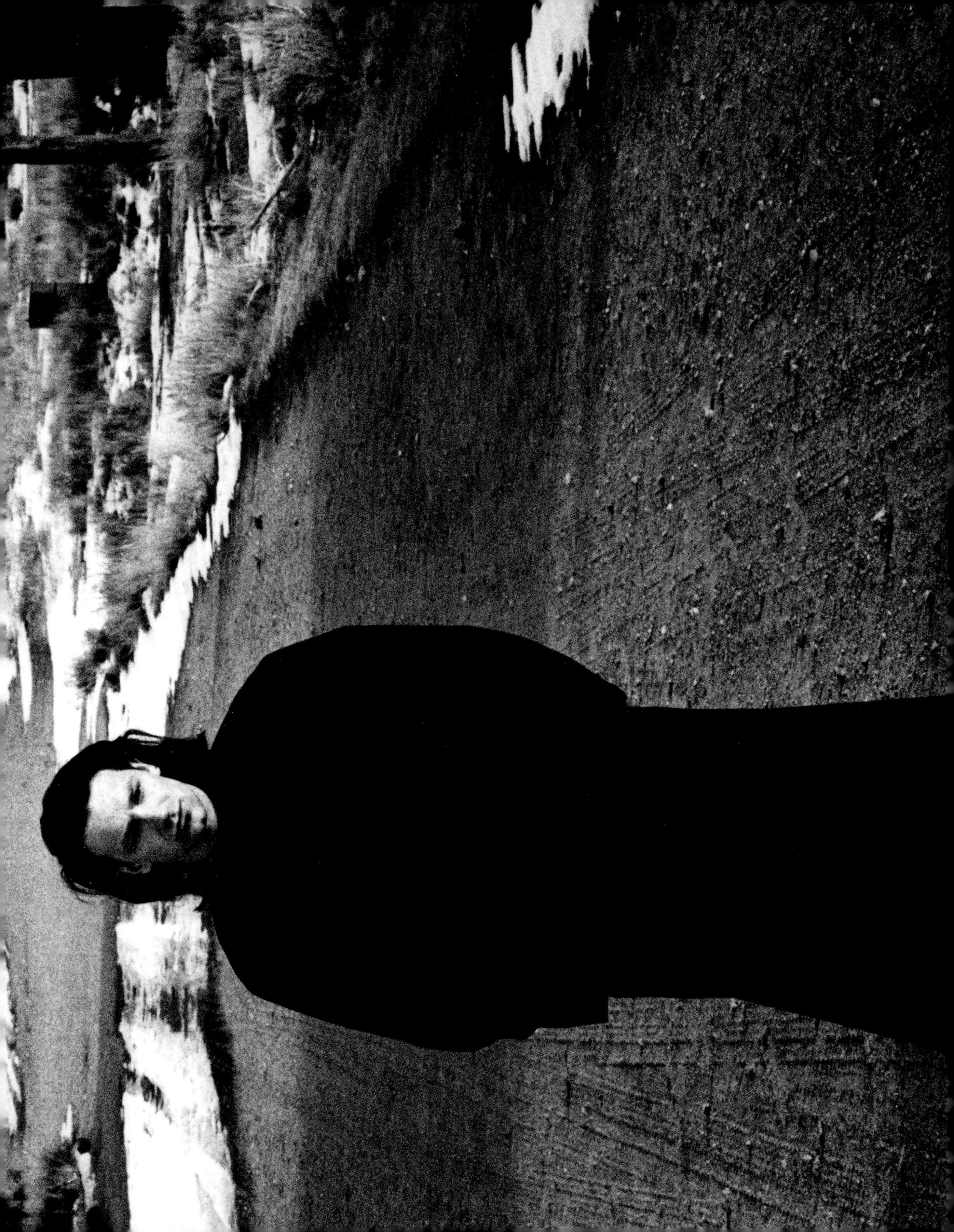

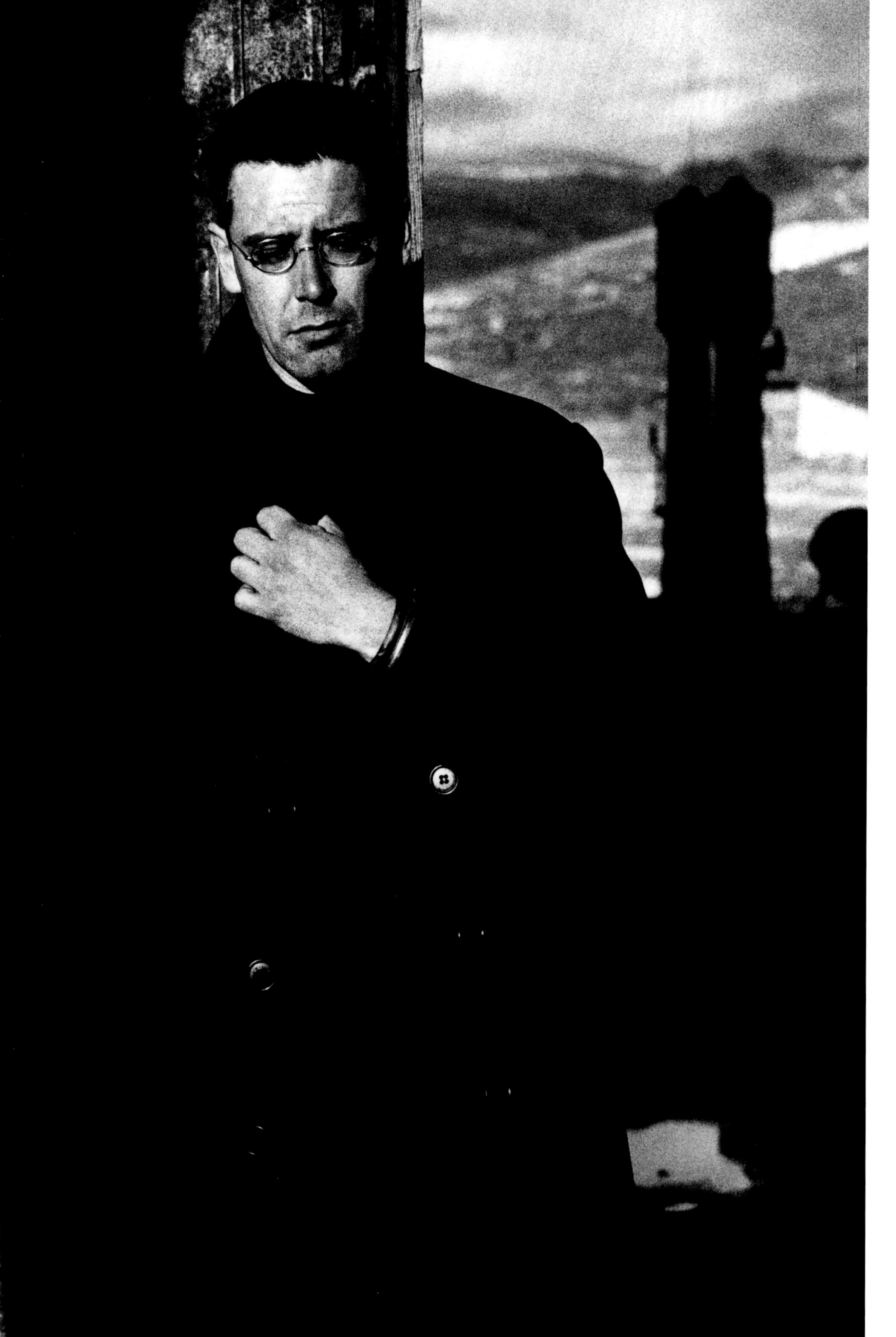

'The Joshua Tree' trip 1986
december

Bodie

1986

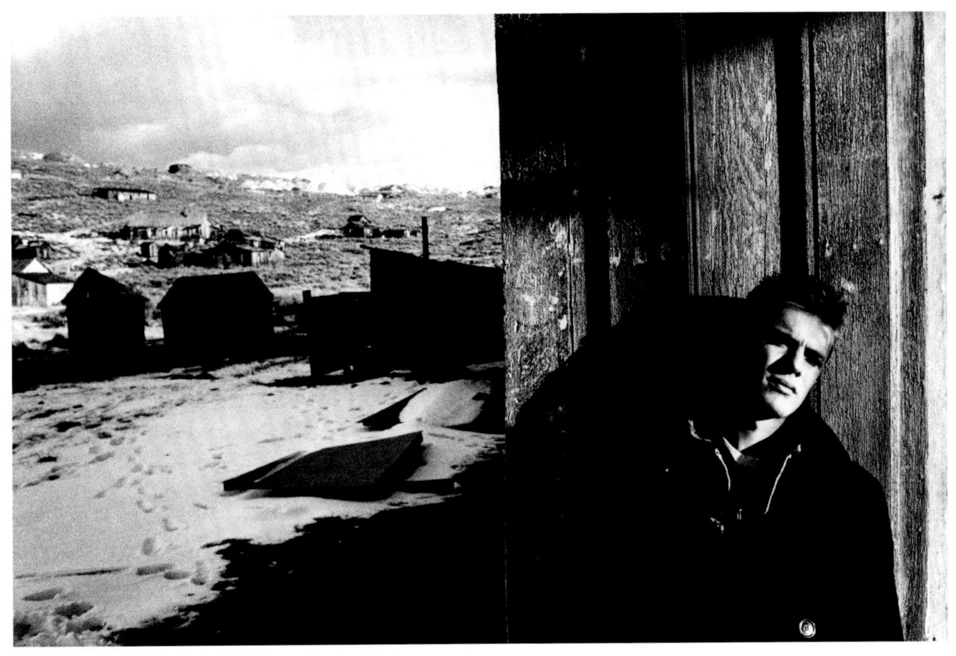

in order to find a location for new photographs i travelled from reno in nevada to palm springs in california. the working title of the new record was 'the desert songs' and also 'the 2 americas' and i was looking for desert locations. after i believed i had found some interesting places the band came over and we went on a 3 day trip, repeating my original journey which brought us to bodie as our first stop. Bodie is a deserted goldmine town and it looked fantastic in the early winter period. it was graphically interesting and had a sense of hope and disillusionment which i felt was appropriate.

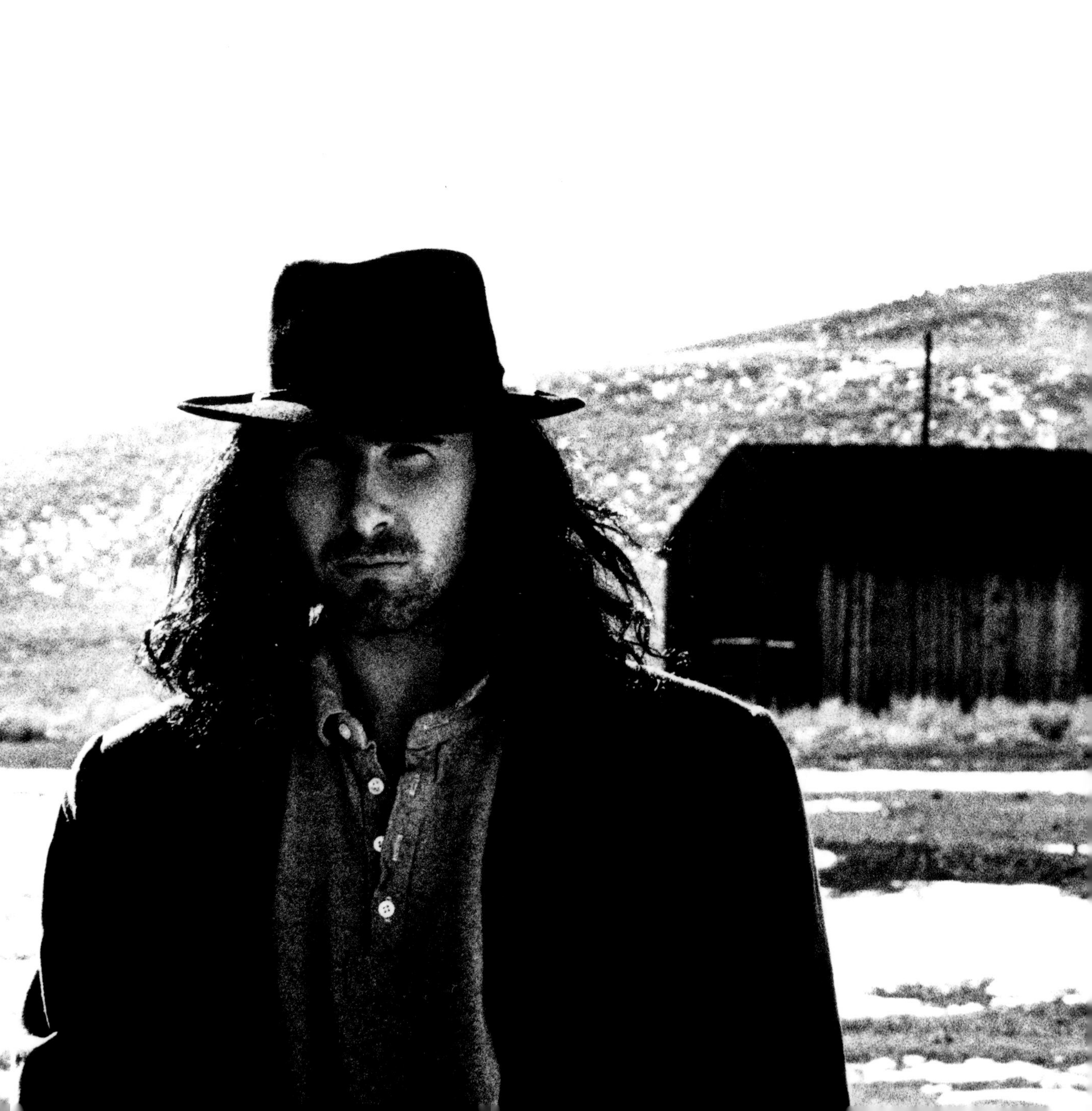

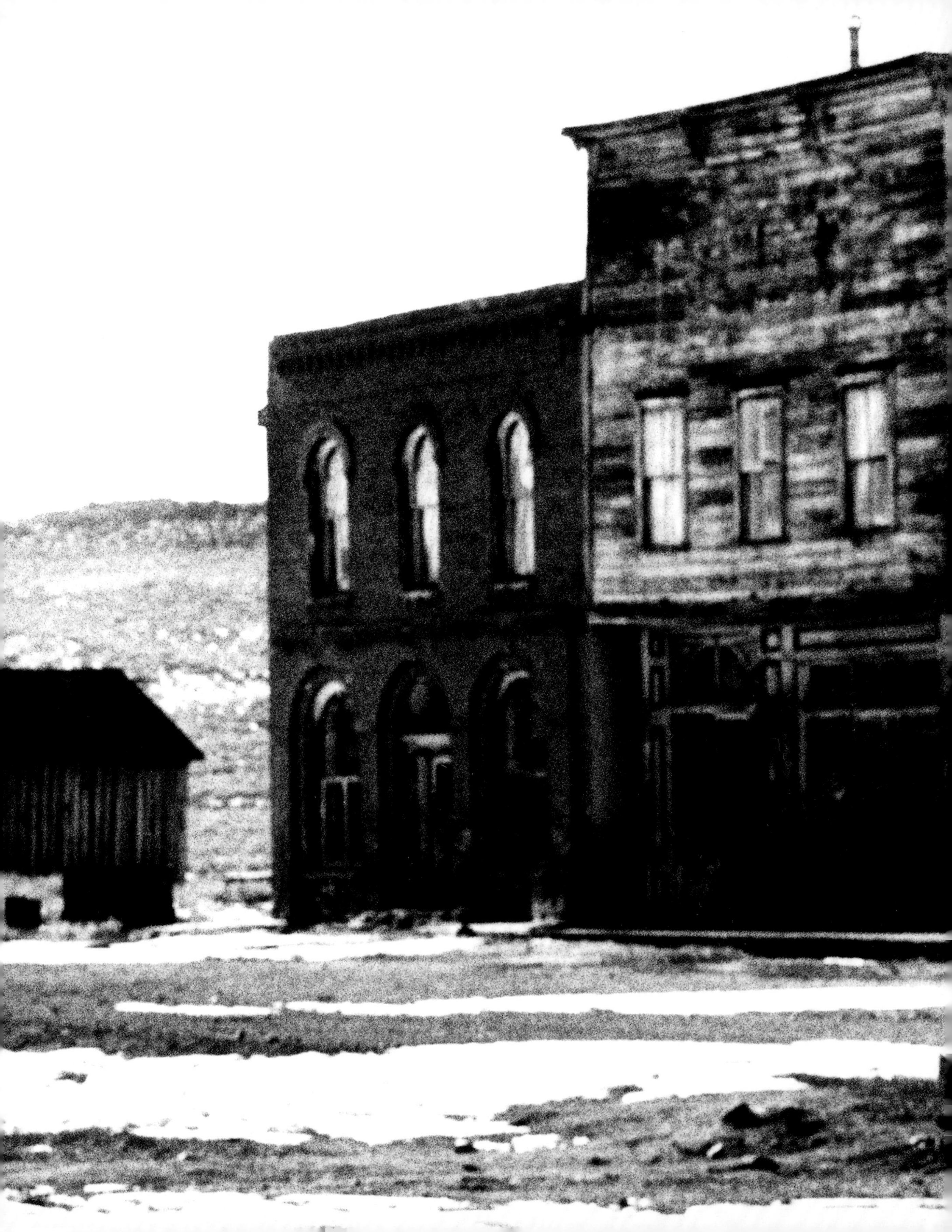

DEATH VALLEY

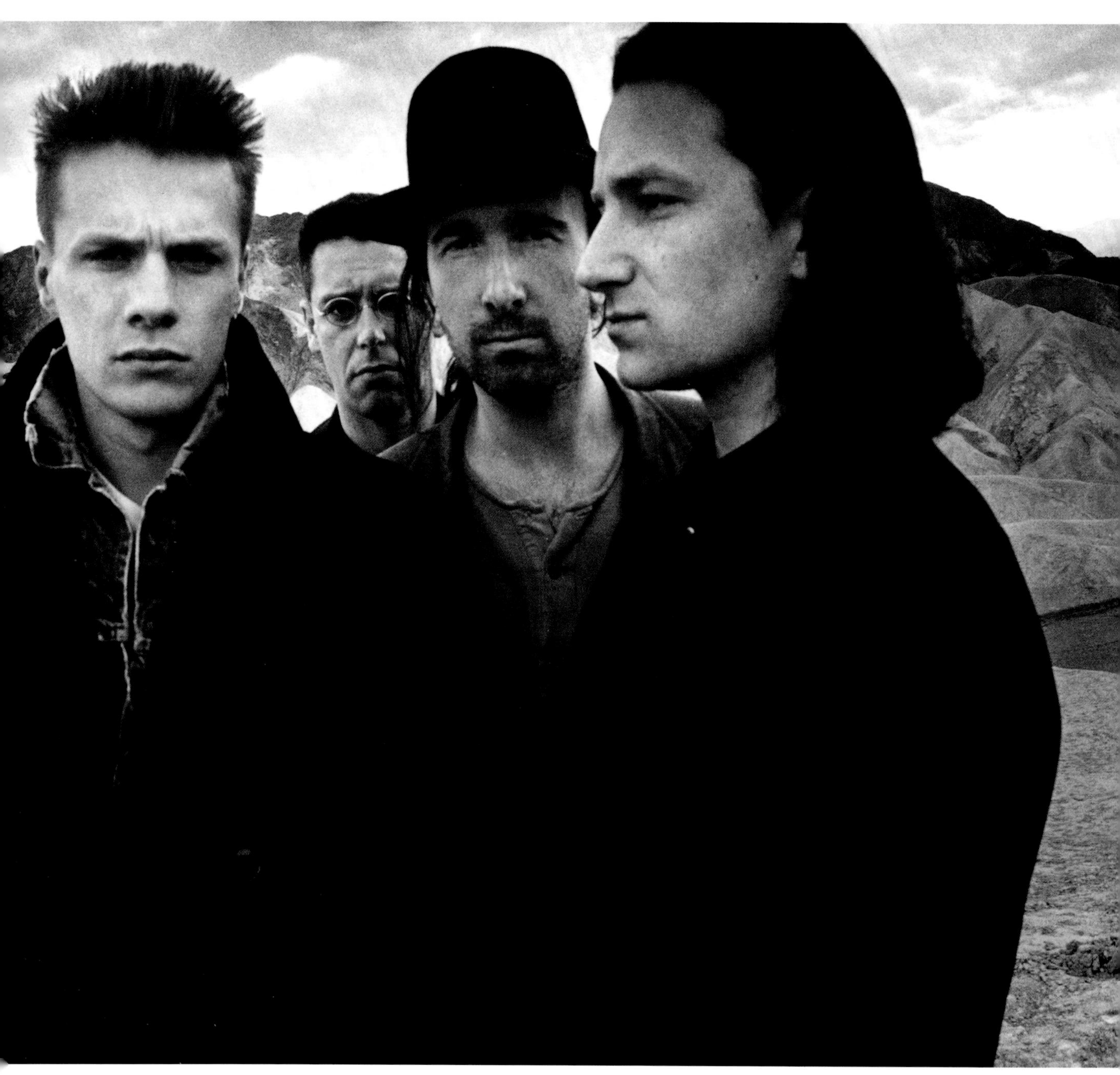

this photograph, taken at Zabriskie Point (Antonioni, Monroe, Manson etc.) ended up on the vinyl cover of 'the Joshua Tree' record. it became my most well known photo for years to come and we tried, successfully, to destroy part of its impact it had, as showing U2 as a band that looked like it ~~take~~ took life and itself too seriously, with the images for Achtung Baby years later.

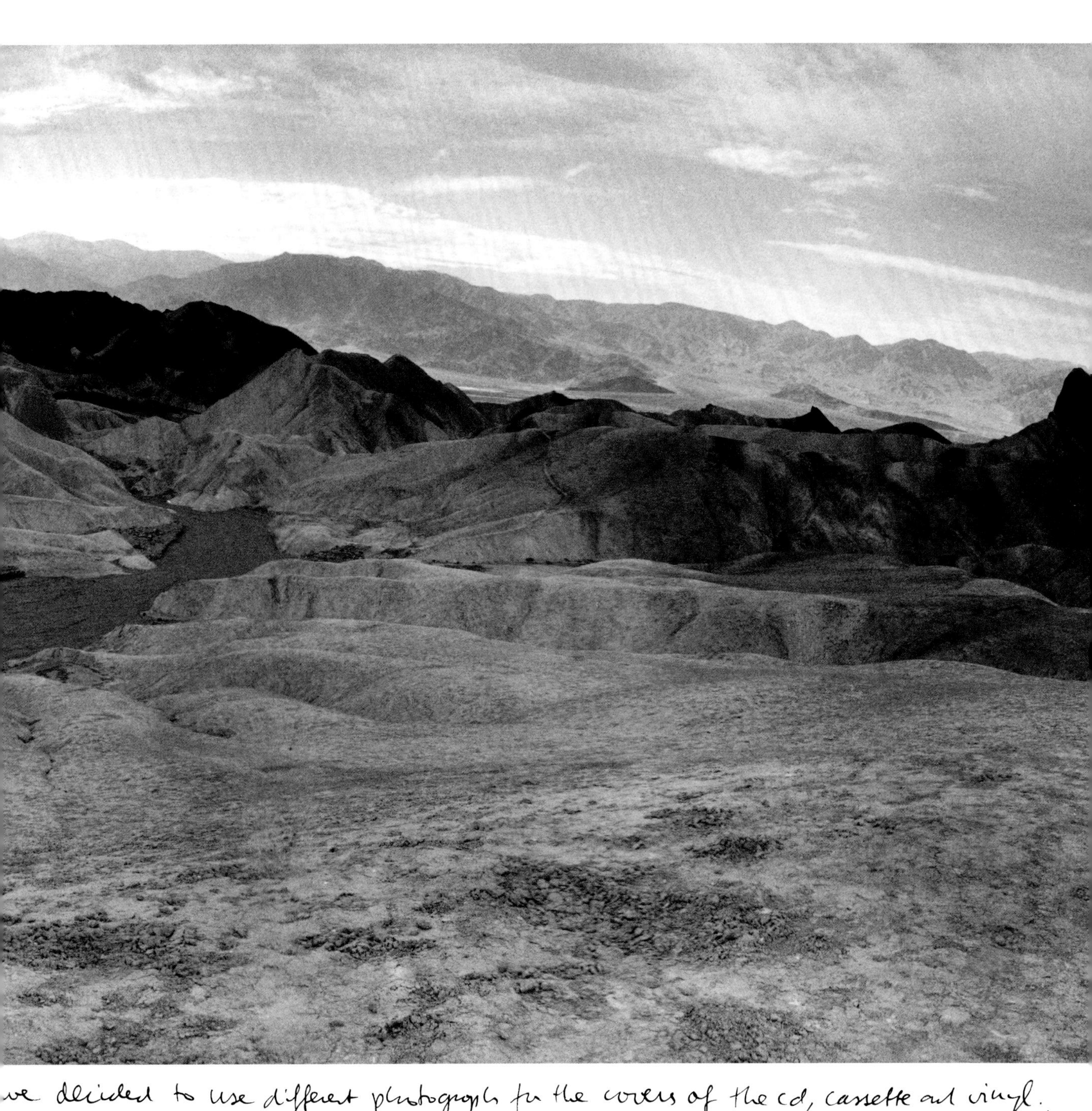

we decided to use different photographs for the covers of the cd, cassette and vinyl. it being the 80's we focussed on the vinyl as being the main output and that ended up looking fantastic. in sharp contrast to the cd for which we used a moving shot of roughly the same image and i regretted that decision enormously in retrospect. the cd cover has now been changed to roughly 85% to what the vinyl looked like. fighting to go 100%!

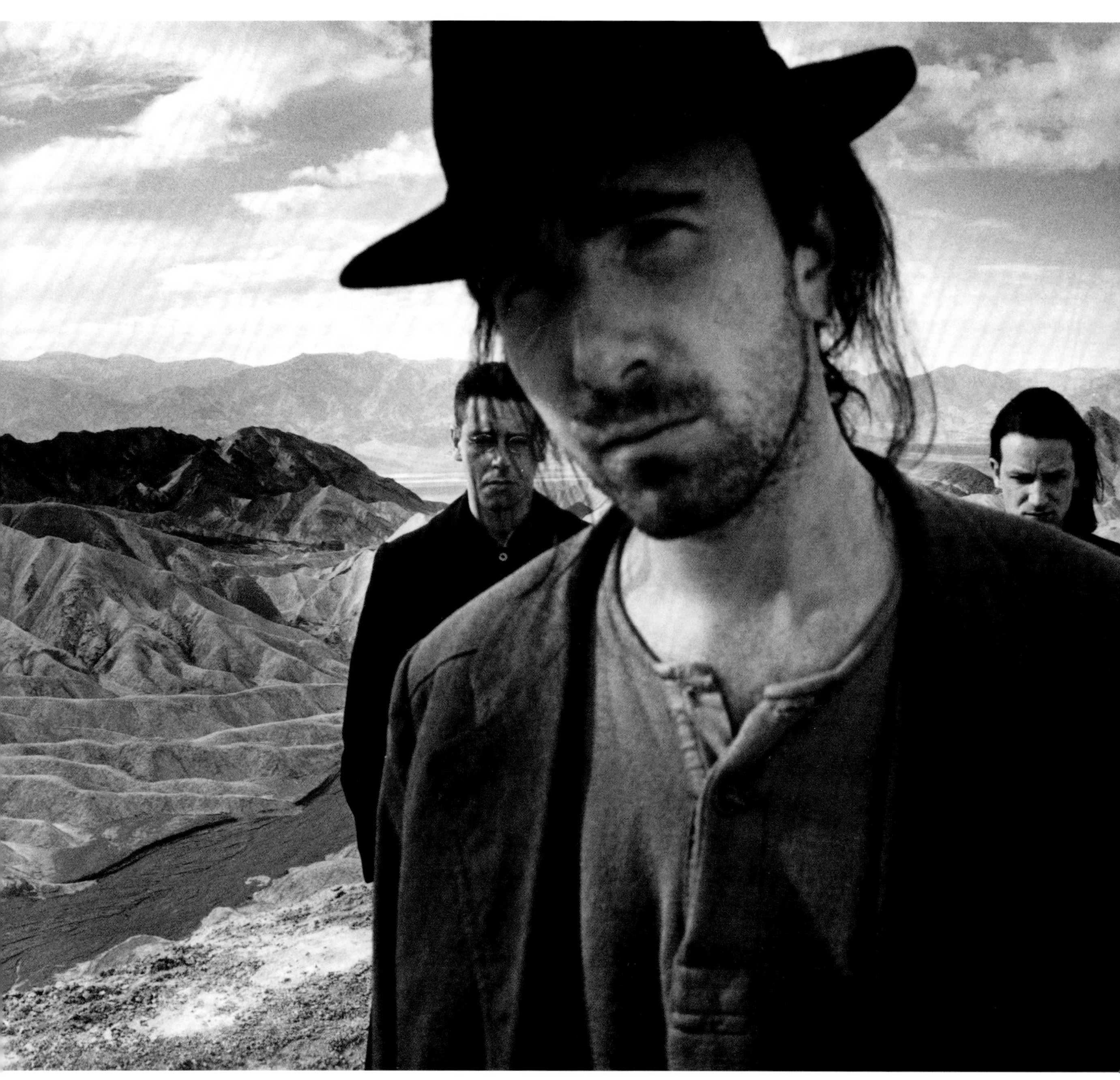

a variation at Zabriskie point – edge
in front and it makes the photo look more
like an outtake of a sergio leone movie

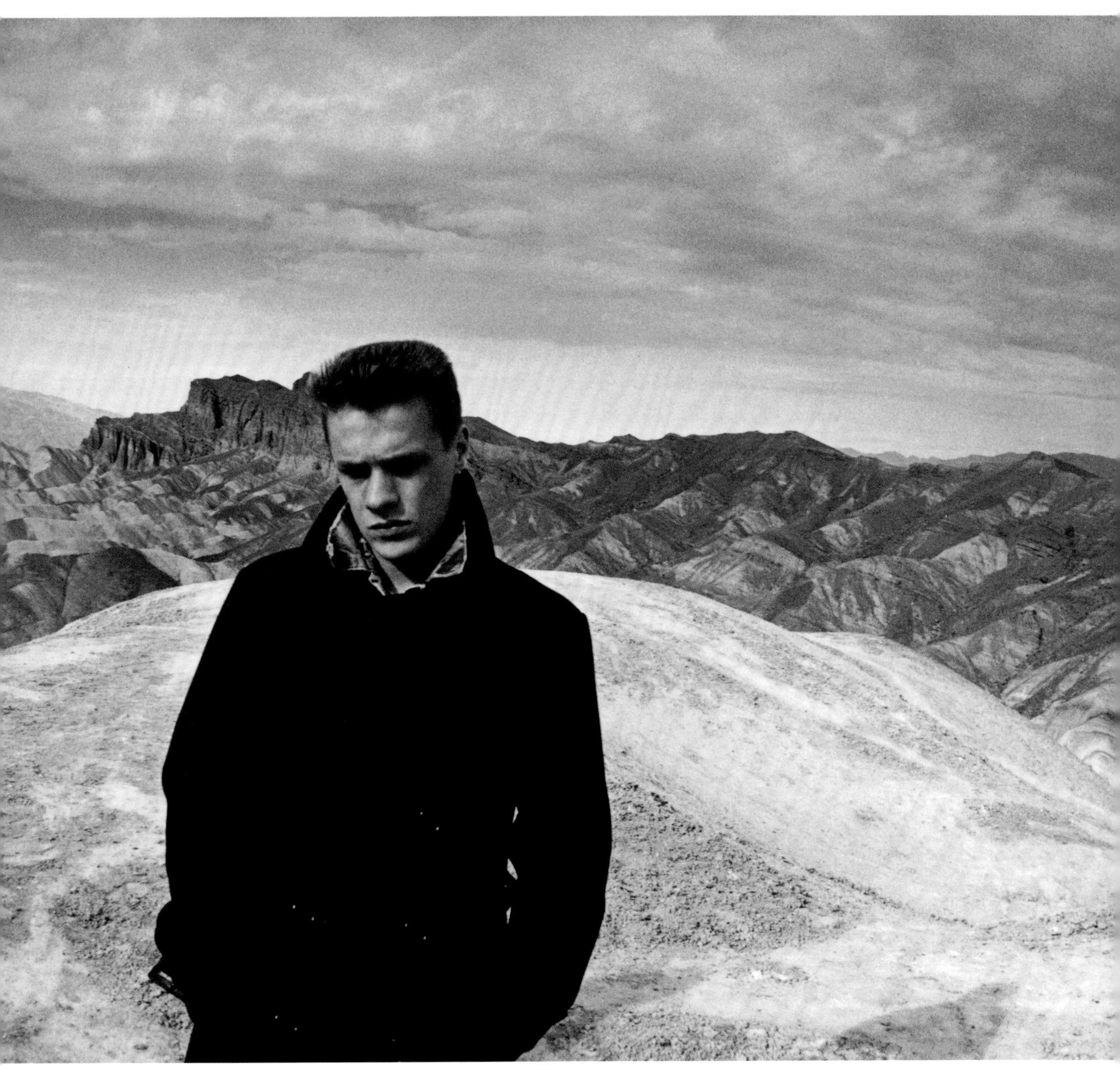

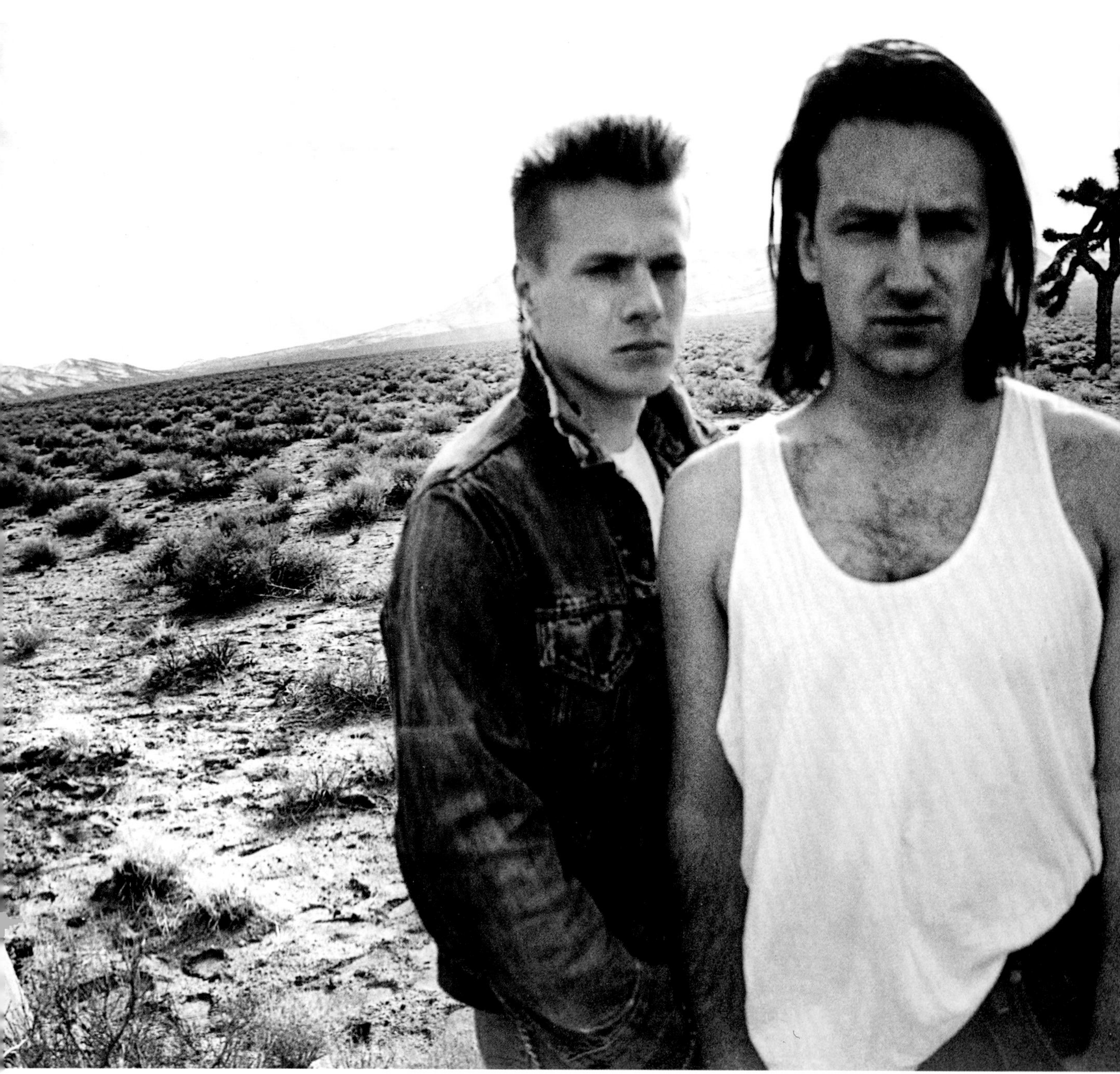

confession time – my inexperience with the panoramic camera became
obvious when i got the film back – it only focussed on infinity
so the tree was sharp but not the band. all good in the end
as was the round horizon which i hadn't foreseen either.
or the light flare at the bottom. or my camera case in the corner.

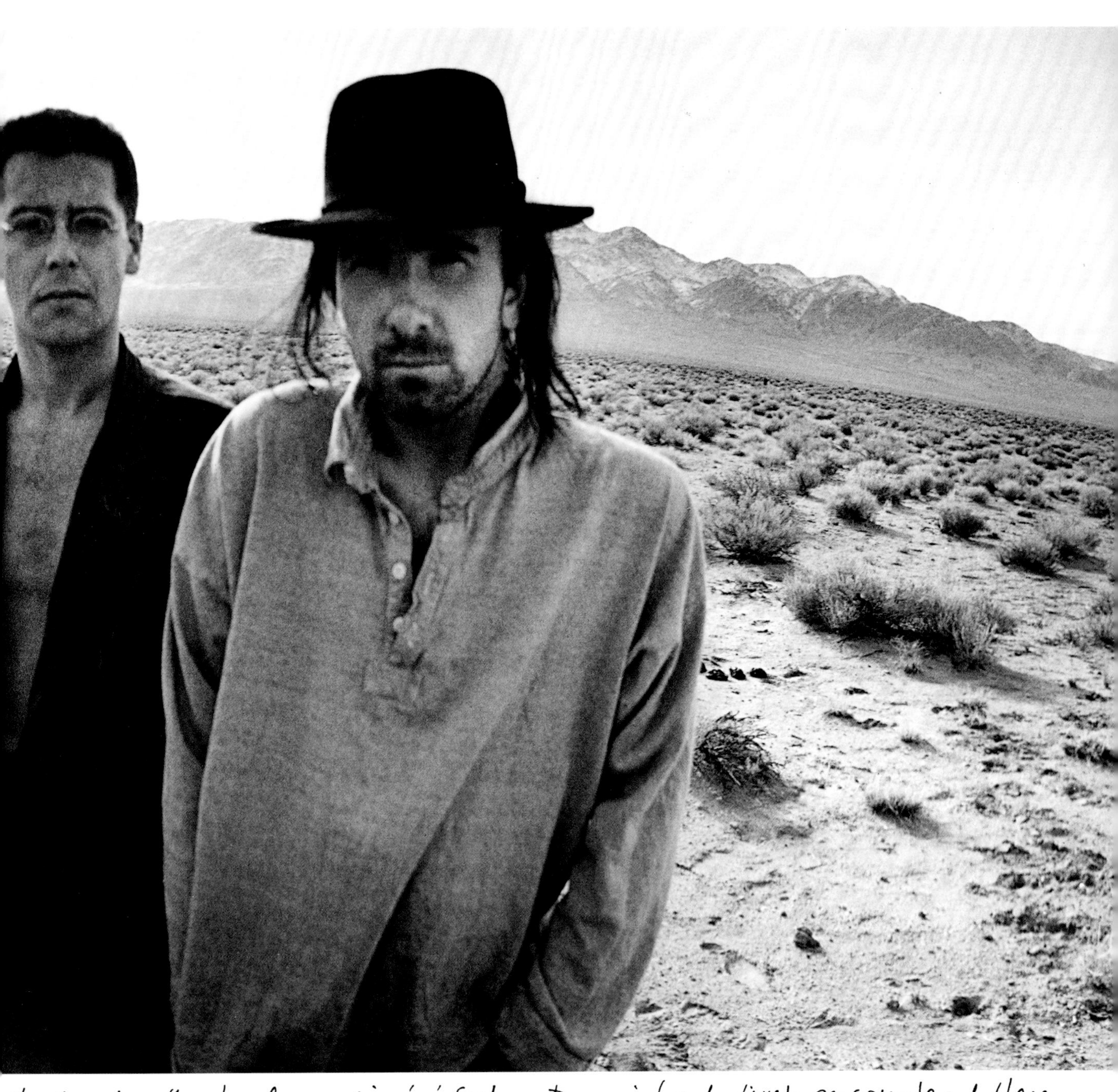

The tree in the background is 'a' joshua tree. i had first encountered these
1980, photographing Captain Beefheart in the desert. when i described this tree
to bono one night prior to entering death valley, he listened carefully and the
ext morning it had become a logical title for the album and we were all looking
t of the windows of our bus to spot a lonely tree as they normally come in groups.

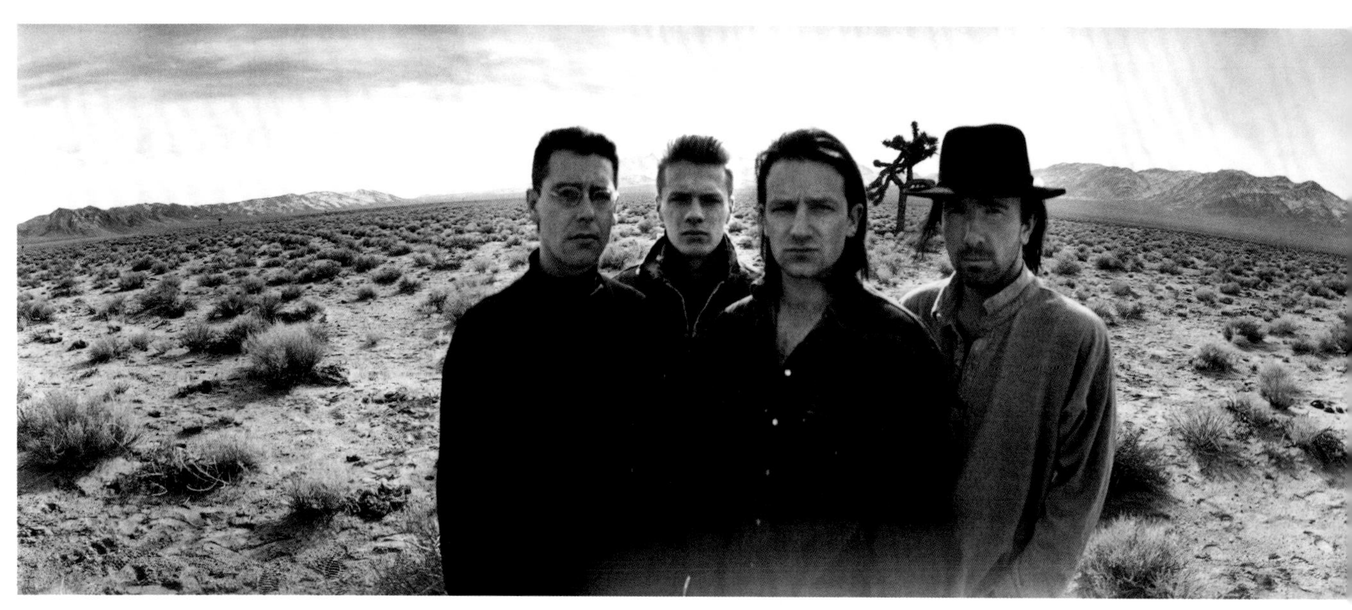

some alternative takes

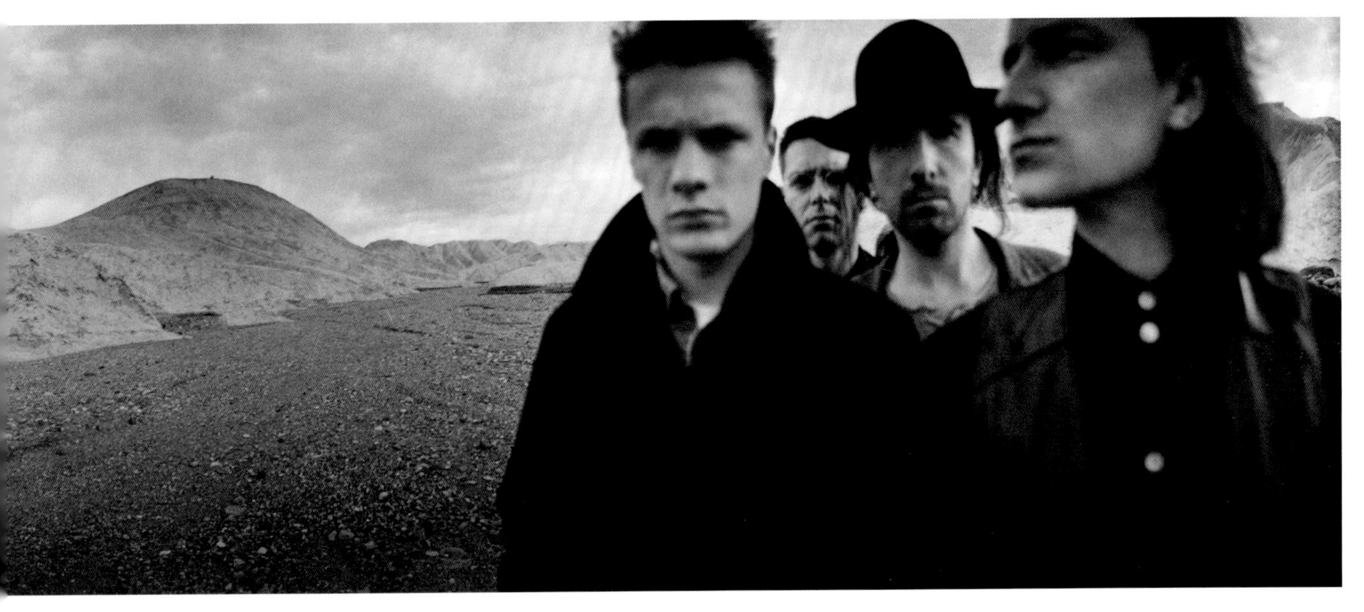

next spread.
bono during a
stop late in
the day outside
'our' bus.

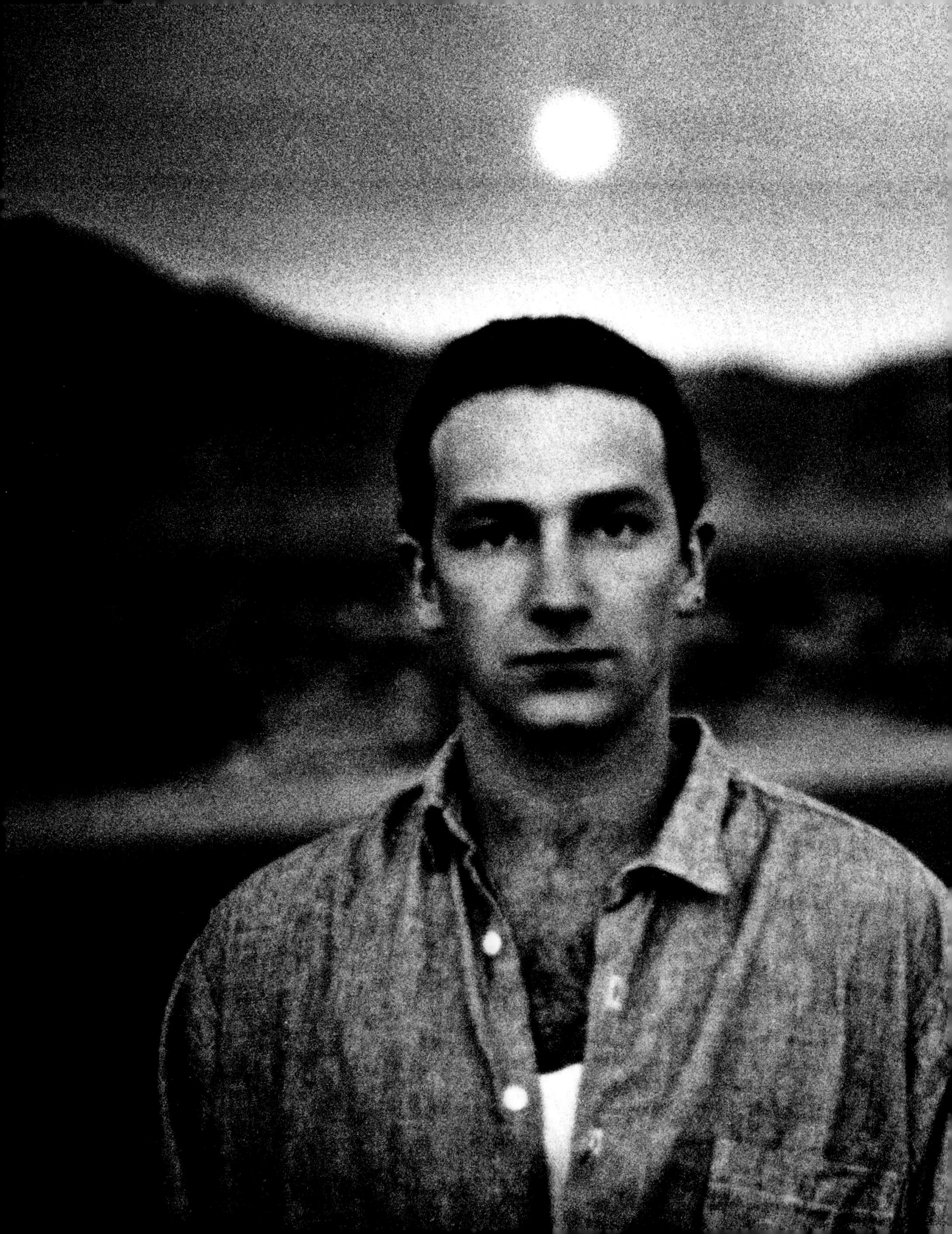

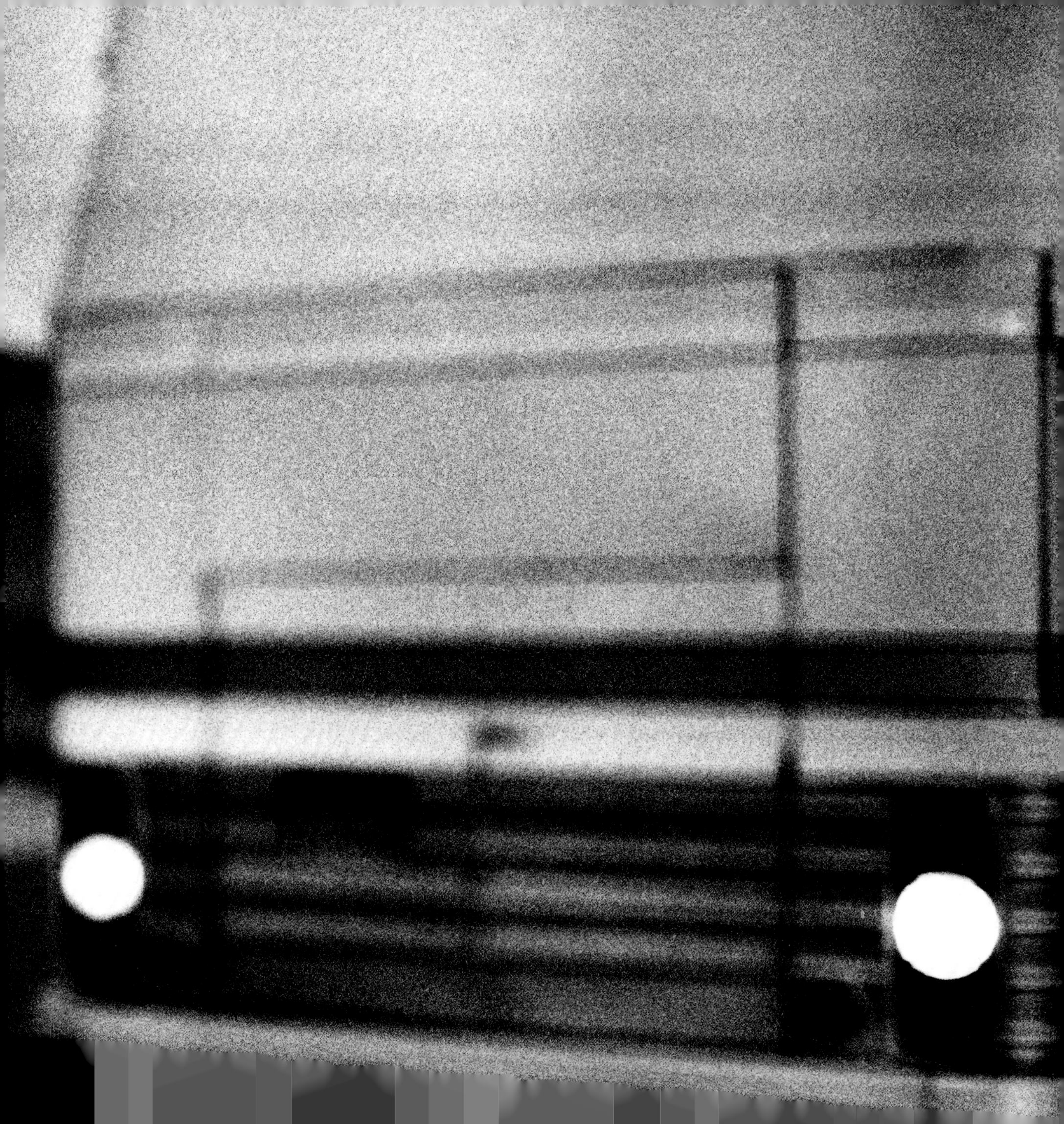

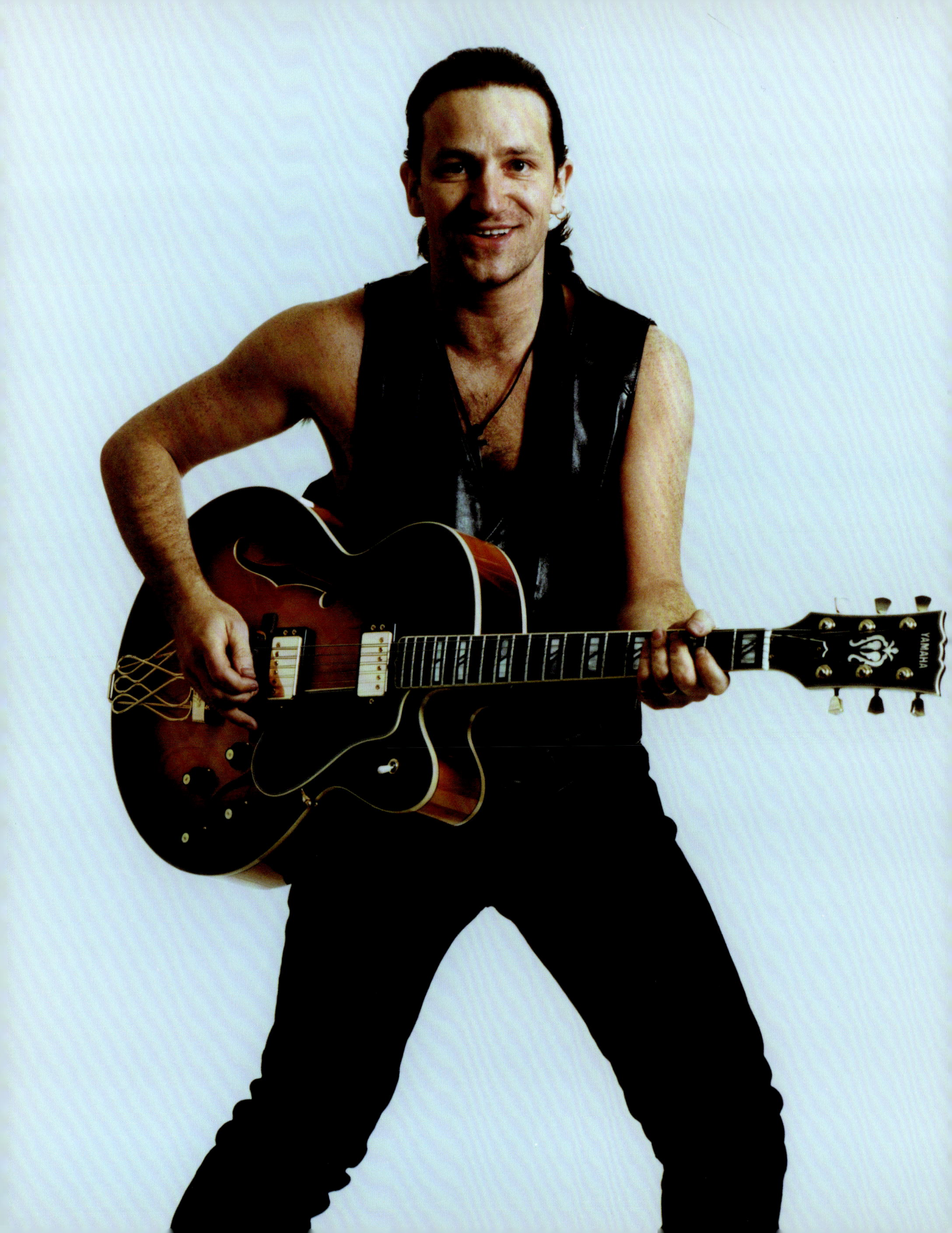
YAMAHA

DUBLIN 1987

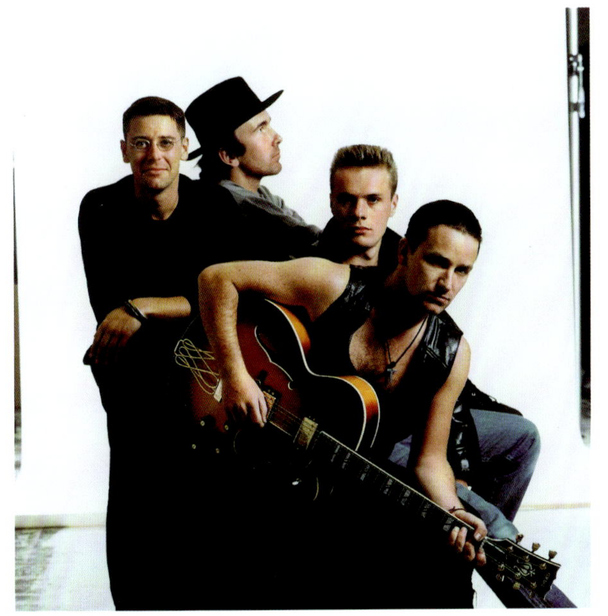

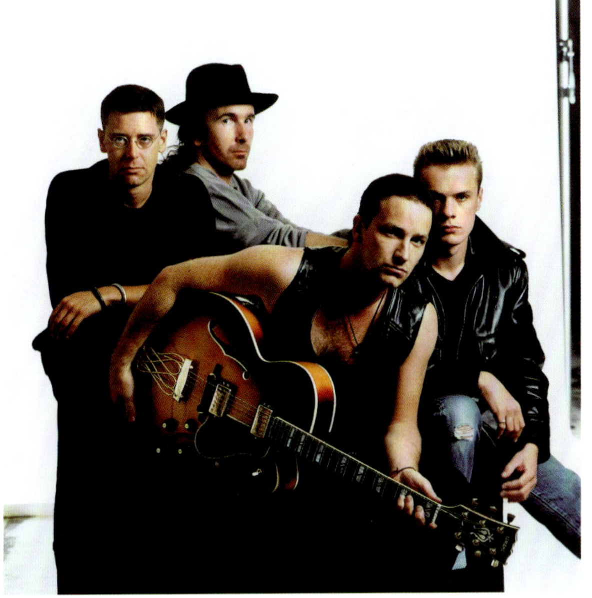

my first cover-shoot for Rolling Stone magazine and naturally it had to be done in a photostudio so that is me like a fish on dry land. The issue of RS came out in march '87 to coincide with the release of the Joshua Tree.

Los Angeles 1987 march

downtown

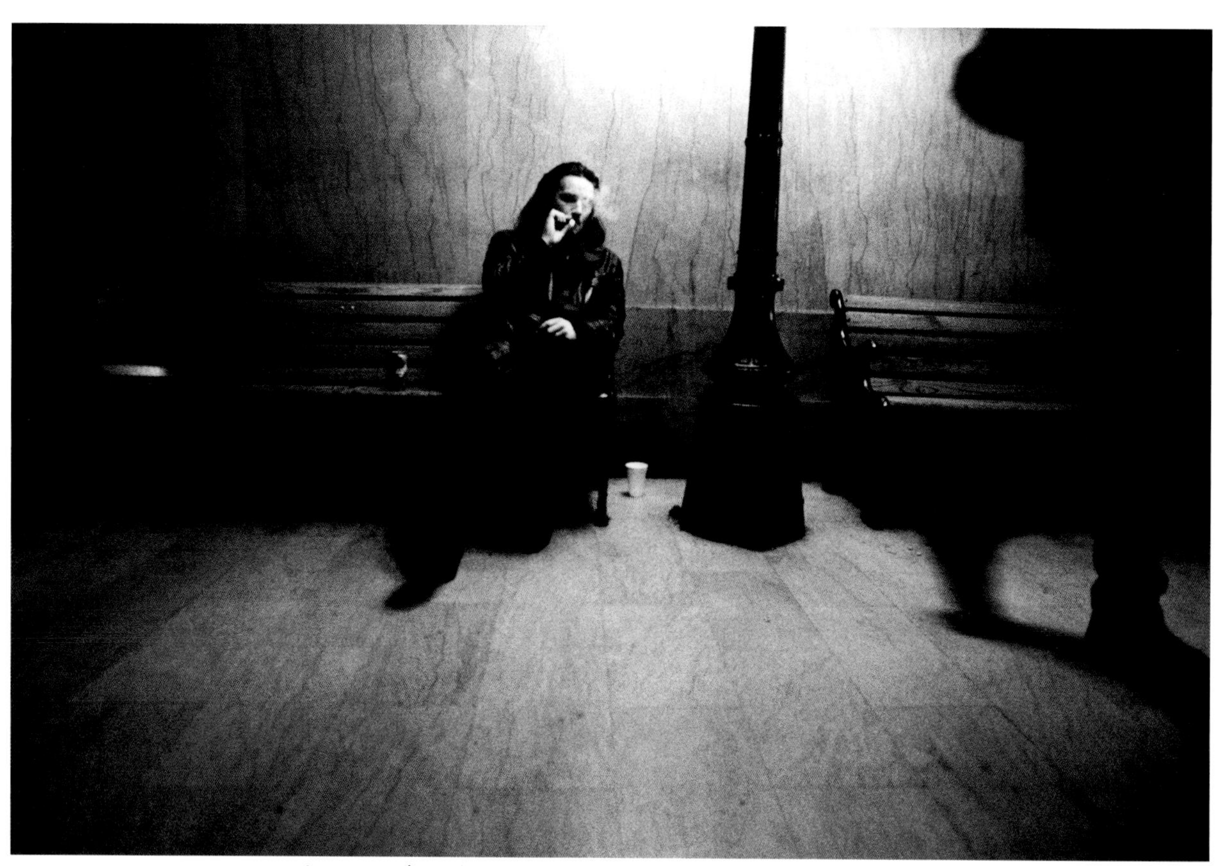

U2 came to Los Angeles to do some promo and a video for the Joshua Tree release and i came over with them to shoot some new press photos. Meiert Avis, the video director, had some photographs from a location scout that i saw and one of which was the roof of a hotel. i went to investigate it as a possible photo location and this hotel was called 'Million Dollar Hotel'. i was very impressed and subsequently told Bono who came back with me to have a look and was so taken by it all that it sparked off a movie in the end directed by Wim Wenders. the photo above and on the right shows Bono sitting in the lobby and taking it all in. it was a wild place, bit like bus stop with a fortified hole in the wall to collect your keys from.

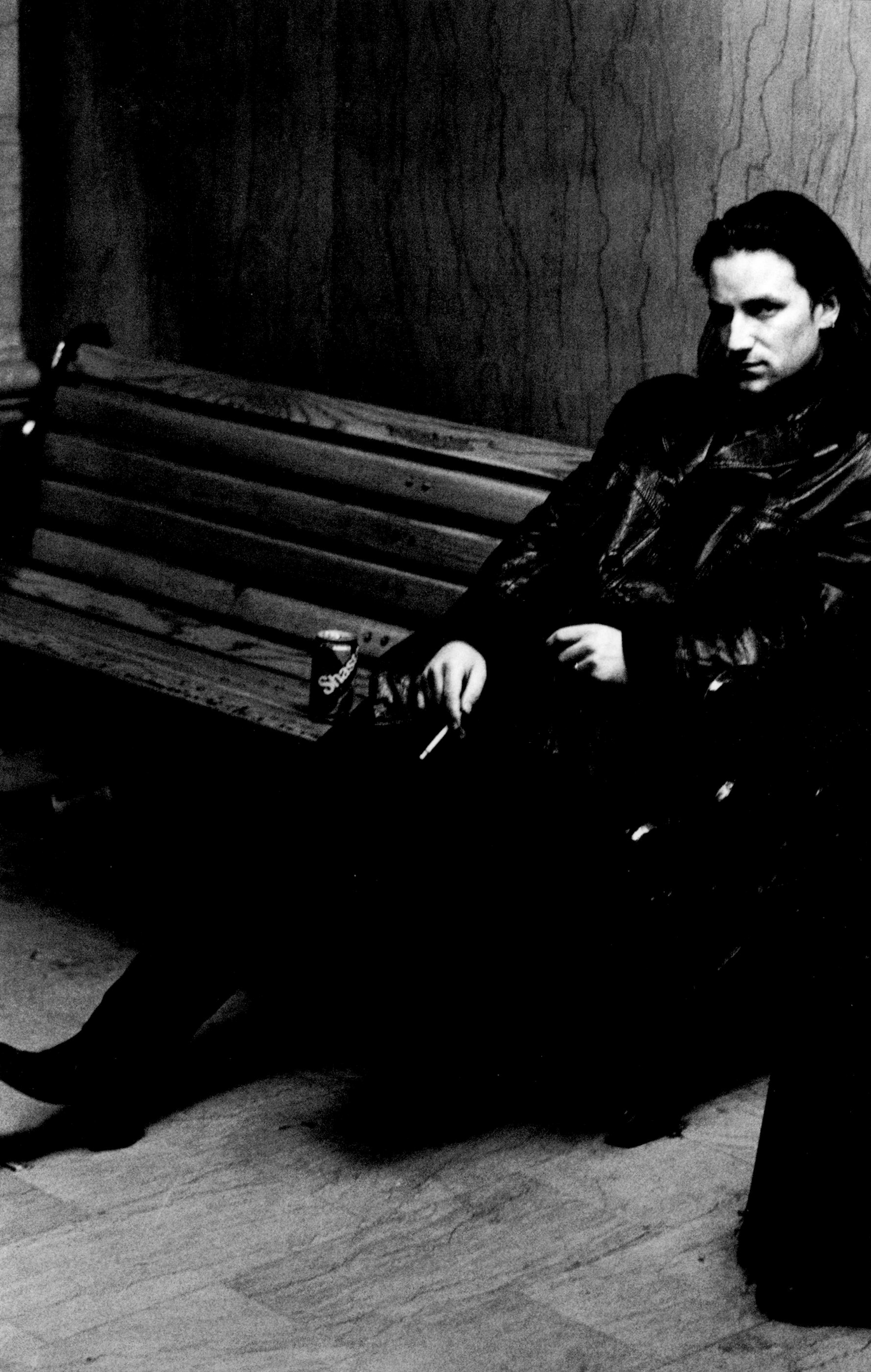

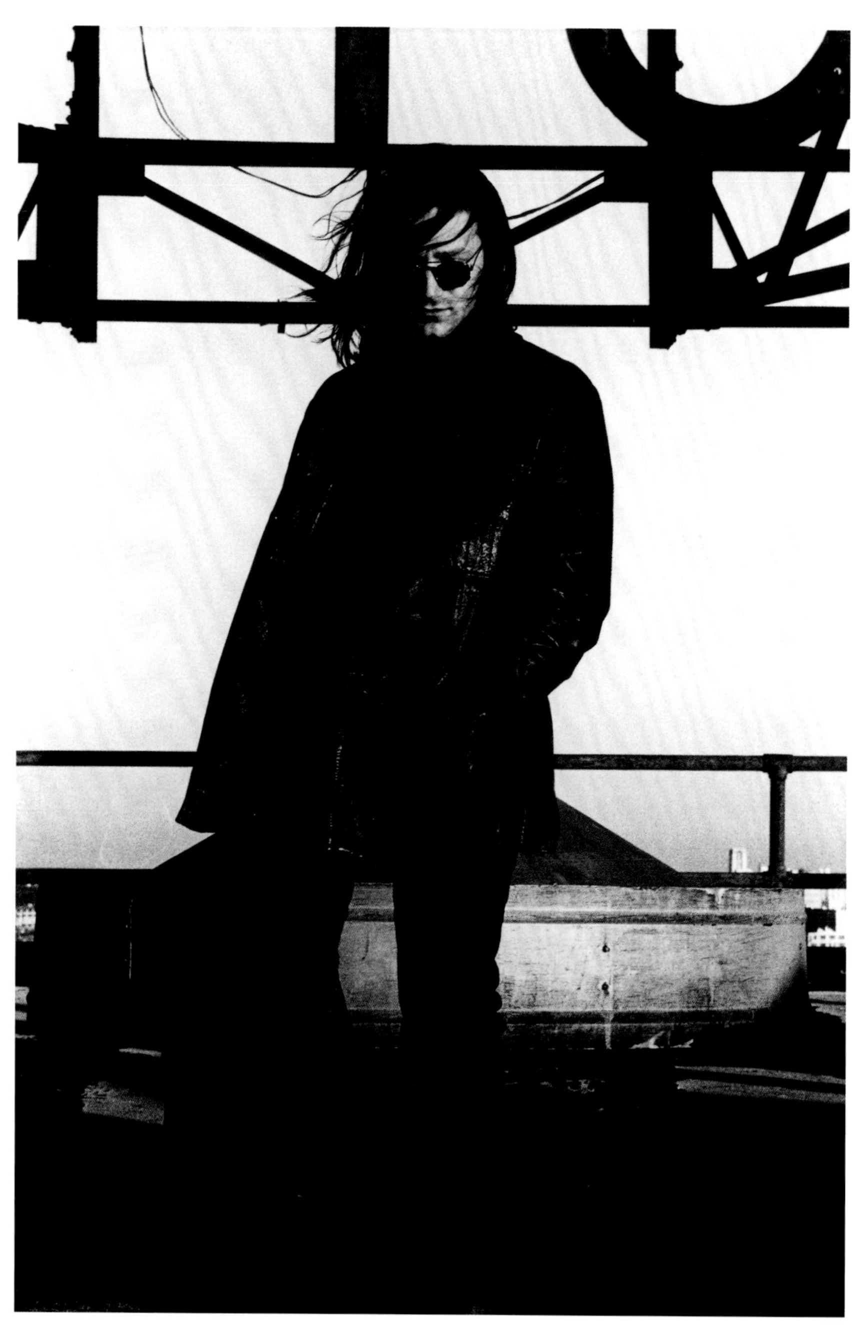

the photos for press we took the following day and didn't use the lobby of the hotel but the hotelroof which was its biggest asset. bono looks a bit 'lennon' like here and in the movie there is a john lennon type character as well.

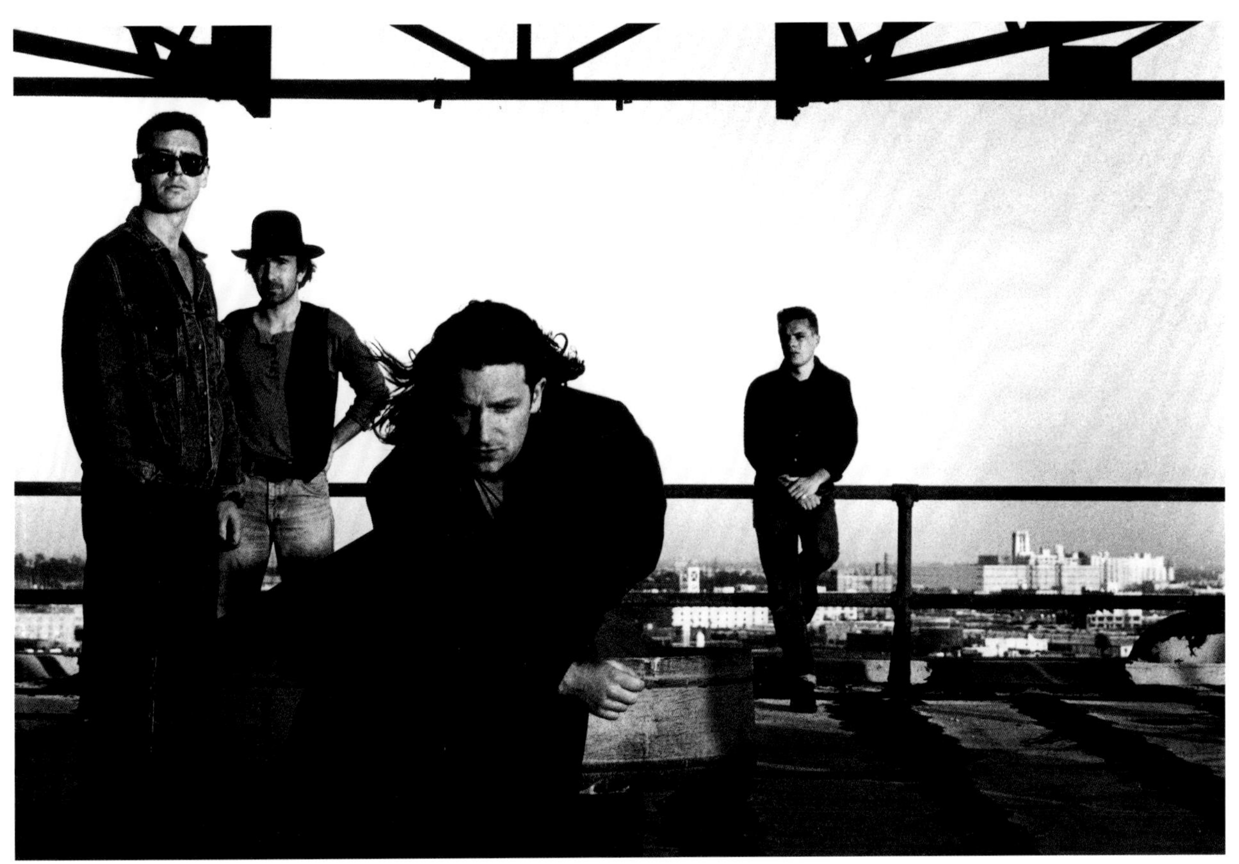

late afternoon sunlight.

on the photo overleaf is a great photo of bono and edge towards the end of the day. it looks quite old fashioned and they look strong and vulnerable at the same time - some innocence captured.

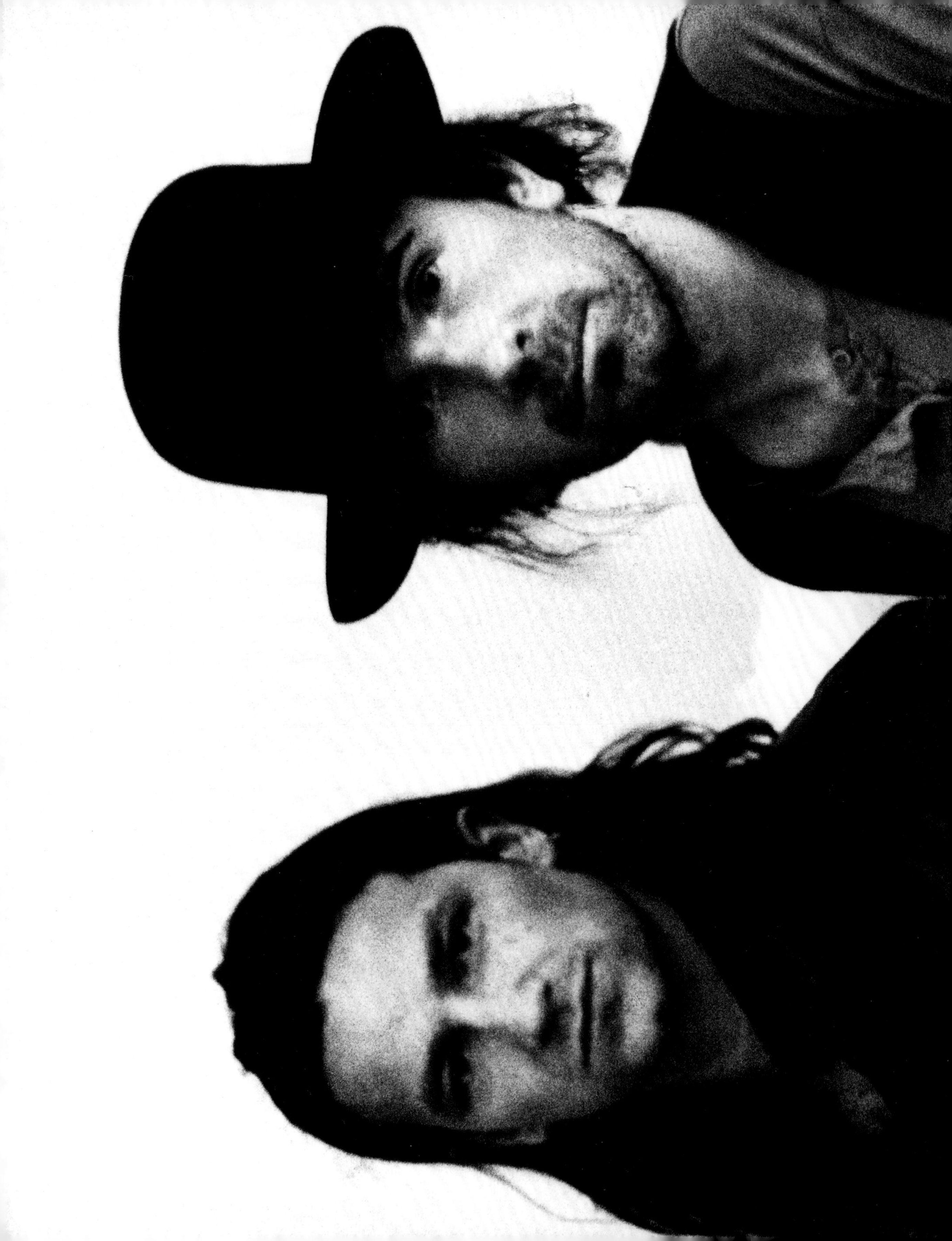

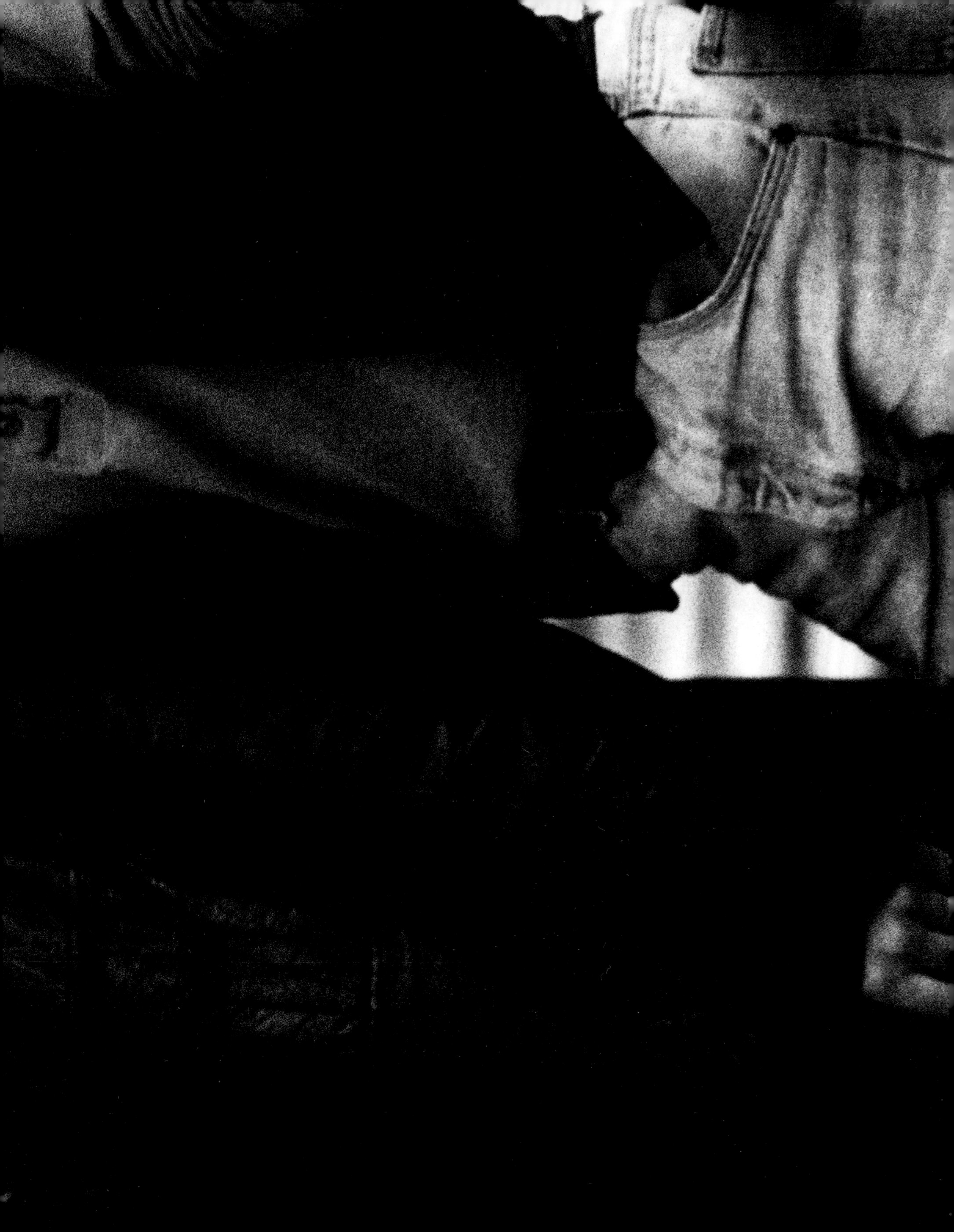

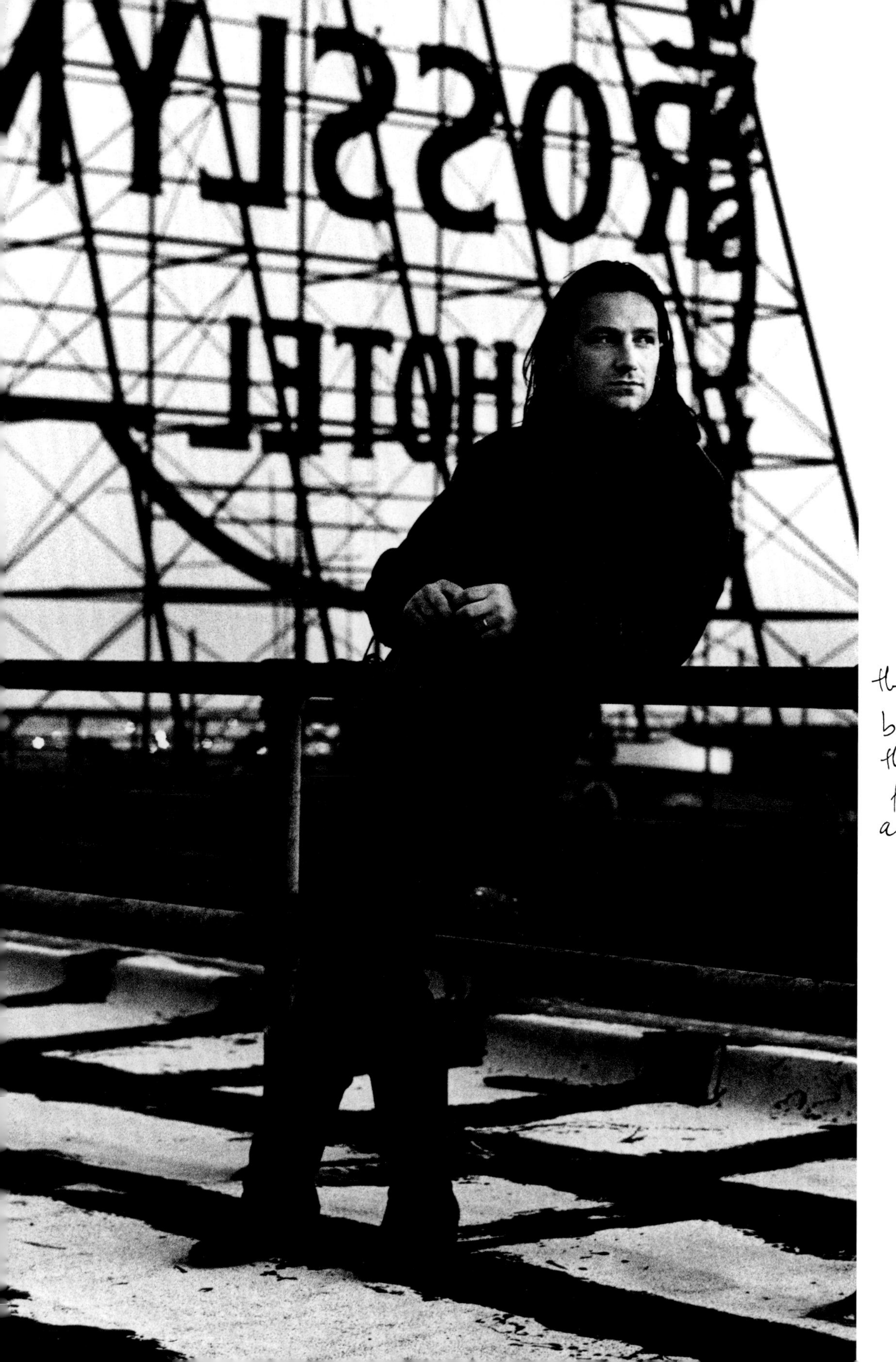

the sign behind
bono is actu
the hotel sign
from a hote
across the roa

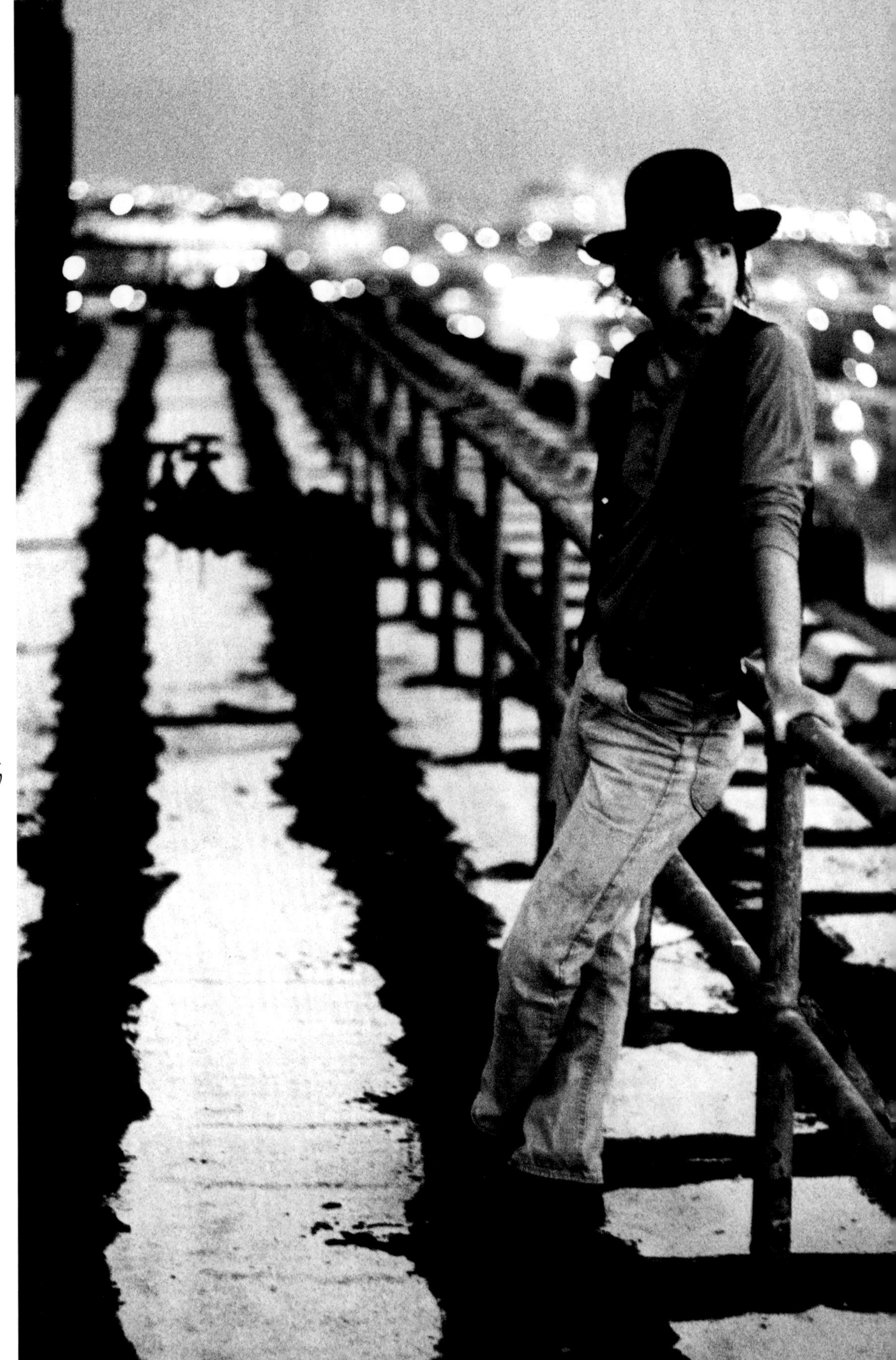

edge ~~at the~~ looking
out over
downtown LA;
last shot of
the day.

Los Angeles 1987

March

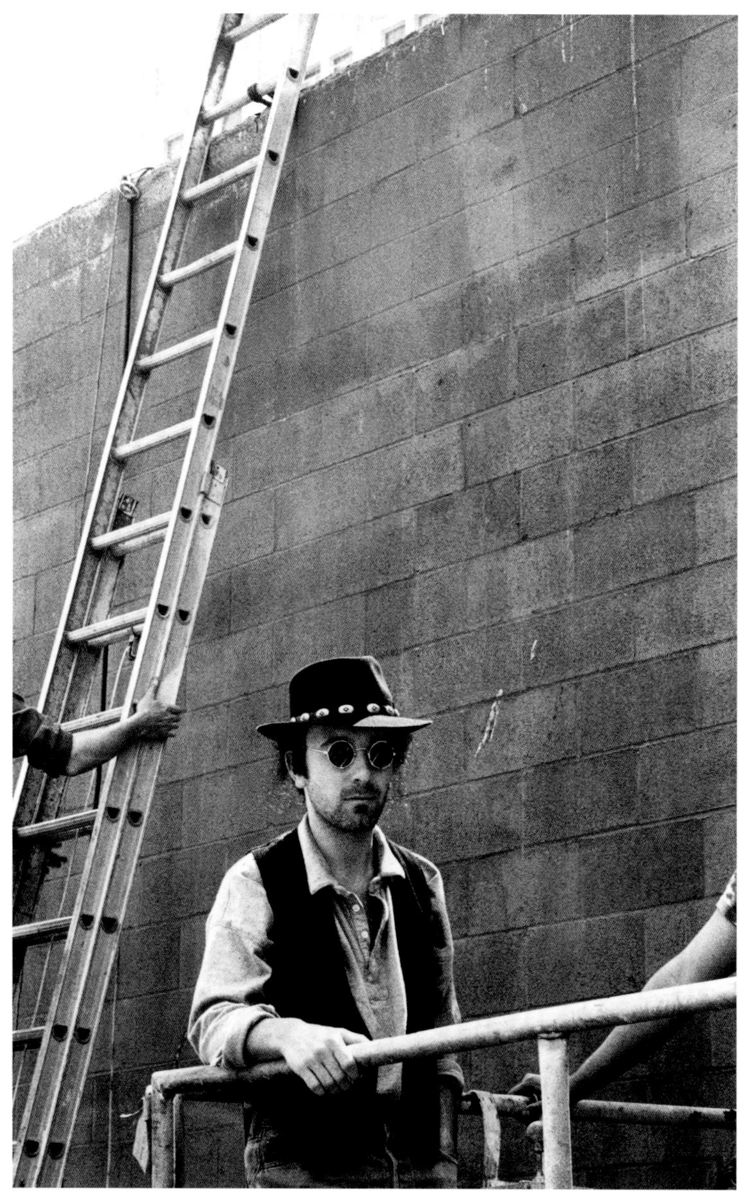

a photo of edge going up in a lift rather than the ladder - this is at the back of the building where the 'streets with no name' video is going to be shot.

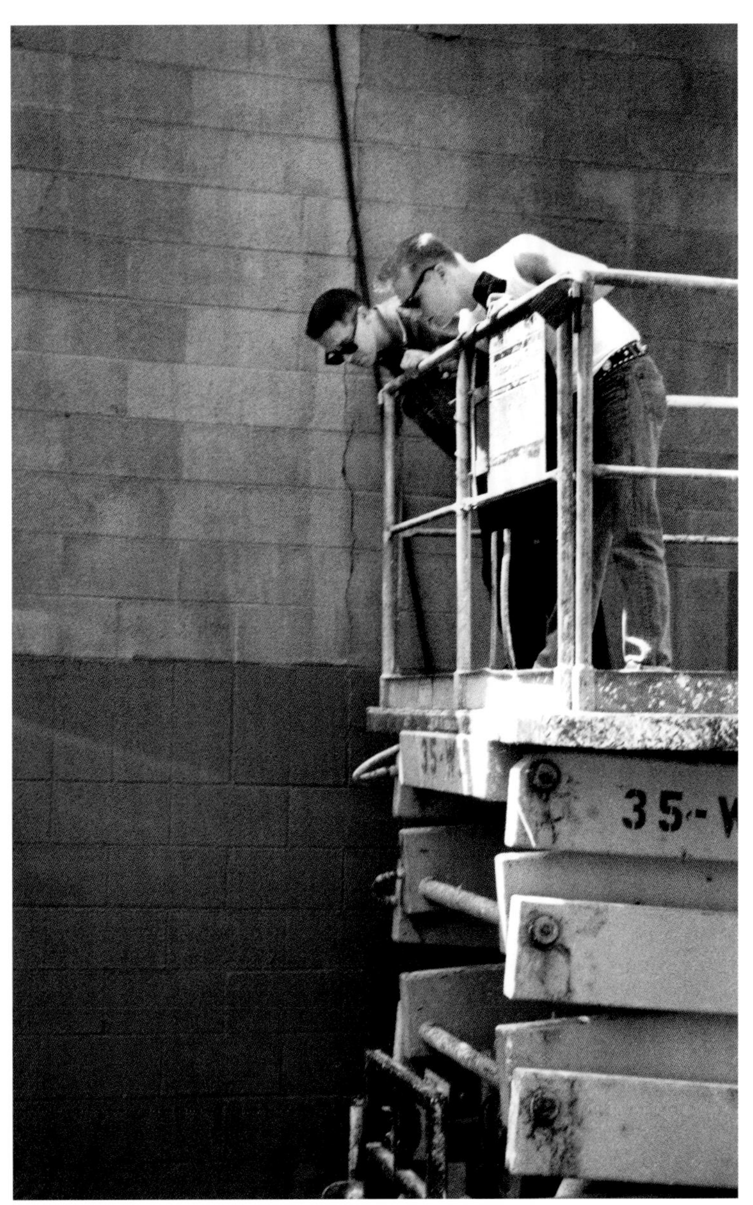

adam and larry in the same lift, 17 years prior to the release of 'vertigo'.

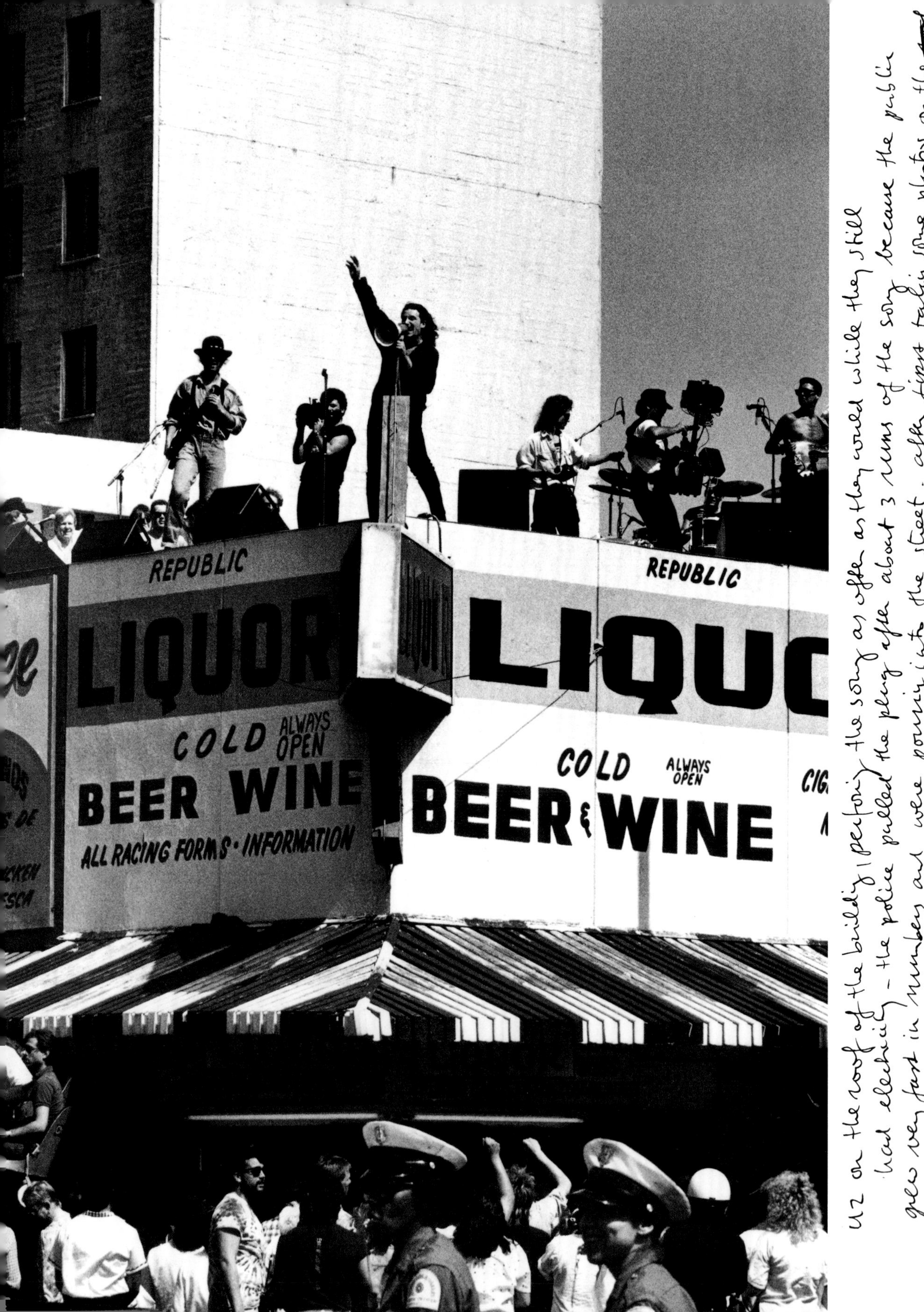

U2 on the roof of the building performing the song as often as they could while they still had electricity – the police pulled the plug after about 3 runs of the song because the public grew very fast in numbers and were pouring into the street. after first taking some photos on the roof itself, i went down to the street level but the police stopped me going back towards the building. if you don't blink you can see this moment, when i get sent back by the cops, in the video.

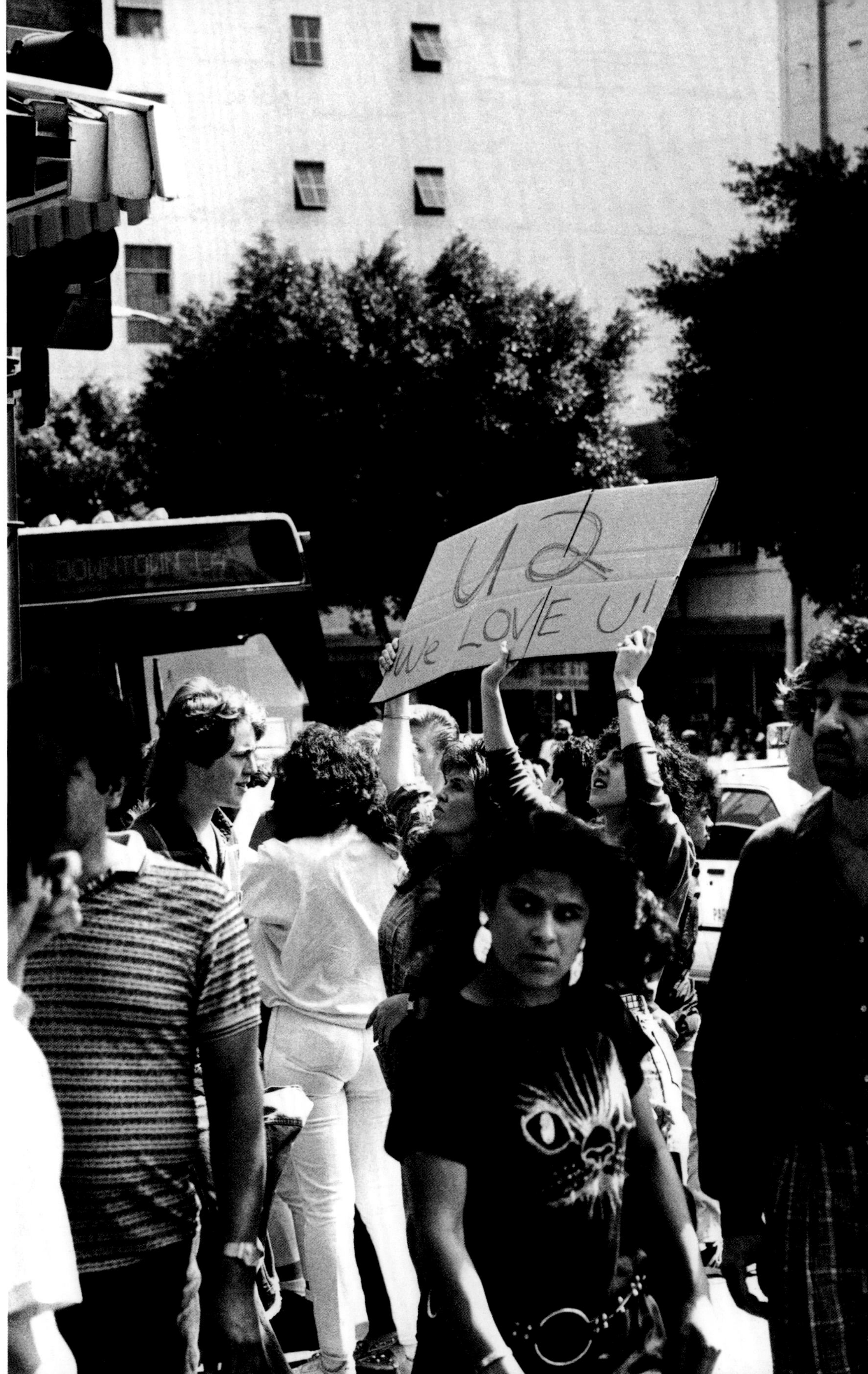
U2
We LOVE U!

SANFRANCISCO

april

1987

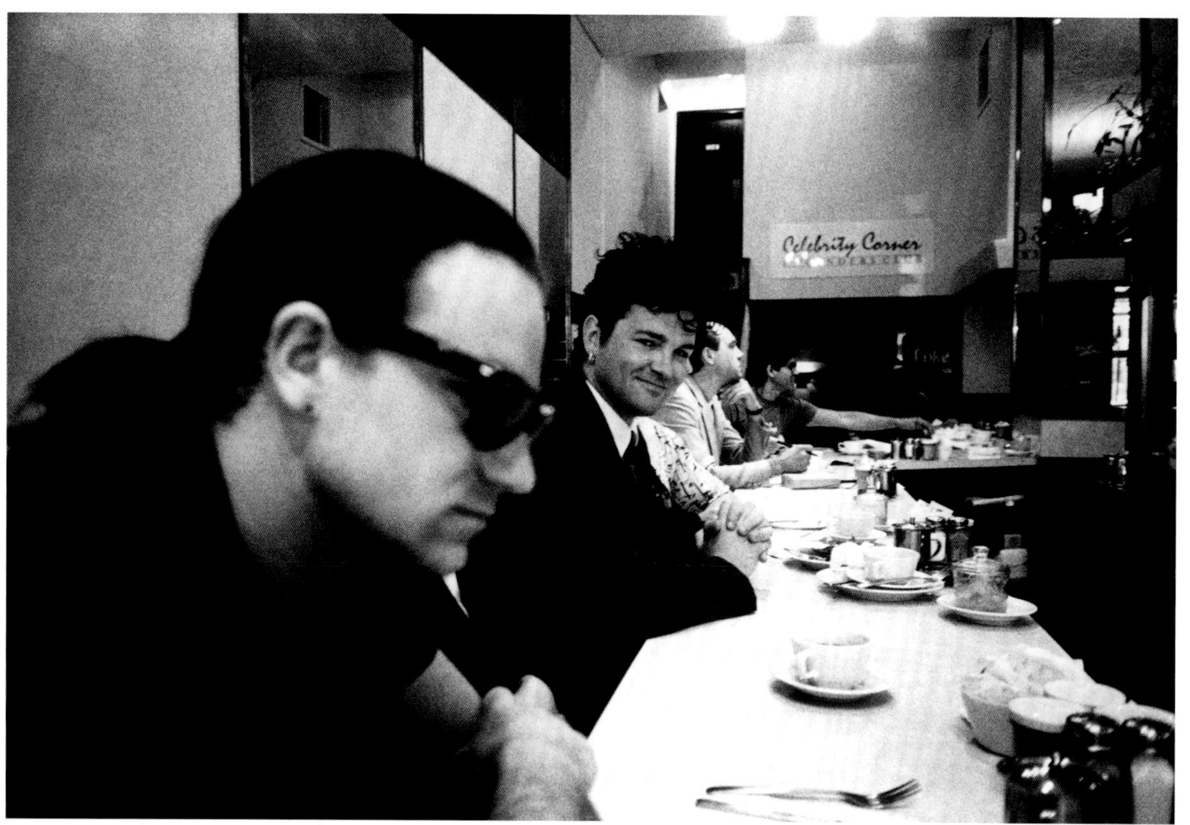

gavin friday and bono having breakfast in SF during the joshua tree tour.

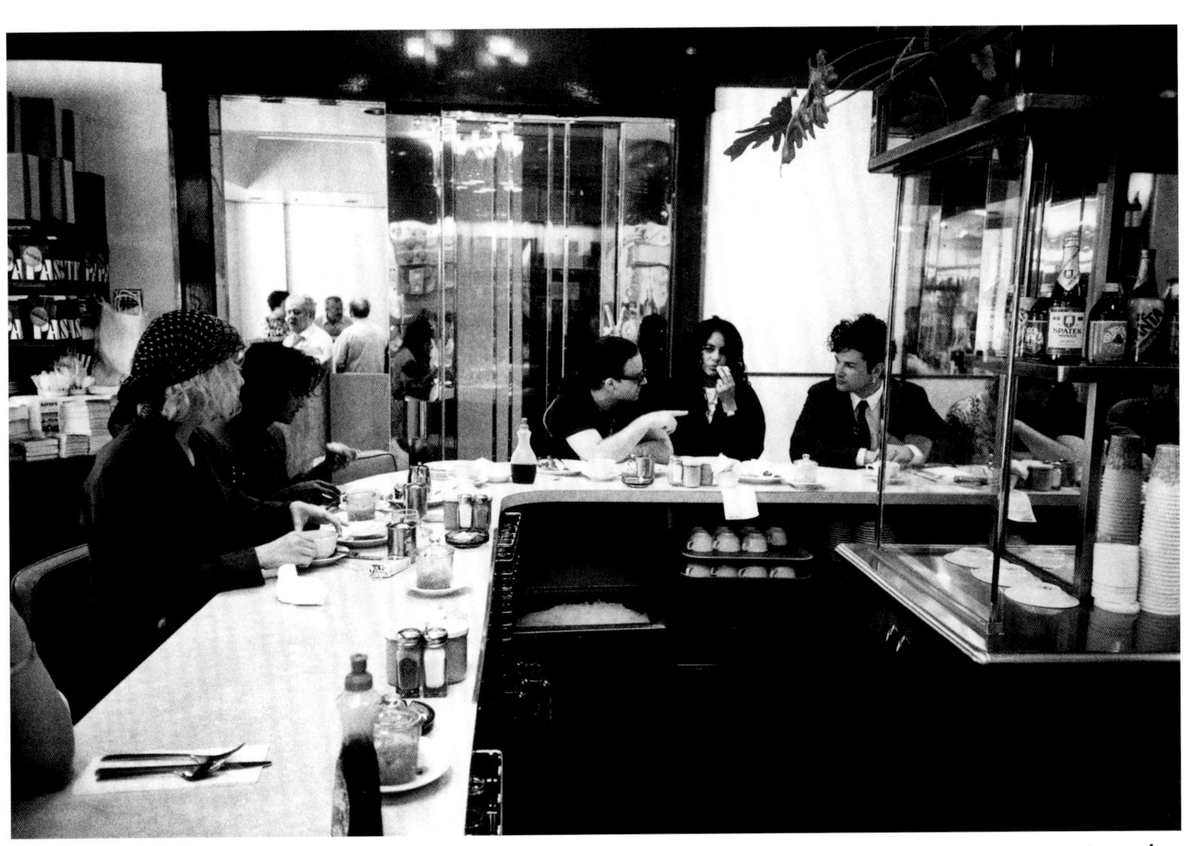

others who joined for breakfast are maria mckee, nassim khalifa (my then girlfriend) and a friend from SF sitting between bono and gavin.

PARIS 1987 summer

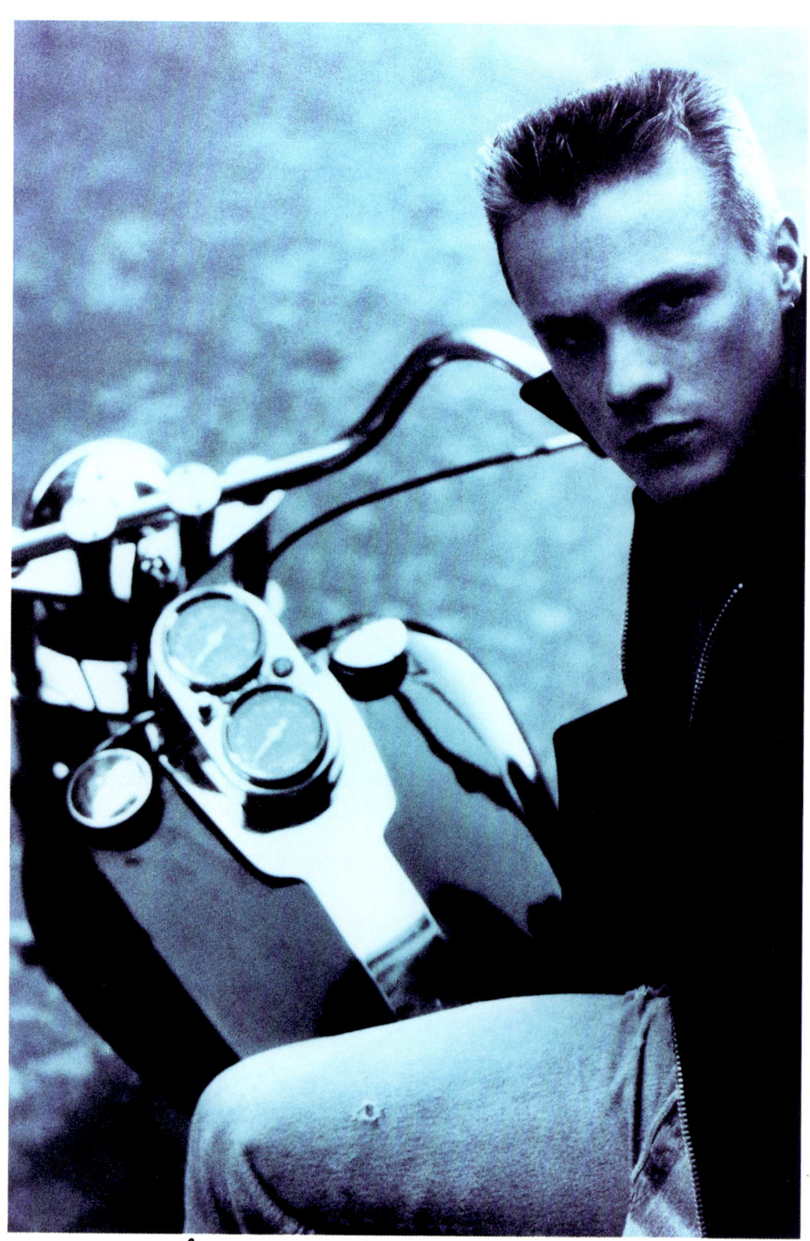

larry on a harley davidson

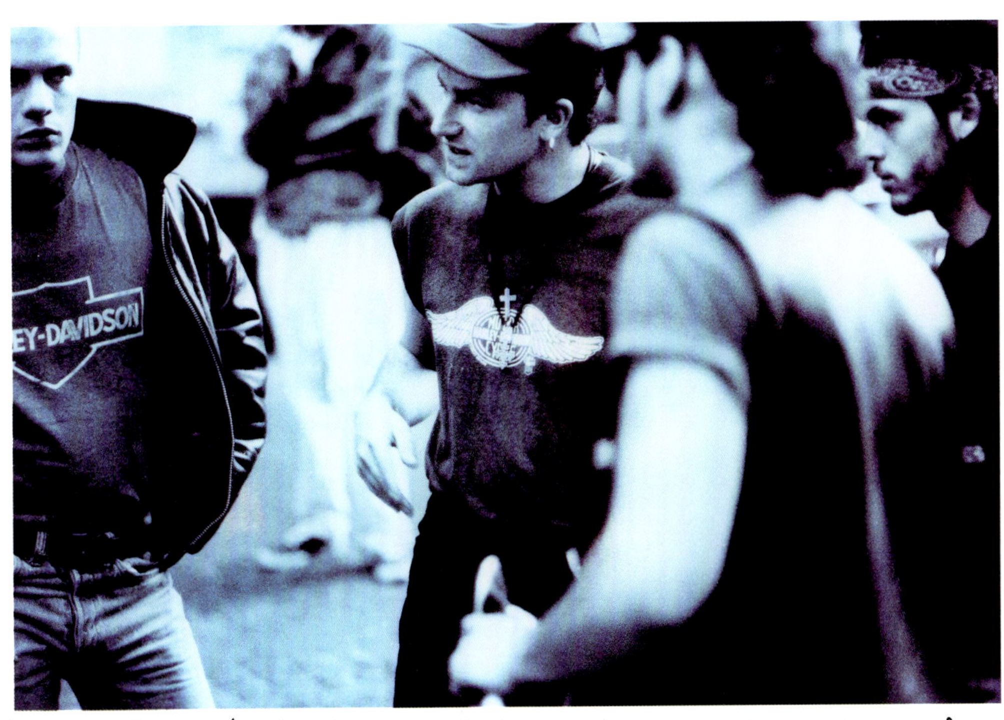

i came to paris to do some photos of larry with maria mackee
for InStyle magazine and i assume it was the first time (more or less)
that i used this polaroid film and used its beautiful grain and color.
we met a group of bikers on the street and bono and larry got talking
to them and i just took a few photos of it.

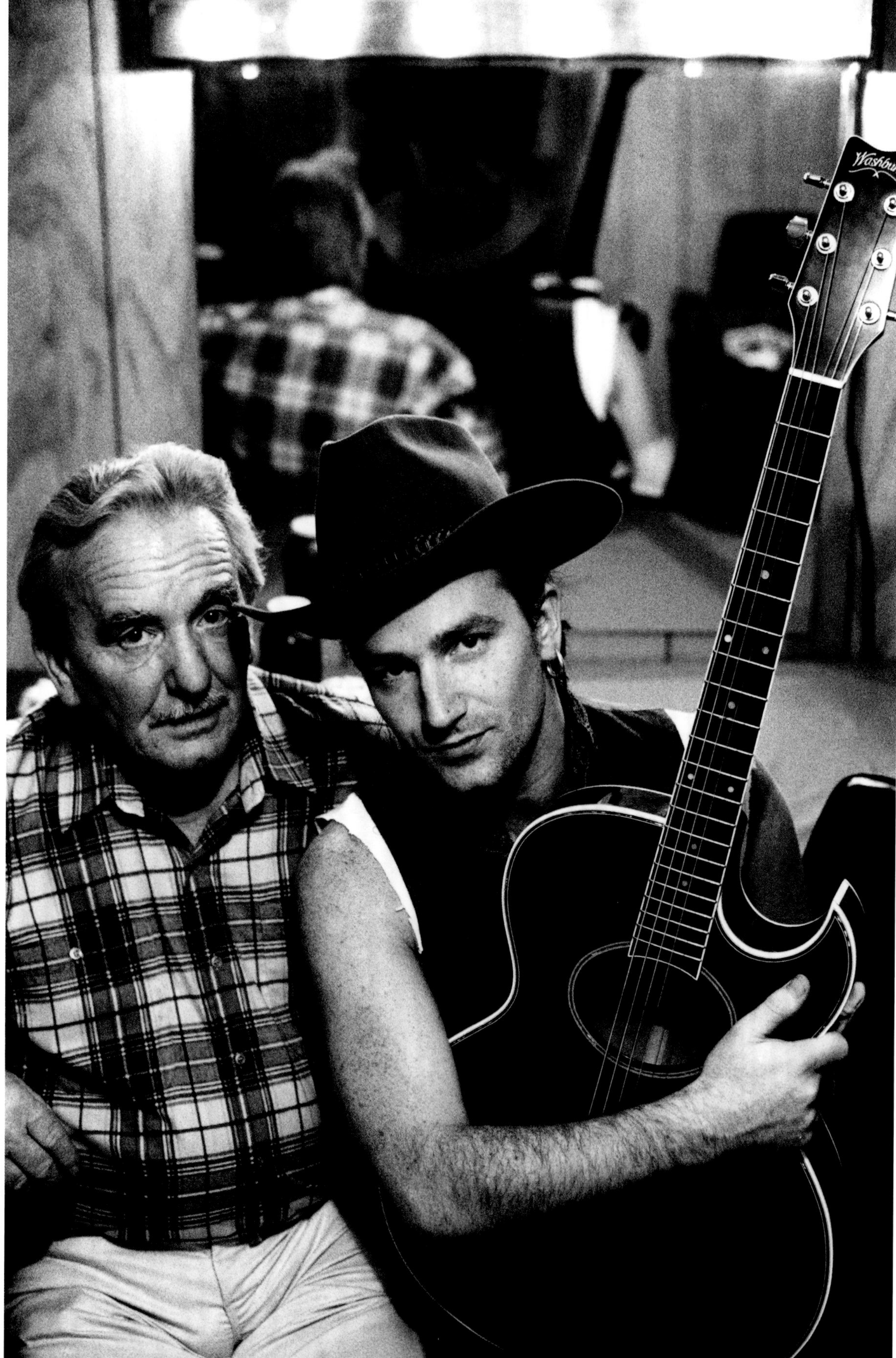

MONTREAL 1987

october

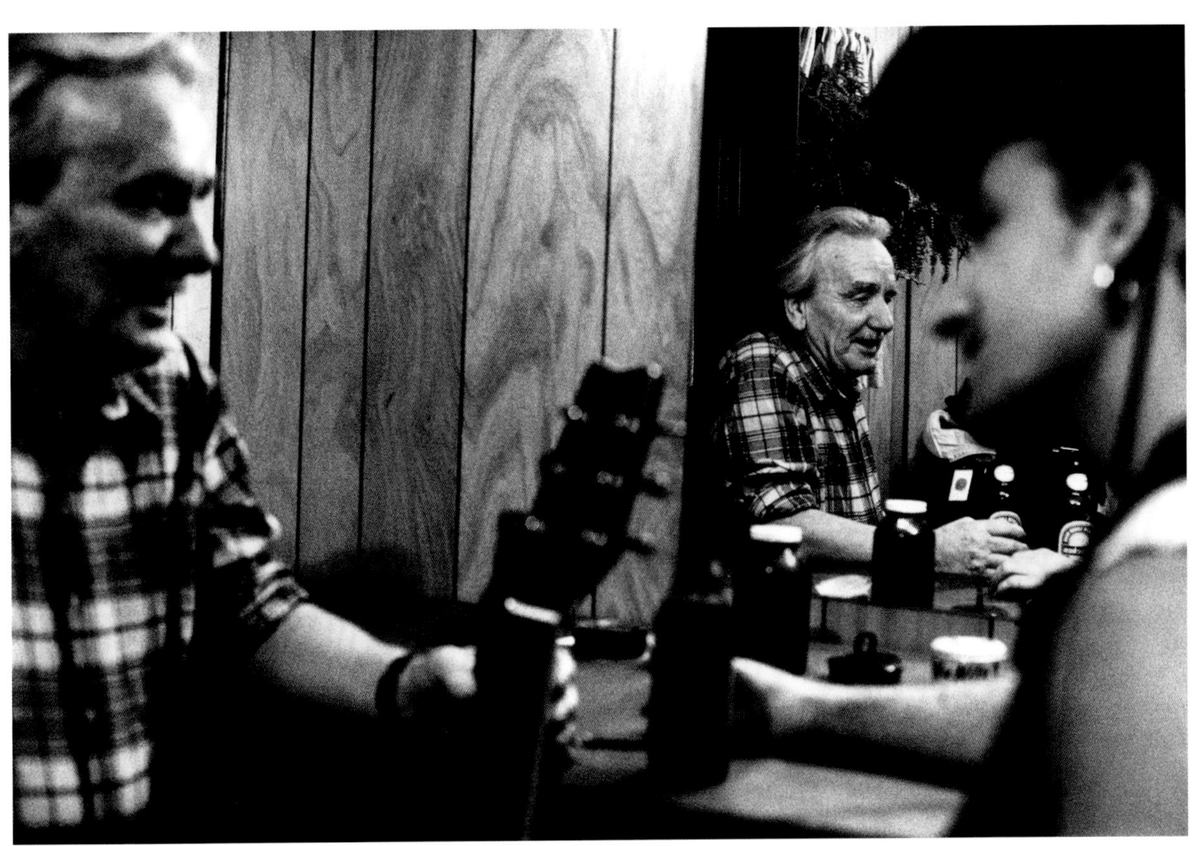

Bob and Bono sharing a drink and a conversation after the show. bono had invited some family members over to montreal from dublin. it was the first time i'd met bob and i liked him immensely. very witty man.

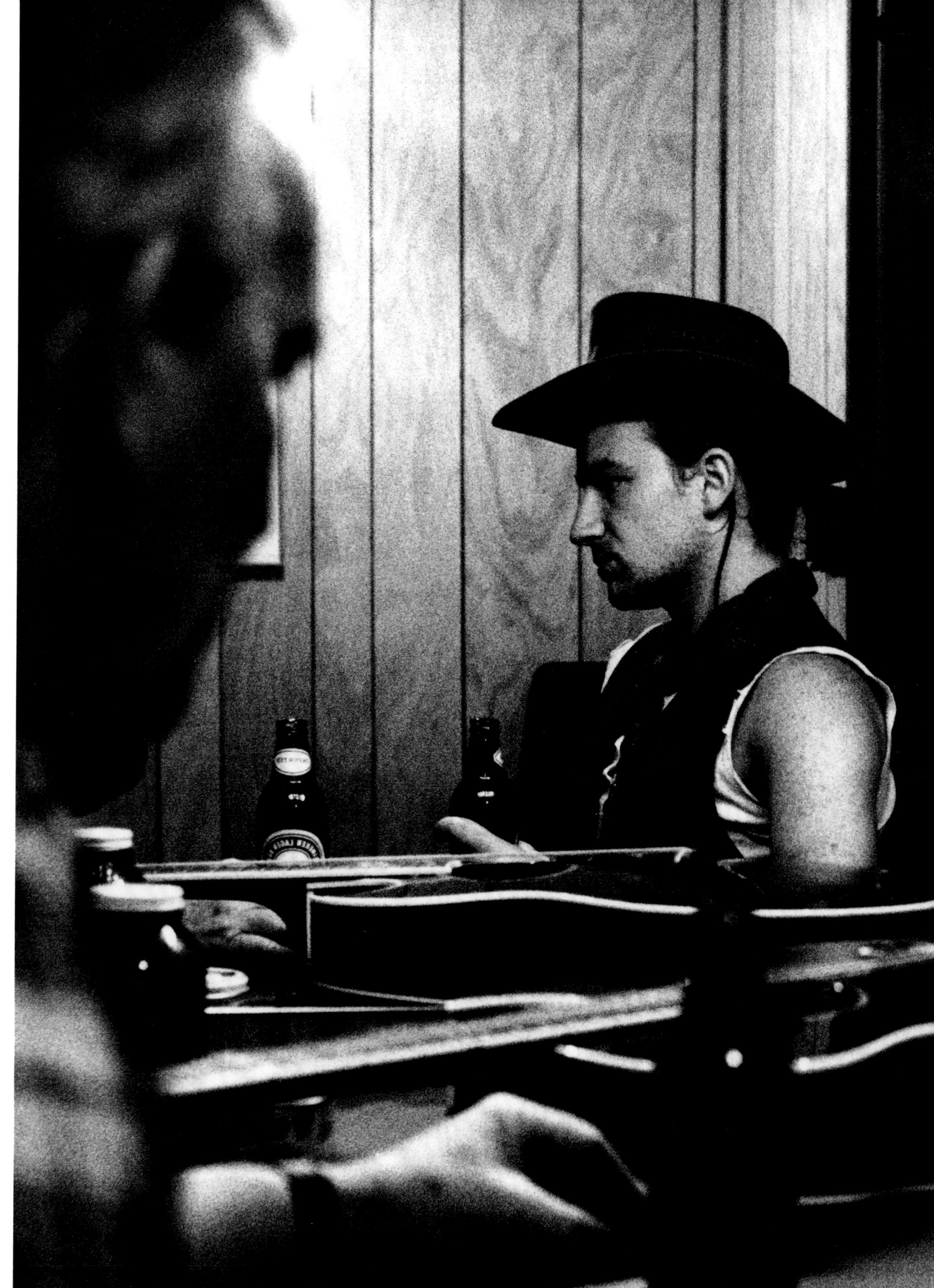

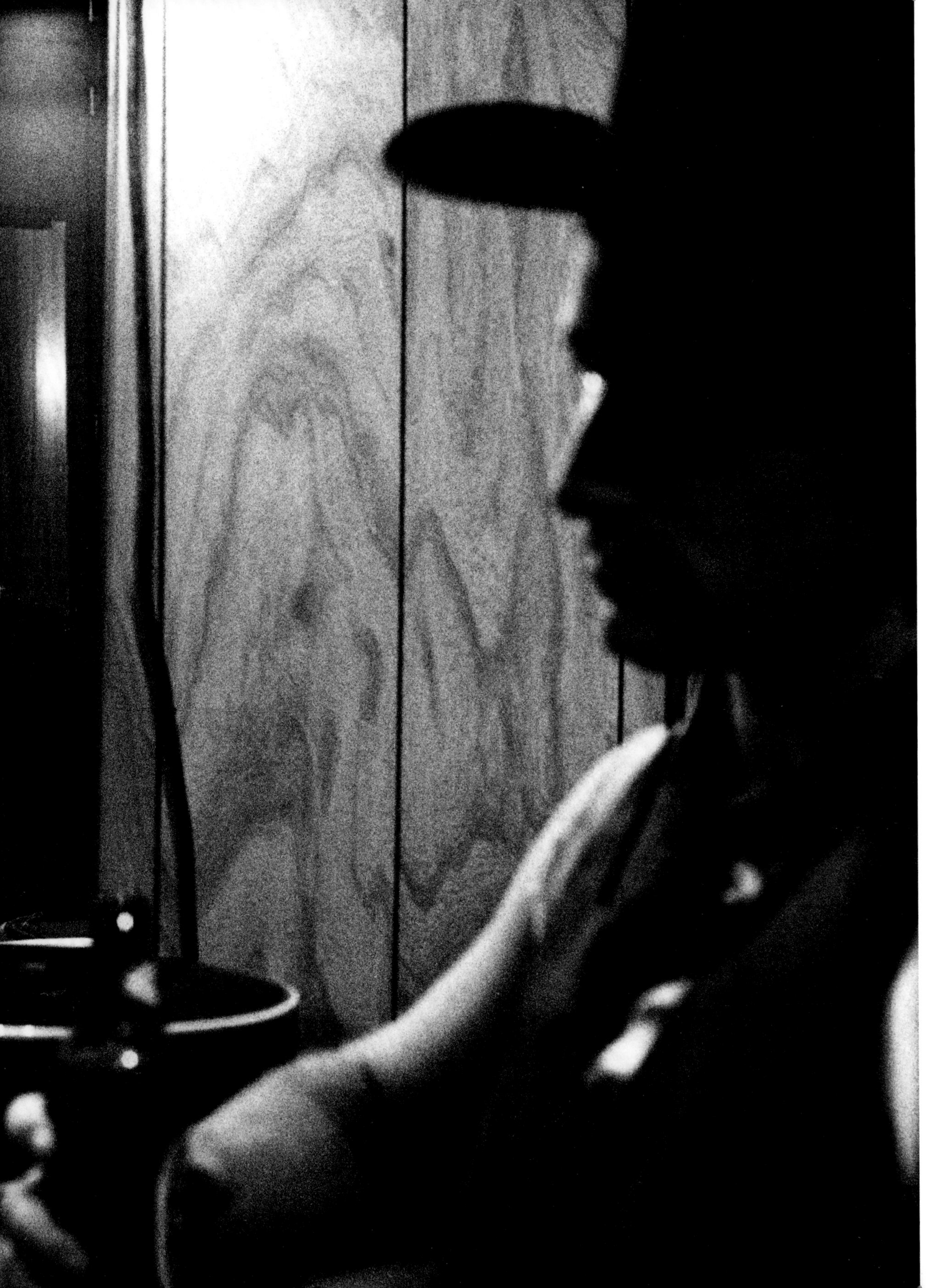

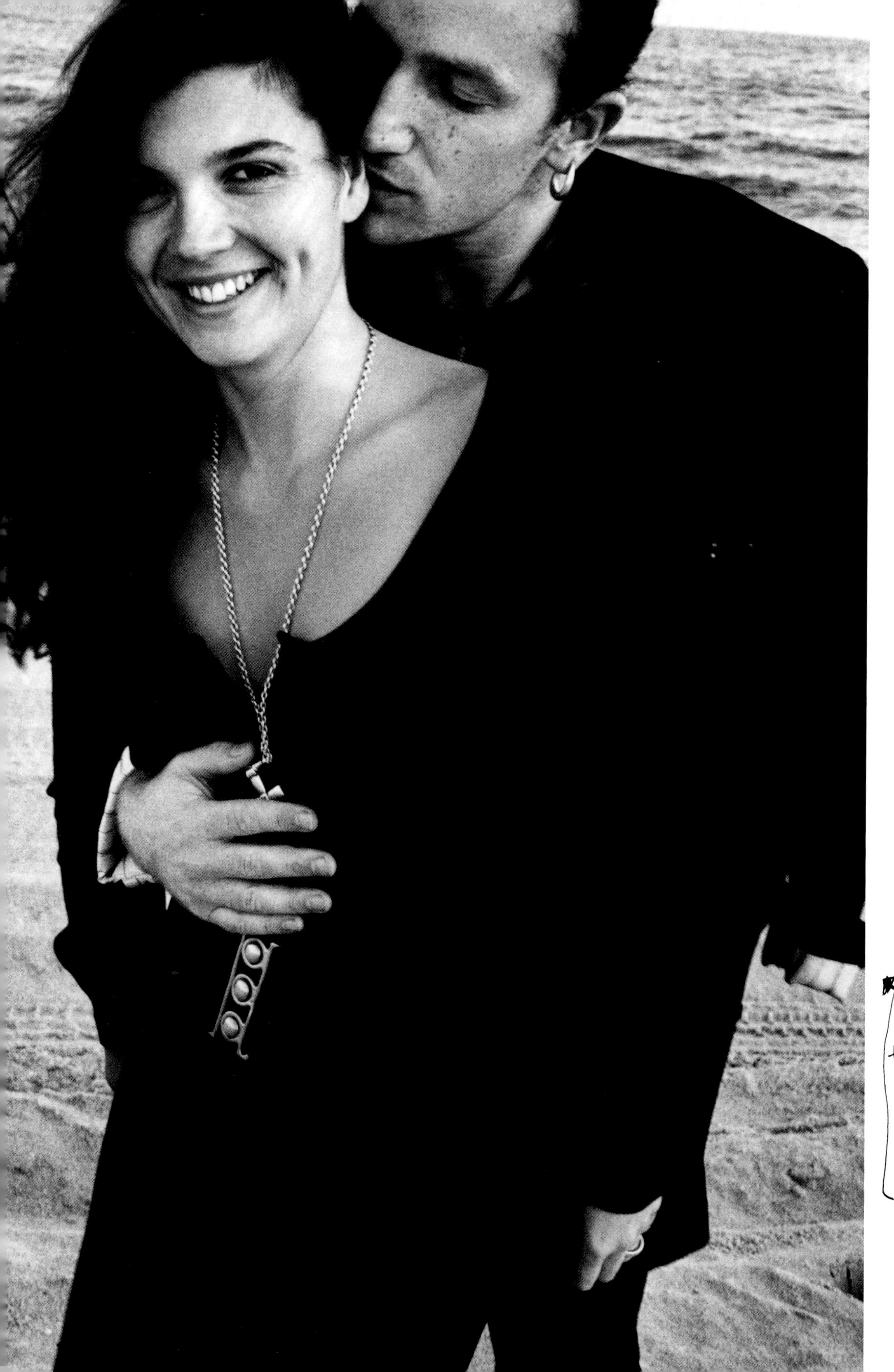

this was the fir
time i photogra
bono and ali
together.
where is bono's
left hand?
answers
overleaf -

LONG ISLAND 1987

september

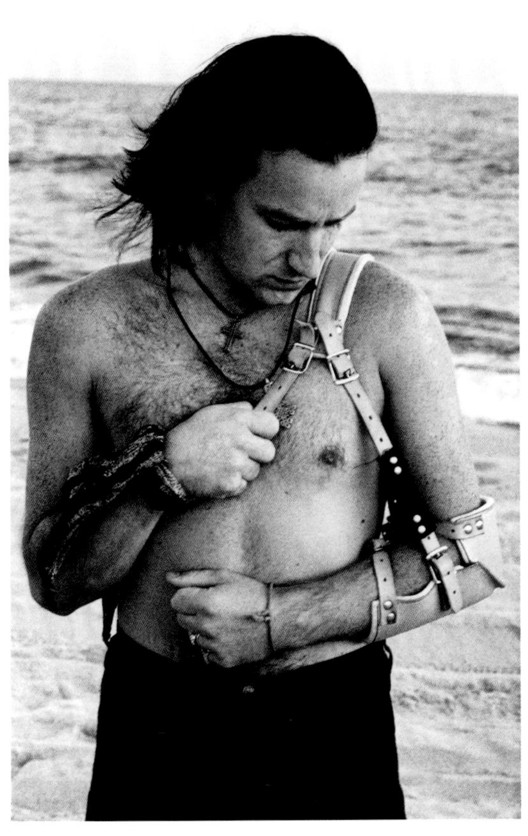

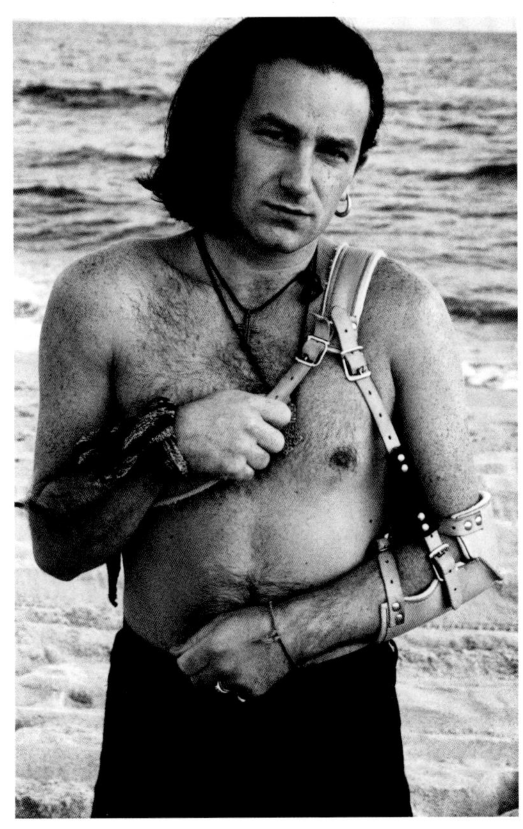

i came out for a few dates on the joshua tree tour east coast USA part and bono and ali invited me to stay with them in their rented place on the beach in long island where they would fly back to after the gigs. one afternoon we just walked out onto the beach and took some nice photos of them and of bono's injury. he had fallen on stage and had to walk around like this for a while. hard for a man with so much energy.

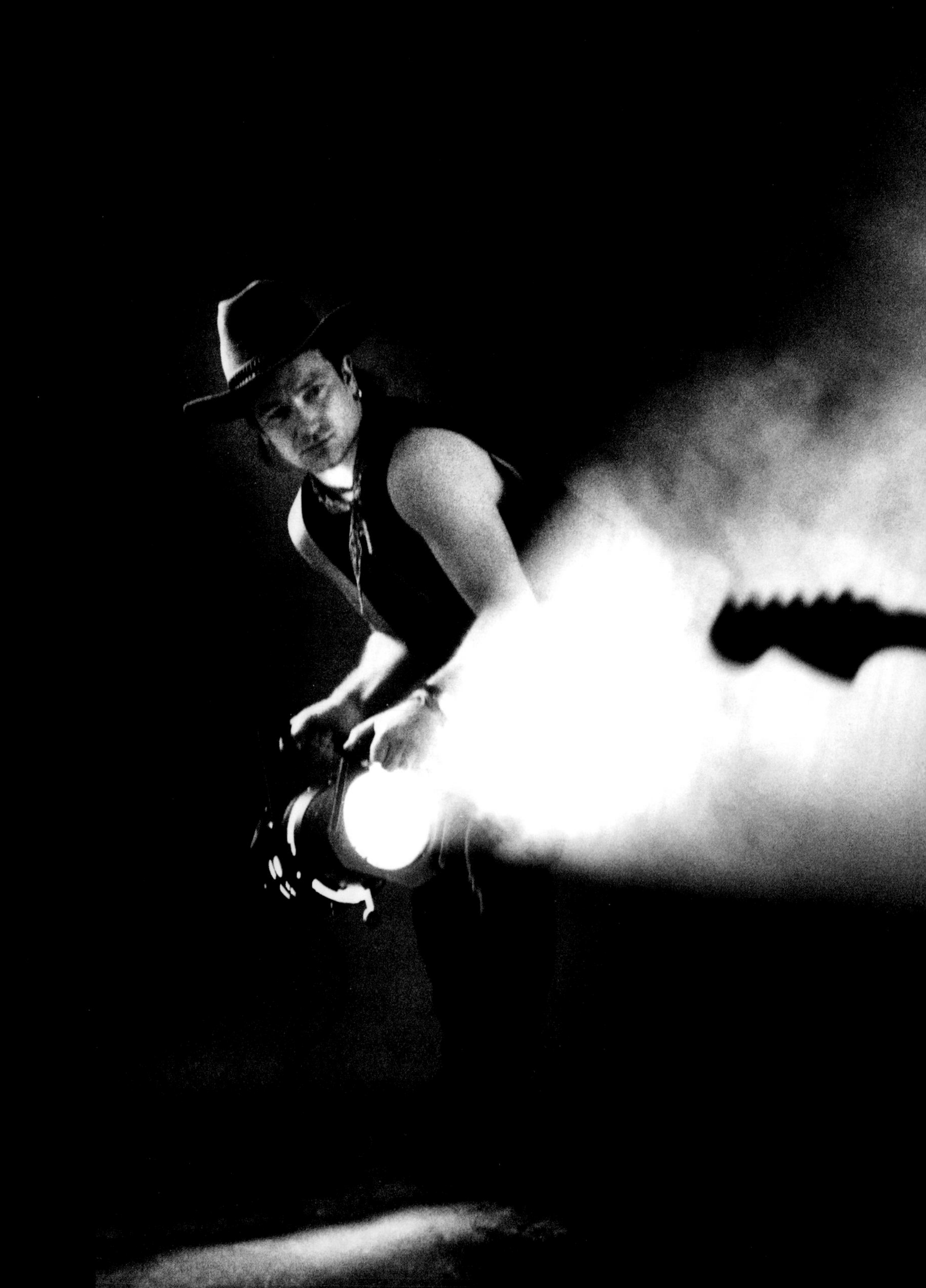

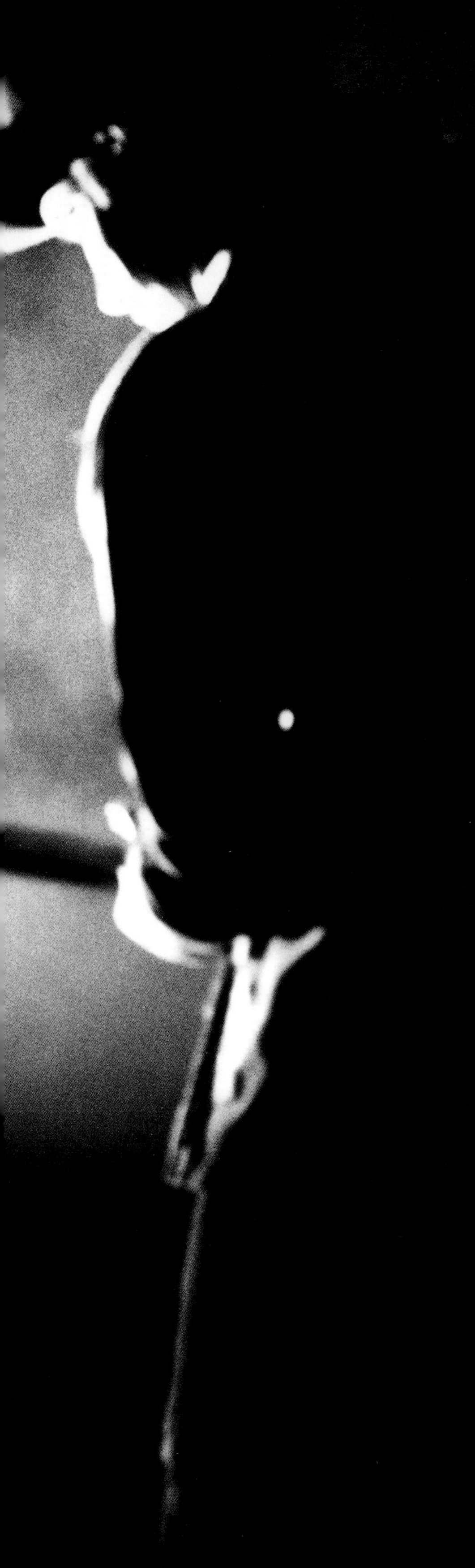

Los Angeles 1988

Rattle and Hum was not a project that i was closely involved in at all. i just came over to LA for about a week to do some pressphotos and to have a go at the albumcover. We ended up travelling to SF for the pressphotos ~~in the end~~. i rented a photostudio to recreate a moment from U2's stageshow – the moment where Bono shines a spotlight on to Edge's guitar during 'bullet the blue sky'. an attempt had been made to use a live photo of this act but that hadn't worked out. the owner of the studio, a very nice french photographer living in LA, helped saving the day by supplying me with some smoke during the shoot as i had forgotten that basic rule: no light visible without smoke! you could say i was a little stressed out.

← on the left is a shot from that studioshoot and the actual shot used on the cover is on the next page.

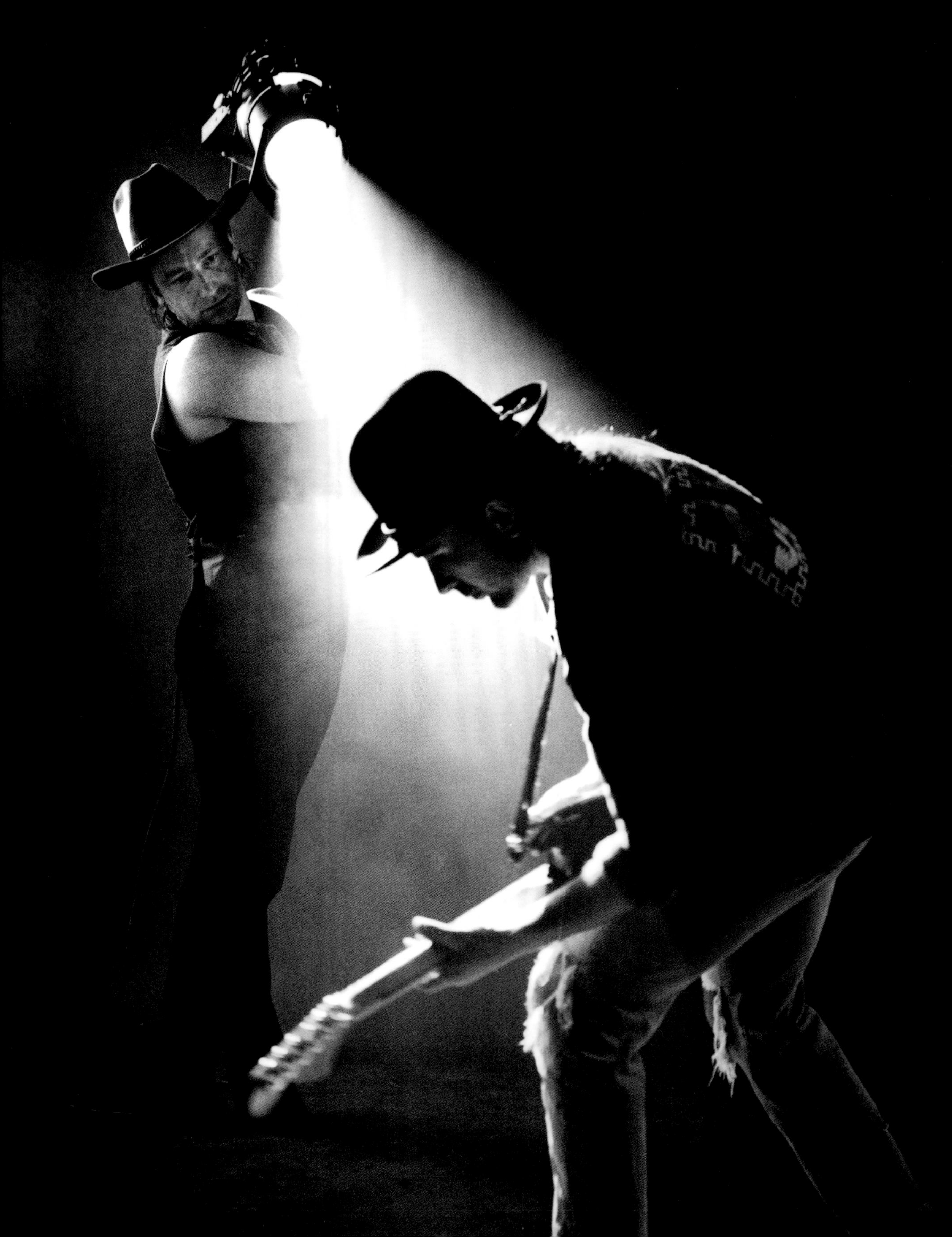

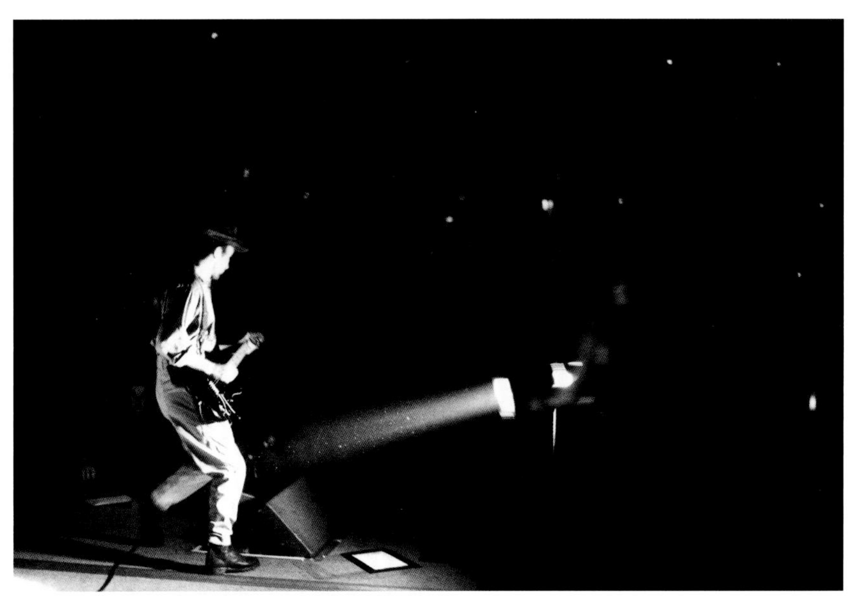

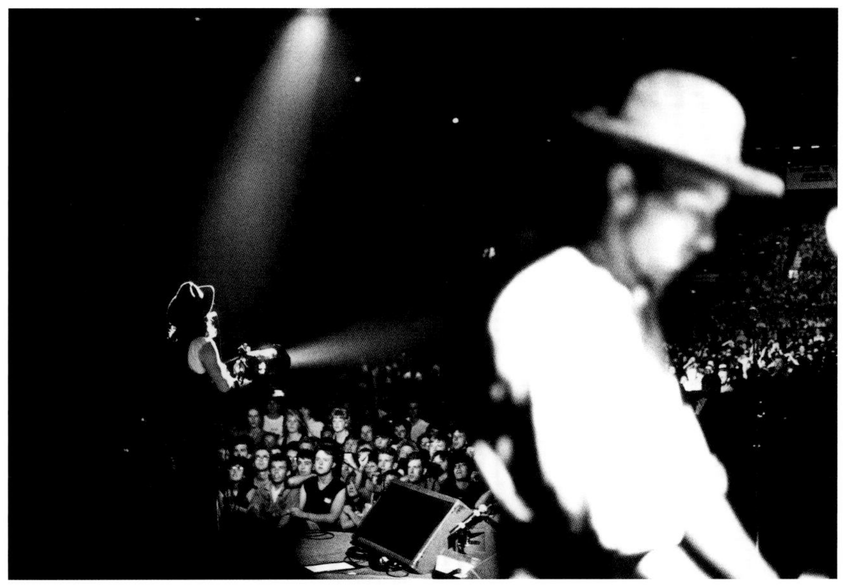

Some shots from the Joshua tree tour showing
Bono lighting up Edge and the audience.

SAN FRANCISCO 1988

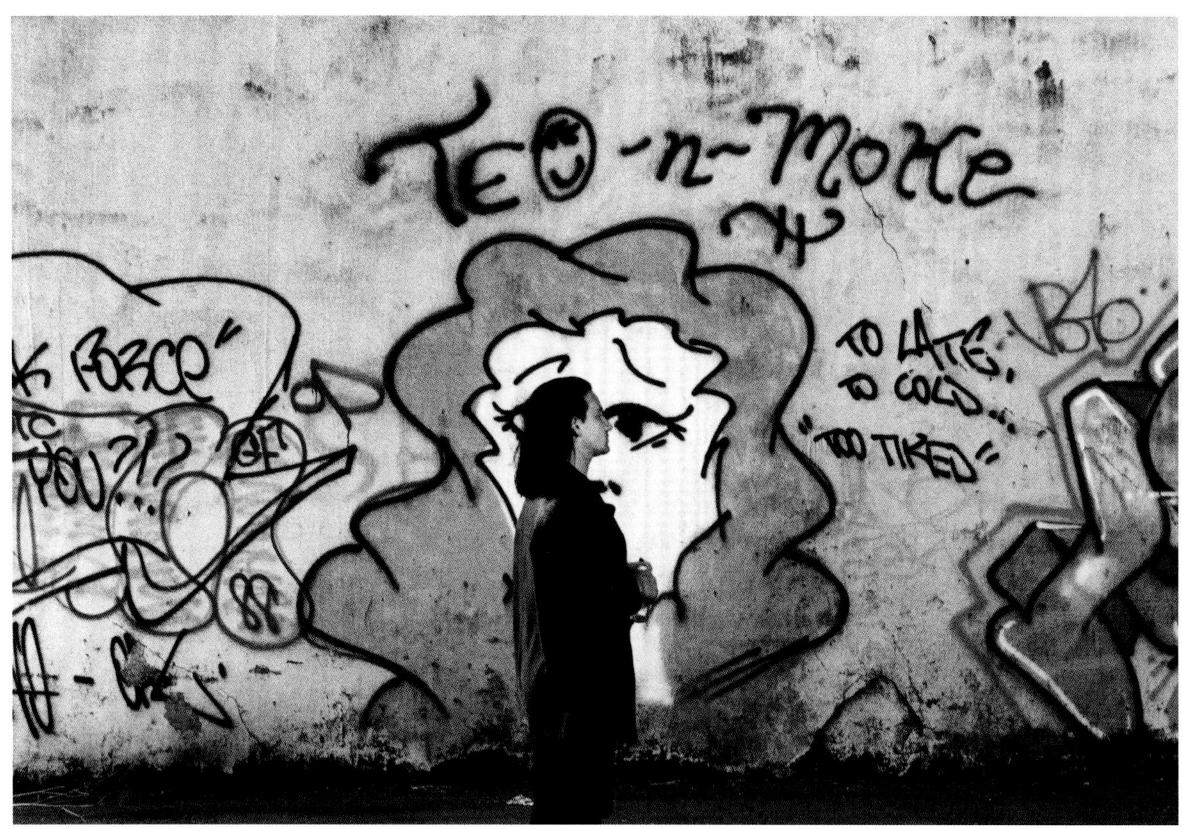

there were two reasons to go to SF for the press photos – one was to get away from their recording environment in LA and the other was the street graffitti in SF that bono so loves.

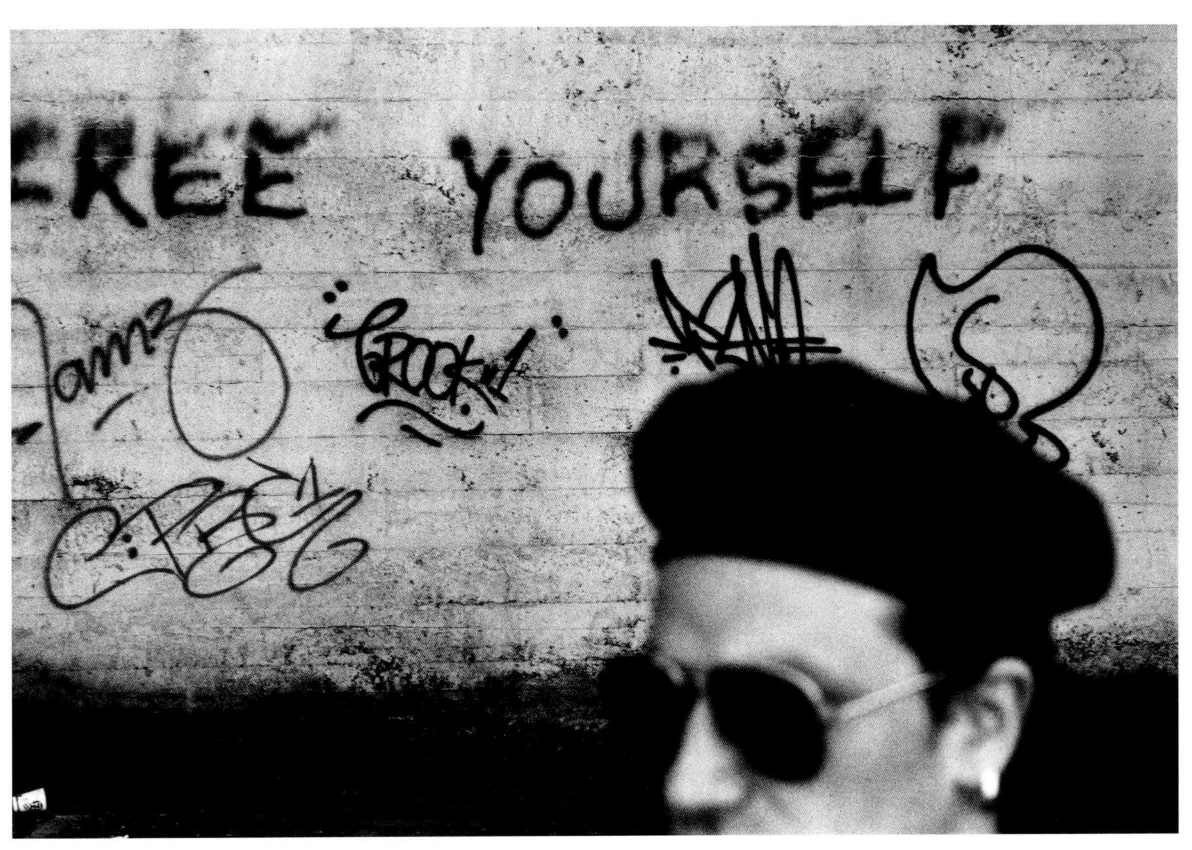

bono had previously met a (graffitti) artist named Rene Castro in SF and overleaf is one of his works visible next to the band. his work was more that of a political motivated painter painting in public spaces than that of a graffitti artist.

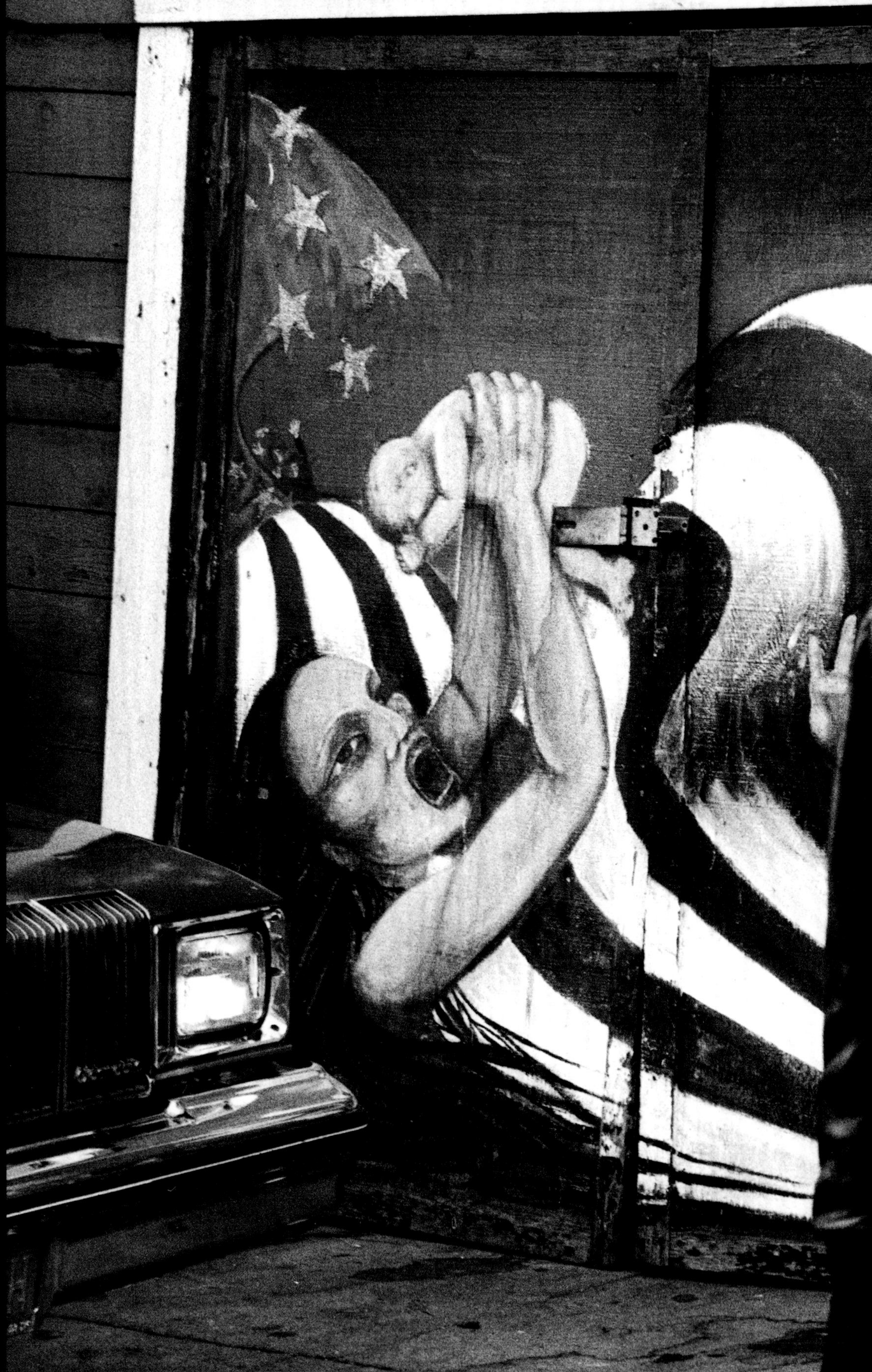

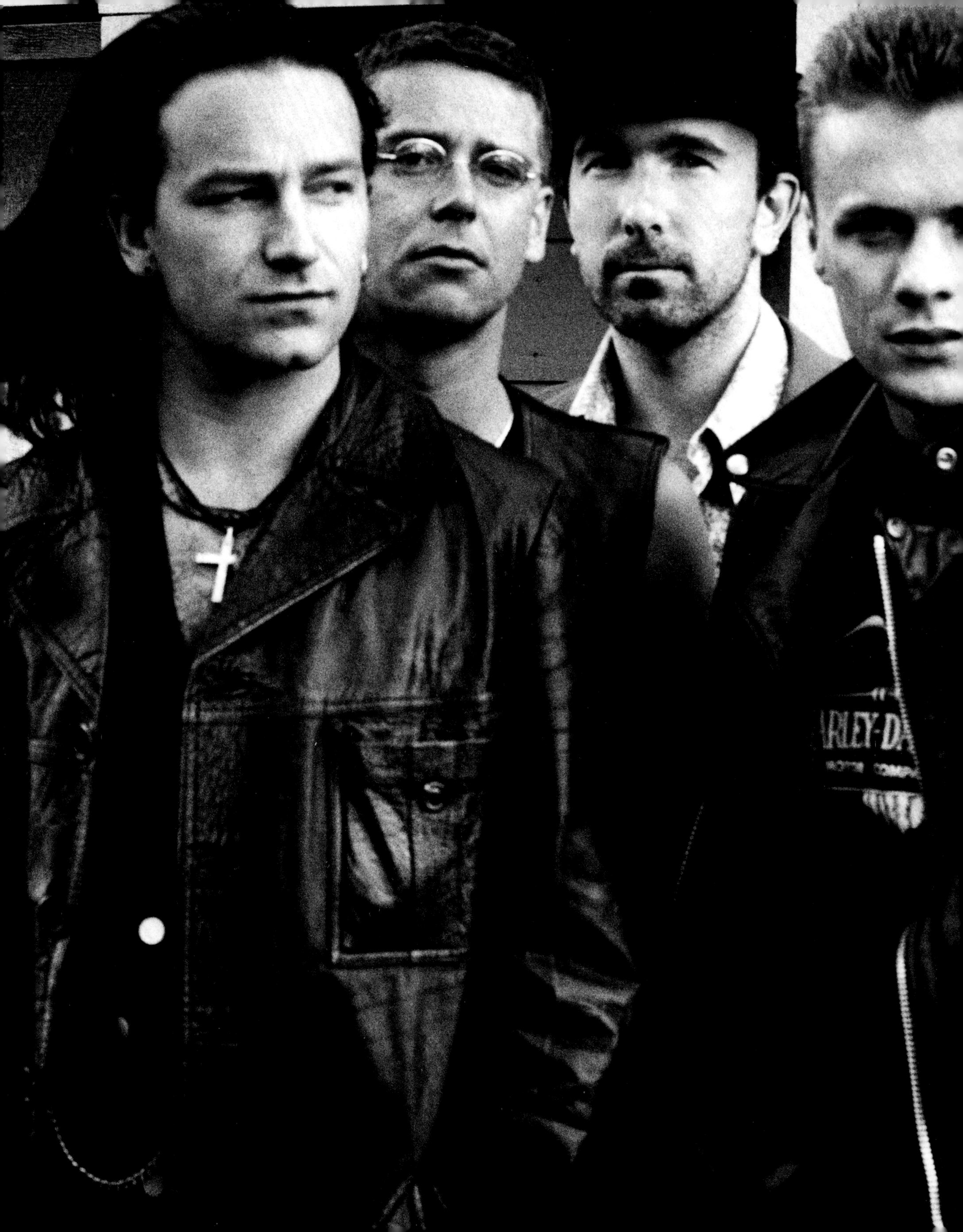

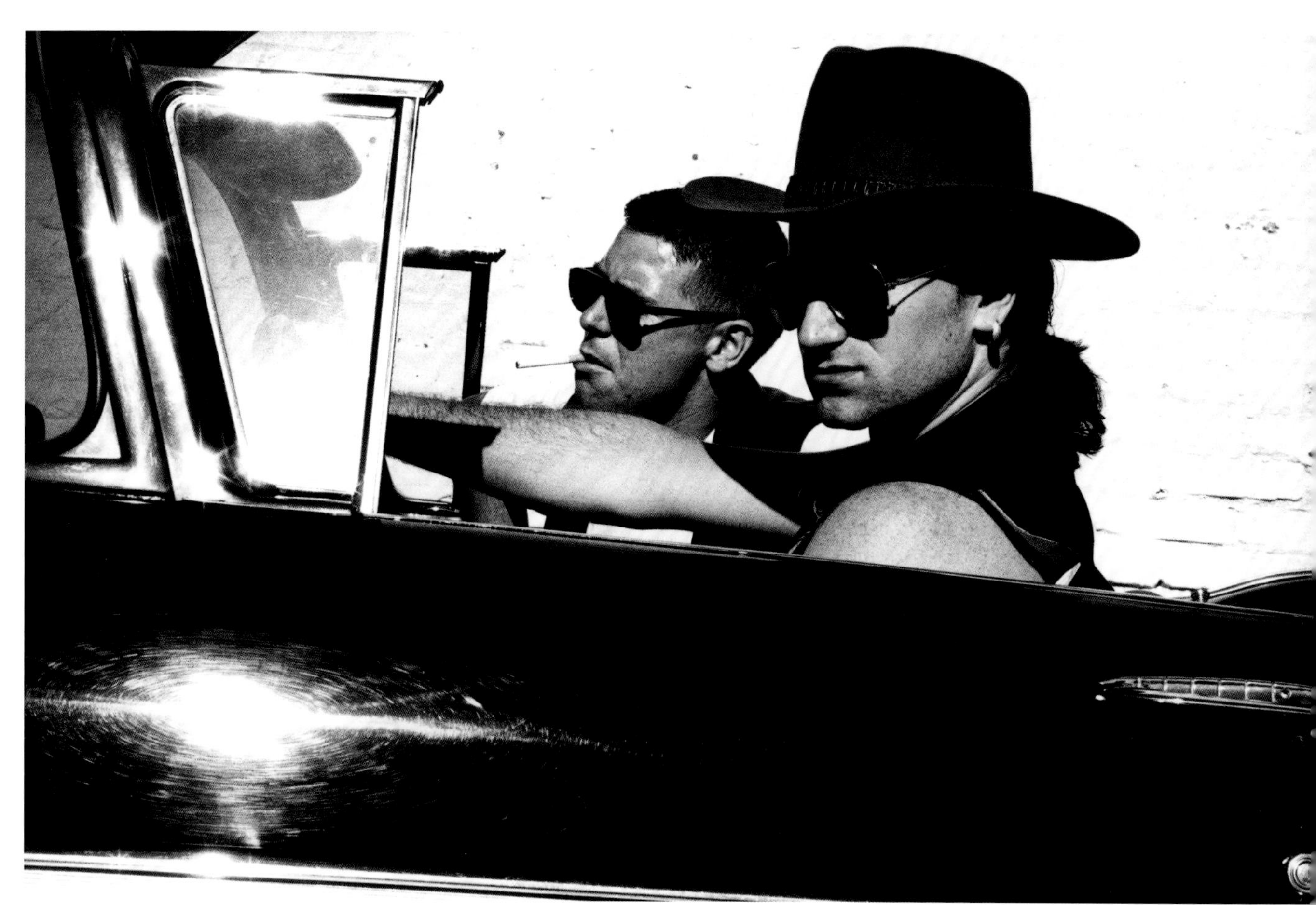

always very tempting to use old american cars for photographs, they just look sóó cool and so does anyone sitting in them.

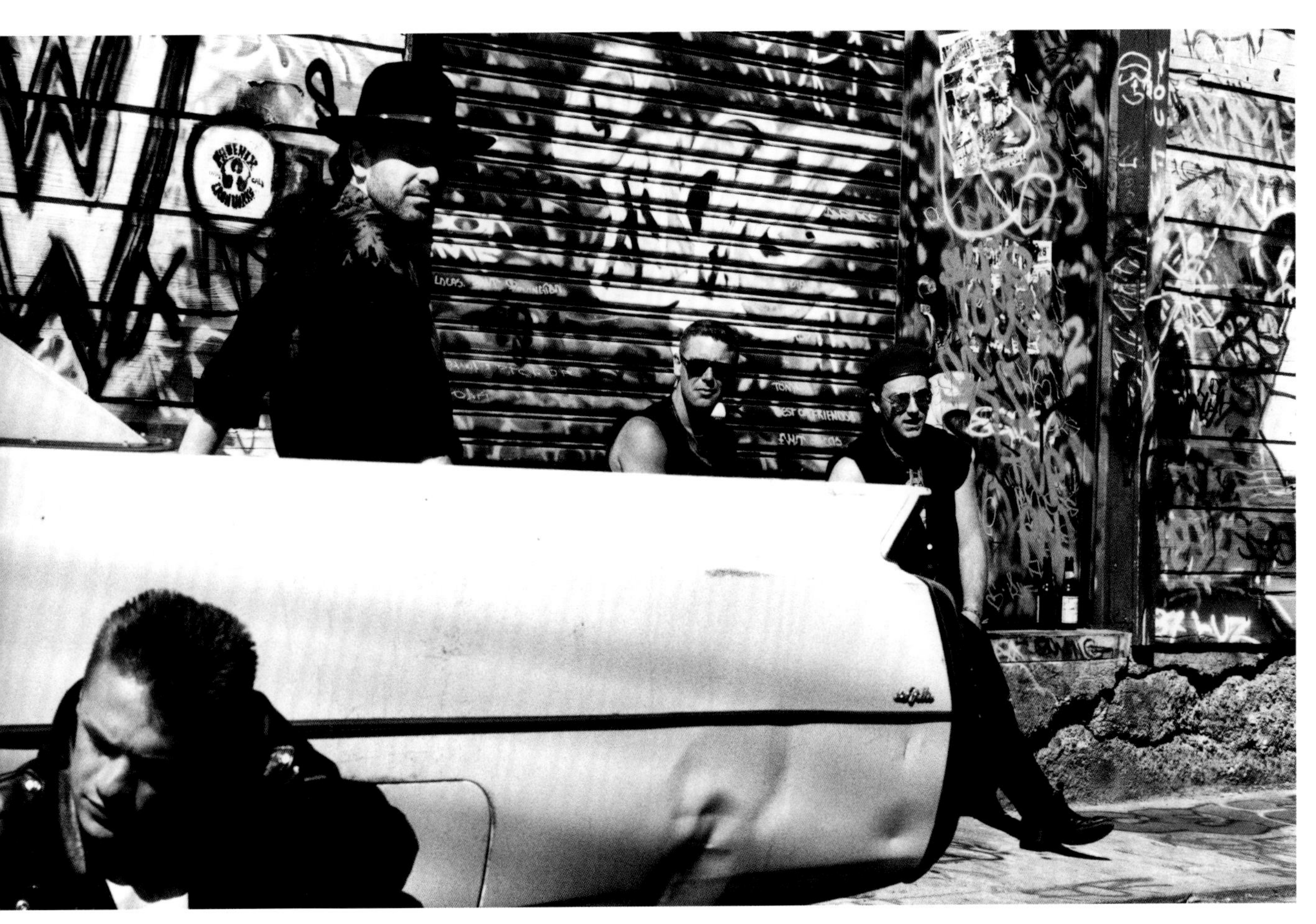

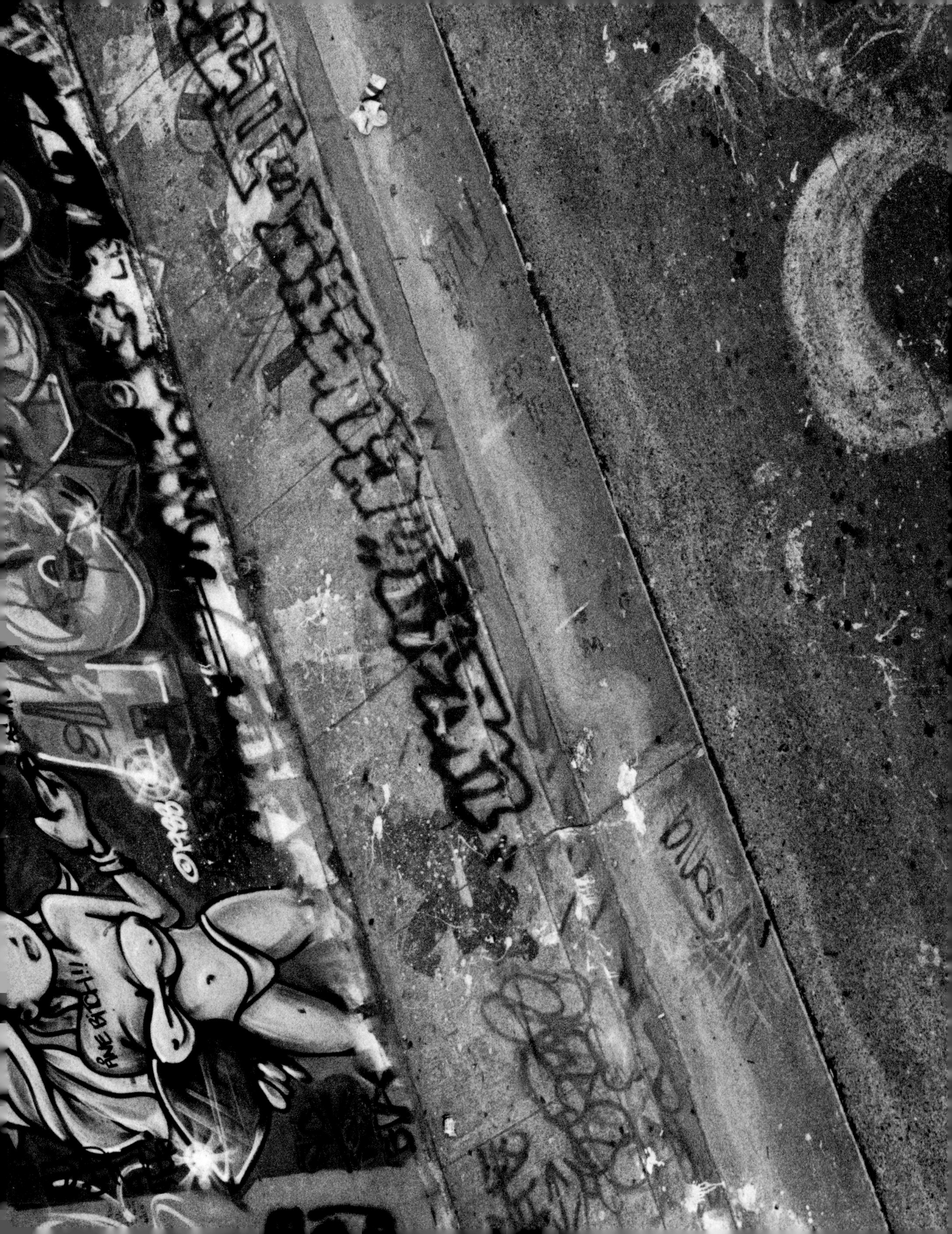

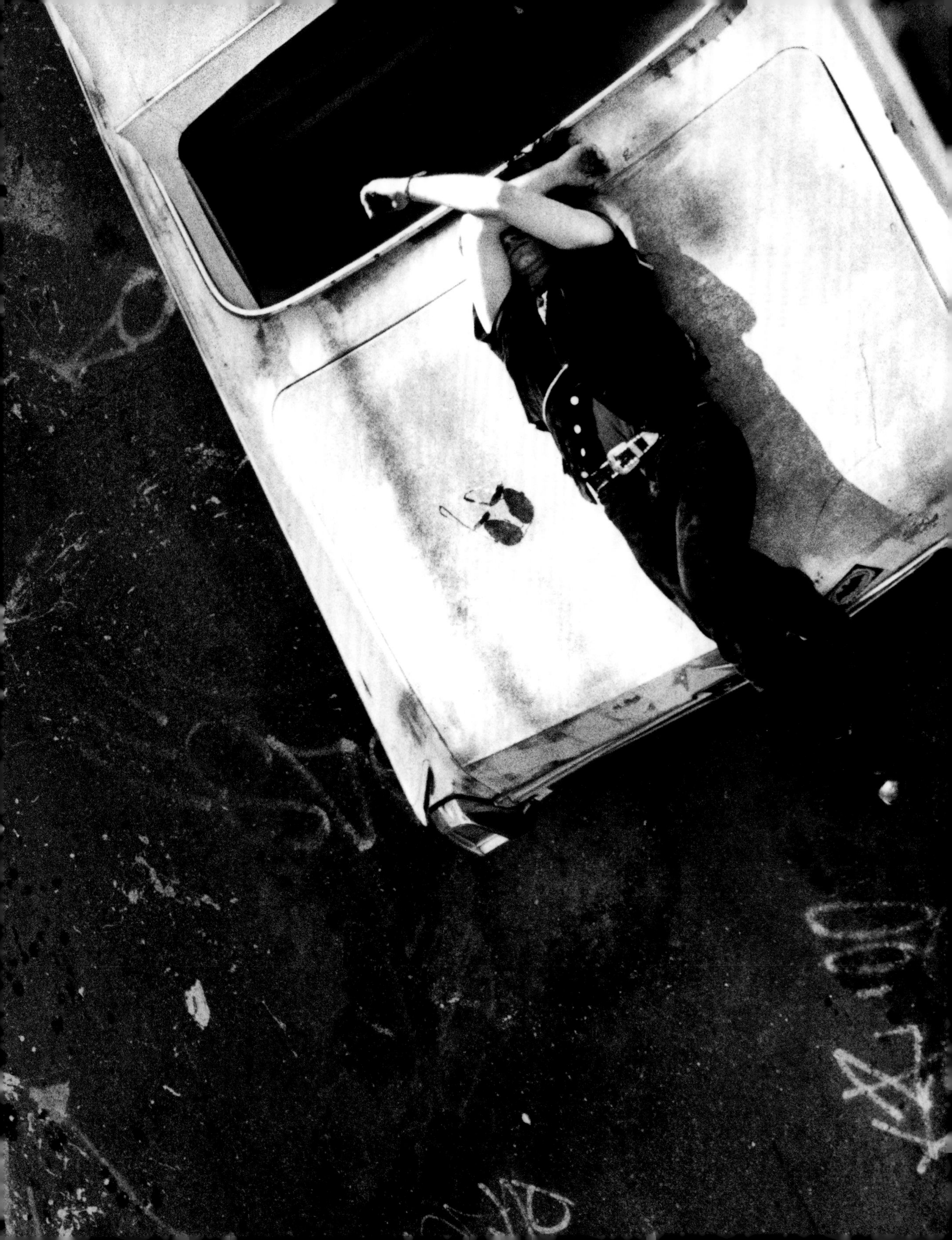

the next day we've havin' breakfast in the cafe across from the hotel old style american b'fast.

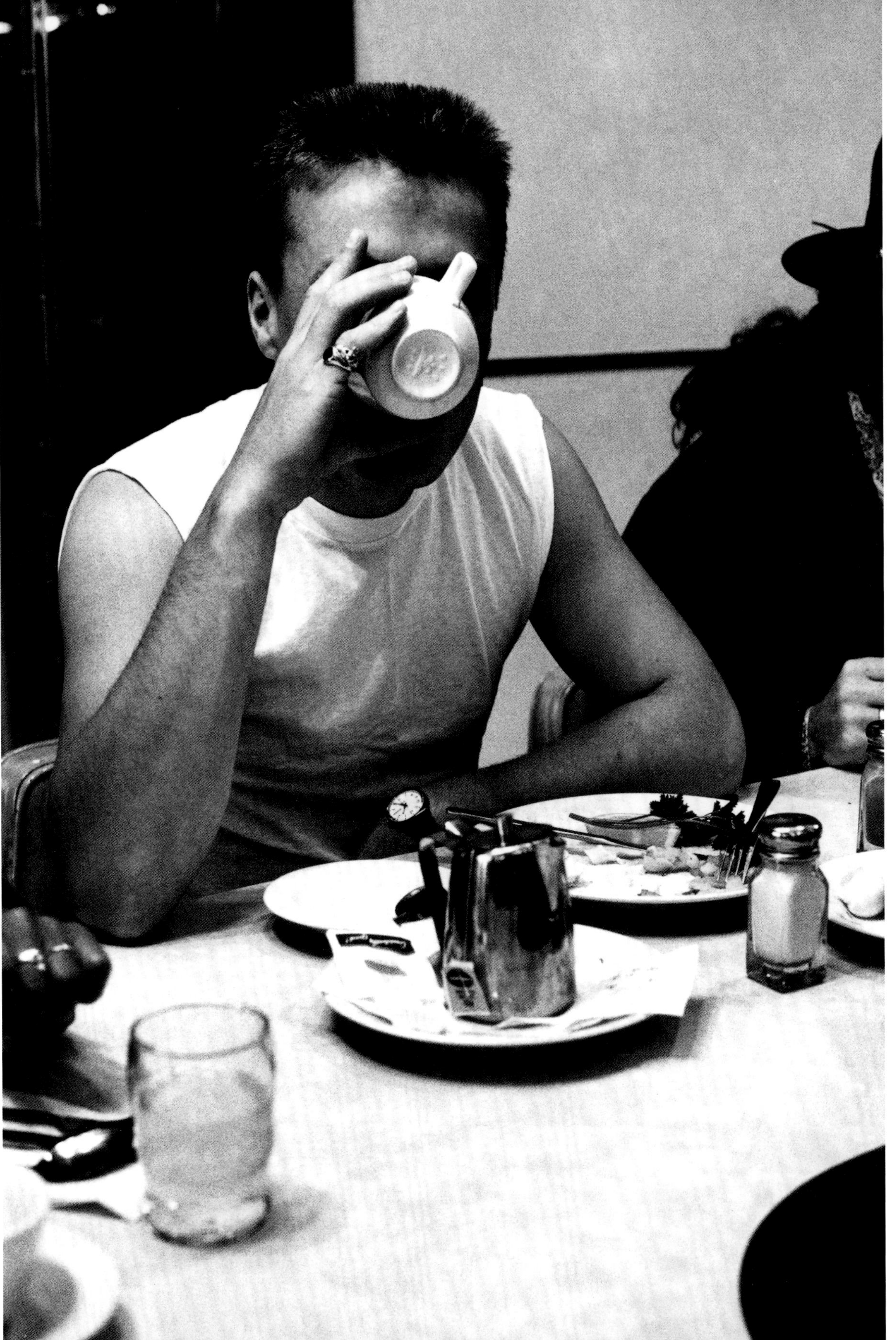

HOLLYWOOD 1988

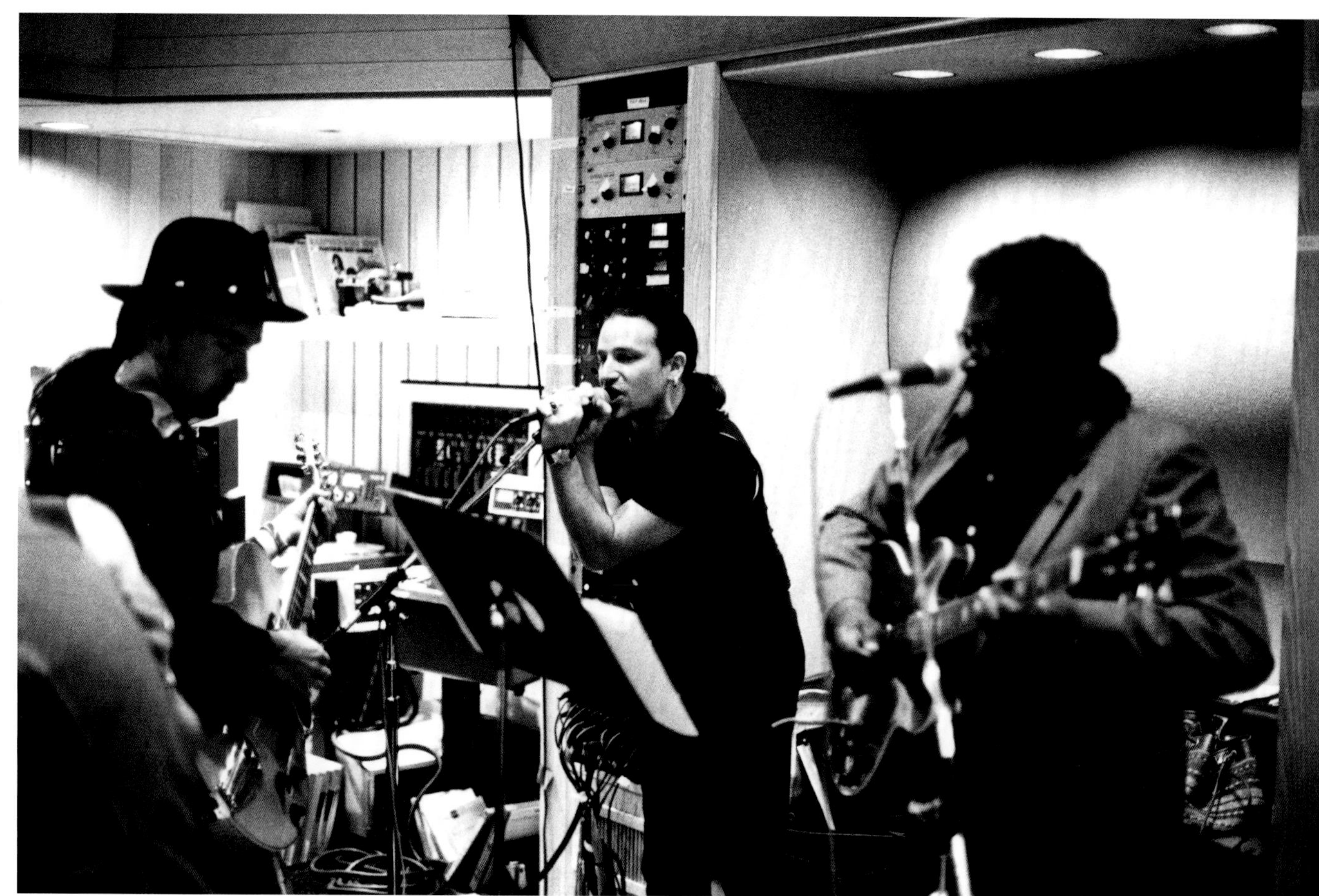

at A&M recording Studios in LA – BB King and U2 putting the final touches to the song 'When Love comes to town'!

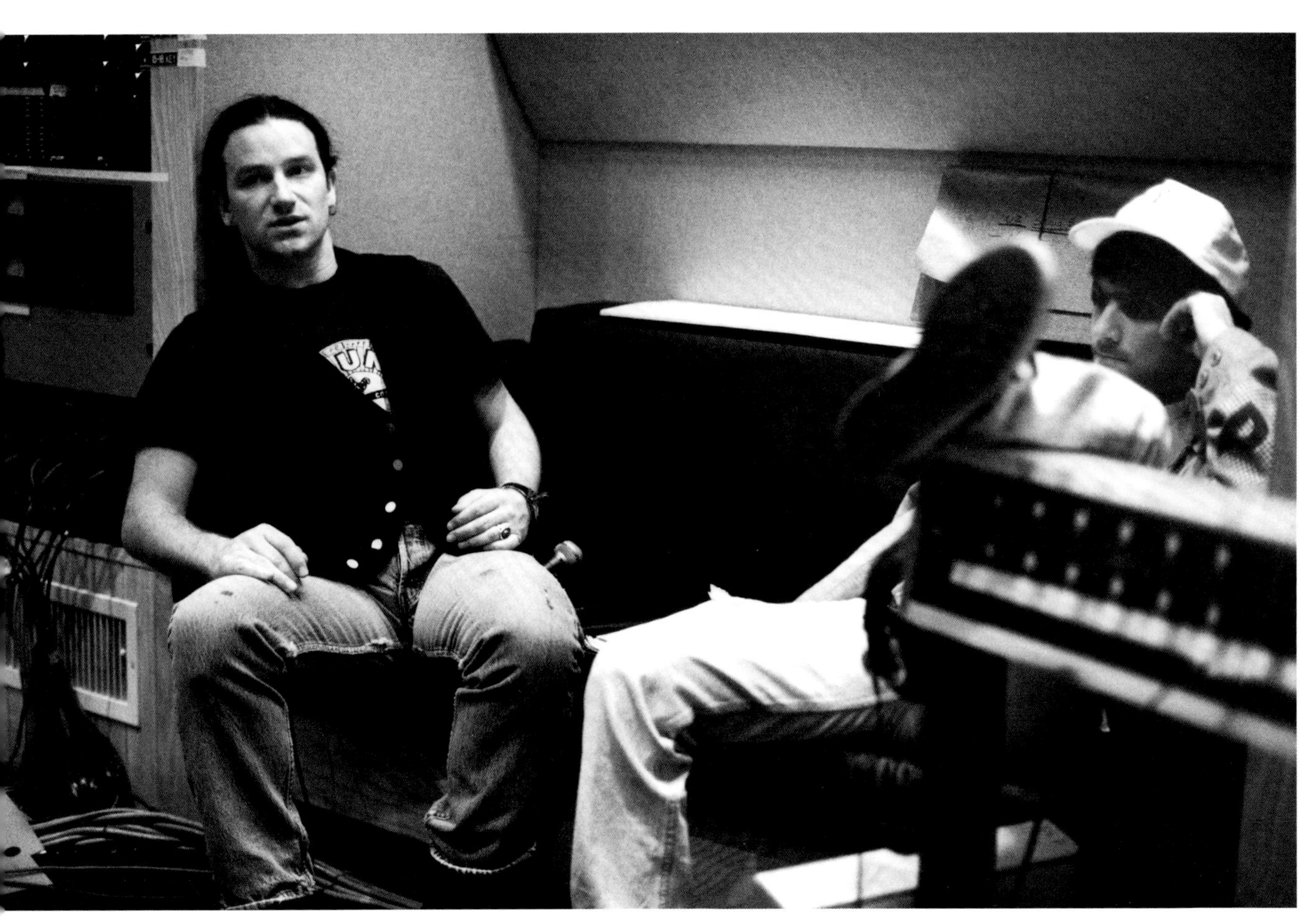

producer jimmy iovine ↑

LONDON 1988 october

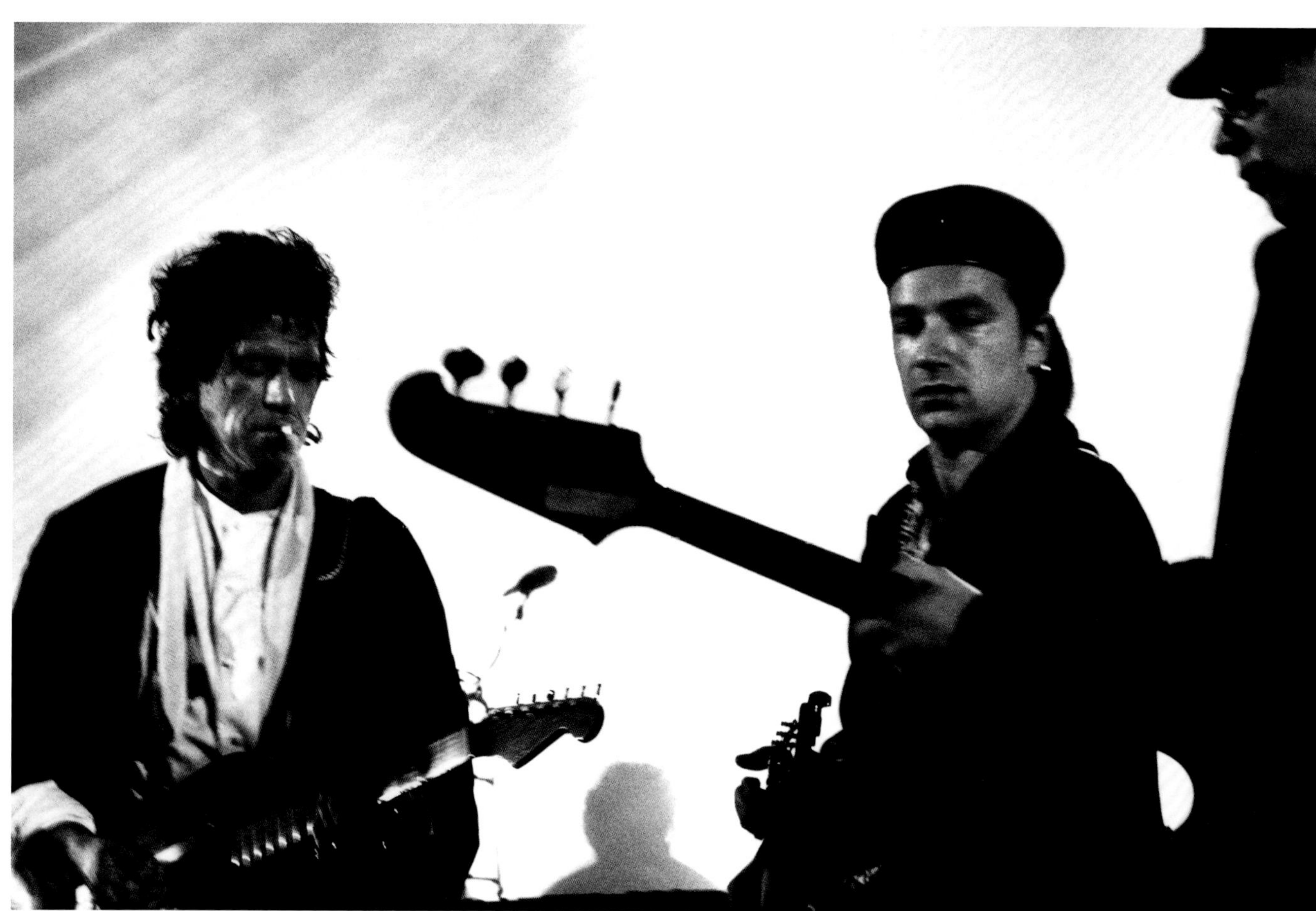

keith richard, bono and adam are rehearsing 'when love comes to town' for the gig that same evening. it is a benefit concert to support the victims of hurricane gilbert that destroyed a lot of homes in jamaica.
keith played a few songs with U2 during their short set – there were several other artists playing that night such as ziggy marley and robert palmer

'smile jamaica'

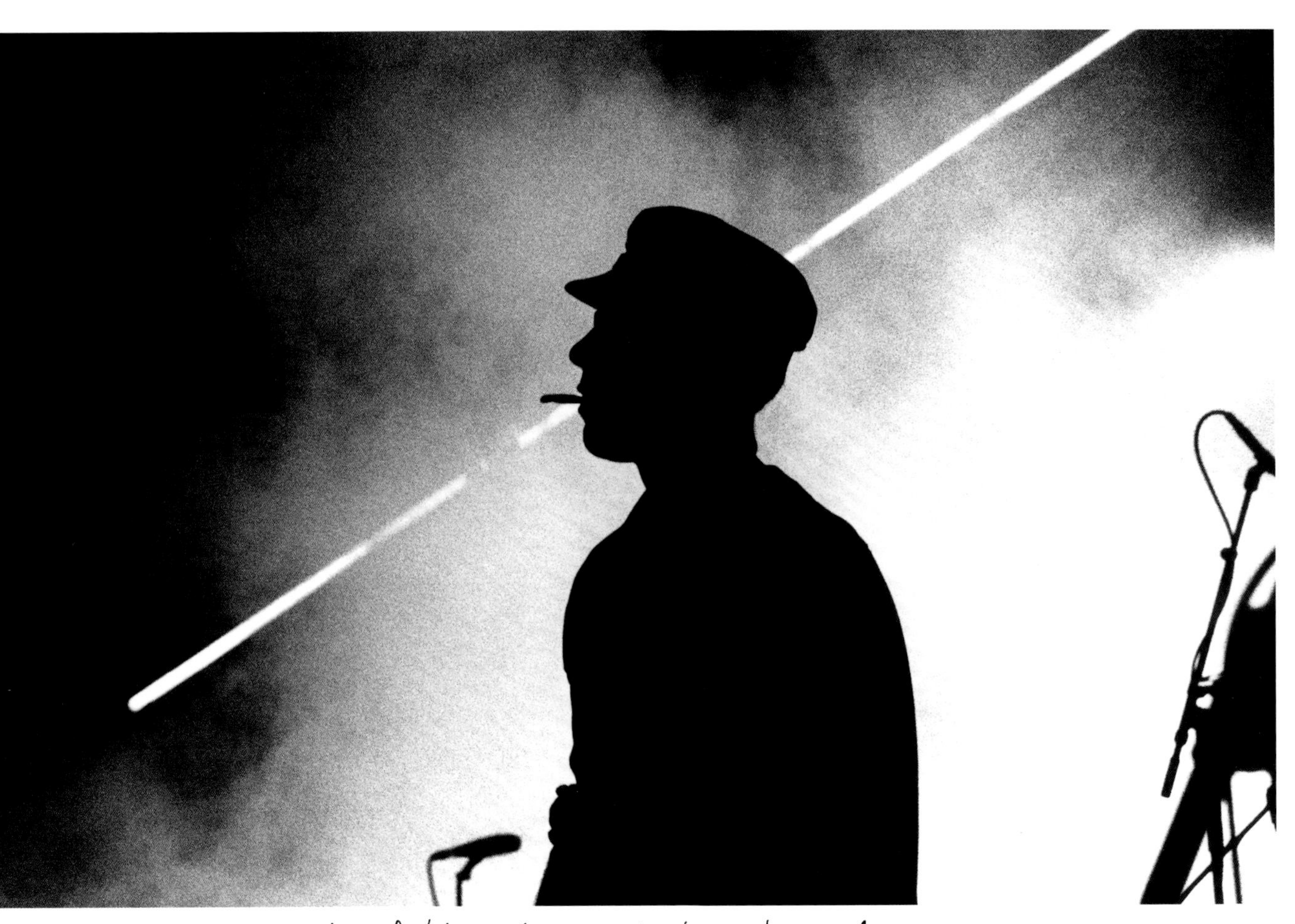

unmistakebly adam, during rehearsals.

DUBLIN 1988
december

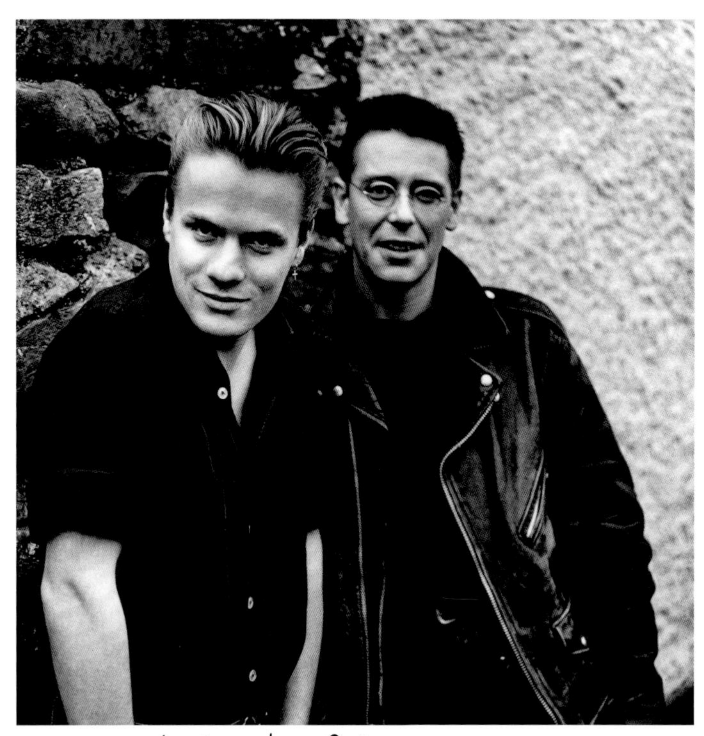

photographs taken for Rolling Stone magazine as they (U2) topped their polls. the cover photo was the shot overleaf on the left and when bono saw that photo on the RS cover he got really unhappy and kind of angry. he so didn't like that photo to be a cover but as it turned out it was an incredibly succesful cover for RS and they got a real positive response to that issue so bono was a lot happier with that knowledge. the RS covers at the time were all color and all devoid of any reality so i felt it was a welcome break of that pattern.

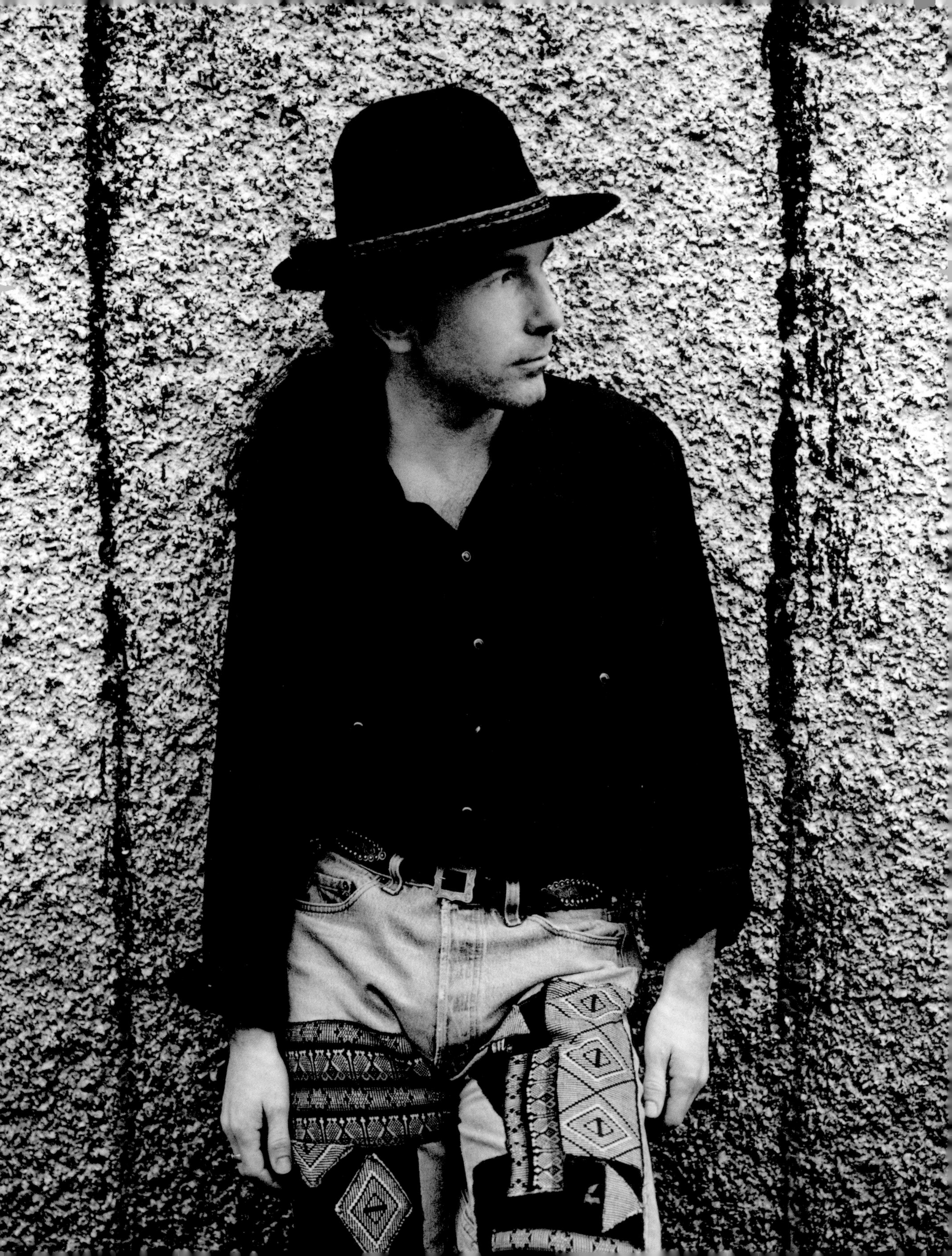

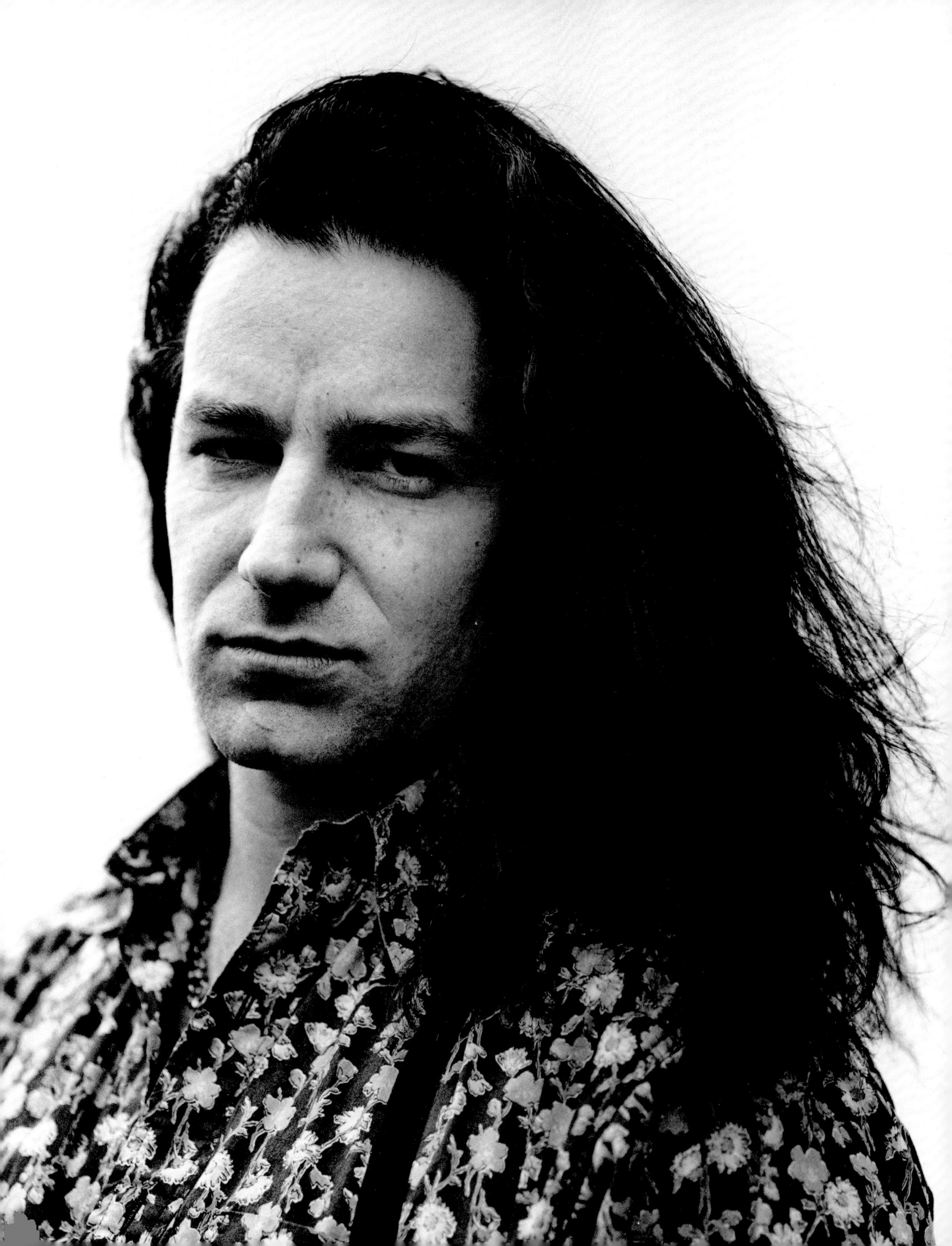

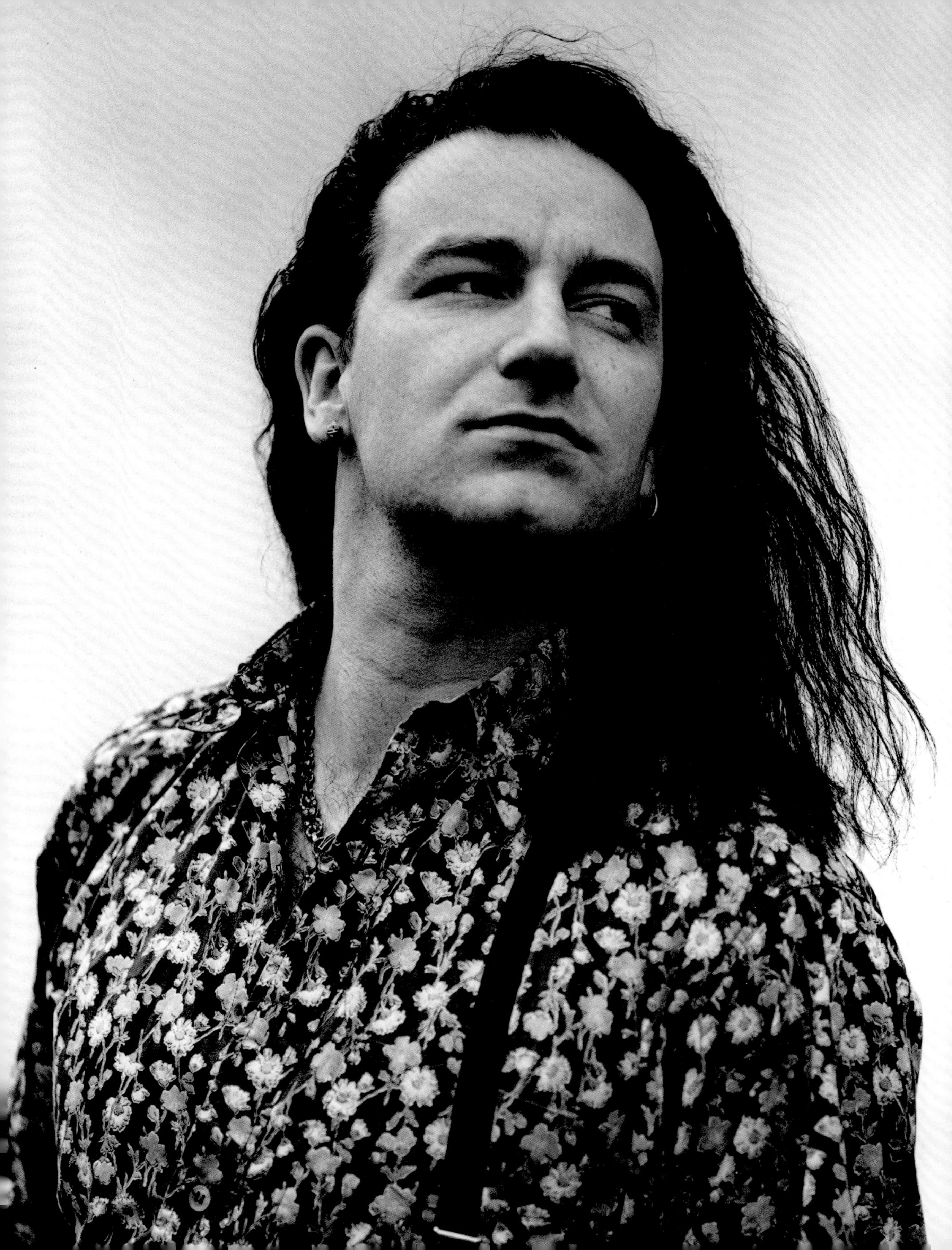

DUBLIN
1989 february?

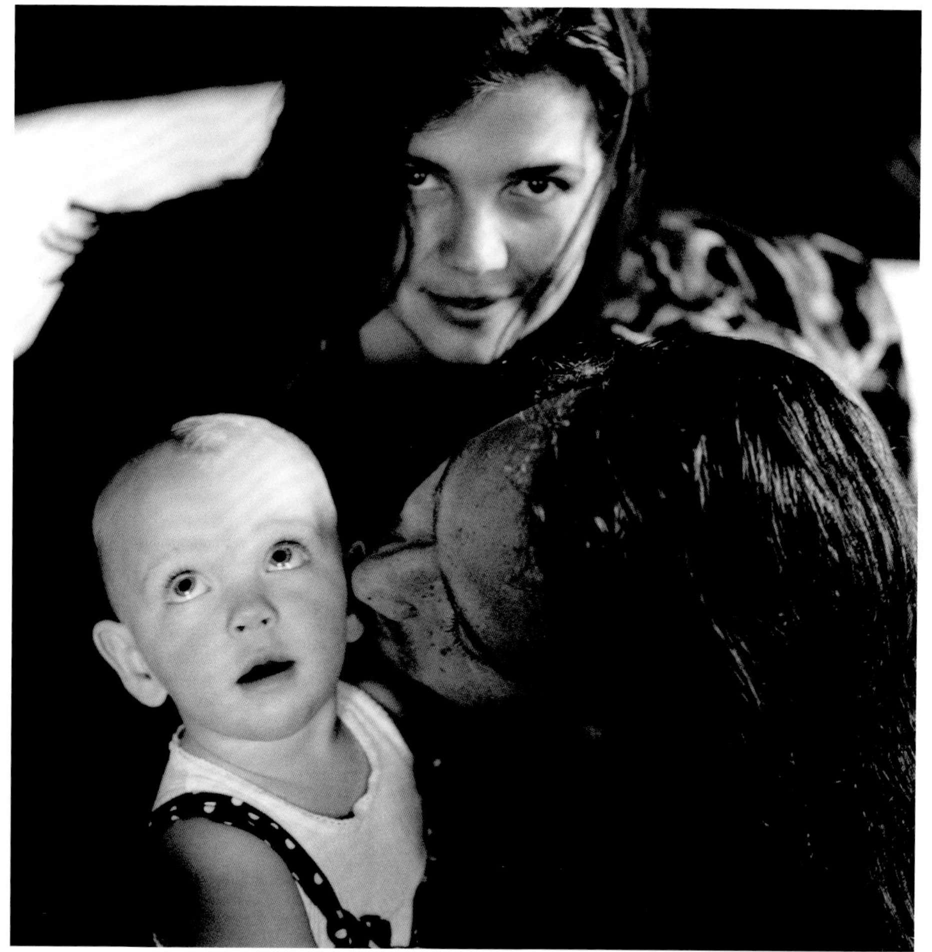

bono at home with ali and their first child: jordan. we did the photos after waking up in the morning hence bono's bathrobe.

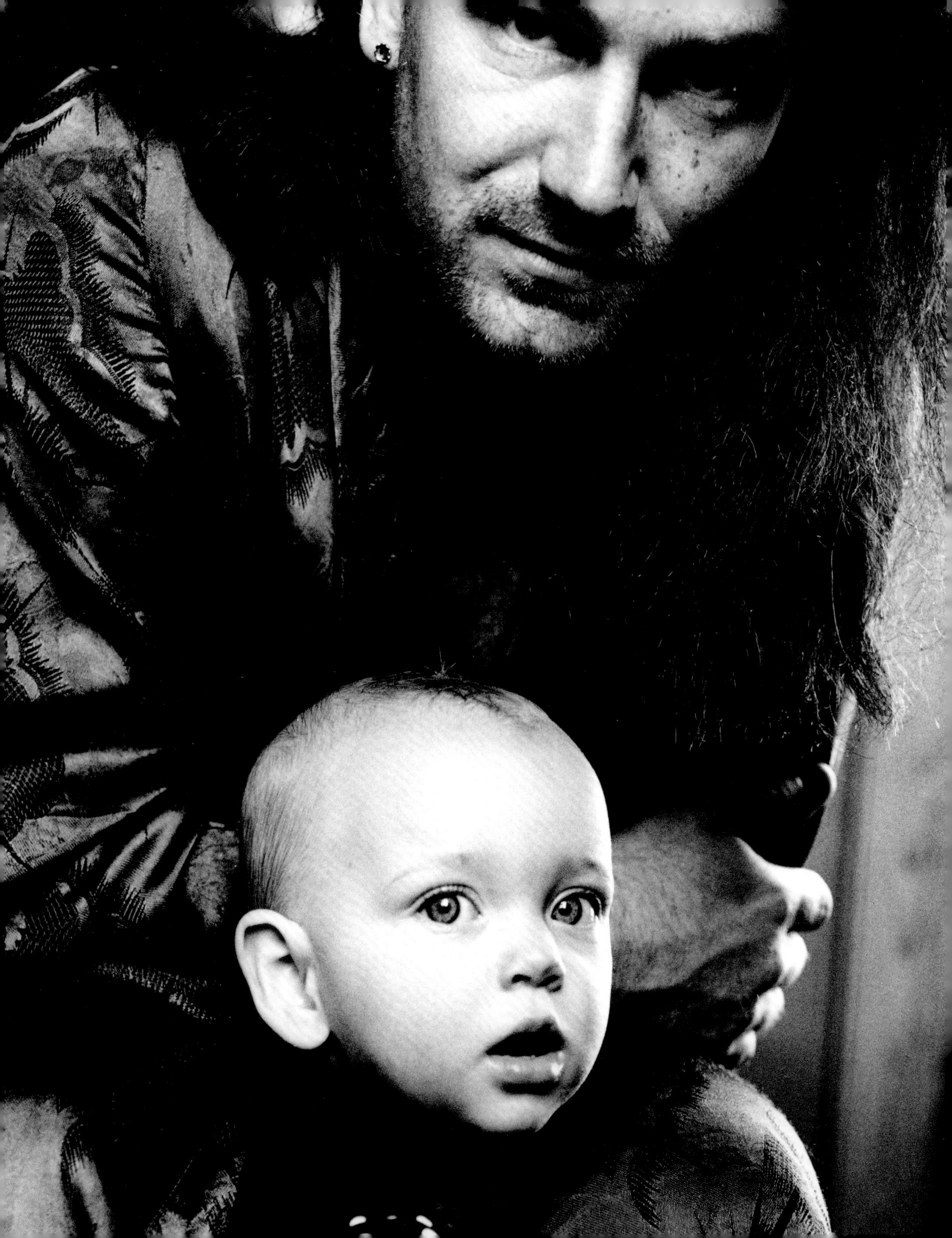

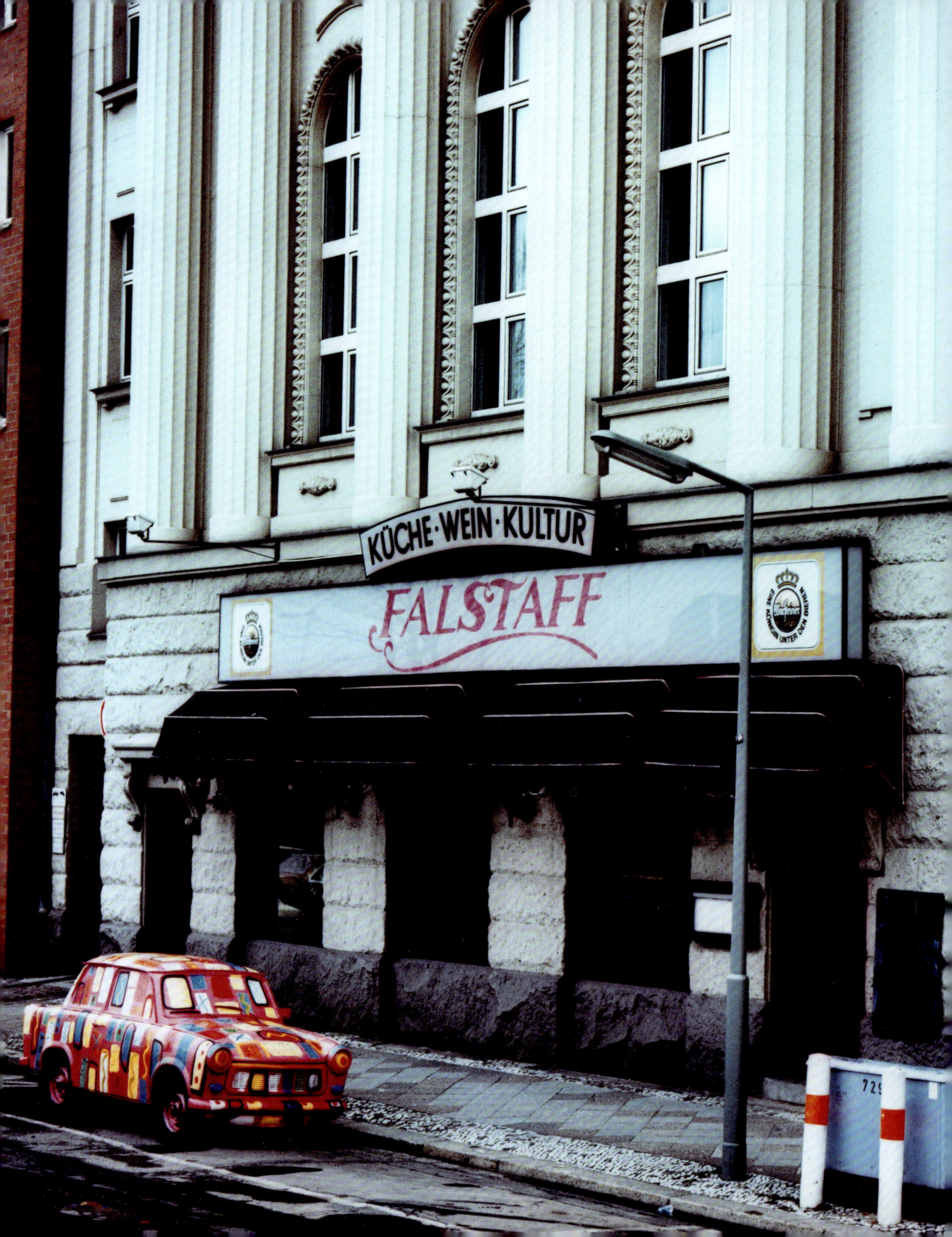
KÜCHE · WEIN · KULTUR
FALSTAFF

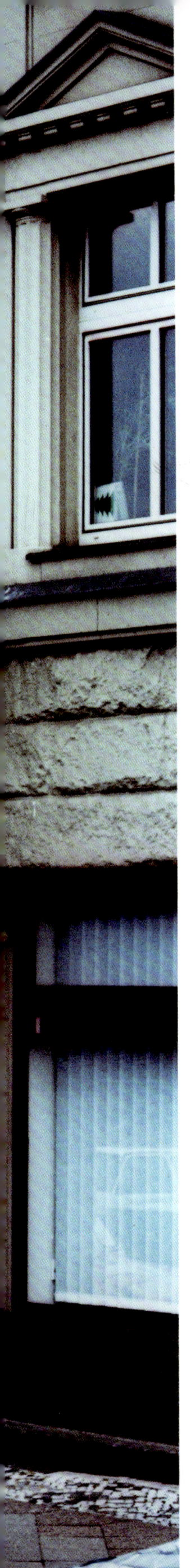

BERLIN 1990

december *

* actually, these two photos of the car were done at a later date, in 1991.

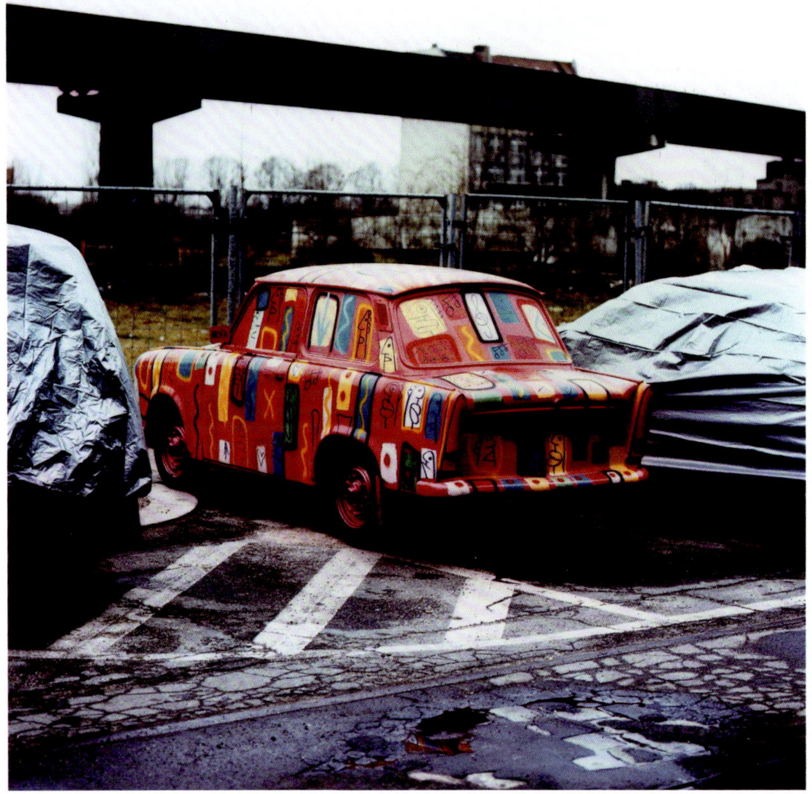

December, again, an album covershoot. after 1982 in sweden and 1986 in the american desert we ended up in the cold again. i'll come back to that on the next pages.
these photos of the trabant symbolise Achtung Baby for me - i suggested to use the trabant (an east-german car) in photos as a 'leitmotiv' if you like - edge then suggested to paint the cars and that how this came about. The photo on the left is the car parked in front of the building that housed Hansa studios and 'falstaff' was its restaurant.

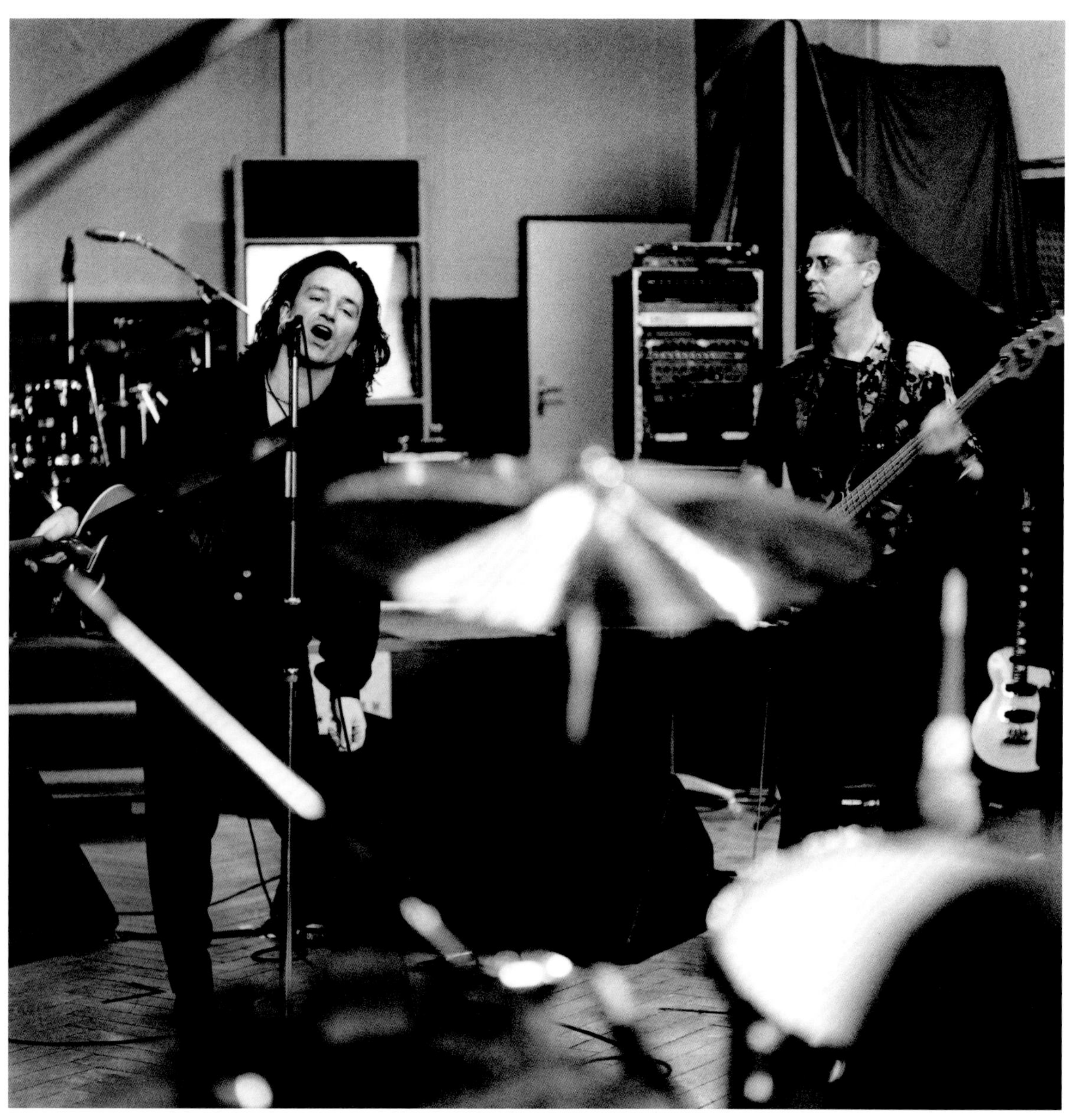

inside Hansa studios during the recording of Achtung Baby.

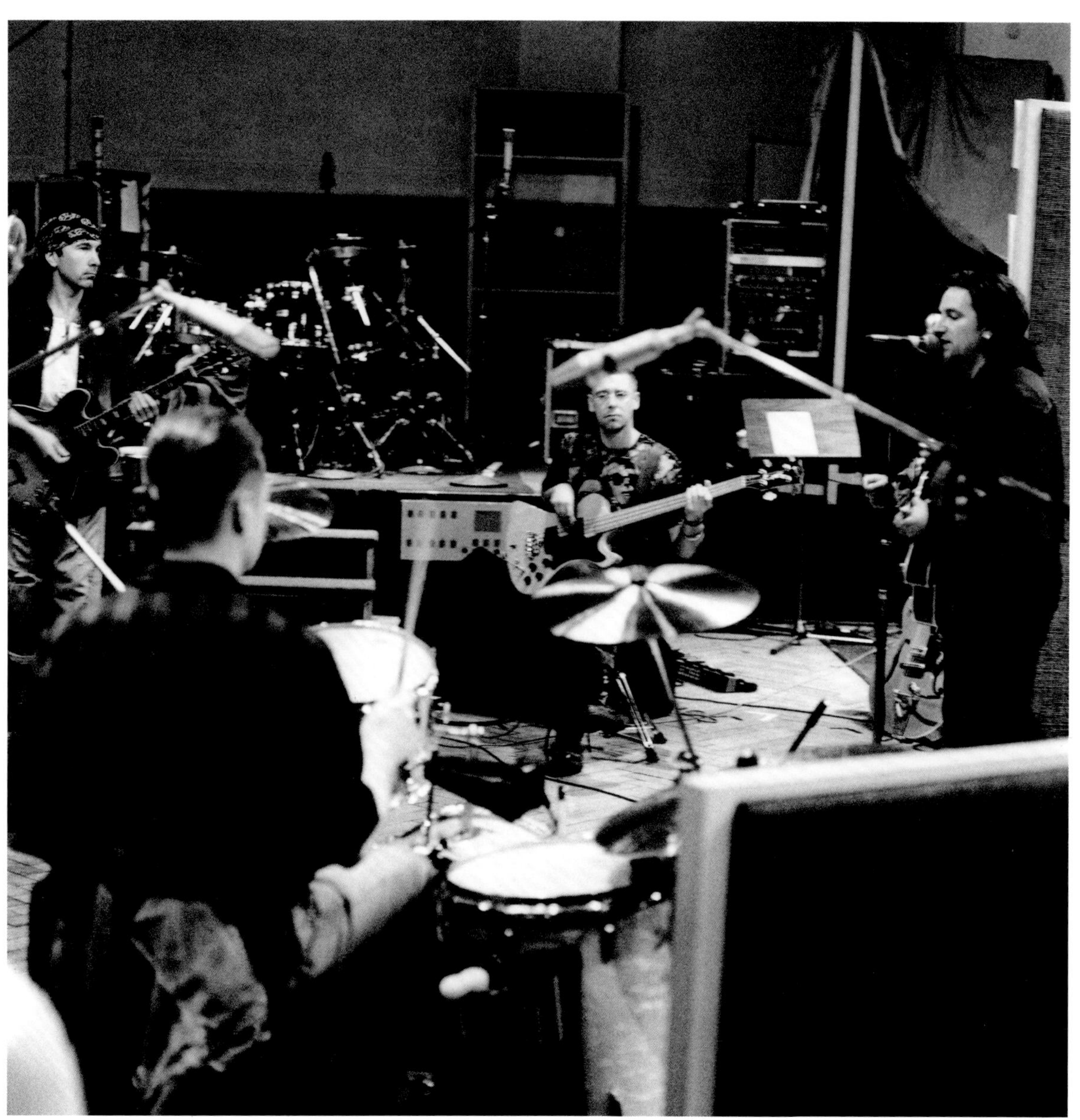

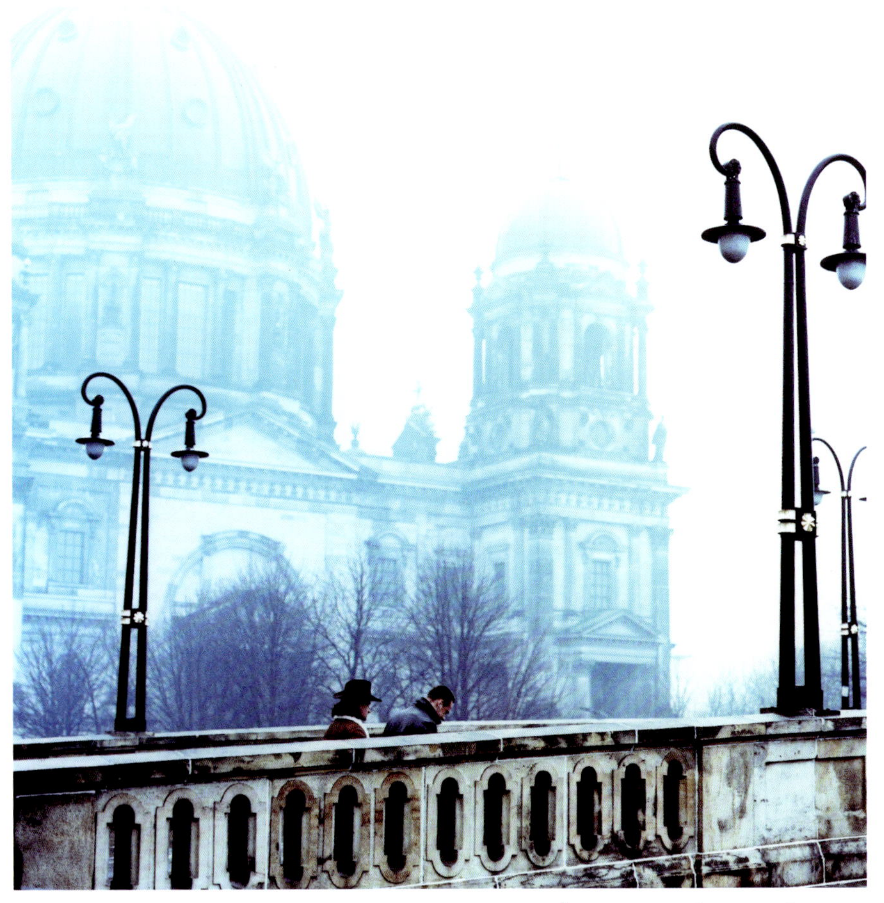

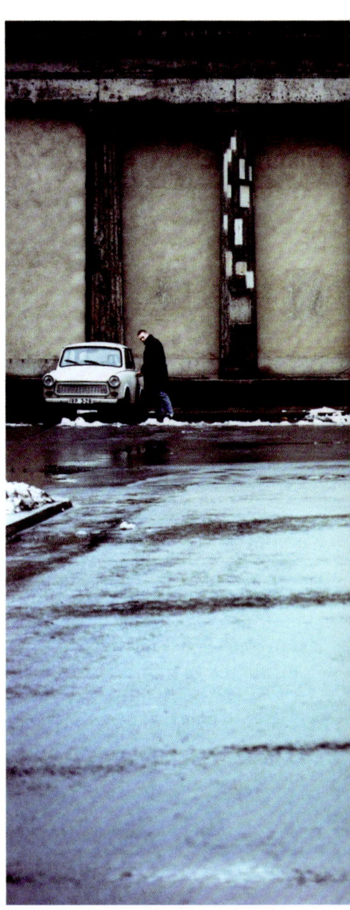

the winterlight was very beautiful for the photographs but it did mean that U2 were going to have to wear thick wintercoats and this being the first proper album after the Joshua Tree, where we see the band very serious in thick coats, it didn't seem a great idea to me to indicate the change in the music that was happening.

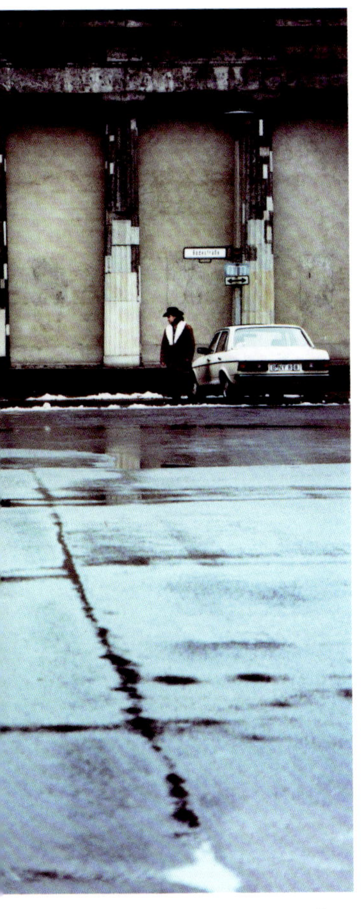

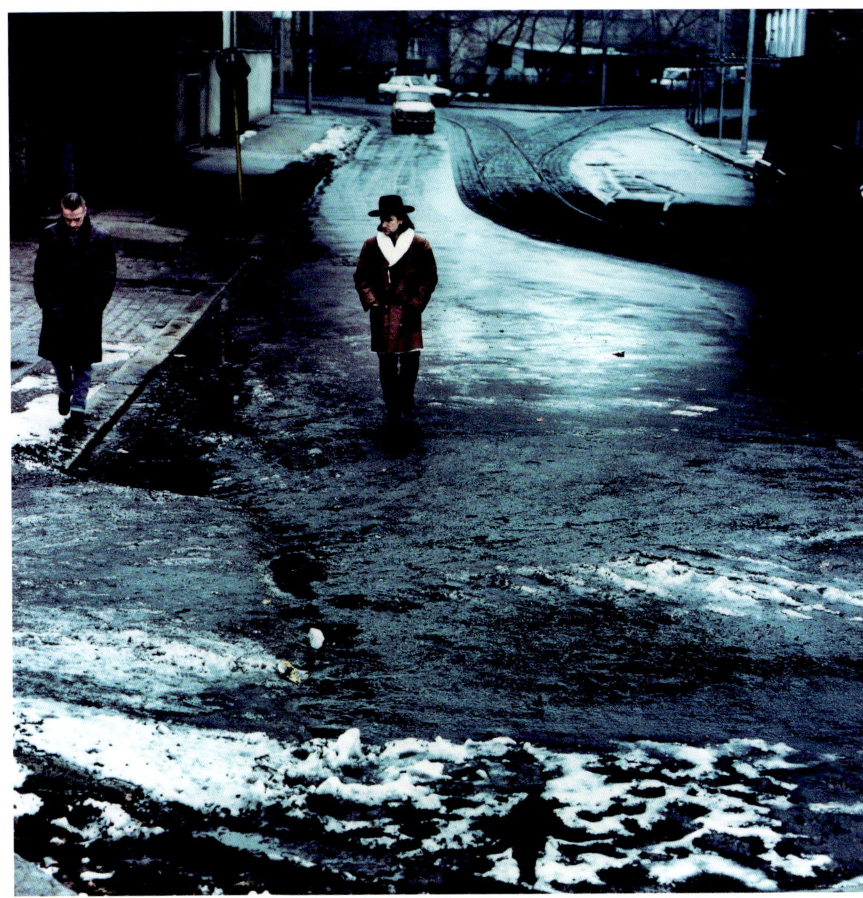

despite these misgivings we did do some photographs since i was there anyway. there seem to be a lot of shots i took of larry and bono walking around the hotel area and very few of edge and adam. i am very fond of the shot on the right ⟶

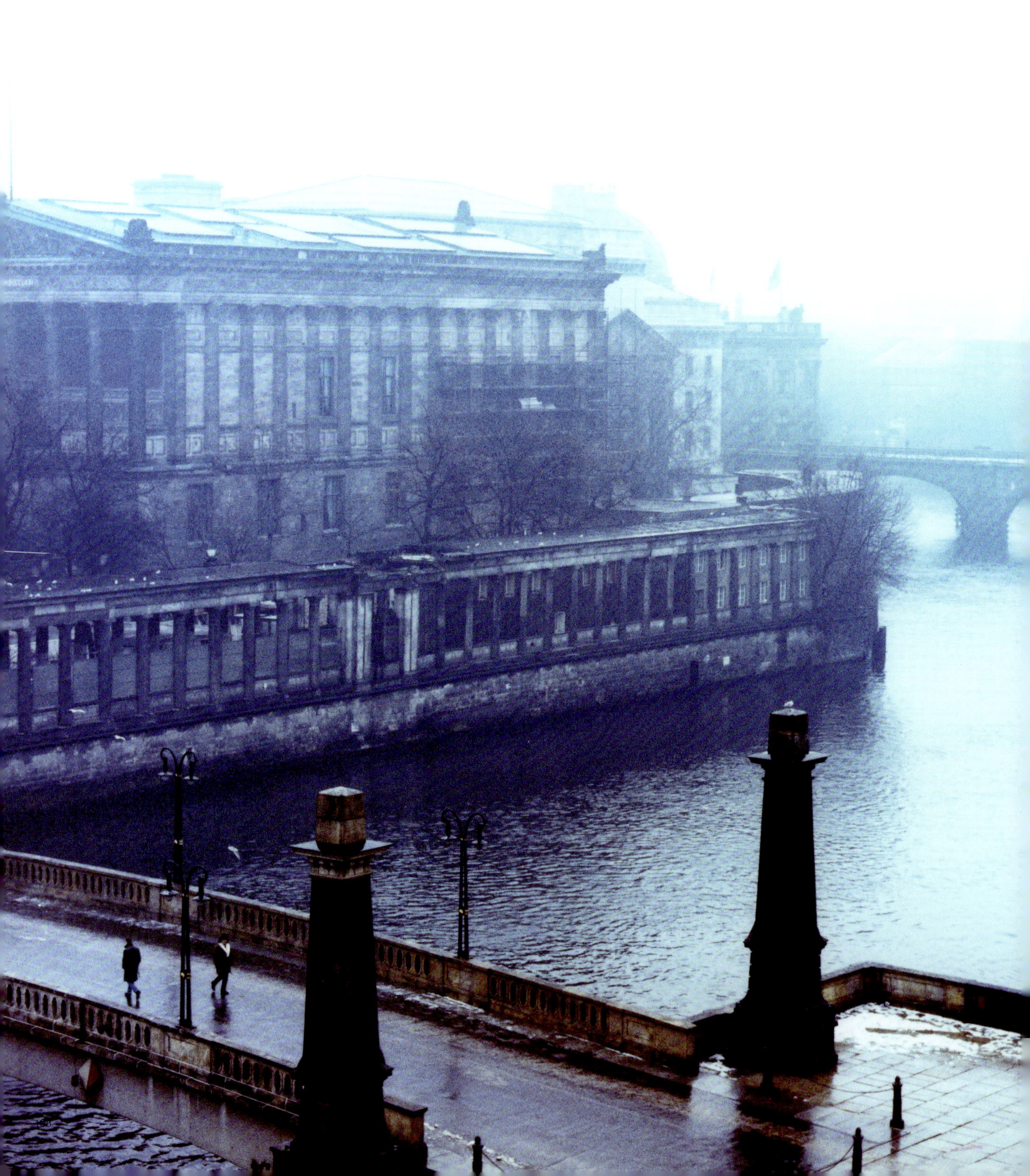

again, a photo of larry and bono walking outside - shot from the safety of bono's hotelroom.

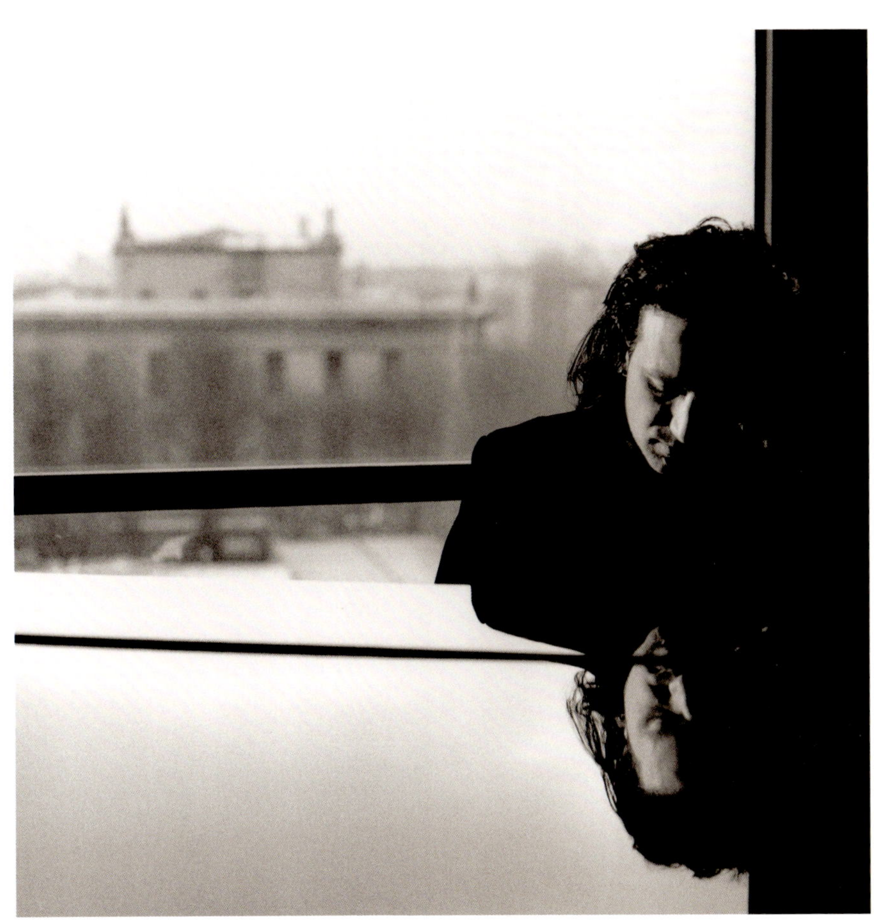

and this is the hotelroom from where the left photo was taken. bono is playing the grand piano that he had in his suite.

same room again, with larry looking out

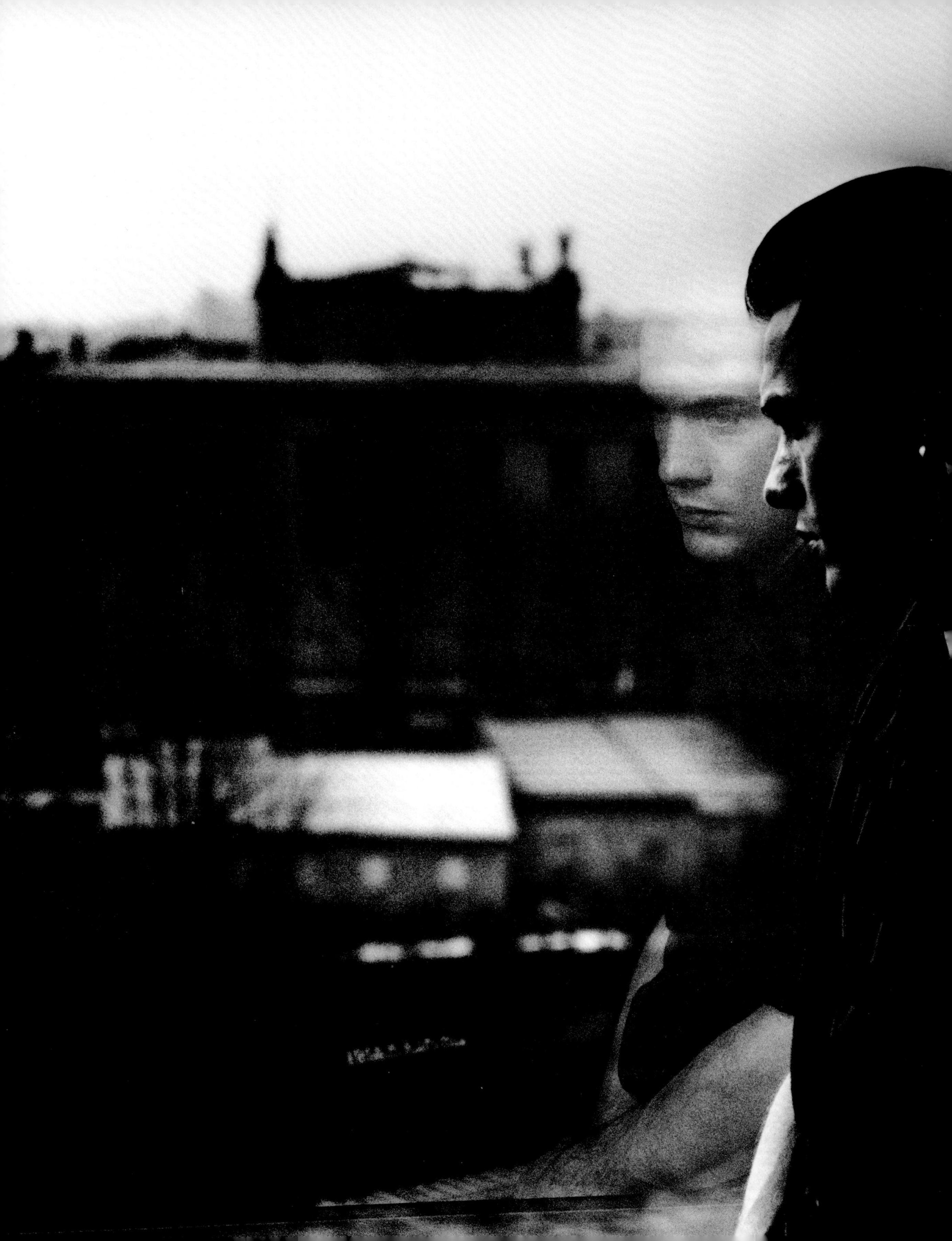

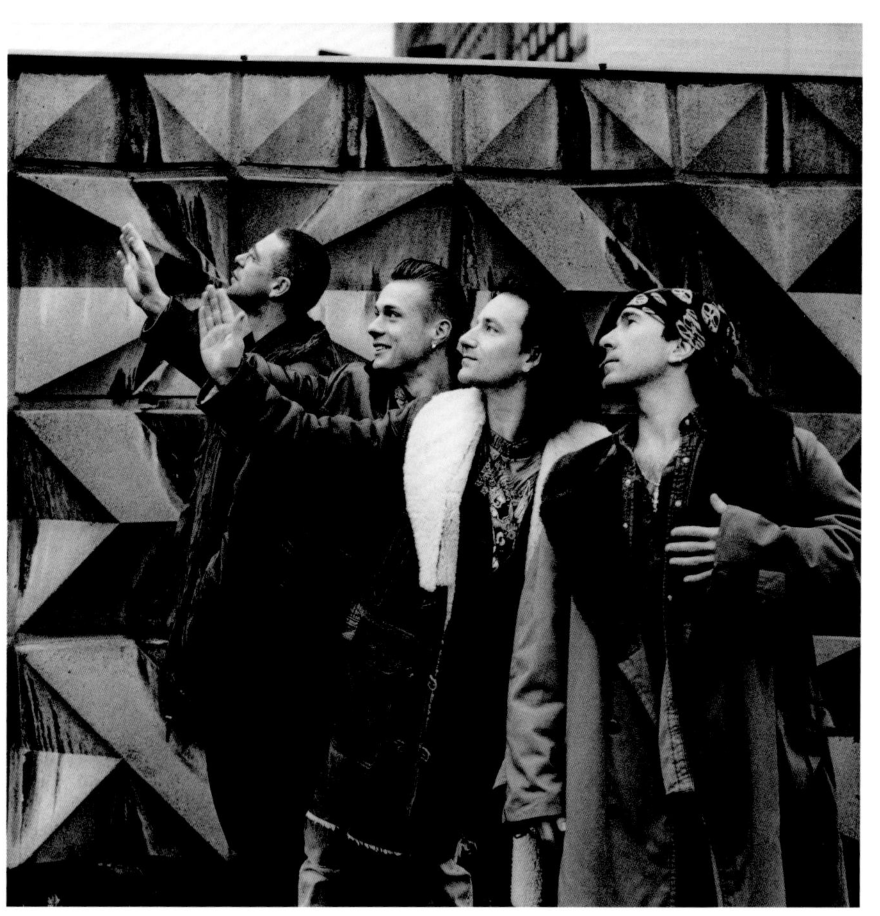

the band imitating a lenin statue in the east part of berlin.

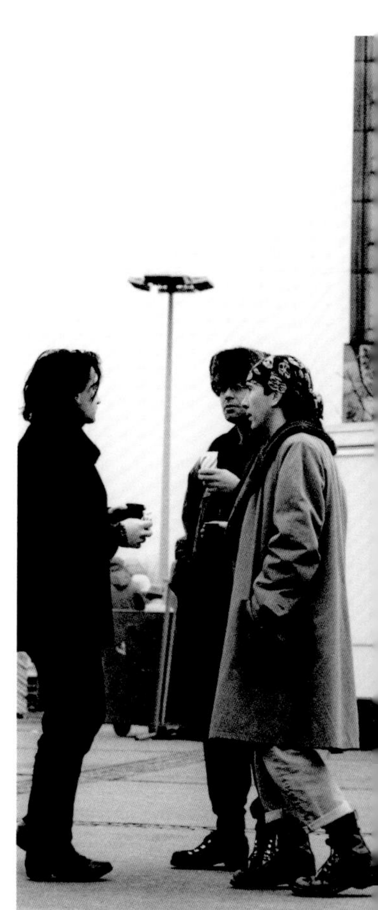

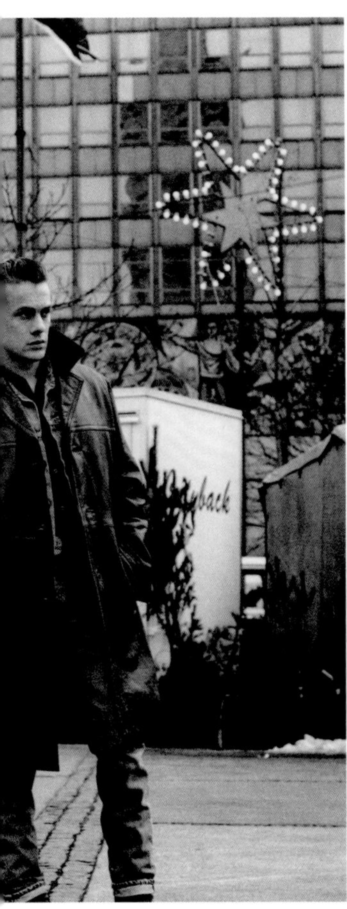

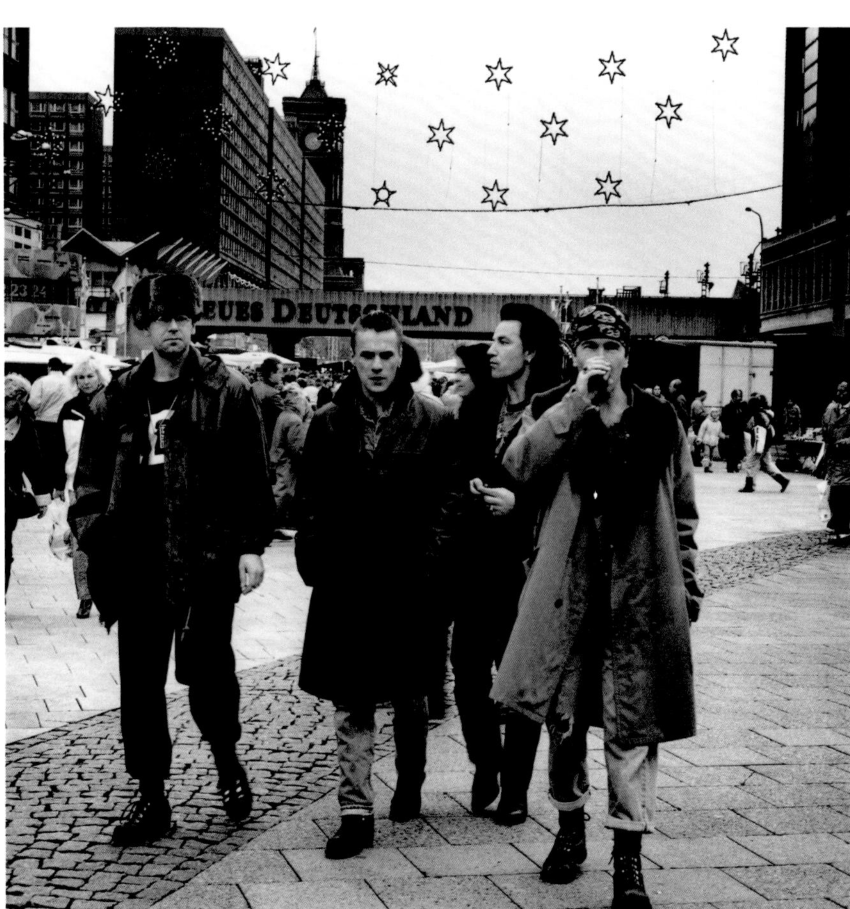

these photos are taken around Alexanderplatz and it is obviously around christmas time.

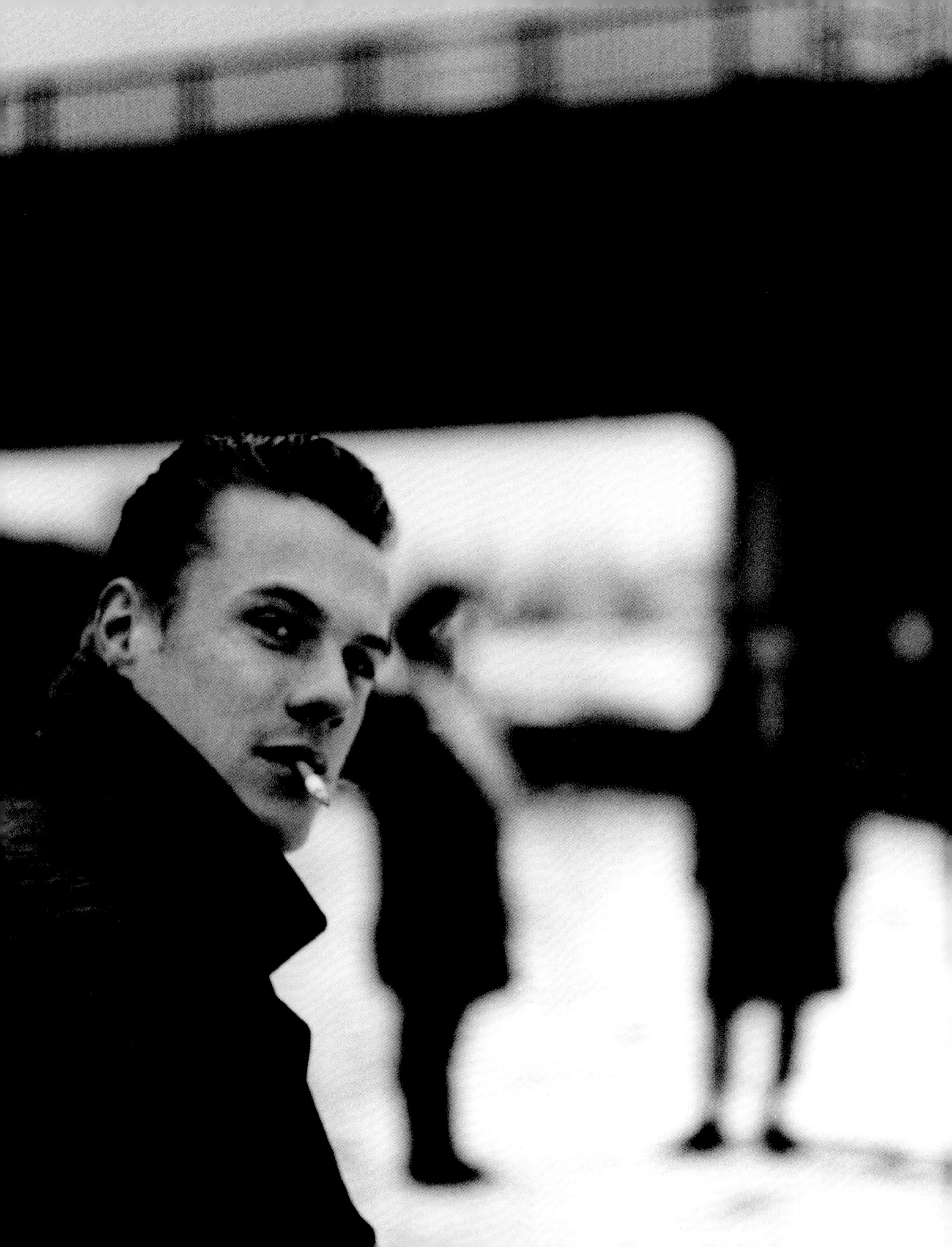

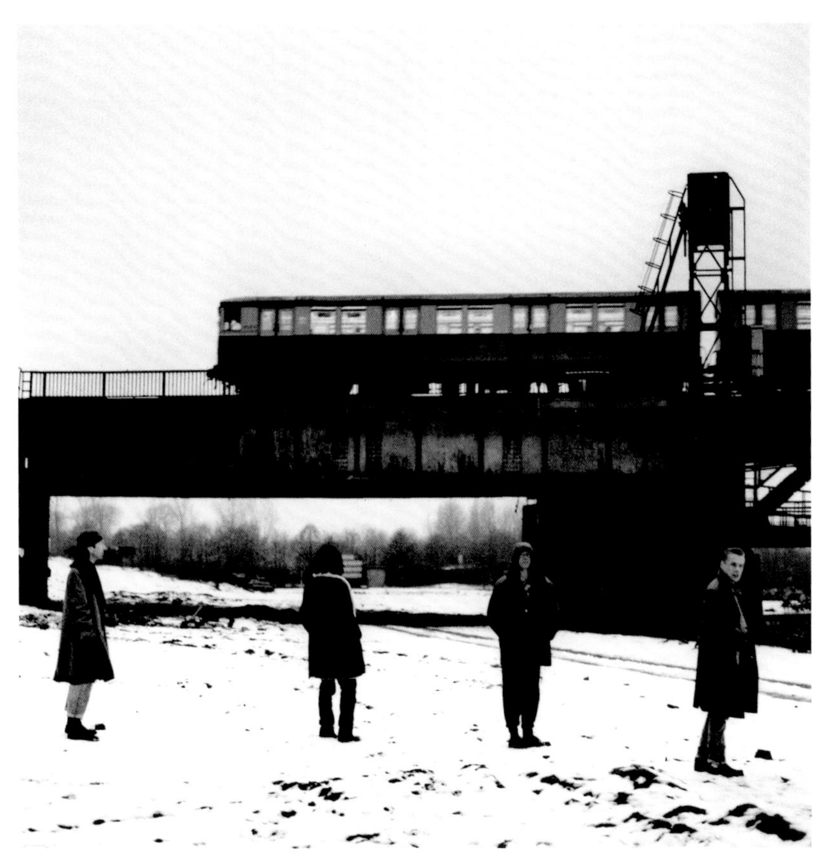

← this photo is reminiscent of beatles/hamburg period i find.
but anyway, the bleakness of berlin as a location
in the winter is plain to see. so we moved ON.

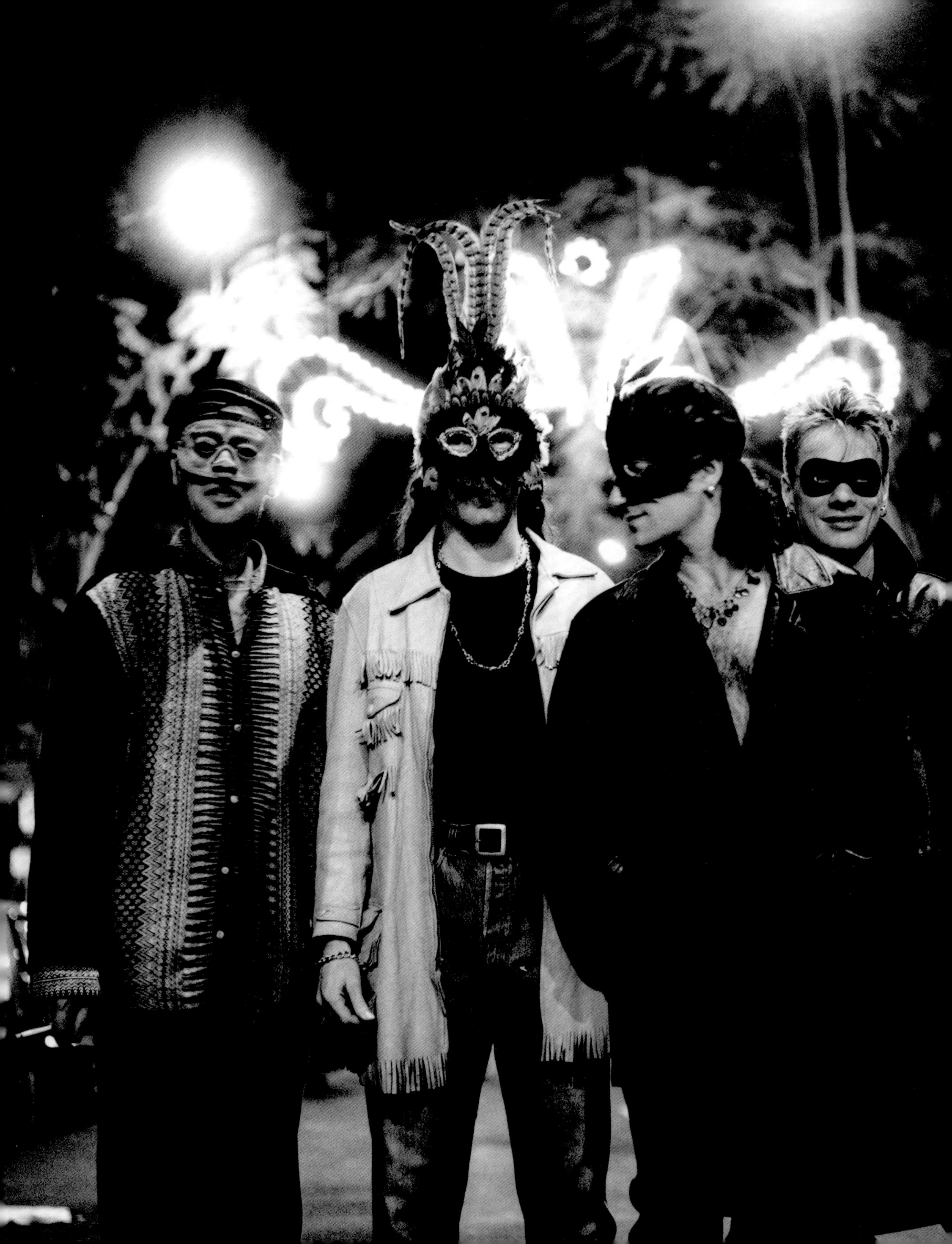

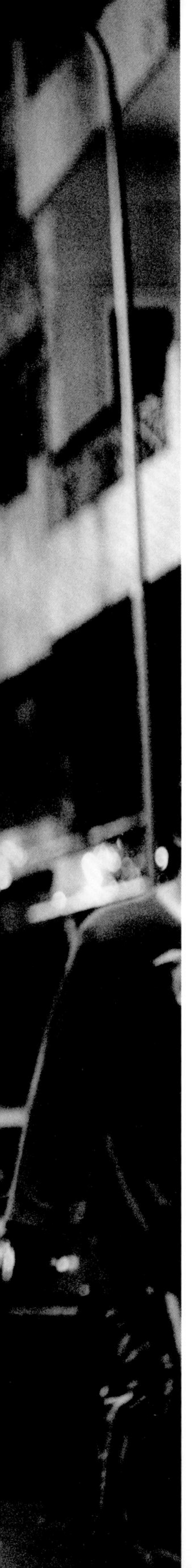

TENERIFE 1991

february

after berlin we were trying to come up with a plan for the photographs and ann-louise from the management had the suggestion to go for the carnival in santa cruz. it would be a different and warmer environment was the idea behind it. once we got there, there was a bit of a panic and i got asked by bono 'why are we here?' and thus the idea came up to dress up so as to get lost in the crowd and try a wilder side of the band in visual terms. Nassim flew over from london having collected lots of dresses, wigs etc. and off we went into the hotel lobby and then into the night. we photographed most of the night and came back to the hotel around 7 AM. we did a lot of great photos i think, too many to show here but you'll get a good impression.

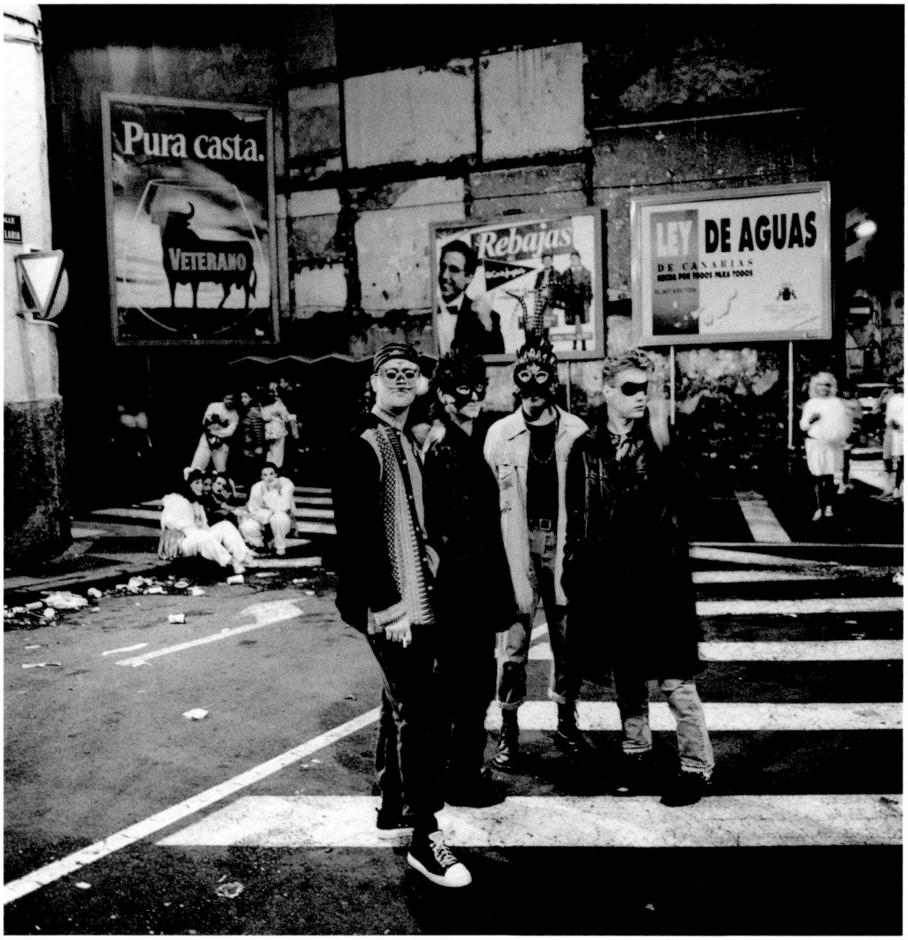

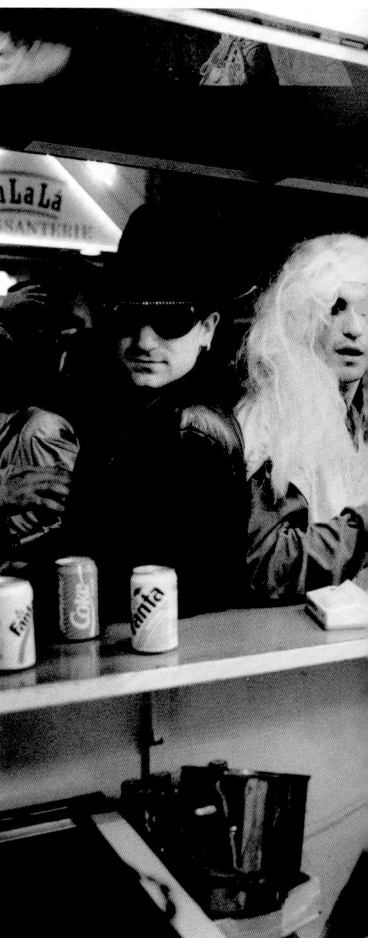

we stood on street corners, hung out at streetbars and became gene
an invisible part of the crowd. the band got recognised now
and again but mostly we got on without too much bother.

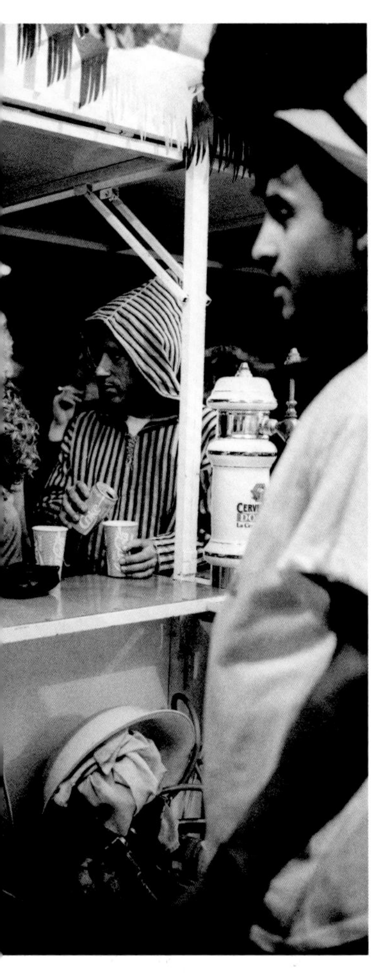

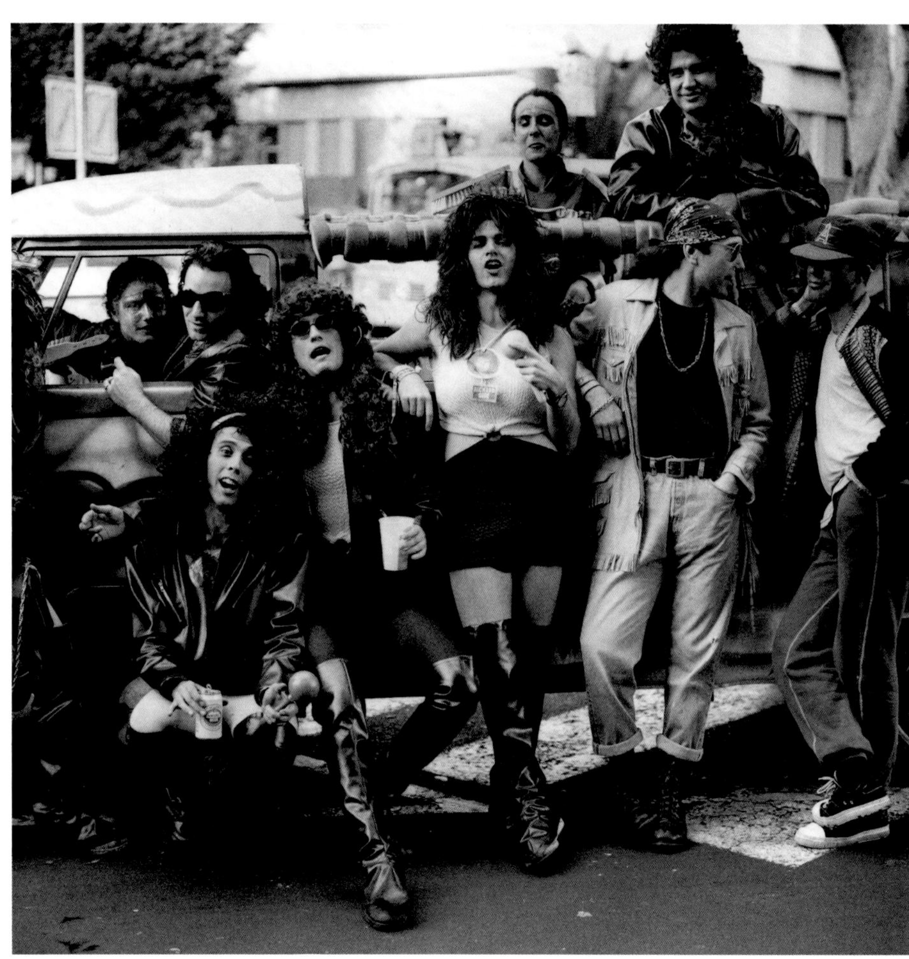

early morning, on our way back to the hotel.

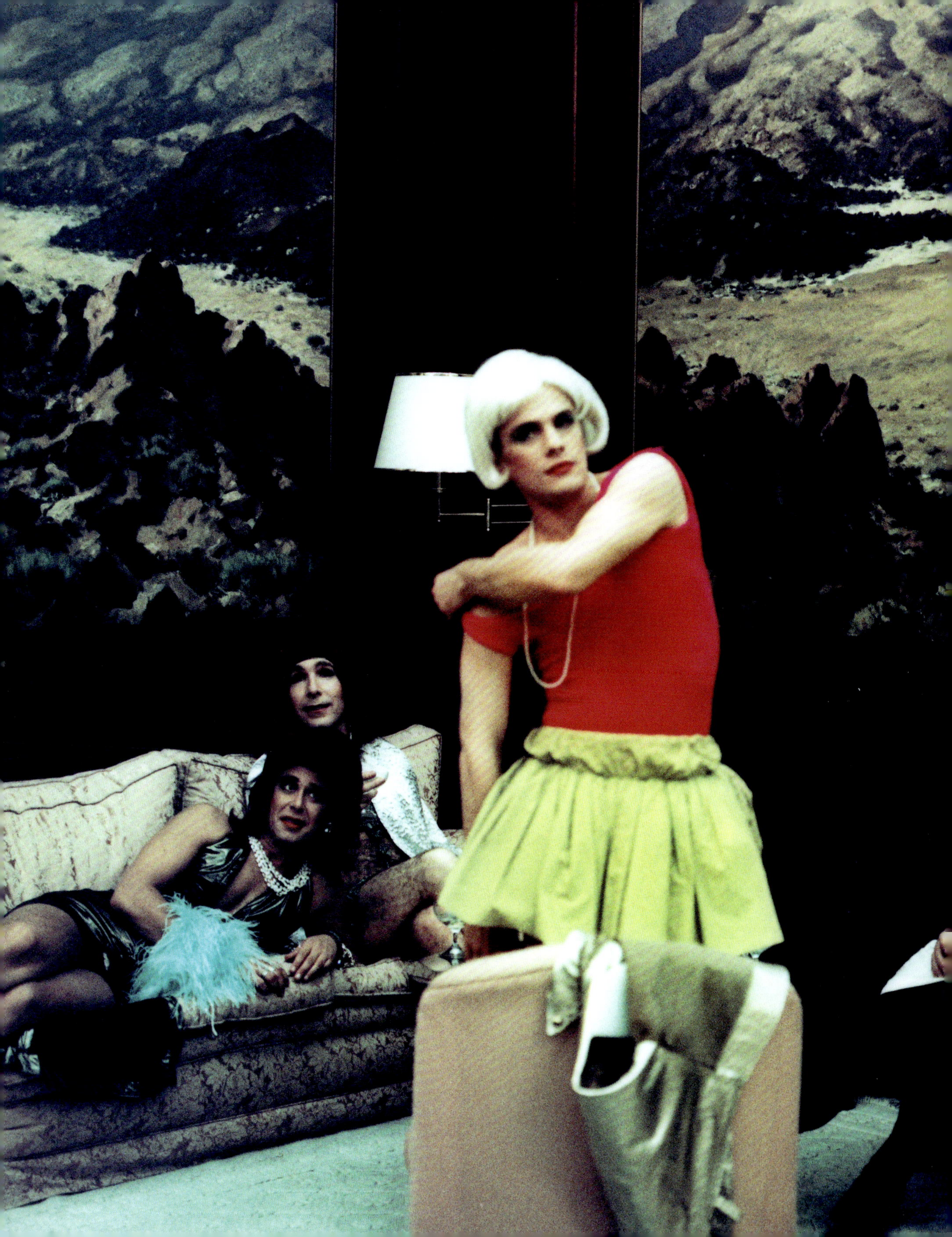

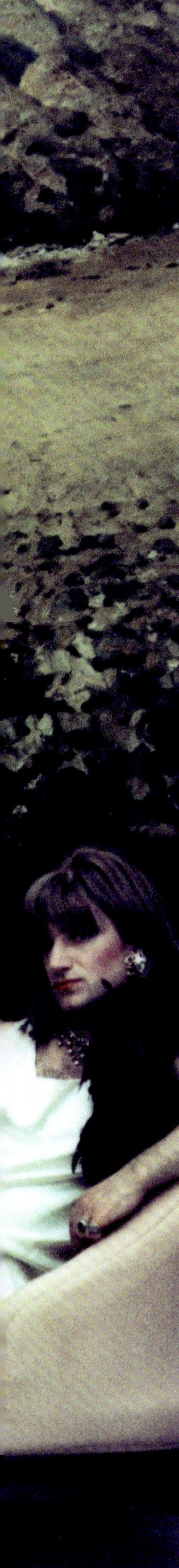

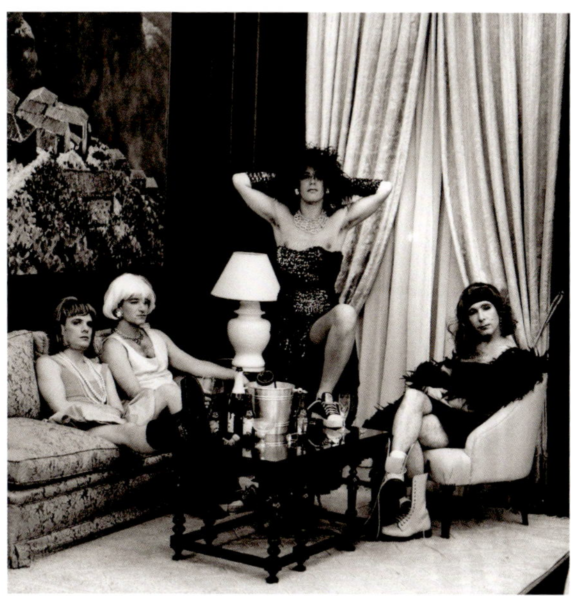

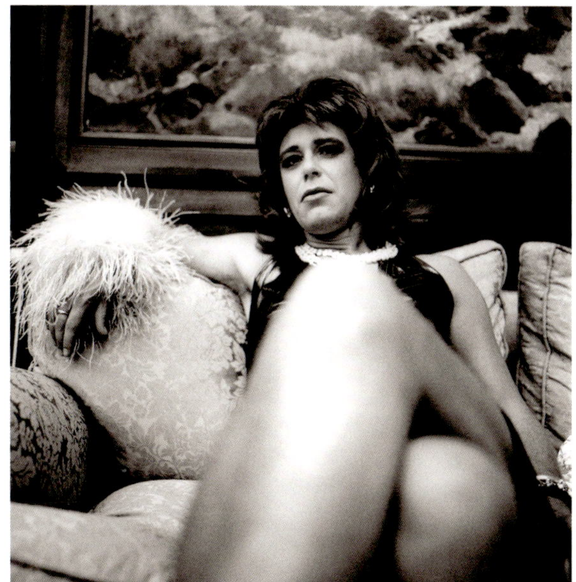

the hotel had this amazing lobby where we tried out lots of different looks. some more convincing than others but the mood was very positive.

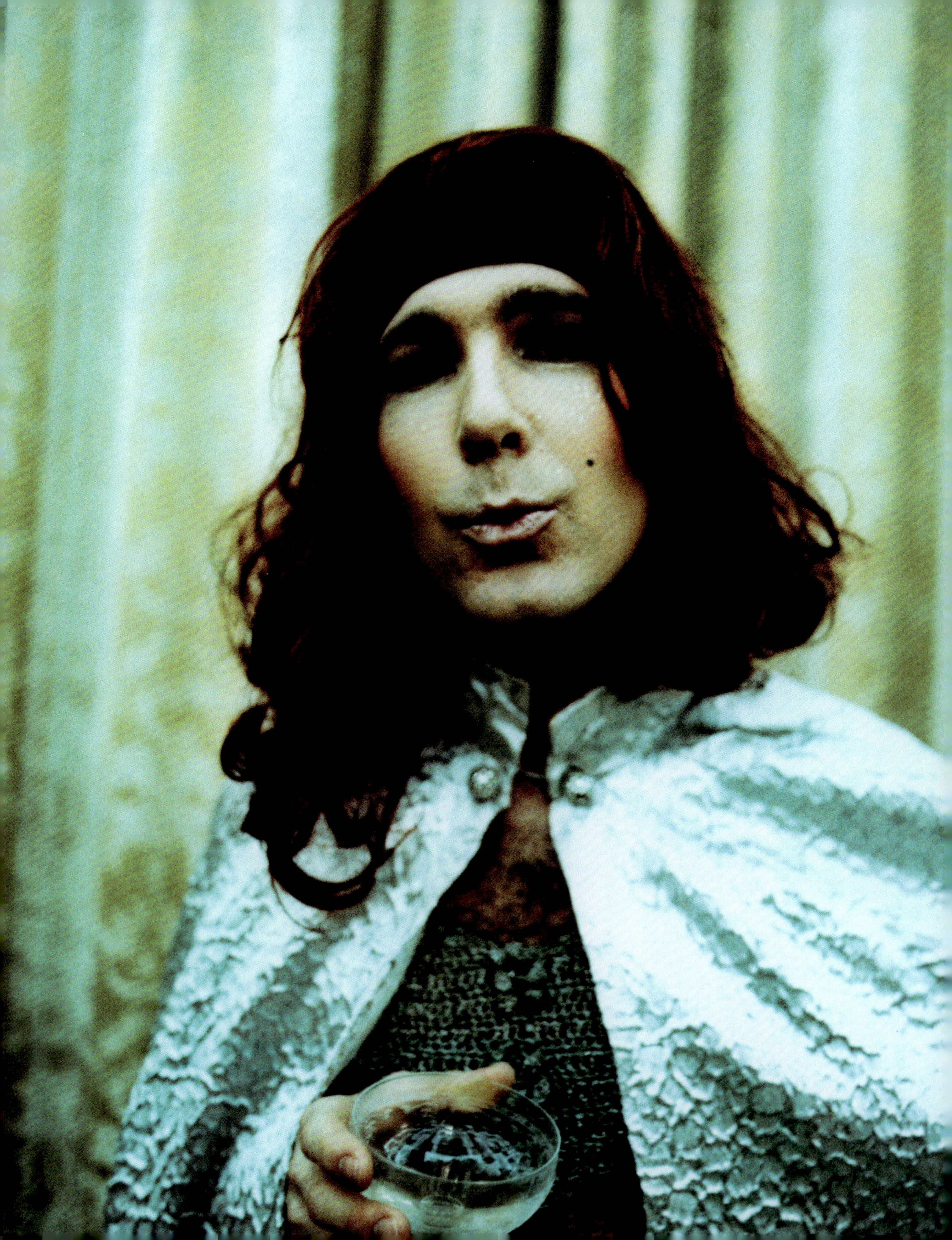

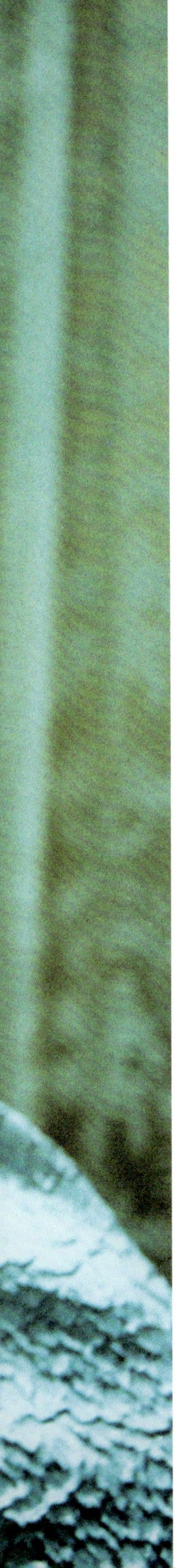

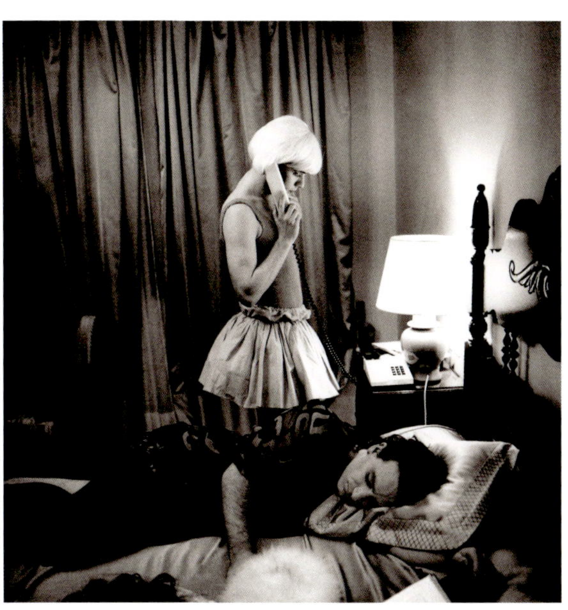

pretty hilarious - larry ordering room service while bono is taking a nap. he tends to fall asleep now and then 'en public' but this was his room after all.

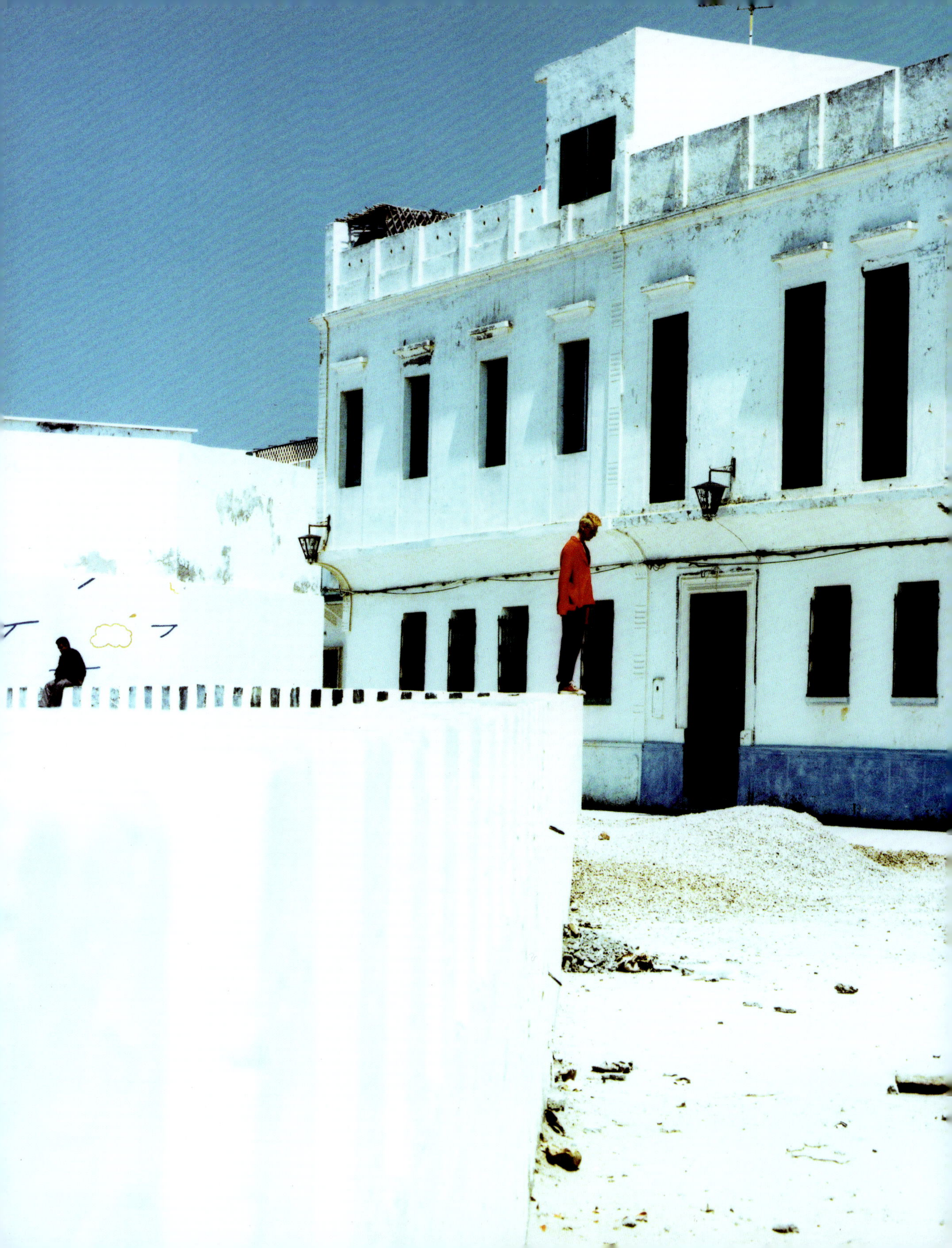

MOROCCO

1991

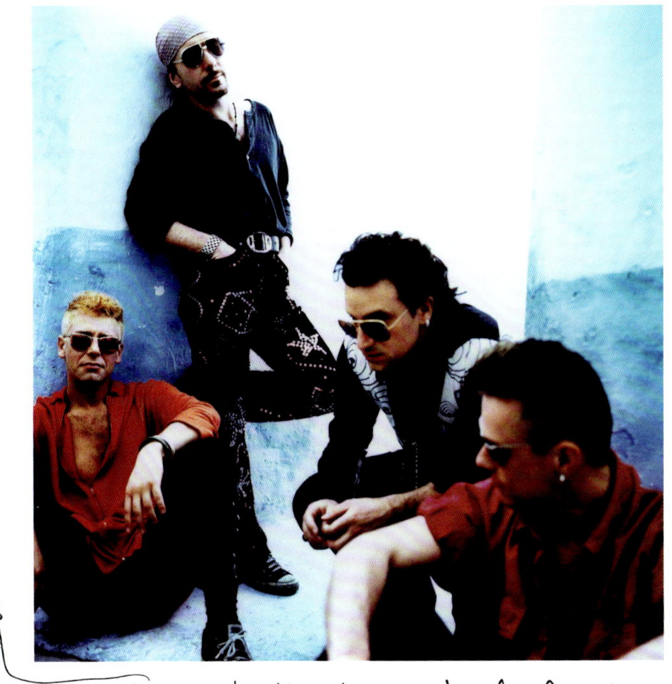

and the roadstart in santa cruz.

after the coldstart in berlin, i went to check out some places in the south of spain and ended up taken a boat to Tangiers and loved it – colours, ambience, food! i called bono and they all came over for a few days to take 'serious' photos. it was a great choice of location and the heat and the place itself, relaxed the band enormously. i took mostly colour photos and that set the tone for the cover of 'Achtung Baby'!

the band wore pretty colourful clothes as well and specially edge had some madly designed stuff – trousers, rings etc. which you can see quite clearly on the next couple of pages. on the left page is adam contemplating gravity in morocco.

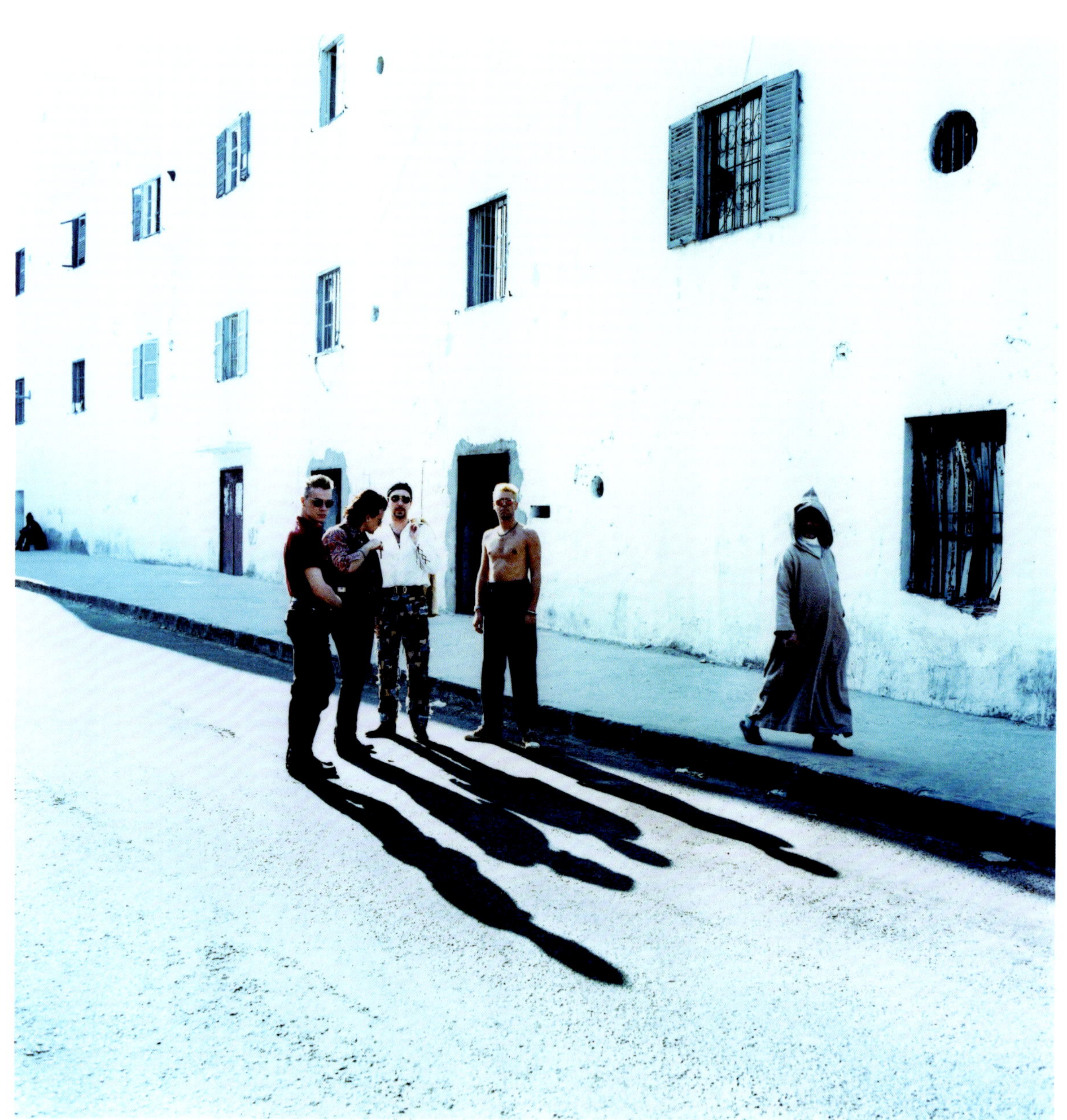

a streetscene above and on the right page the band are taking a break while looking at some polaroids. i love the name cafe maroc for a hole in the wall. the architecture, the light and the difference in dress-sense all added up to a great mix of cultures in the photos. on the last spread you can see that U2 even dressed up with some make-up but Not to the extent of total cross-dressings as we'd done in Tenerife.

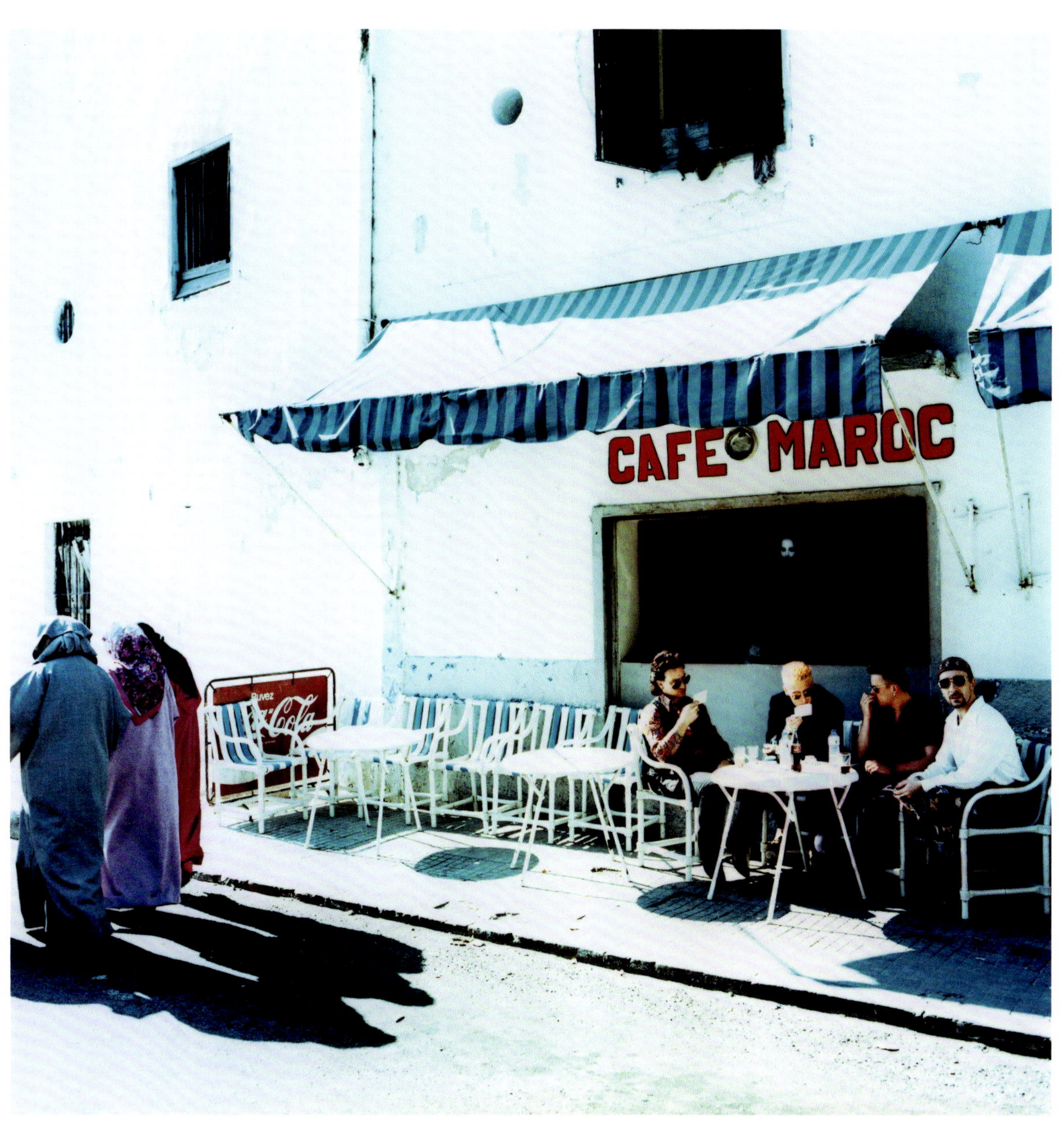
CAFE MAROC

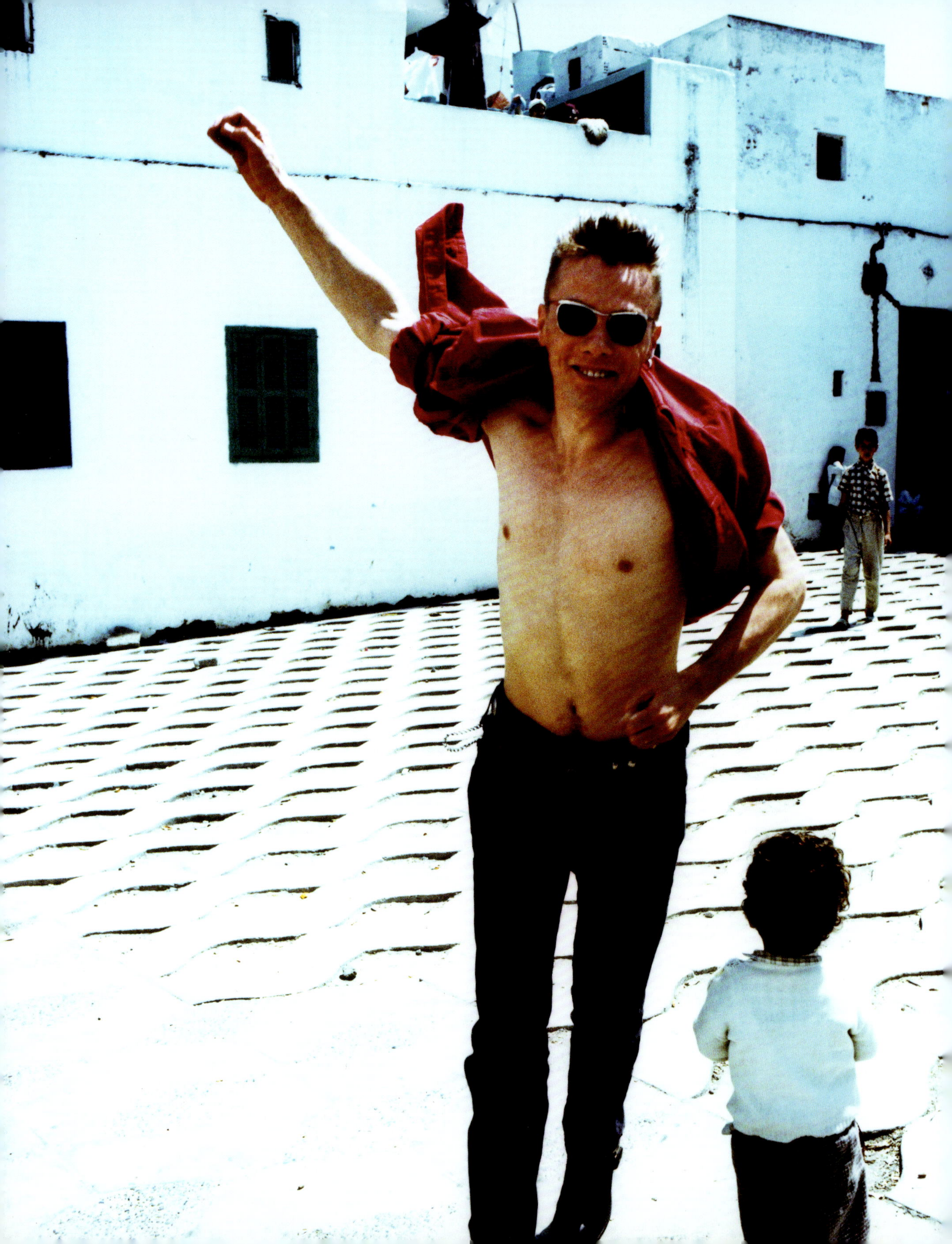

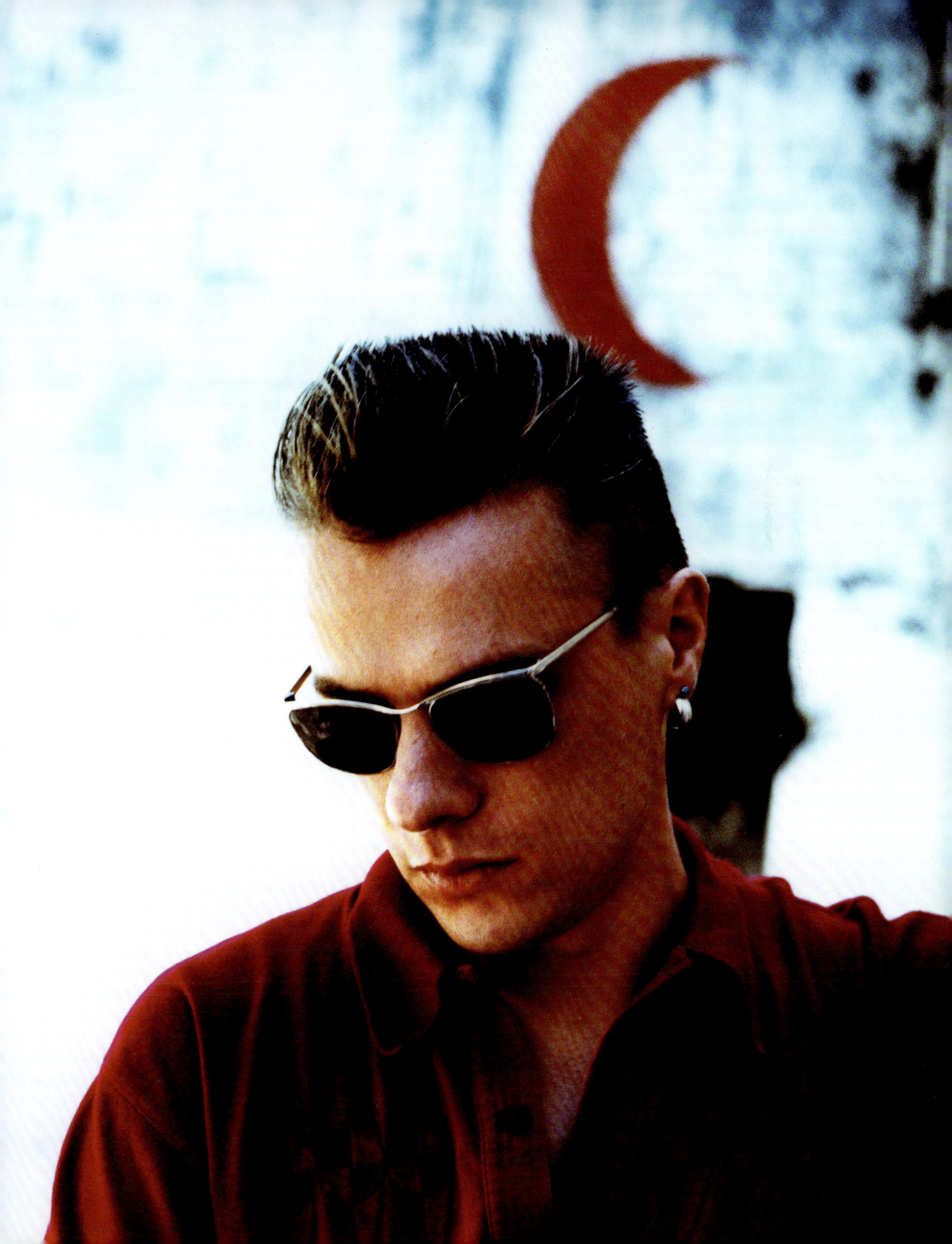

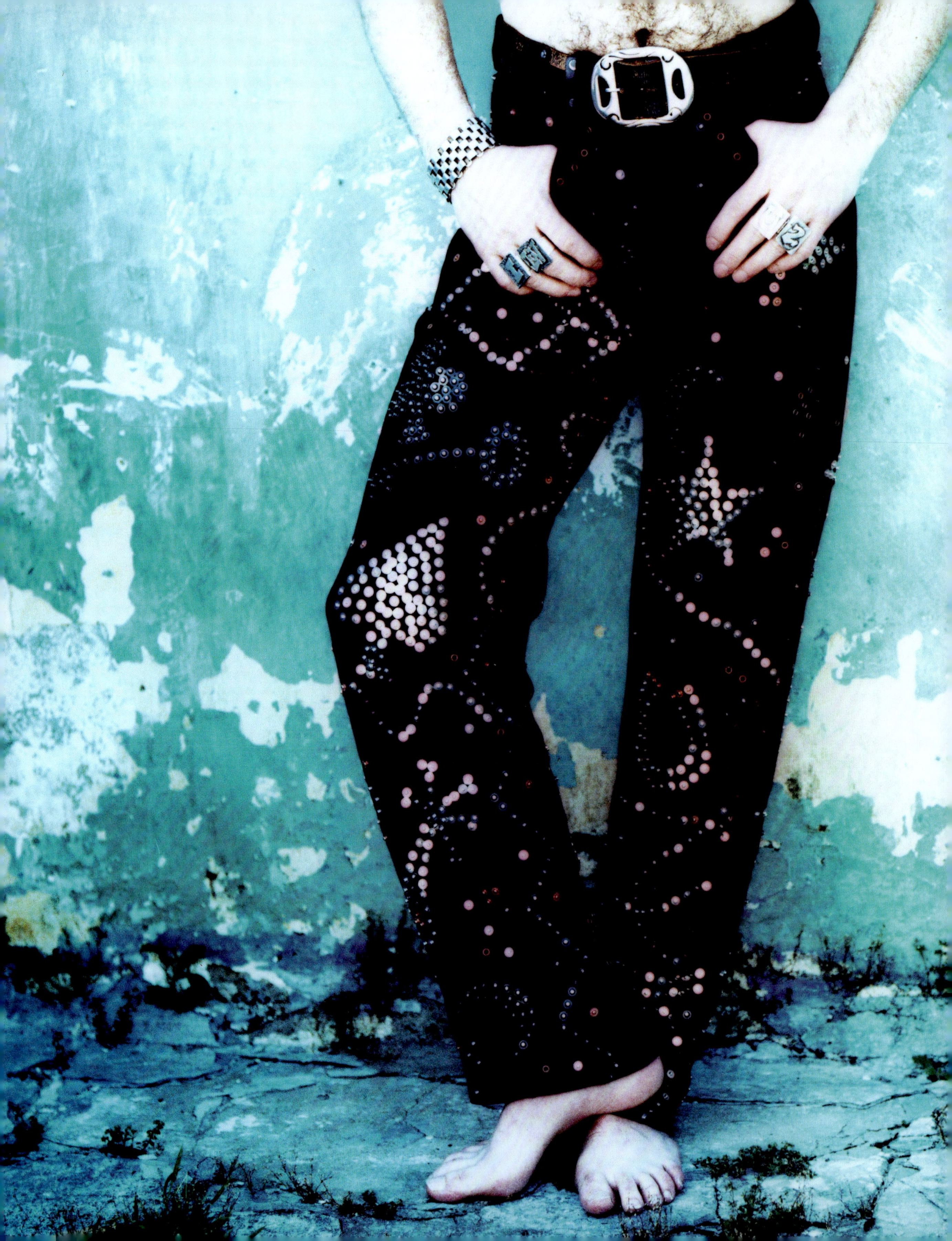

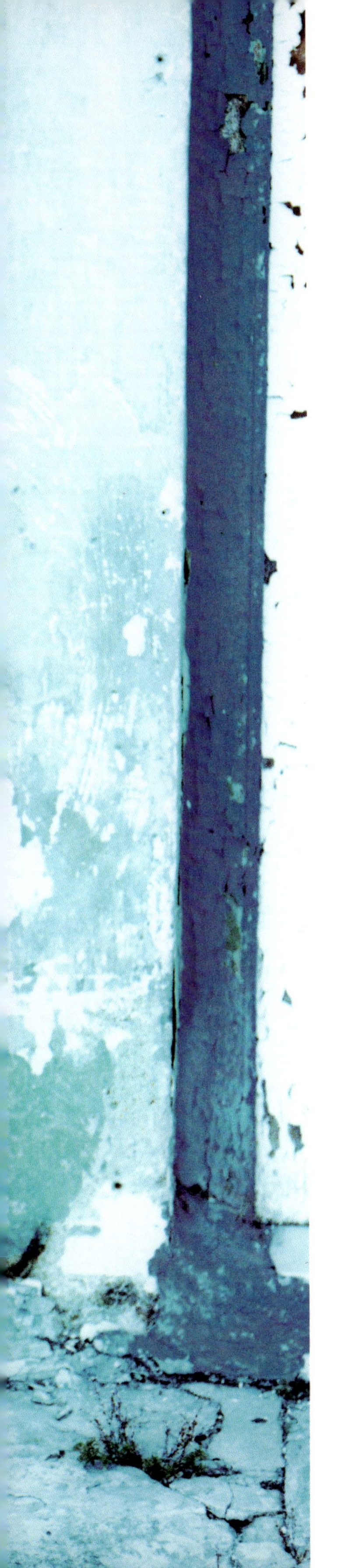

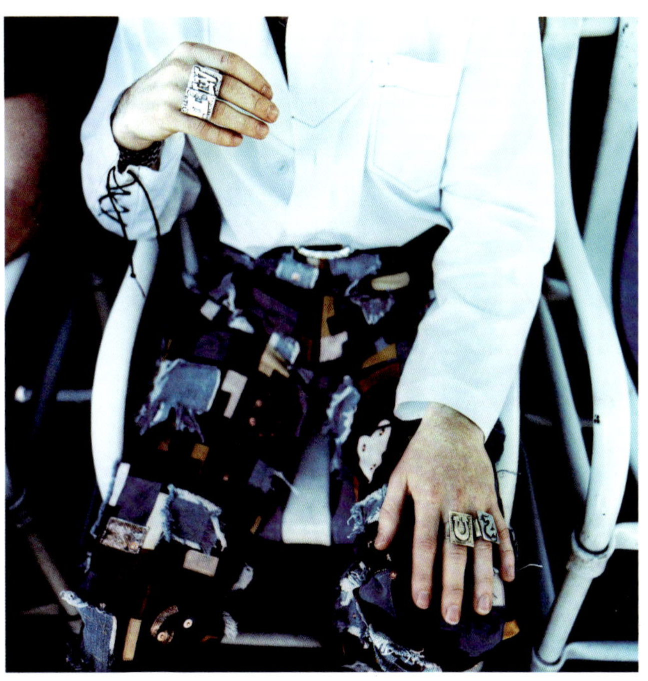

edge is showing some wild trousers and your
~~the message 'i love u2'~~. thoughts on
his rings.

overleaf, dusk in
morrocco
brings out the
best in some.
→

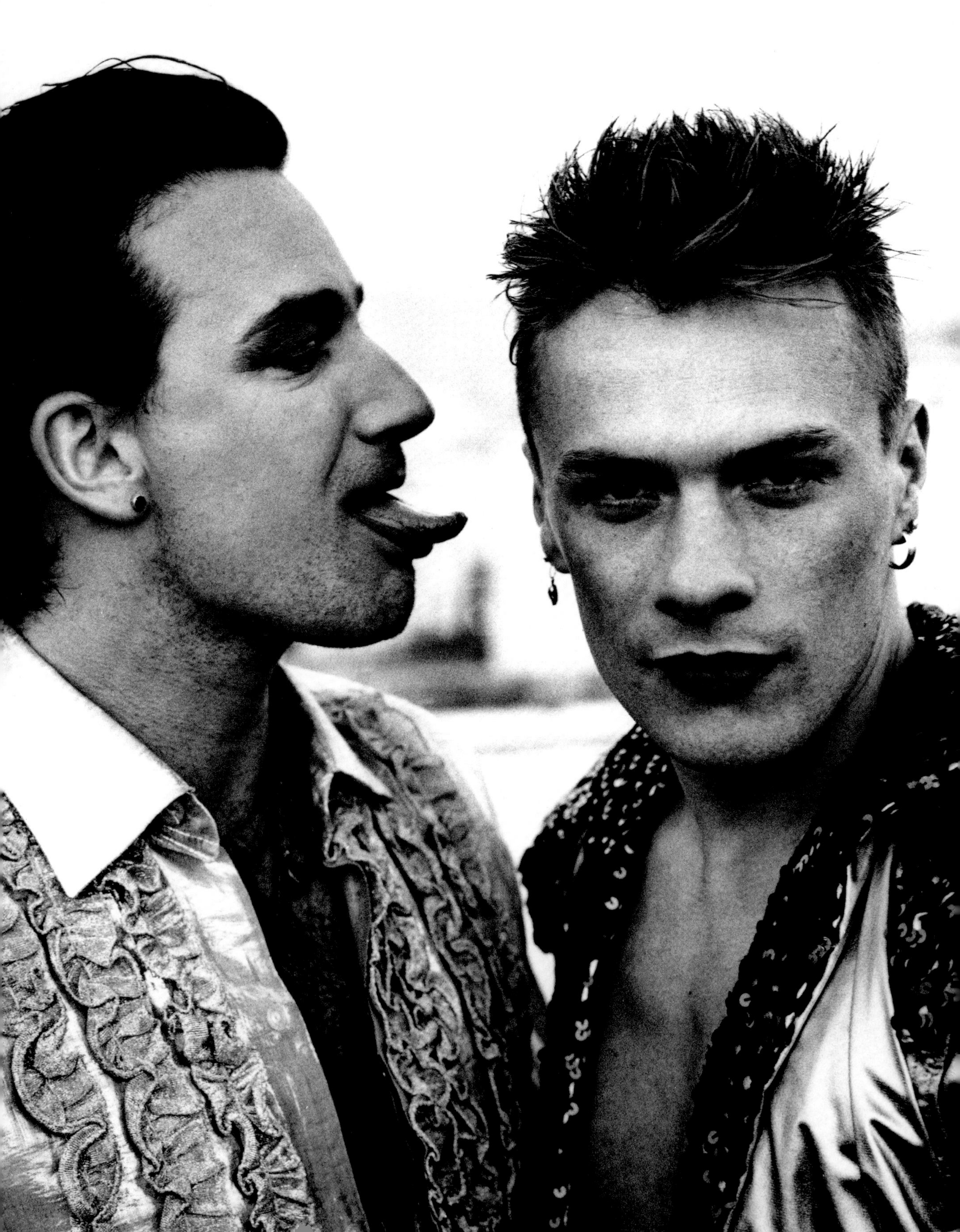

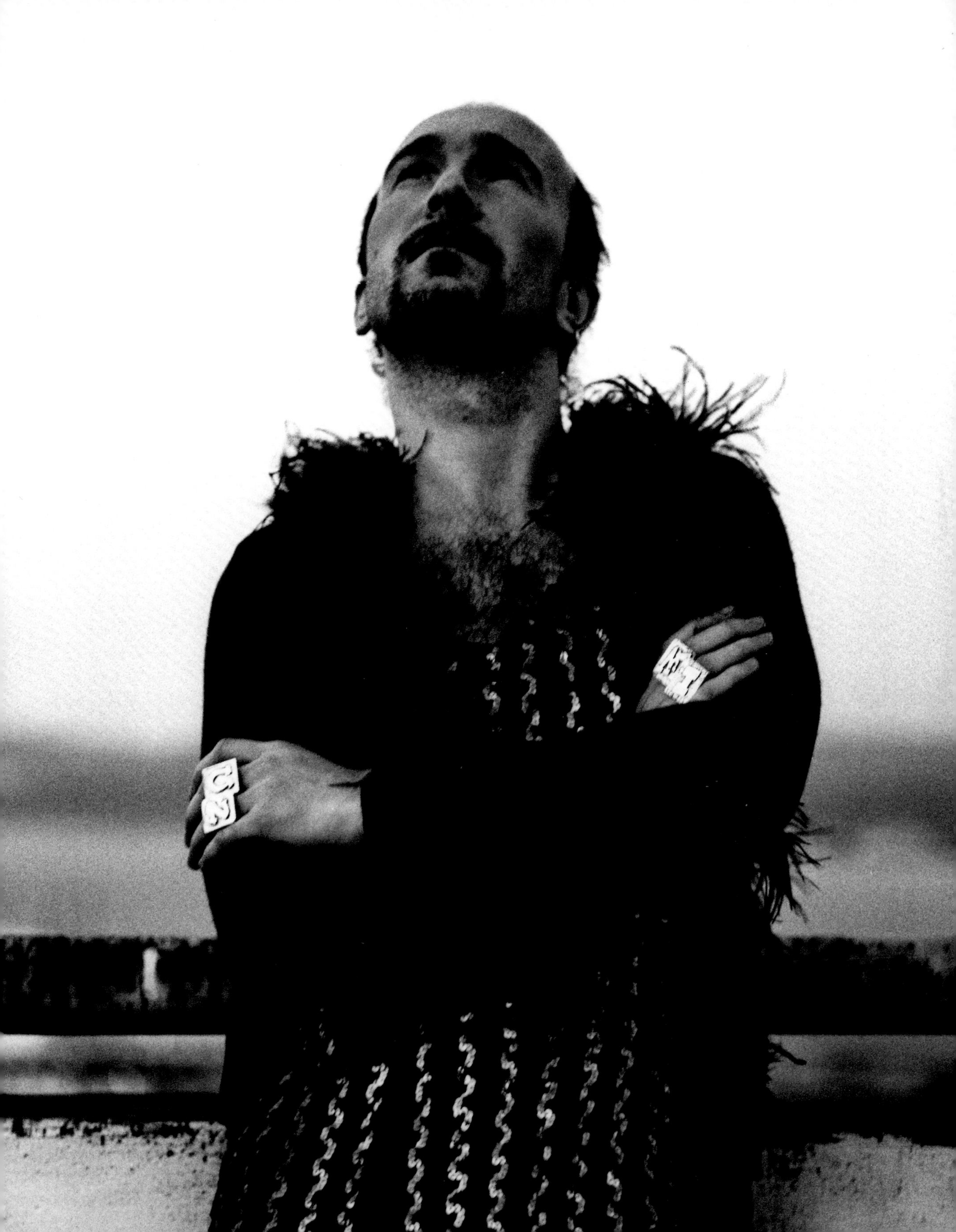

DUBLIN 1991

june

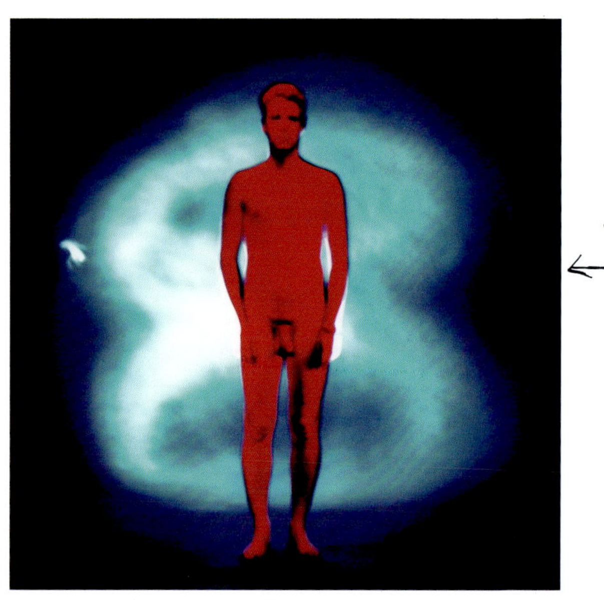

red ←

→ bulls / probably cows actually.

after the shoots in berlin, tenerife and morocco, there is still a feeling we haven't gotten a photo for the front of the record! slightly panicked i go to ireland to shoot some more conceptual stuff of which the above shot of adam is quite well known in europe at least (in the USA adam had to be covered up!). It was shot, as were the photos on the next spread, in a specific way, using a handheld flashlight in complete darkness and let the camera accumulate the exposure while you paint away with your light. this → photo was never used – maybe it was considered to sexist to go with the title? maybe just not good enough?

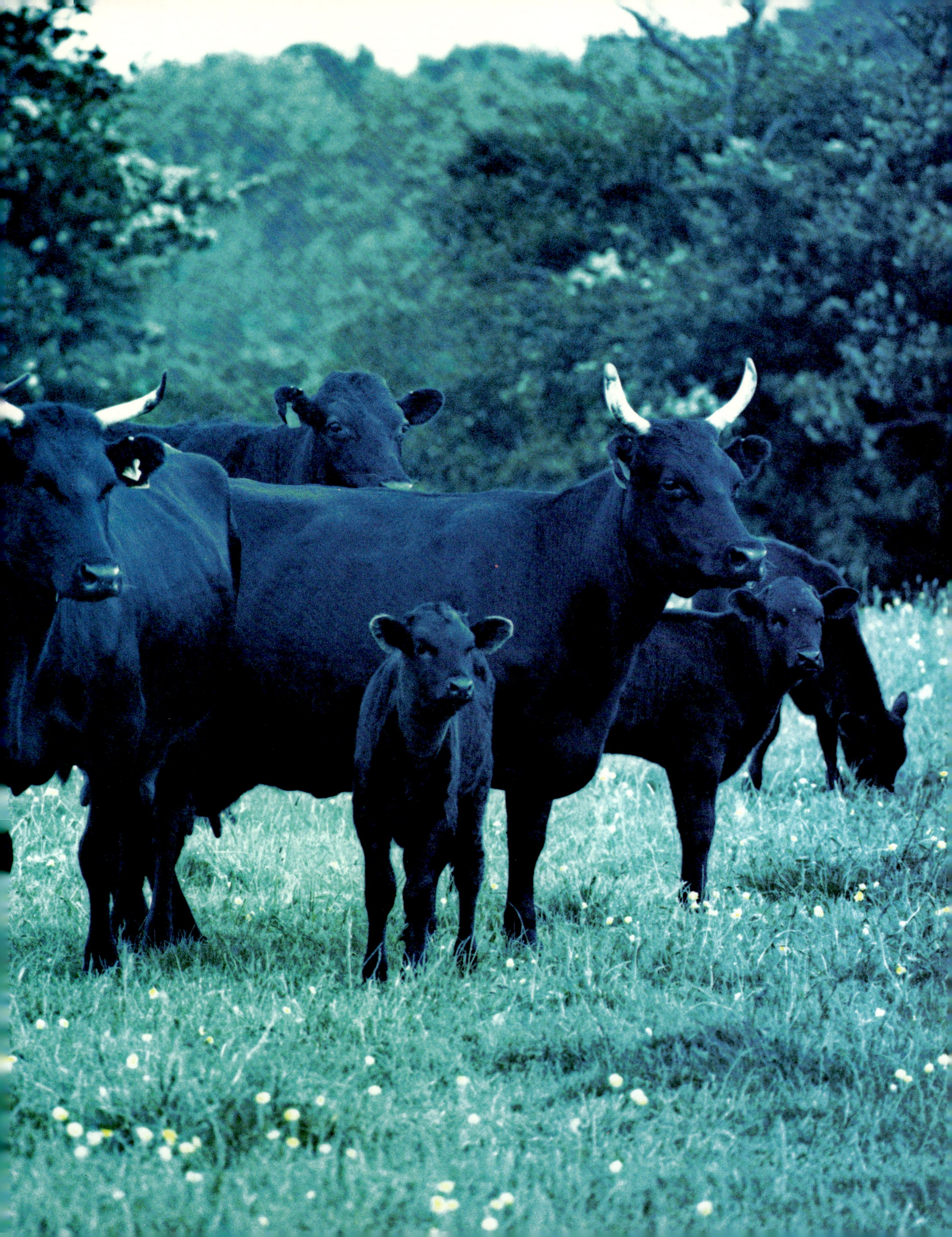

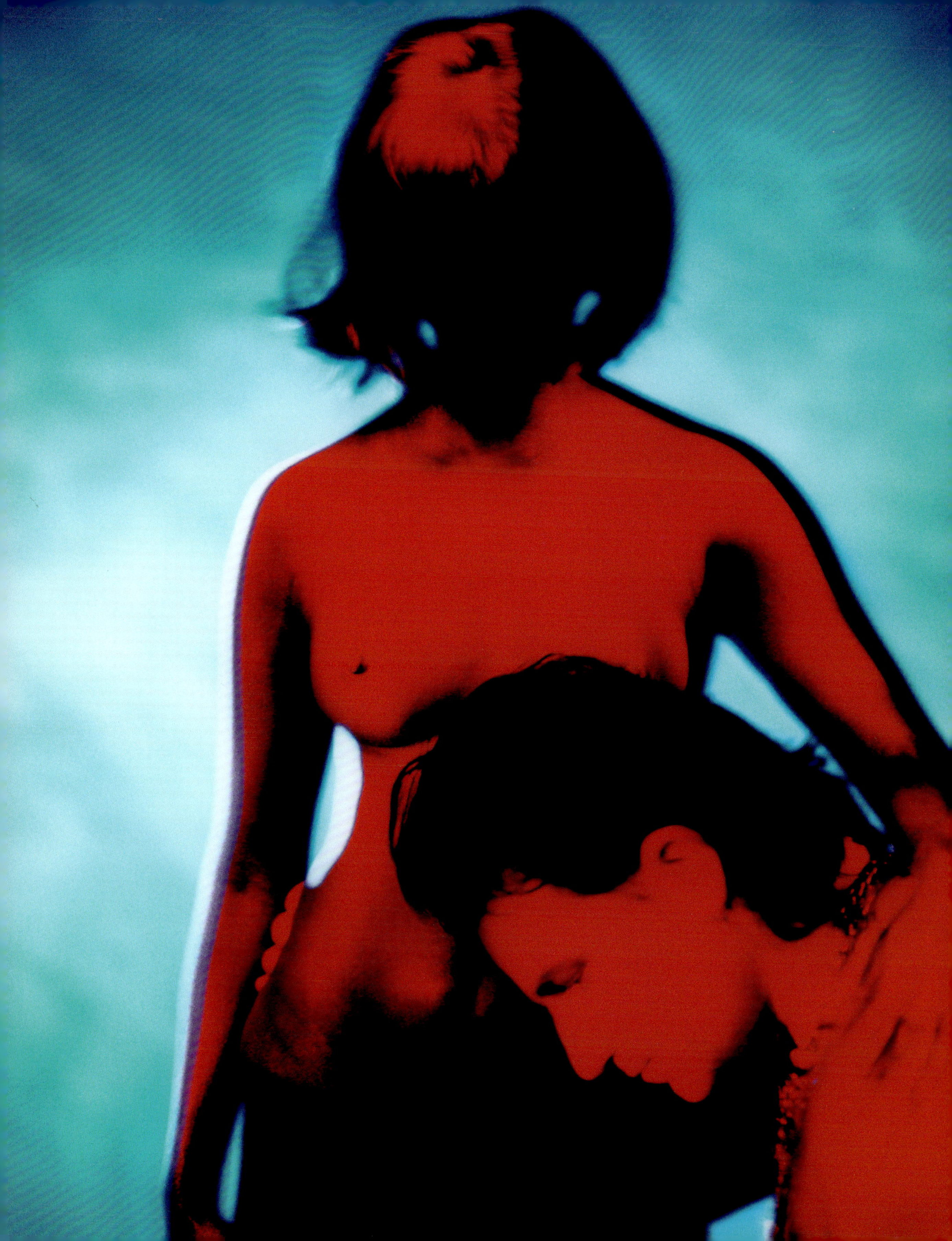

this photo features Nassim, at the time U2's make-up person and my then girlfriend, with Bono. this never made the final cut either but we used a different version of the idea on the record somewhere – a shot we'd done in Santa CRUZ earlier that year.

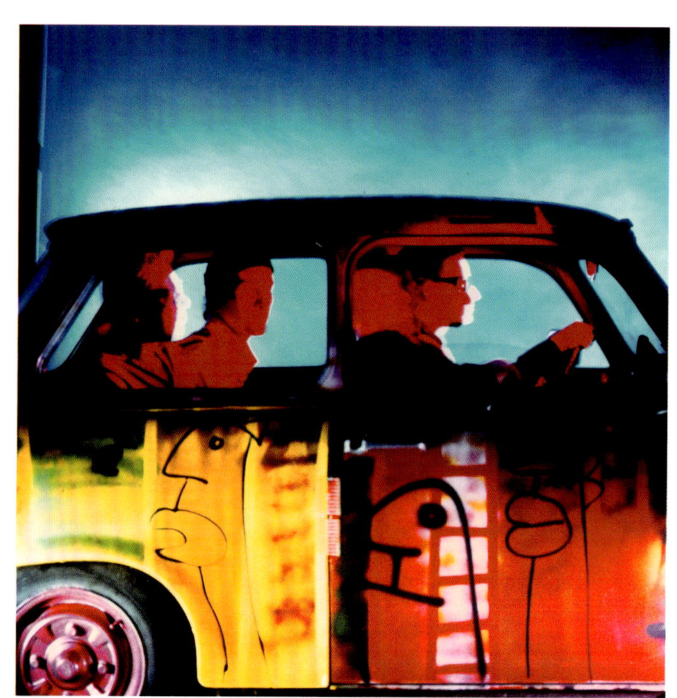

this trabant goes places – in the studio here with the whole band on board and it would have made a great cover too but ended up being cut into 4 pieces to become 4 individual single sleeves. Bono had this pre-conceived idea about the cover and no matter what i brought in to show, he would never acknowledge that a single photo was good enough to be the front and he ended up getting his way, which was using a grid with loads of photos on the cover. I fought it but had to admit later that he was on the ball – it was a marvellous sleeve and still stands out as one of the greatest record sleeves in R'n'R (i think that says Rock and Roll).

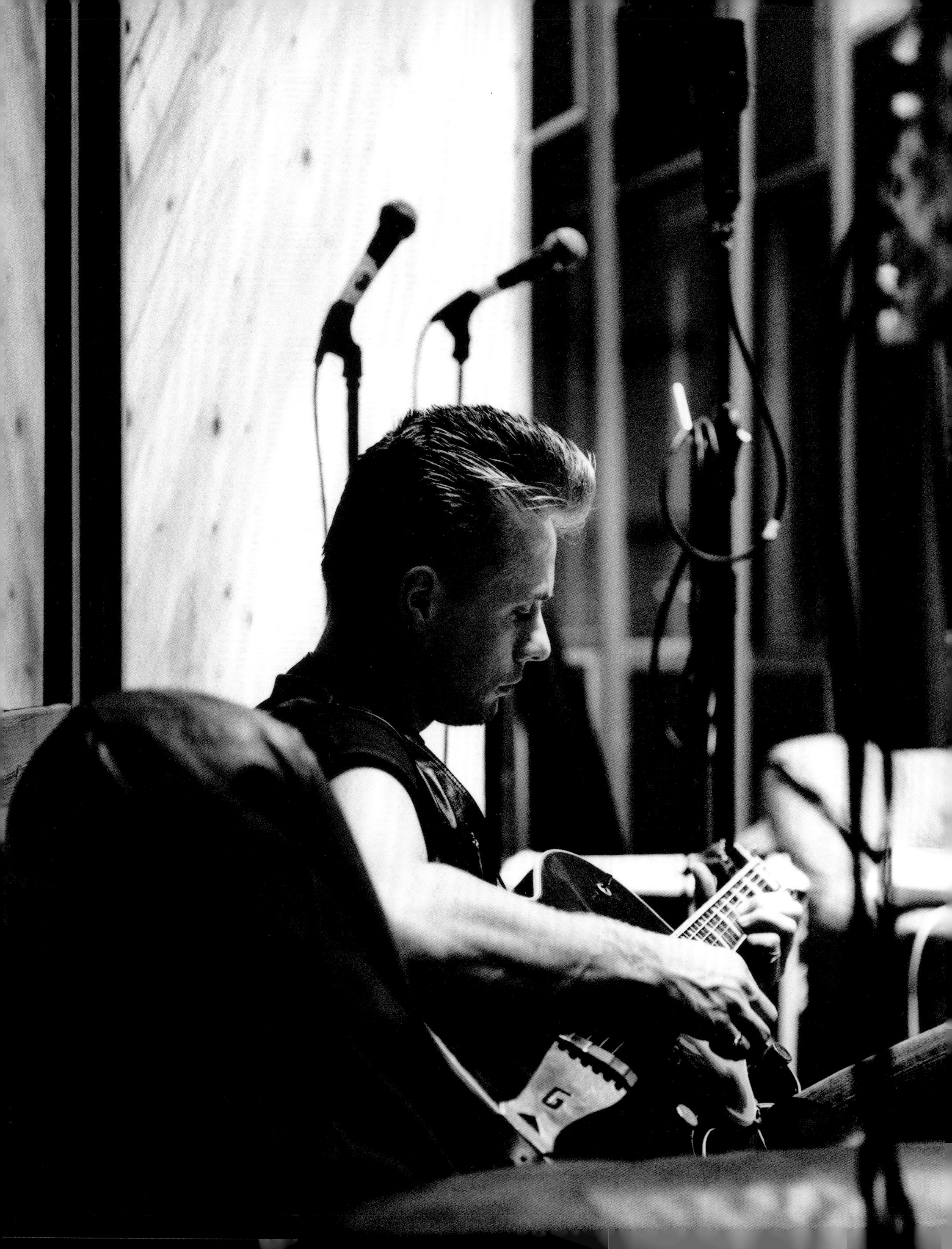

DUBLIN july 1991

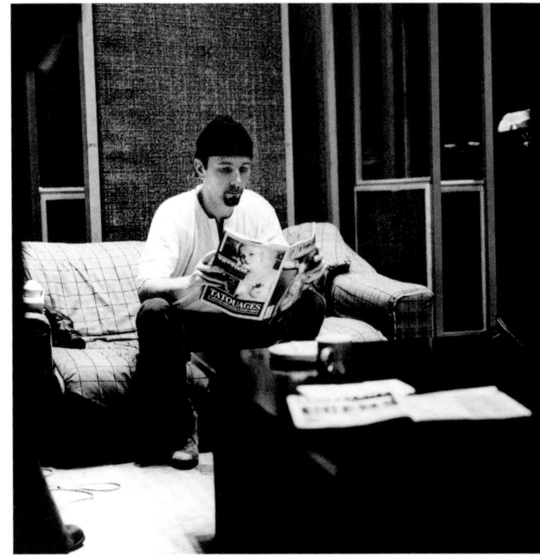

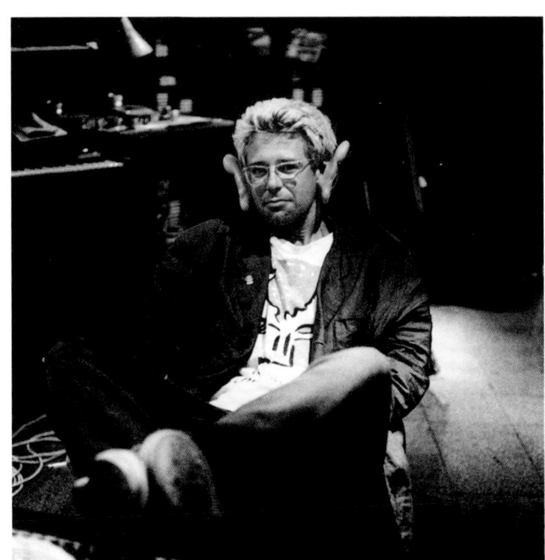

the last days in the studio in dublin _ while the record is being mixed and bono still adding vocals to it, the others have a lot of dead time on their hands.

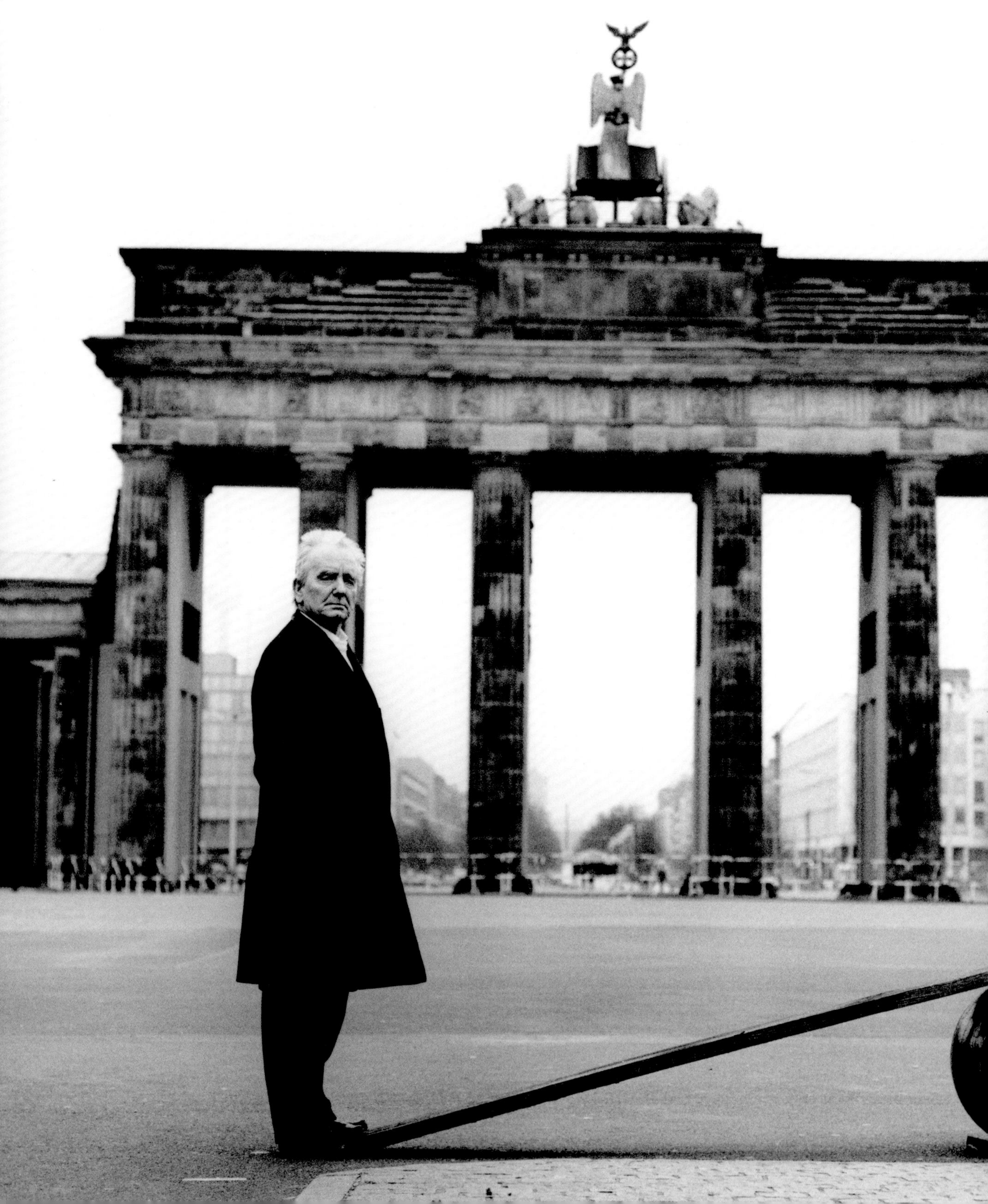

BERLIN 1992
february

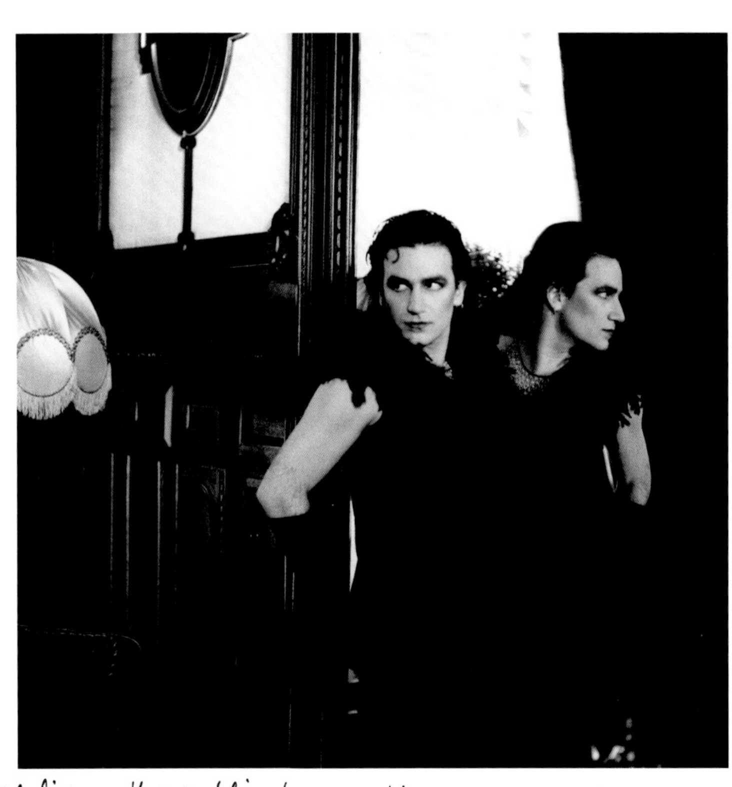

bono →

bob
←

berlin – the setting for my first real video for U2 : 'ONE'. it seemed an ideal place for this song as it ~~was~~ just lost its dividing wall and had become 'one' city once more.

Other references to 'one' were (at least for me when i thought of ideas for the video) man and woman are one, father, son and holy ghost, a circle is one, a seesaw is out of balance if used by one person etc..

I was very fortunate to have bob hewson (bono's dad) agreeing to be in the video – for me the strongest moments of the video. I also painted 2 trabants myself – it took me 2 full days and no idea where they have ended up.

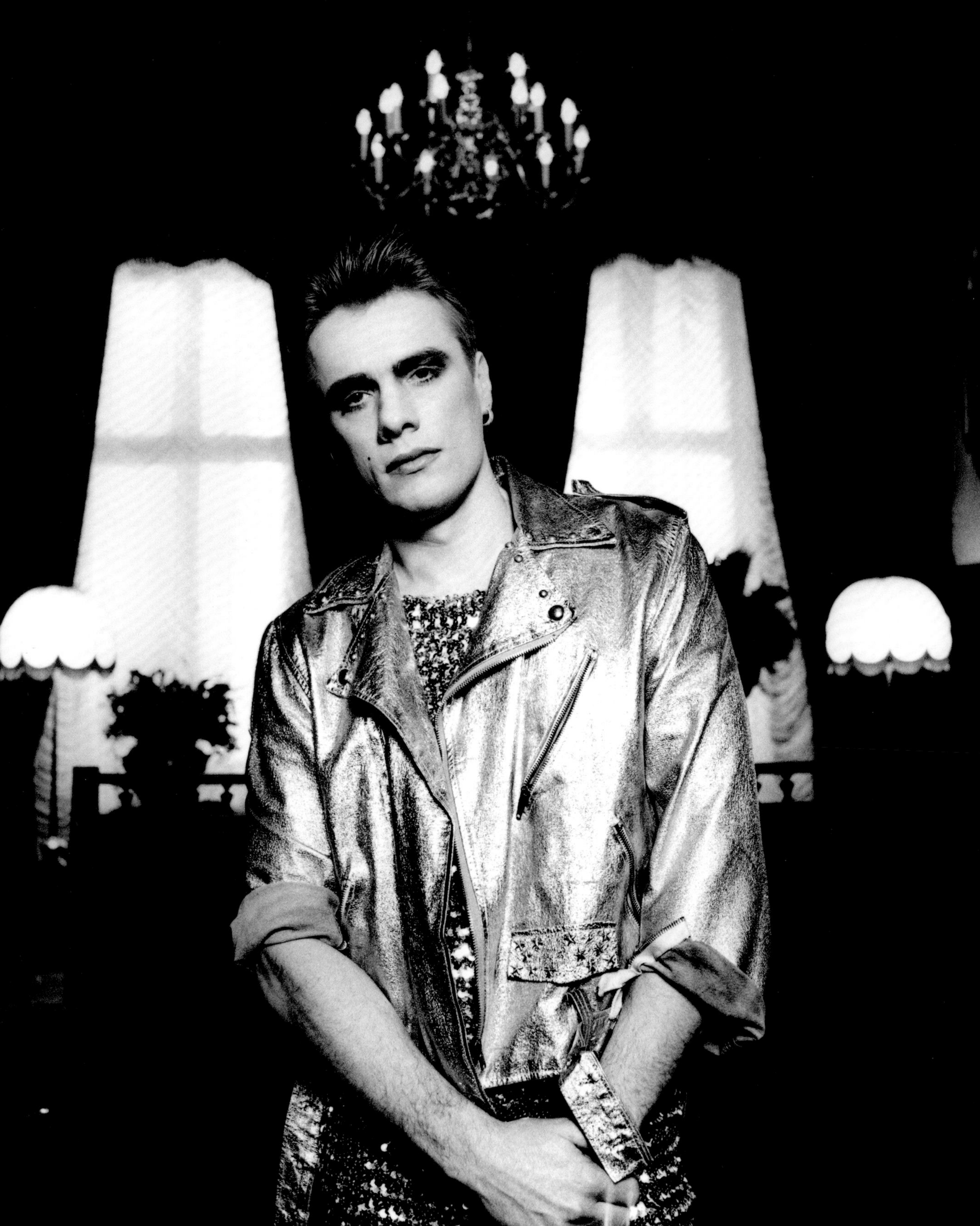

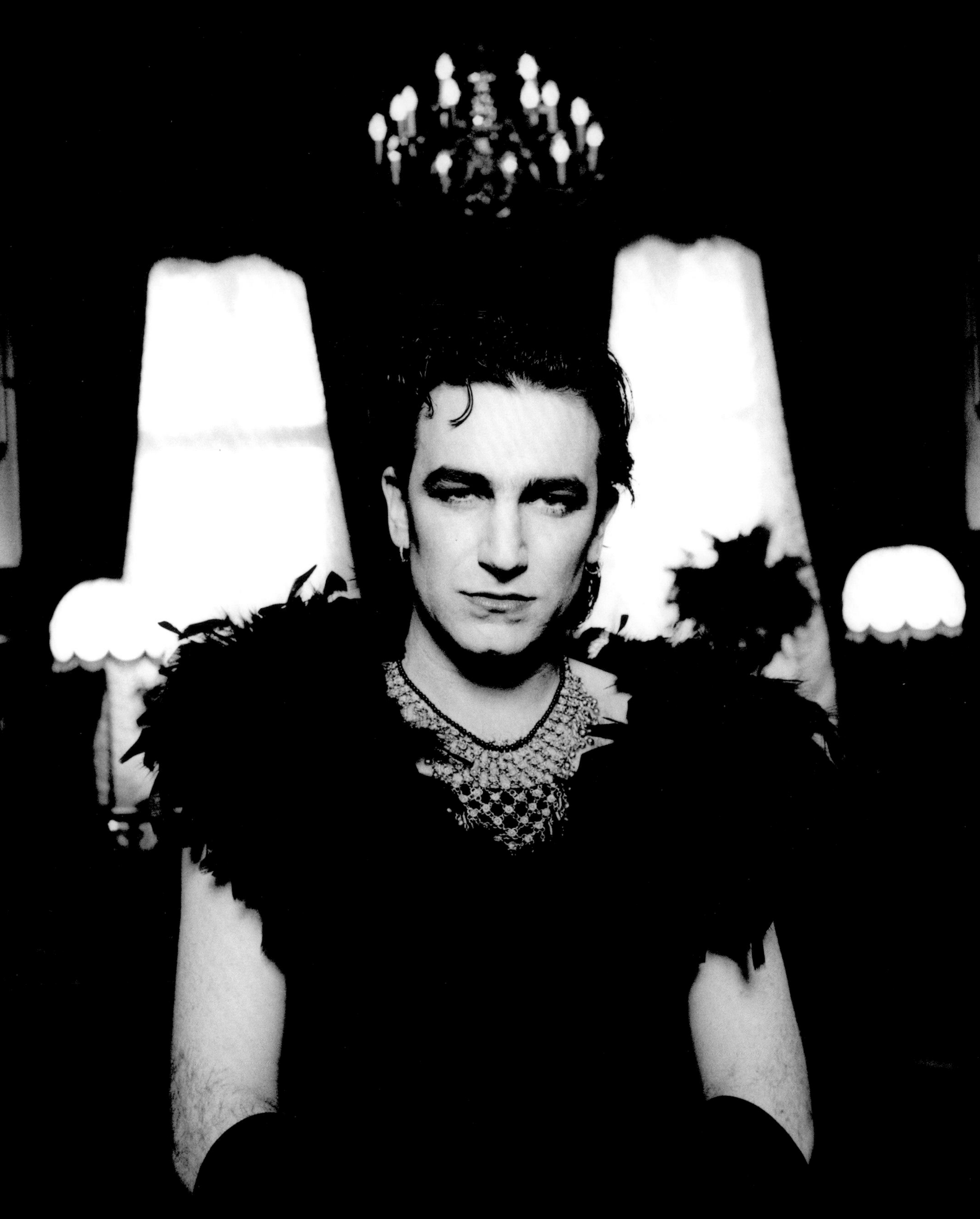

the other interior was the hansa studios.

we filmed a lot of the interiors in an old brothel on the former east side of berlin.

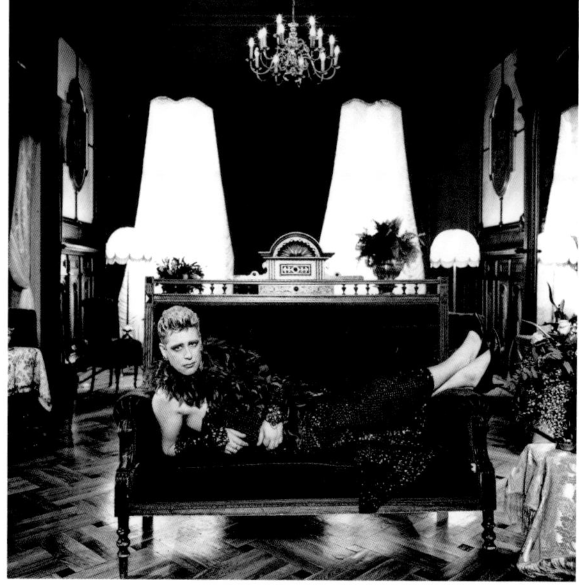

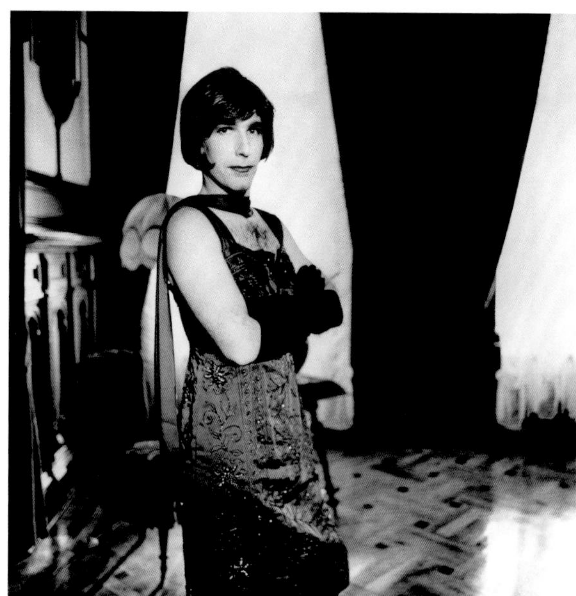

the female version of adam with the male version of the trabant.

it is all good and just did a director's cut for a dvd release.

of course, in the end the video was held back for 4 months due to some sensitive issues but once the single had died down in the charts, it was given to TV stations as an alternative version. i had put a lot of effort into this film and was devastated when it was shelved for a while, but now

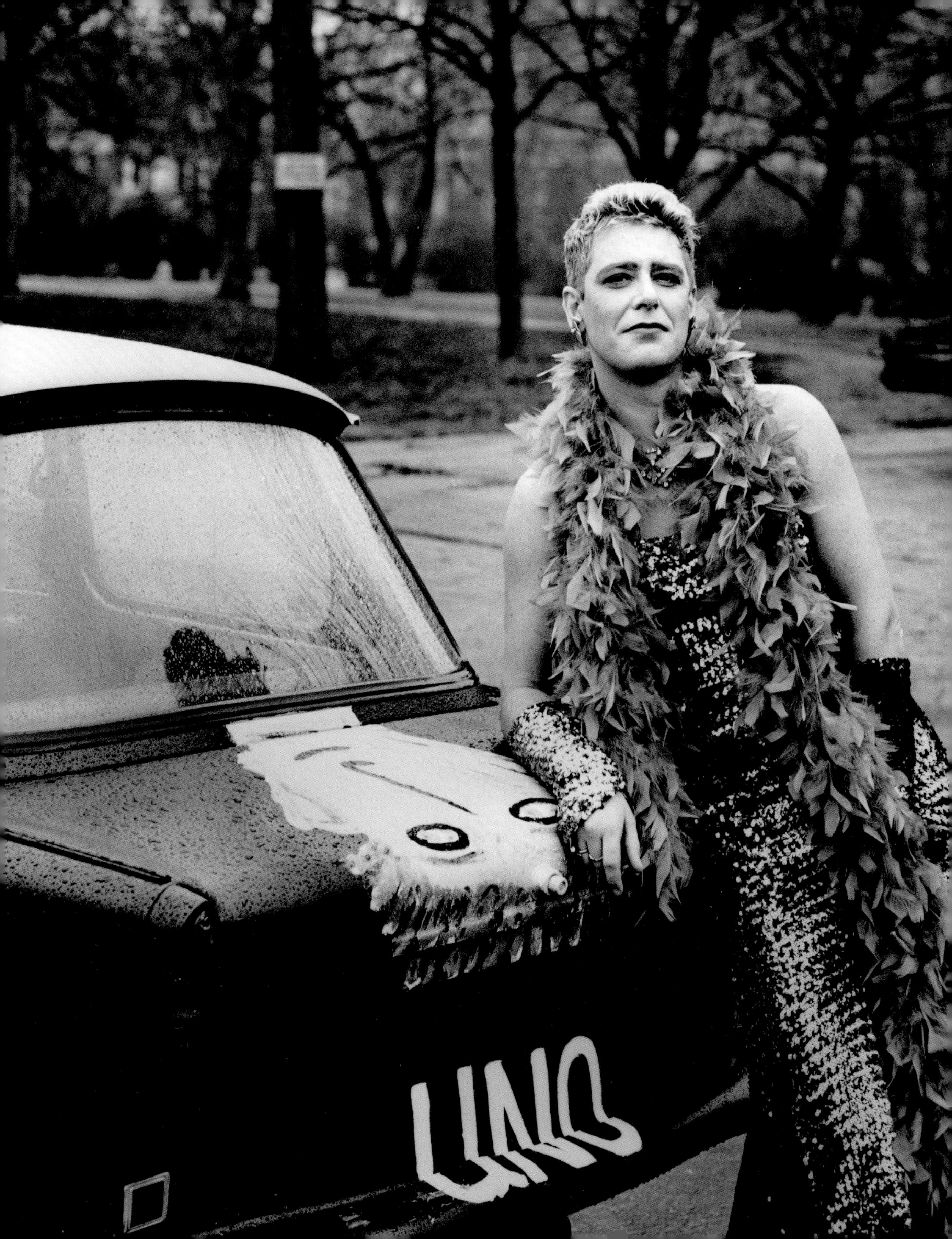
UNO

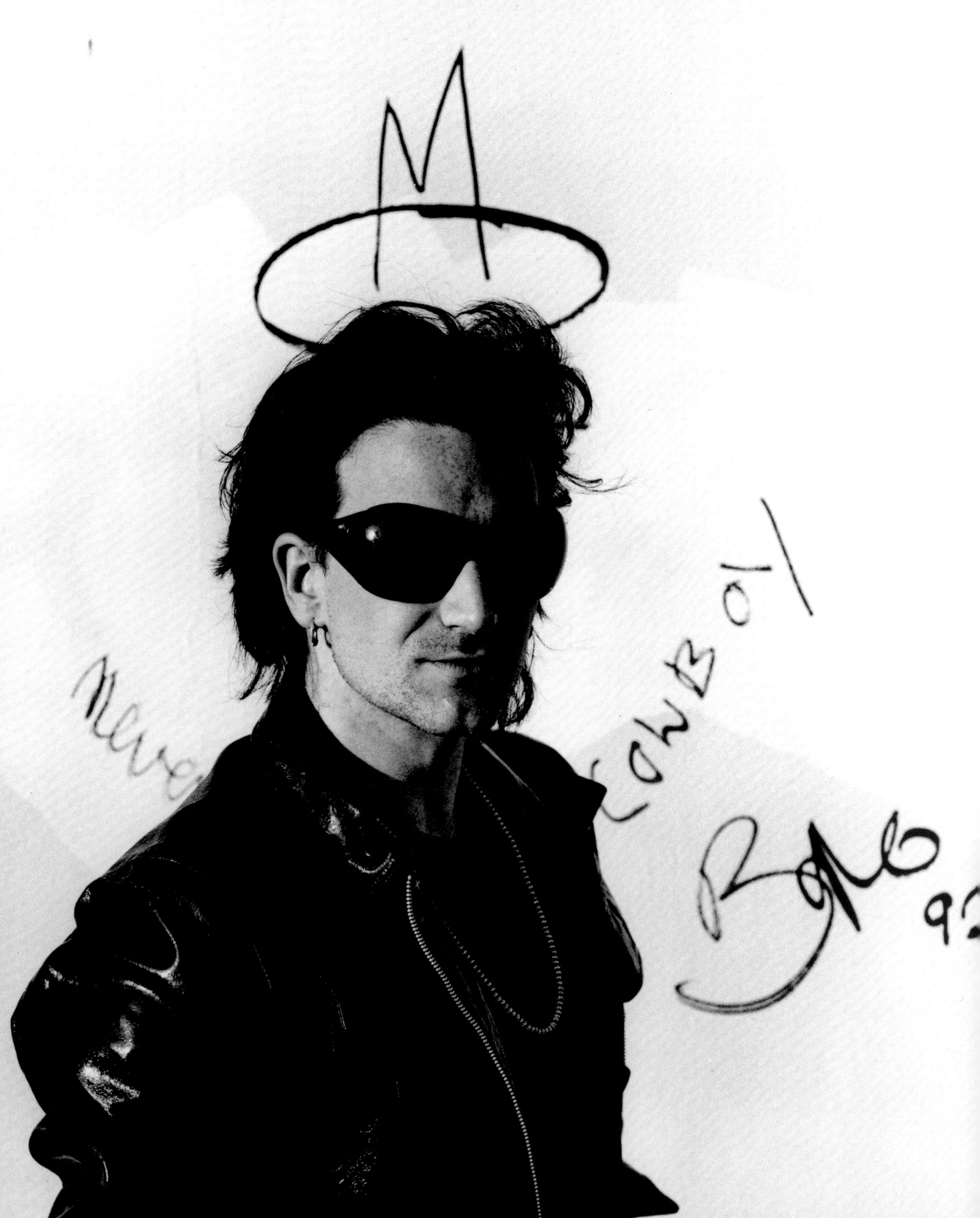
M
COWBOY
Bono

MIAMI 1992 march

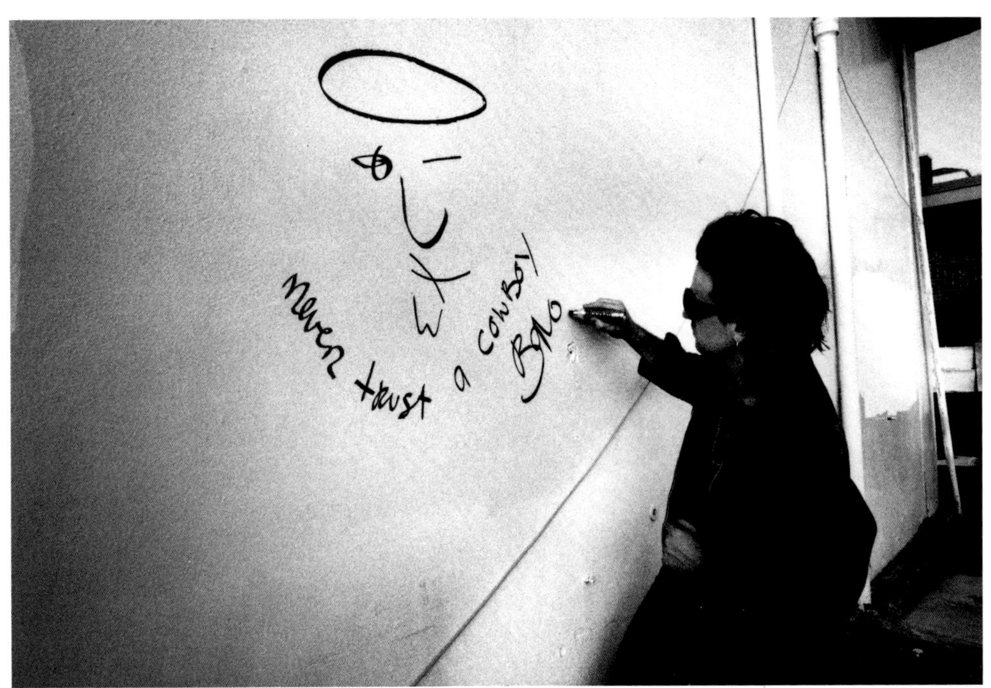

inspired by graffitti artists, bono adds his bit to a wall in miami to use as a backdrop for a photo we are doing for the FACE magazine. this ~~was~~ the first or second city on their ZOOTV tour and the first time i saw them again after they shelved my 'one' video but there were no bad feelings that i could detect. i was ~~prob~~ probably a little anxious though. Bono looked really strong and the fly outfit was a fantastic look for him.

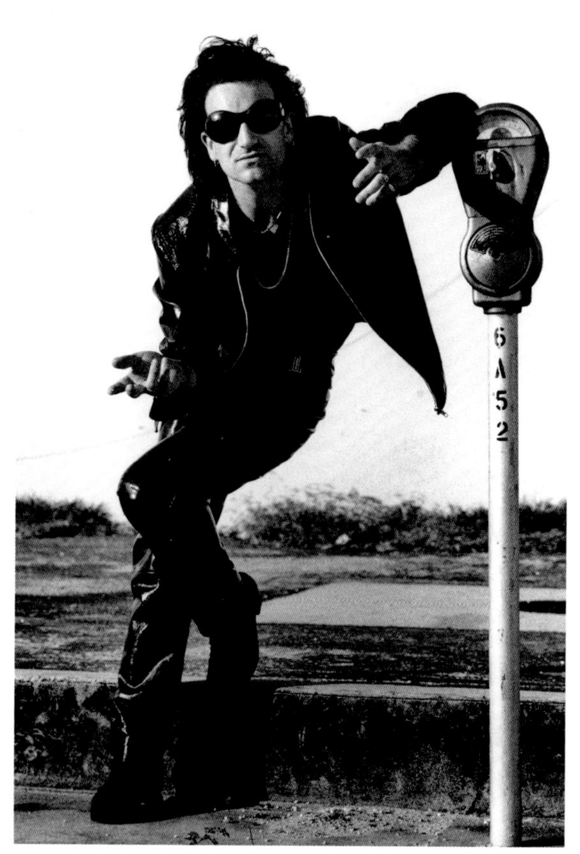

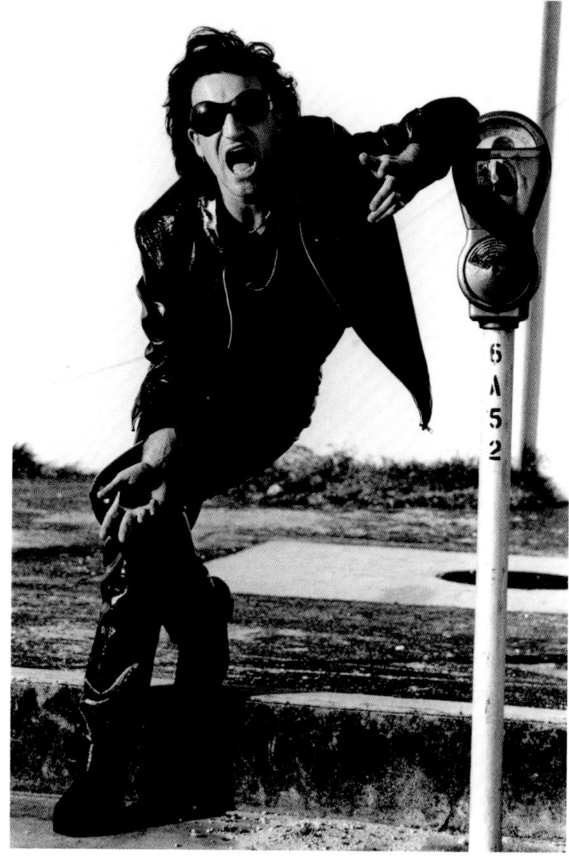

couldn't choose between these two photos so here they both are.

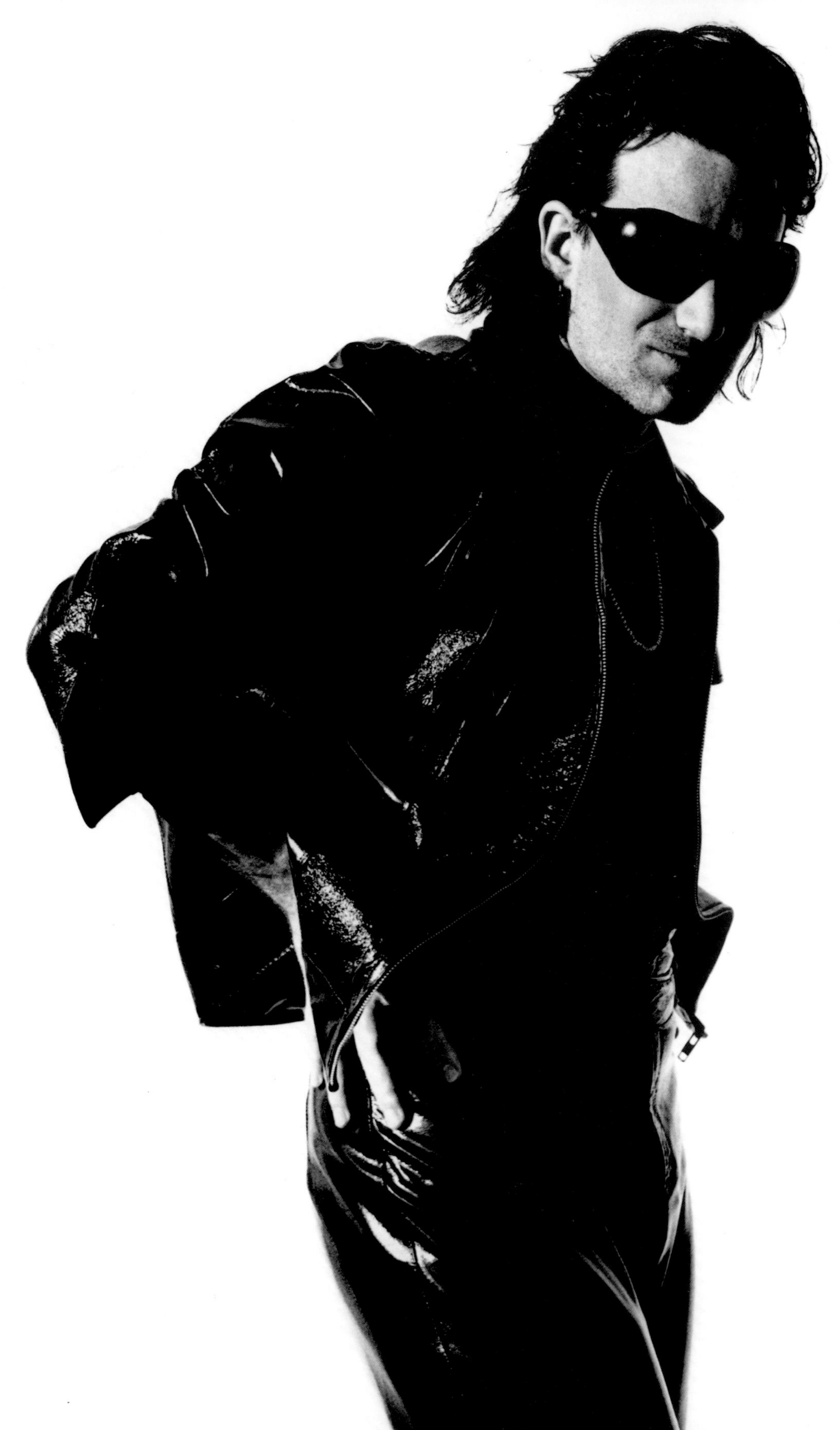

CHICAGO 1992 ~~March~~ march

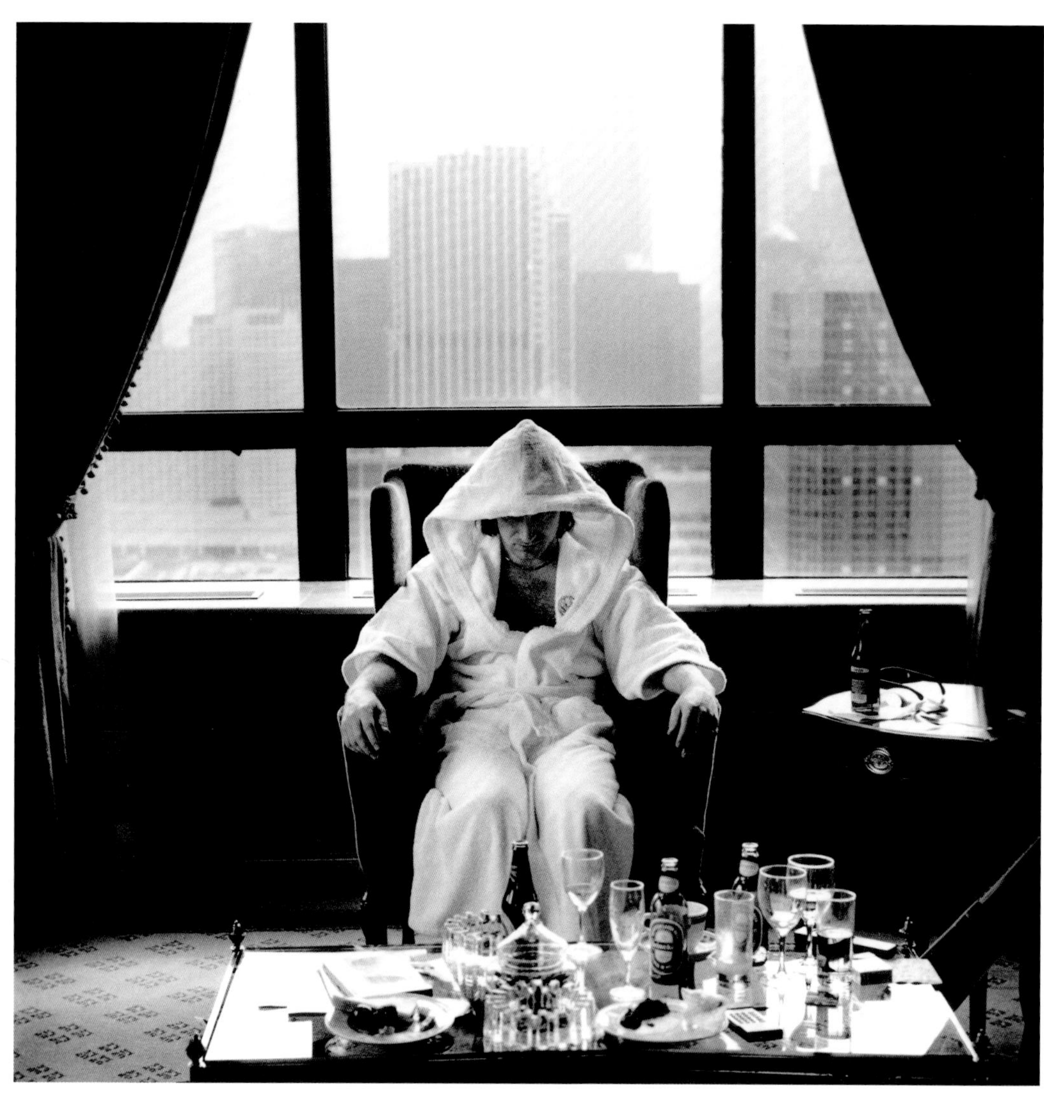

this is the morning after the night before. we were staying in a Chicago hotel where the then governor of Arkansas, Bill Clinton, was staying as well. Needless to say, Bill and Bono met up in Bono's room and this was the scene i found entering Bono's suite in the morning.

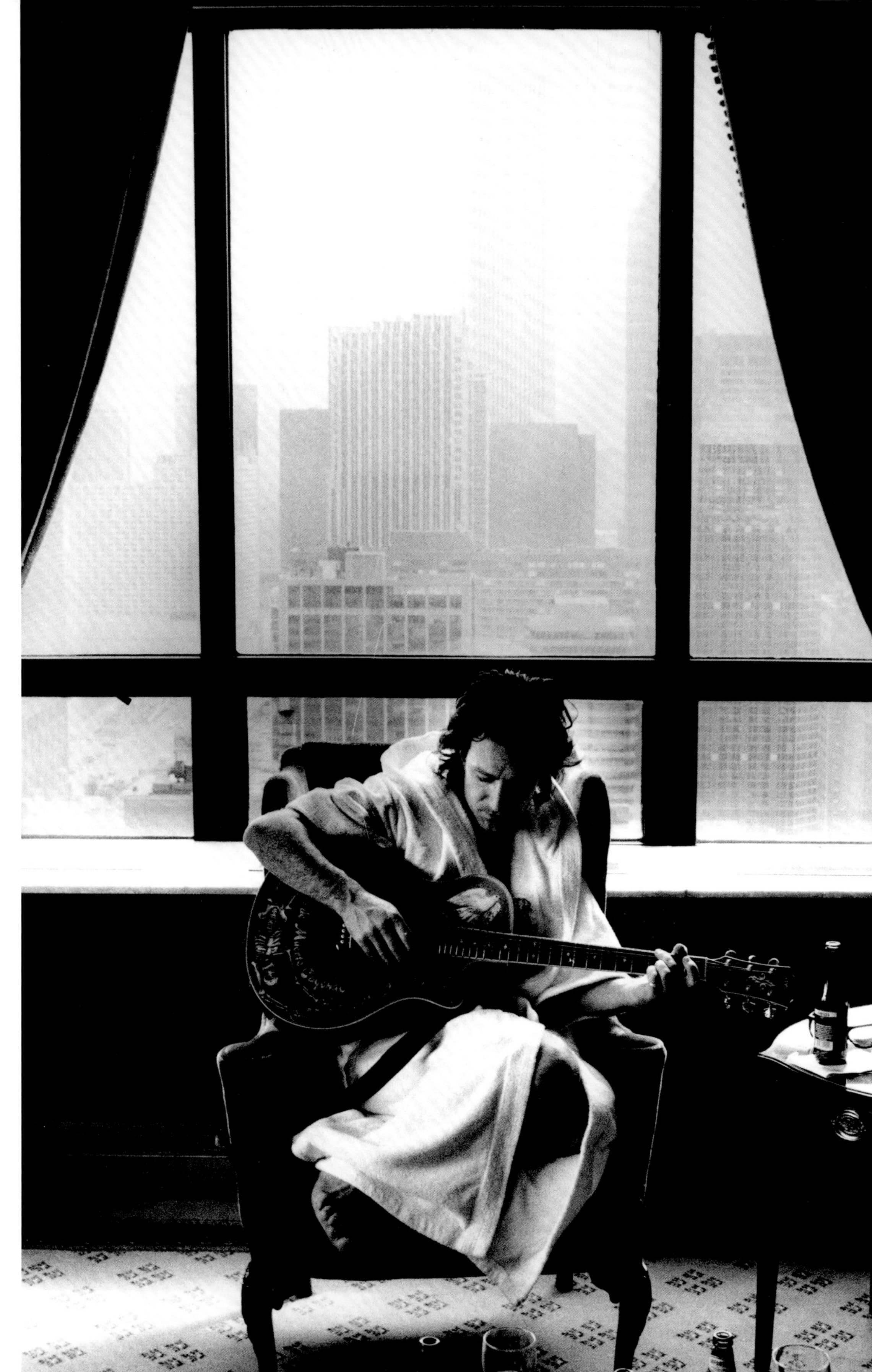

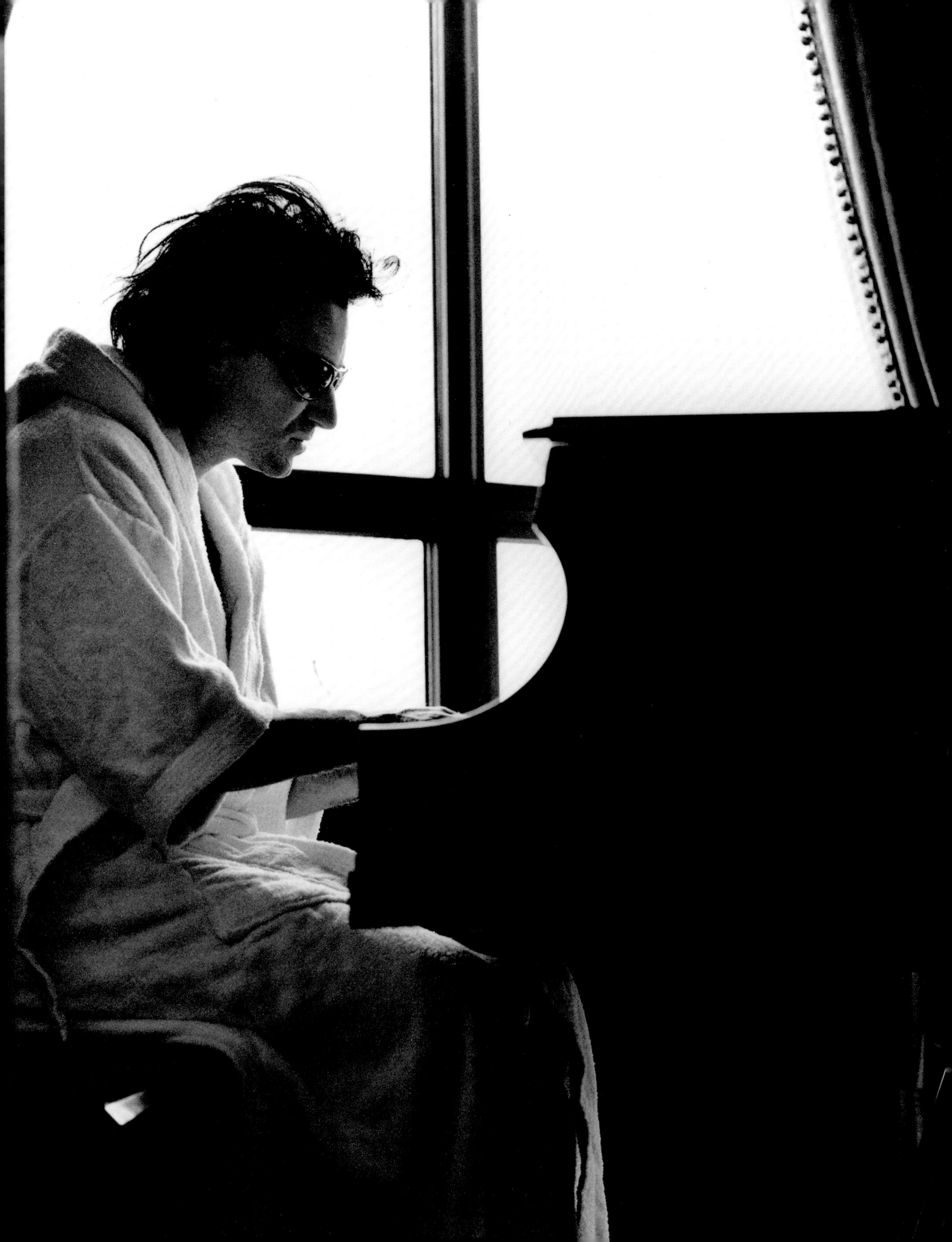

this was a very large suite, consisting of two floors and a grand piano.

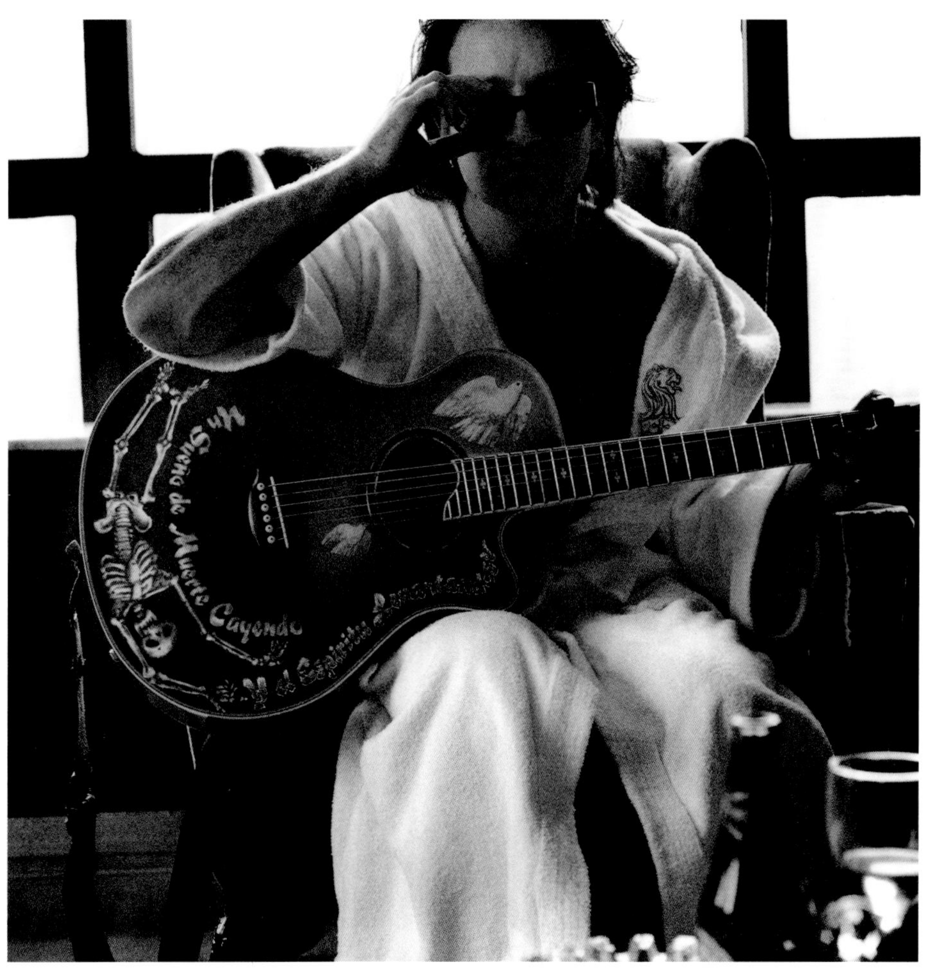

up there, in the air 1992 march

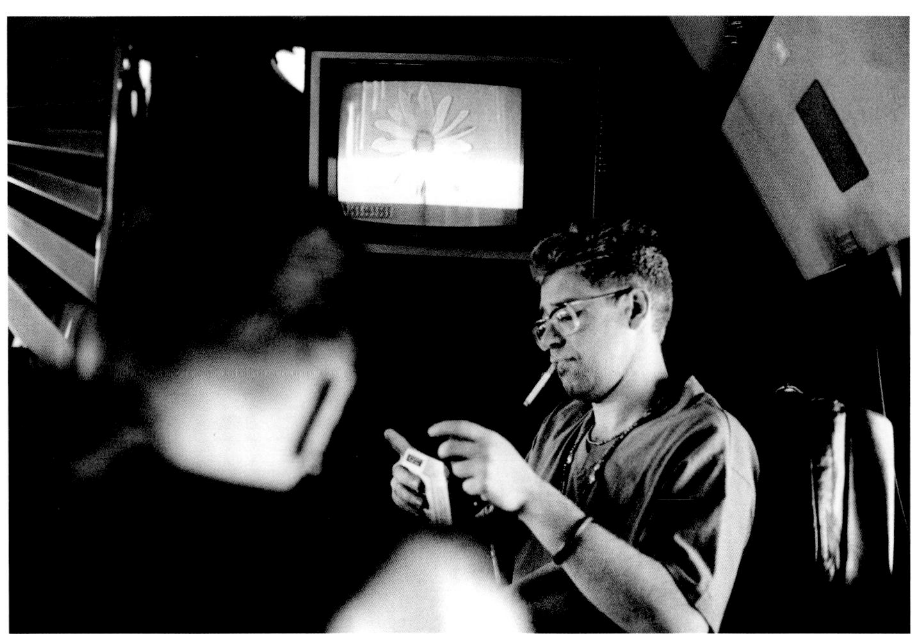

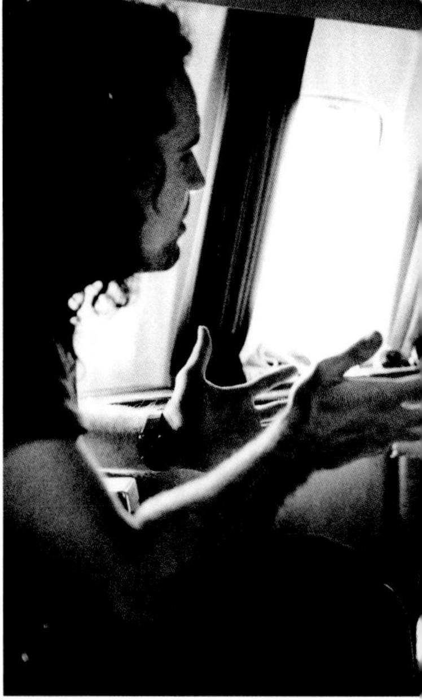

i seem to think that this is on the U2 plane travelling from Chicago to minneapolis, where the band will be playing a concert before flying back to Chicago. Just a snapshot of life on a plane with adam and larry reading, edge in conversation with Jason Patric and Bono listening to Julia Roberts.

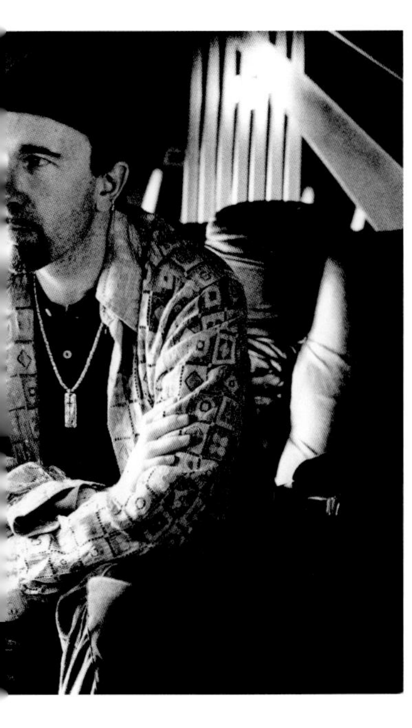

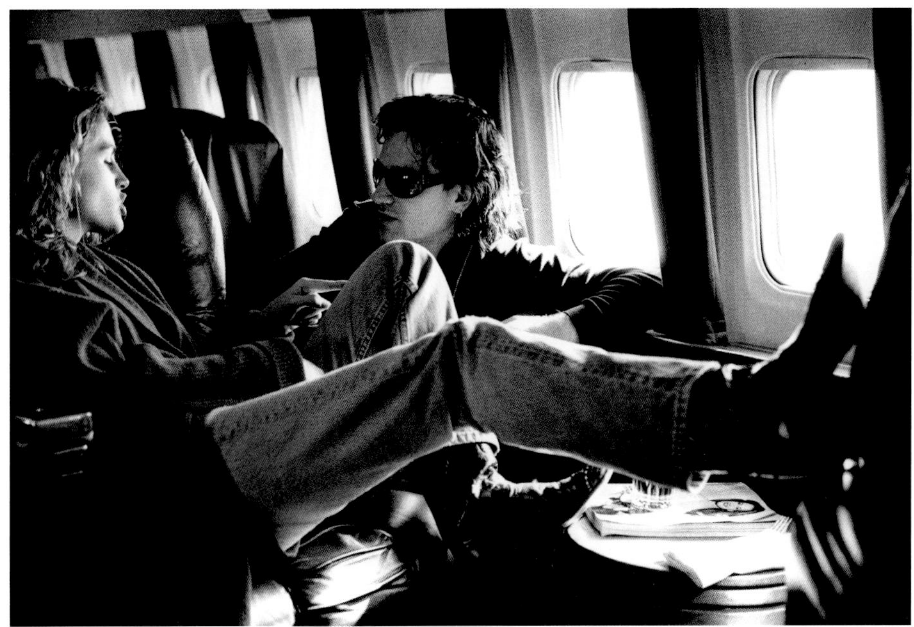

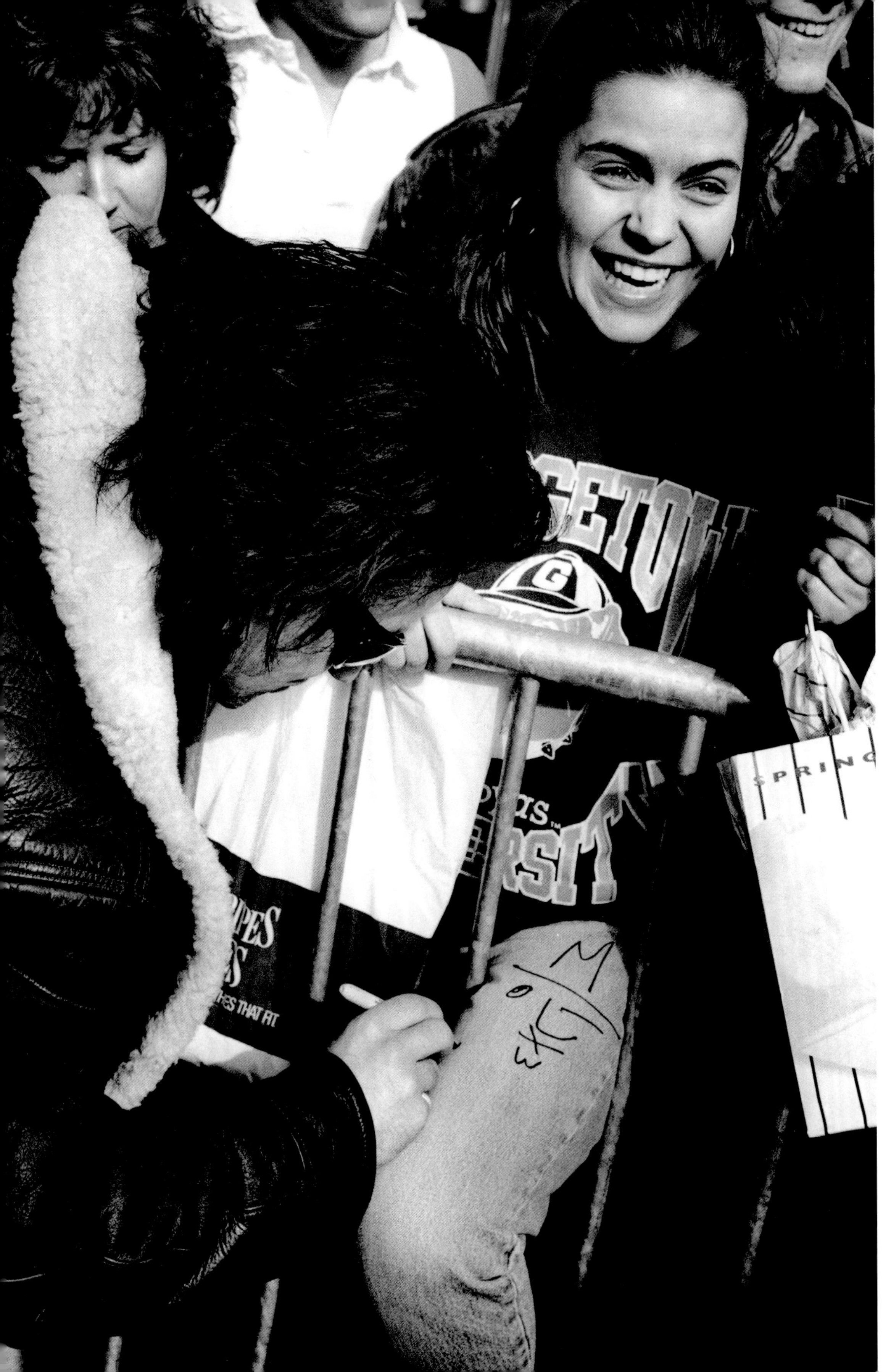

MINNEAPOLIS 1992 march

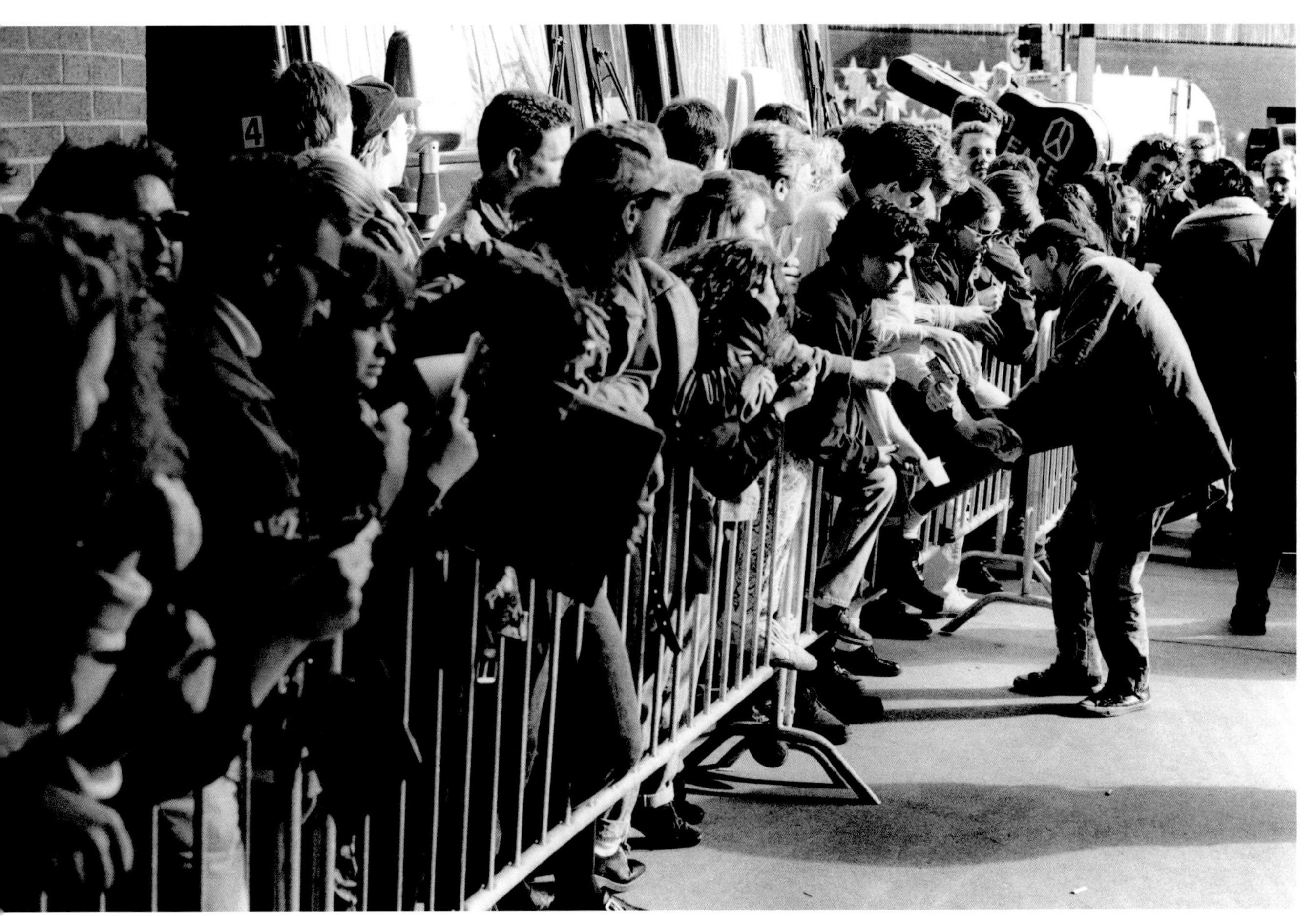

U2 arriving at the venue in minneapolis

boredom/routine/tension,
all probably alive and kicking

Bono and dress hanging around backstage

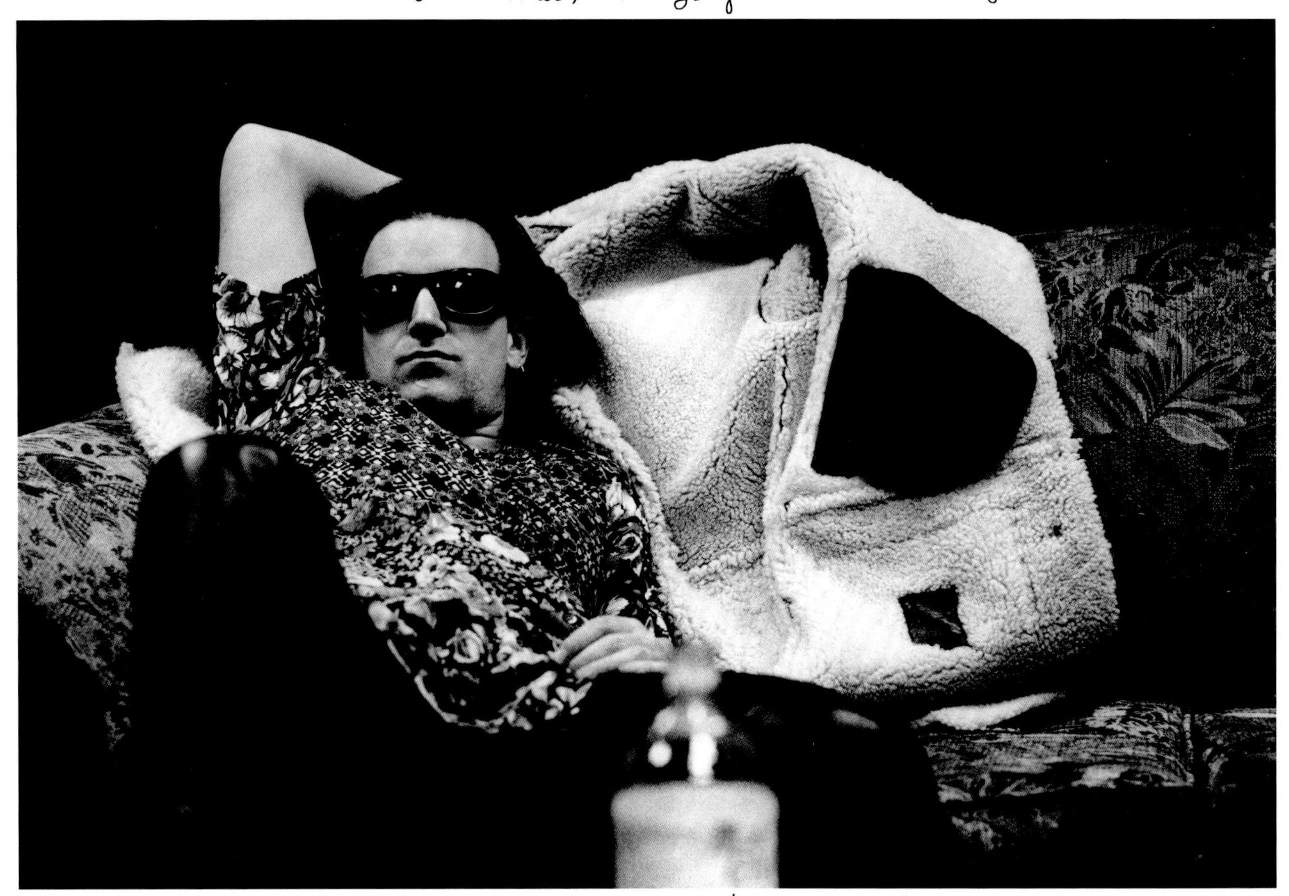

i cannot remember where this floral dress came from - pretty mad though and we did some more photos with it the following year.

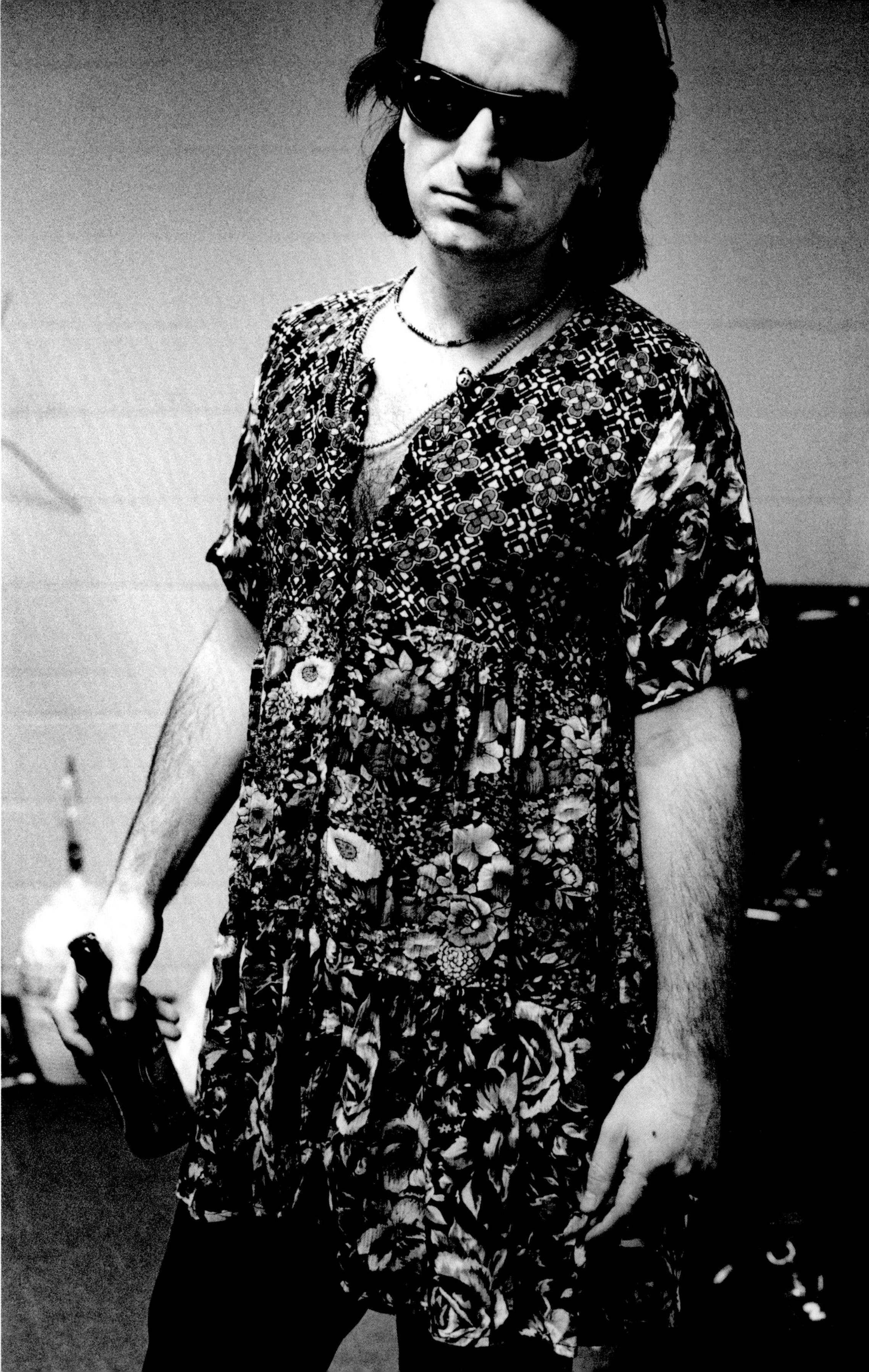

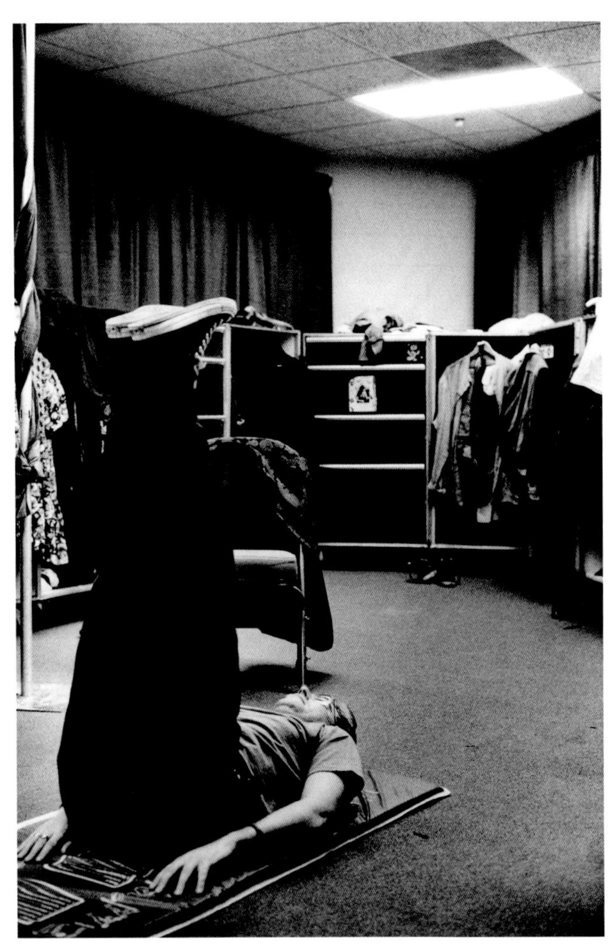

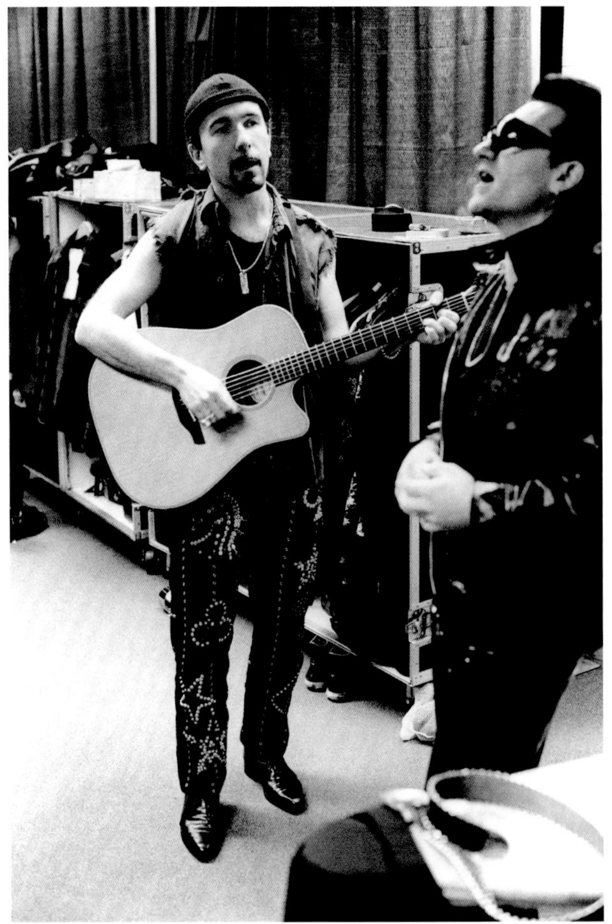

(out of sight)
larry and adam are physically preparing for the concert while
bono and edge exercise their voices. on the opposite page,
is the band waiting and ready to walk to the stage.

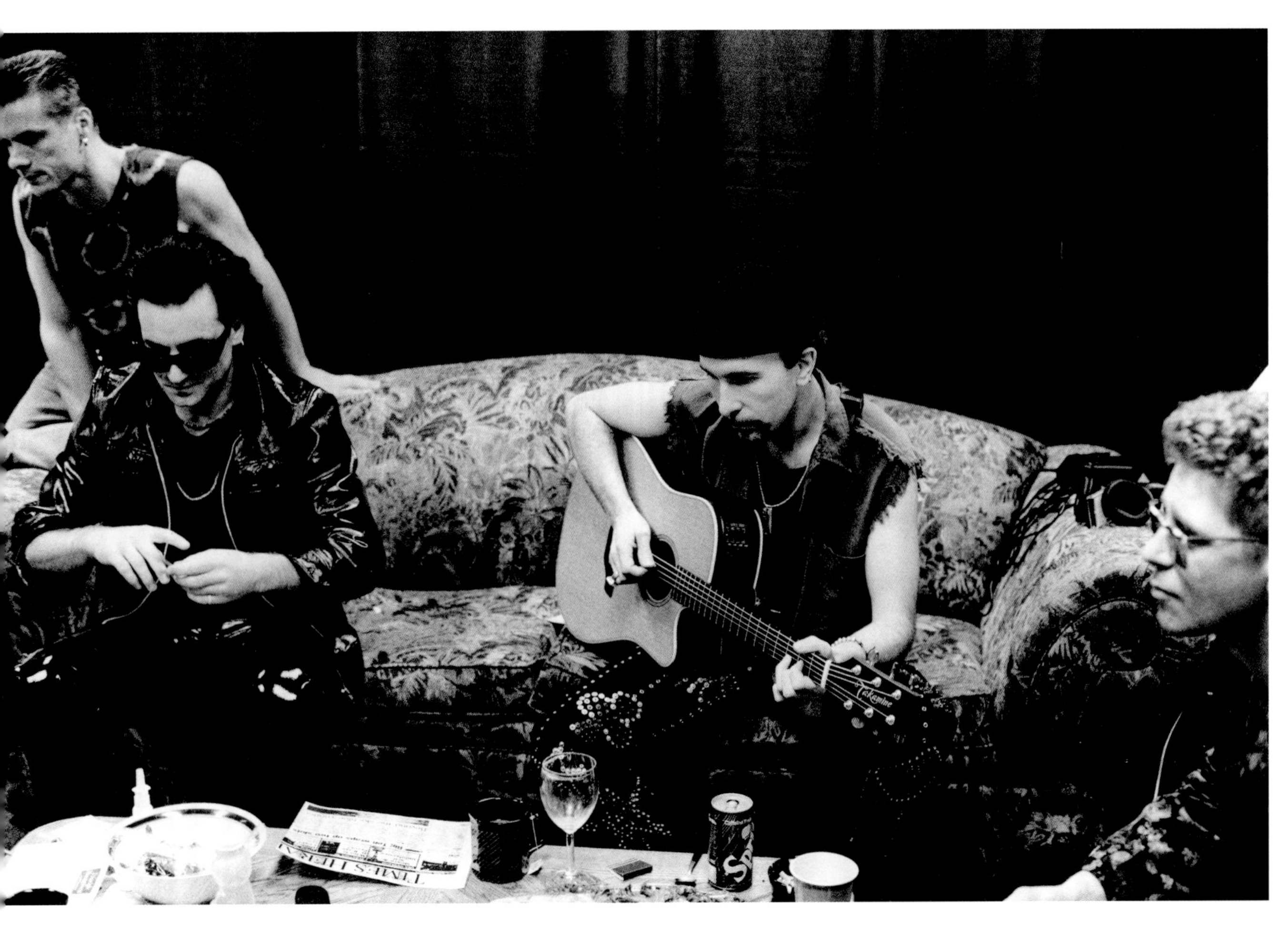

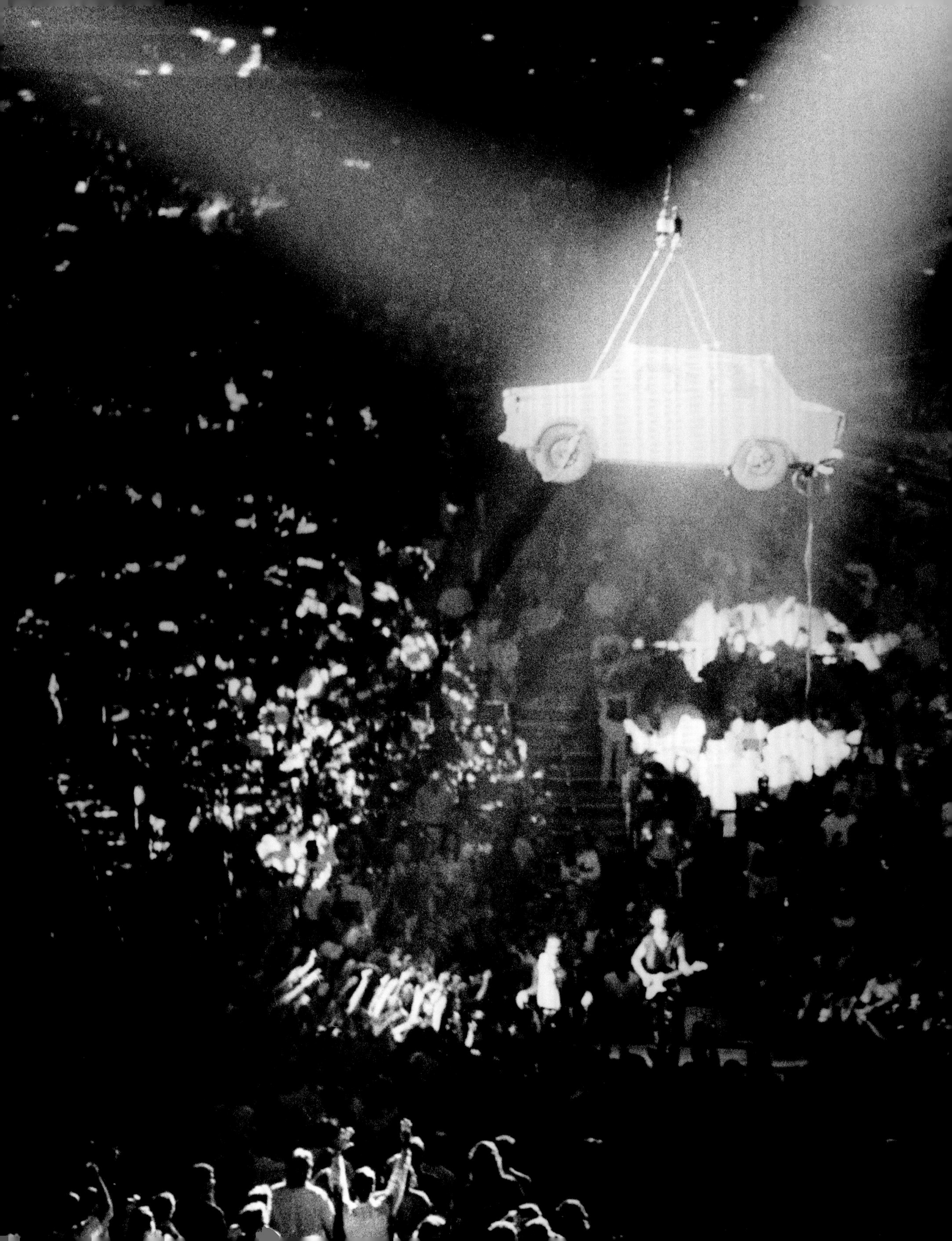

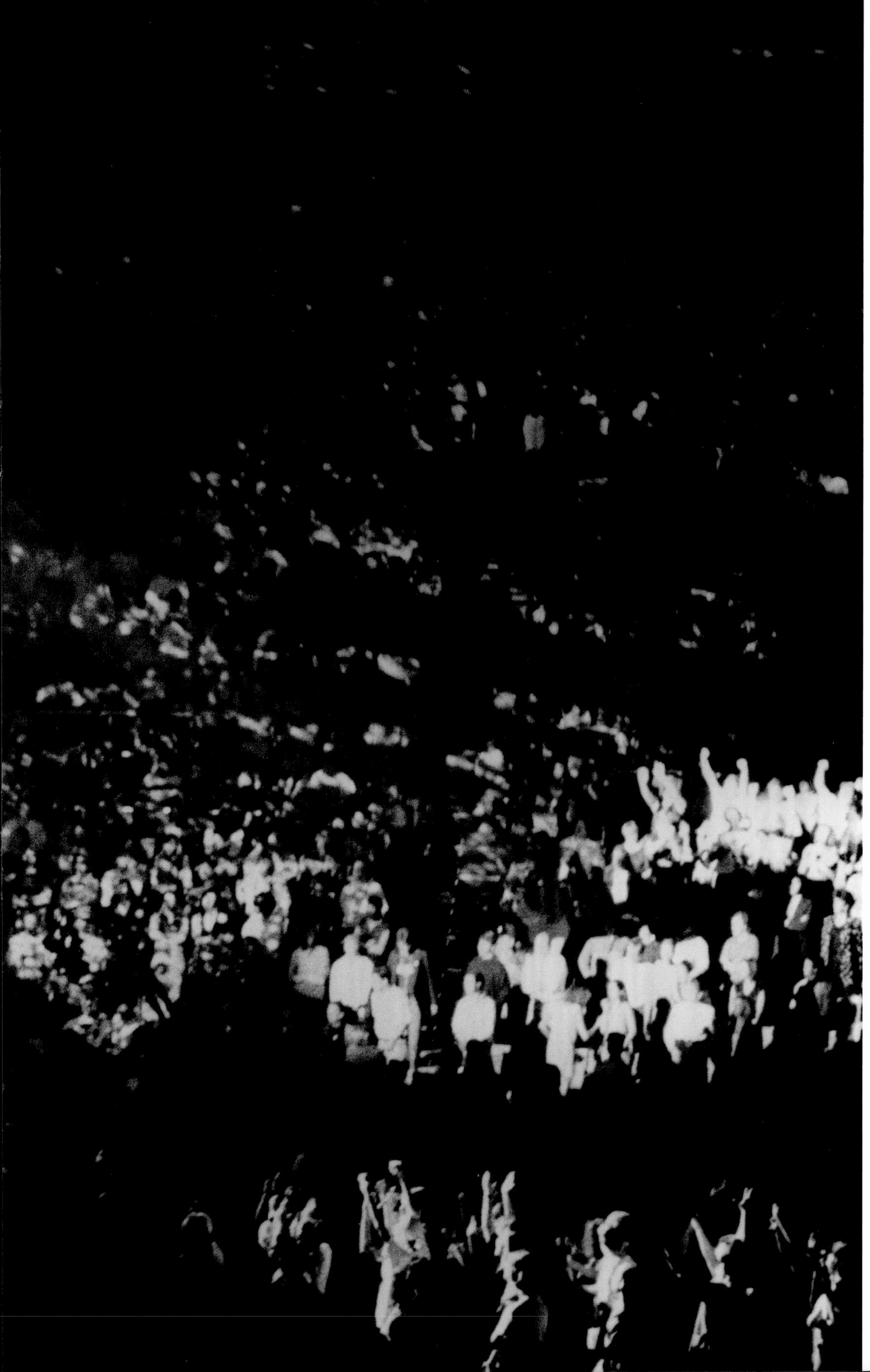

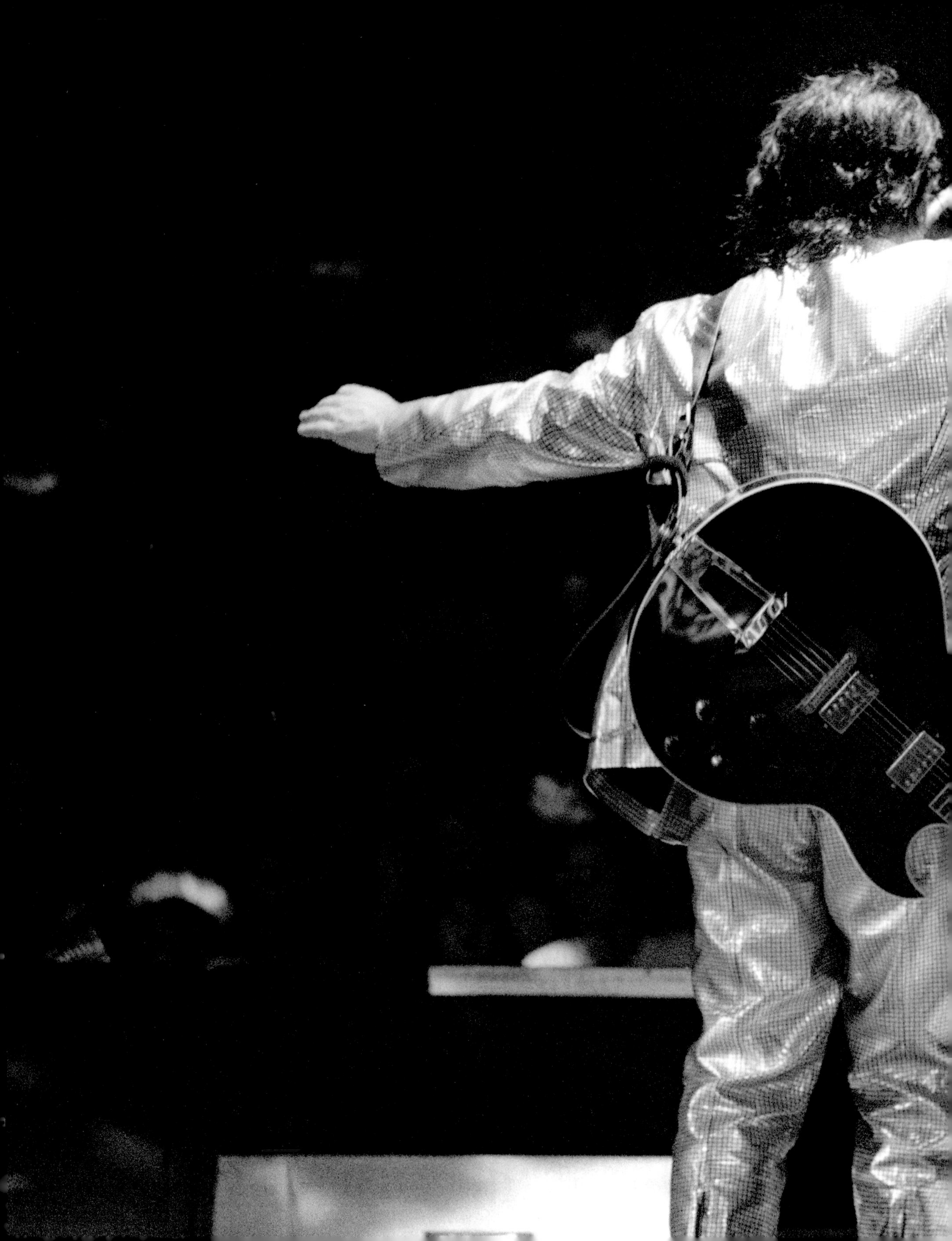

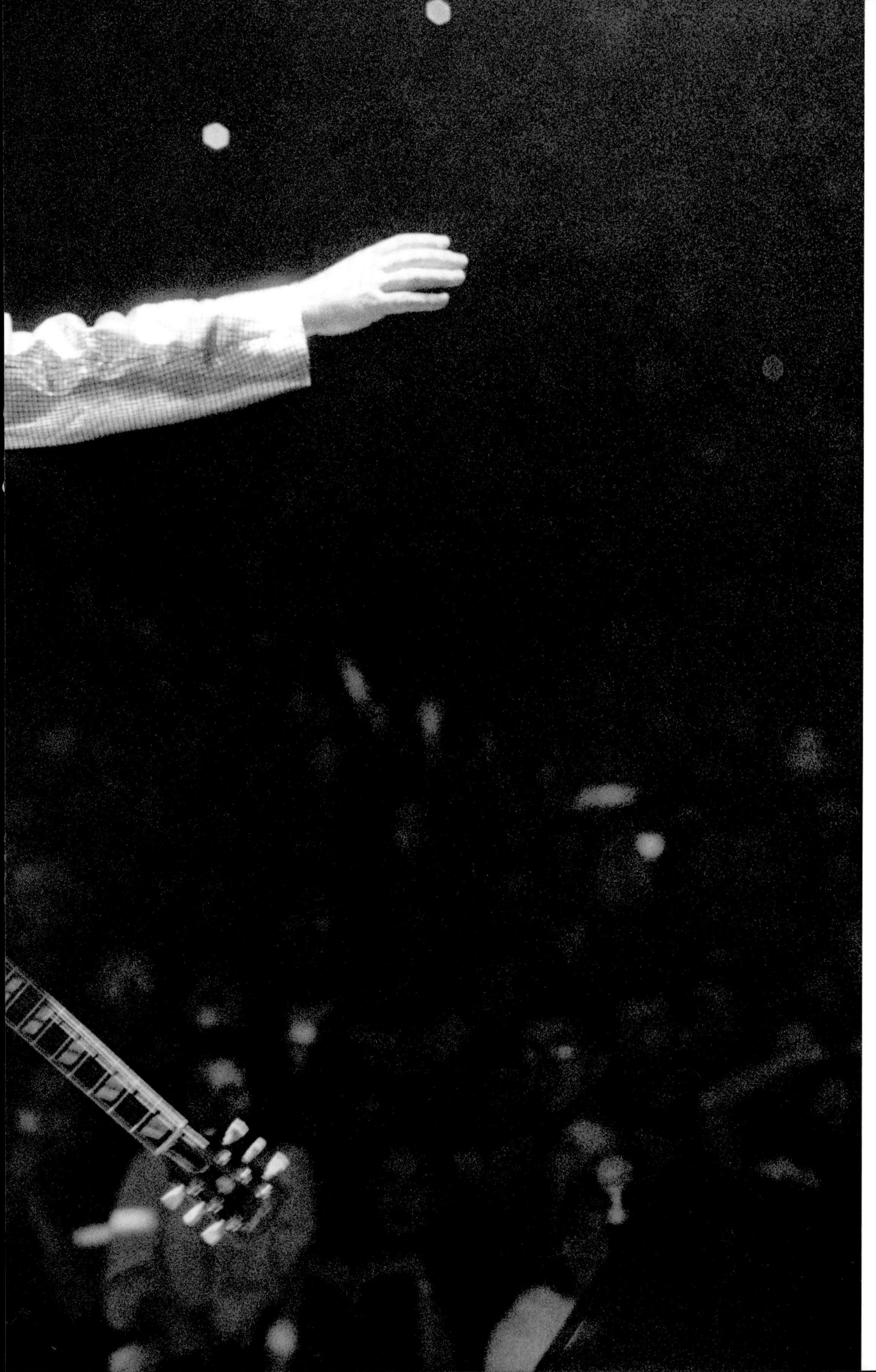

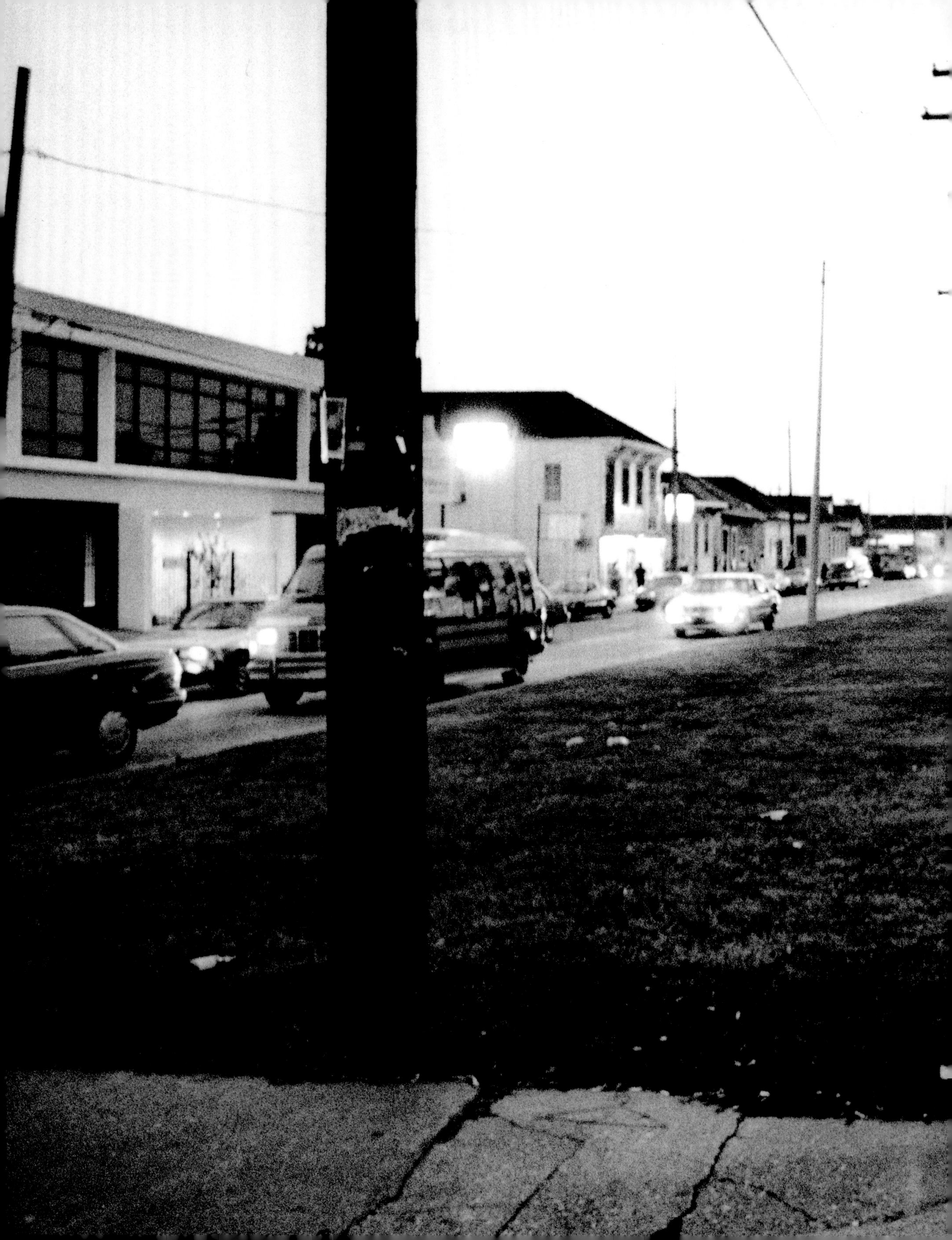

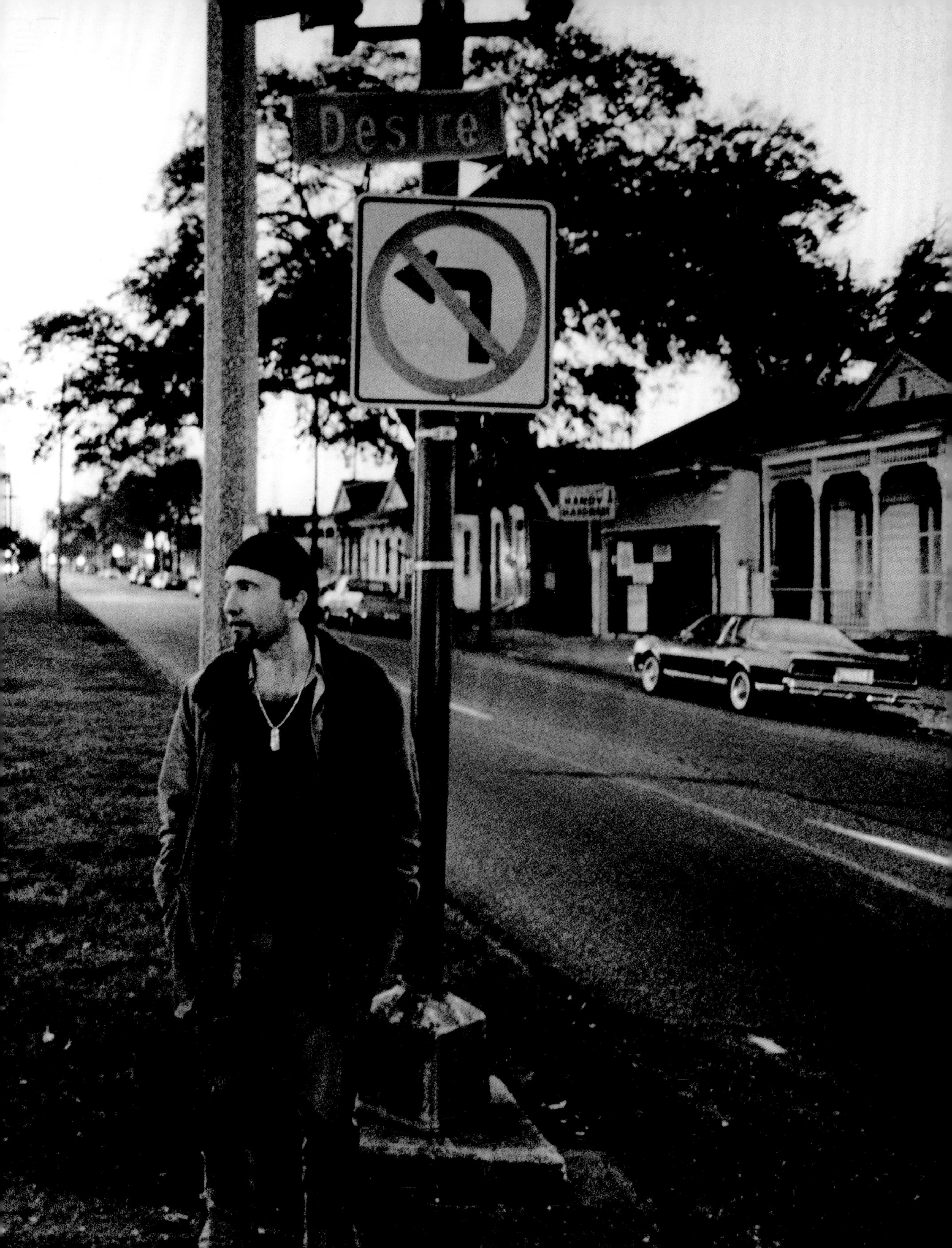
Desire

HOUSTON 1992

april

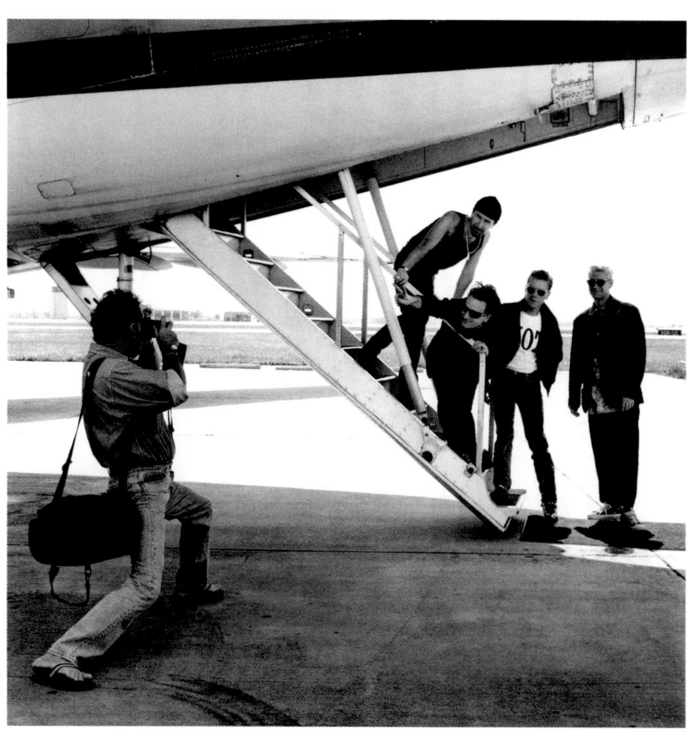

chris blackwell, founder of island records, takes a photo of the band posing on the steps of their airplane. and so do i. →

1992 march
NEW ORLEANS
previous page

edge on a day off between 'gigs' in different places choose to spent it in new orleans.

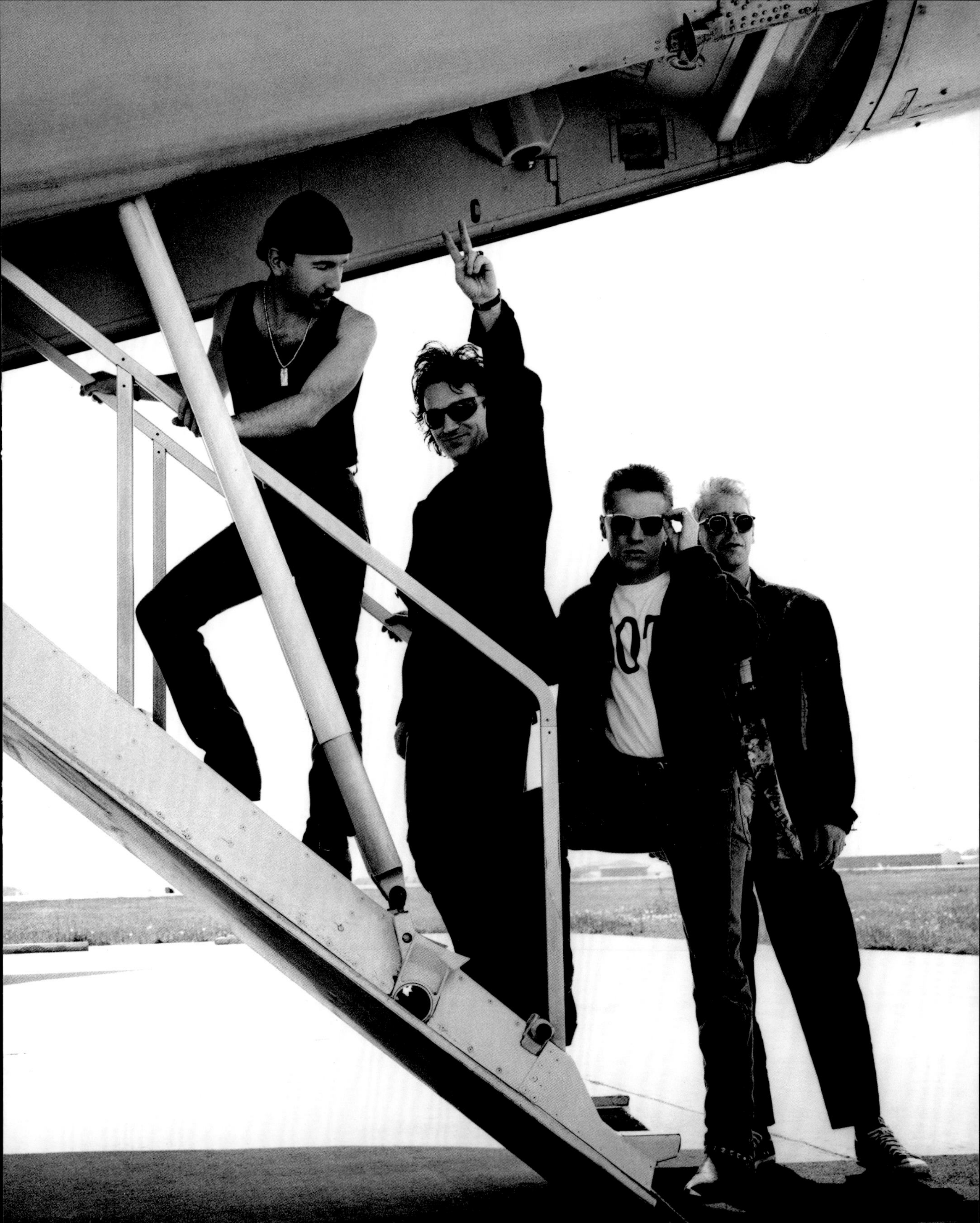

SWEDEN 1992

june

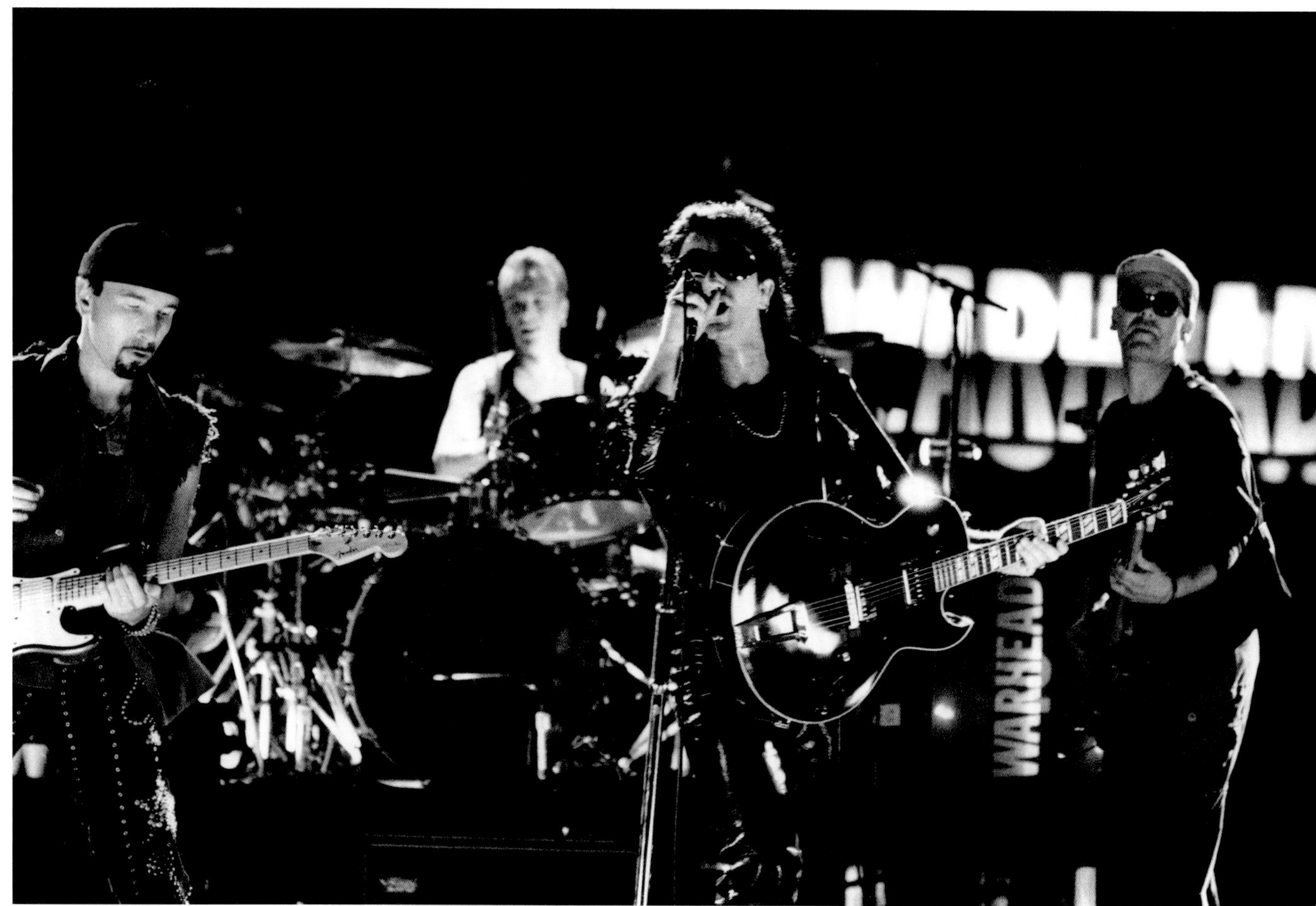

during a show in a smaller venue, possibly Gothenburg, the band were supposed to all look at the camera at some point during a certain song while i was standing in the audience. Edge forgot!

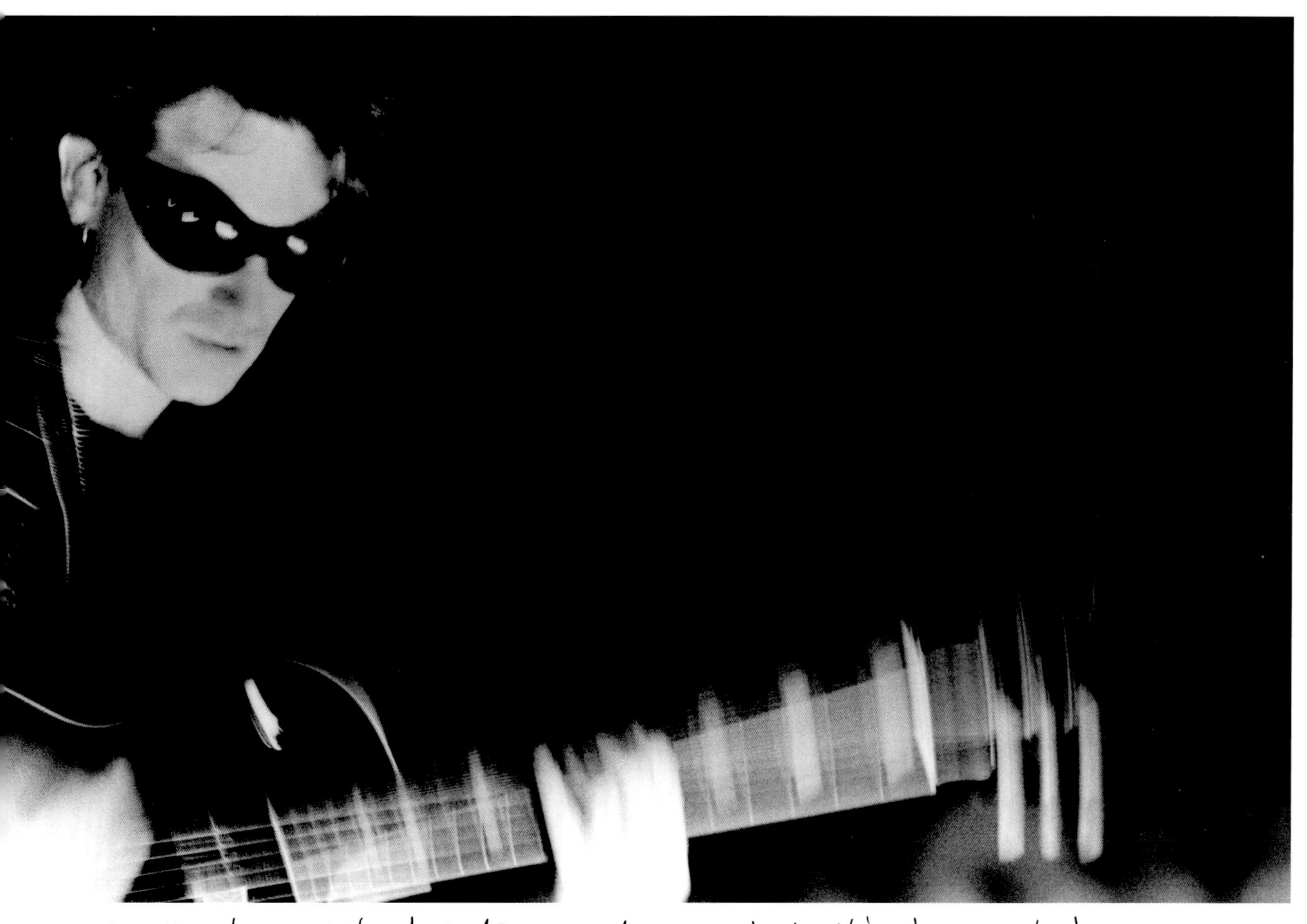

very much a velvet underground moment in this bono photo.

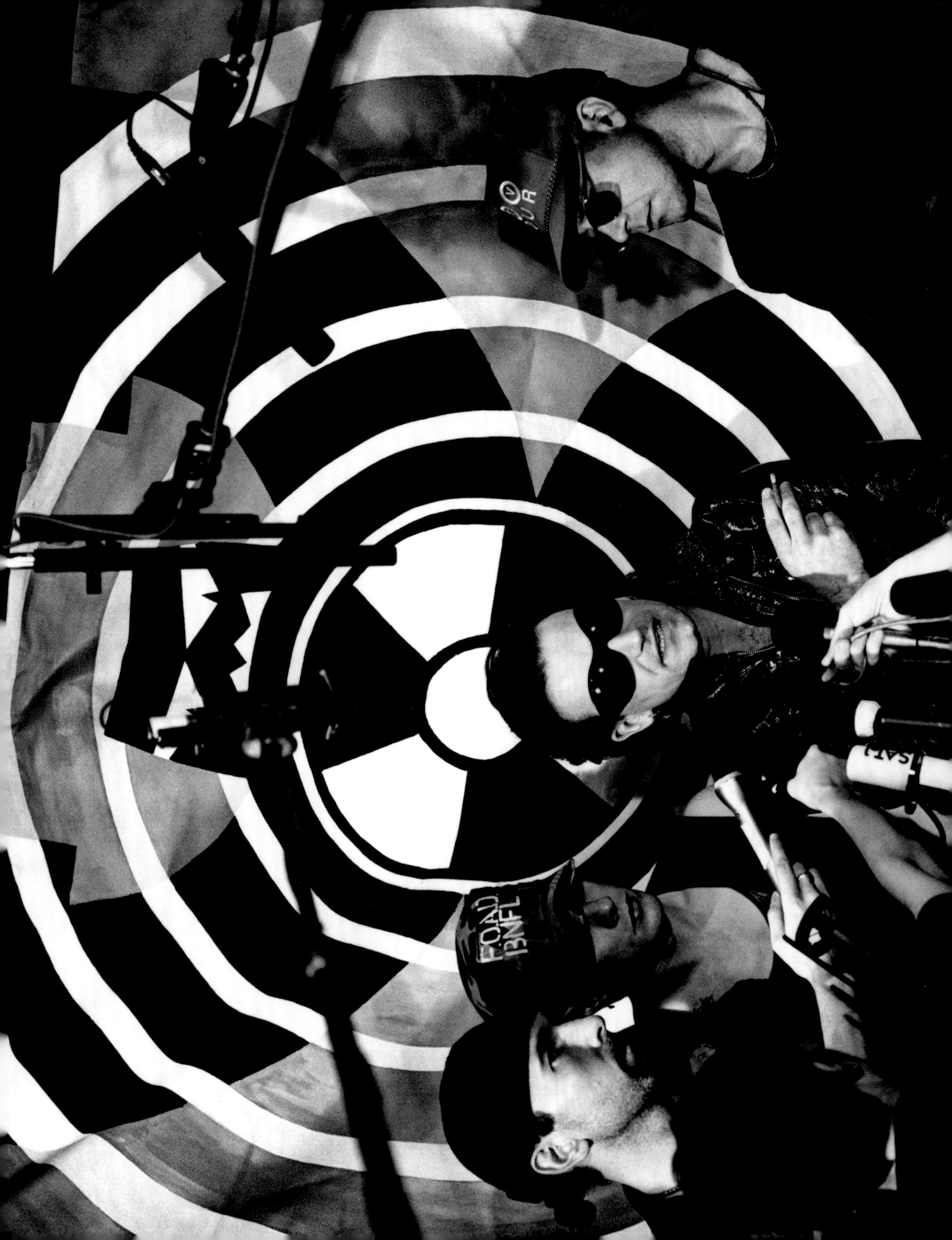

MANCHESTER 1992 june

on the 19th of june there was a concert in manchester to raise the issue of the nuclear powerplant of Sellafield, on the westcoast of England, and one that is effecting health of people as far away as Ireland.

It was a U2 show i think but it had a lot of acts on the bill. Kraftwerk played as did Public Enemy and Big Audio Dynamite!

and Lou Reed joined U2 onstage for Satellite of Love.

the photo above shows U2 doing a pressconference in front of an anti-nuclear banner.

the next spread shows paul mcguinness, instructing the band how to say 'help' with their little flags, aboard a greenpeace ship, which we boarded at night after the show and took it us overnight to the Sellafield plant.

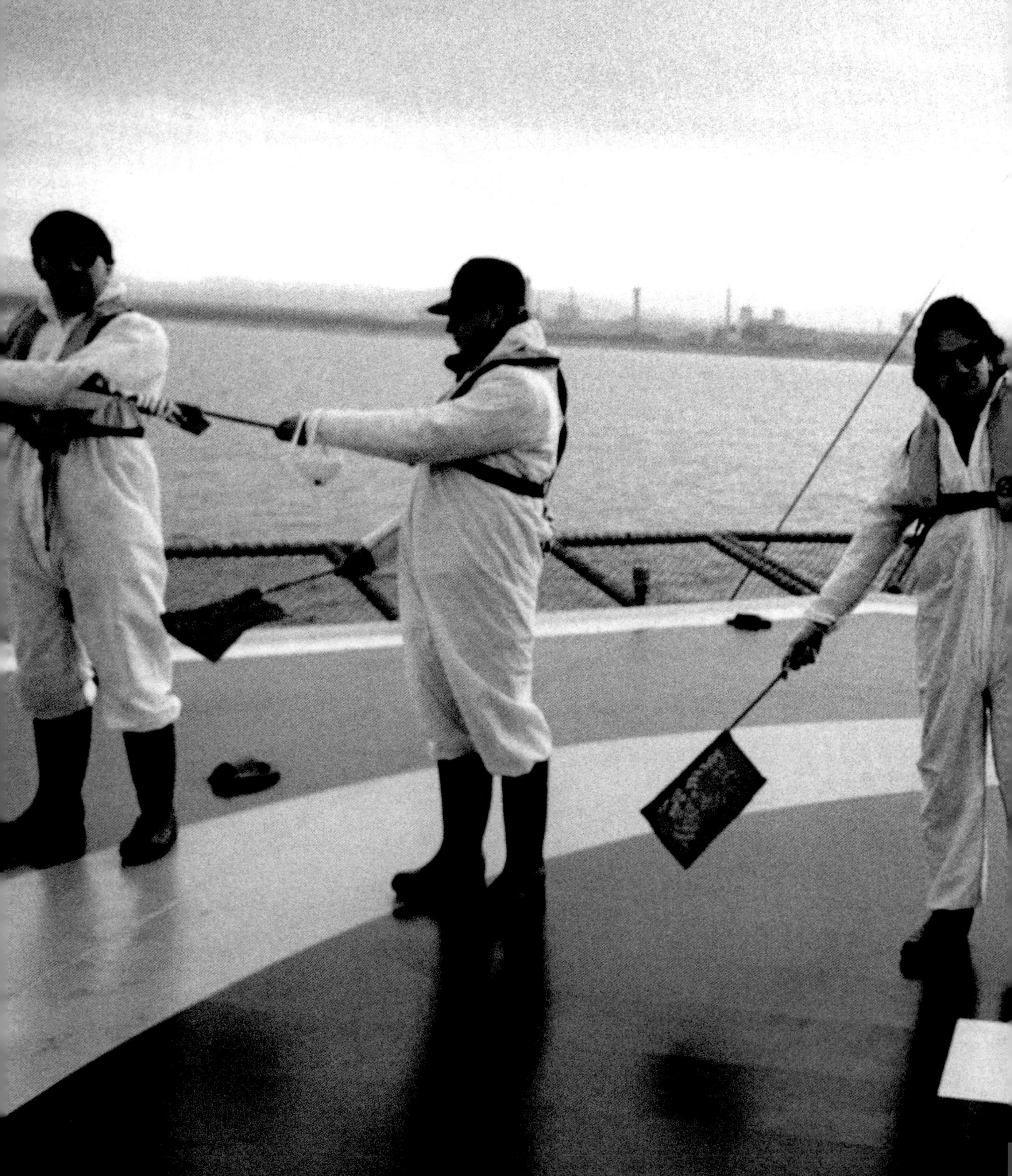

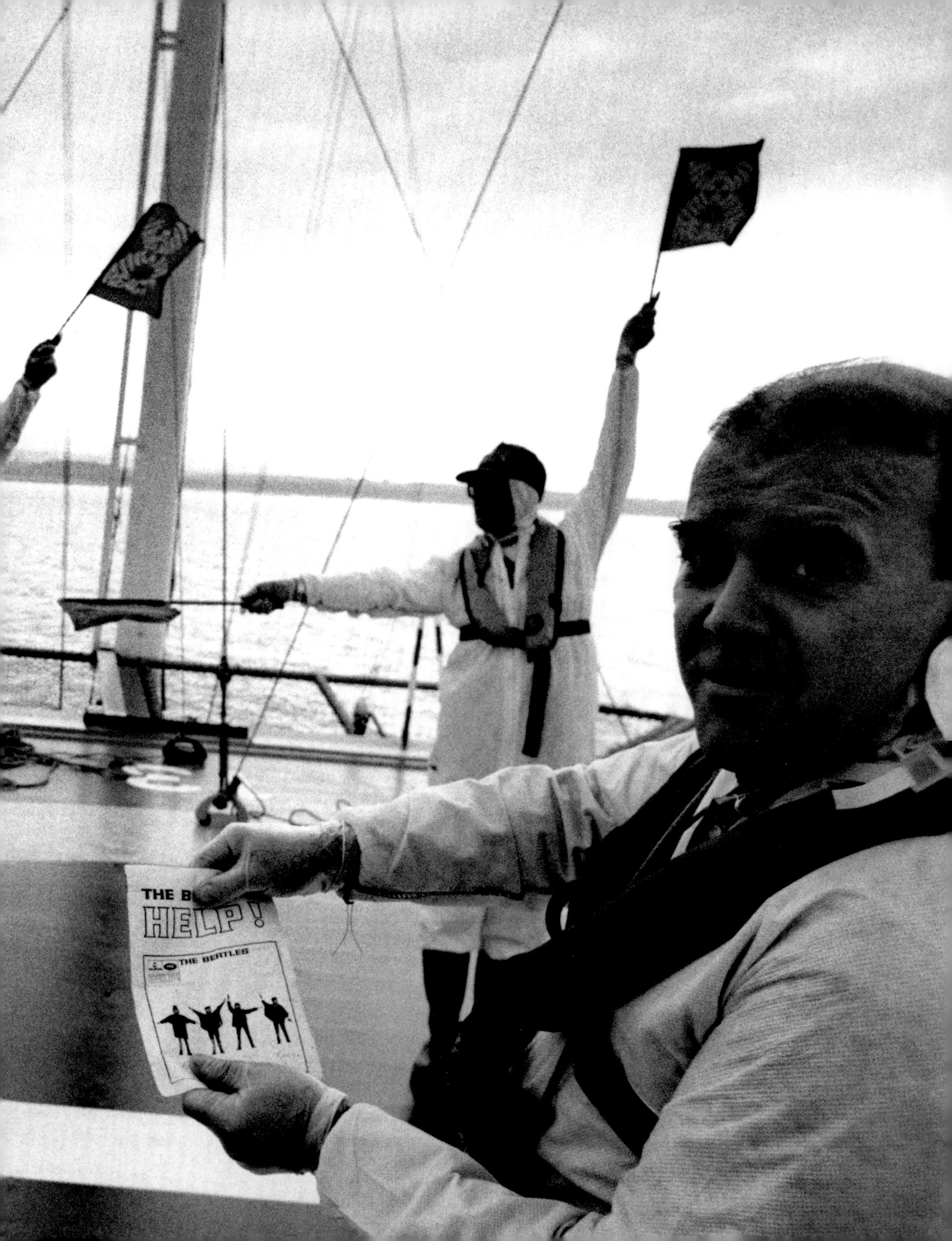
HELP!
THE BEATLES

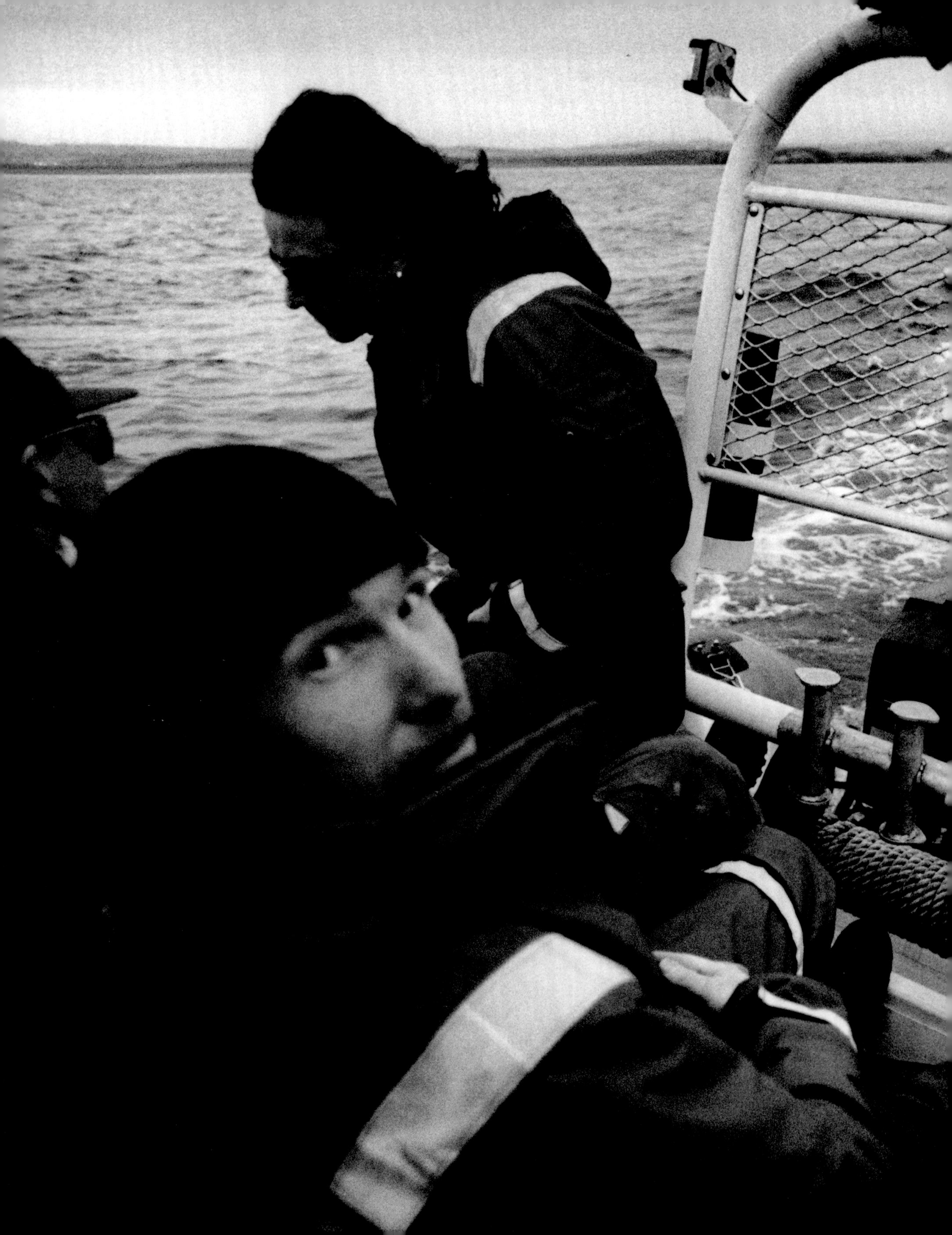

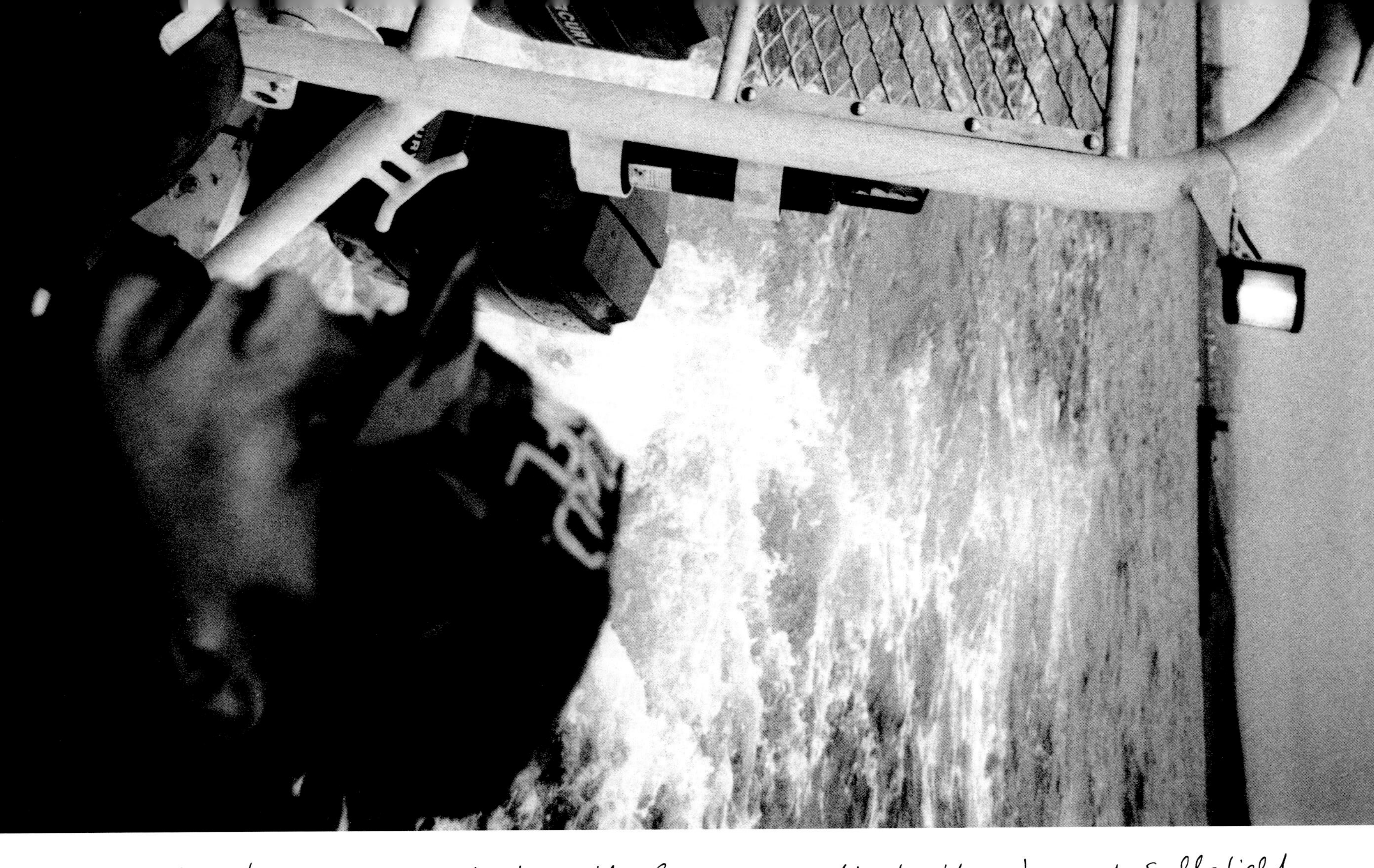

the band en route from the Greenpeace ship to the shore at Sellafield. The whole enterprise was secret of course so we would not encounter any security guards on the Sellafield waterfront.

Sellafield 1992 june 20th

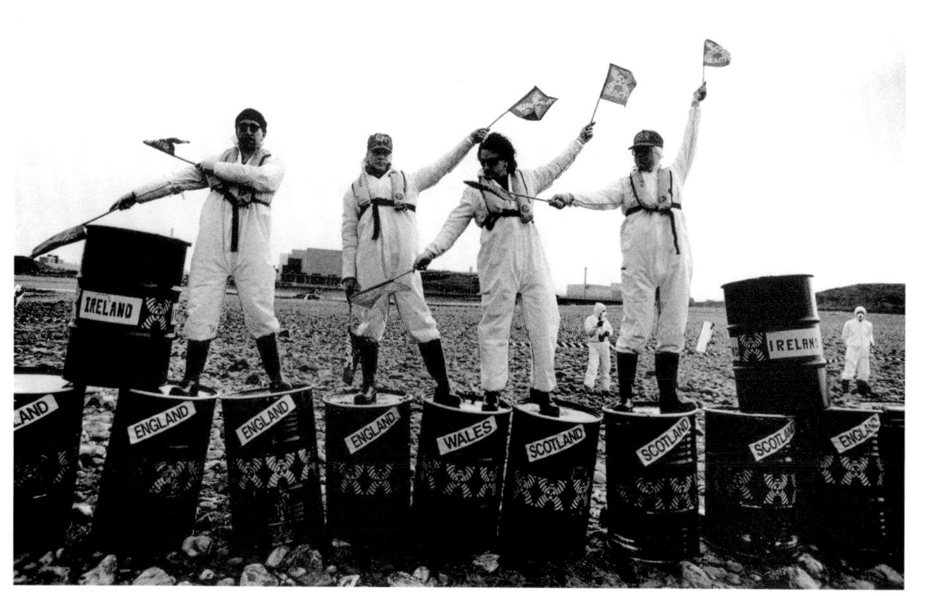

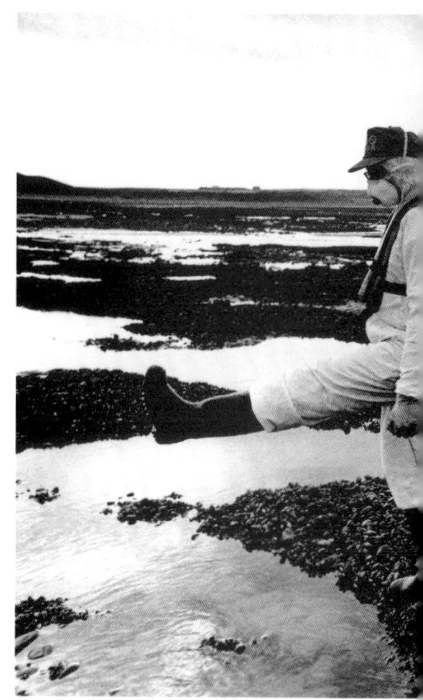

i don't think it says 'help' actually but it probably came quite close and standing on those sealed drums displaying the names of the immediate effected areas, the message came across very well.

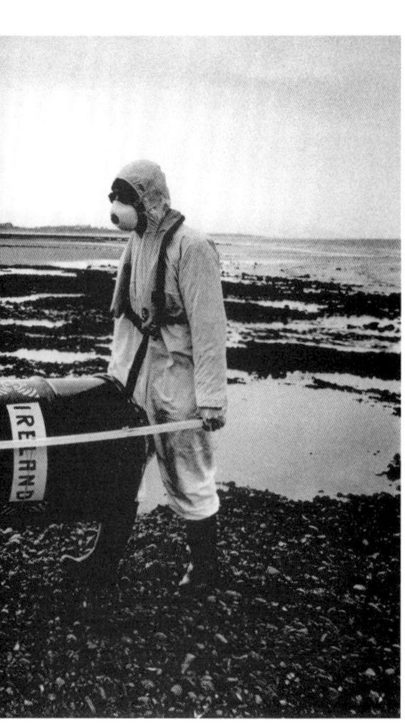

adam and edge

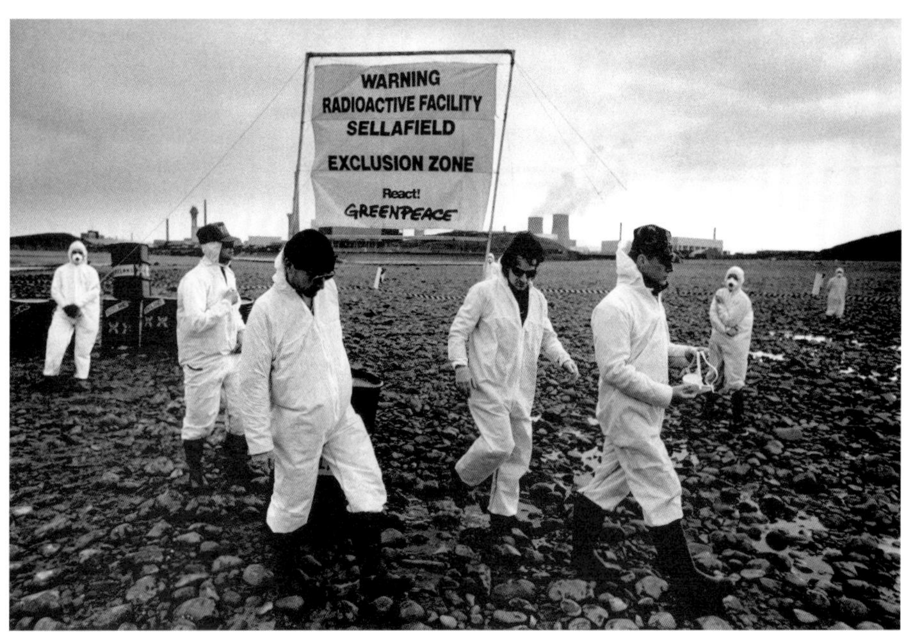

around 8 am we all go to the hotel to get some sleep.

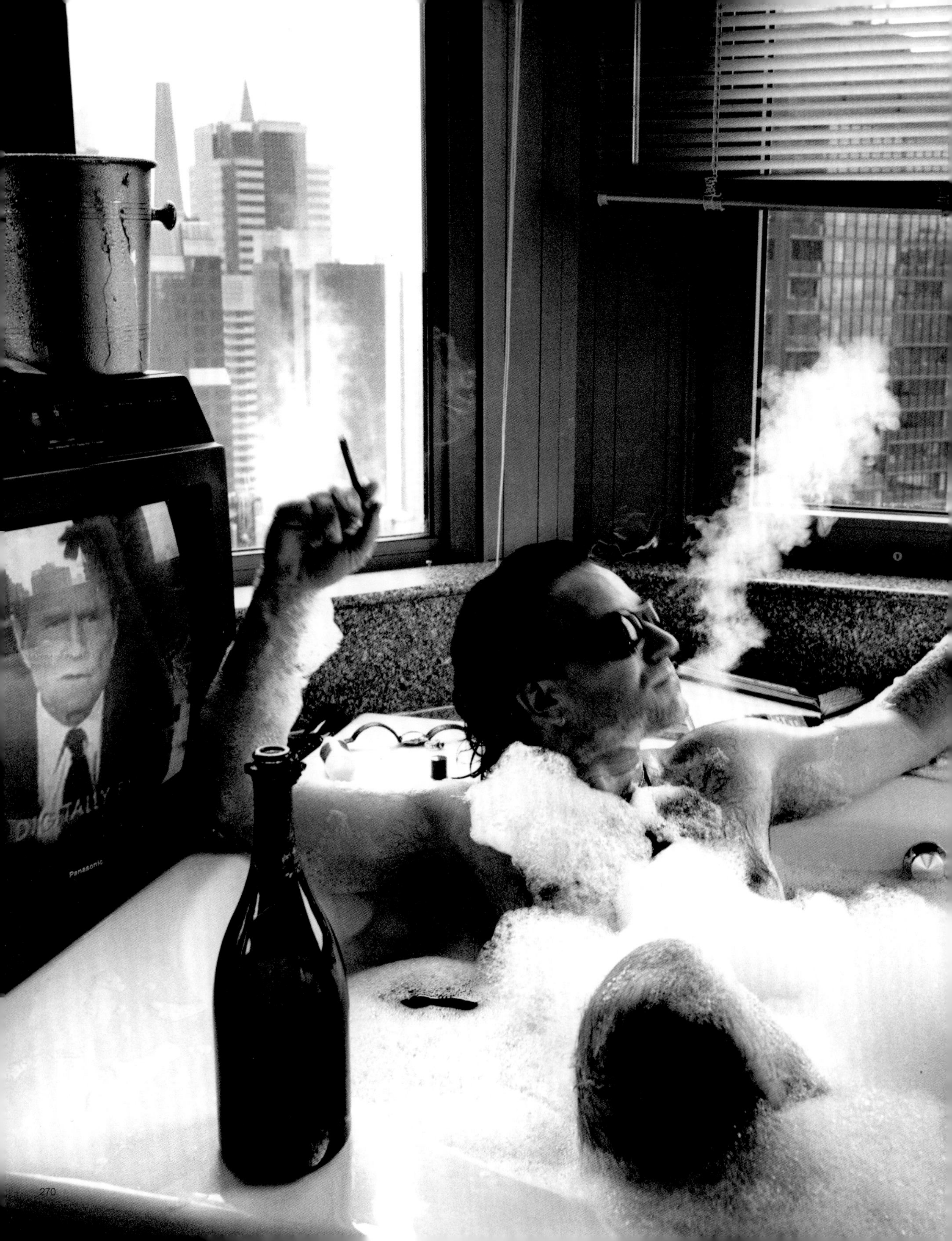
Panasonic

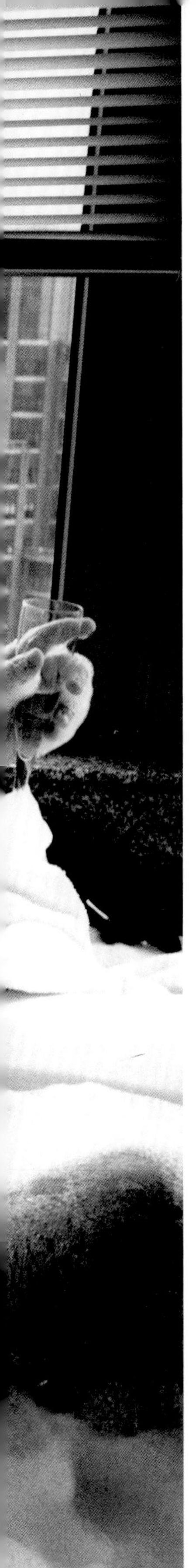

NEW YORK 1992

for some reason bono always ends up with the biggest hotelrooms, and when we were in new york he had this great idea to do something with the bathroom in his room. he wanted to create a persiflage of the ultimate rockstar's lifestyle, ignorant of the world's problems or the man on the street. the view, the champagne, a videotape of Bush SR., a cigarillo and bubbles was all we needed to surround bono with to get this result. fyi, it was just him and me in there.

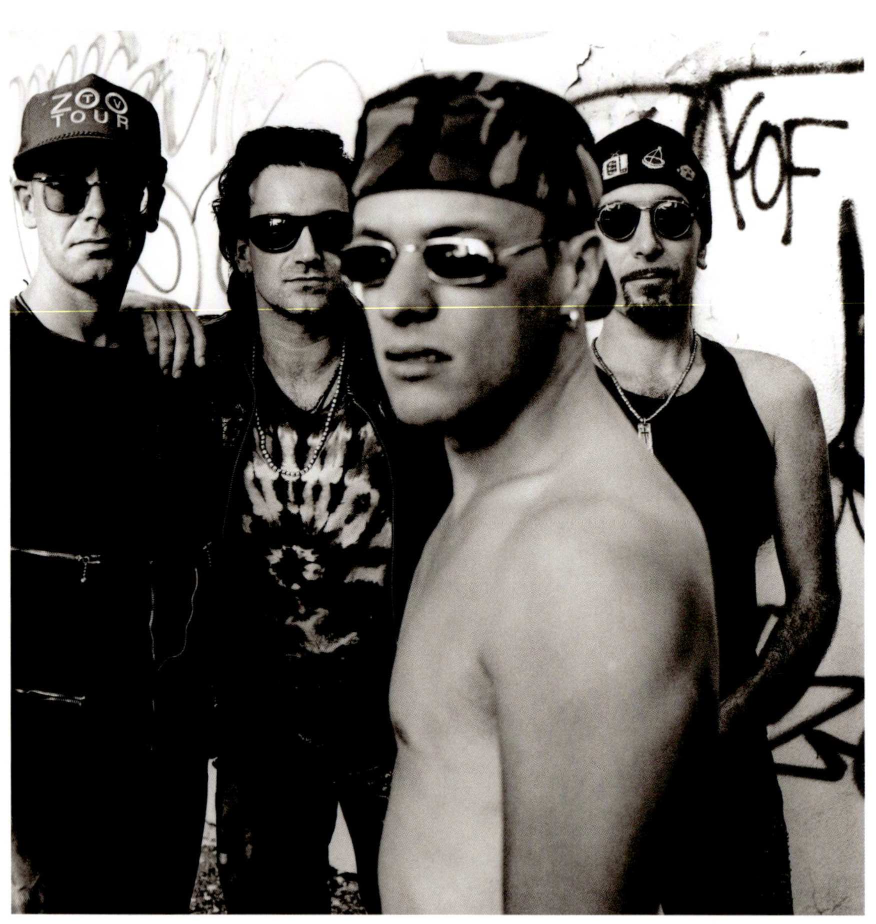

over the next few pages some photos we did for press around harlem

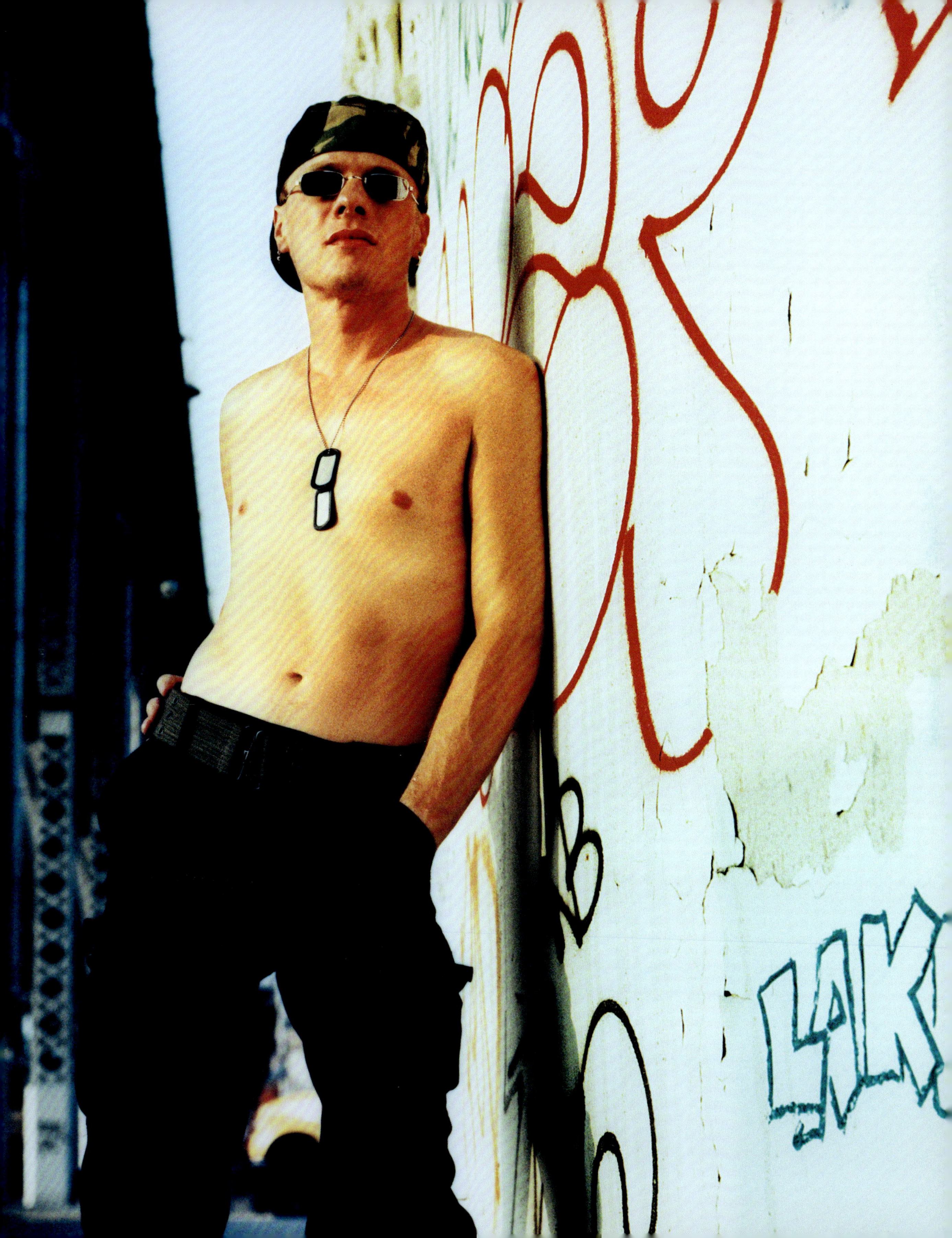

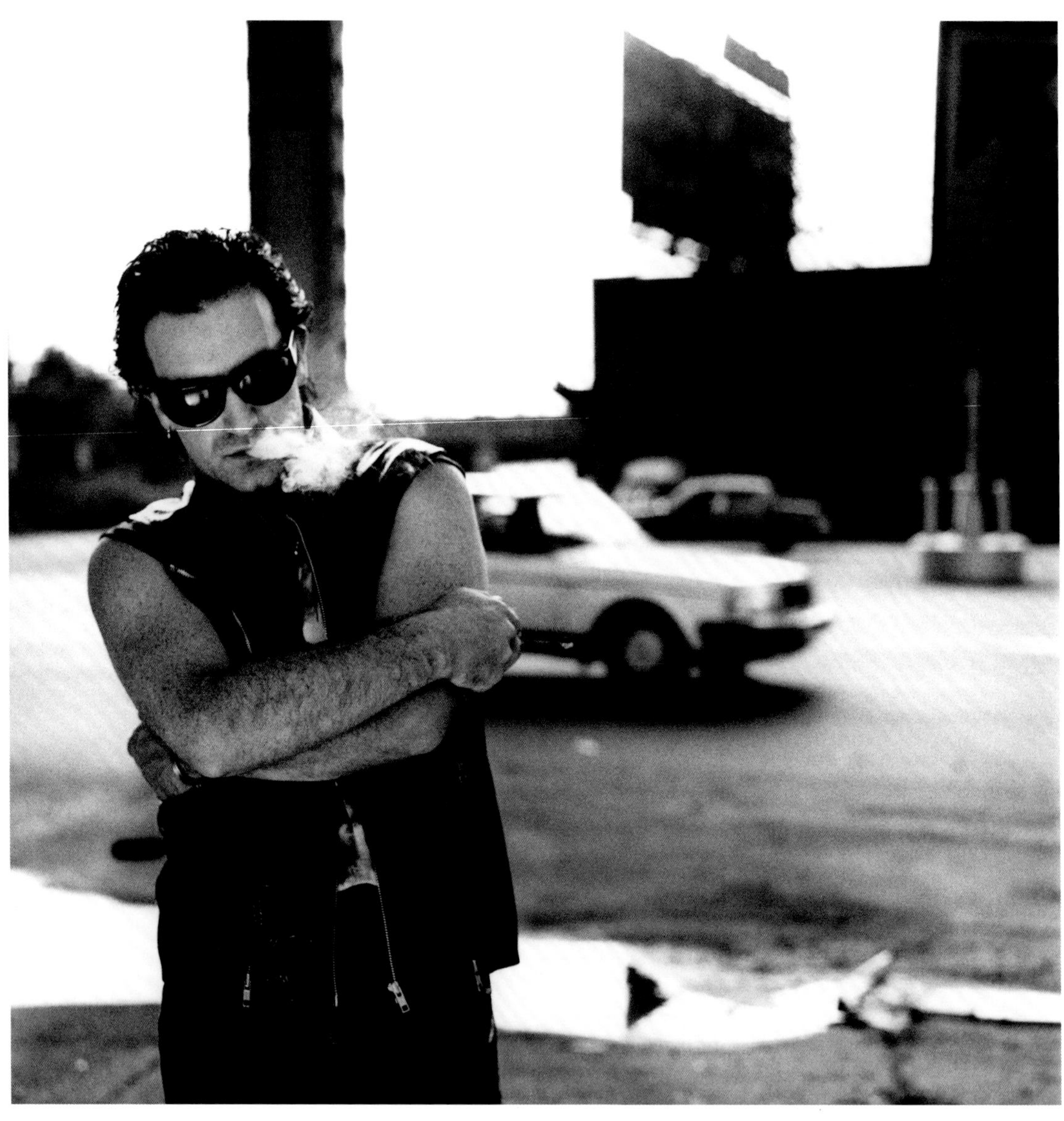

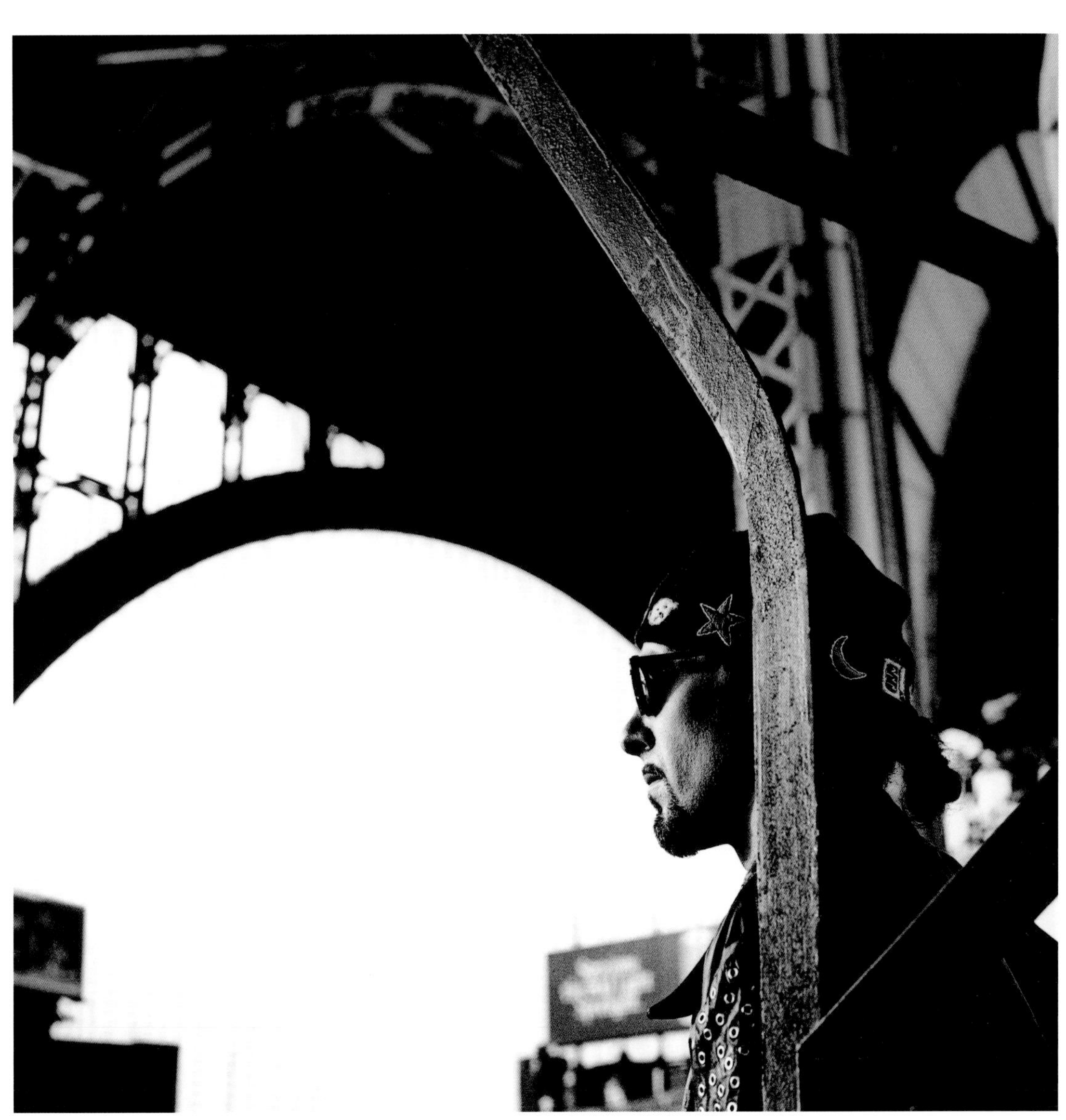

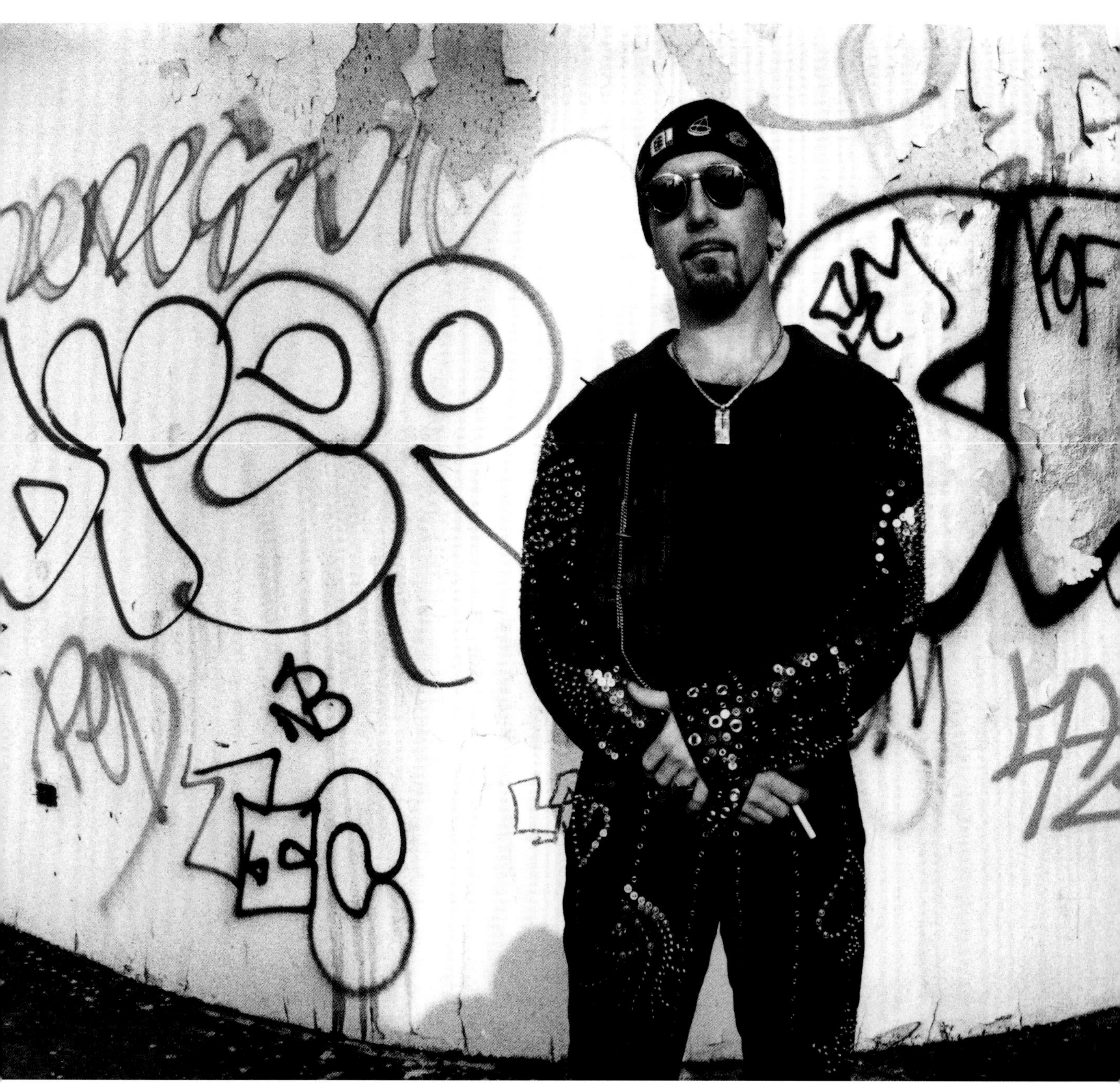

for the first time since the Joshua Tree, i used a panoramic camera again for U2. slightly more in focus on this occasion, but i made an exception on the next spread.

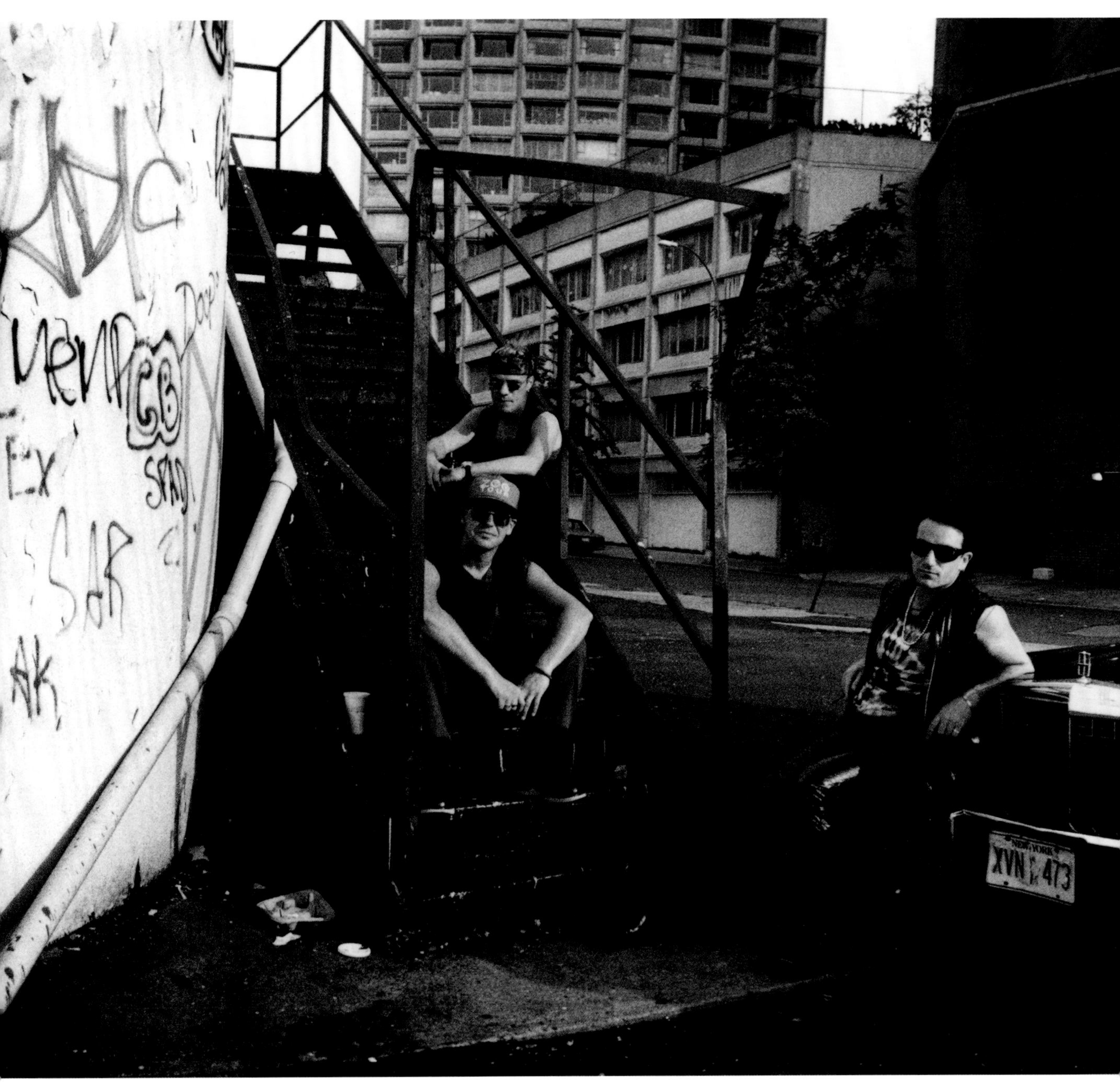
NEW YORK

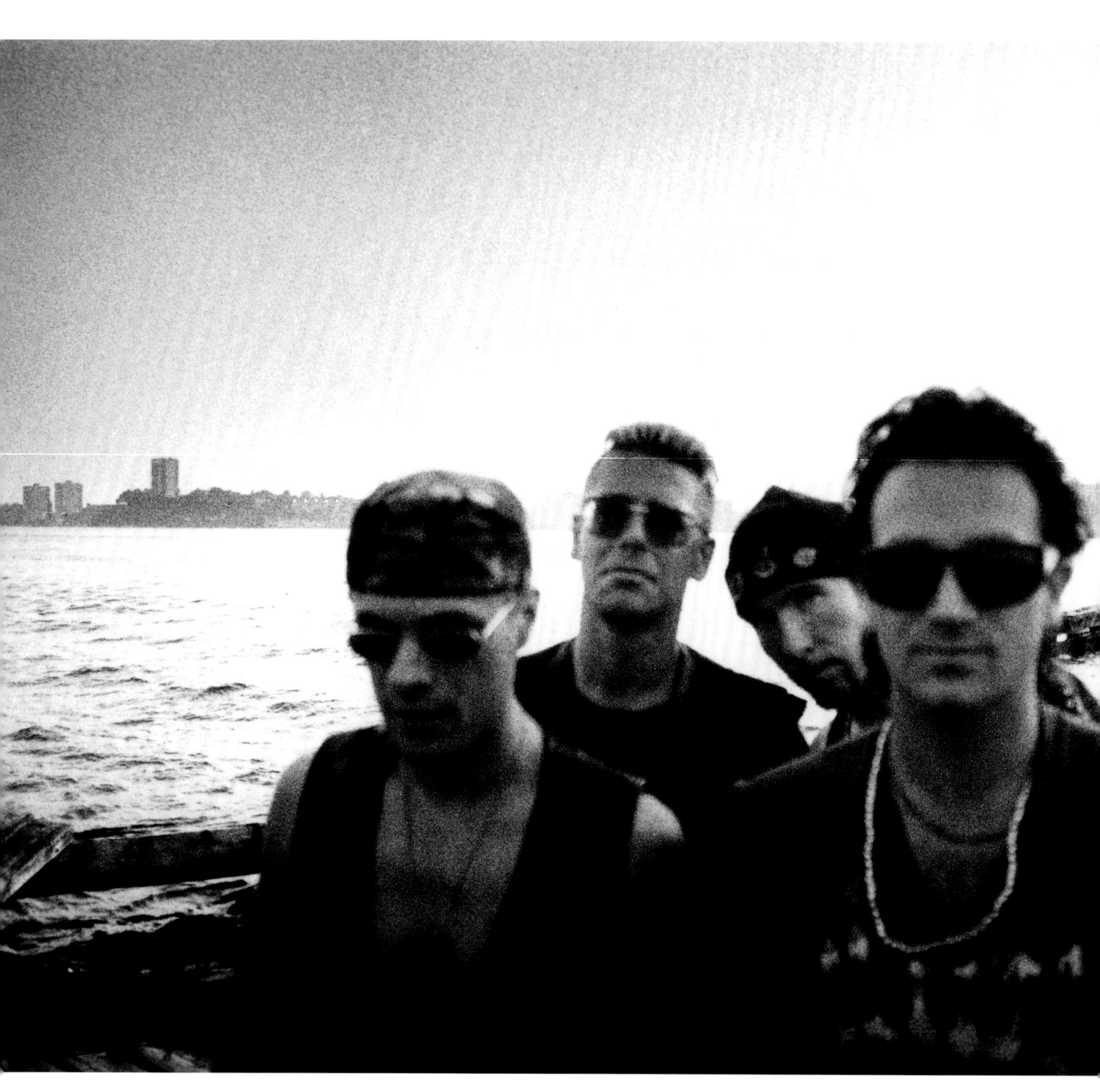

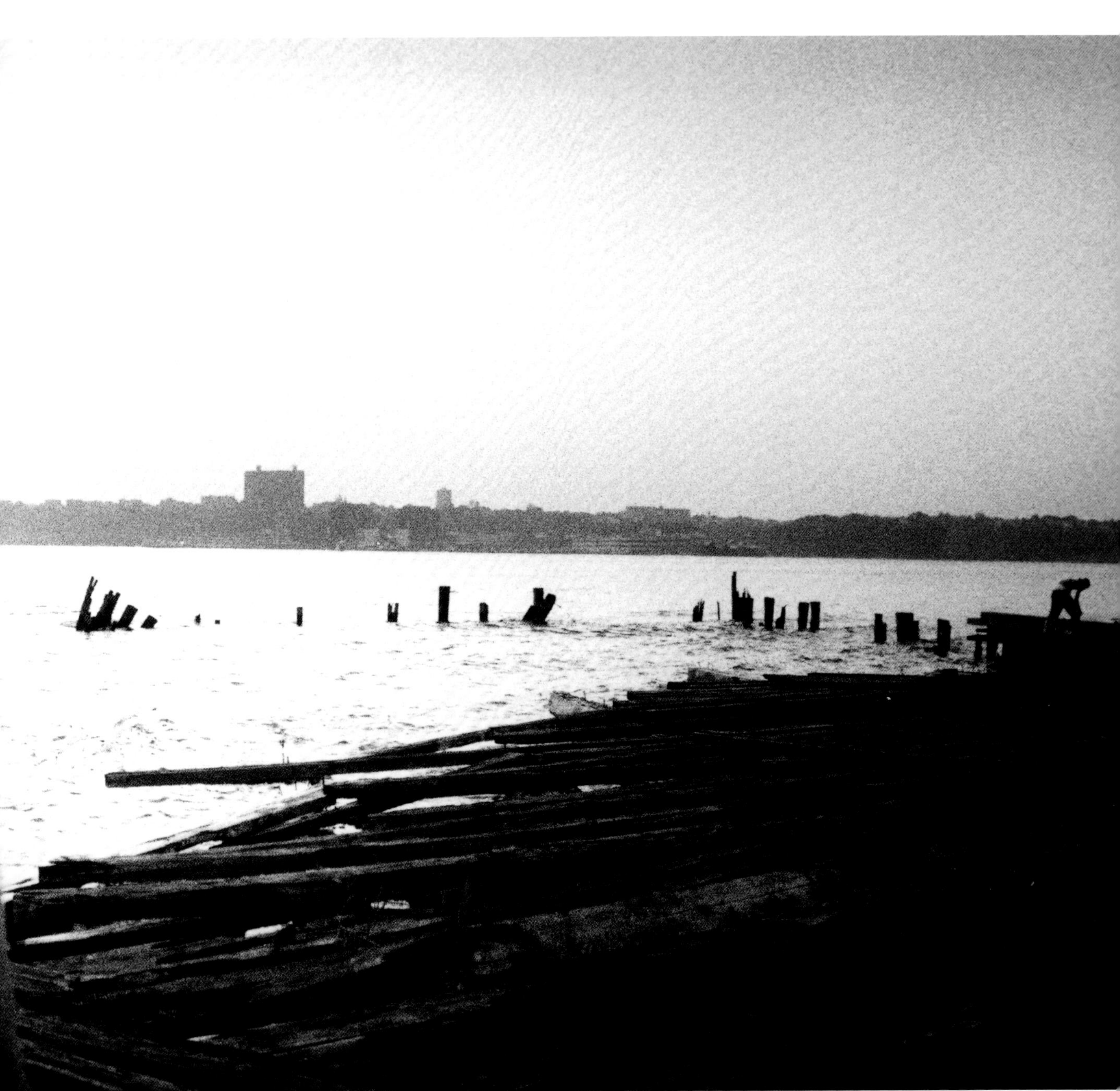

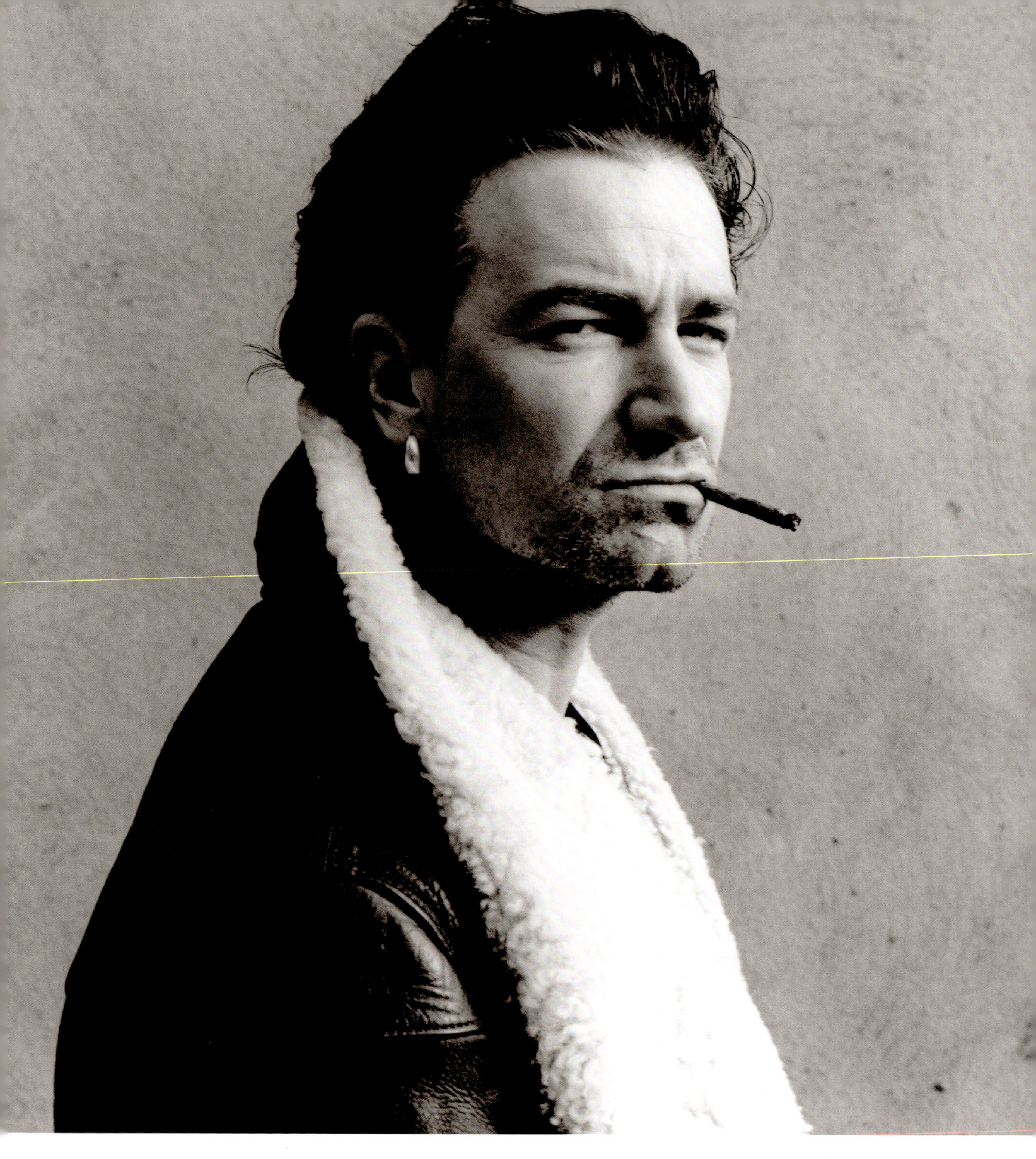

DUBLIN 1993 march

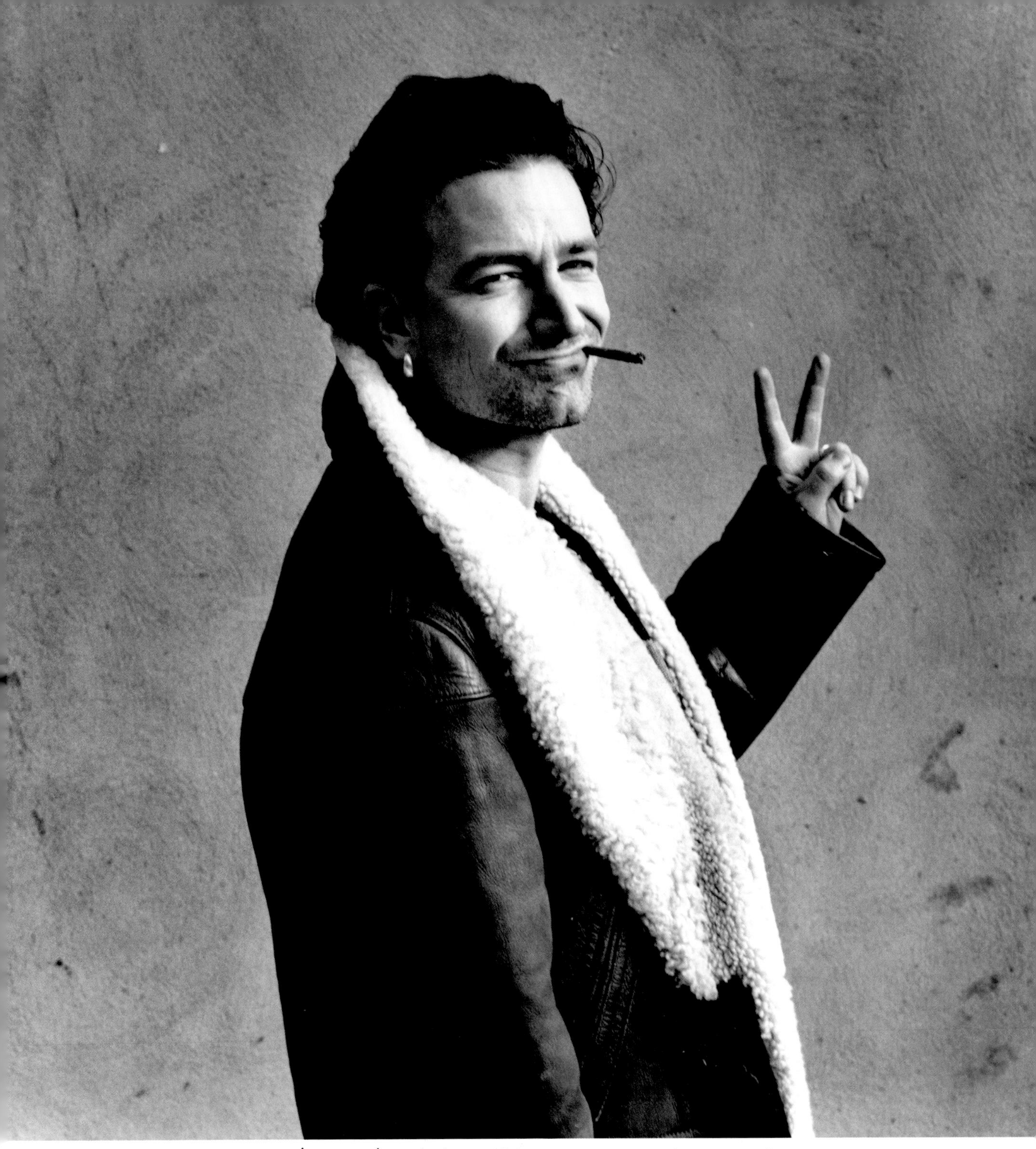

as i remember it, bono had forgotten i was coming over to photograph him for Details magazine. I went to his home and discovered him by himself as the rest of the family had gone away for a couple of days. I don't think he had had a lot of sleep.

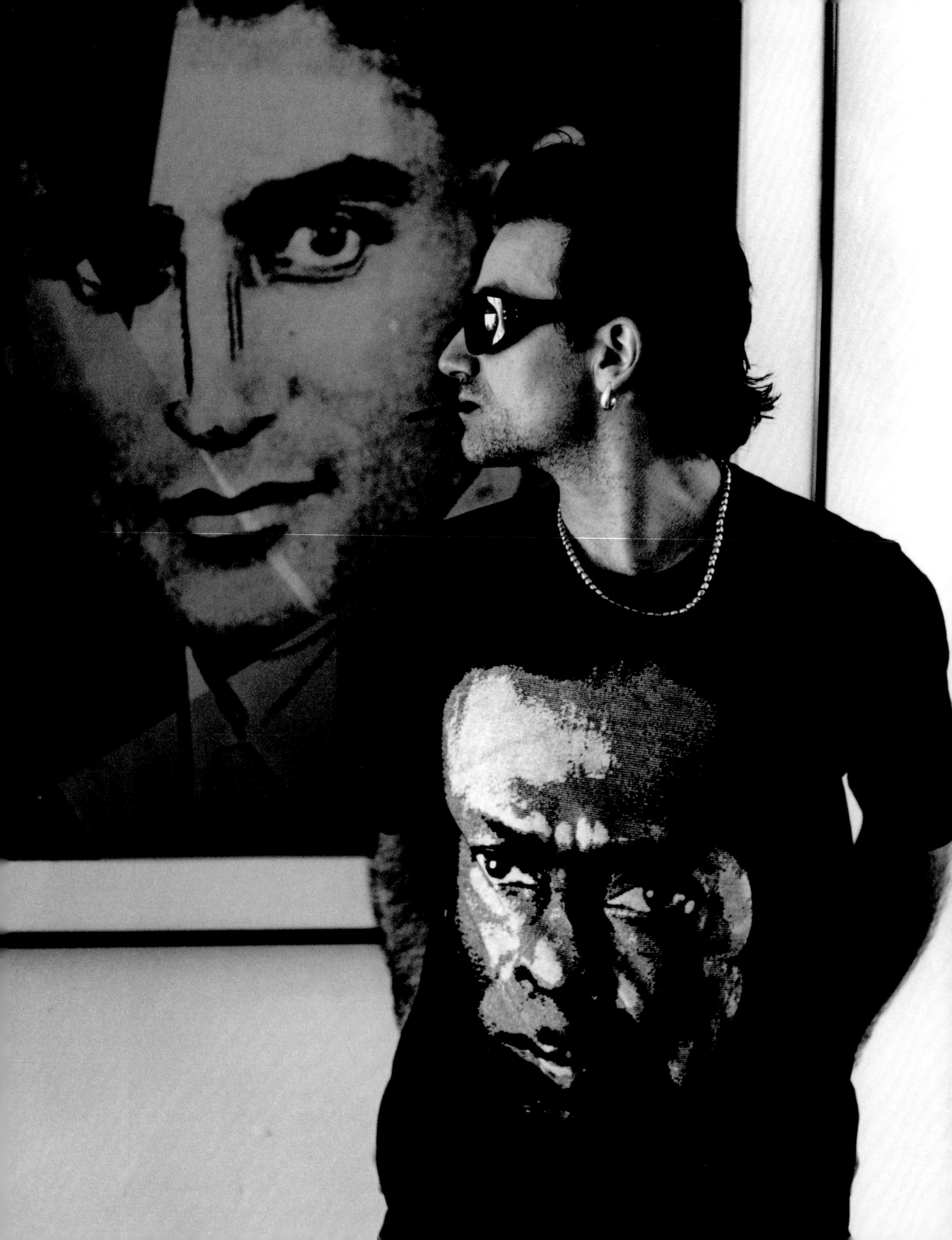

he photo of the three faces - kafka, miles and bono - is one that is nearly 3 dimensional.

this is bono throwing a few shapes for the camera in a spare bedroom

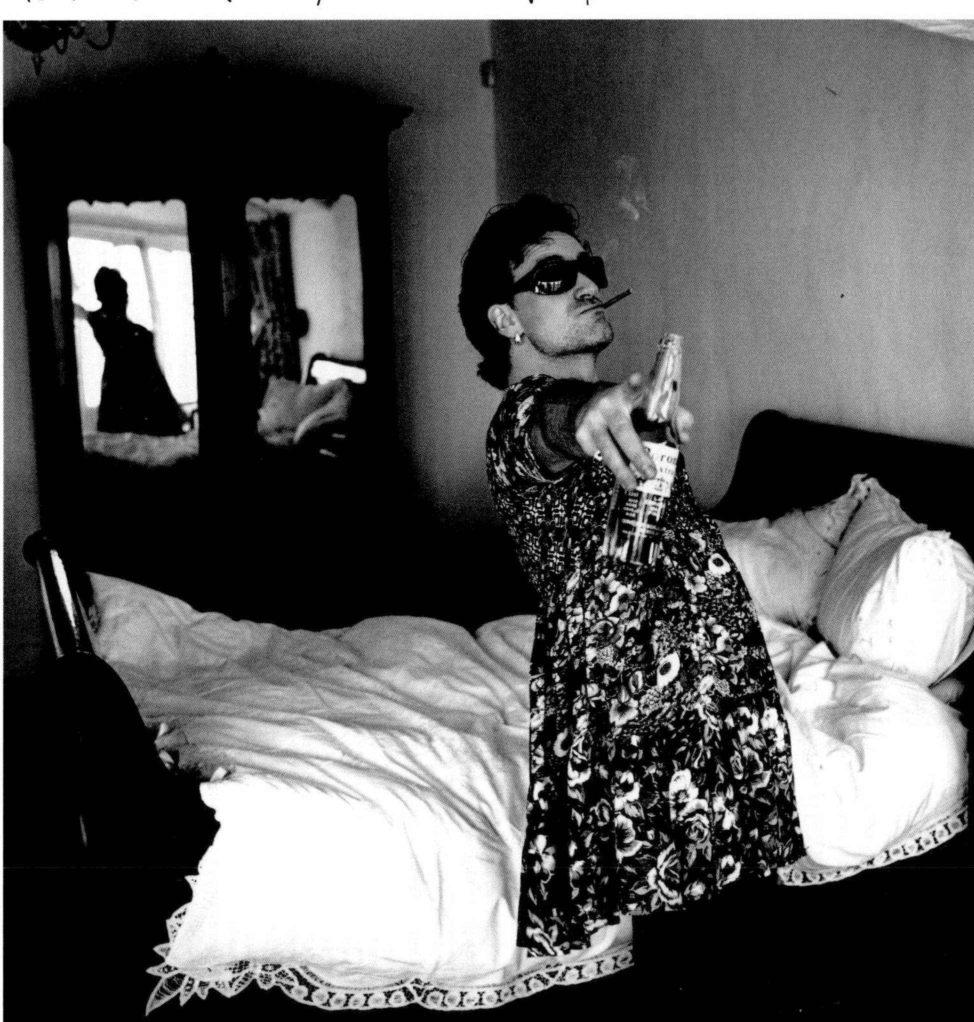

sleep or no sleep, he is such an entertainer. can't help himself.

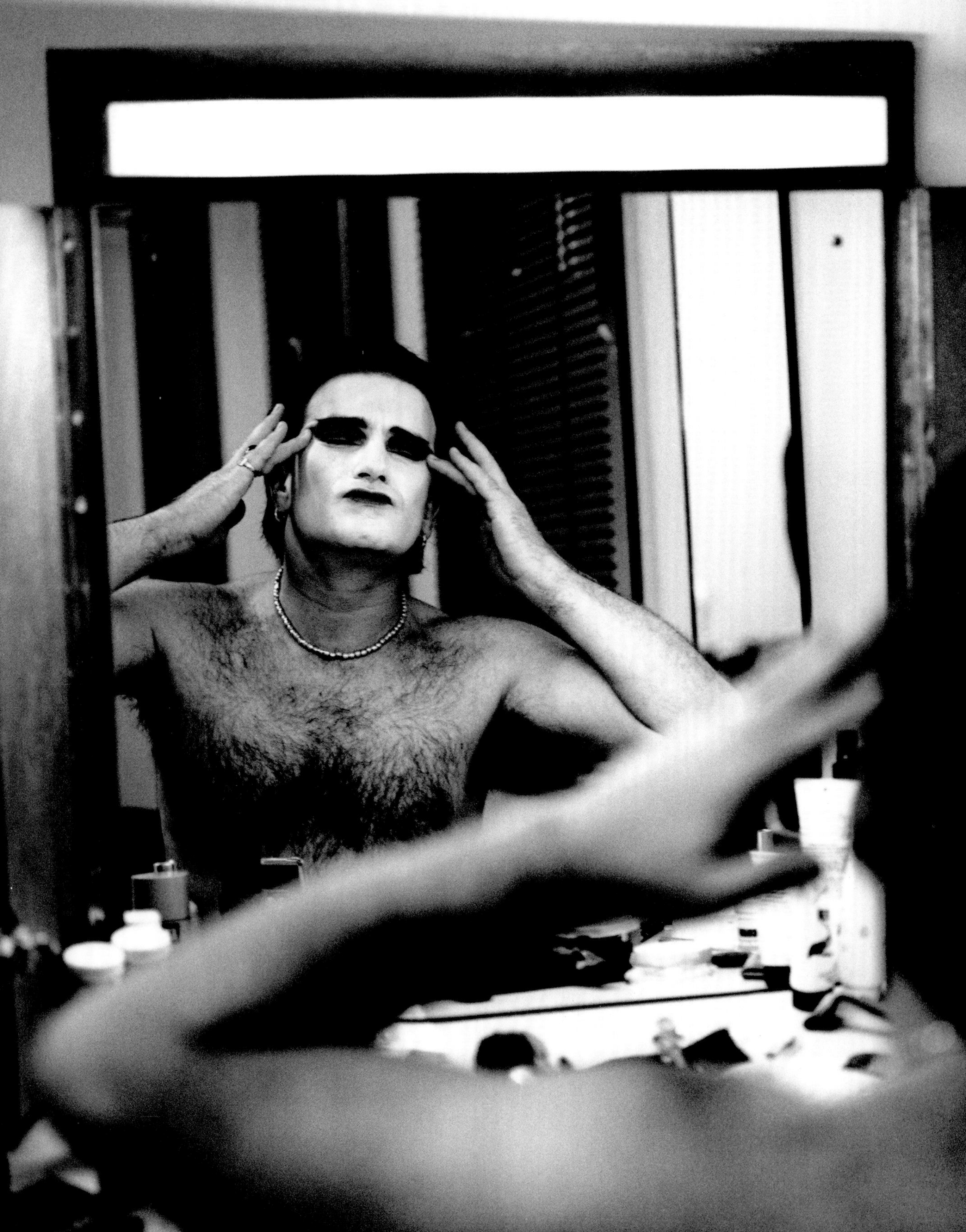

LONDON 1993

august

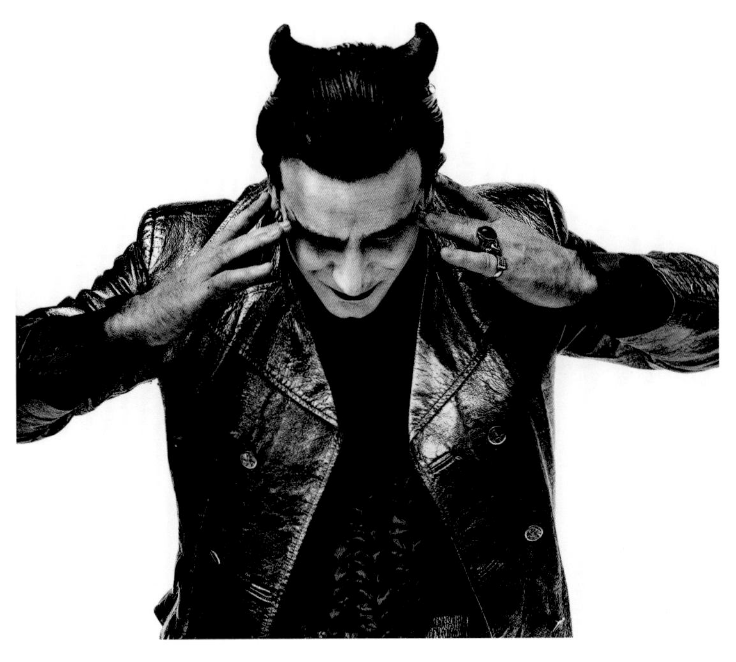

these are some stills i took during the making of the 'LEMON' video, which featured bono in the macphisto character.

although it was a very successful look for bono in terms of publicity, it wasn't one of my favorite ones. it photographs really well i have to admit.

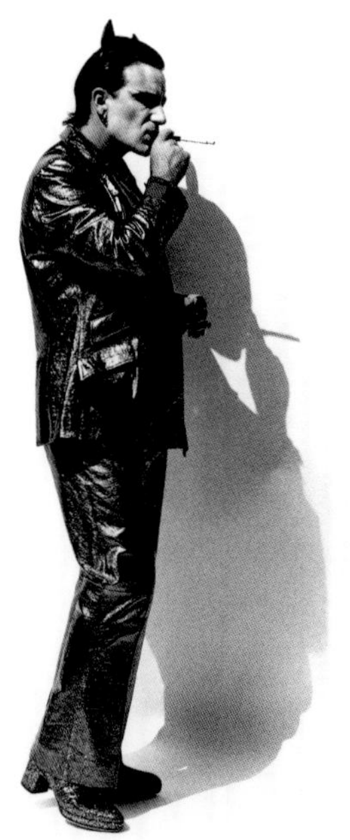

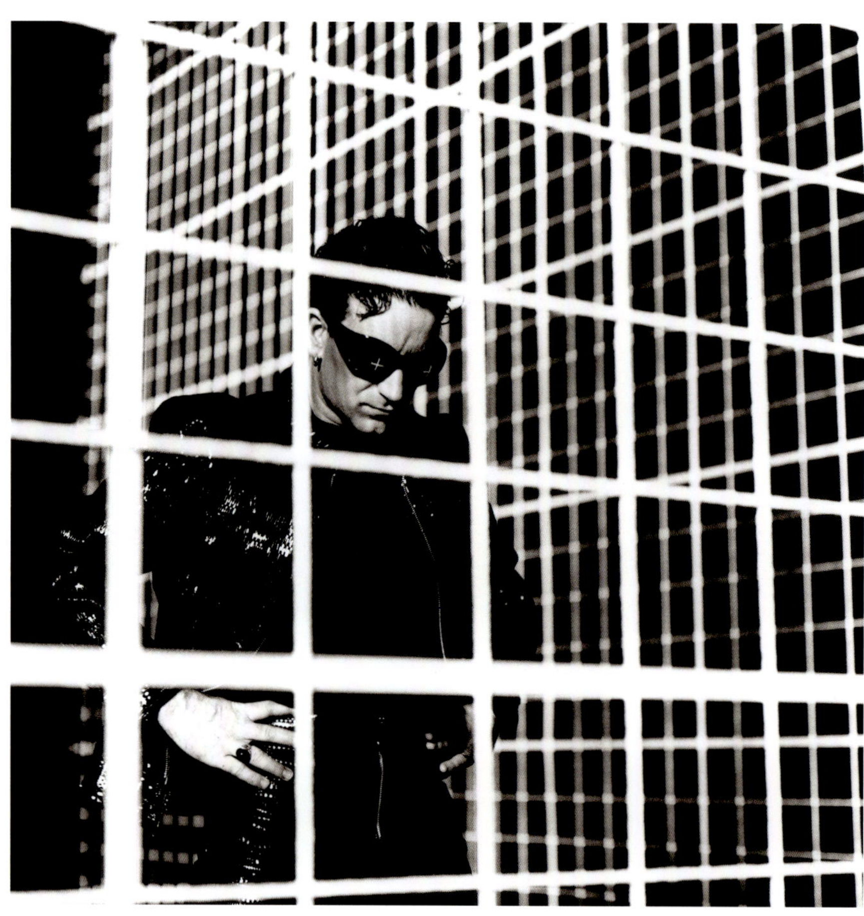

part of the video was based on muybridge photos
showing human locomotion.

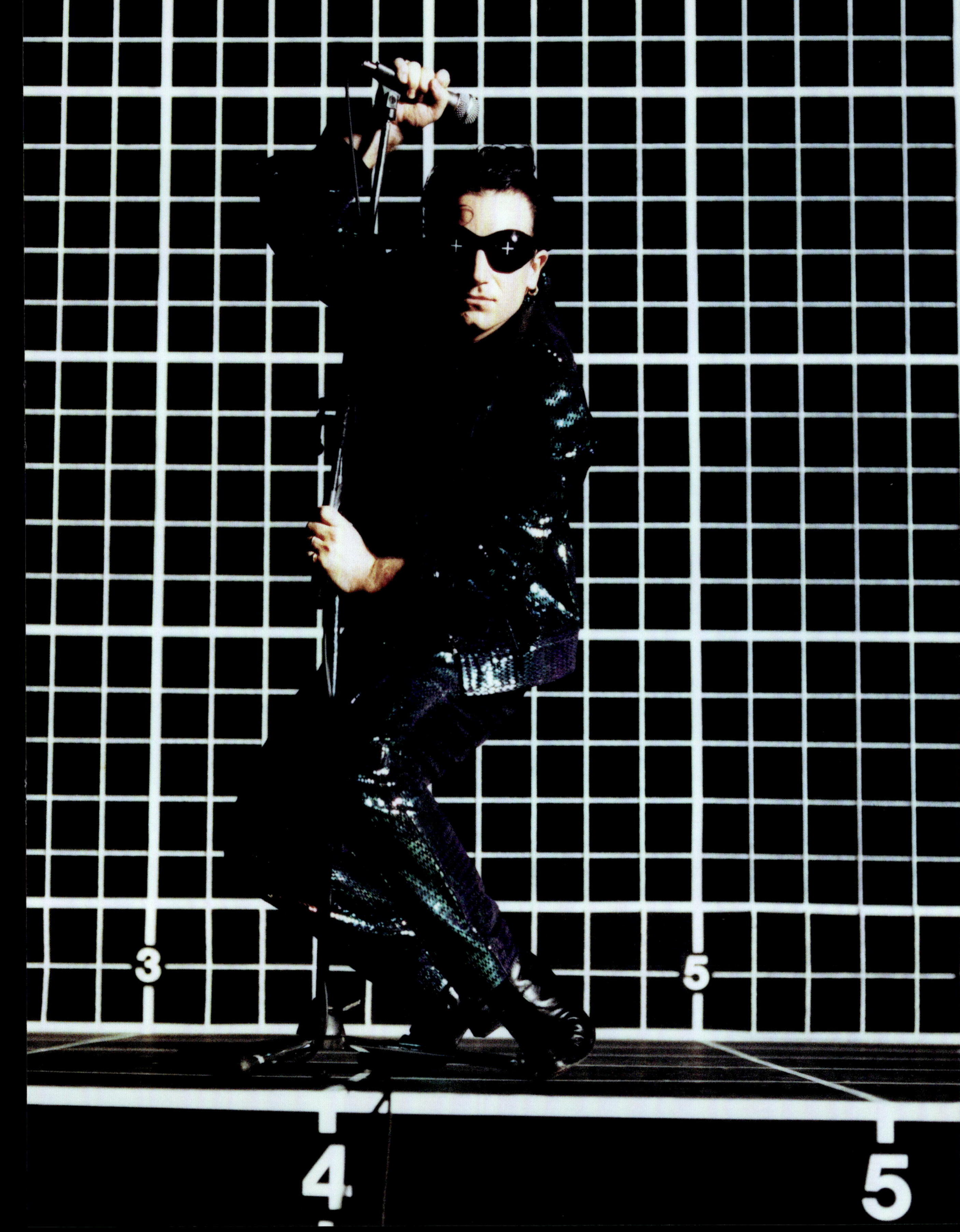
3
5
4
5

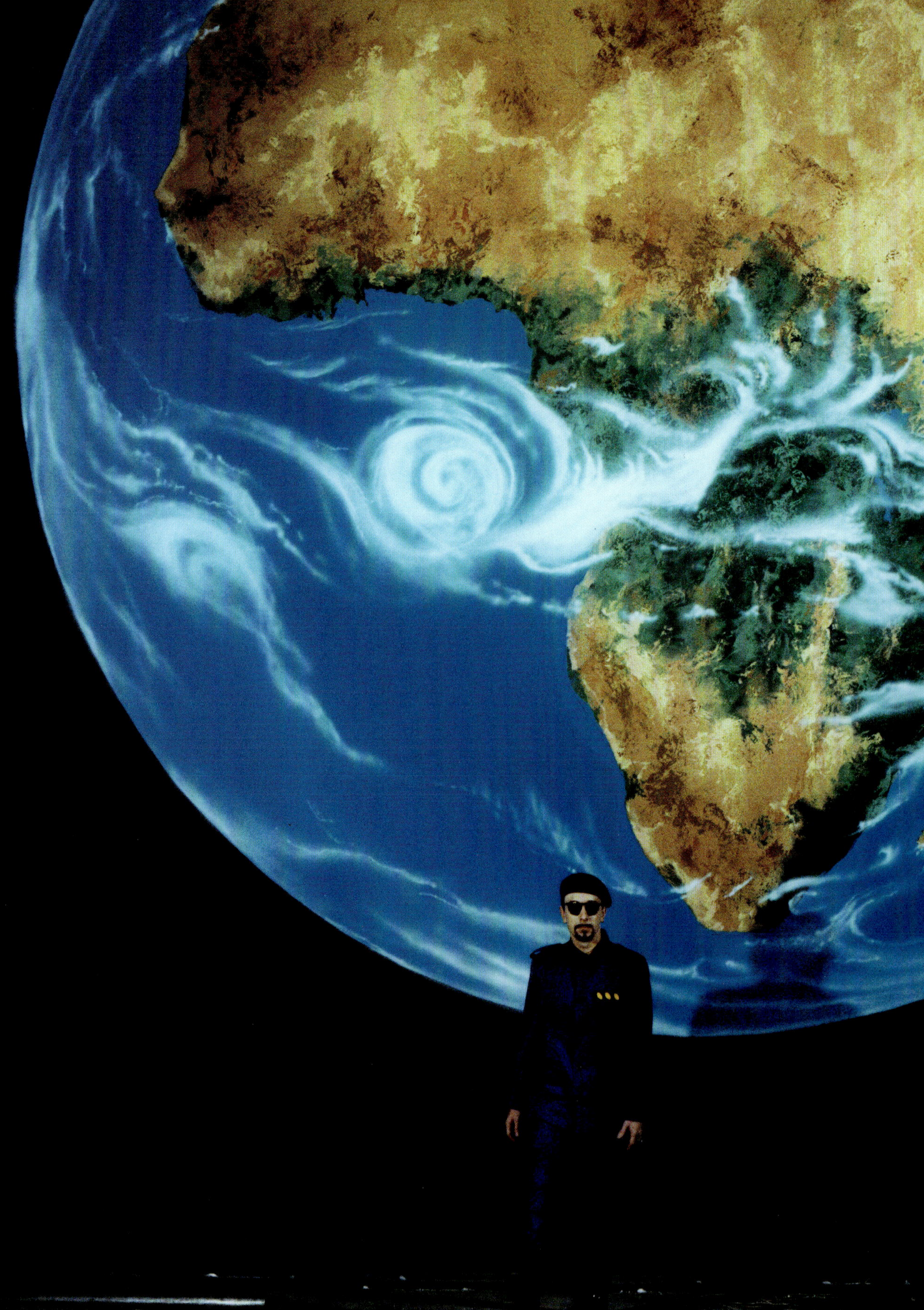

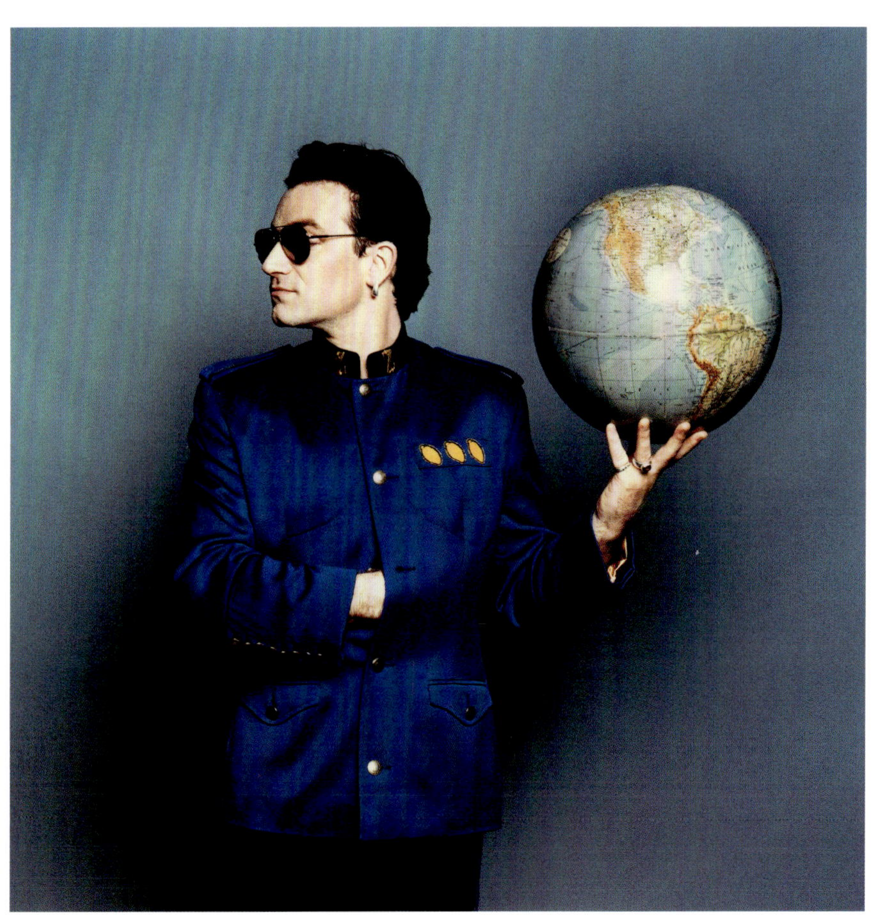

note the lemons on the jackets

contrary to what you might read elsewhere,
the globes in these photos are models, not lifesize ones.
small scale

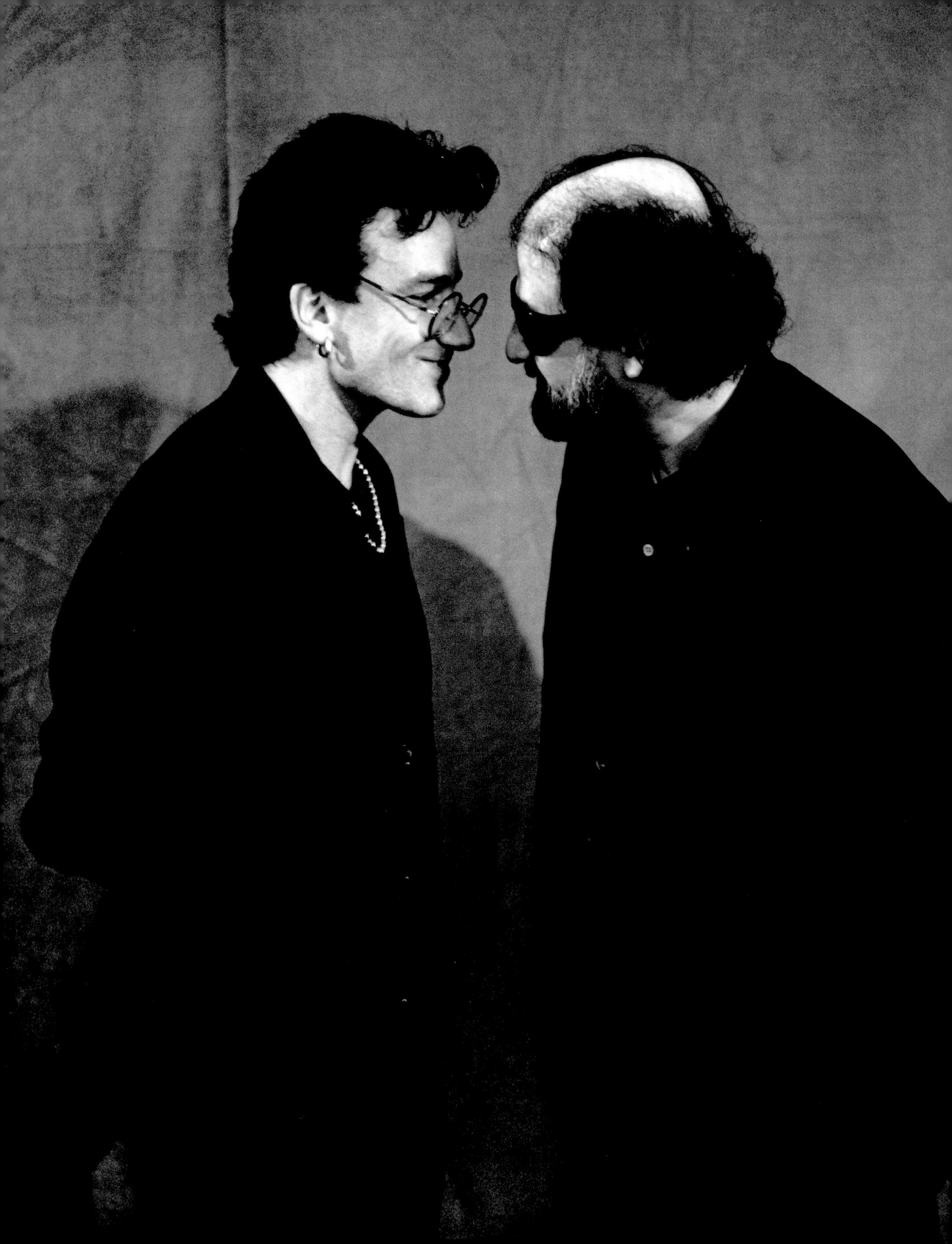

LONDON 1993

august

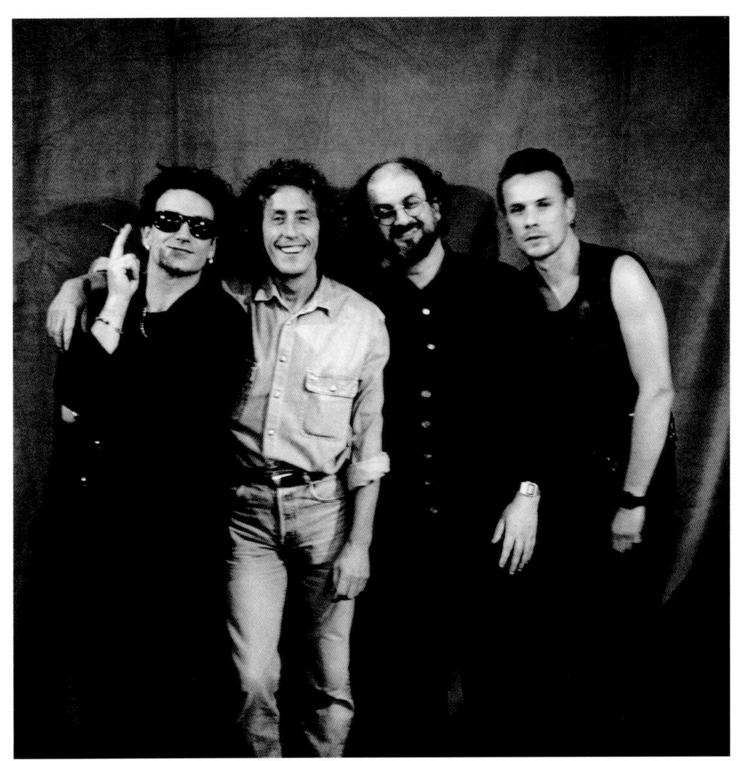

backstage after the concert at Wembley Stadium which saw Salman Rushdie on stage with U2. the photo on the left (the glasses) shows again bono's trick of swapping clothing items for a photograph. what i like about the photo is the similarities of their postures with their arms behind them and the graphically interesting heads with opposite parts of light and dark. Above a typical posing backstage photo with from left to right bono, roger daltrey, salman rushdie and larry.

PALM SPRINGS 1993

november

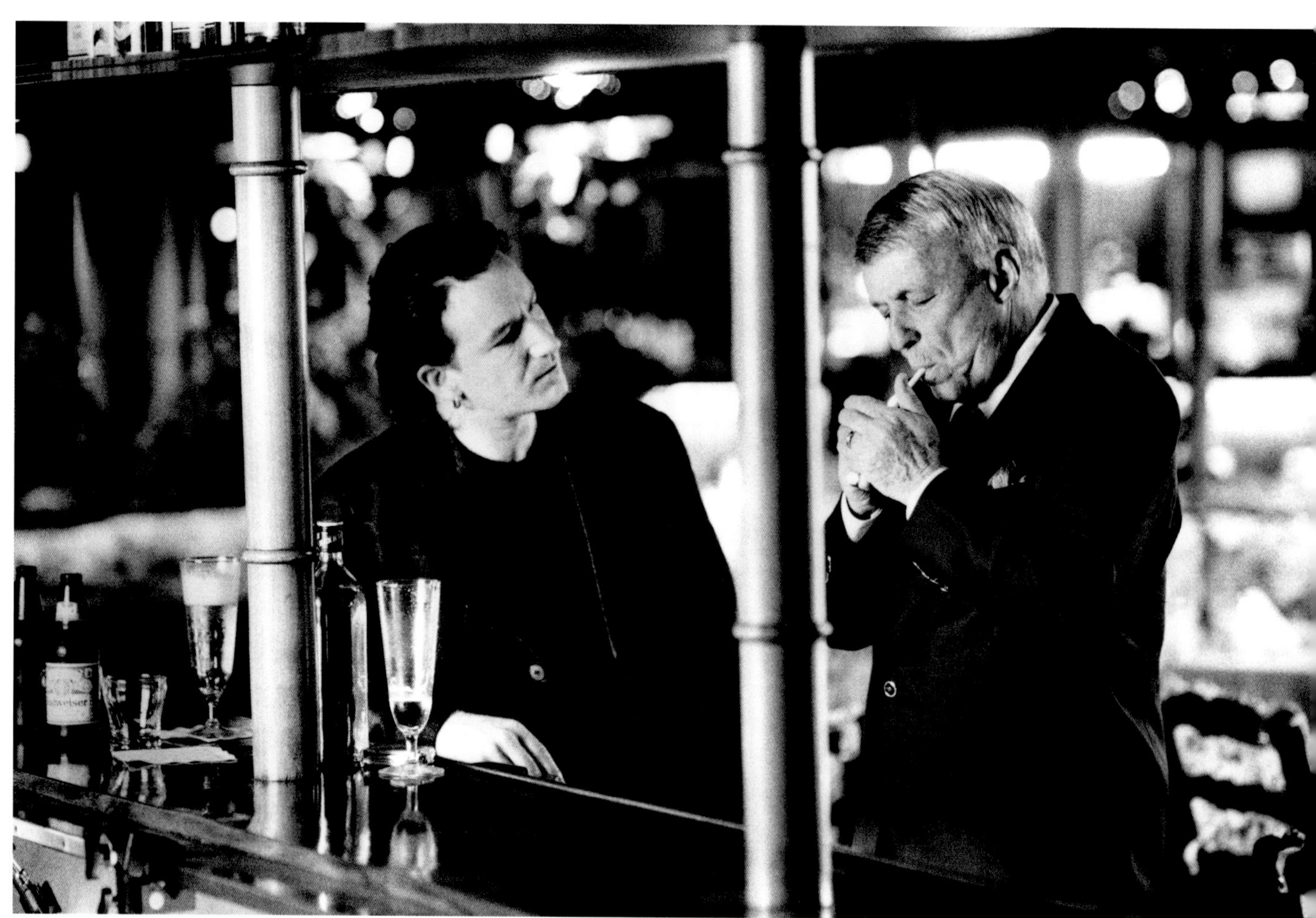

these photos are actually stills of a video that never materialized. it was for a duet bono had done with frank sinatra and the idea for the video was for frank to sit at a bar, bono enters and gives him a present (a bottle of something) they sit together and at some point go to a table and eat.

the idea never made it past the bar and then frank left and invited bono to his own place. can't blame him.

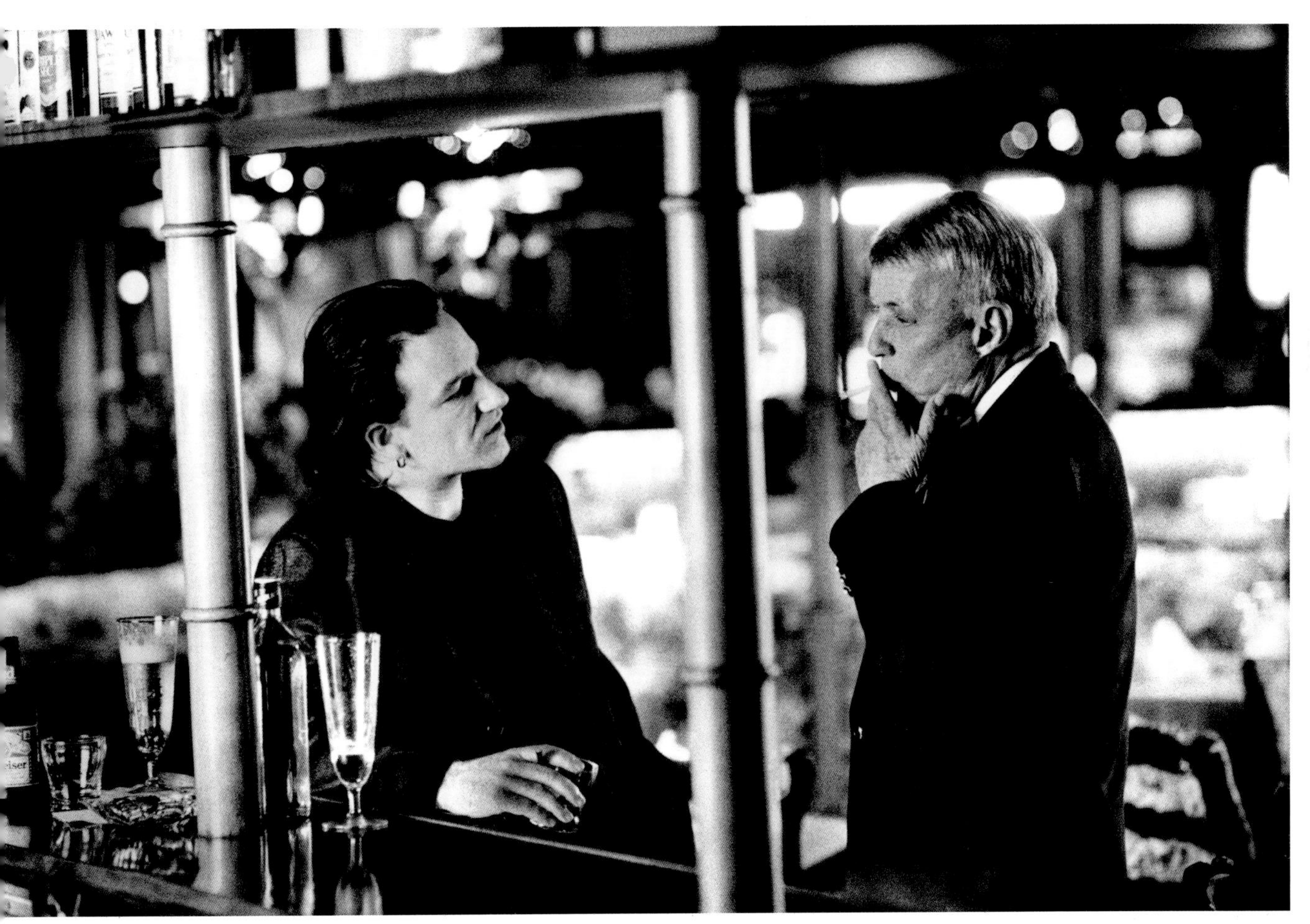

TOKYO 1993

december

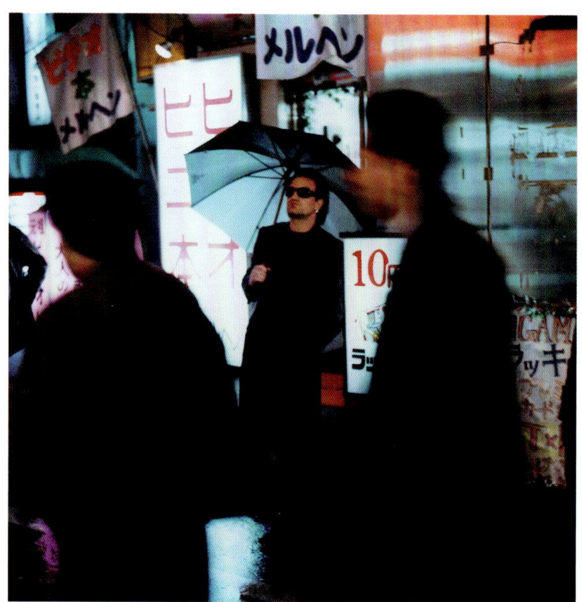

the zooTV tour finished its run in december in Tokyo and we walked around a bit to get some photos in the streets. Noodlehouses, neonlights, rain, umbrellas, massageparlours – it was all good to my eyes. The low tech vibe.

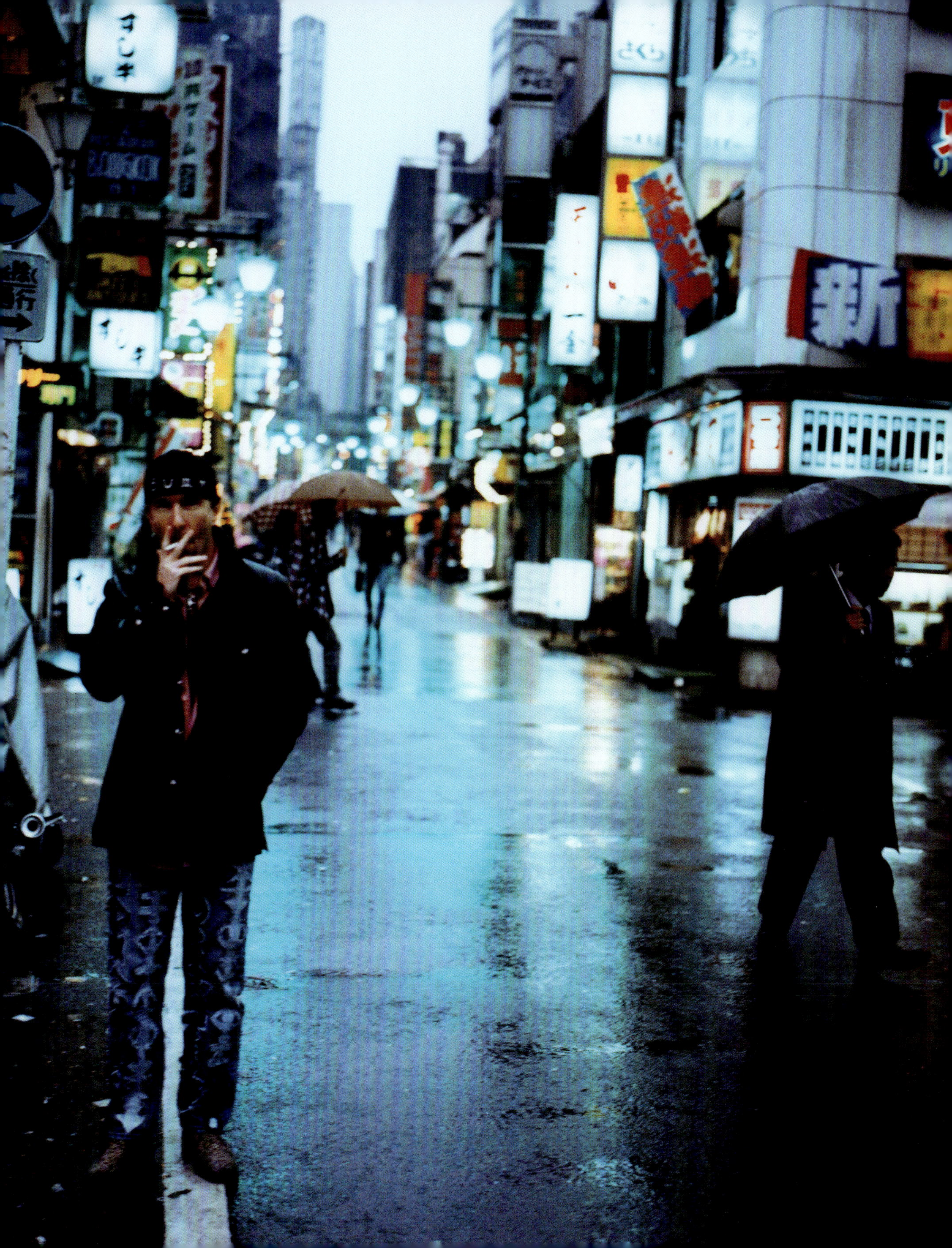
さくら
新

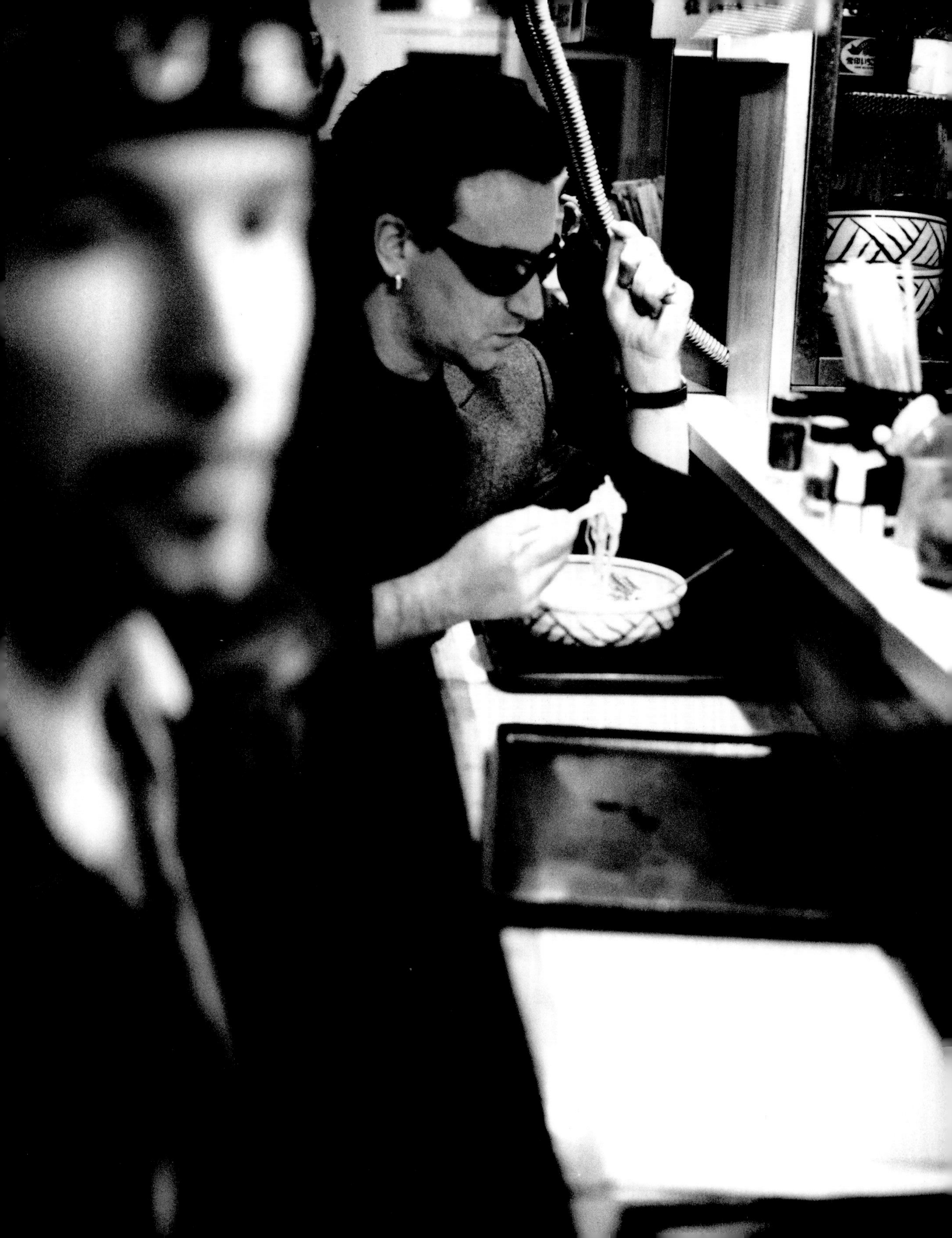

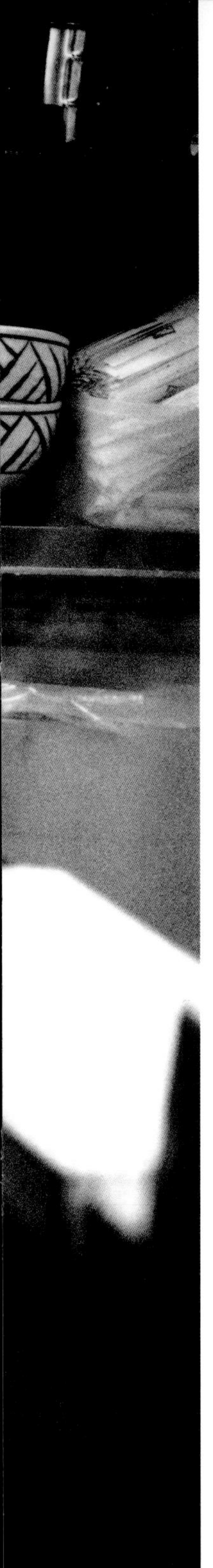

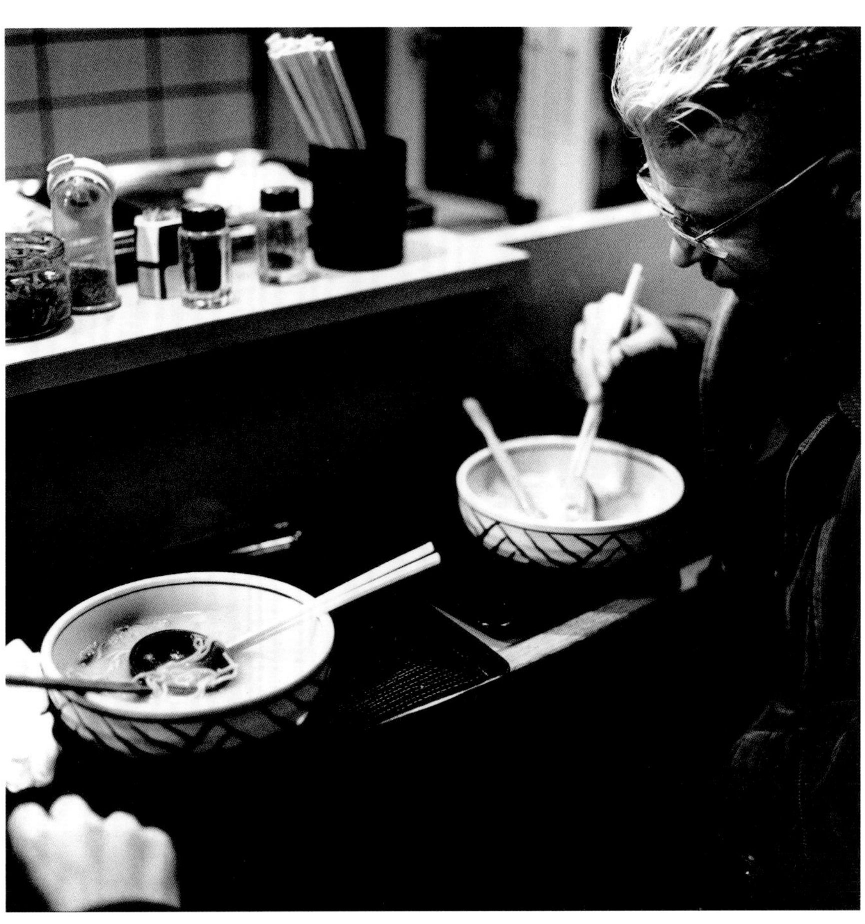

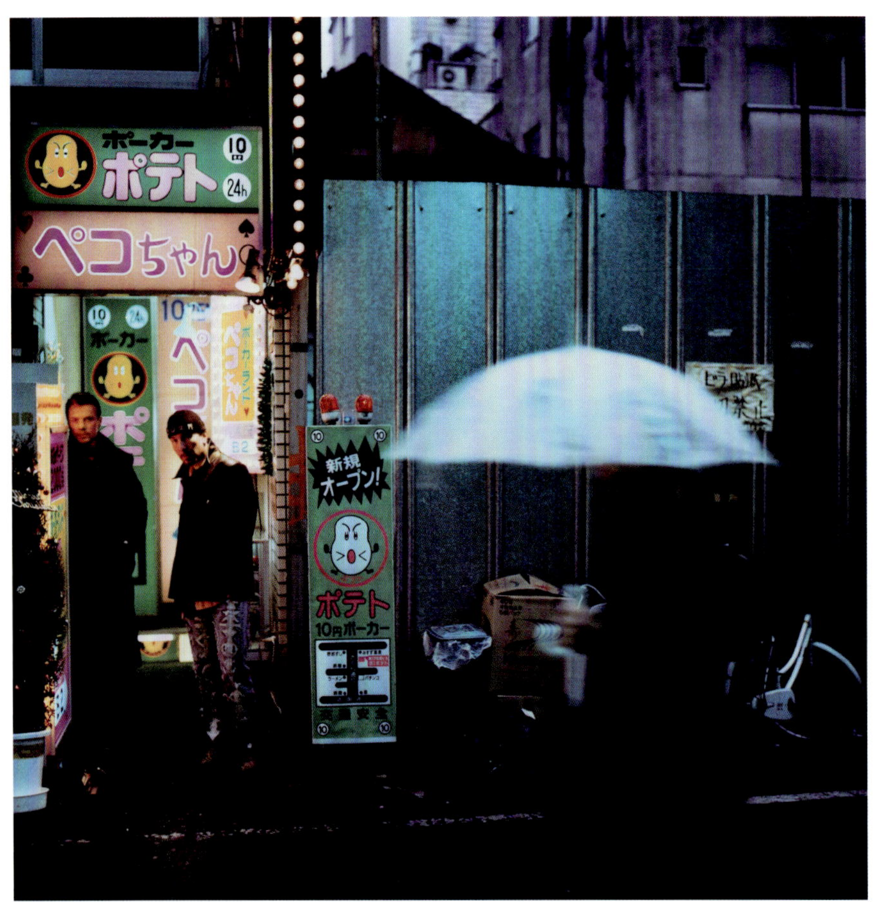

we stood in front of a lot of colourful neon, not knowing exactly what it advertised but there was the suspicion it might be of a sexual nature.

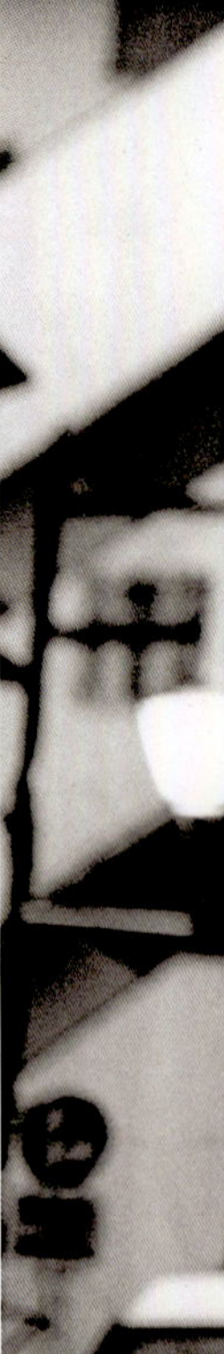

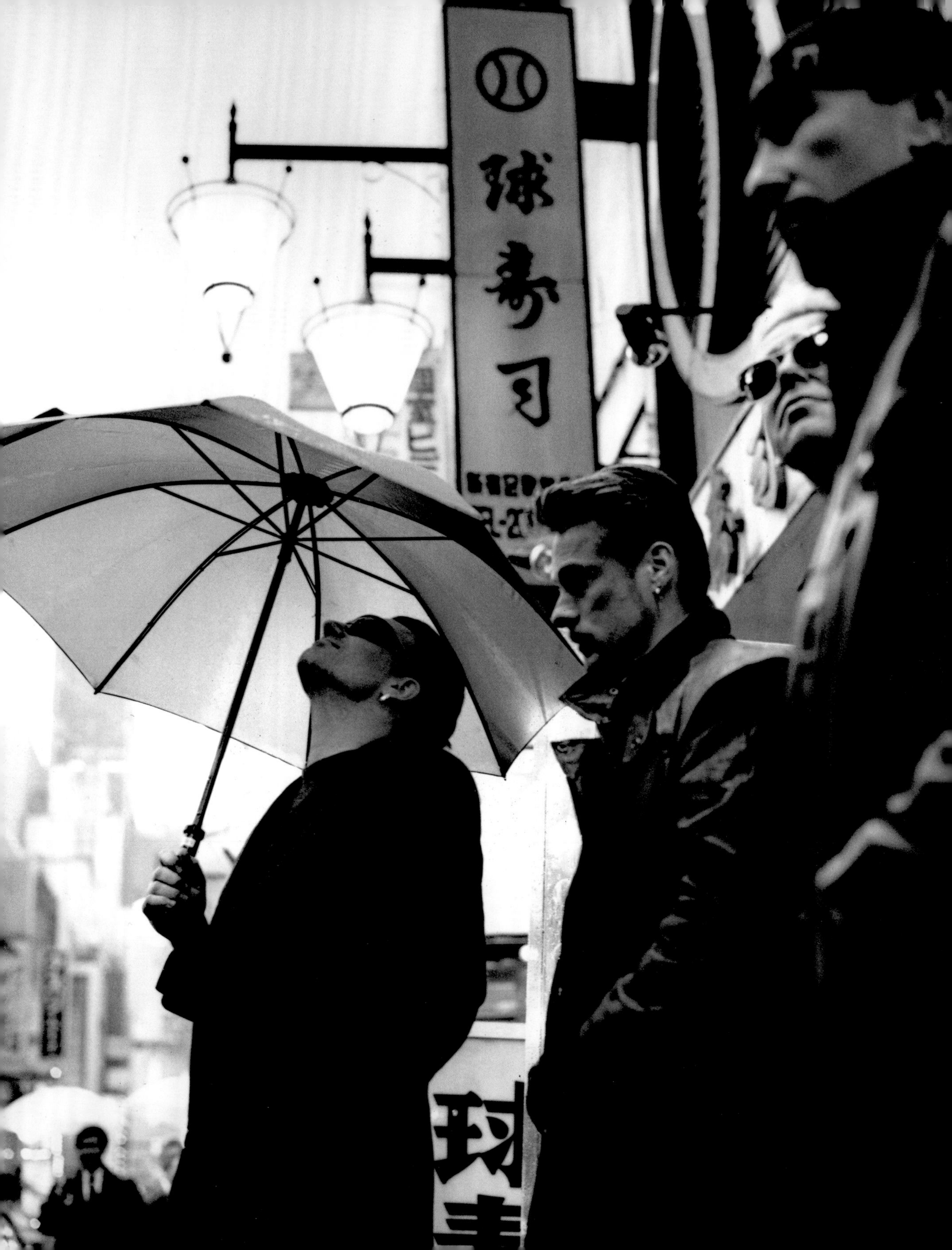
球寿司

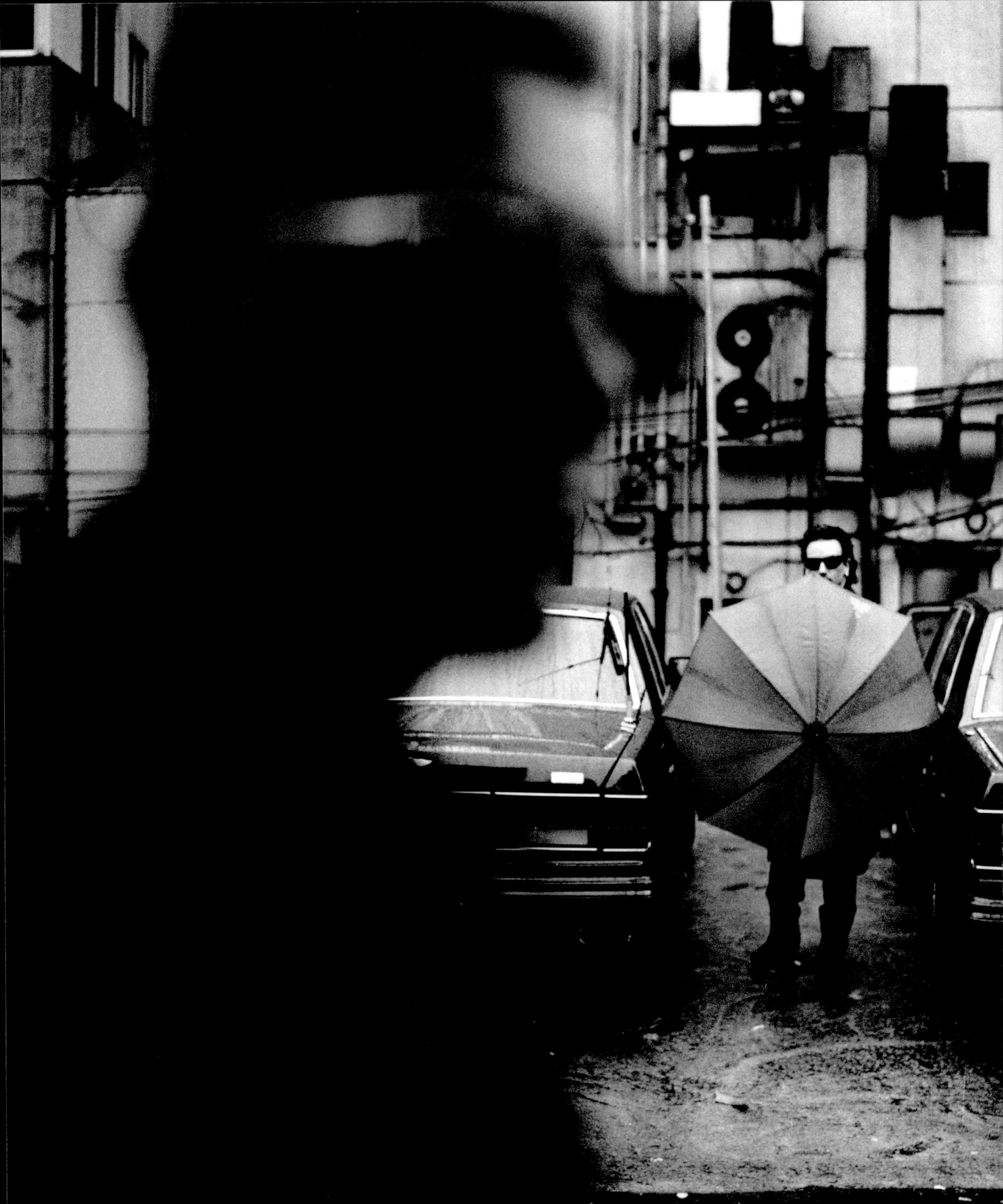

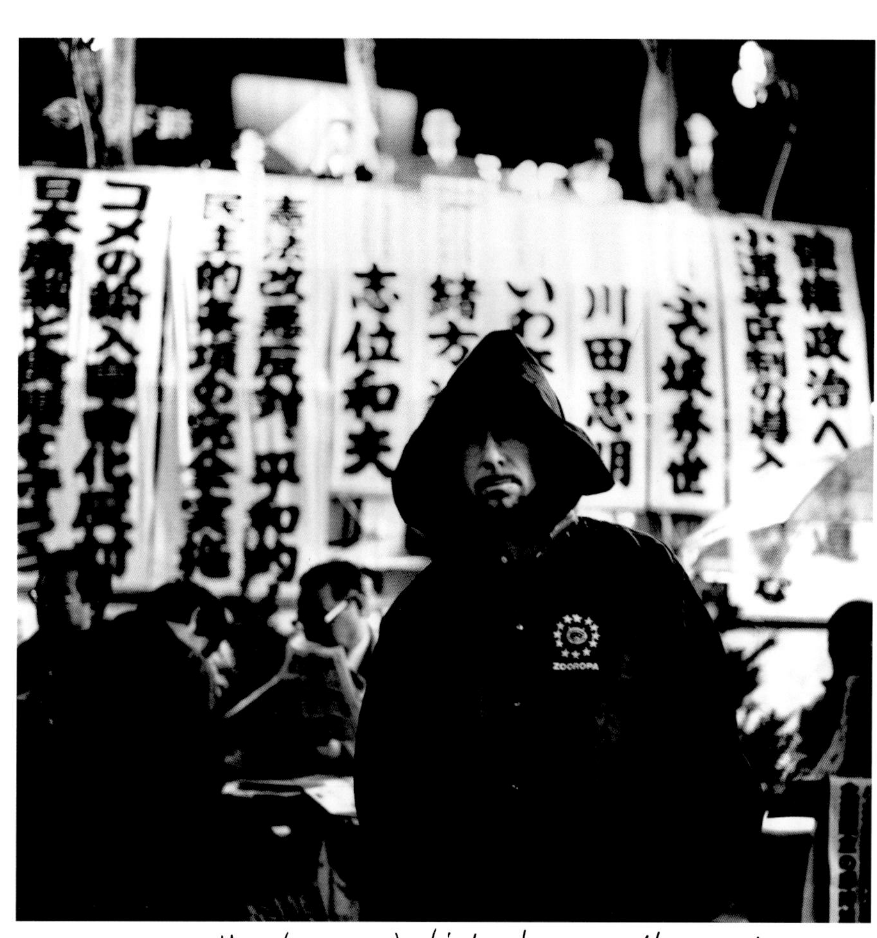

the slogan behind edge are those of a ~~political~~ political party, selling their ideology on the street.

adam and bono and 2 Rolls royces – surely that spells danger.

NEW YORK 1994

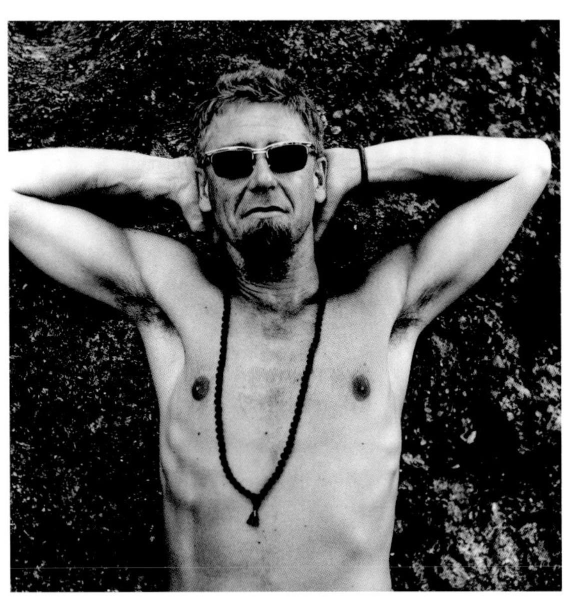

i happened to **Be** ! i happened to be in NY at the same time as adam who had just bought a place there and was spending time in the big apple. so we killed some time in central park.

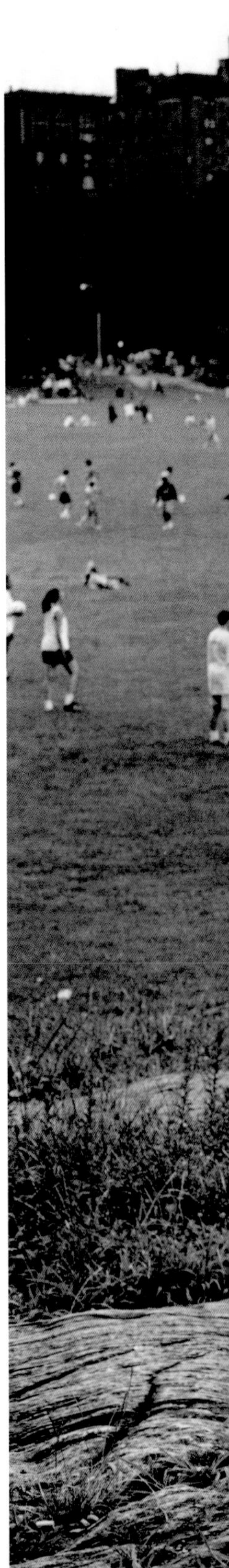

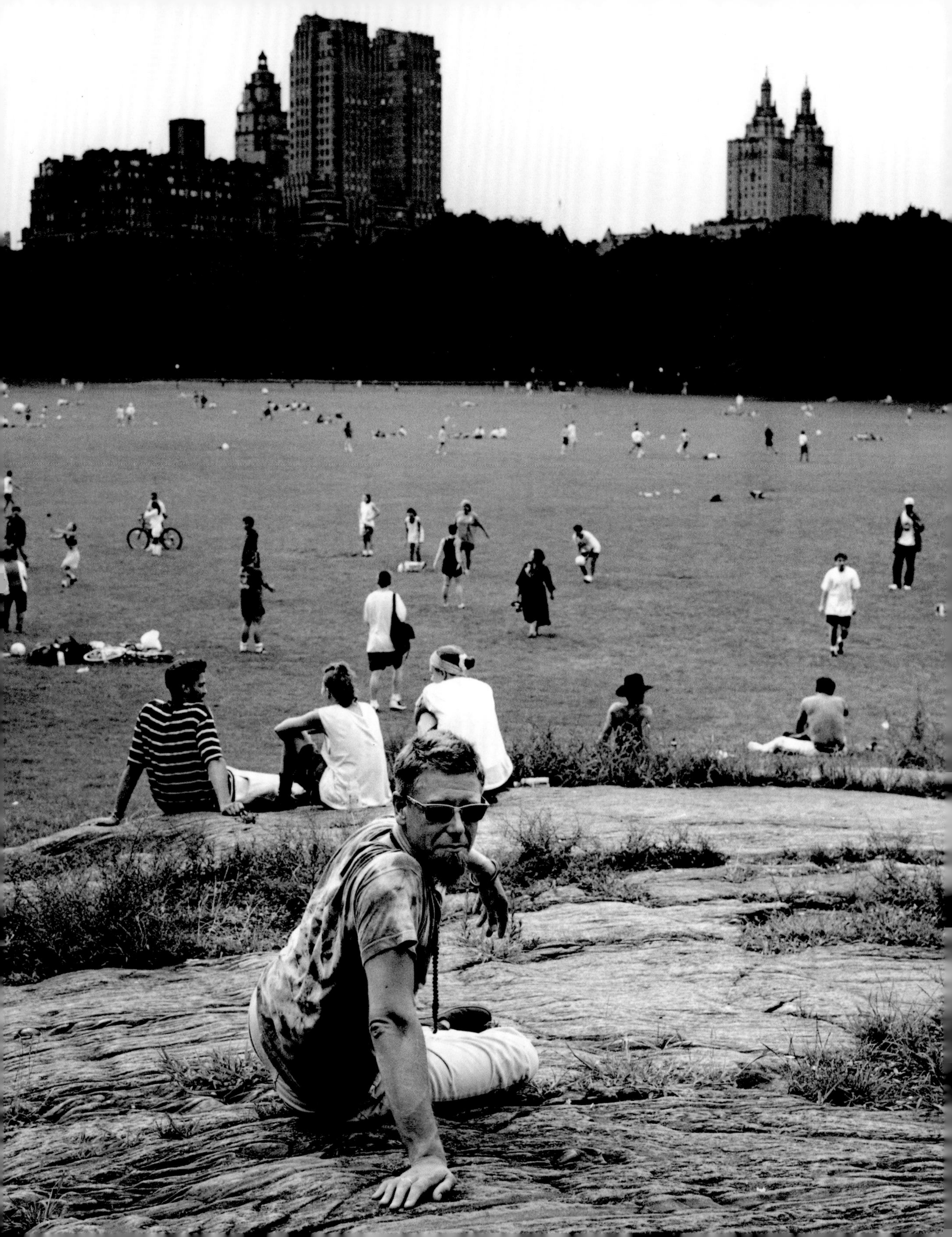

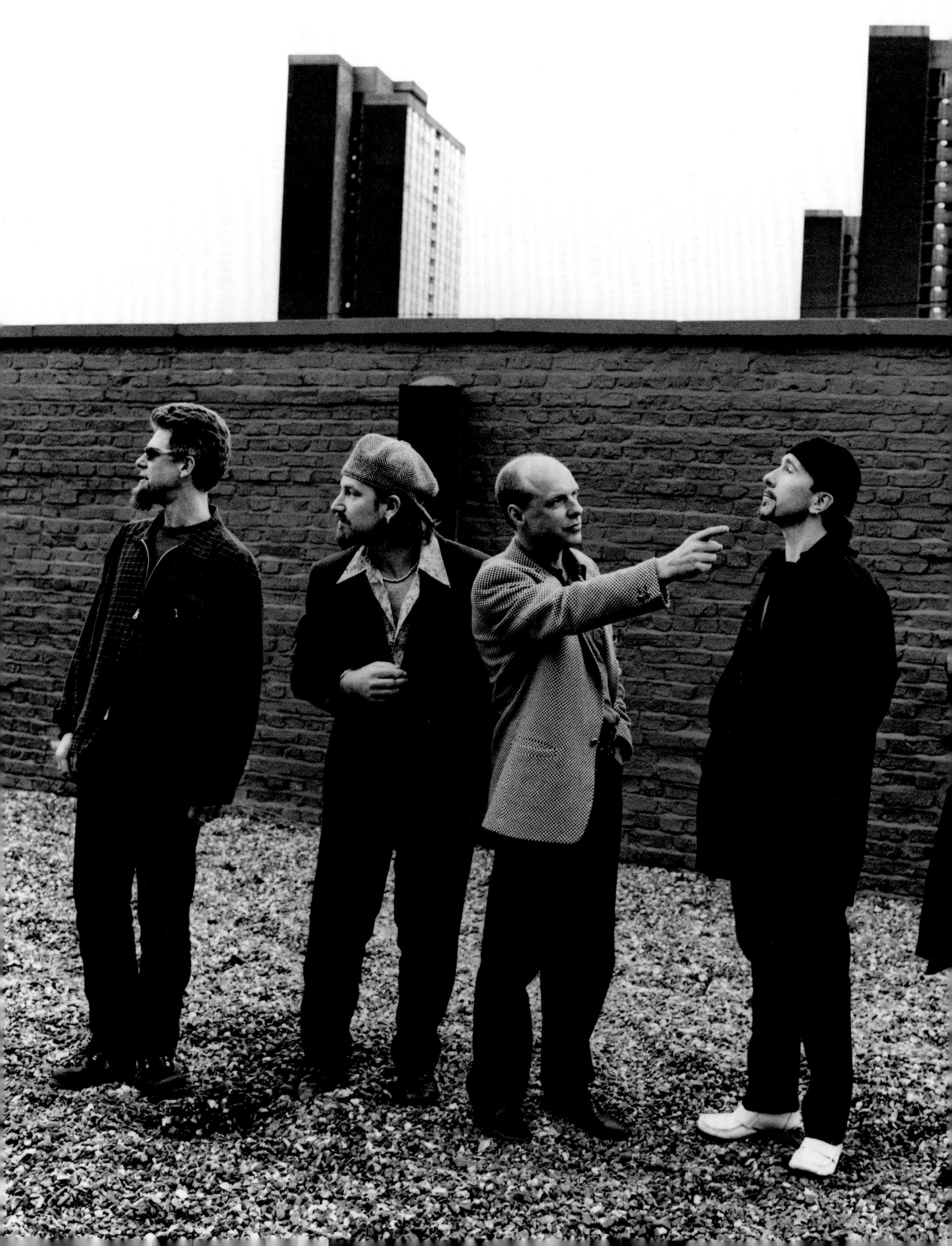

LONDON

1994 november

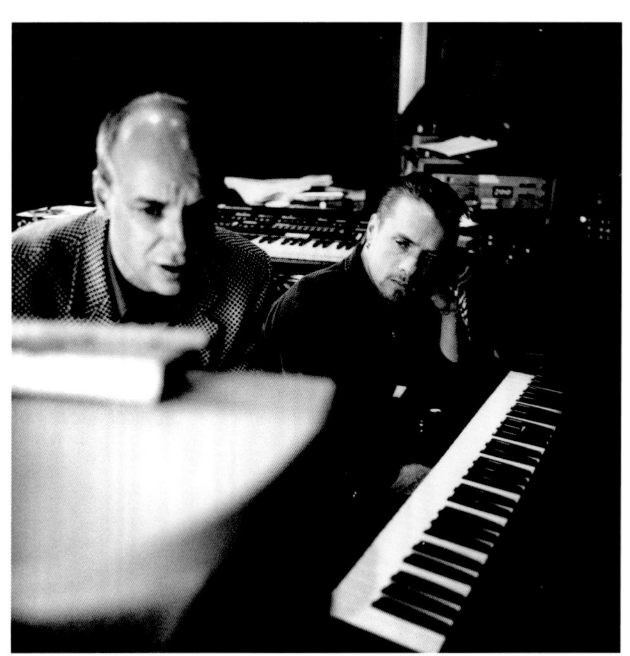

U2 and Brian Eno started rehearsals for their collaborative project 'Passengers' in London and i popped in to disturb the pace. i never done a photo of brian with the band so that was my goal. the photo of them together is set up obviously but not totally bereft of reality. the songs were soundtracks to imaginaire films and brian wrote the linernotes with the records detailing the imaginairy scripts of these films and many of us found ourselves making an appearance in these stories. supposedly i am the driver in one script, my alias being TONY CORBIN.

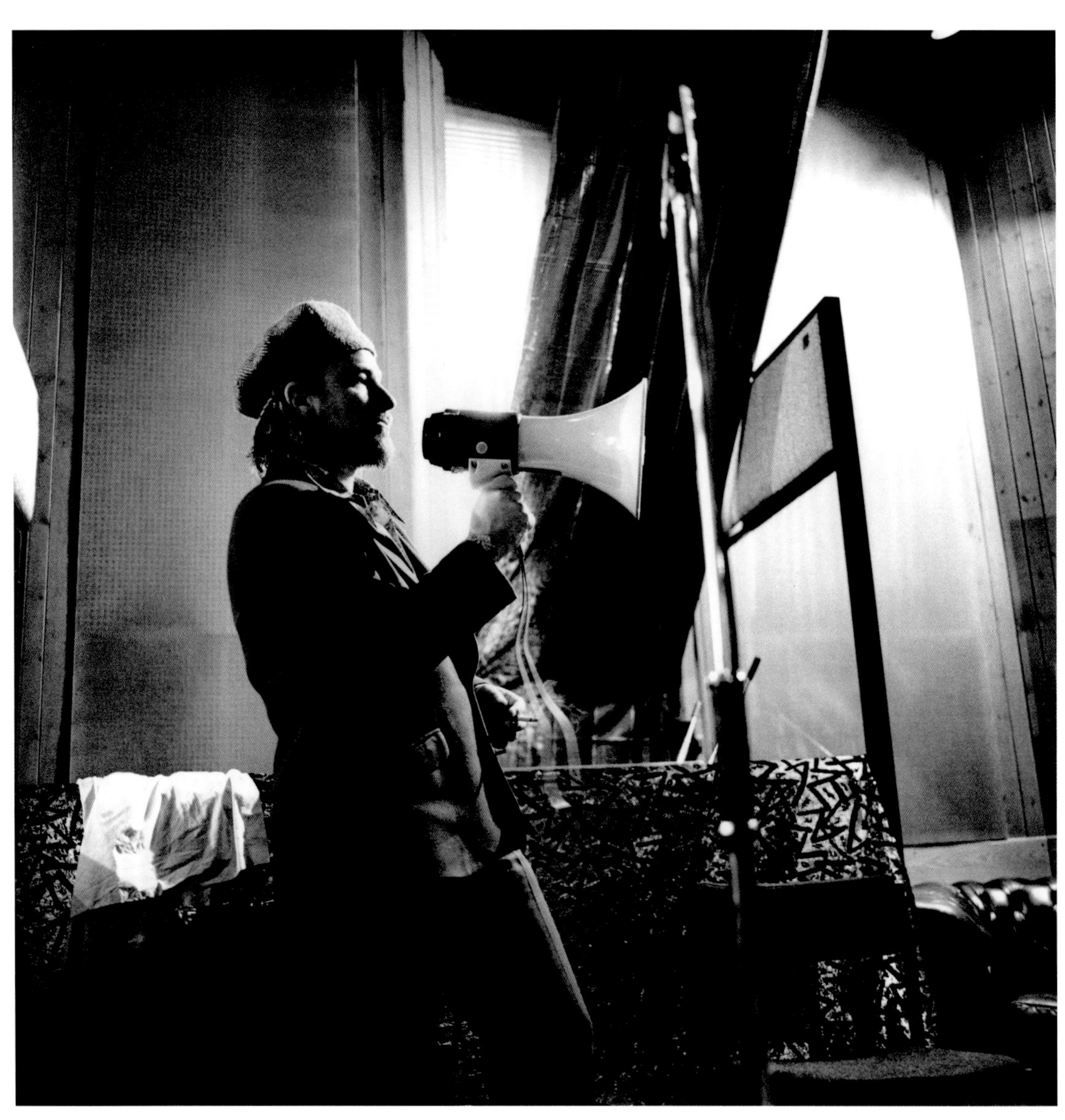

brian encouraged unorthodox approaches to songwriting, be it megaphones or playing to several TV screens all showing different films.

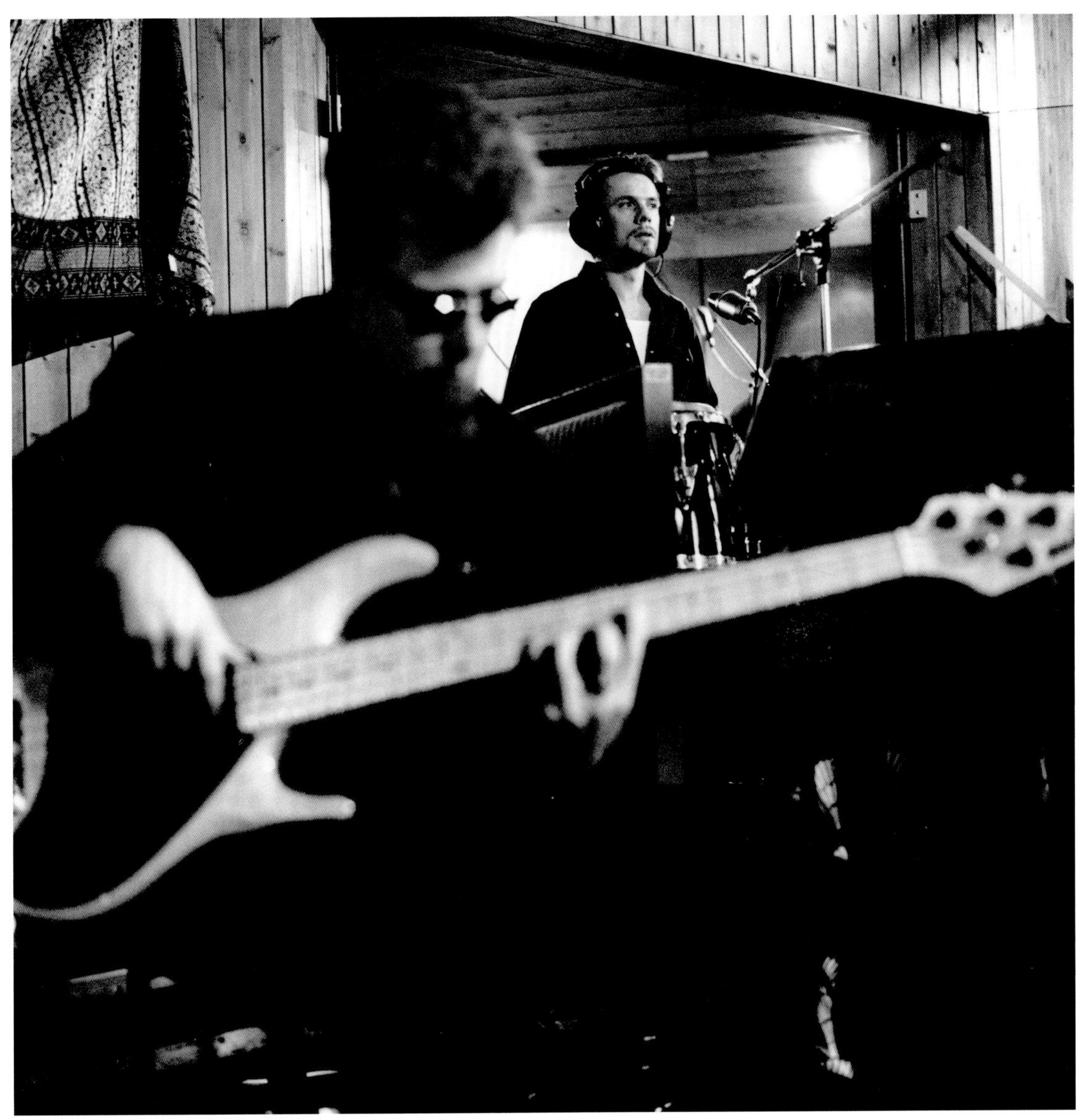

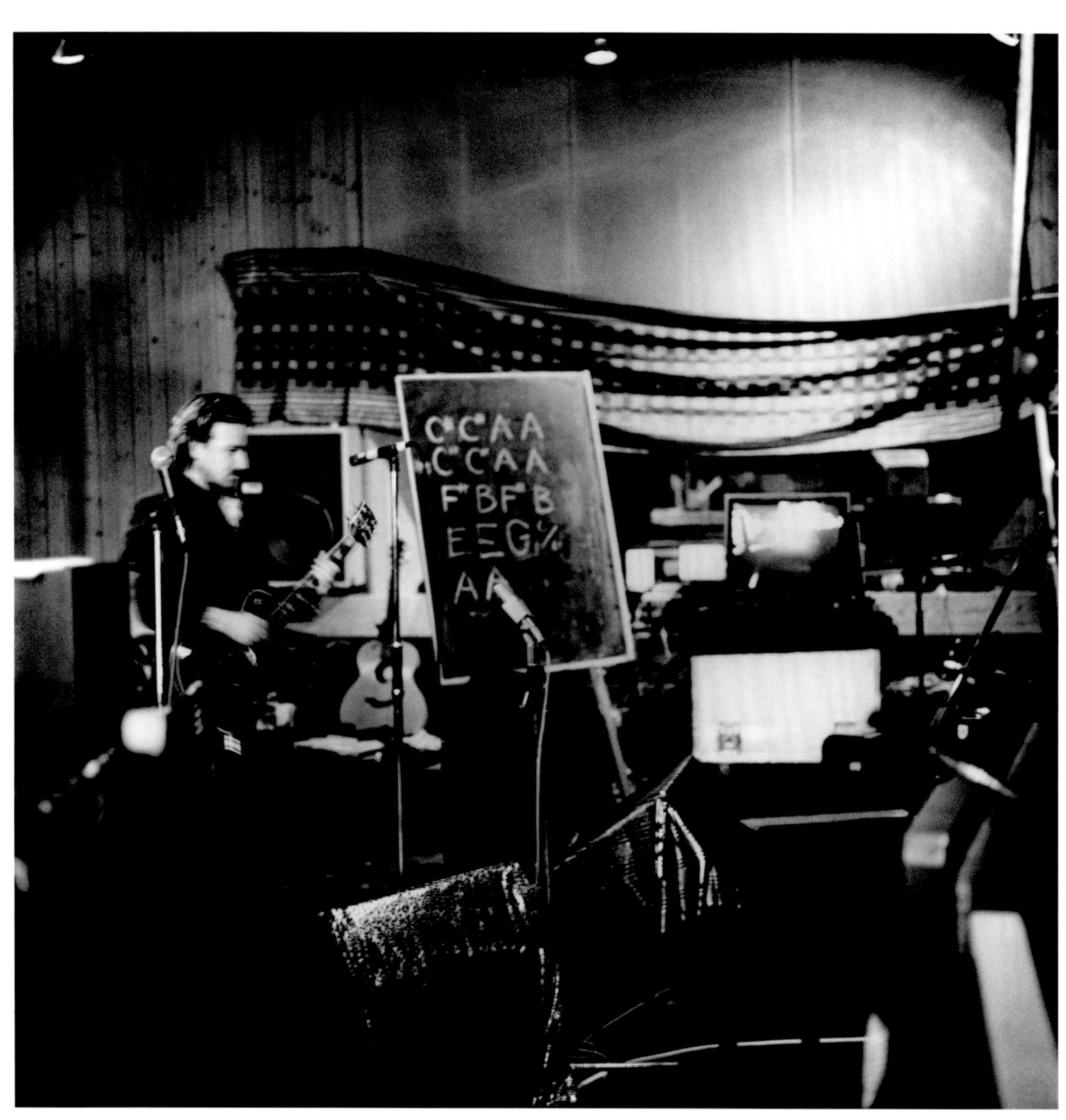

brian + i recently tried to work out for which song these
END chords were and he figured it would be a very
early version of miss sarajevo.

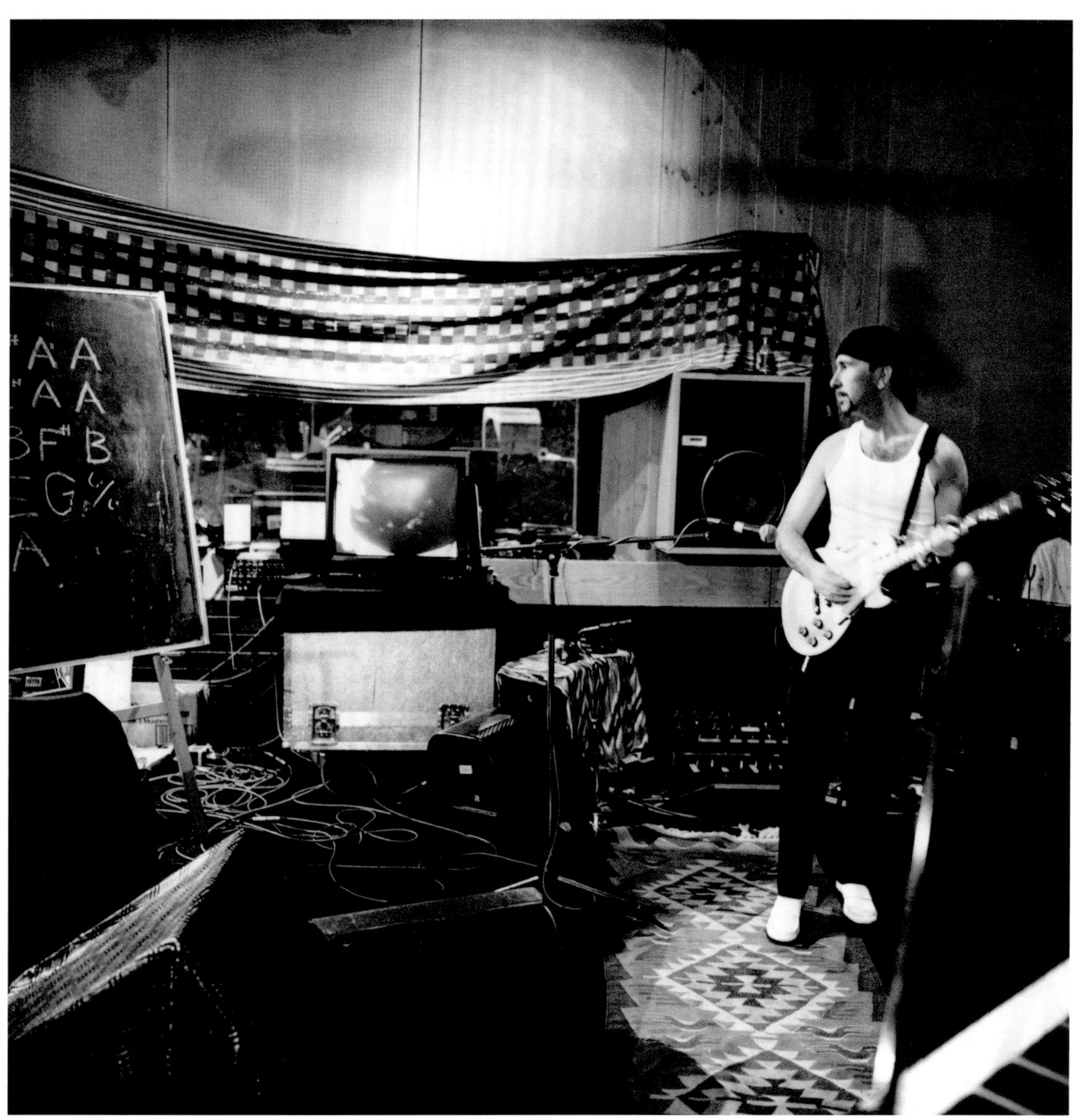

the carpets and other pieces of textile were put in the studio for atmosphere and inspiration rather than for soundquality. at least, that is what i deducted from the proceedings.

JAMAICA 1995

january

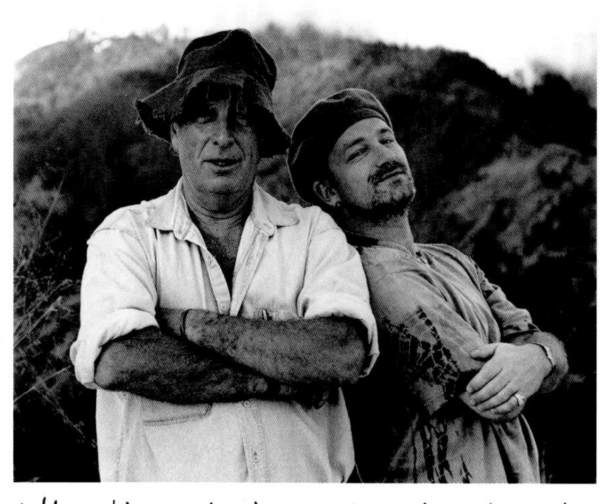

chris blackwell

i went with a friend of mine to jamaica for a few days and we ended up spending a lot of time with bono and ali who happened to be there also. these photos were taken in strawberry hill near kingston at a place owned by chris blackwell. it was a fantastic place which comes as no surprise if you know chris; he's got a great eye for things that make you feel good. apart from being the founder of island records and bringing bob marley into our lives, he produced one of my all time favorite records, 'one world' by john martyn. acquired taste possibly but you will be richly rewarded.

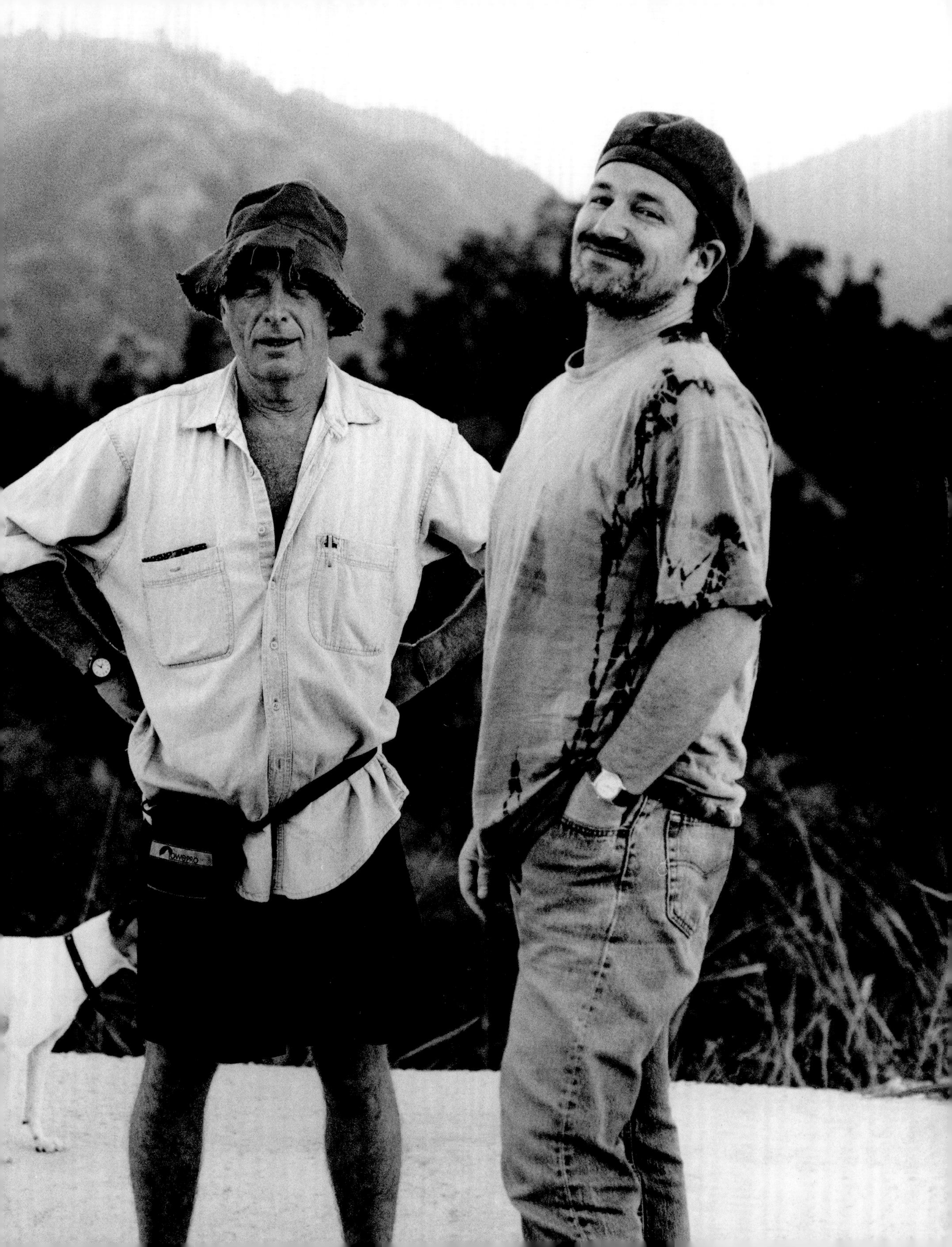
LOWEPRO

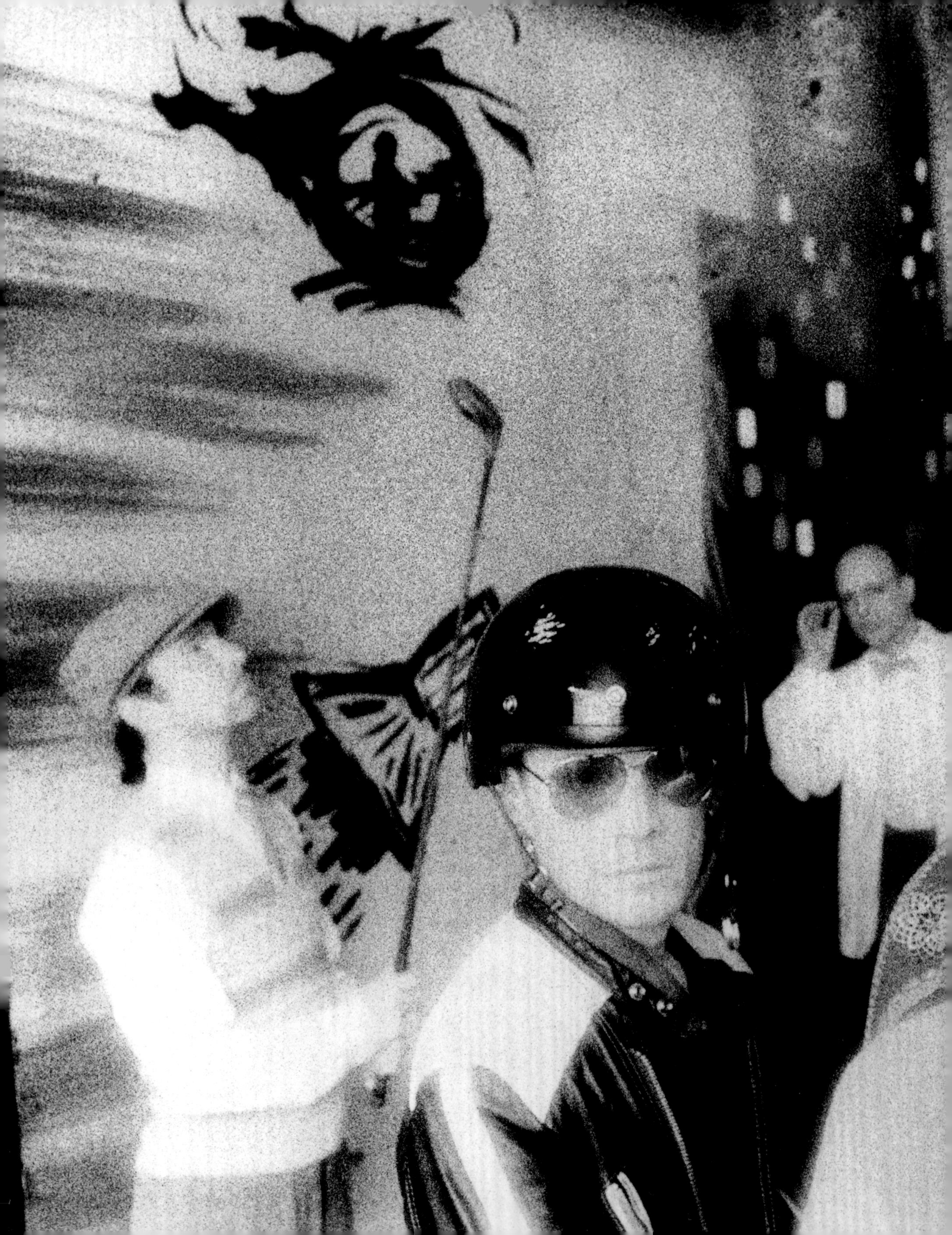

DUBLIN 1995

'the Passengers'

brian eno + u2

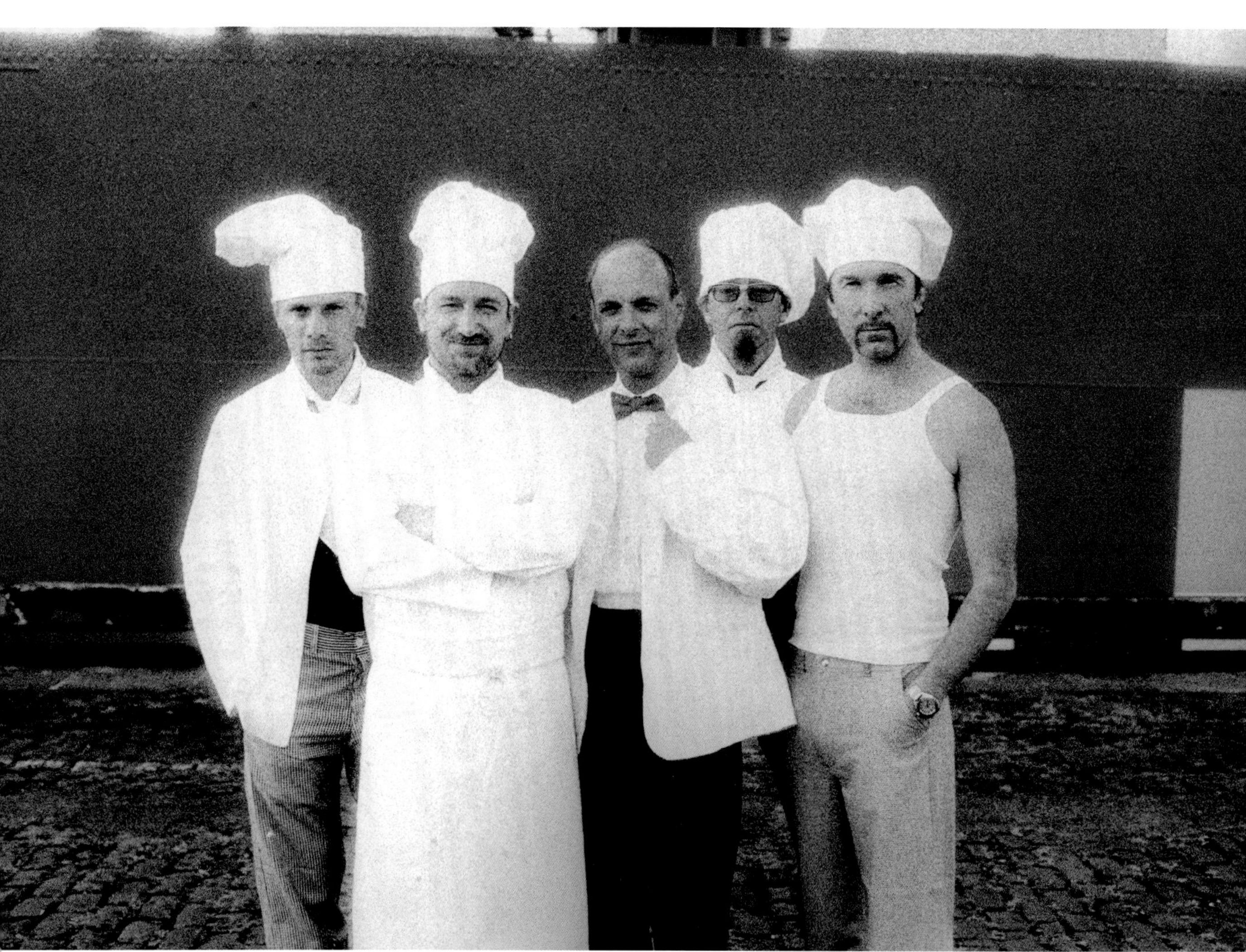

i know, it looks like the crew but they are the passengers. i used infrared film to get the photos to move away from the band + brian eno just looking dressed up. we shot in the recording studio where i had ← someone paint a massive backdrop which i had sketched on a small piece of paper. then we did the photos on this spread on the waterfront just 100 metres from the u2 studio. the interior shot looks like a mixture of a horny holy underground movie and a community theatre-actor

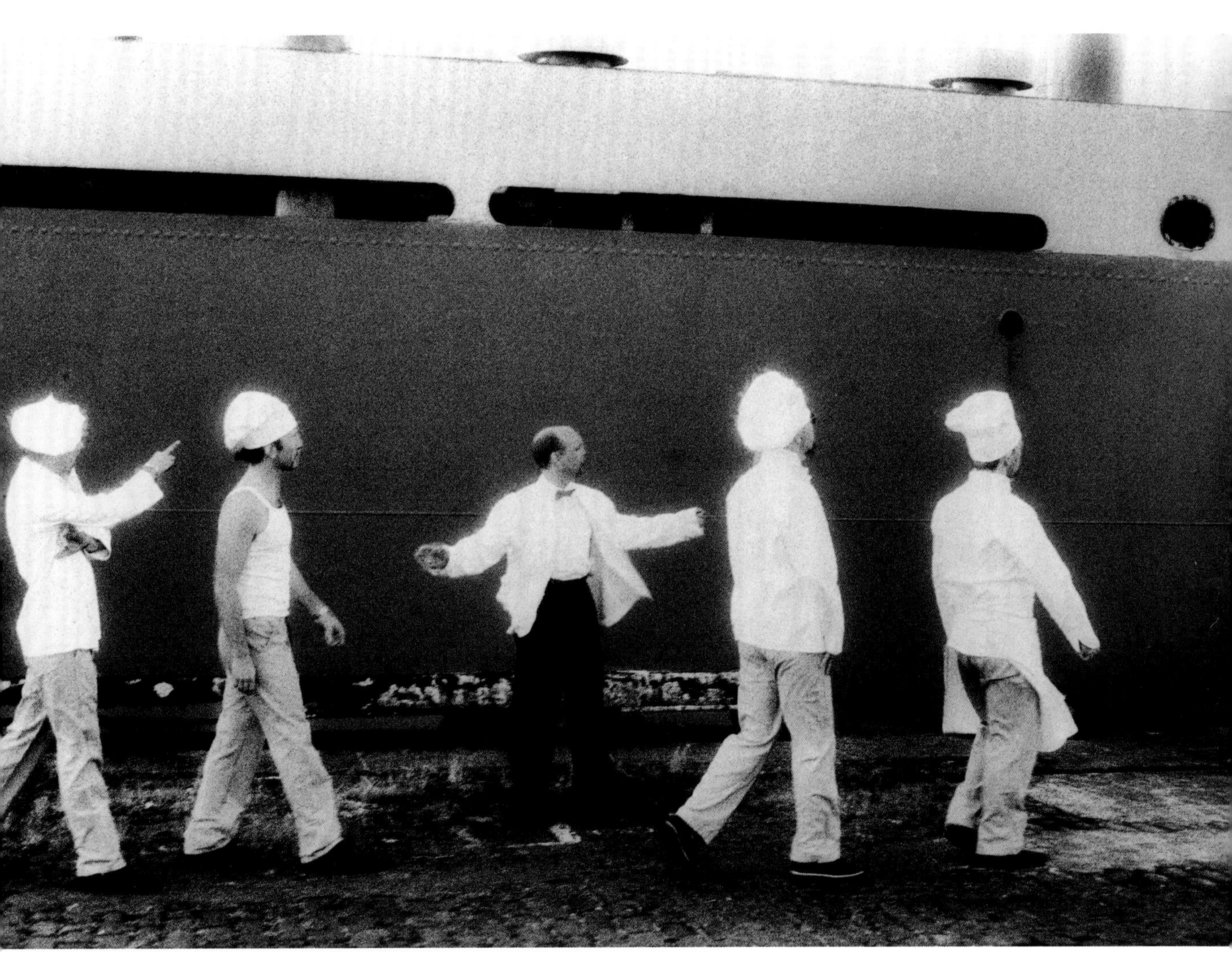

LONDON 1995 november

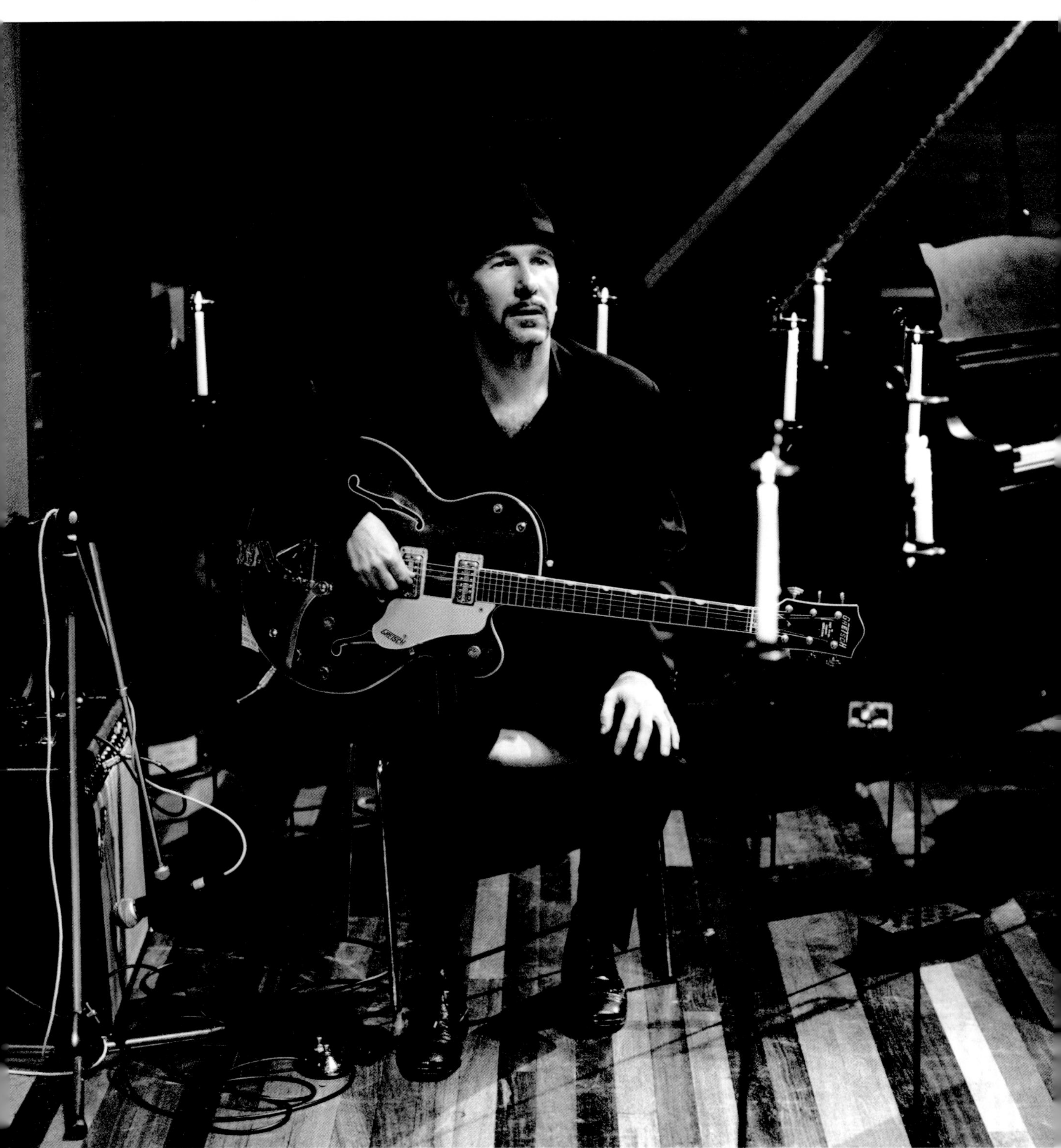

bono and edge
with a string-
orchestra in
a recording studio
in the south of
London. they
played and
recorded a
version of "Two
shots of Happy,
one shot of Sad"
for Frank Sinatra
whose birthday it
was i gather.
it was late in
the evening as it
was broadcast
live in the USA.

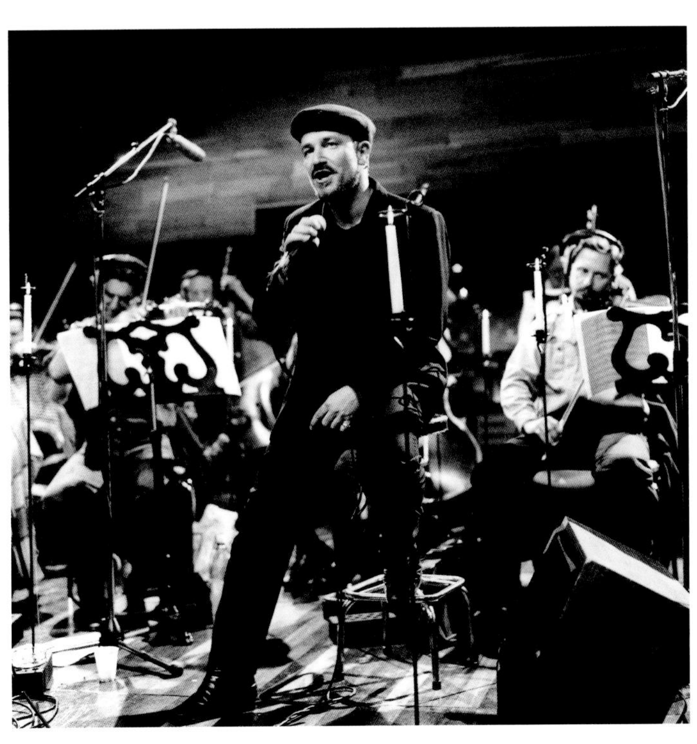

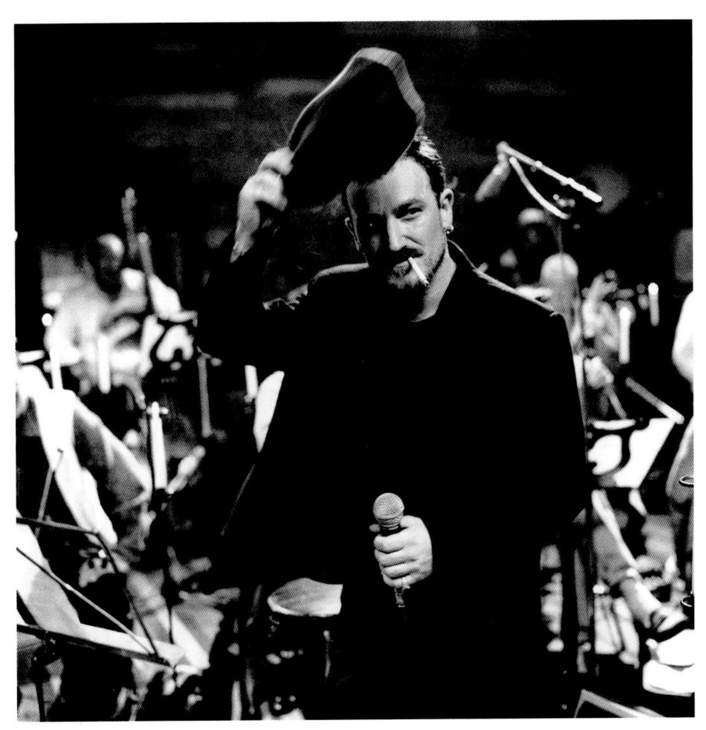

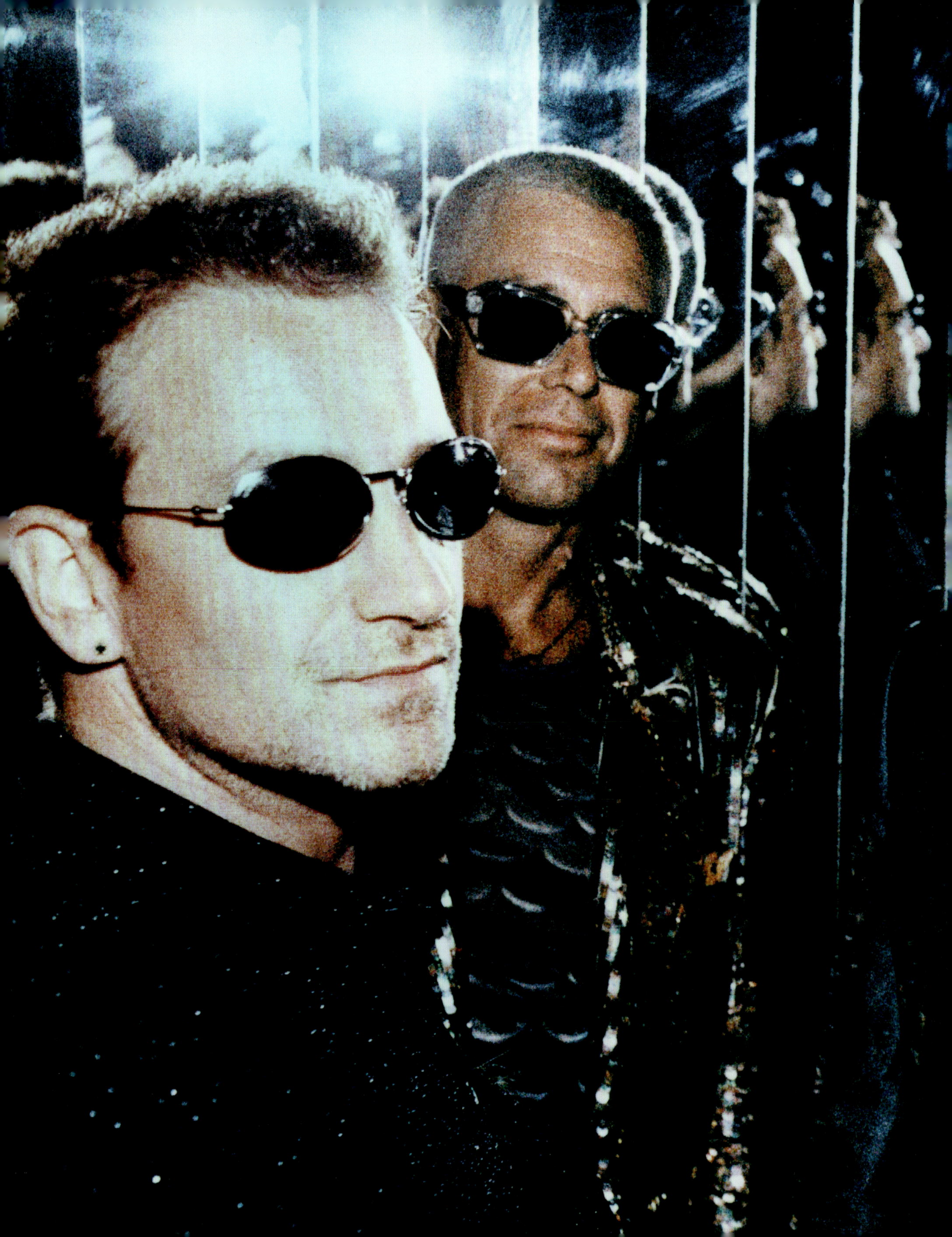

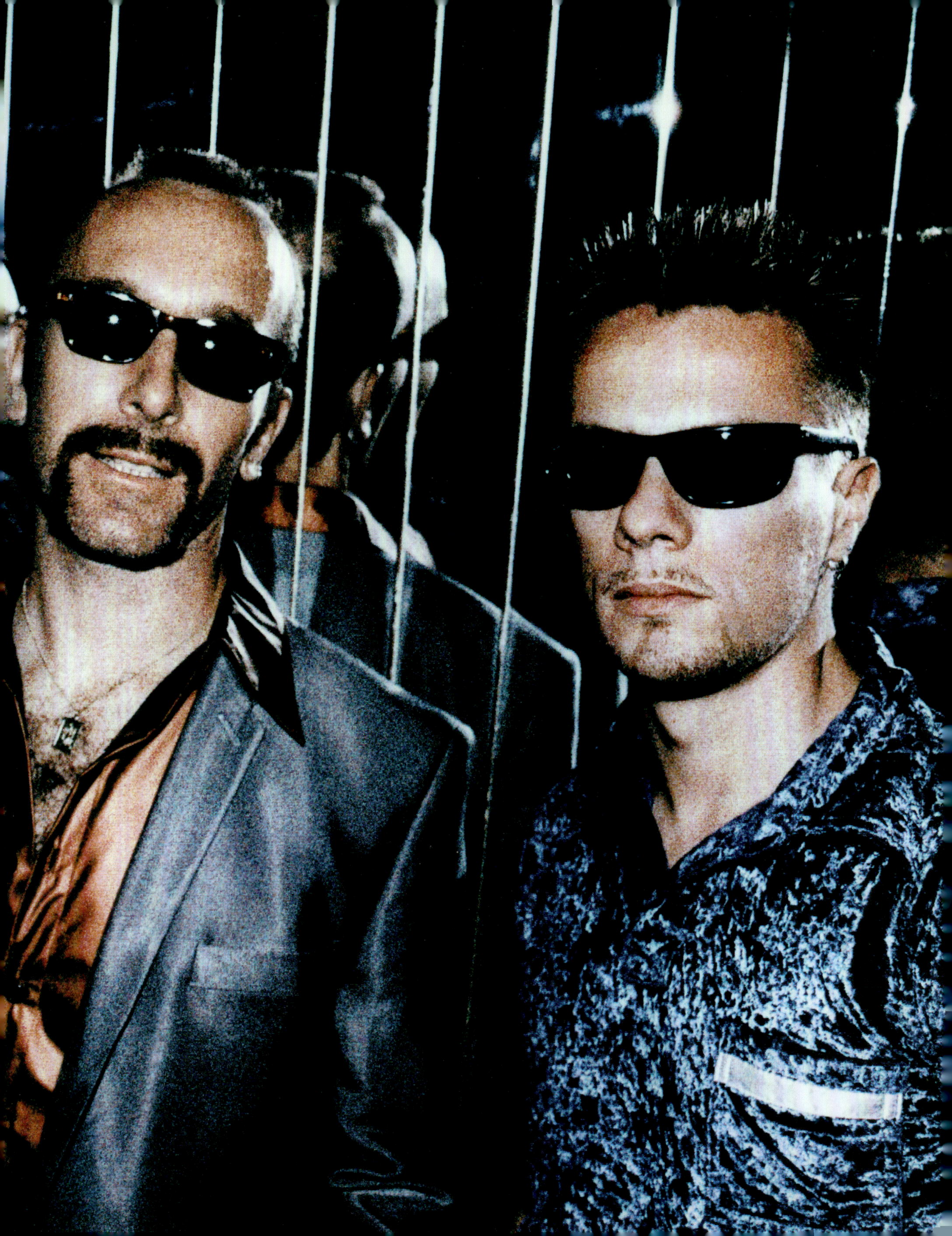

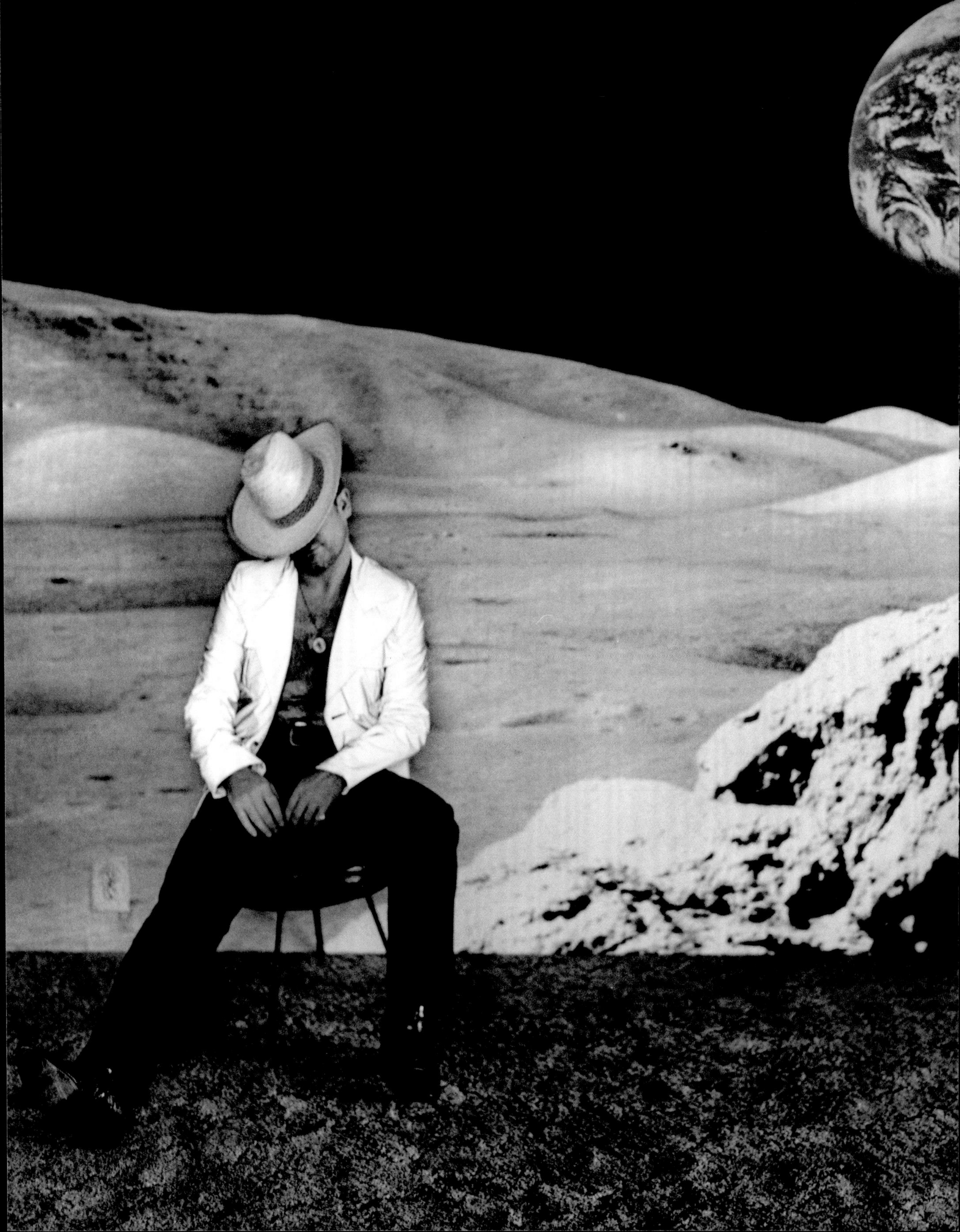

MIAMI

may 1996

← 70's →
wall
paper

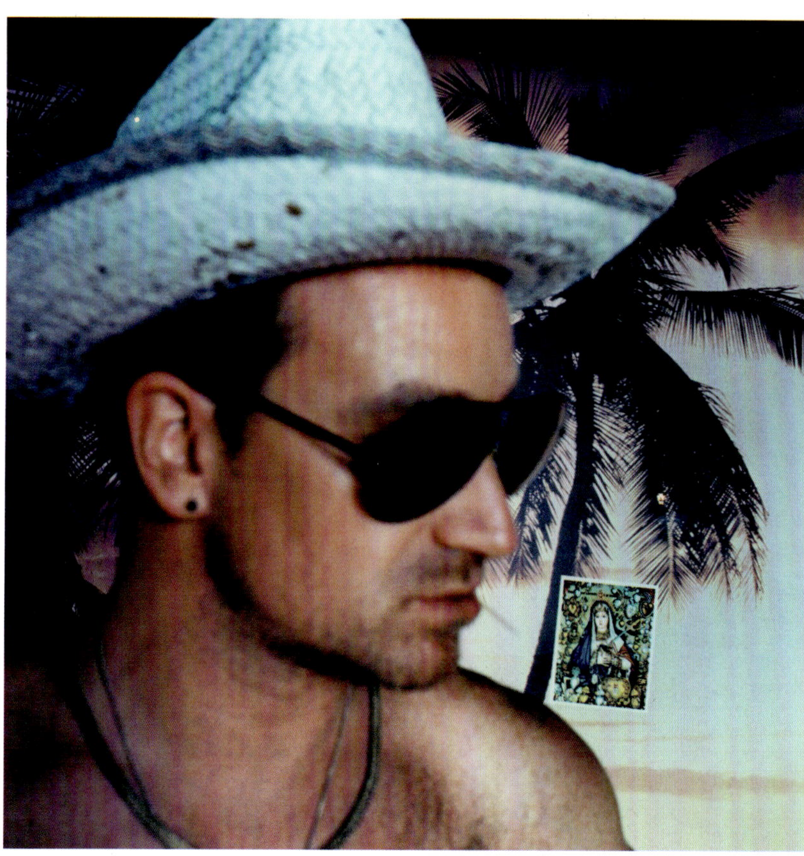

the band recorded part of PoP in miami and it was decided to shoot there for the album cover also. the mix of american and hispanic cultures was of interest visually as much as the actual atmosphere there. we shot for 3 days at various places, including a disco (previous page), hotel lobbys and photostudios, and the streets. the band looked really strong and we got some great photos out of it but the cover of the record became 4 individual portraits in the end.

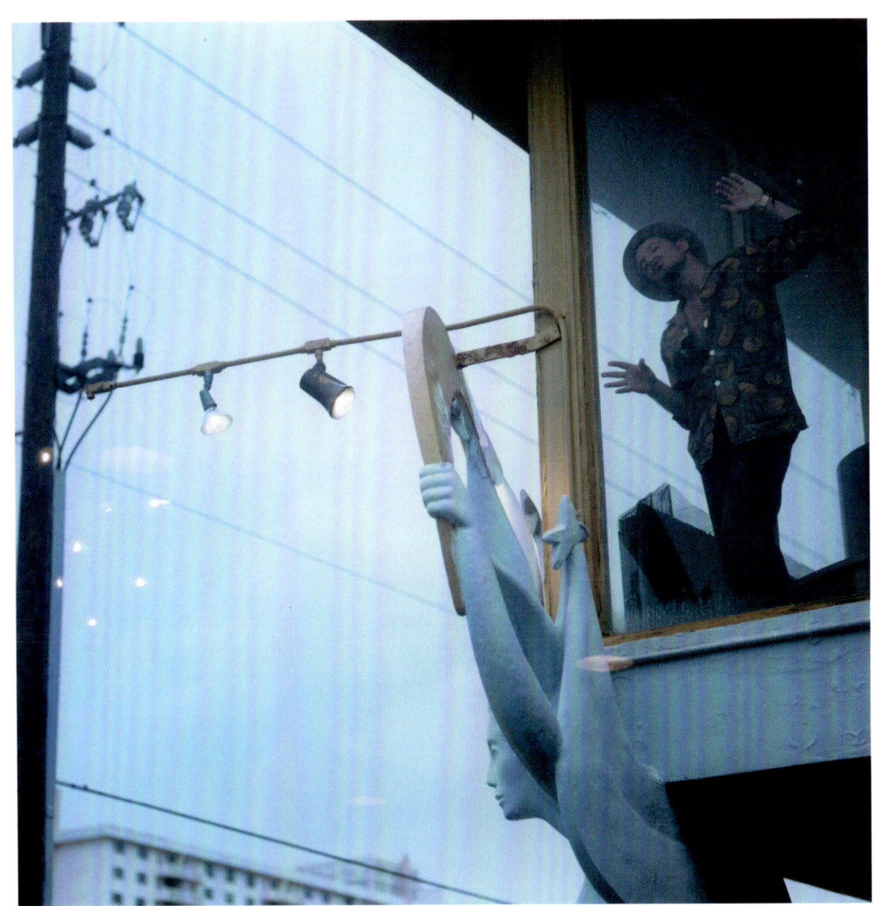

many of the old art deco
hotels have a lot to offer
visually. specially the motel ones.
the photos on this spread and
the next are all taken
at such a place.

trying to outdo
kraftwerk but
we ended up with
a cheap fashion
catalogue shot.
good fun
actually.

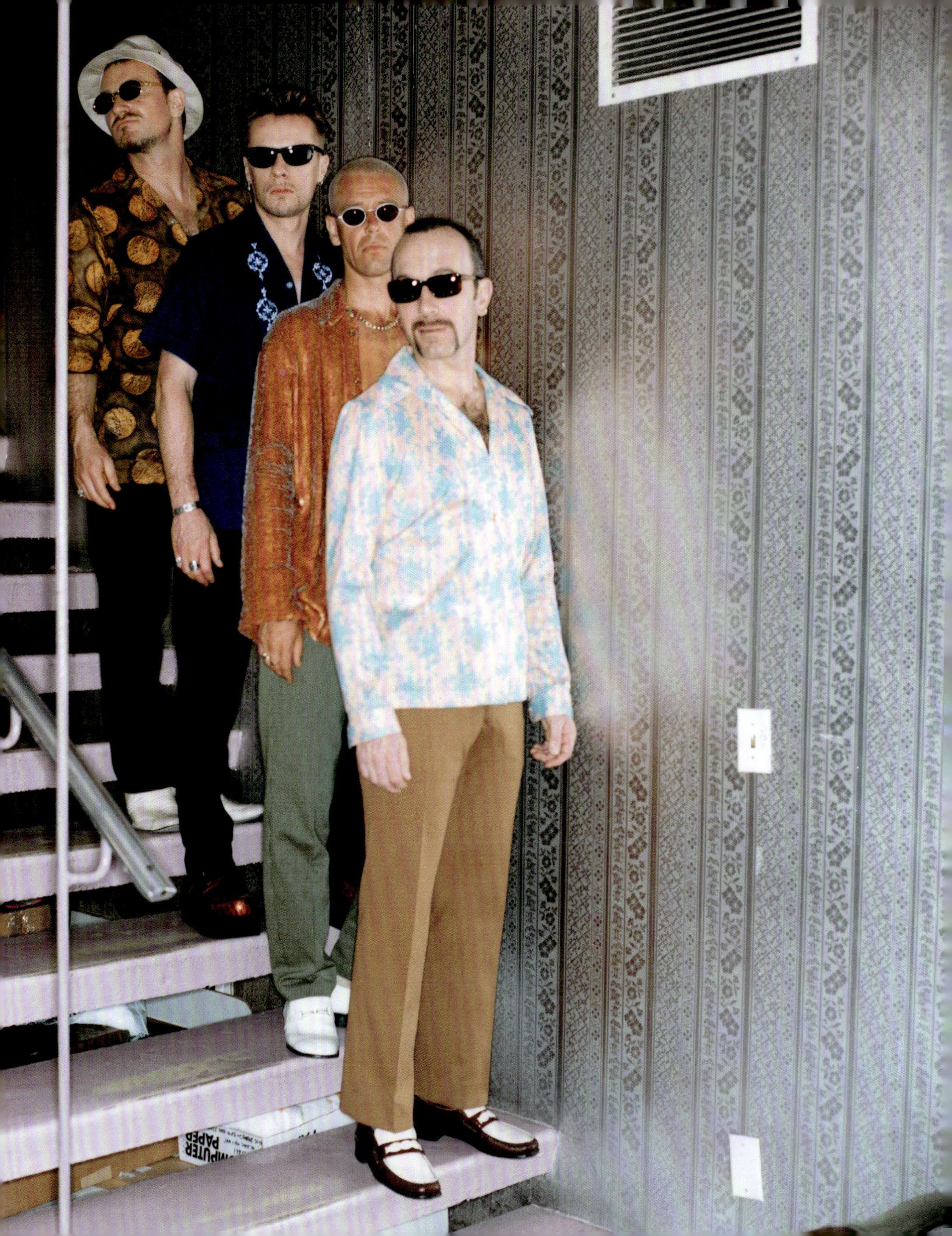

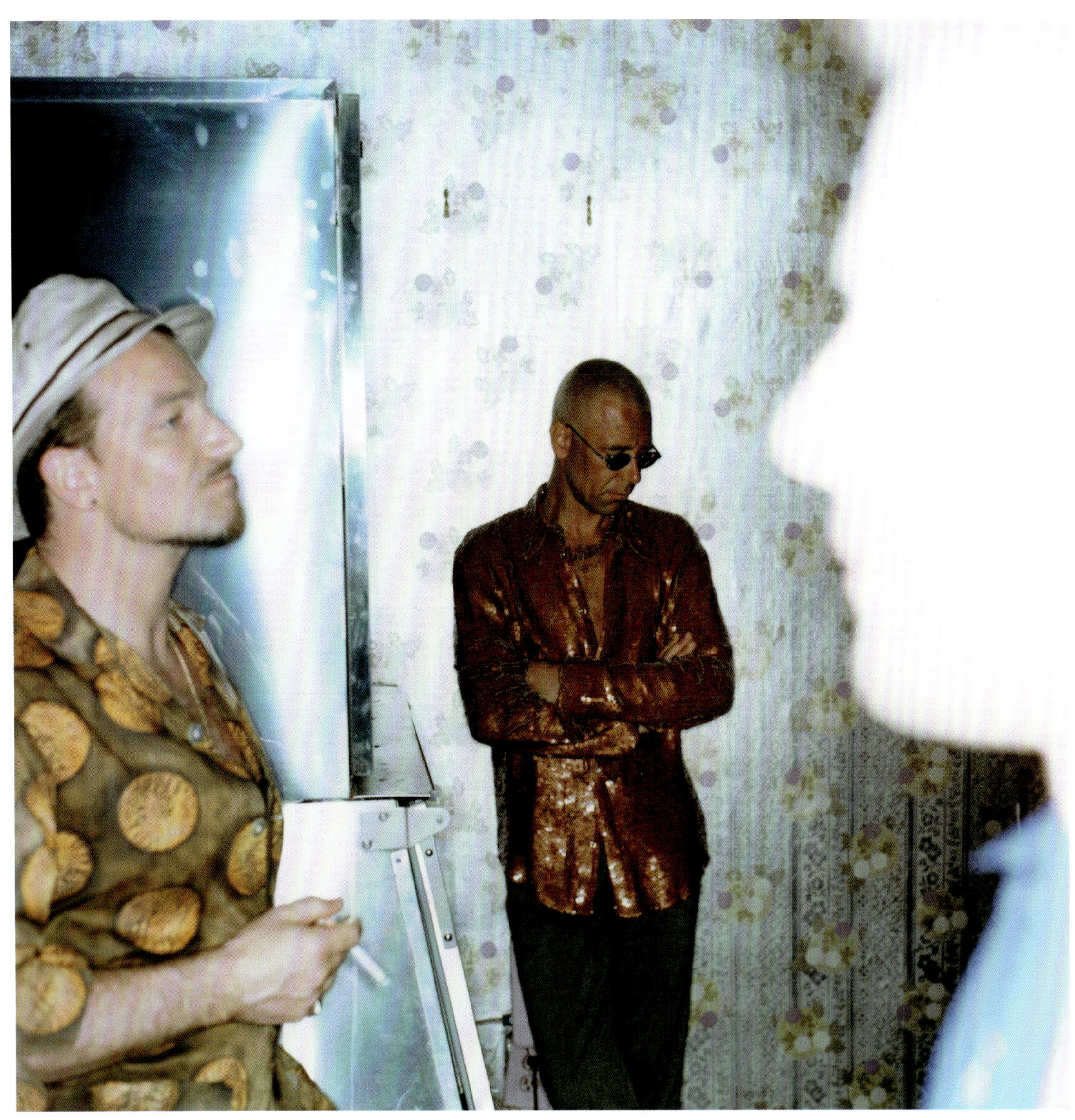

i had an old 'Ringflash' from the 70's which i hadn't used for 2 decades and brought it to florida for the shoot but i forgot that it was meant for a 35mm so i had to rent one in miami that fitted the hasselblad. i used it for some photos to get a more fashion vibe going and to use it for effect as seen on this ~~page~~ spread, overexposing

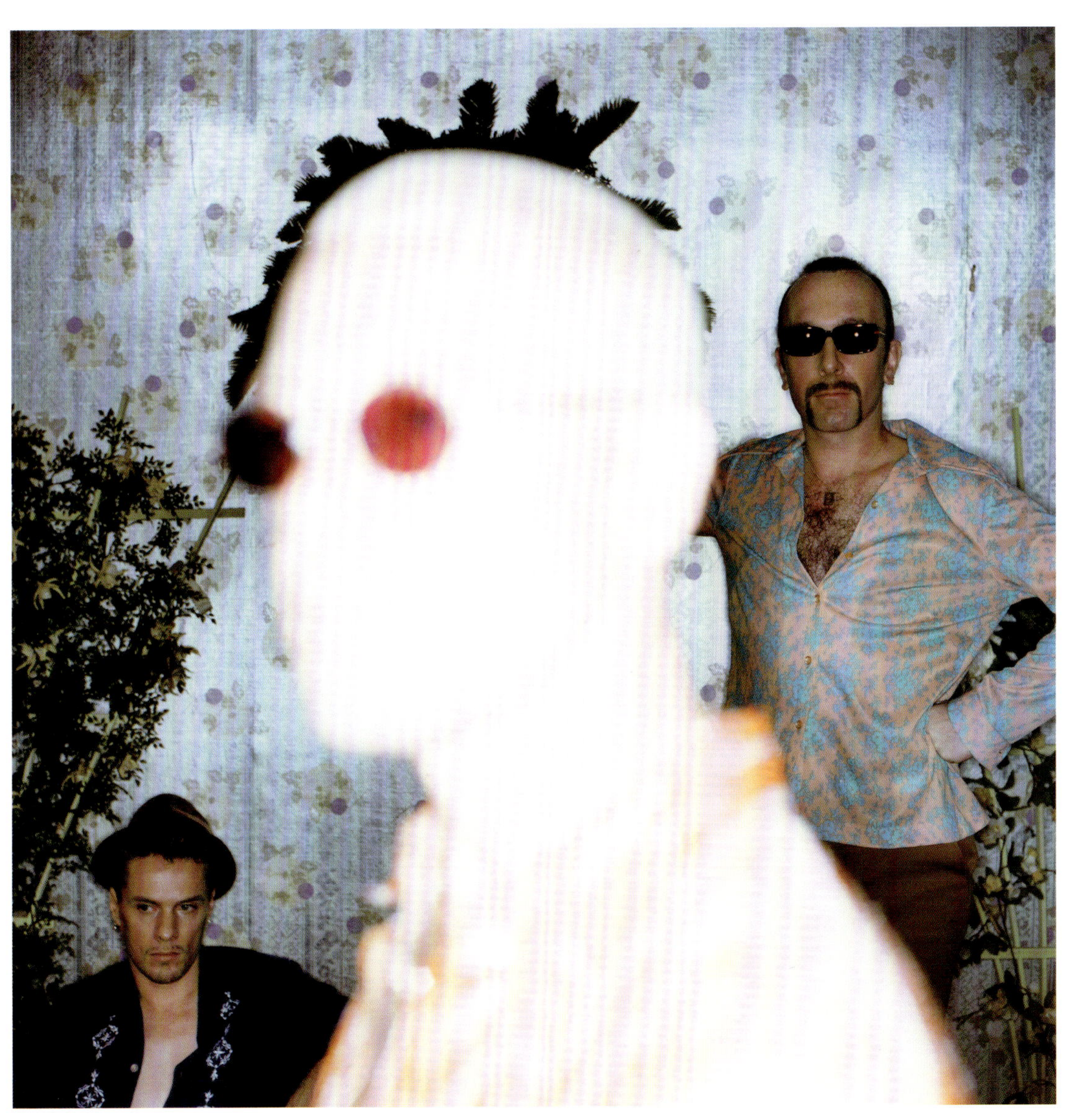

persons close to the camera. On this page adam is too close and opposite it is larry's profile that falls victim to my flash.

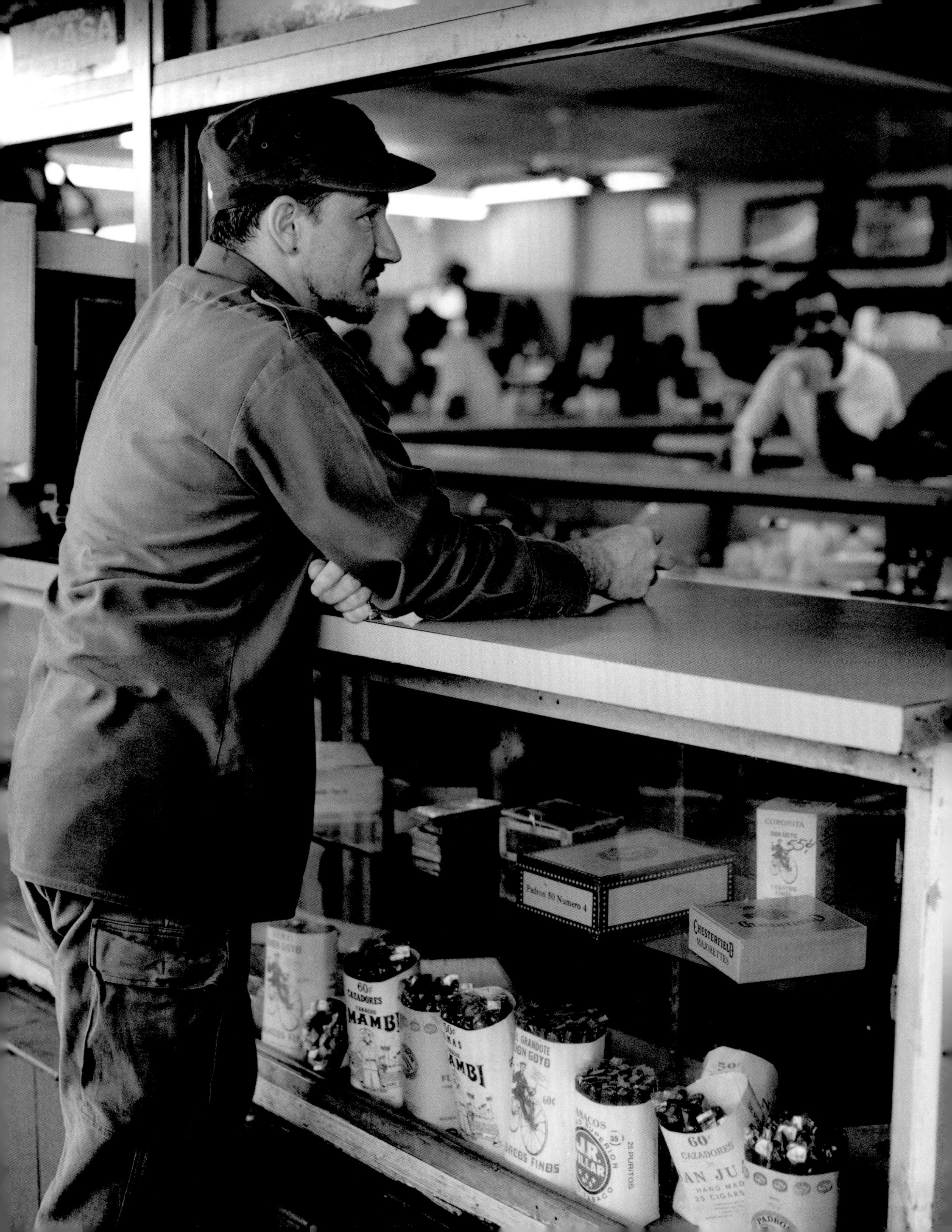

CORONITA
55¢
Padron 50 Numero 4
CHESTERFIELD
MAJORETTES
60¢
CAZADORES
MAMBI
MAMBI
EL GRANDOTE
DON GOYO
60¢
25 PURITOS
60¢
CAZADORES
HAND MAD
25 CIGARS

- found a kind of
uban workshop
where they rolled
igars and after
we had a look around
bono had to buy
some.

i think these
photos were done
just around
the corner of that
cuban place.

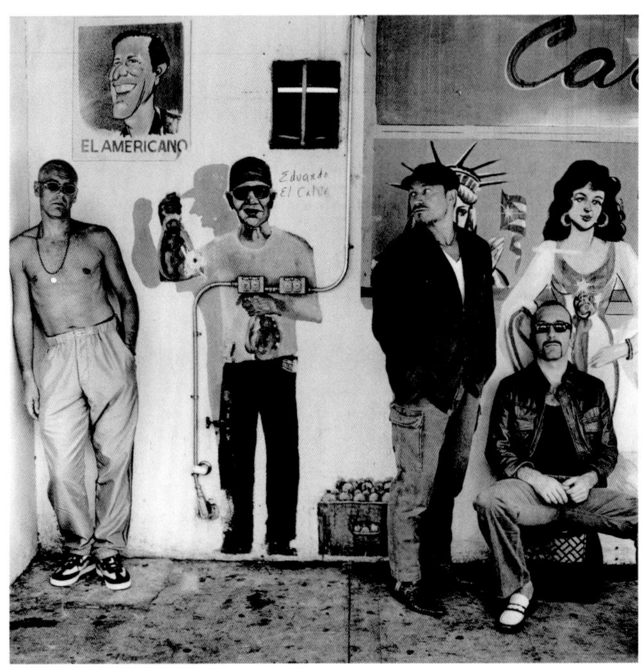

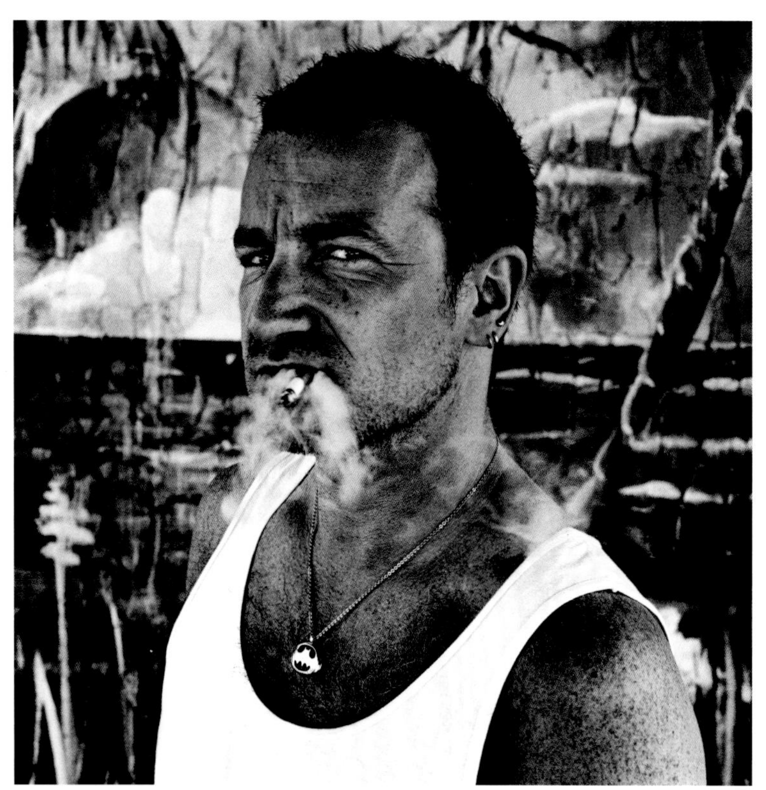

we were trying to play with being
tough characters for this set-up.
street fighters vibe. very convincing edgy
↑ the photo above i call bono-batman

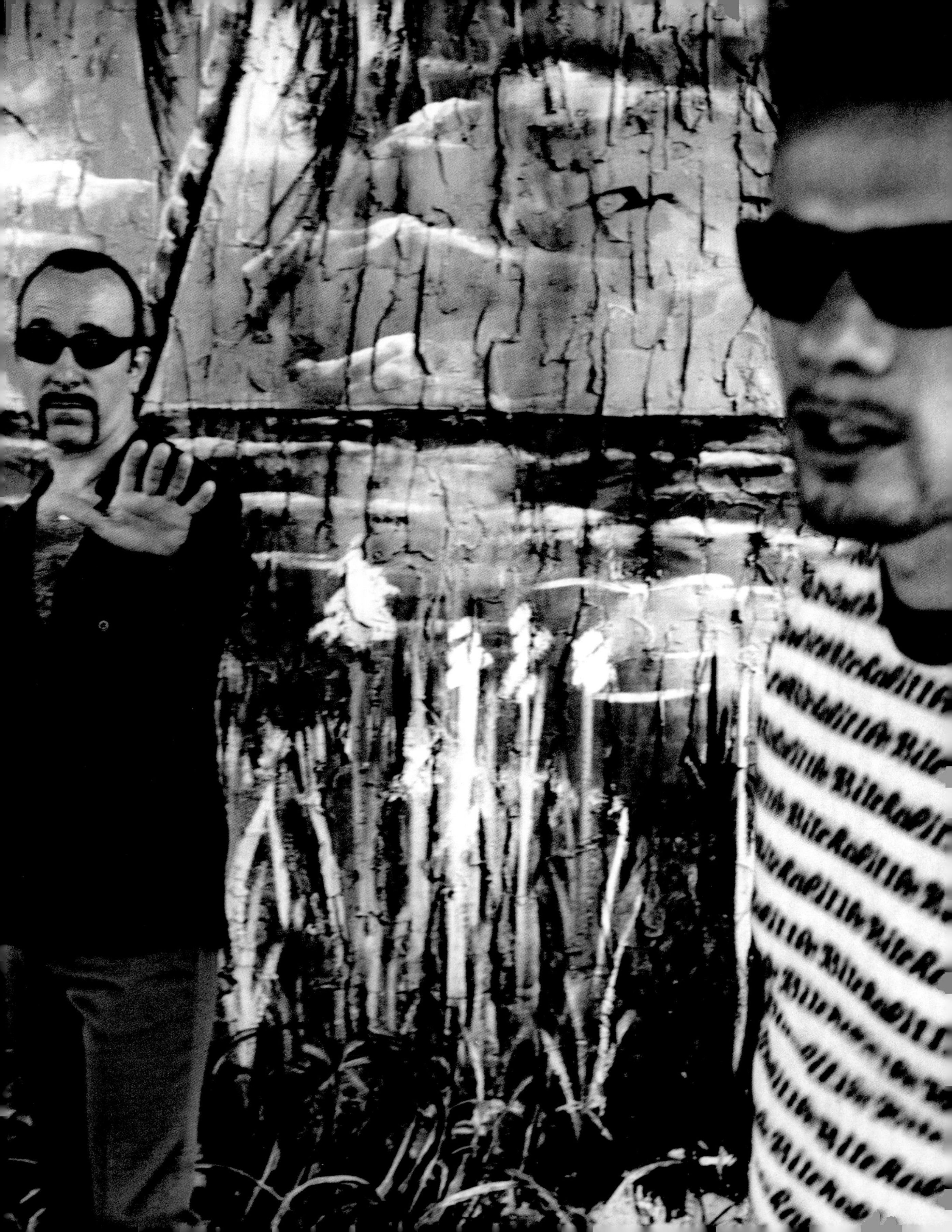

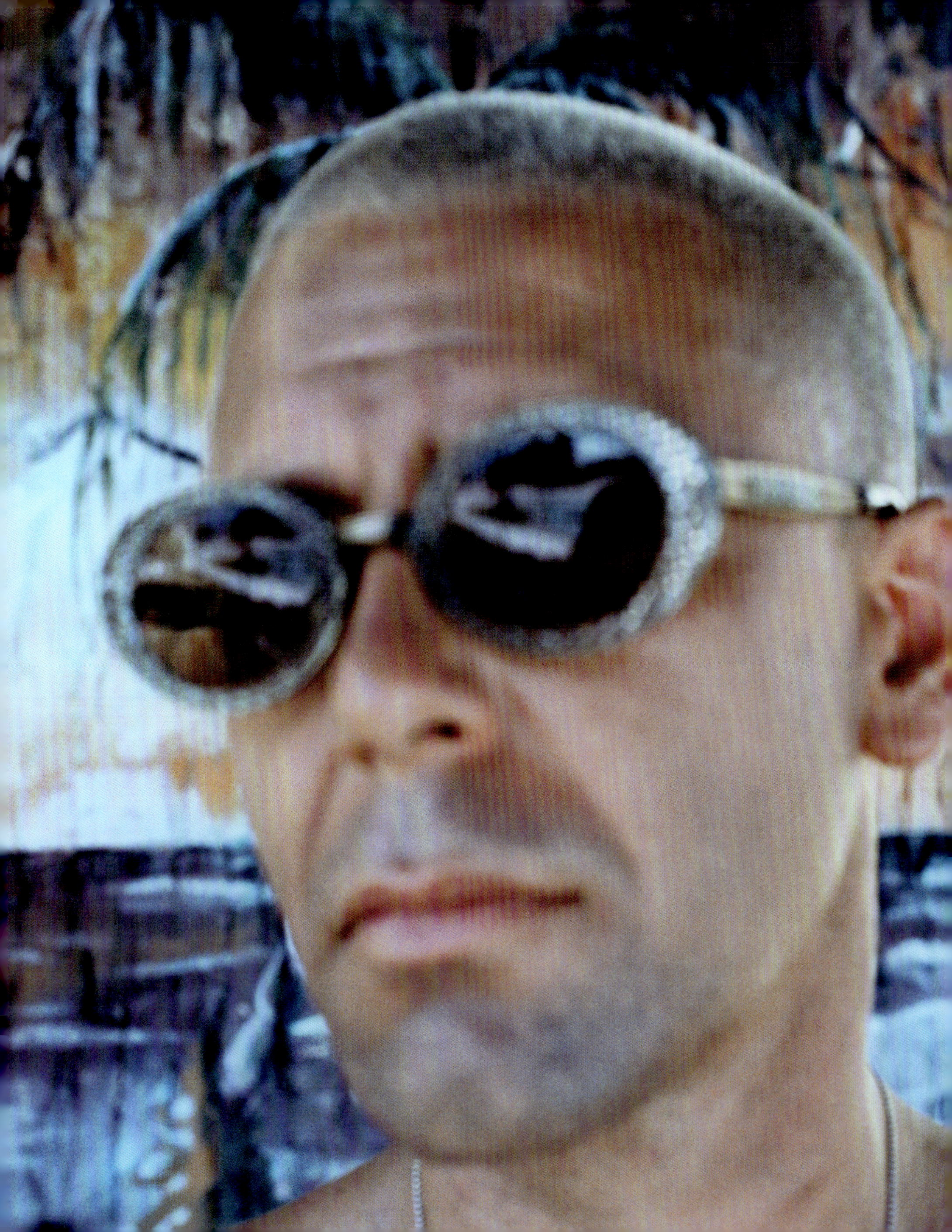

great look for adam

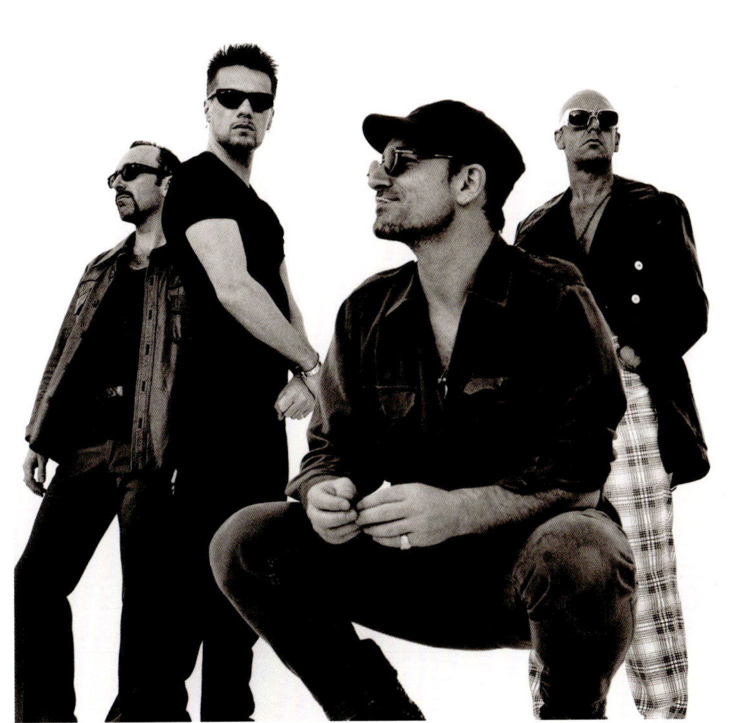

an unusual angle for me, lower than the band.

SAN FRANCISCO 1997 june

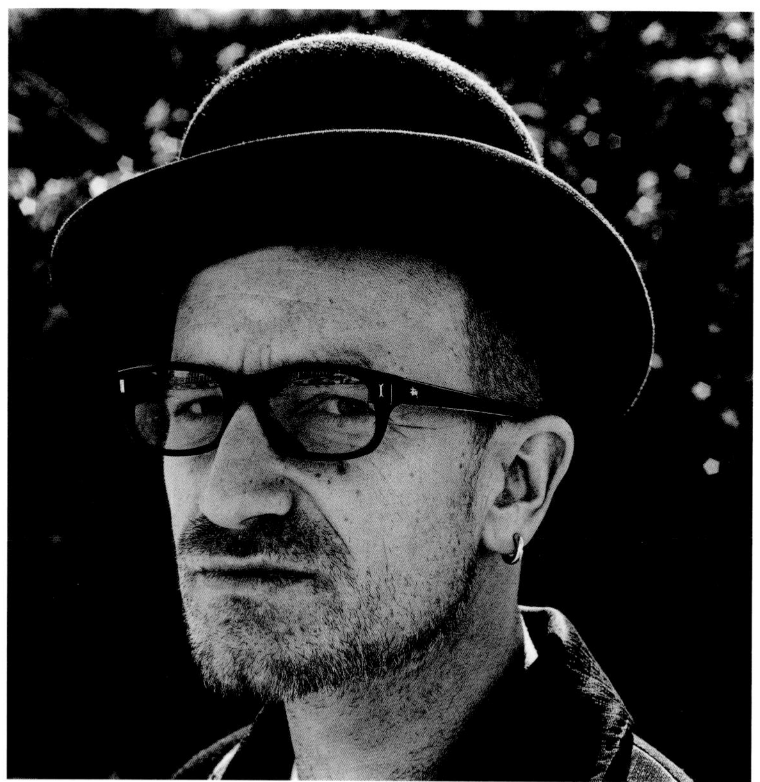

the clothes that the band were wearing on the Popmart tour were so comical and outrageous that they had to be photographed offstage to make them even more absurd. All designed by walter van bierendonck from ANTWERP. Edge as a camp cowboy and bono as a macho fighter took really to the roles of their new personae during the shoot

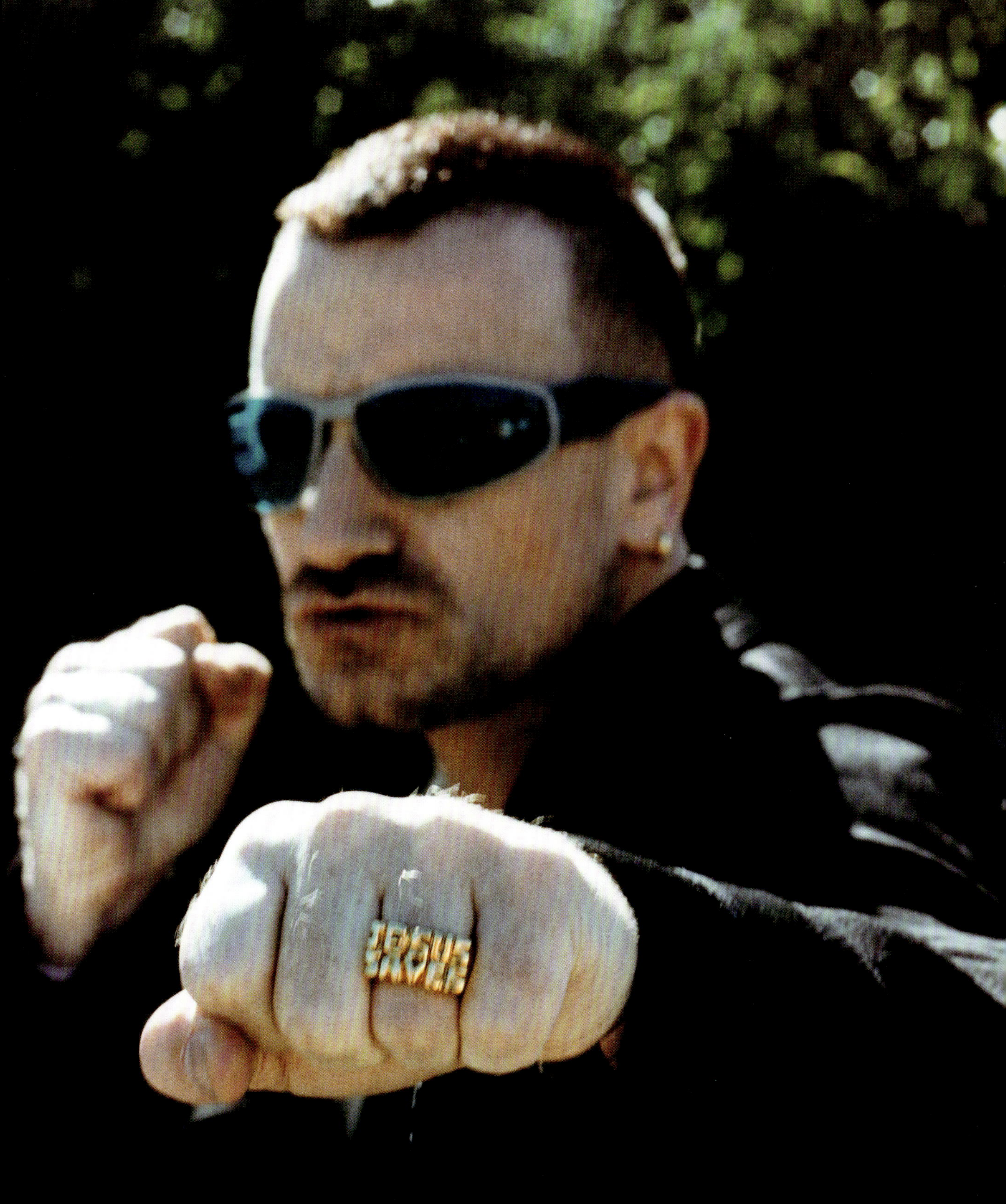

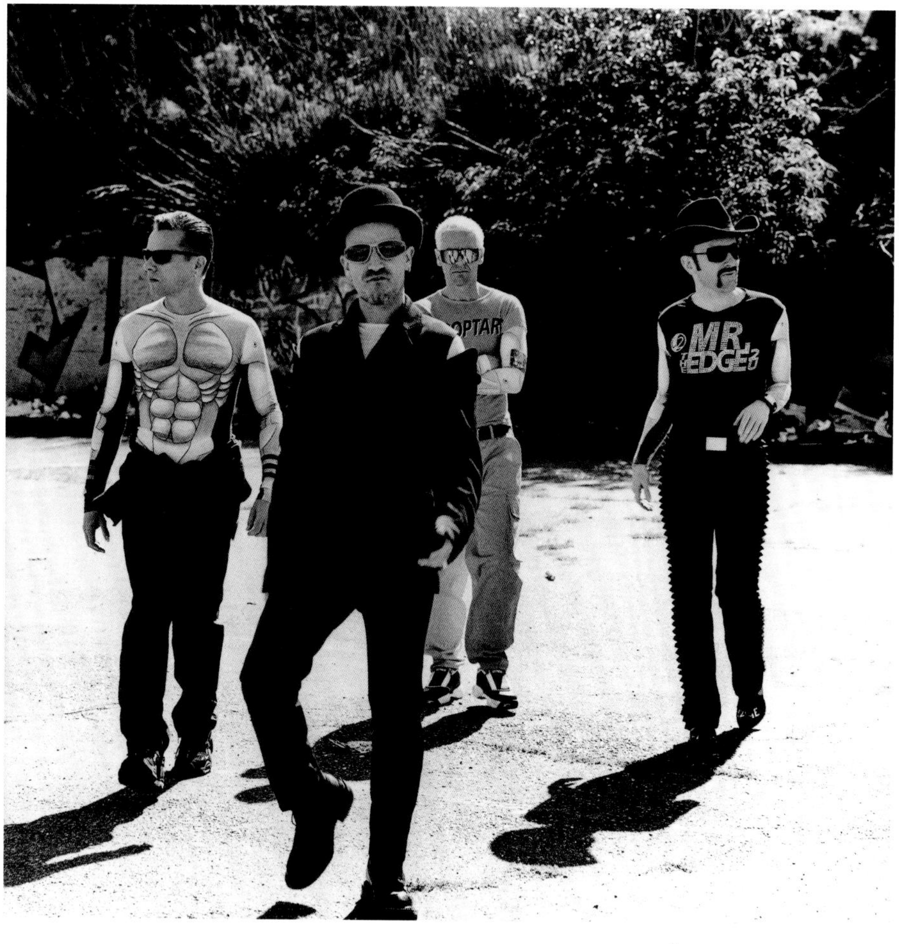

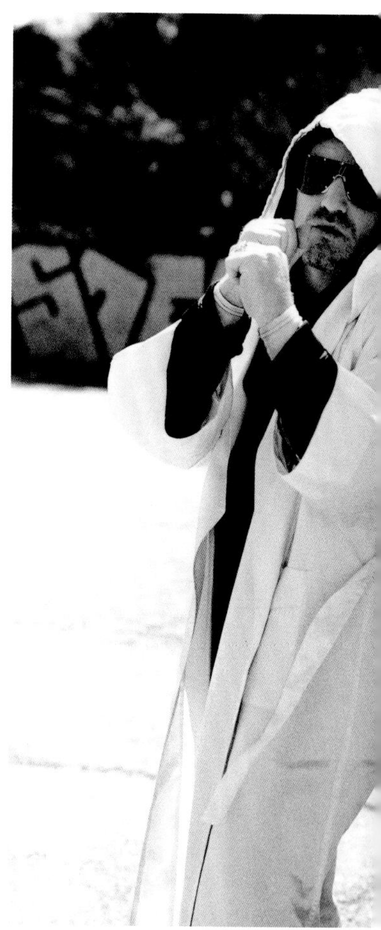

there was a bit of gavin friday in bono's mannerism which is most obvious in the shot on the left.

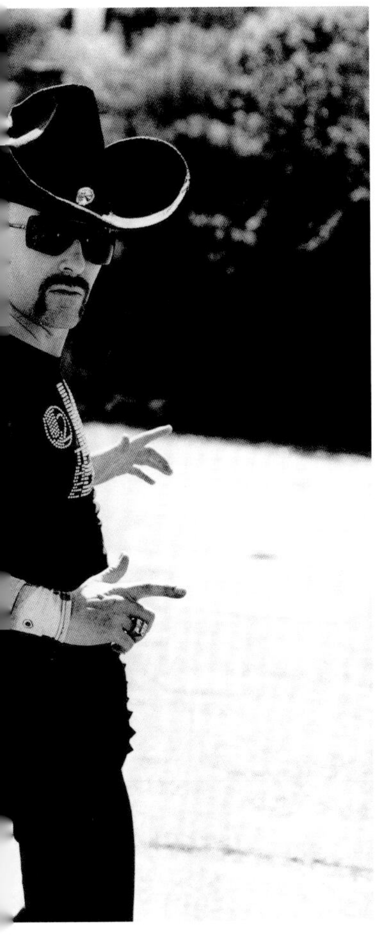

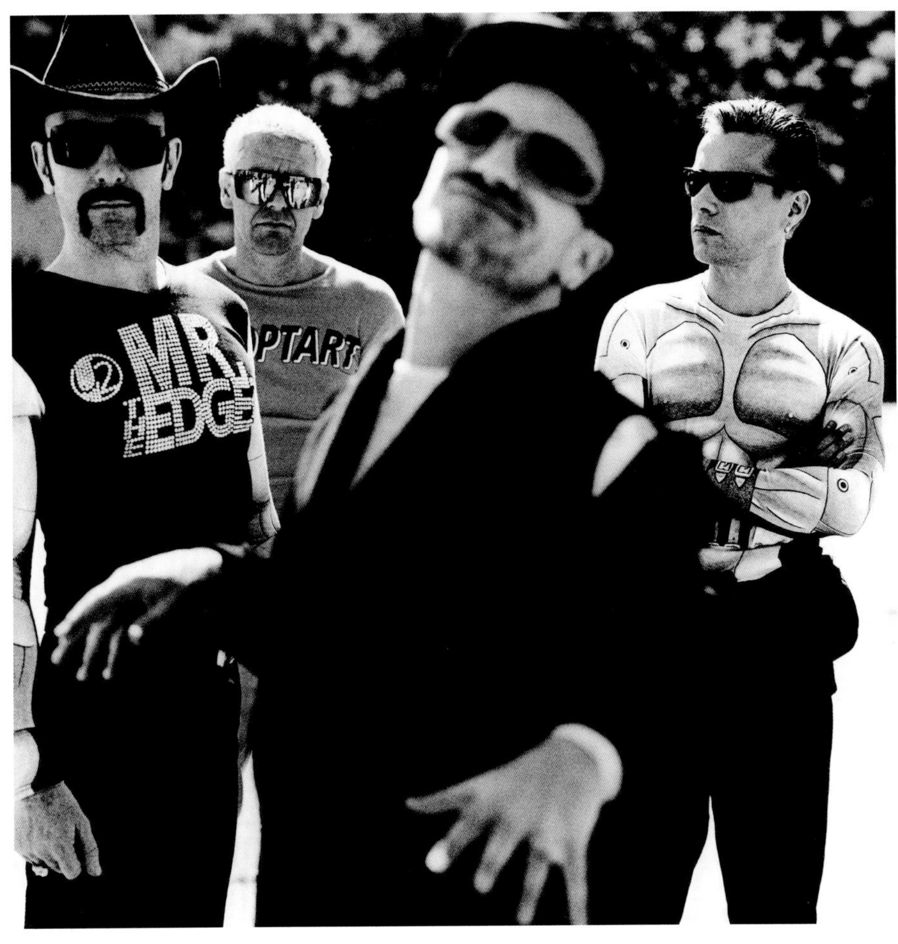

became such a different bunch of guys in these clothes and that was great for the shoot. specially after 15 years of photographs, it was great to get ifferent vibes in group shots and avoid repeat action that way. the shots above were taken (on a sunday) near the studio we had rented for the shoot. it was an industrial area so very quiet on the weekend. overleaf are the studio photographs →

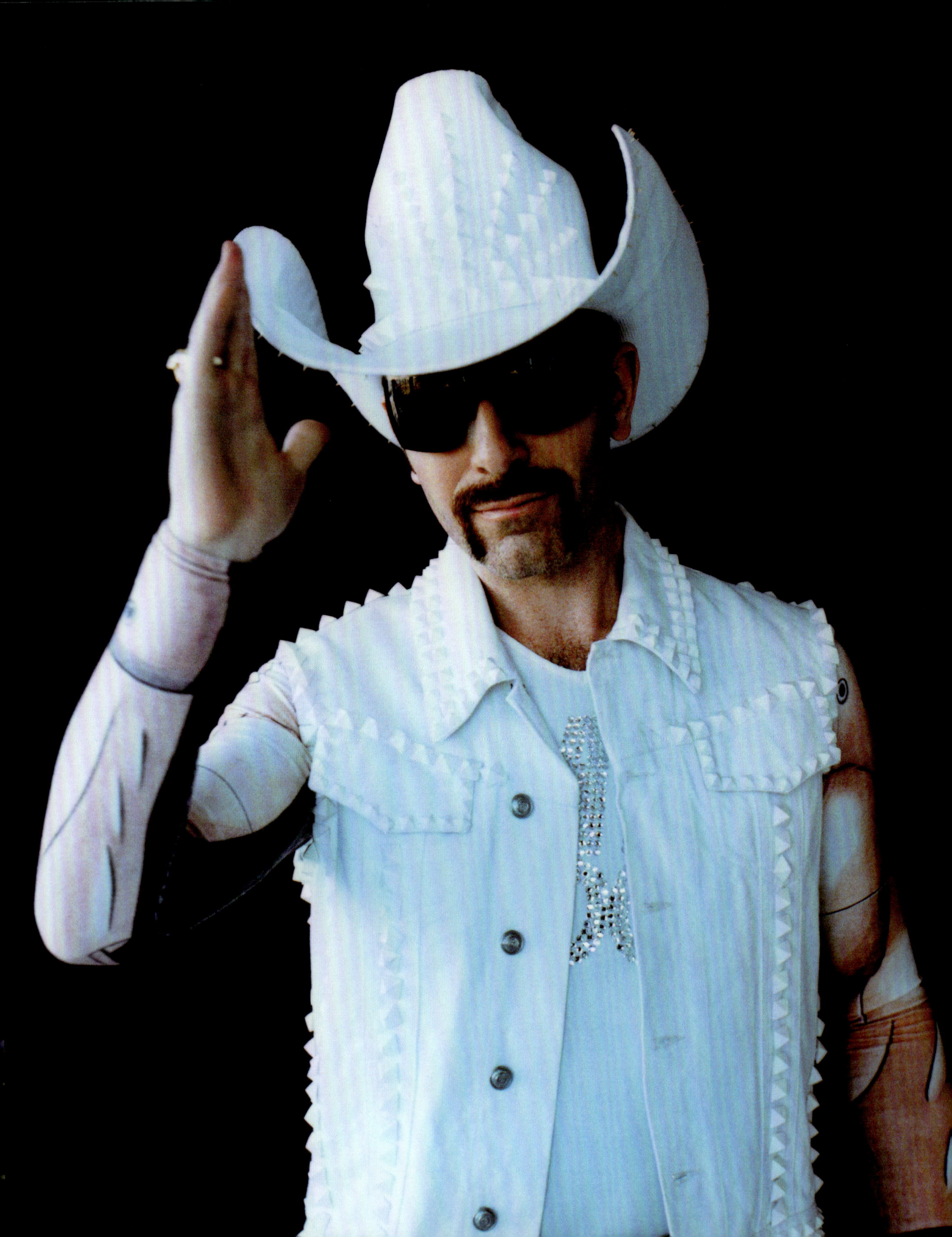

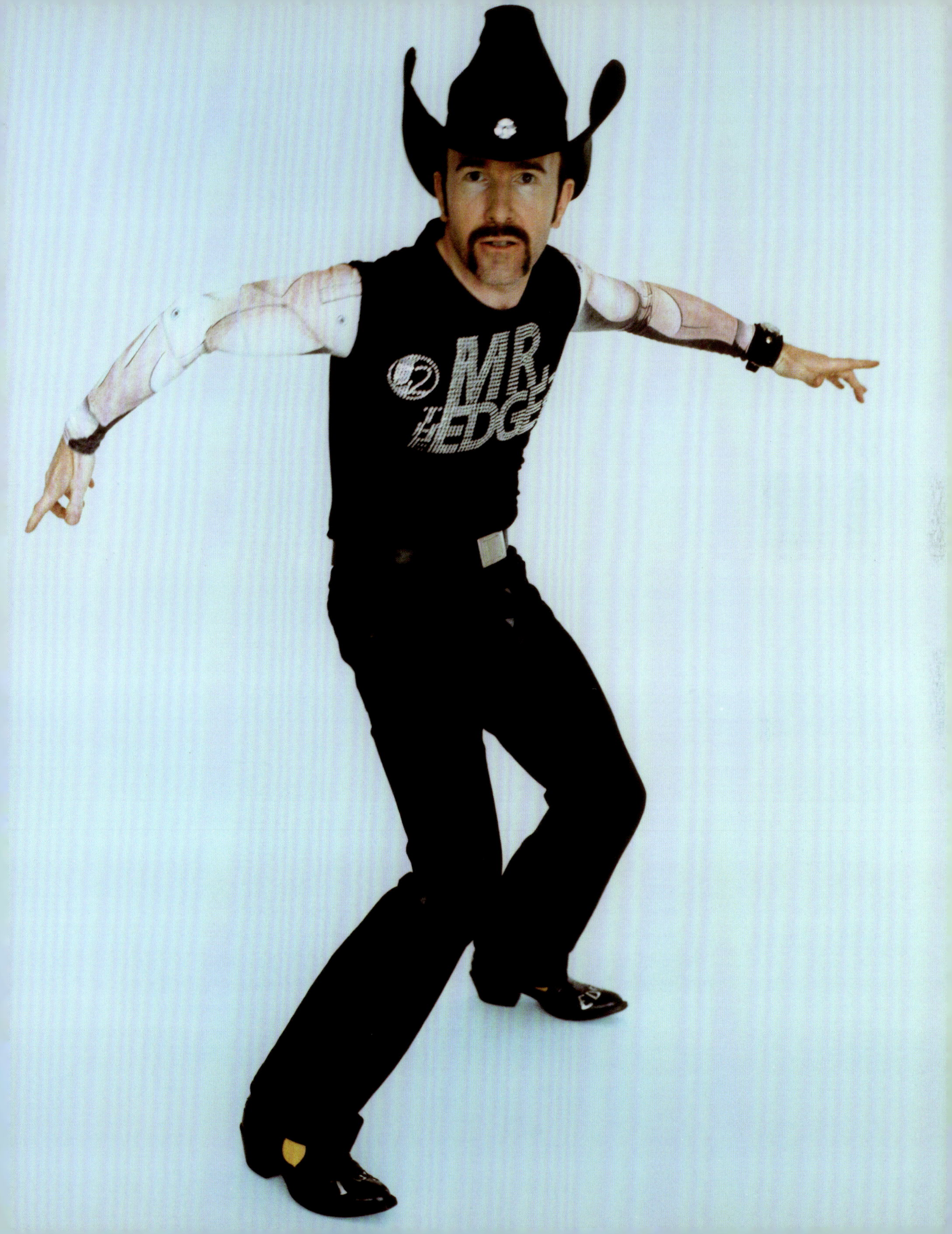

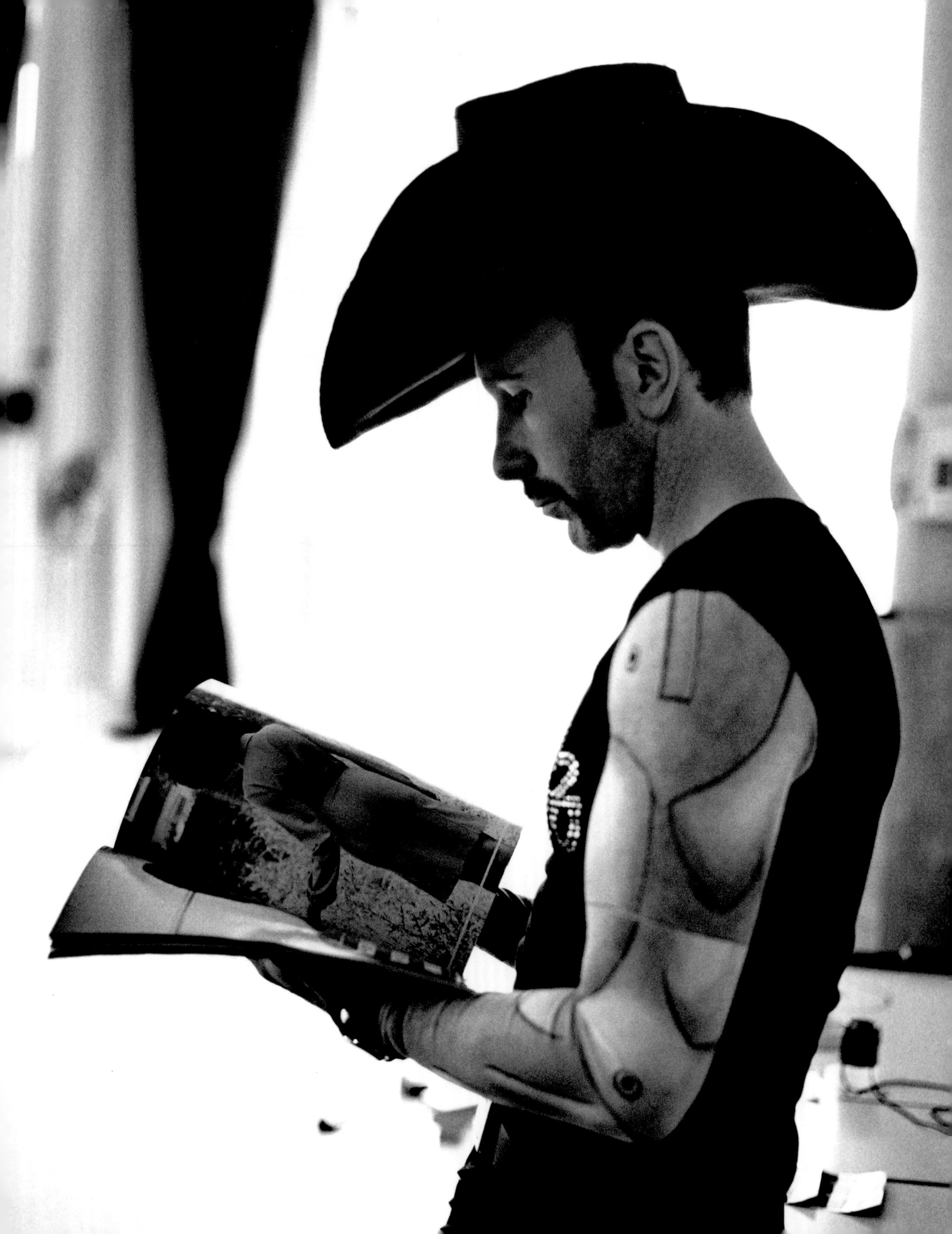

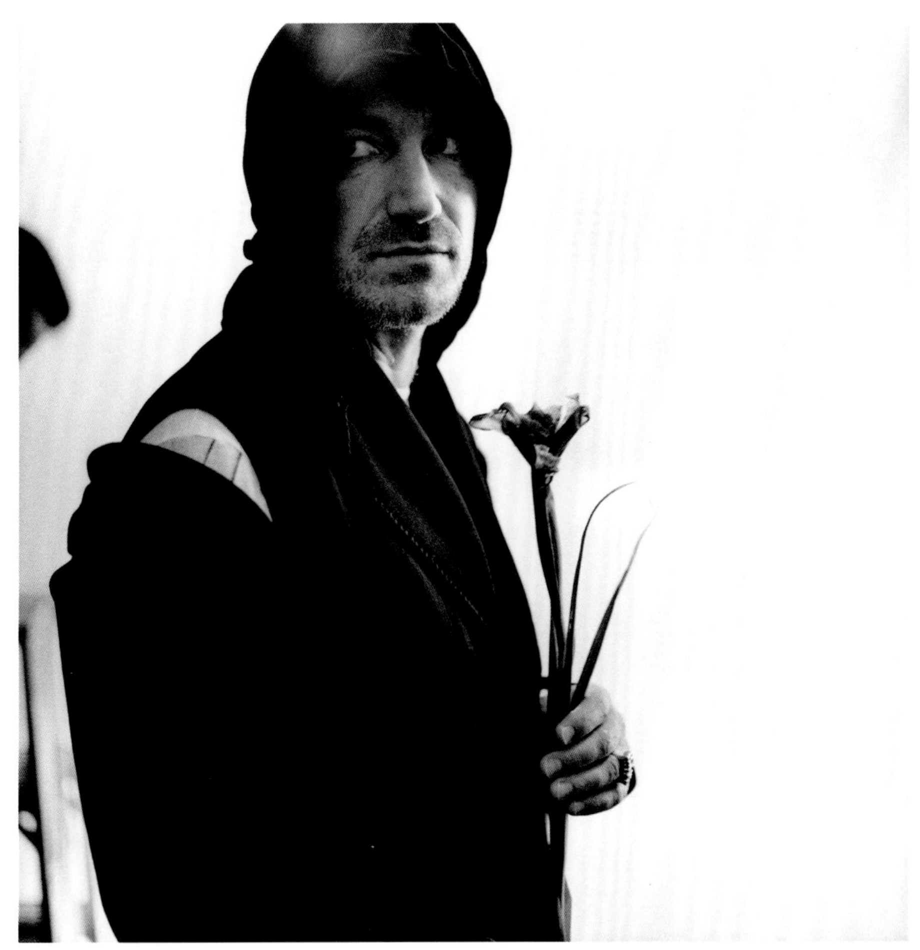

2 moments when edge and bono are not in character acting.

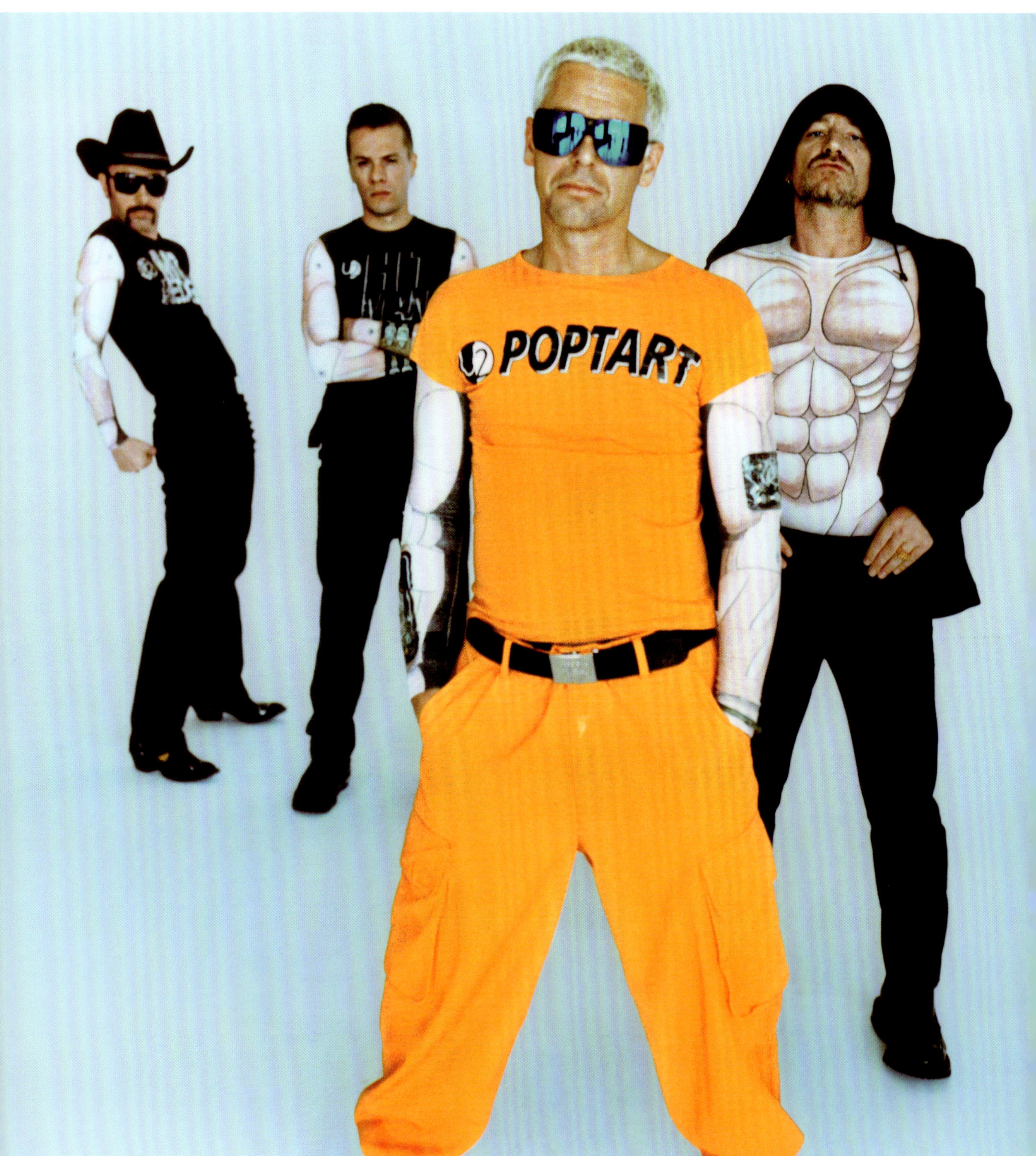
POPTART

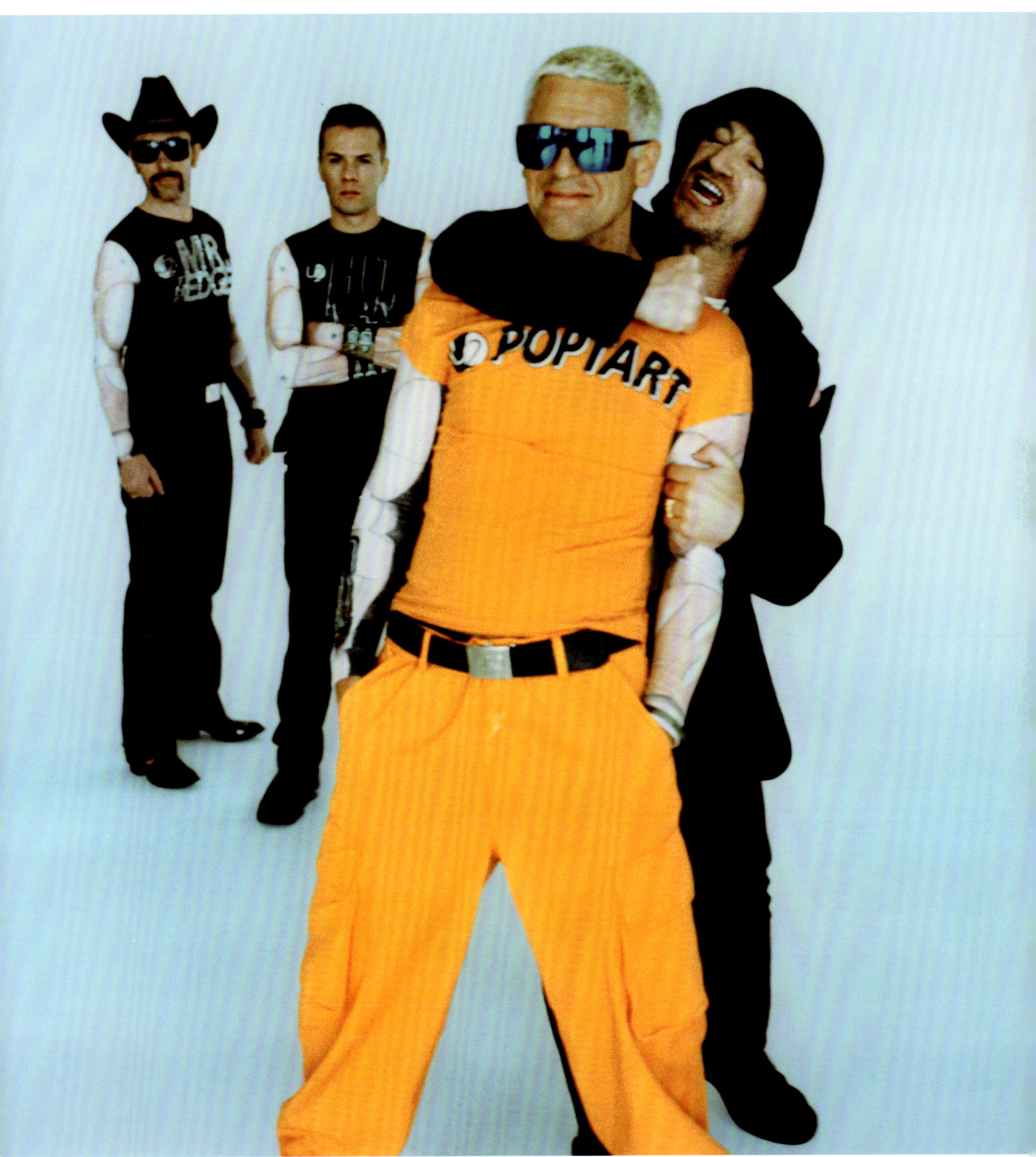
MR
POPTART

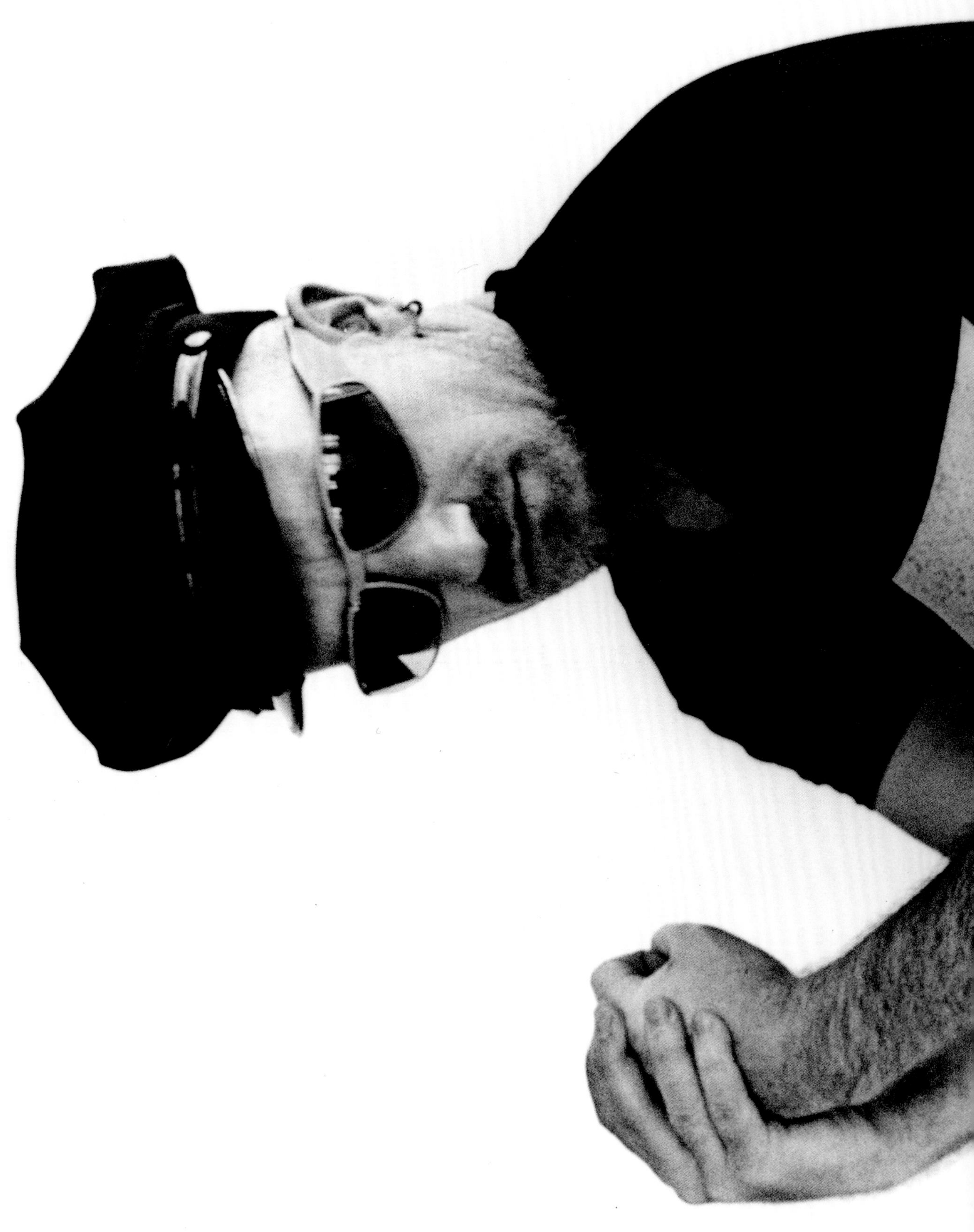

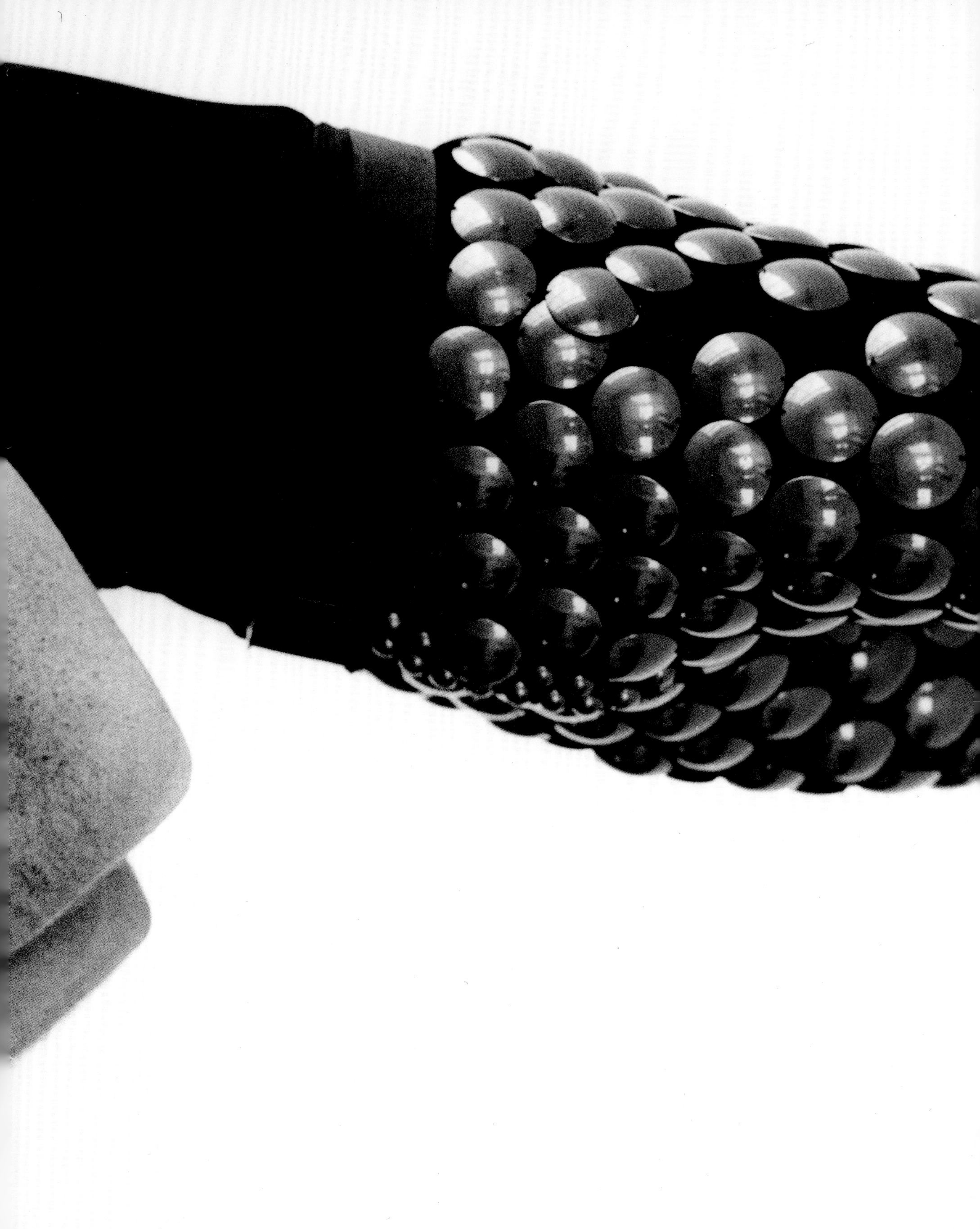

LONDON

1997

august

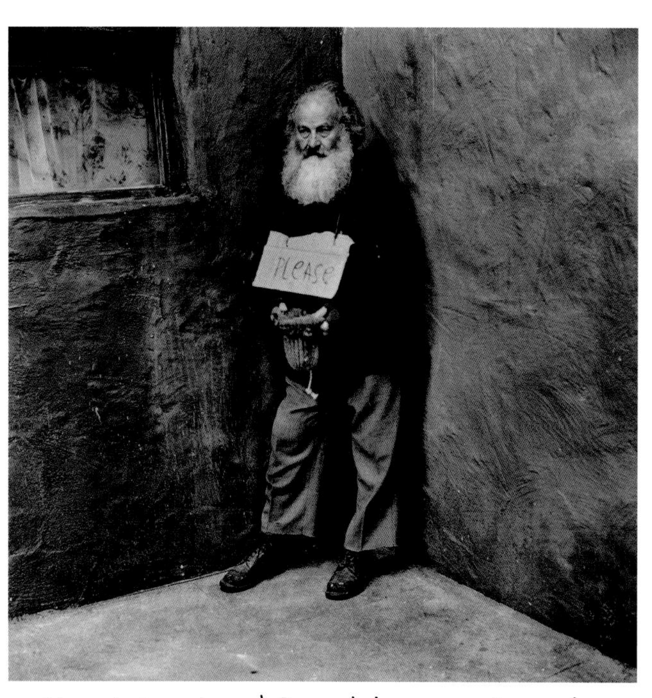

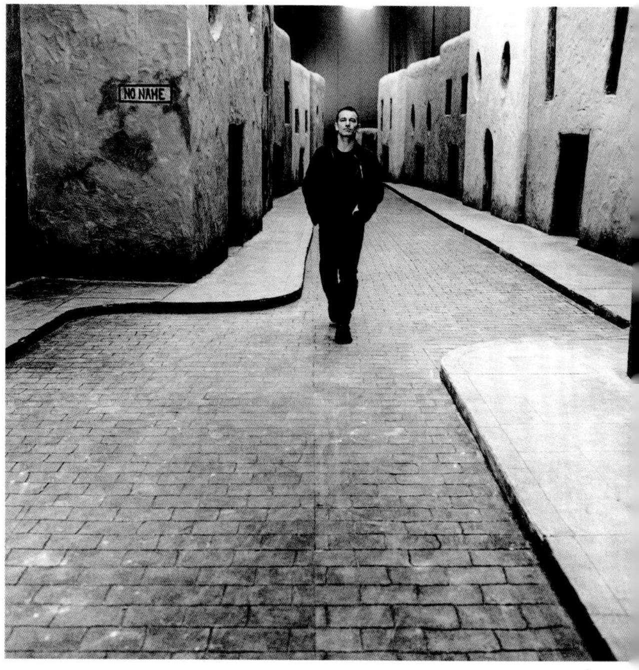

the video for 'PLEASE' is a pretty serious video but pretty funny in places i found. ther
are two kinds of worlds represented - an ideal world and a world based on realit
we shot in a studio in london with a pretty large set that was built for us - lot
of houses with faces on them in a street named "no name". deep stuff!
the man on the left kind of represents God - don't confuse left and right
here. there are two versions of this video and 'my' edit shows bono
crying for real towards the end of the song, which i took as a song about
the religious divide in northern ireland. i remember vividly that
princess diana died during the edit as i had to meet the band
in paris to show them my edit of the video and watching the funera
in a room in paris.

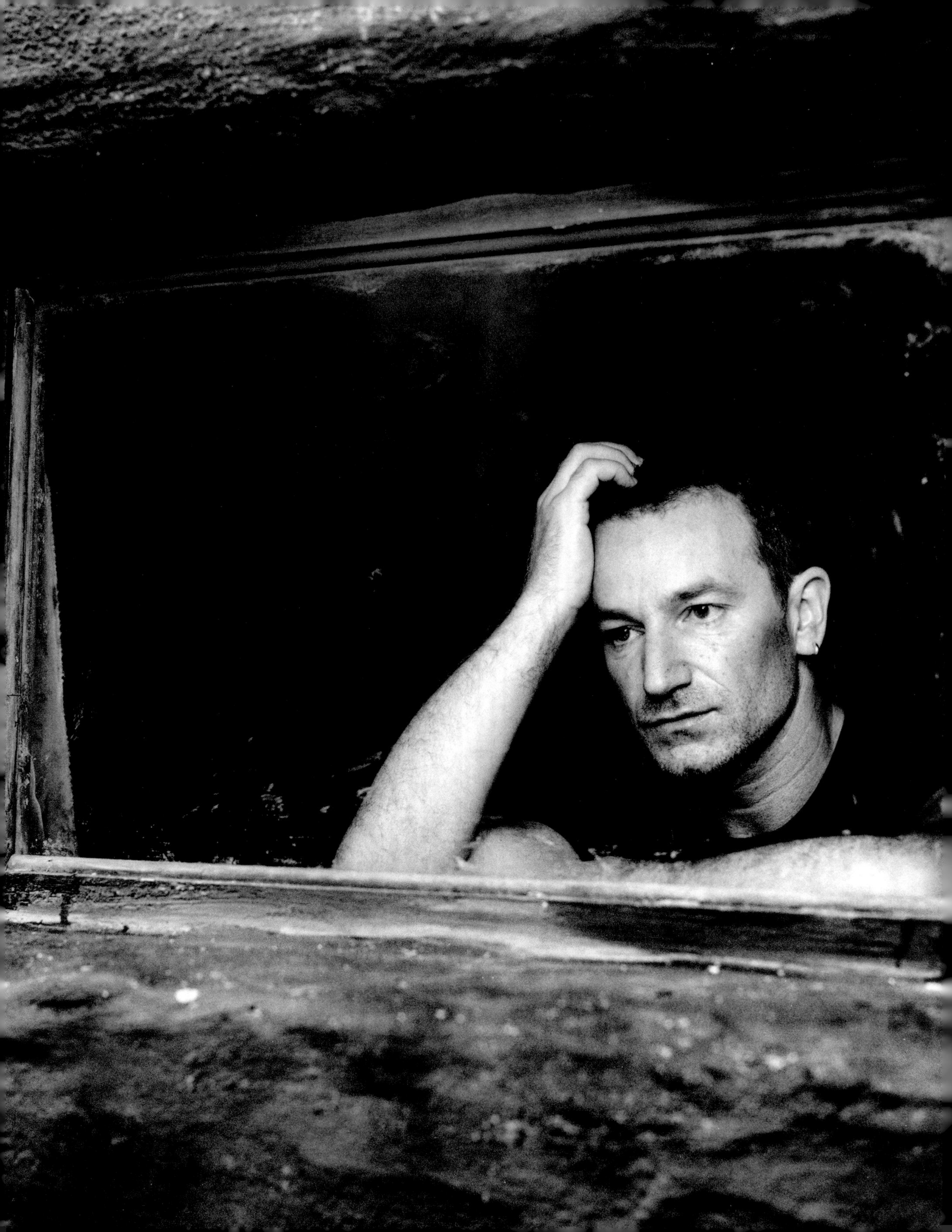

Mexico 1997

december

cabo san lucas
~~or de luca~~?

cactus ↓ ↓ bono cactus ↓

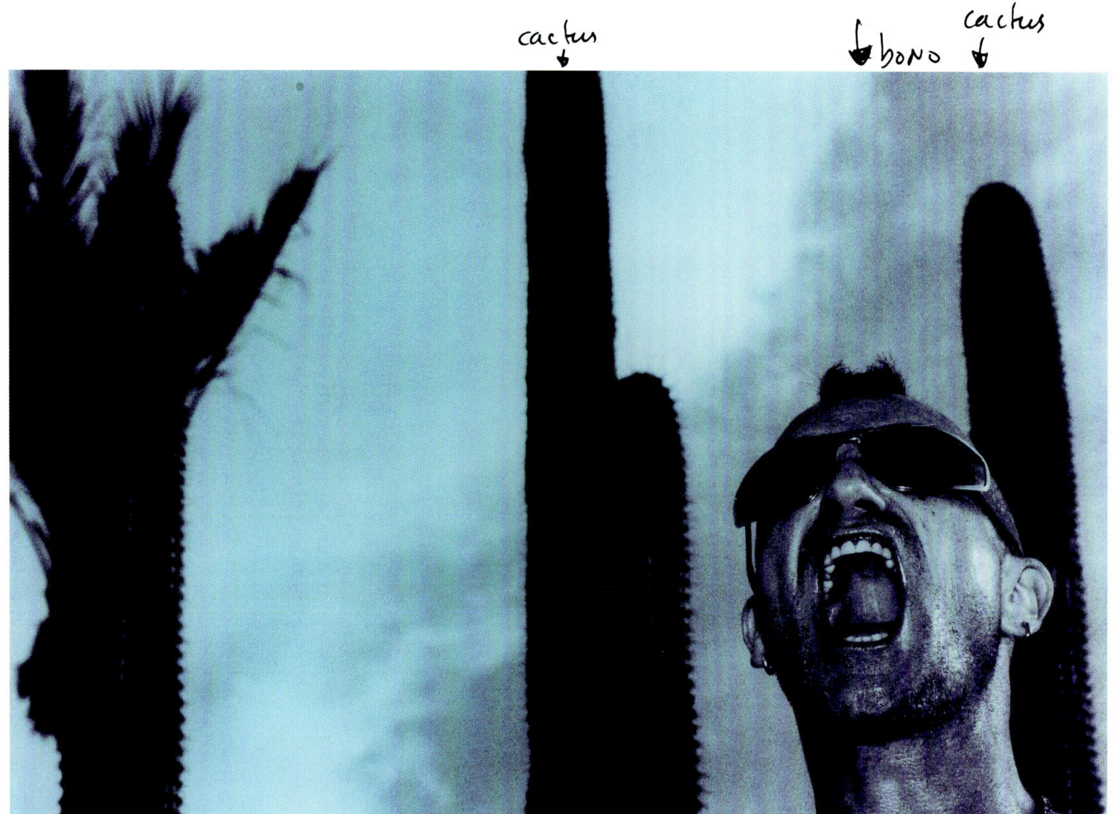

i came to visit U2 in mexico city for their 2 concerts there; i only saw one of these as i fell asleep in bono's hotelroom (jetlag is to blame) on the first night and was woken up by having thrown cups of cold water over me by bono and friends around 3 am. Obviously i made a real effort the next night to stay awake and see the show which was pretty incredible and was filmed for a video-release as well. There was some tension after the show as a bit of wildwest behaviour occurred involving mexican bodyguards for a relative of the president who hit one of U2's security people with a gun. Ola! But the real reason i came to mexico was to take a photo of Bono for my new 'blue' series.

sombrero bought locally by sharon blankson

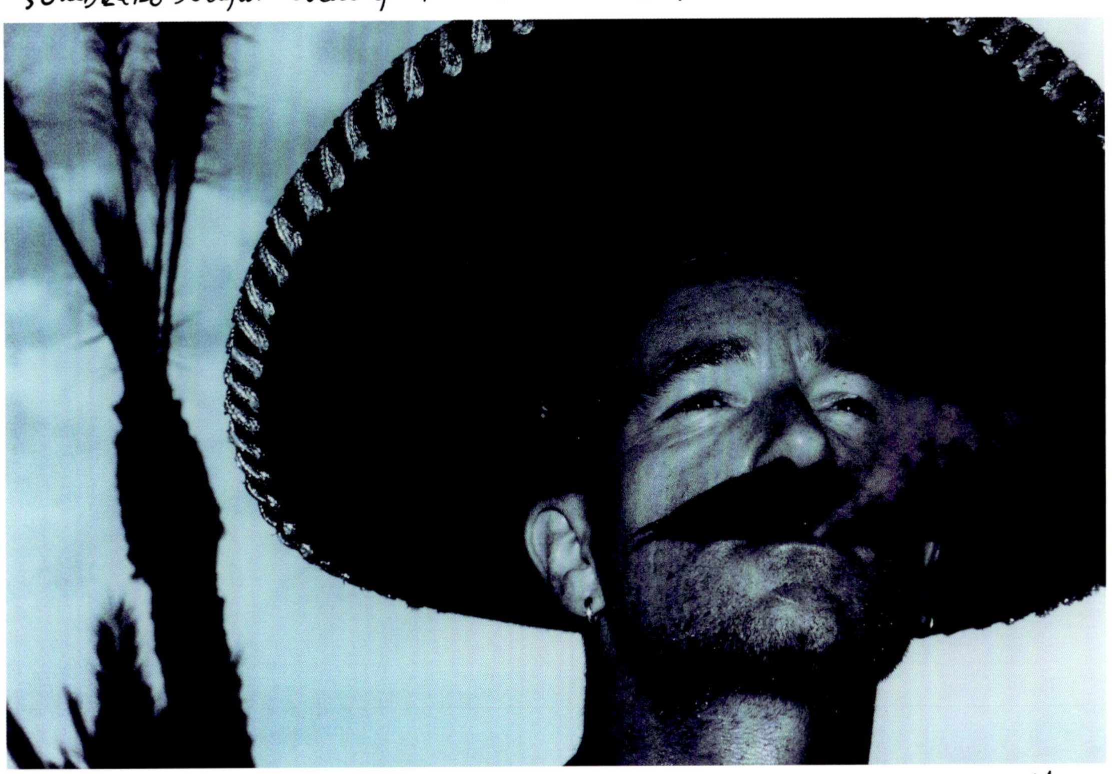

this series was eventually called '33 still lives' and dealt with the way celebrity was being visualised in the media and the role the paparazzi played in this. It dealt with truth and lies. after the concerts in mexico city we spent some time in Cabo san lucas where i persuaded bono to pose for me as a bandito and he decided to go one step further and shave his head to the point of a mohawk with which we did some photos in a golfcart (see my book 'WERK') and also some with cacti (see page left). above a relaxing Bandito. after the shoot he got rid of the mohawk as he only had 2 more shows to do that year and there are some decisions that are made easier when tequila is around.

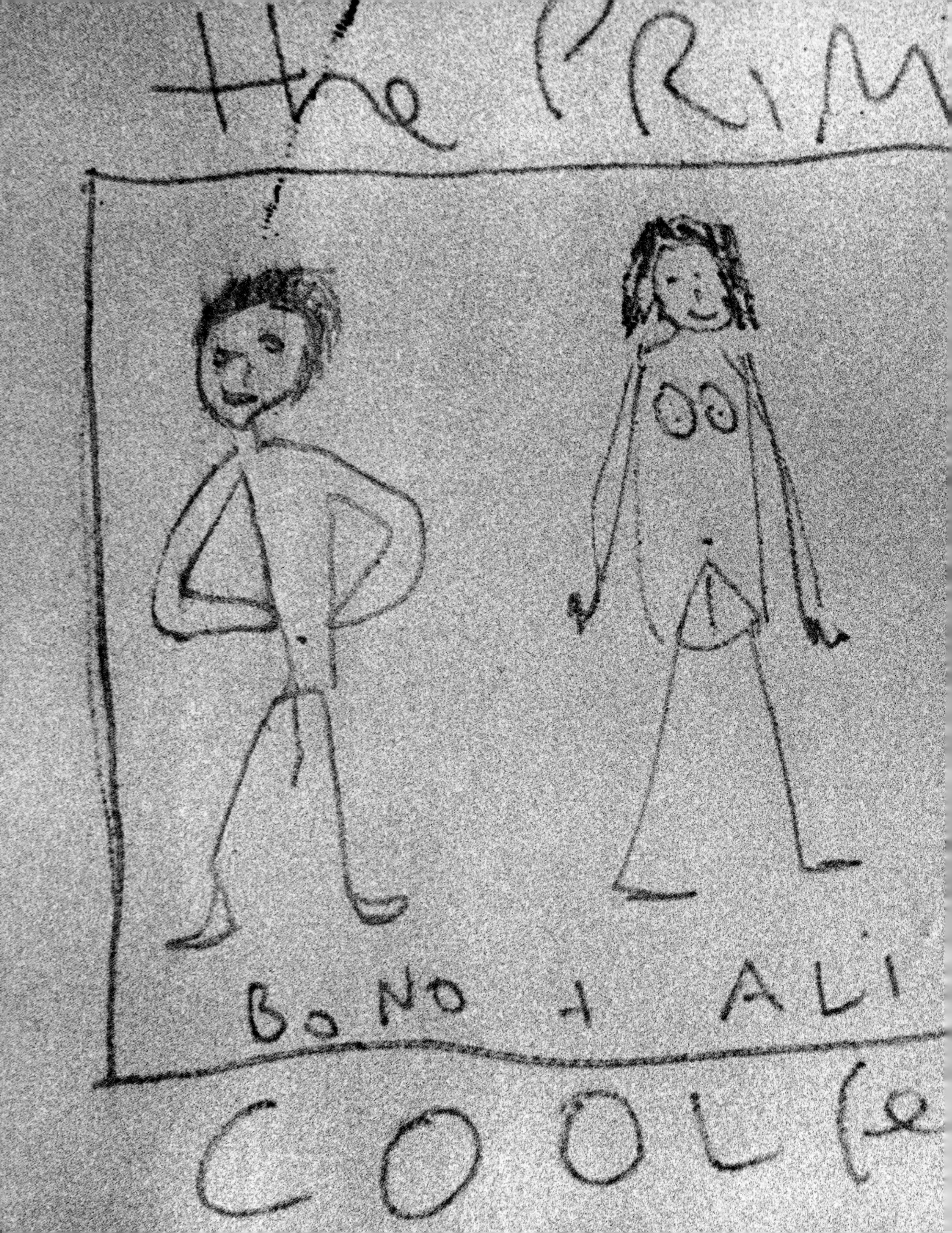
the PRIM
BONO + ALI
COOL

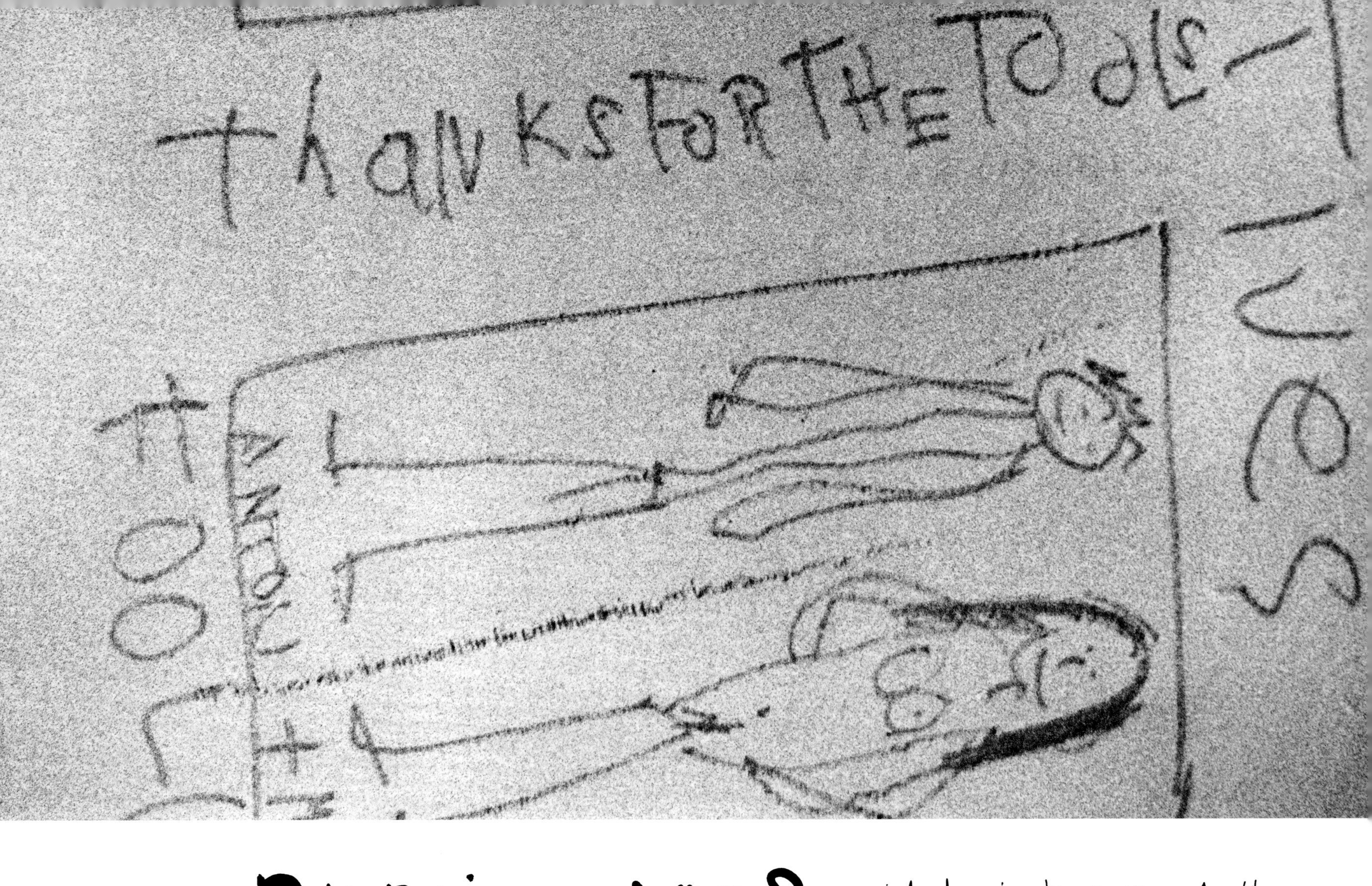

DUBLIN, july 1998

i do drawings too, on request. the one year i didn't take photos of U2 was 1998 – there was little band activity so nothing really was photographed. fortunately, i did stay at bono's house that year and made a drawing on his bathroom wall which is still there. it is quite high up, near the ceiling and even i had to get a chair to photograph this. don't ask me what it all meant.

los ANGELES 1999

bono →

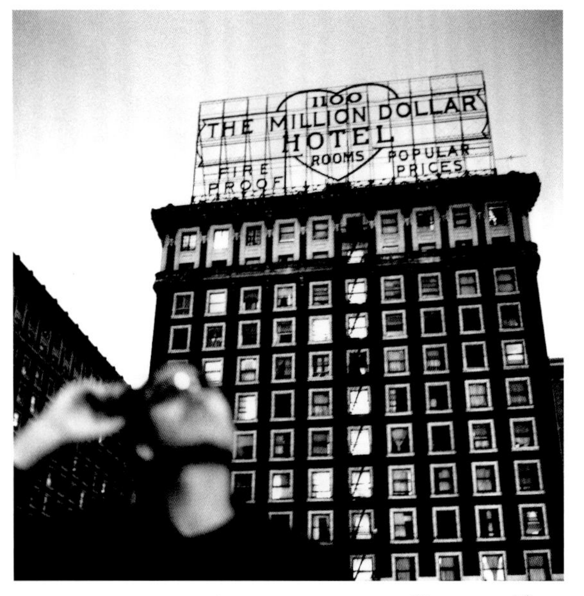

← hotel

on the set and in front of the million dollar hotel. as you might recall from previous chapters, bono & me first came to this hotel in 1987 and it got bono into writing a script about this place which eventually got made into a movie by wim wenders and starring mel gibson and milla jovovich amongst others. even bono and myself are in it for a brief second. the movie looks amazing, as do most of wim's films. we just stopped by a few times - me because i was very curious and bono because he is involved and curious. on the right he is standing next to wim.

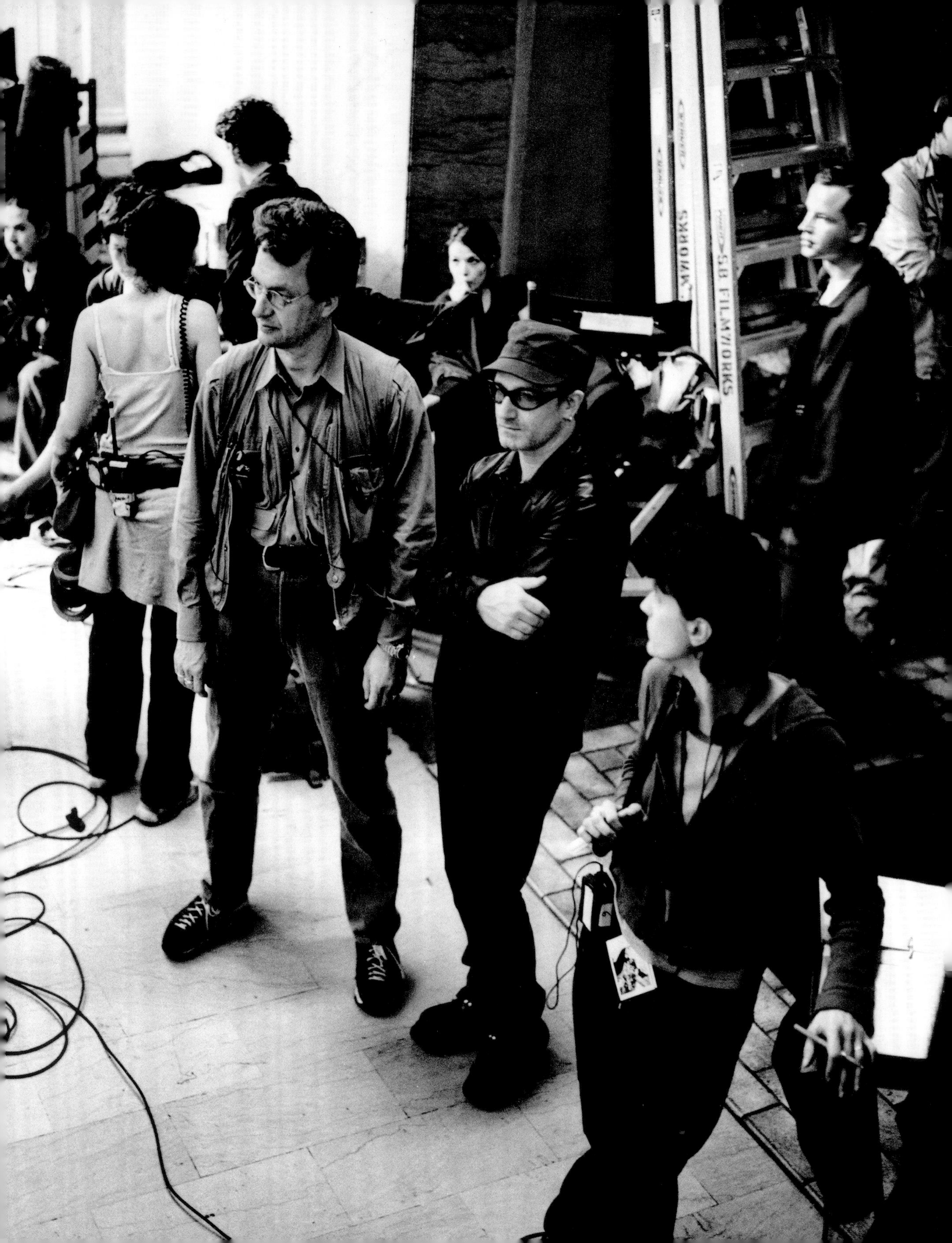
SB FILMWORKS

DUBLIN 1999

november

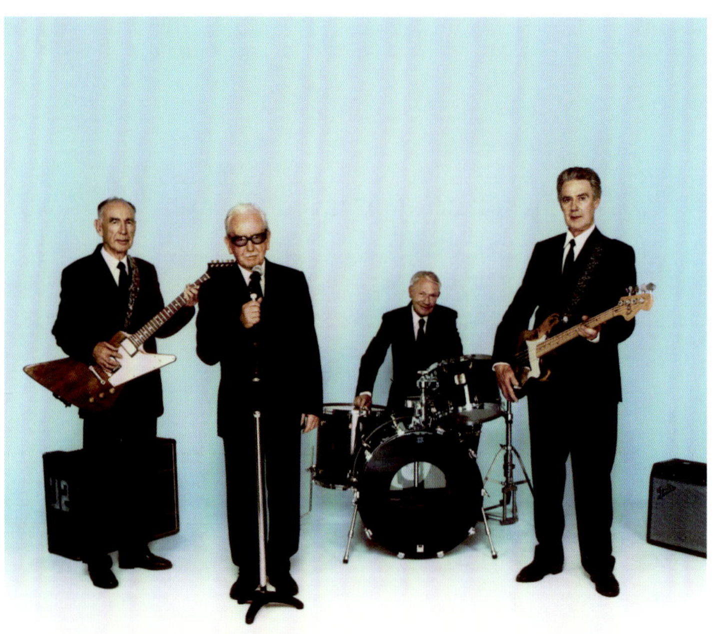

bobo
pau
hews

perhaps the most far reaching photograph anyone could do within the 'rock-photography' framework: the sons and the fathers. as this book deals amongst other issues, with the passing of time, how better to illustrate it than with the past, the present and the possible future. all this on a quiet sunday afternoon in dublin. by dressing everyone similar, the genetics become very visible. i let the photos just speak for themselves, only to say that the shoot was a very moving experience for me. i can only imagine what it must do to the band looking at these photos.

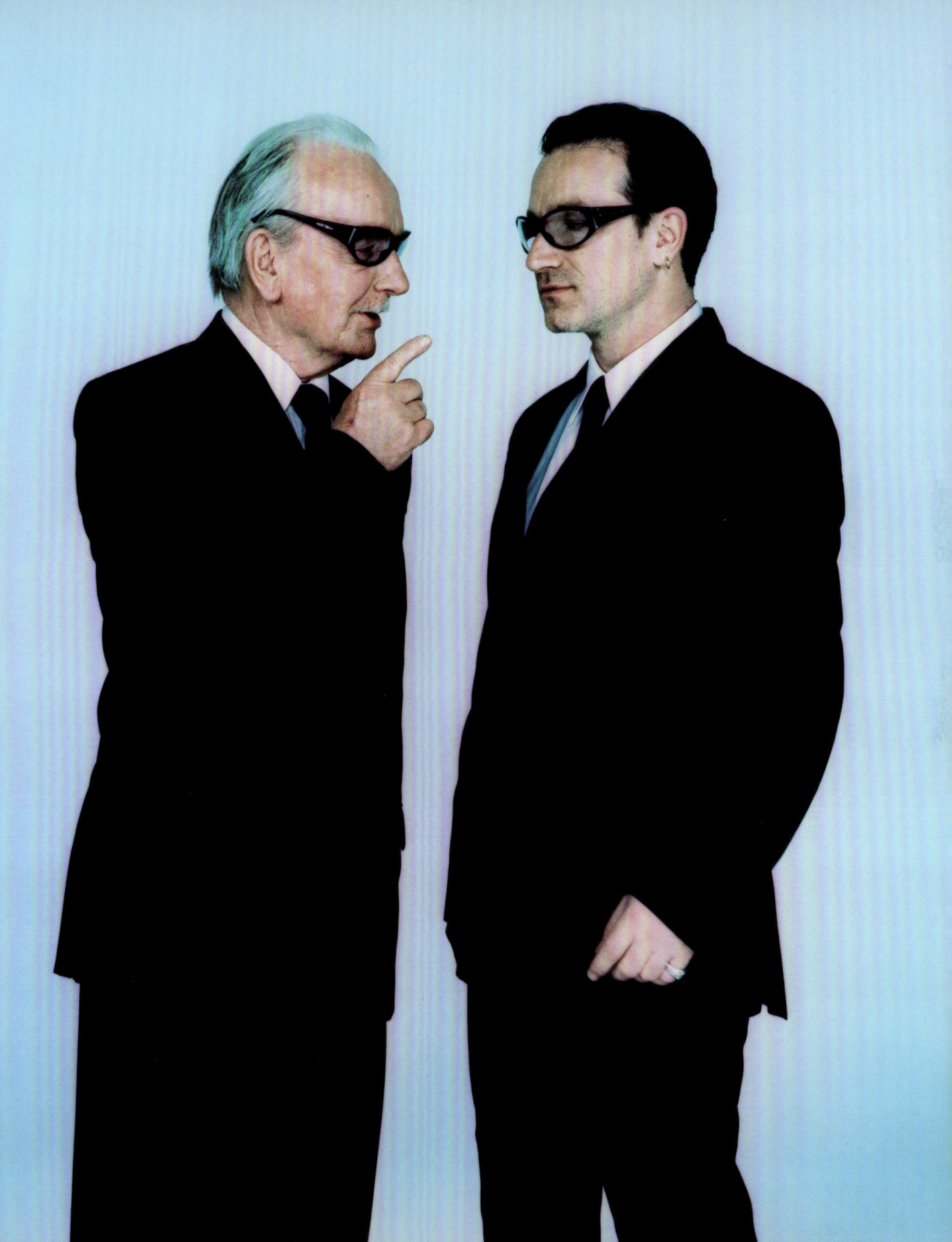

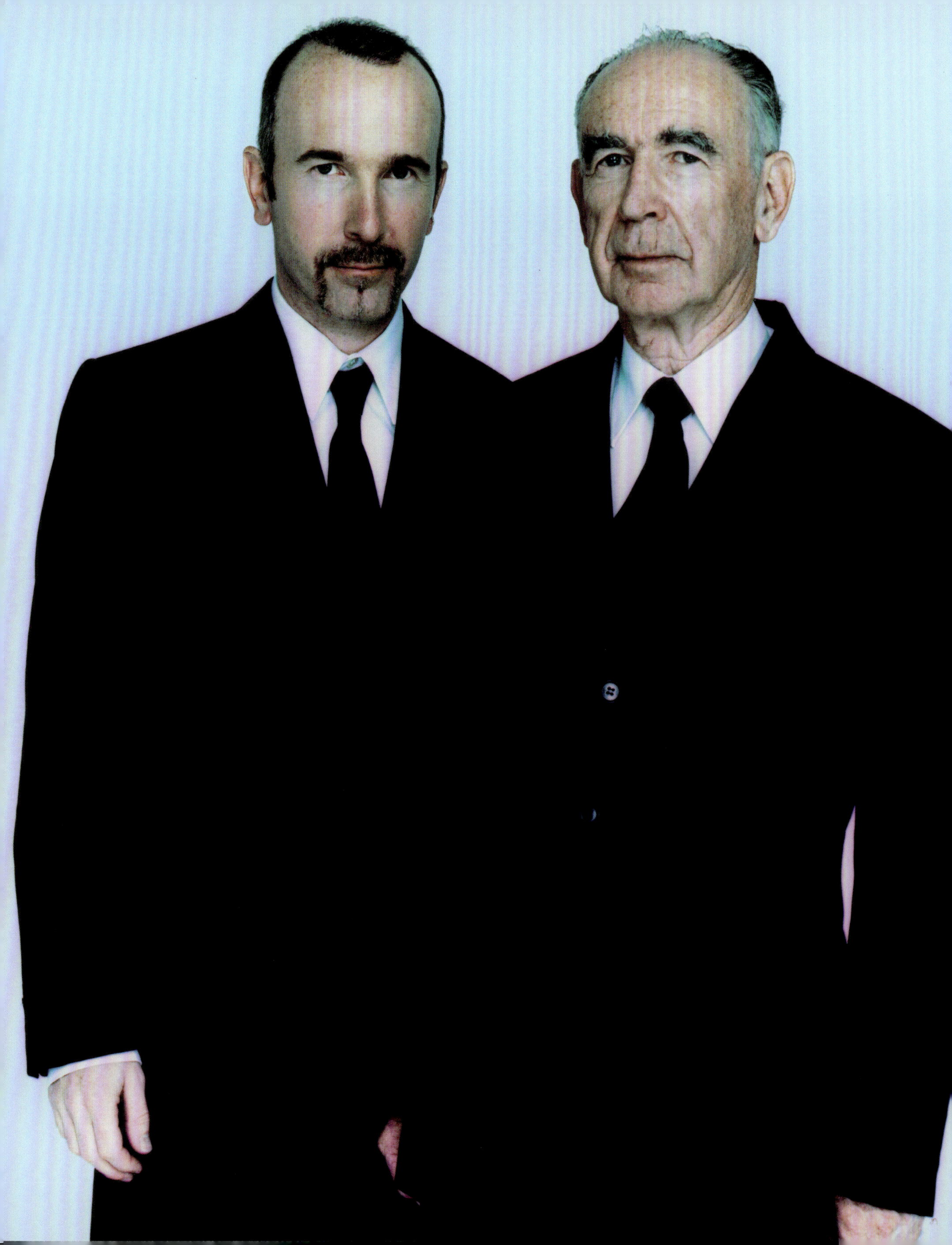

ave and
gavin
evans

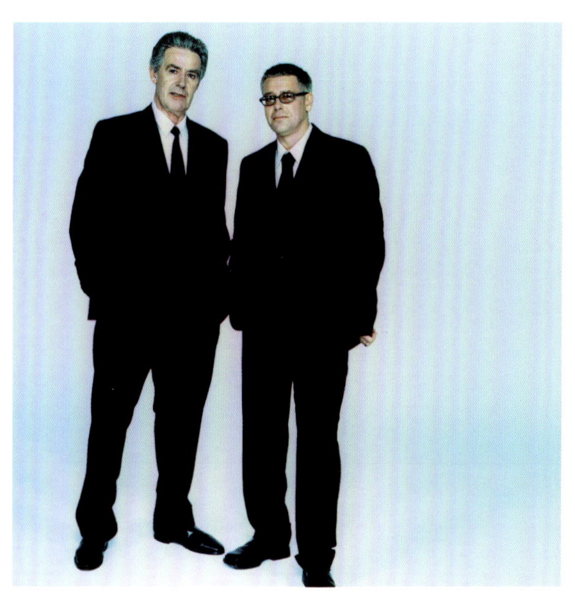

brian and adam clayton

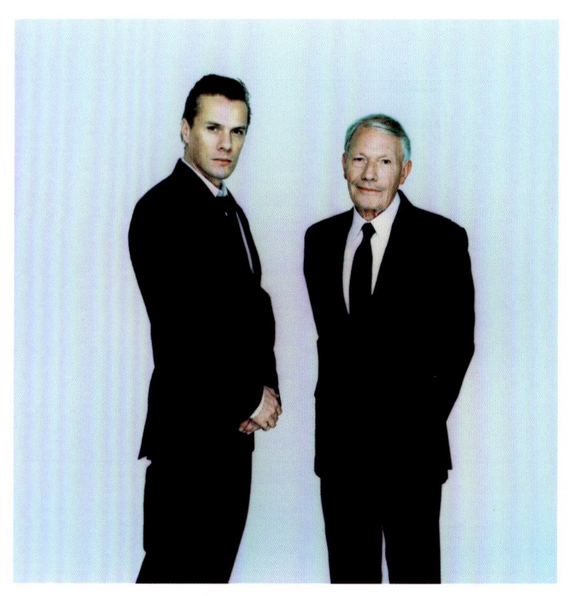

larry mullen jr. and larry mullen sr.

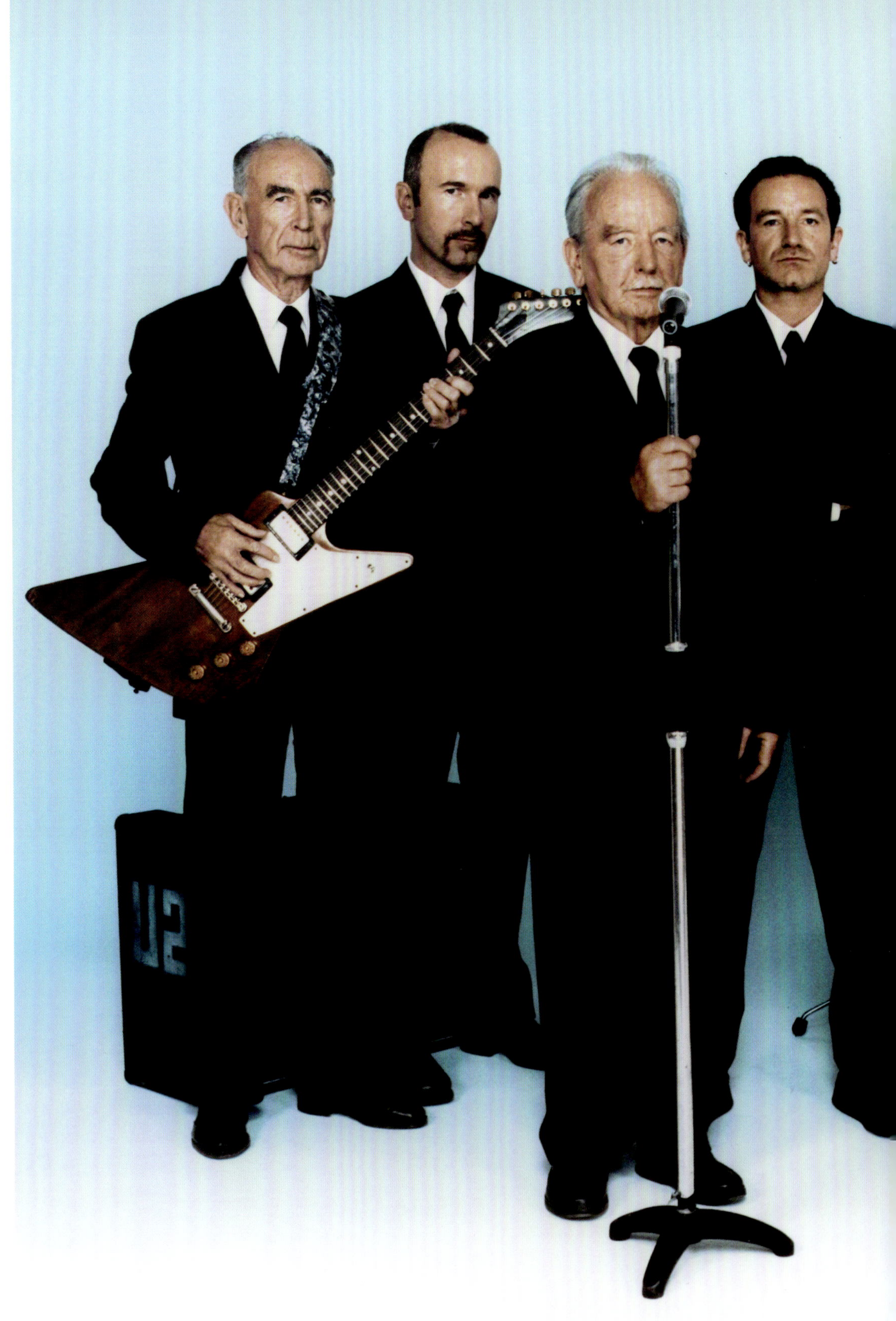
U2

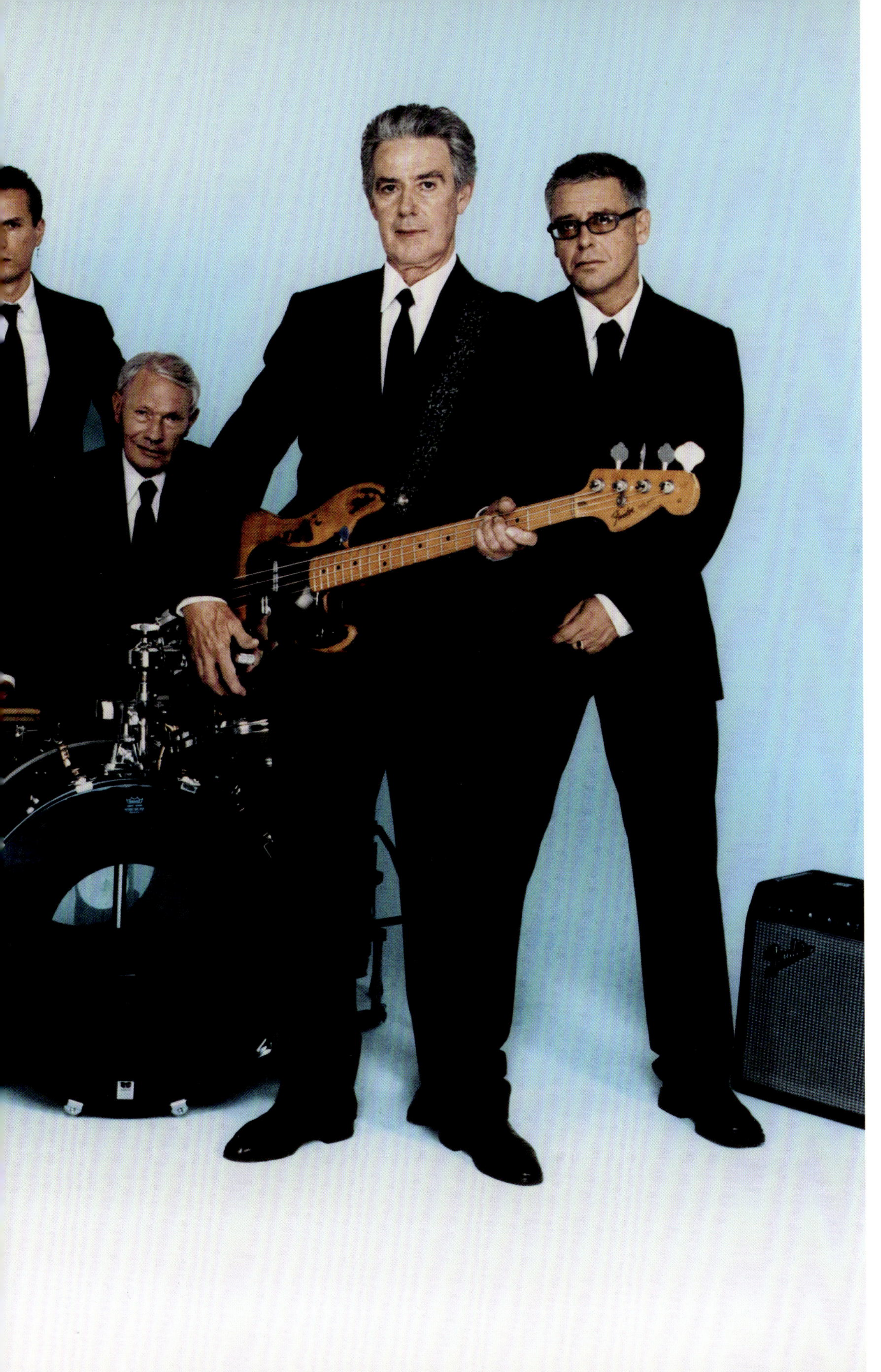

IRELAND & FRANCE 2000

april

"all that you can't leave behind" locations

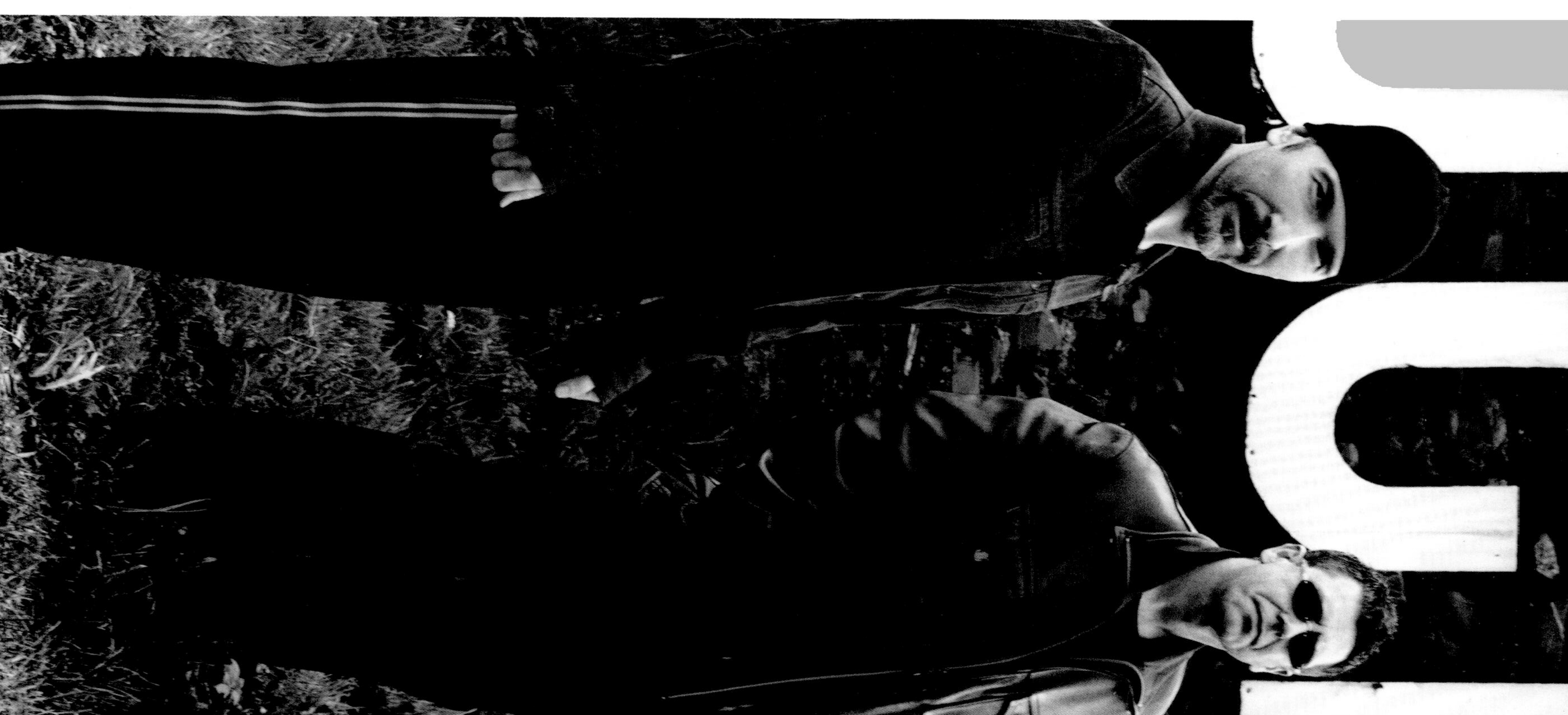

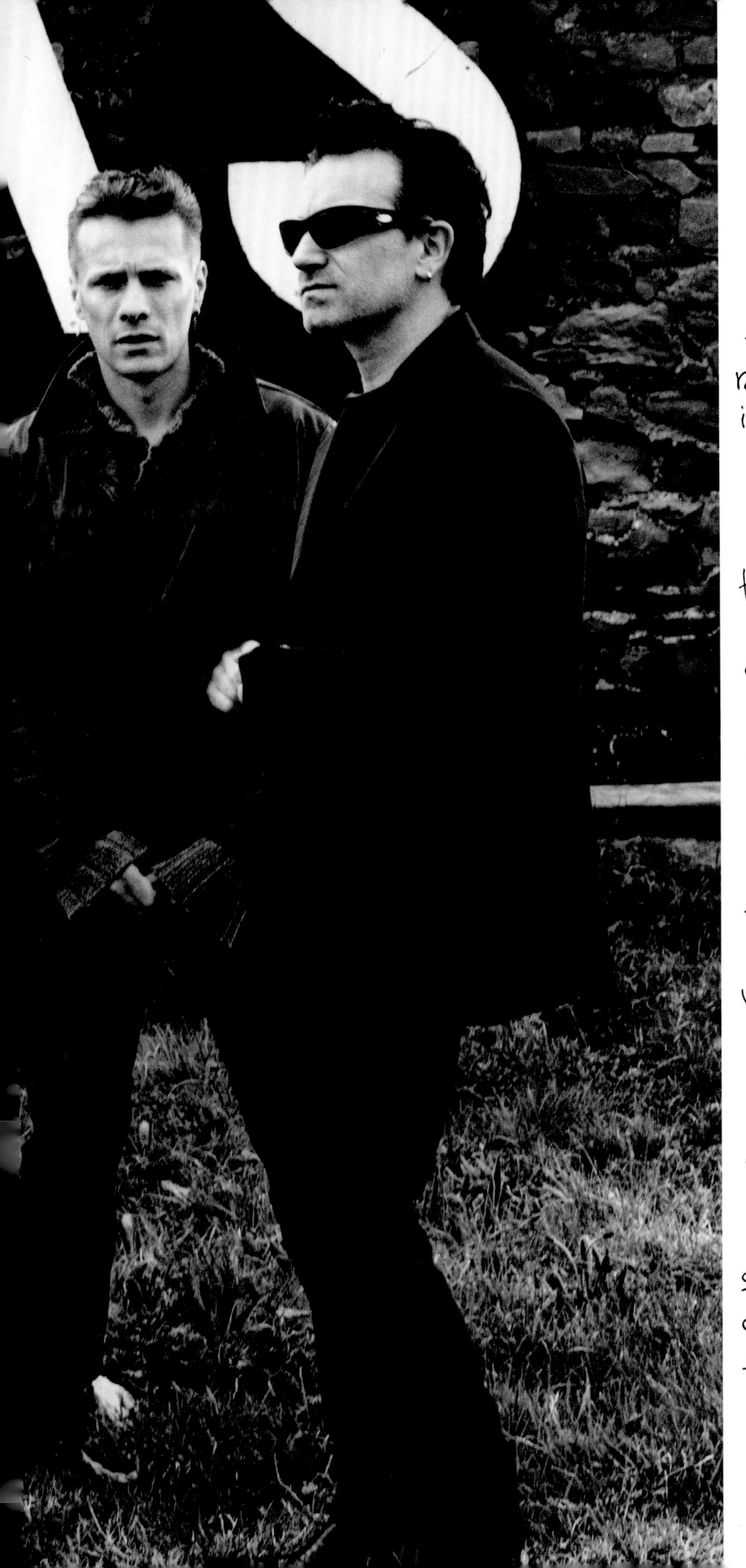

there were a couple of ideas running around for the cover image of this album. one was to shoot on the dublin docks, same kind of place where the photos for 'october' were done. for one shot of the sign at the docks (GRAND CANAL DOCKS) i spent 8 hours shooting during the day, all without the band. a shot which i was going to make into a composite eventually. then we did some pretty fast shots with the band who i have to say were not really ready for a shoot so there is some frustration visible, particularly on bono's face. part of the problem of the photos i had taken here were only obvious once i saw the prints. I had cropped the sign to a degree that it could have read like something far more sexually explicit than seemed necessary from a sales point of view. Anyway, we drove off to the airport from here to catch the last flight to paris that night.

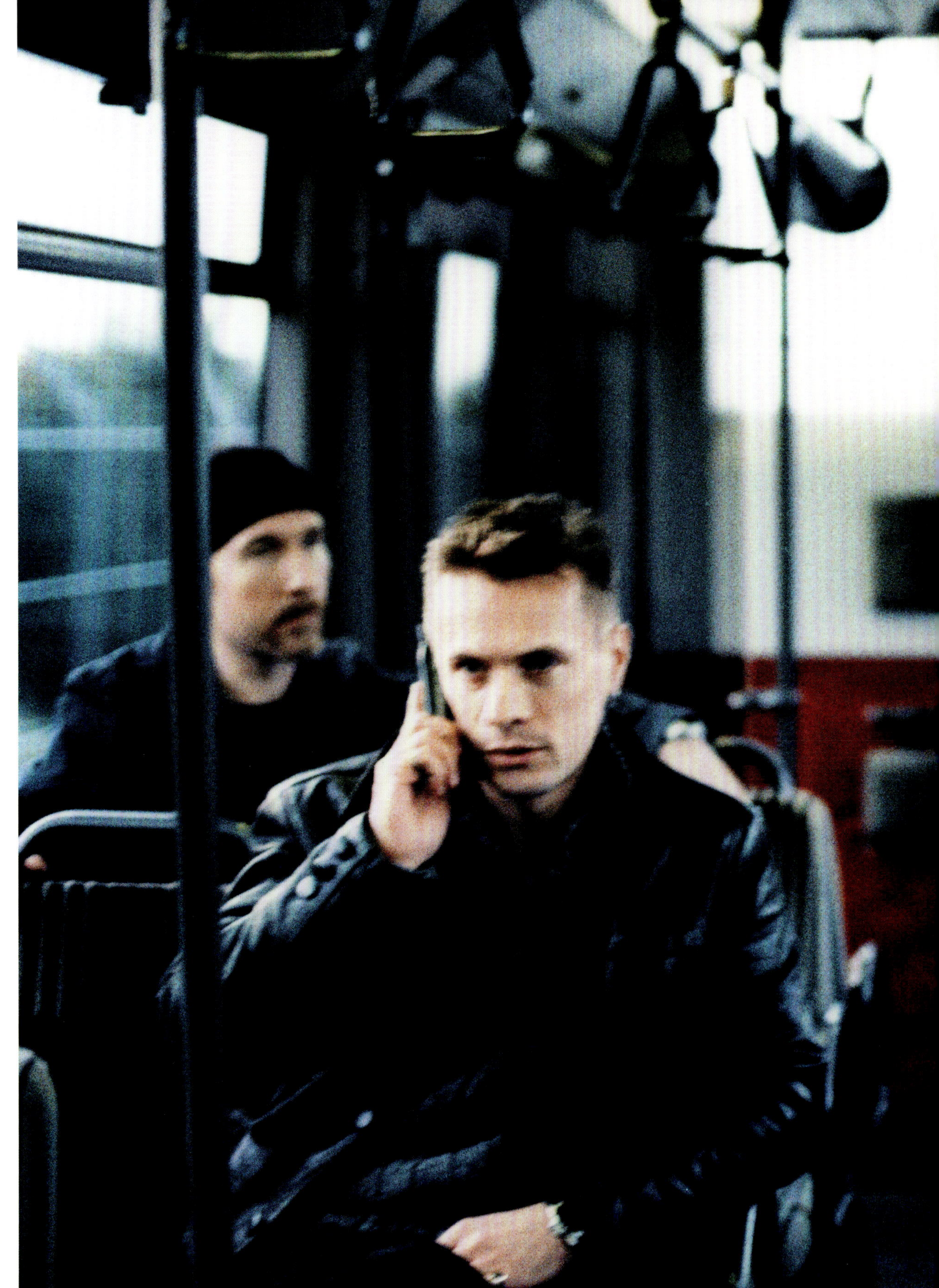

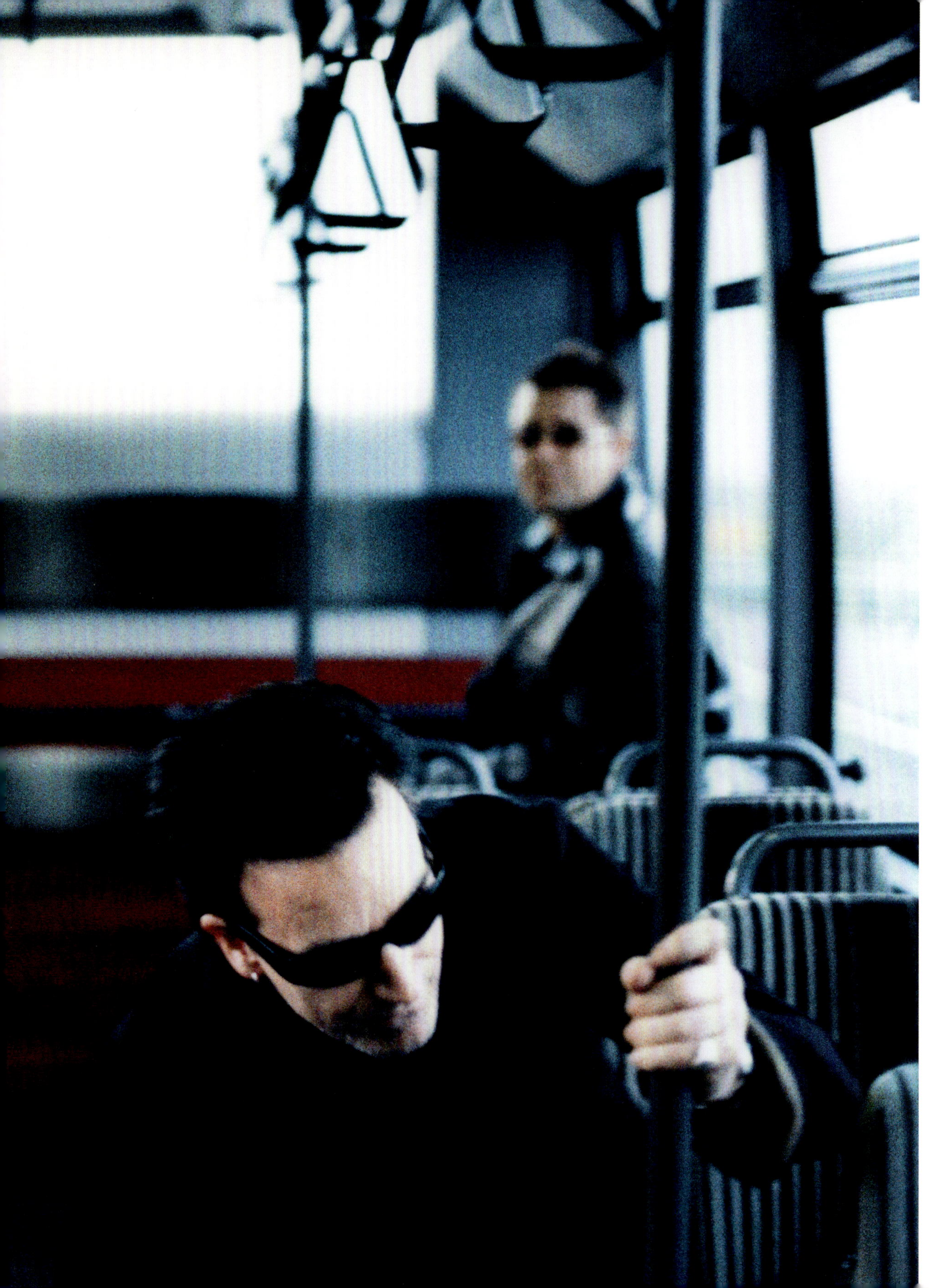

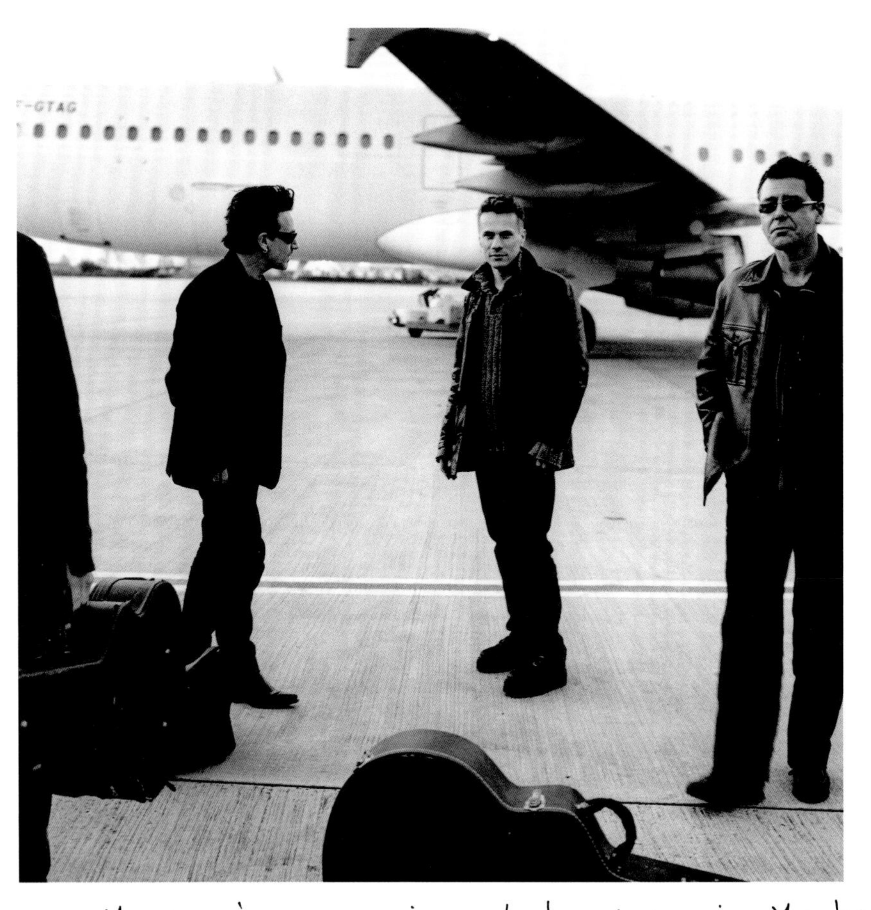

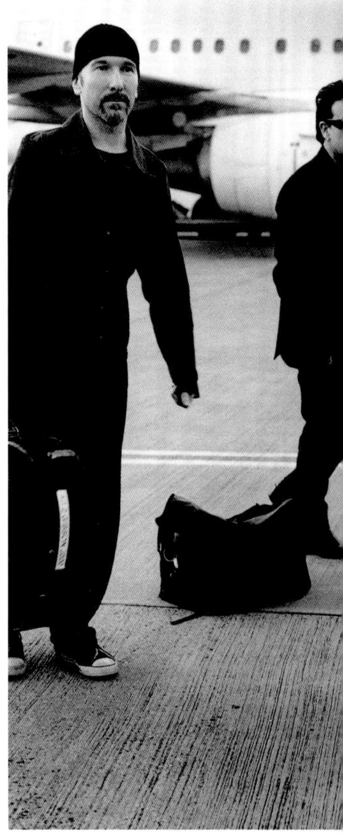

on the previous page is a photo of U2 in the bus
on the airport of Charles de Gaulle which is taken us
to the location above. we were trying to blag
this location as no-one is really allowed to be
on the tarmac without al kinds of permits. the idea
was to show the band as they are these days – well-off and
kind of at home anywhere, always on the move. an airport location
seemed pretty ideal.

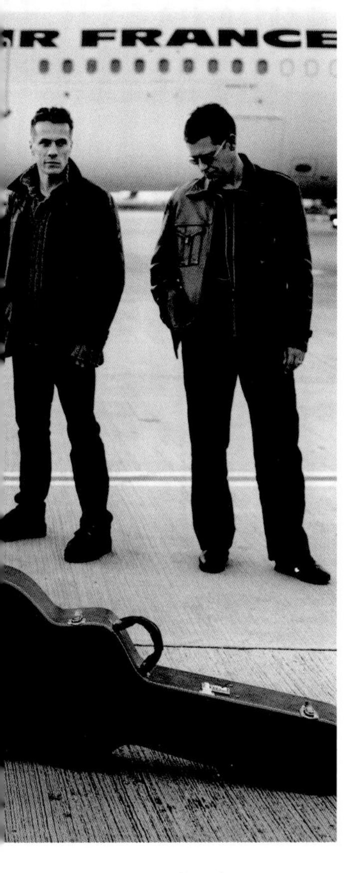

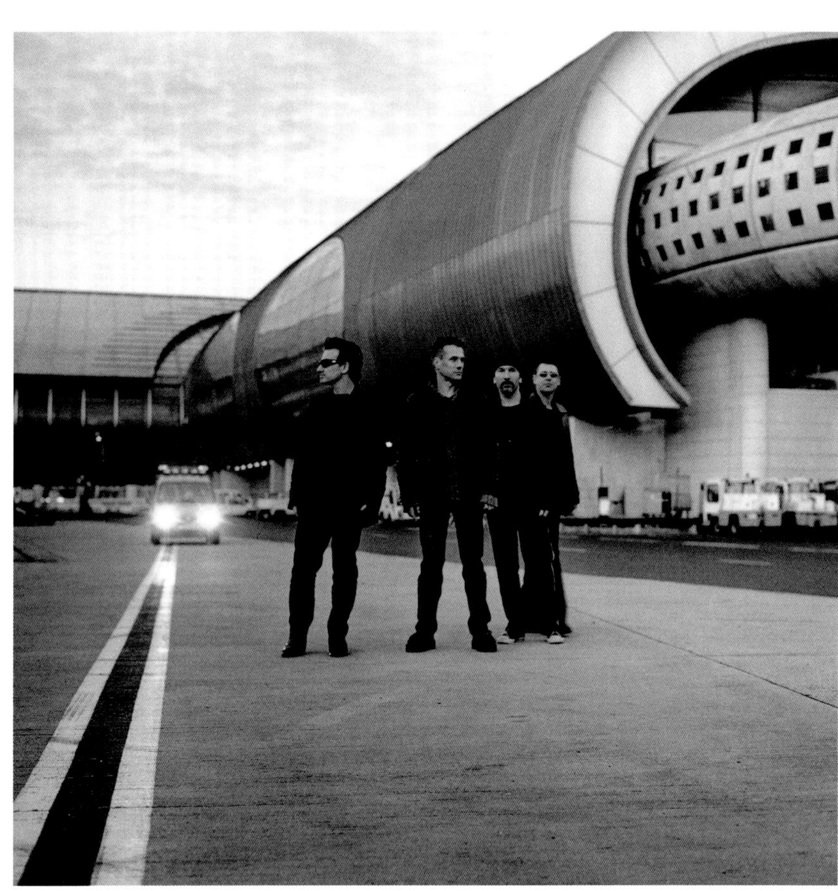

on the photo right ↗ you can see a car coming right at me as we had been spotted very quickly and told in no uncertain terms to get back into the bus and get out. we did and headed for the terminal where we had to catch the next flight, to Nice, and one where we did have a permit to take some photographs.

Spot the differences is a game that could be played with the photo on the right - it is more or less the coverphoto for 'all that you can't leave behind'. It is for sure the basis of the cover - some alterations were made though. main changes are adam, the roof and the signs for the gates. Because we were at such a late time in the evening at this particular wing at Charles de Gaulle airport, there was a distinct lack of fellow travellers which worked great for us. we just took some photographs in the middle of the hall without anyone blinking an eyelid. It became a very recognisable cover despite, or possibly because, the band were such tiny figures. real people in front of an empty futuristic background.

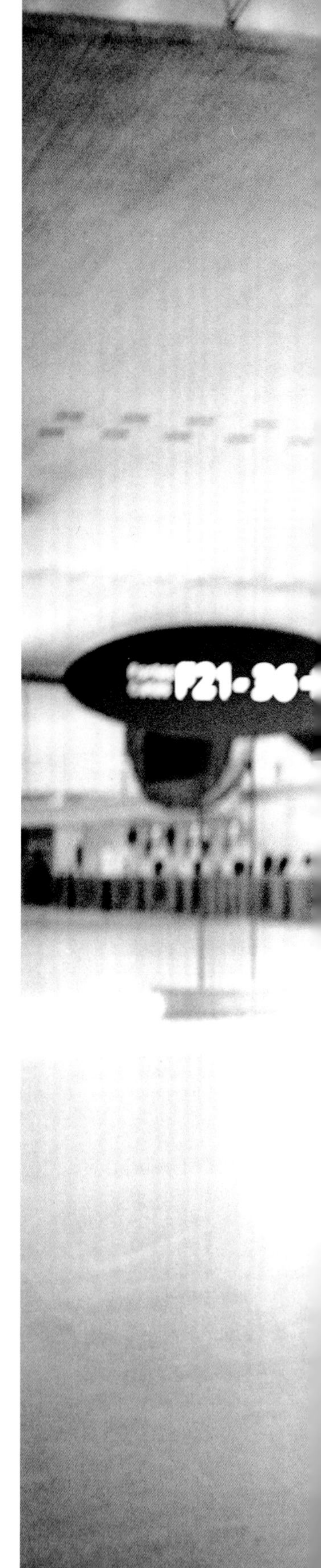

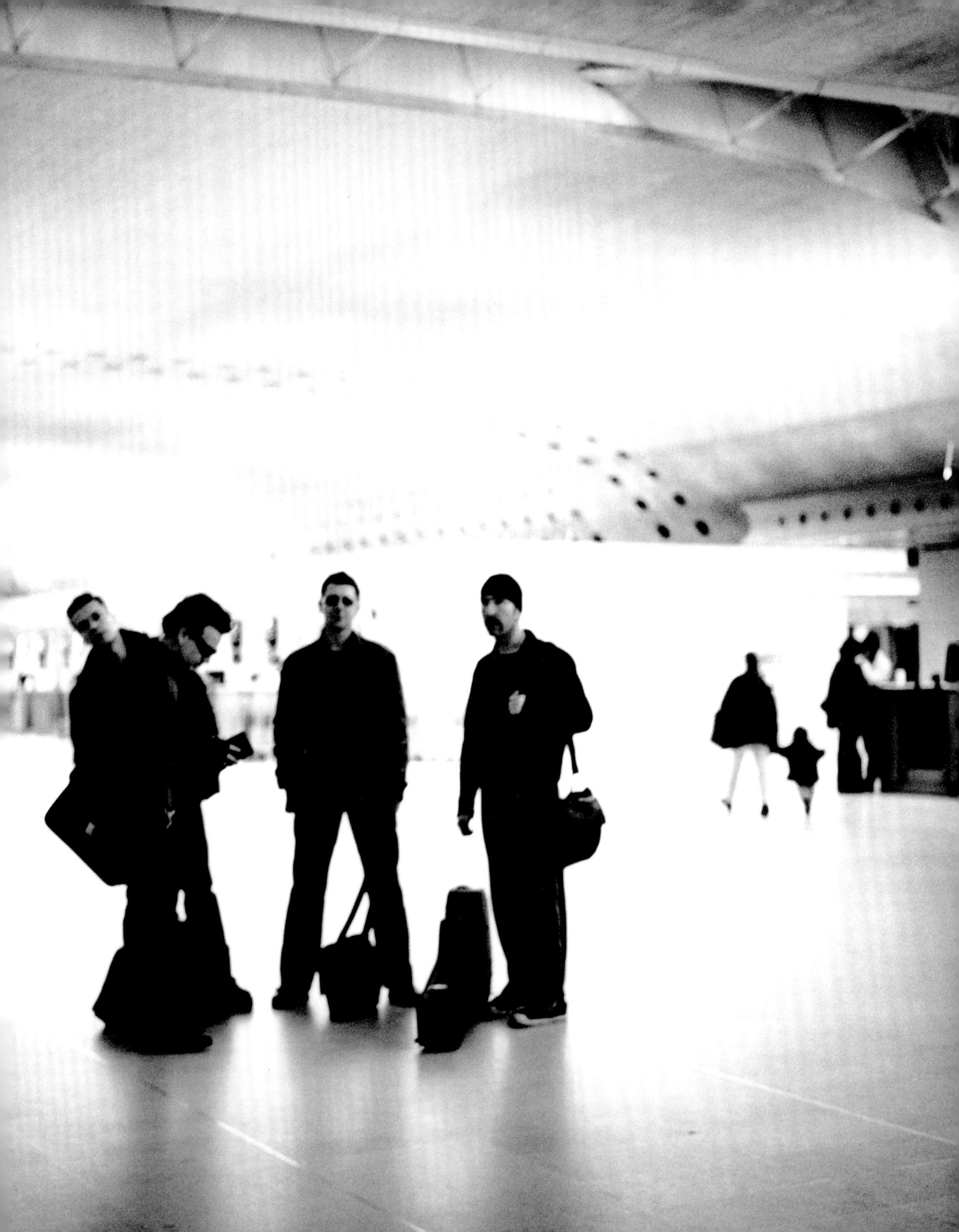

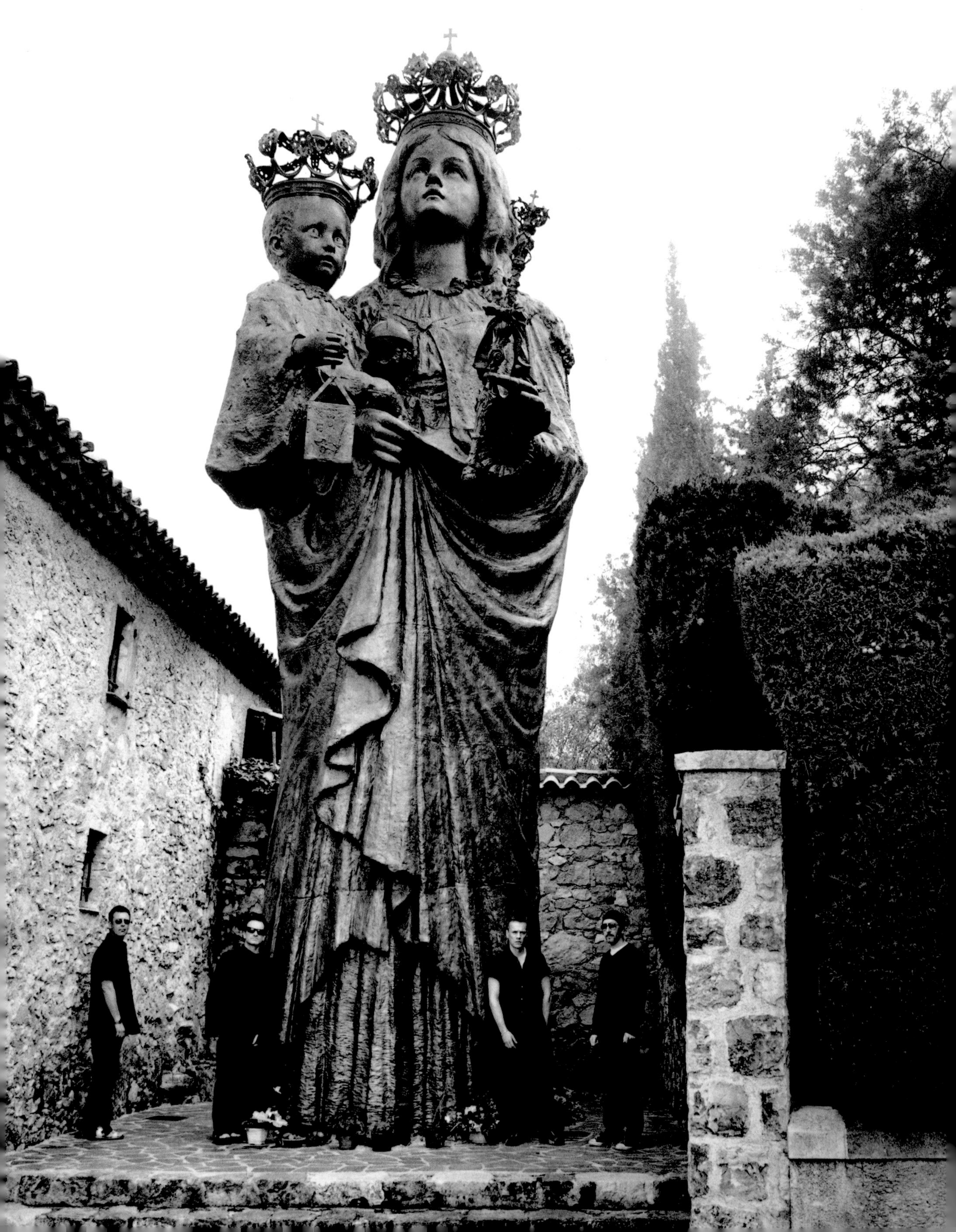

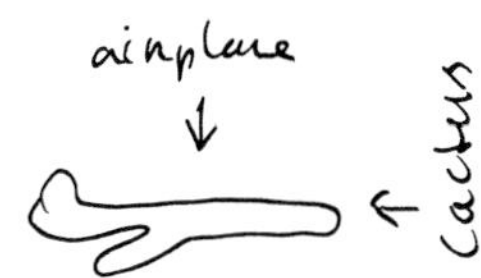

we then flew to Nice and did some photographs near Nice. the band live part of the year in that area so it felt like home, just like dublin does (or an airport hall). in the morning we were kind of lucky as there was a strong mist on the coast and that made a spooky and fairytale like backdrop with the trees. i think we were trying out some beatles vibe on this shot.

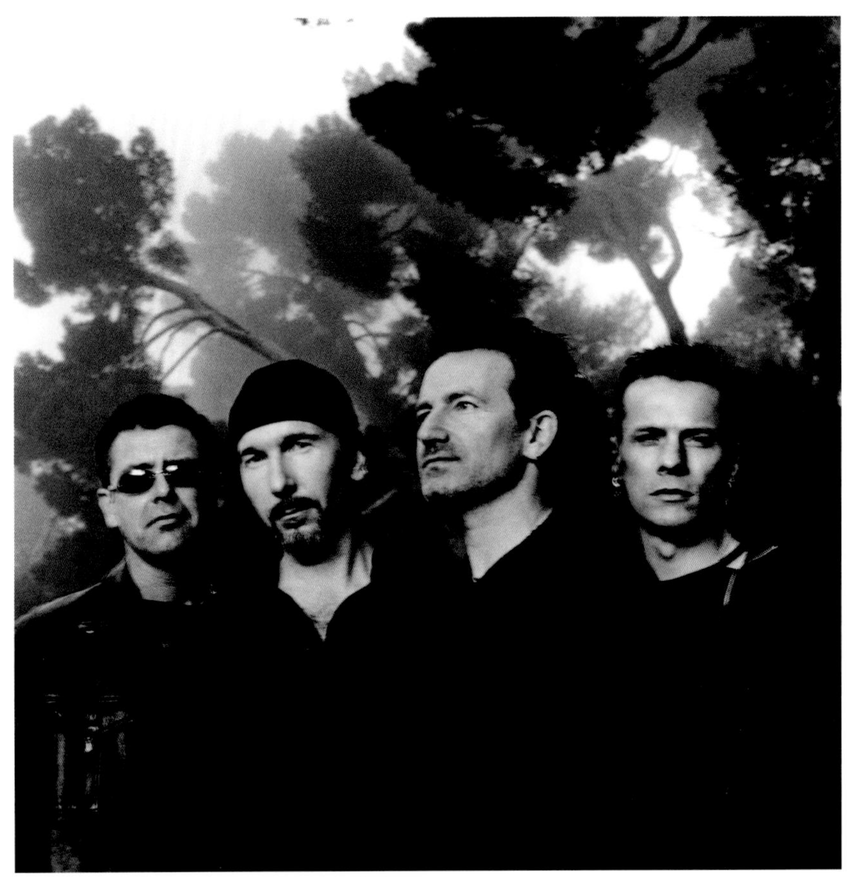

on the next spread is a photo made inside the train that goes to nice – you can open the doors once the train is moving and i used that again two years later for the 'electrical storm' video. It is illegal so do not attempt this yourself!!

when i saw this, i thought it was a jeff koons piece but it wasn't of course. it had been there for quite a while and it made for a 'must use' backdrop.

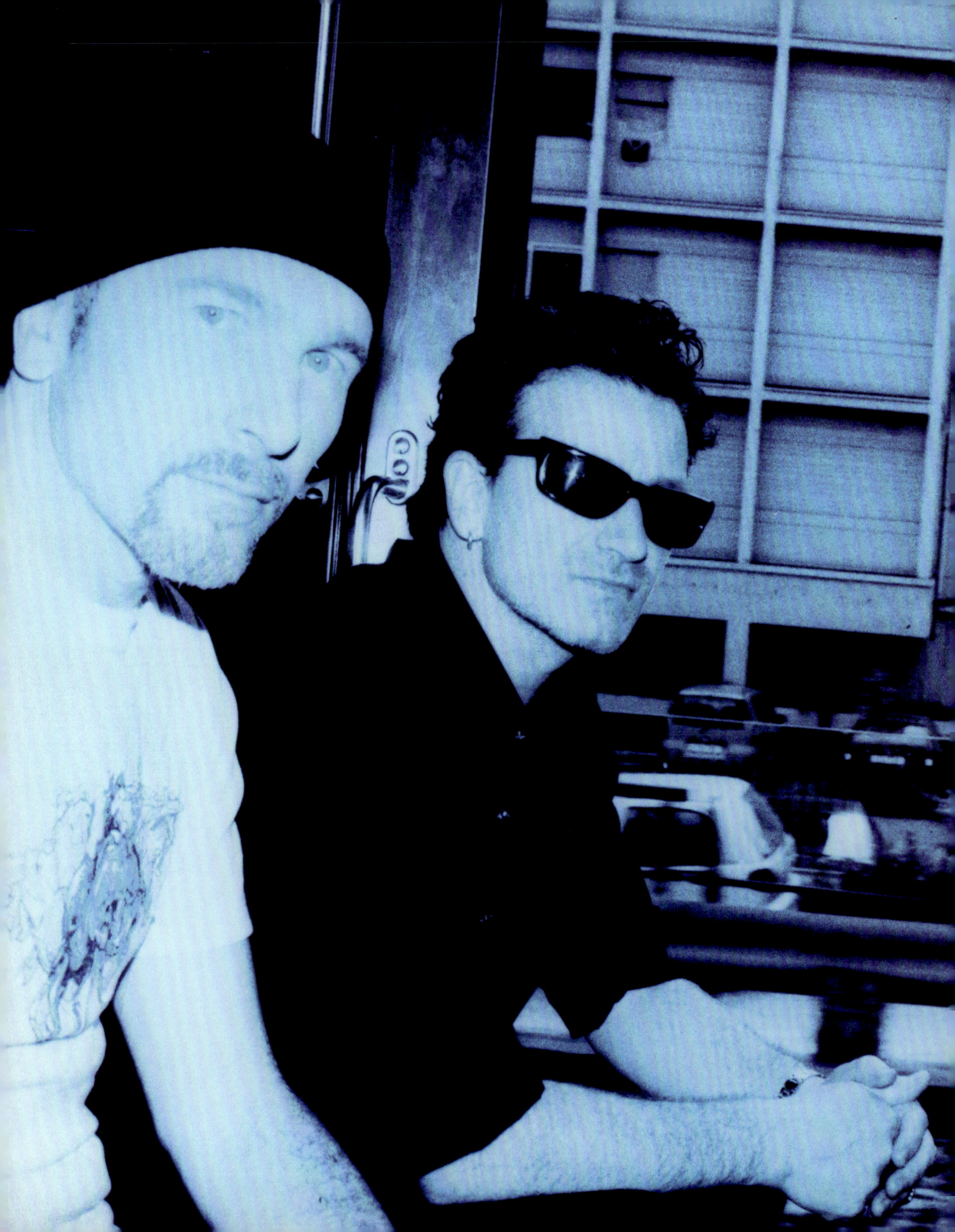

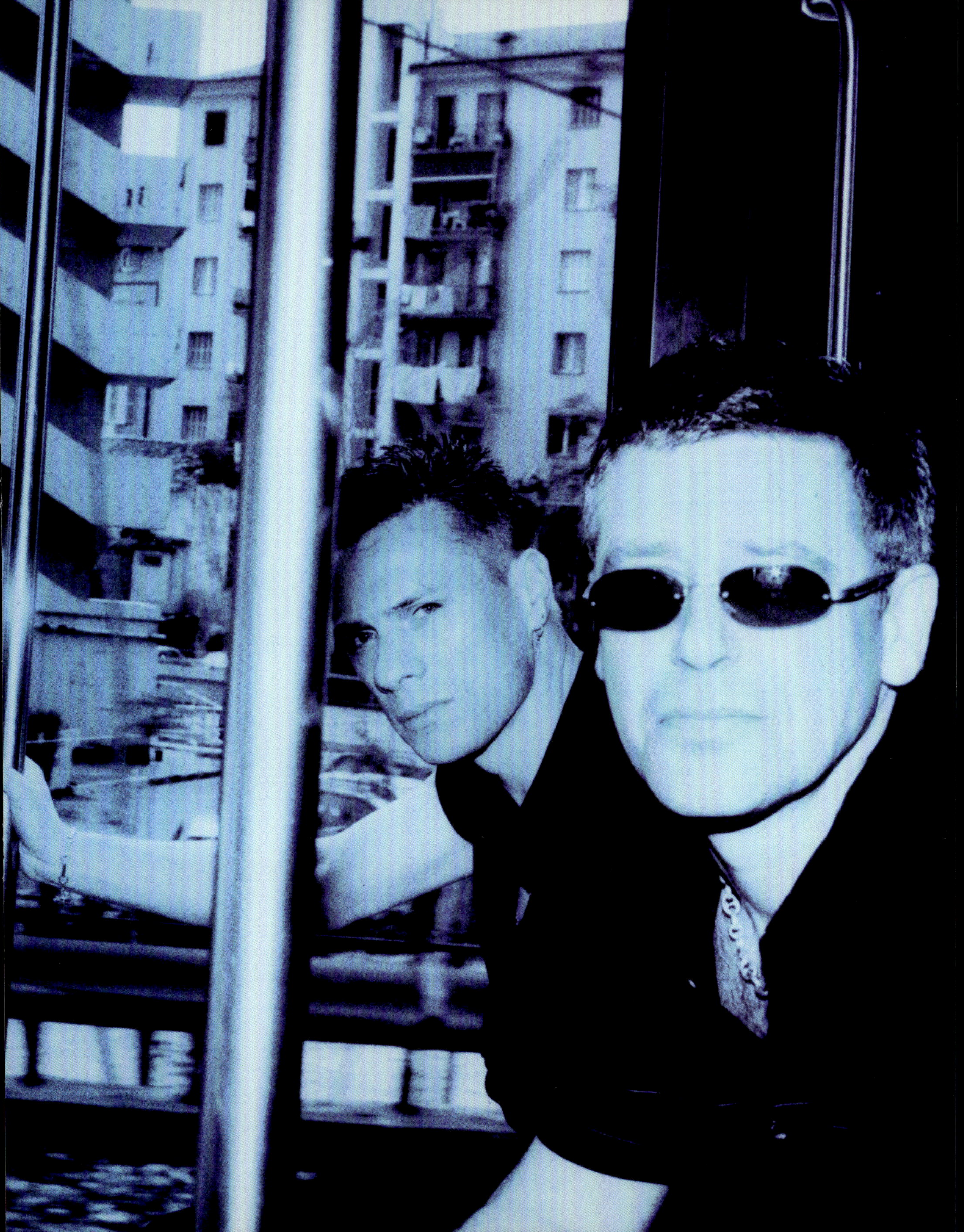

LOS ANGELES

2001 april

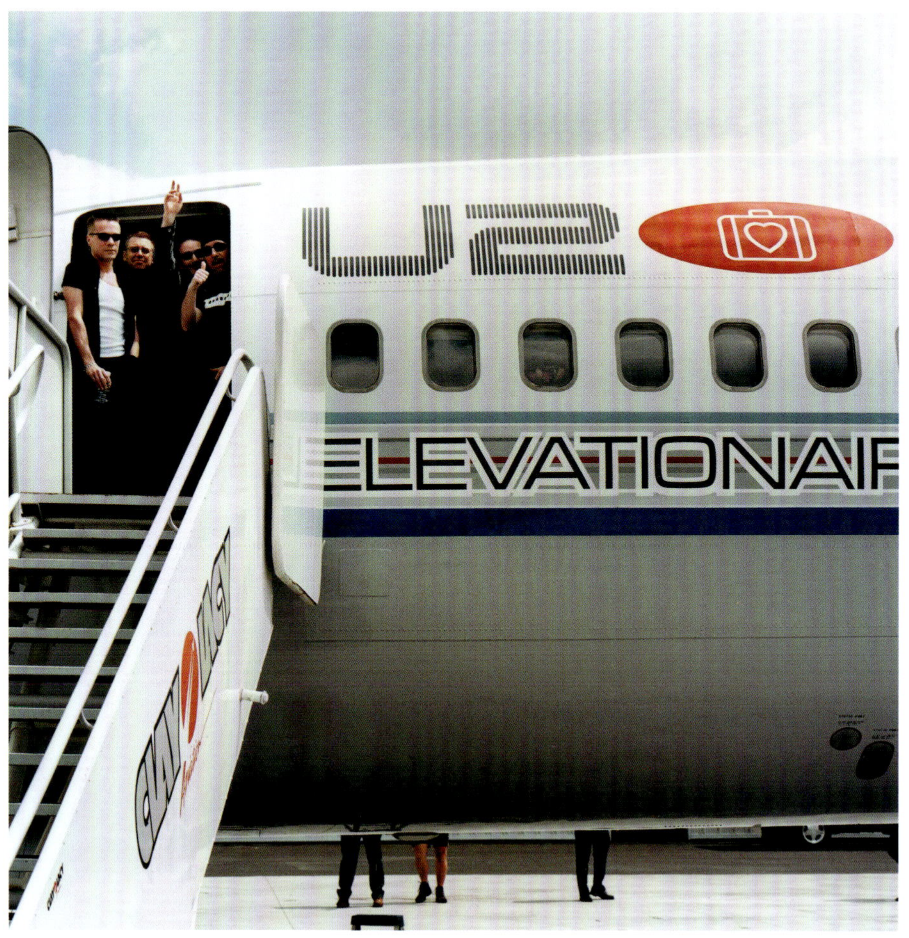

all aboard the plane to fly from LA to Denver – always wondered whose legs we are seeing behind the plane. airport workers, dennis sheehan, security? or are they holding the plane from falling over?

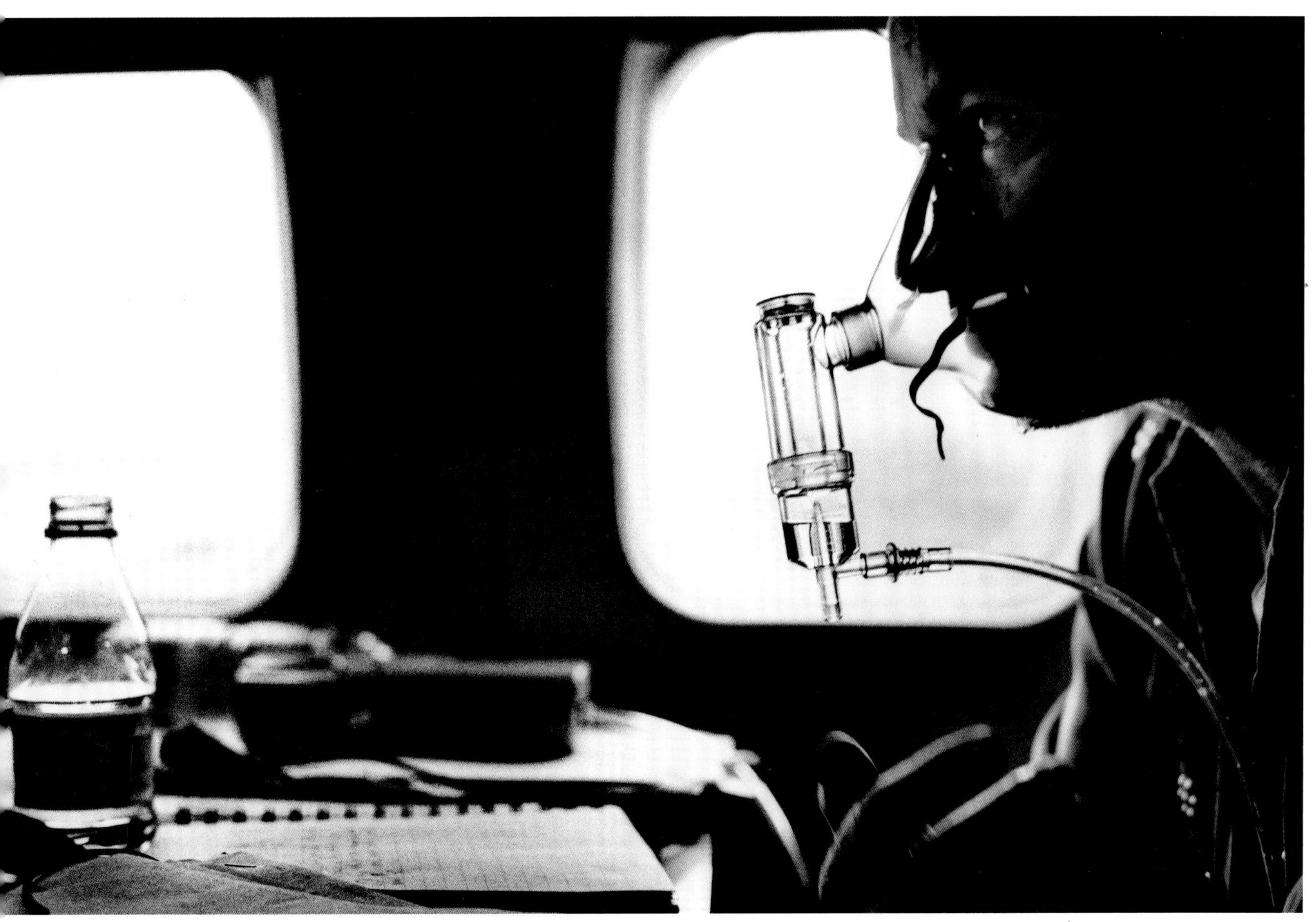

bono's got some problems with his voice / throat, so on the flight he uses this apparatus to inhale some liquid based stuff at this stage of the tour to moisten & heal the throat. and he can't talk this way either.
from Denver, we flew back straight after the show to LA.

DENVER

april 2001

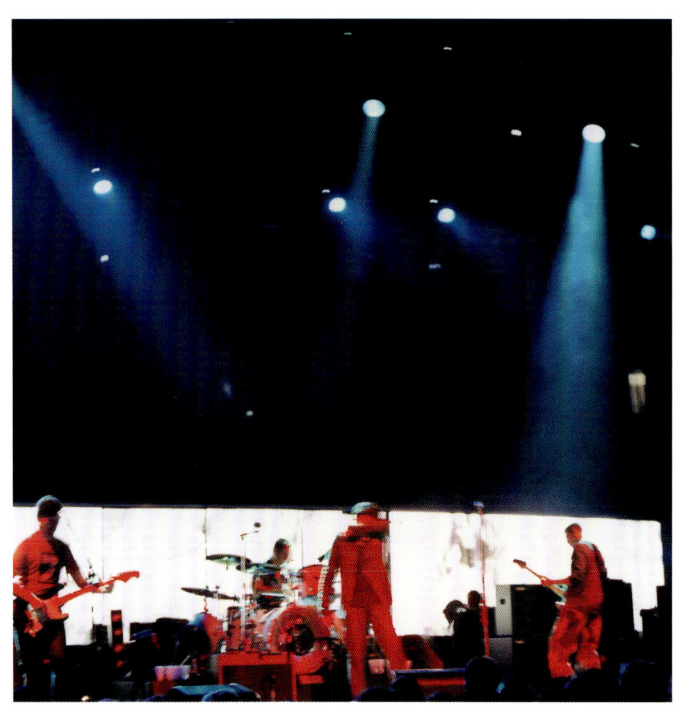

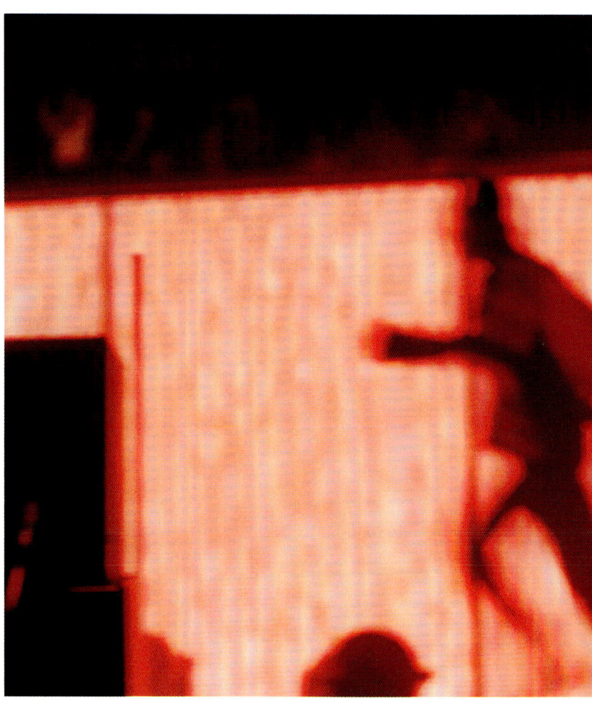

So this is what it looks like if you're out there in the audience trying to take some photographs of the show. i used a slow time to get more the feeling of the colors and movement of the show.

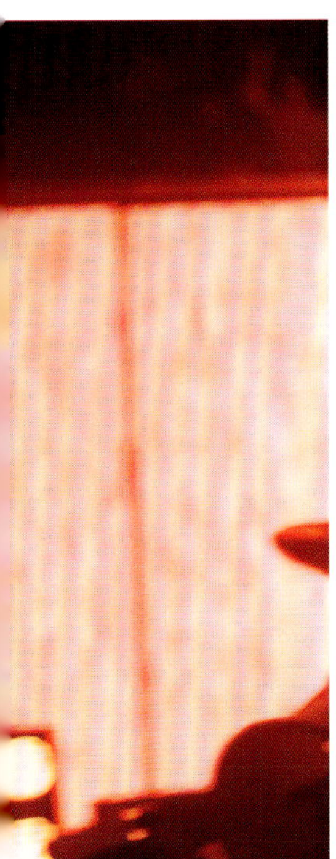

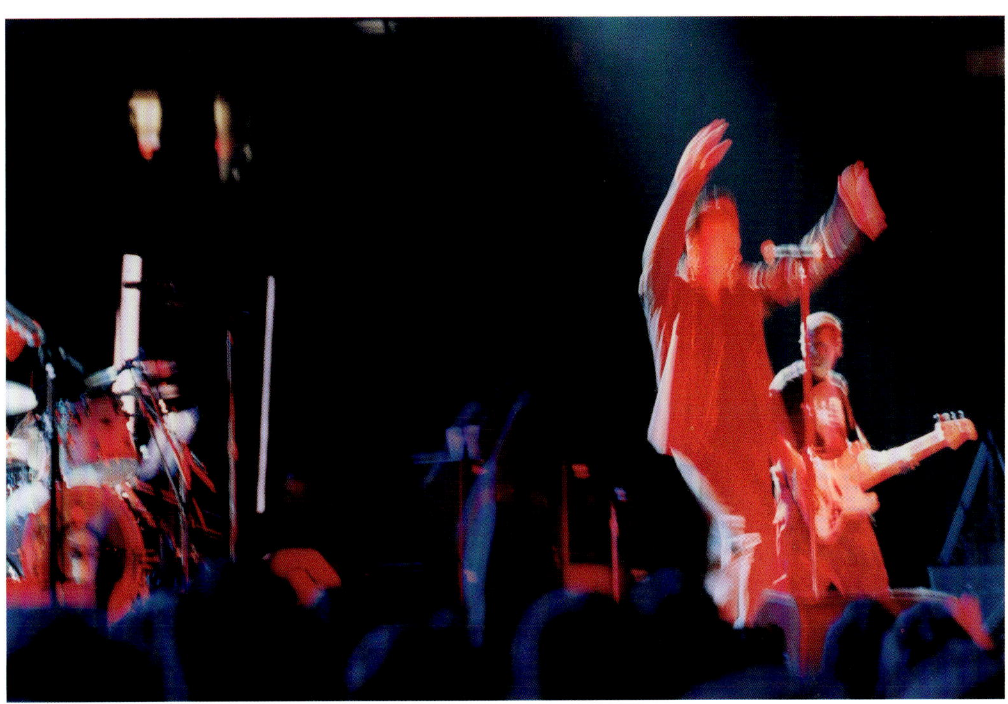

The advantage of being tall was offset by people pushing and moving against me when i was taking photos. no-one likes me to stand in front of them.

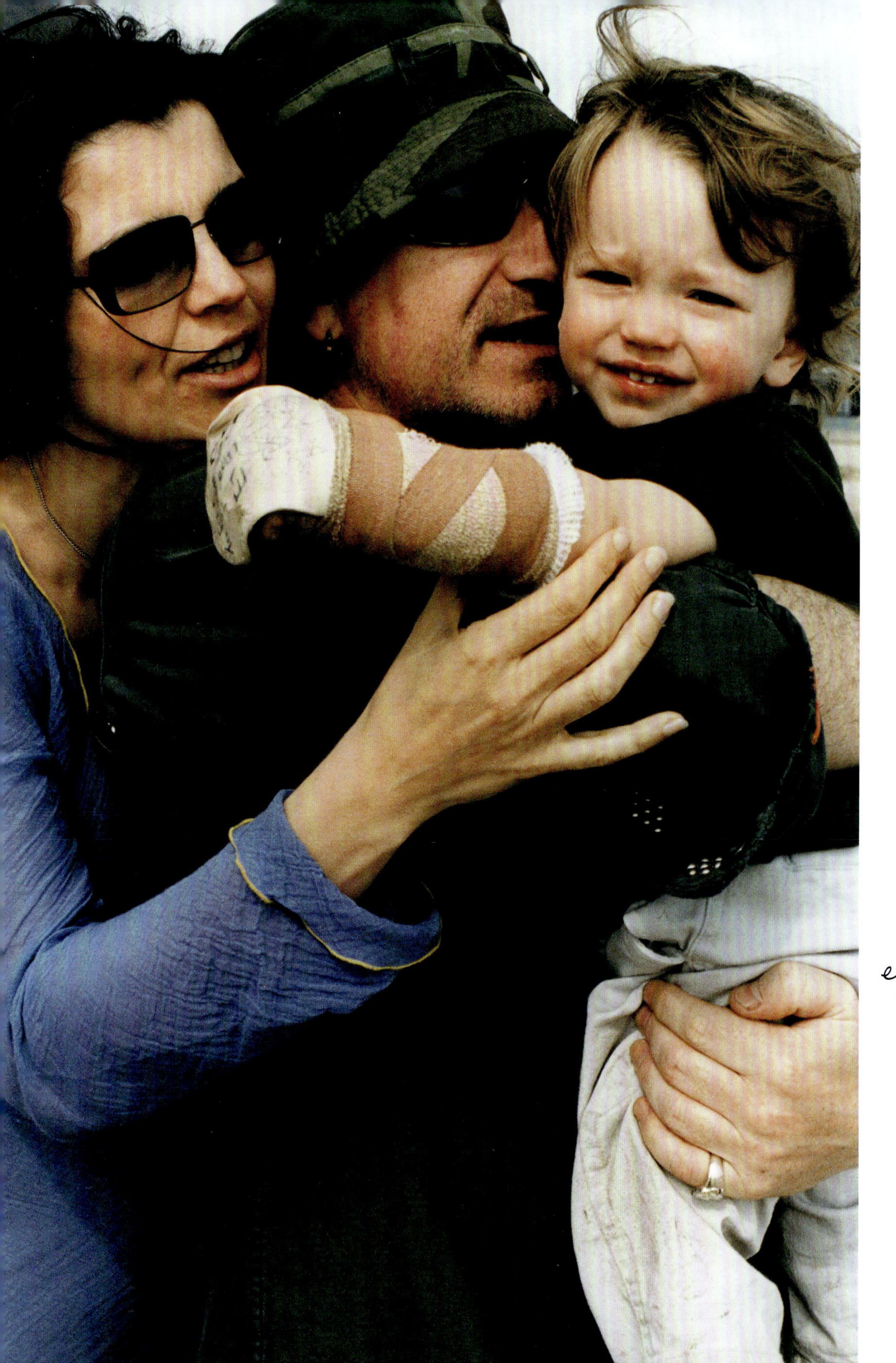

elijah trying to imitate his father anno 1987.

SANTA MONICA 2001
april

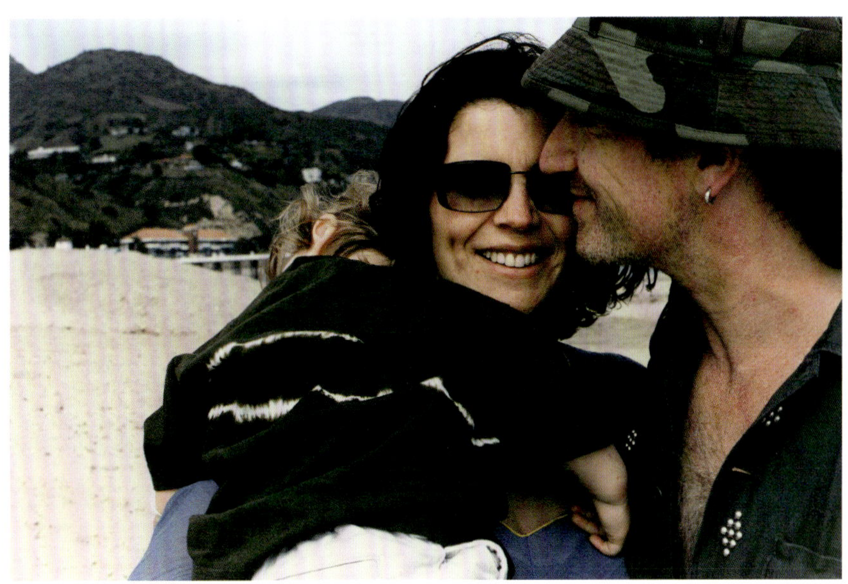

just a few moments on the coast near santa monica with
bono, ali, eli and jordan and eve too but not on this photo.

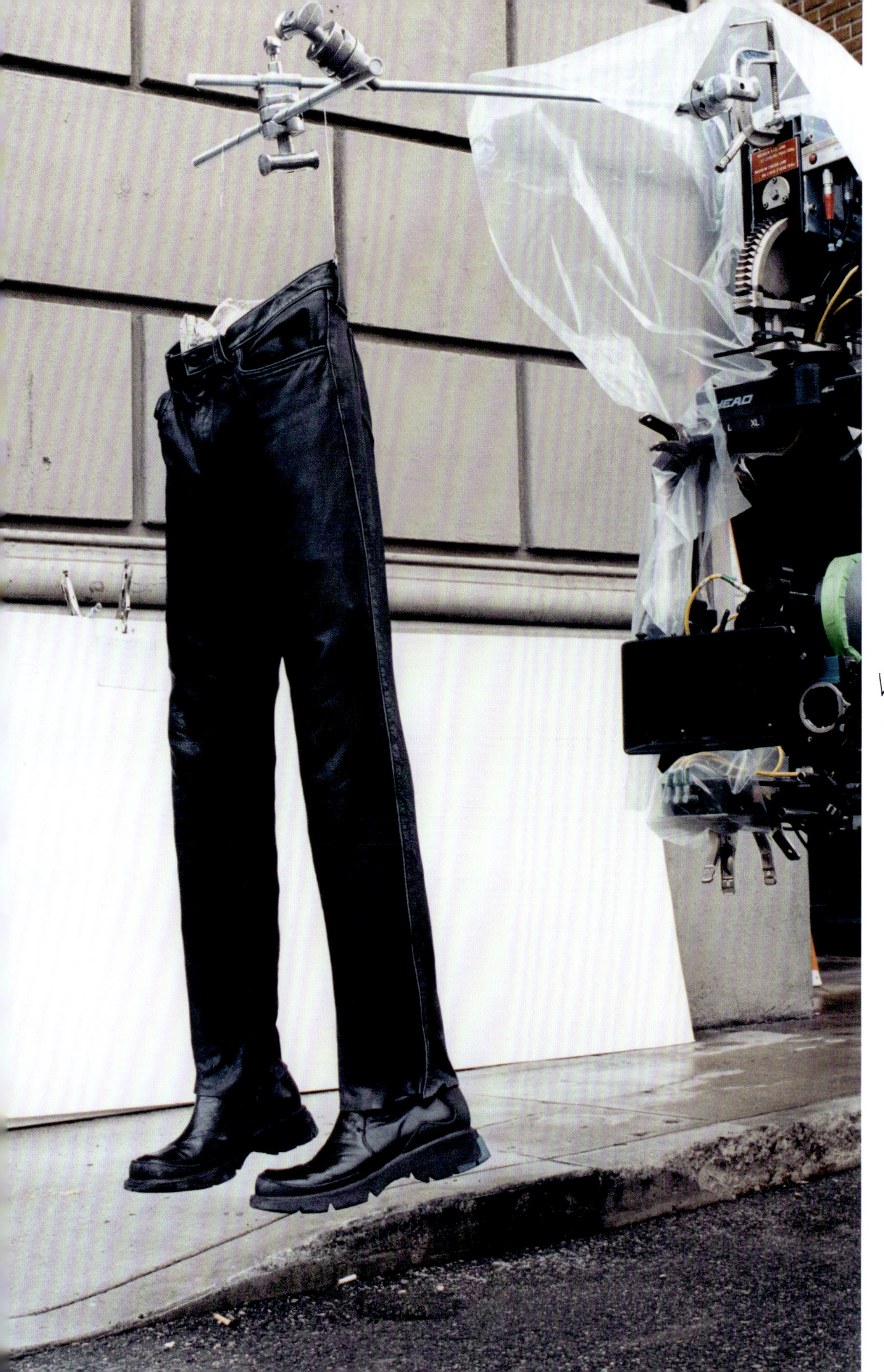

bono's spare trouse
waiting for the
close-up!
the video plays
good U2 off agai
an evil U2 so
suggest both are
the same shot,
kind of tricks ar
used. these
trousers are from
the 'evil' bo

LOS ANGELES 2001 april

the tombraider video shoot

U2 started shooting this video the day after the denver gig.

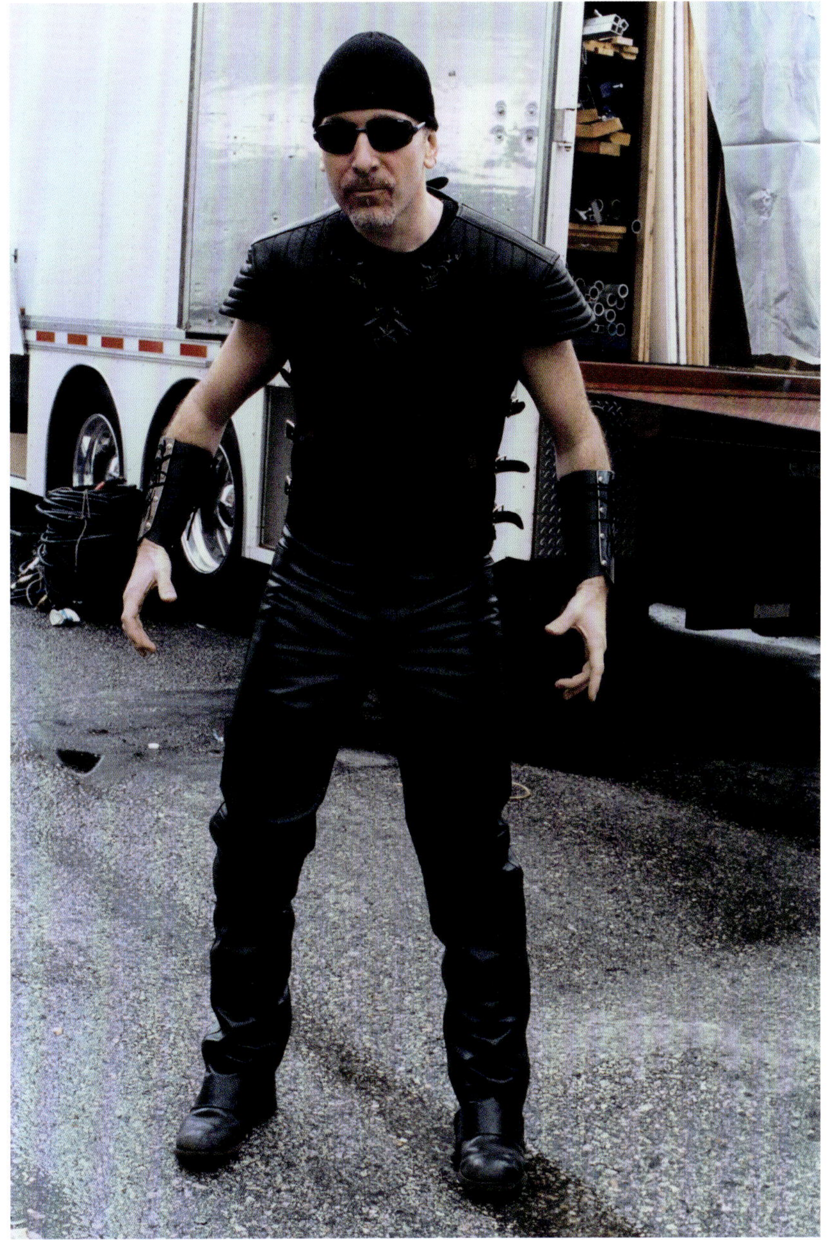

Edge preparing for the role of 'evil' edge for the tombraider video. which was shot on the universal filmset – an entire town made up of hollow houses. great place to be given over to you for a few days.

'evil' bono trousers

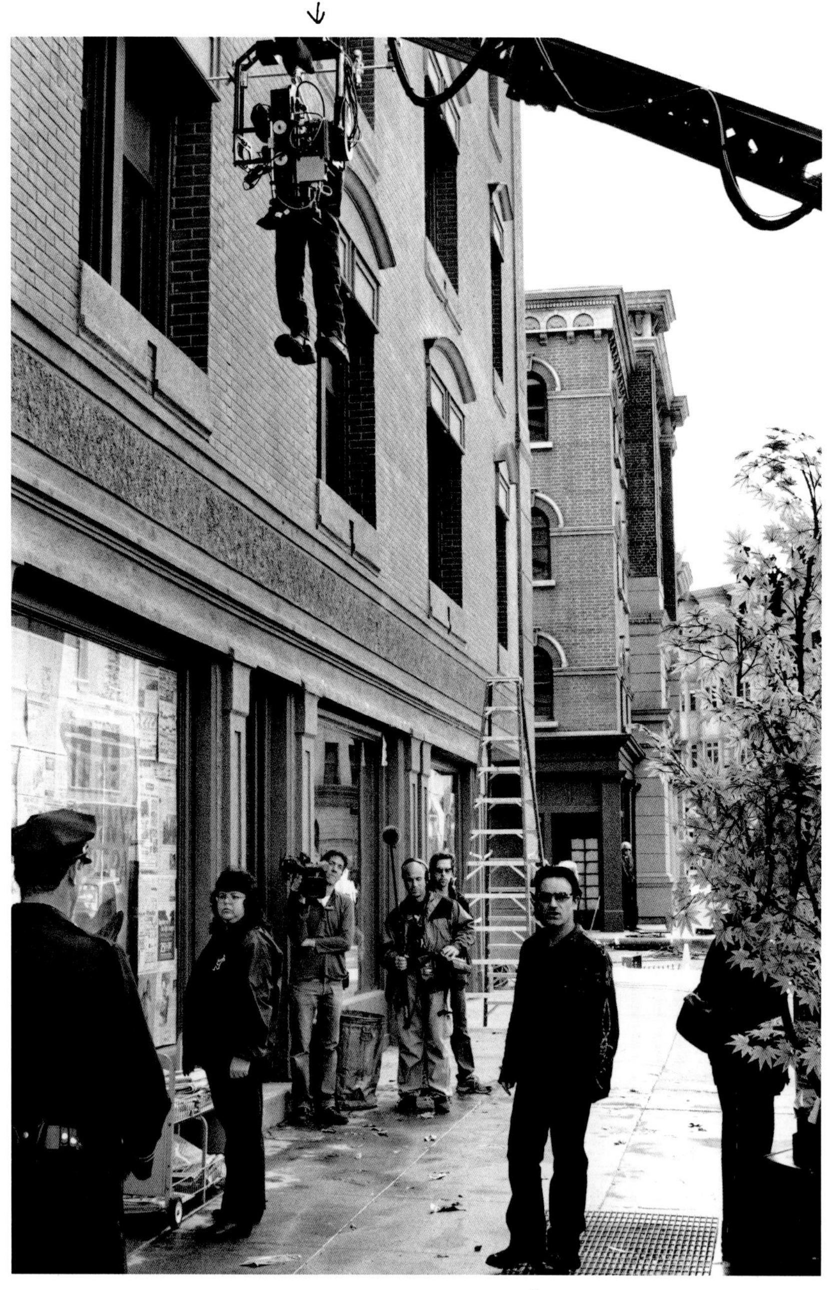

good bono

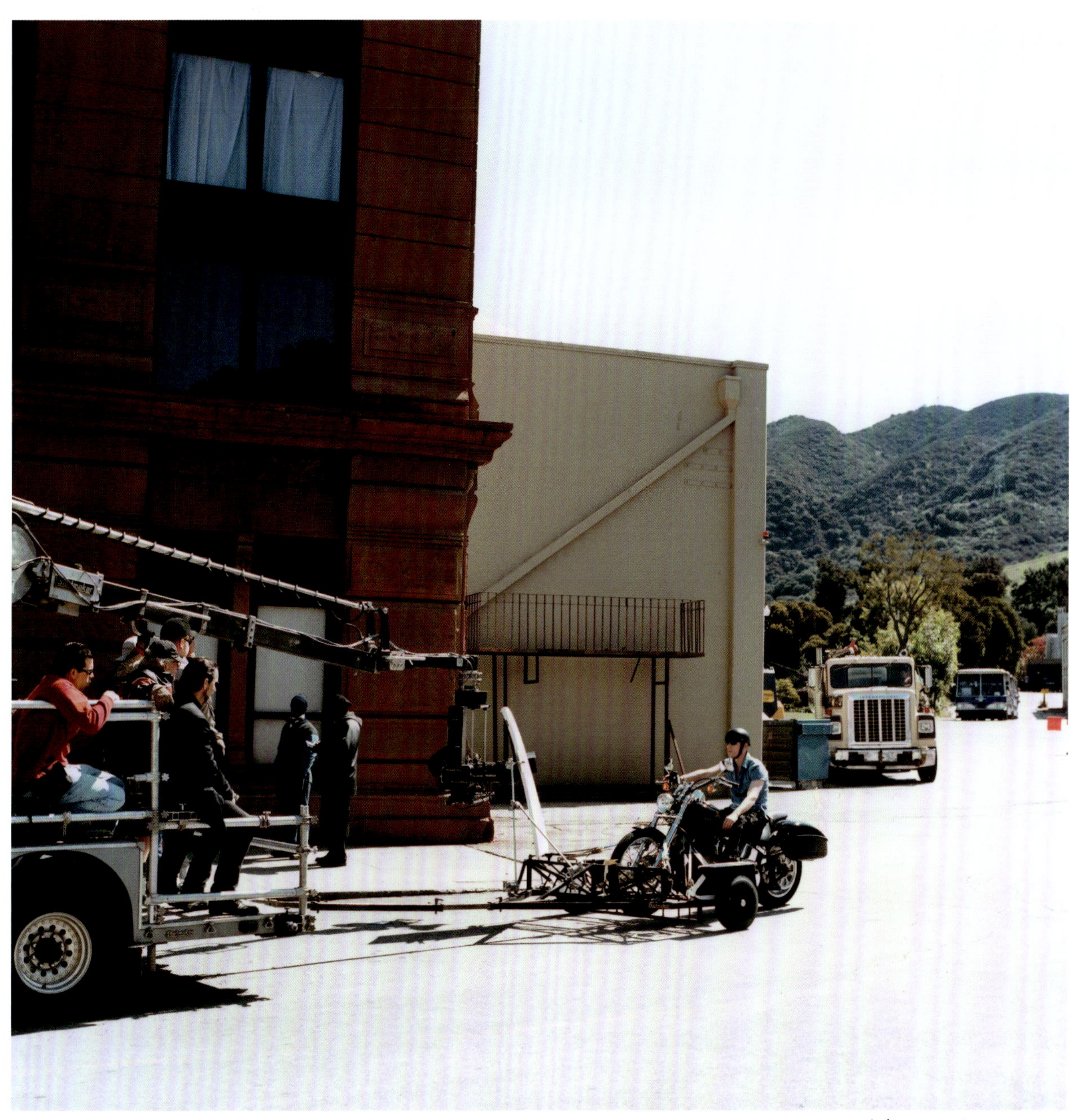

larry being filmed the hollywood way as an 'evil' motorbike rider on the universal backlot.

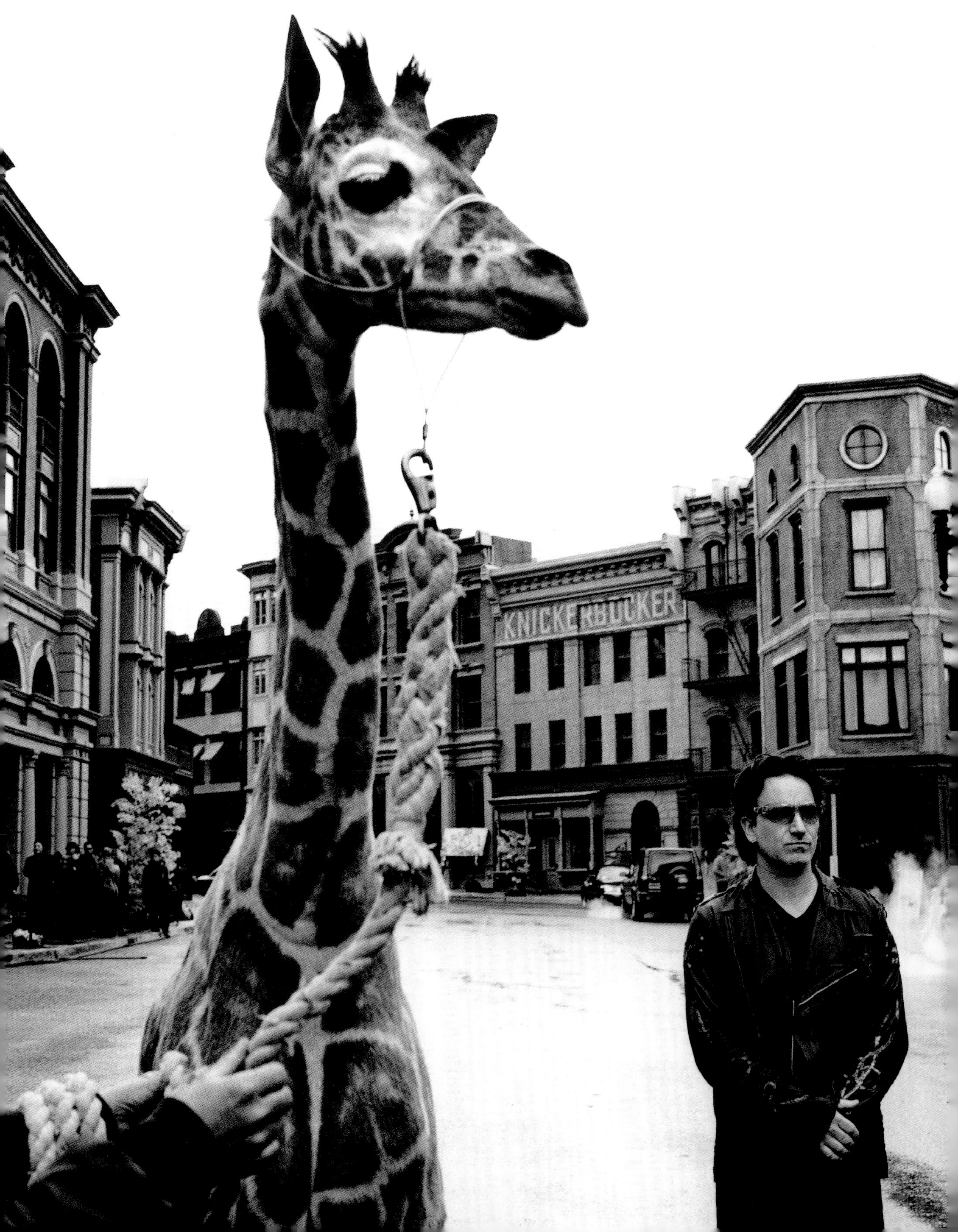
KNICKERBOCKER

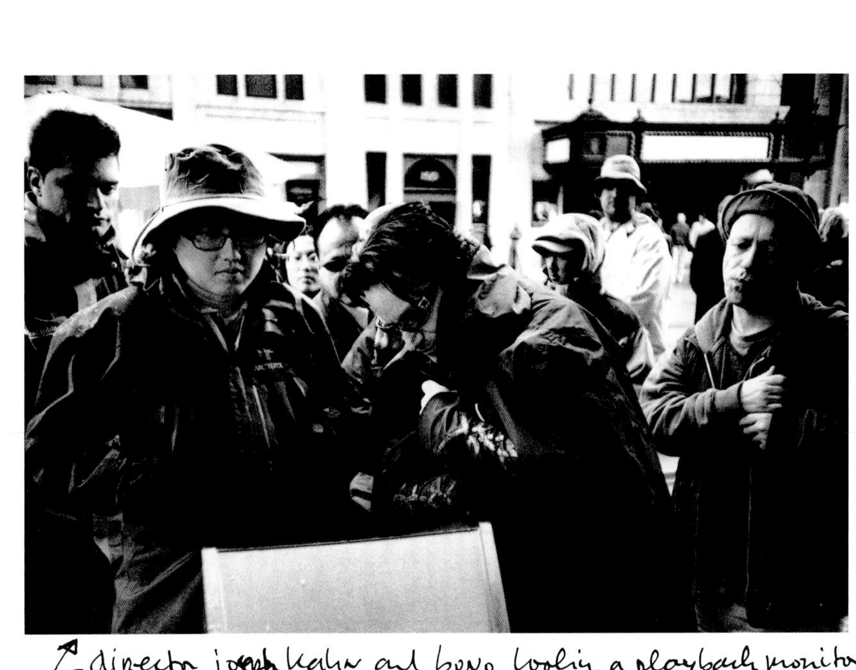

↖ director joseph kahn and bono looking a playback monitor.

the biggest videoshoot i've ever witnessed, with lots and lots of extras, special effects and a 'baby' giraffe. bono looks a little worried here.

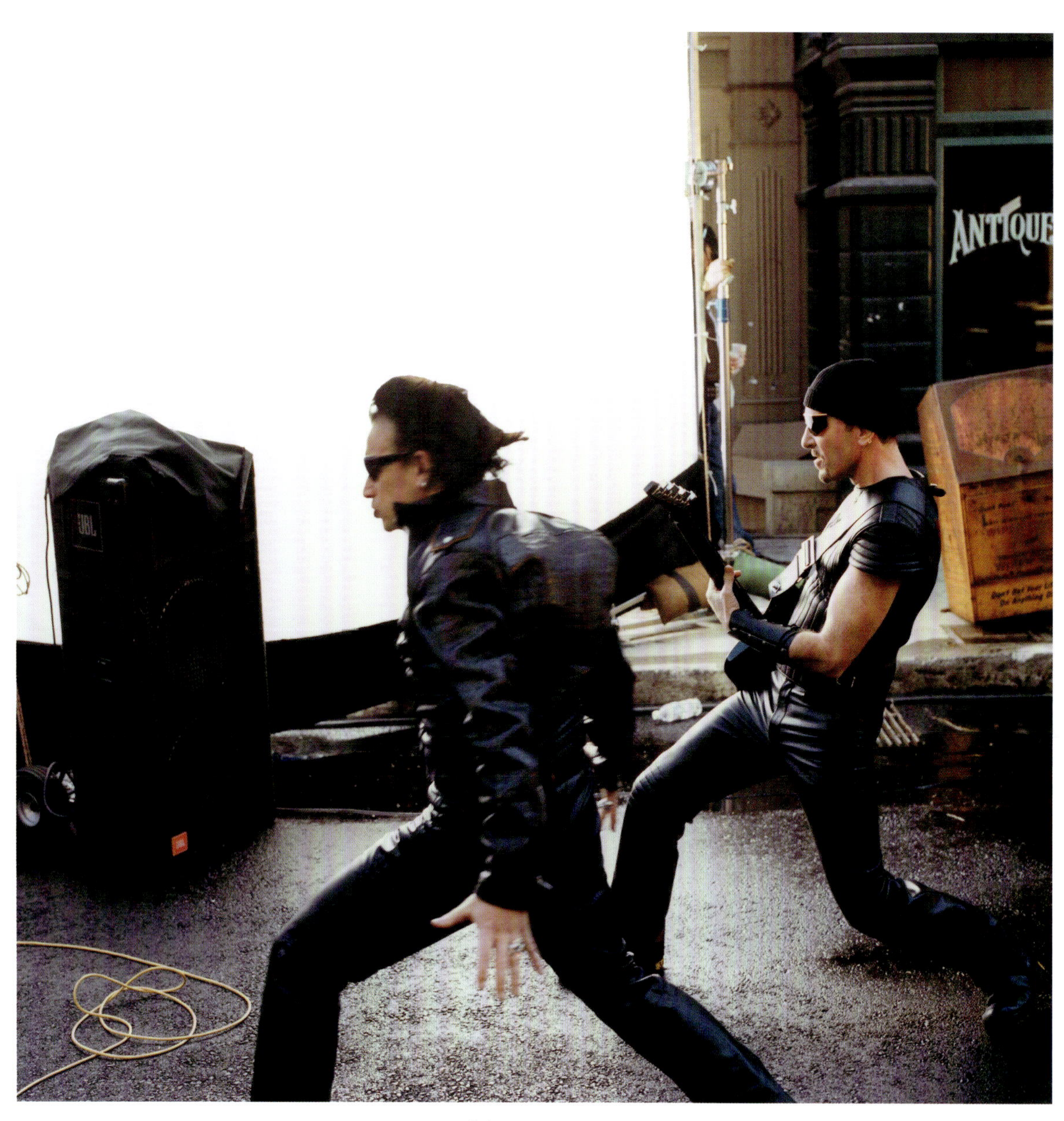

performing as the 'evil' U2

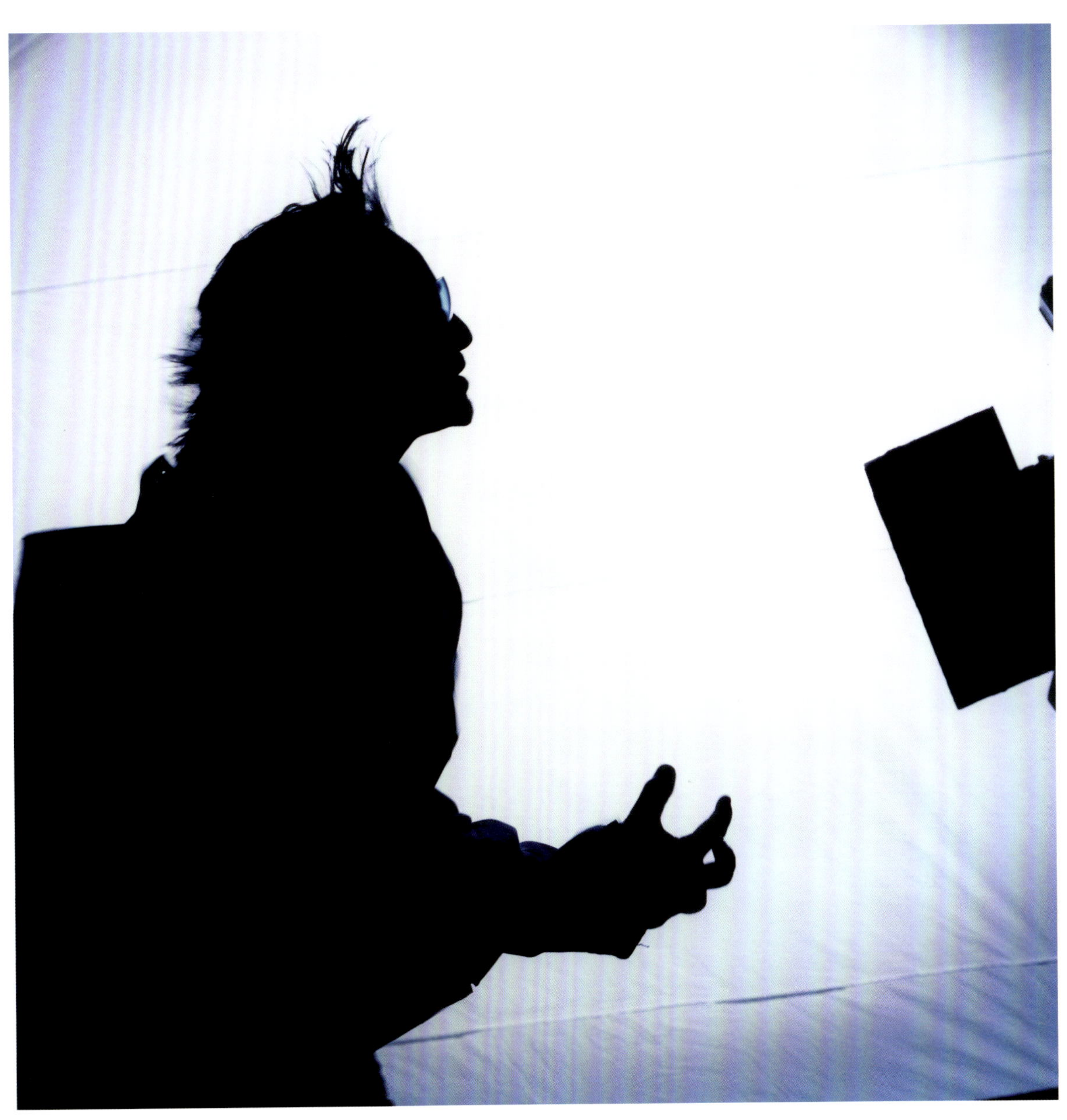

bono singing against a very large windmachine →

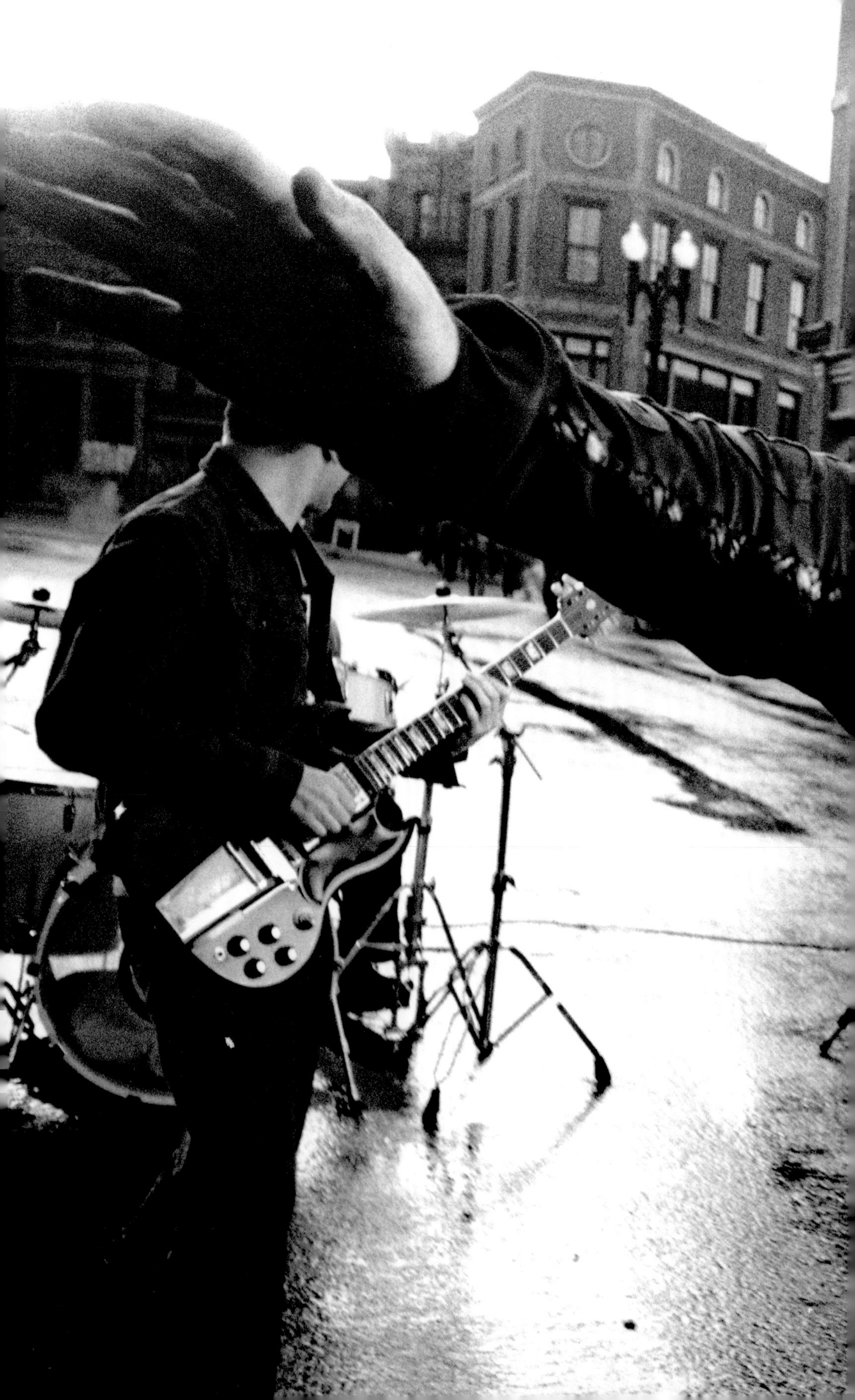

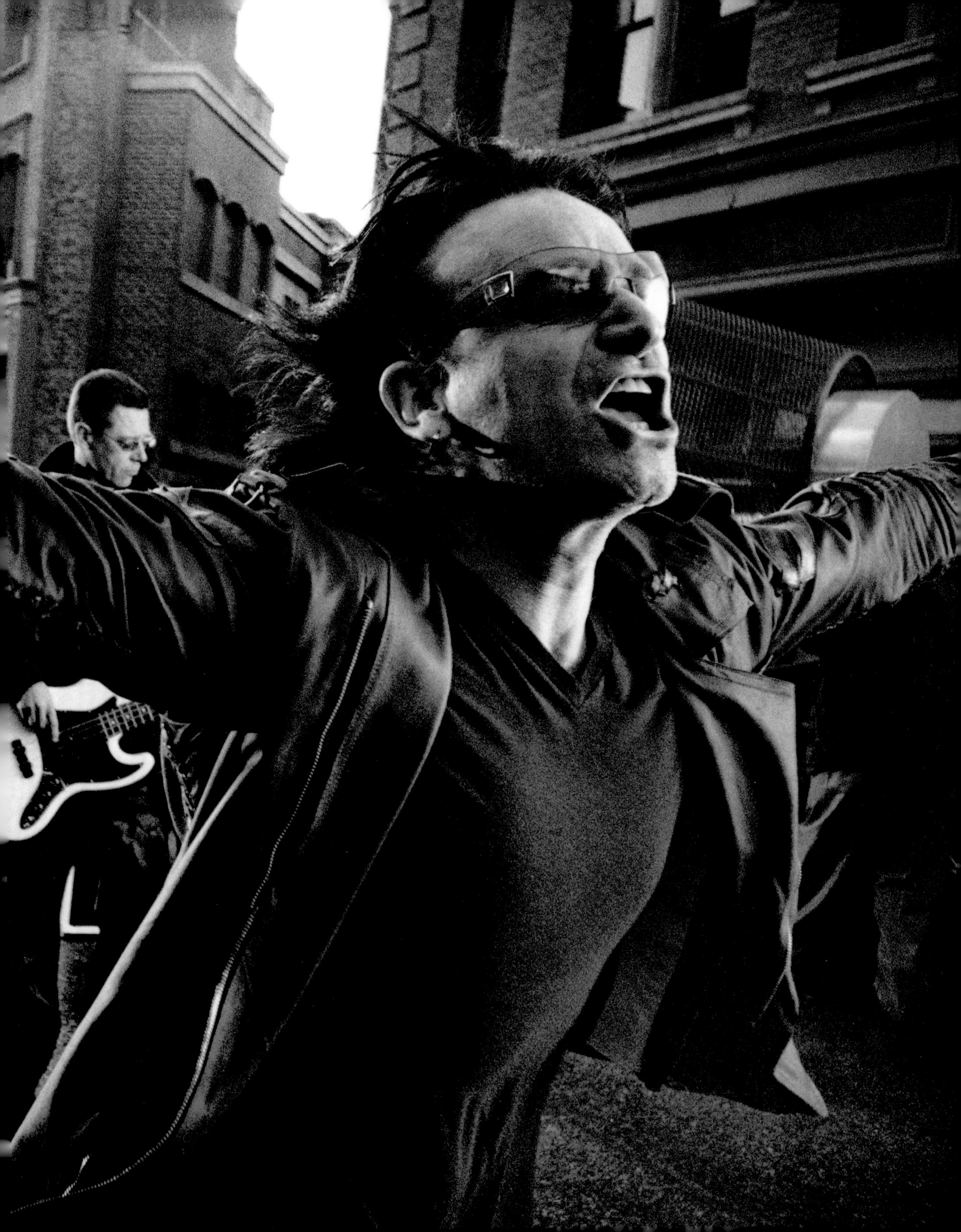

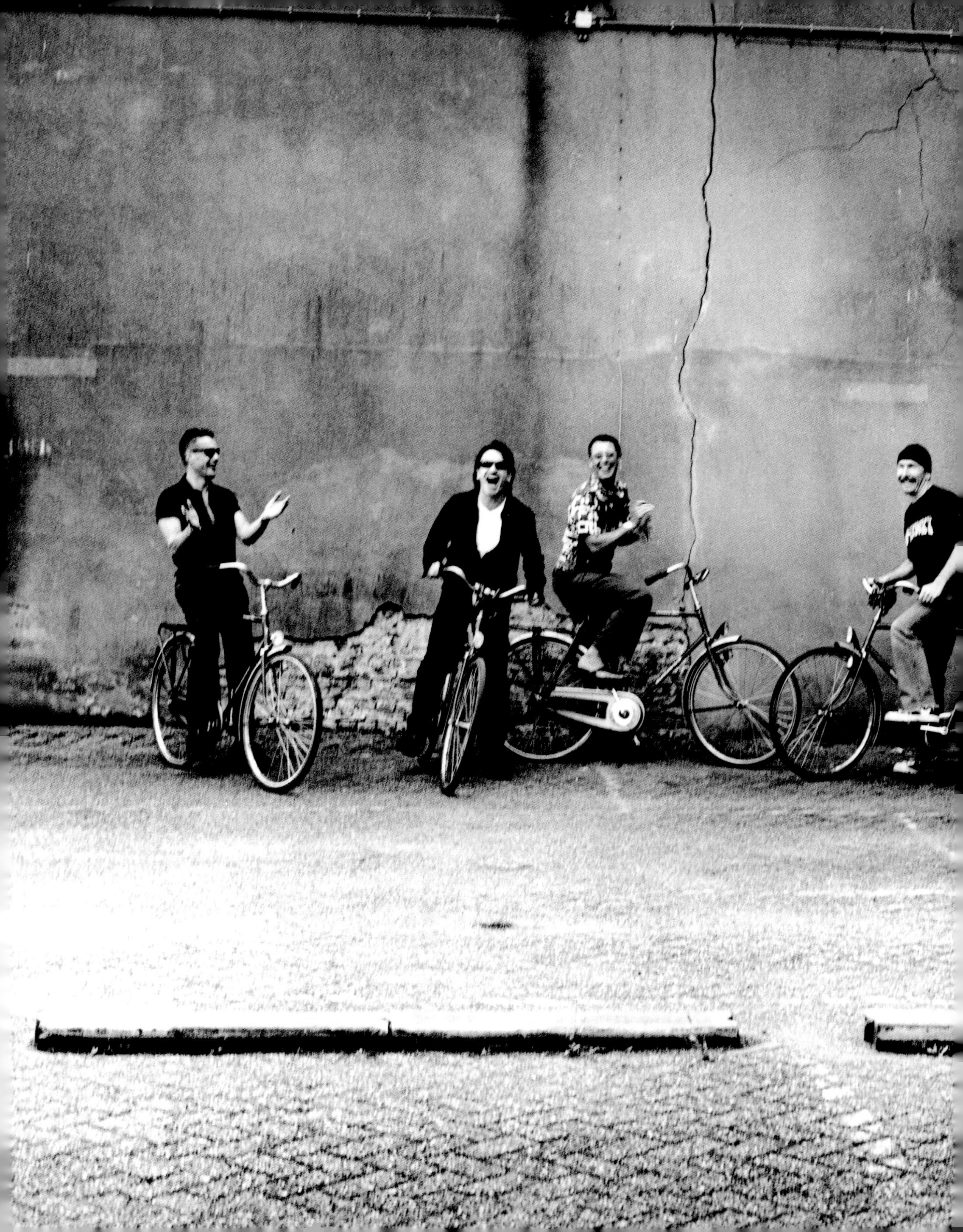

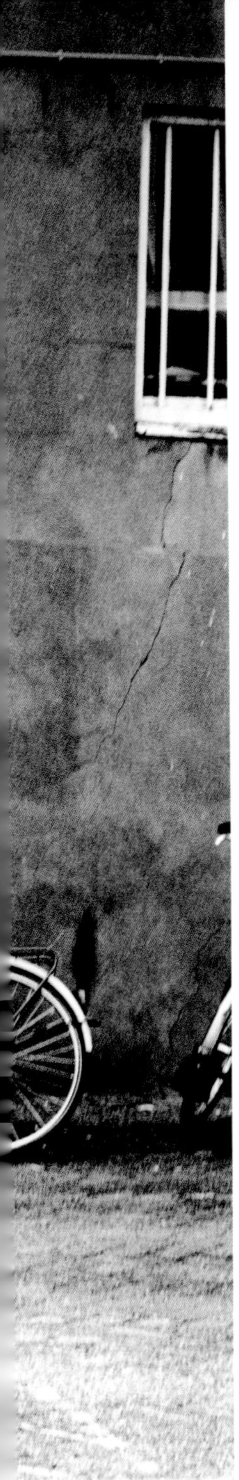

AMSTERDAM 2001 august

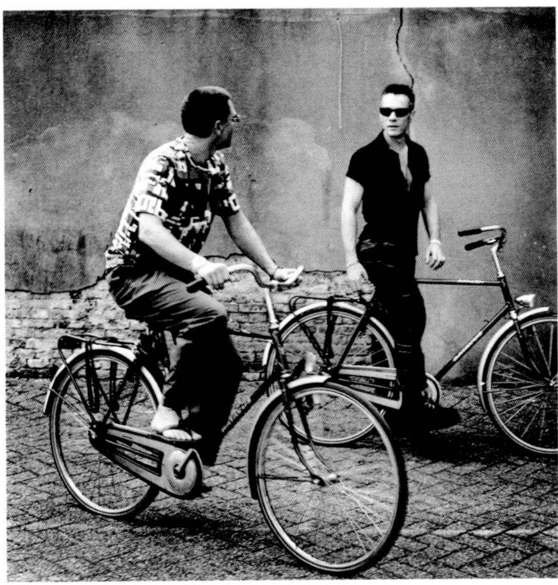

u2 on pushbikes! a dutchman's ultimate wet dream it was not but i had for a long time wanted to do some photos (or film) with a proper dutch pushbike and USA's GQ magazine gave me the opportunity when i was asked to shoot the band while on tour in holland.

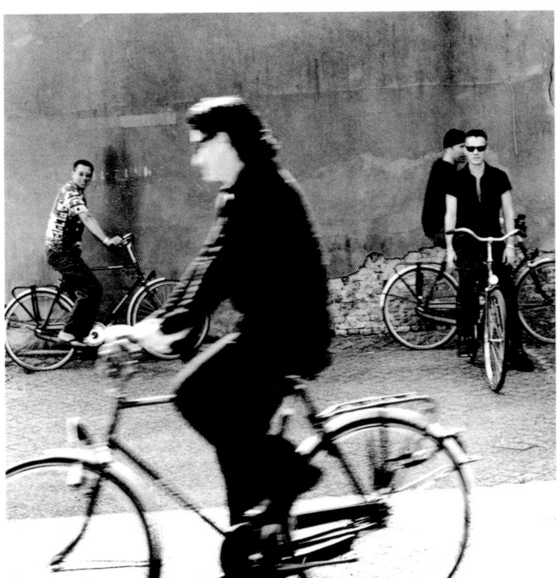

← this photo shows the band having a good time. truth is that initially nobody seemed to warm to the idea of the bikes and it was going a little hesitantly so to get the show going i decided to drop my trousers and that photo shows their reaction. we did well after that but still not sure why they had to laugh that much.

AMSTERDAM 2001
august

it is a long story but here's the short version:

i had a friend called herman brood and i photographed him since 1973. he was to become holland's biggest rockstar and it subsequently brought my photos to a wide audience in the 70's in holland. He was also a very inspired painter, and unfortunately, a junkie, albeit a happy one generally. he was very intelligent and sensitive but also an incredible exhibitionist and attention seeker. he was charming and easily bored. a real lover of women, preferably young women and lover of a full life. a real character.

i introduced him to bono on the 5th of november 1997, which was herman's birthday, in herman's painting studio. they liked each other and started talking about the bible and ended up in a red light district bar with edge, me and a few others. bono sent him afterwards a cactus (on the photo visible →) and sang a line about herman at the MTV awards in Rotterdam the next day. Herman took his own life in july 2001 and i took bono for a last visit to herman's studio one afternoon and that is where these photos were taken. the painting behind bono is one of herman's.

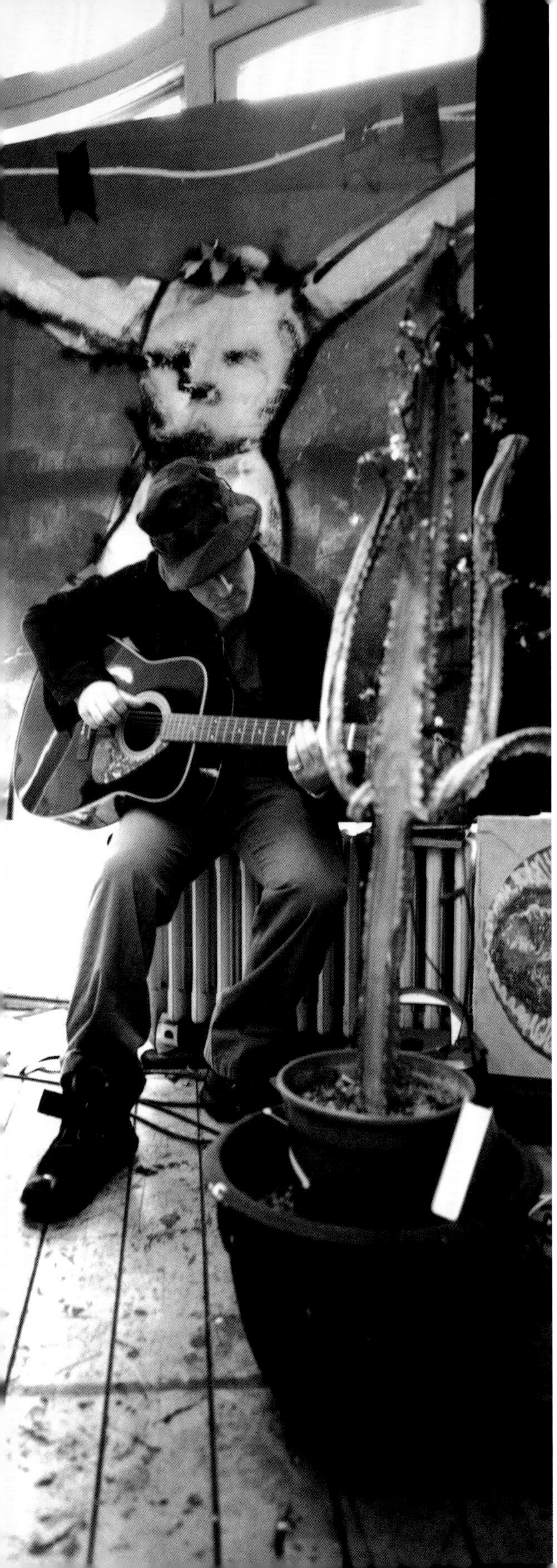

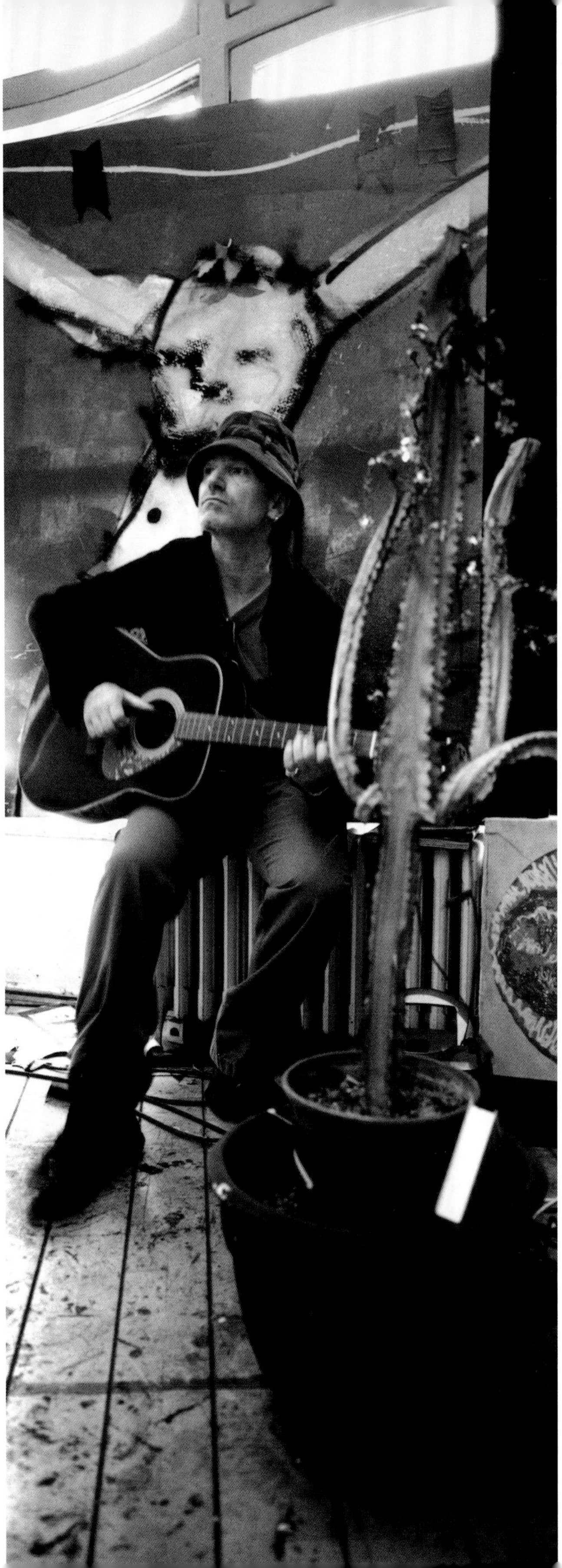

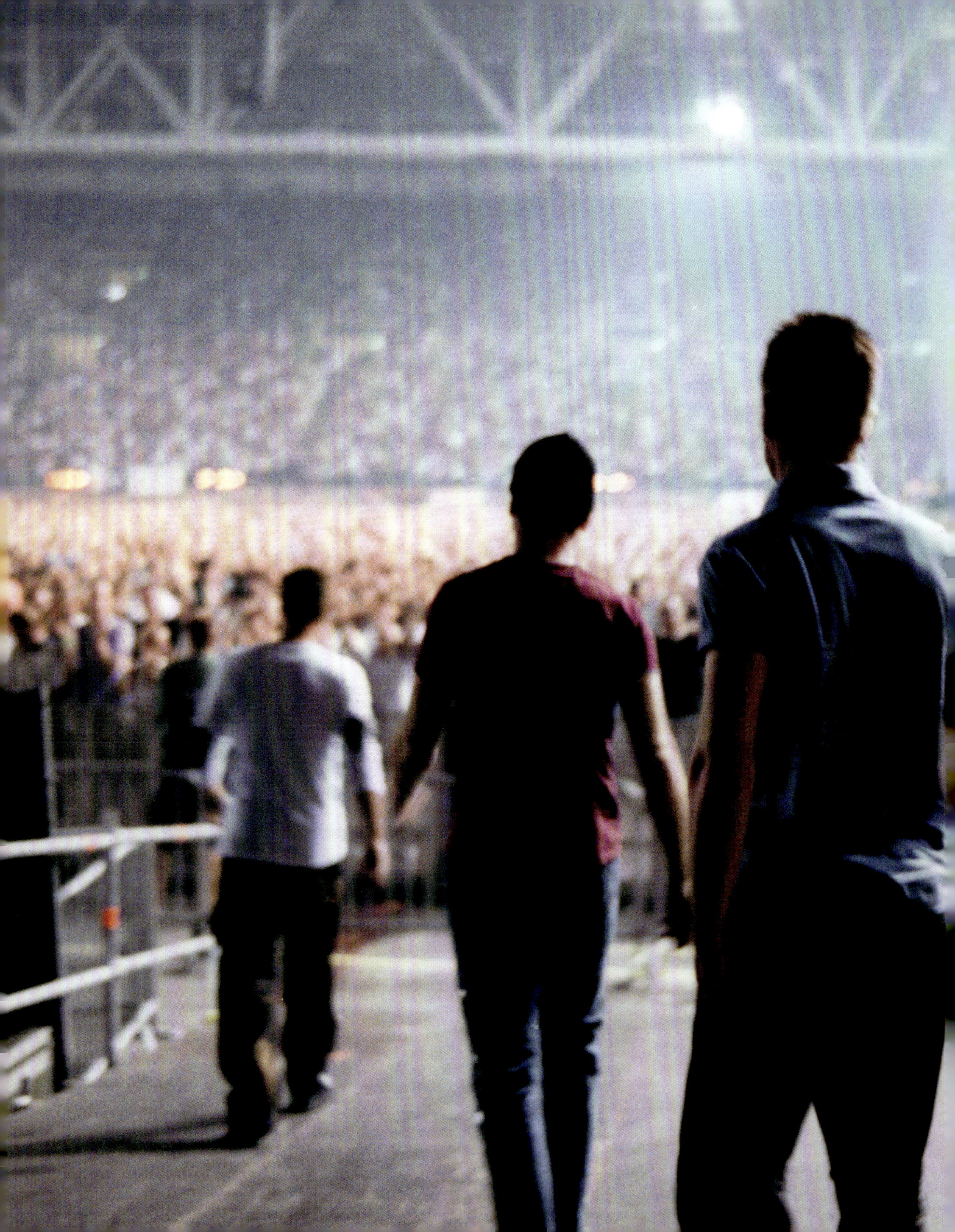

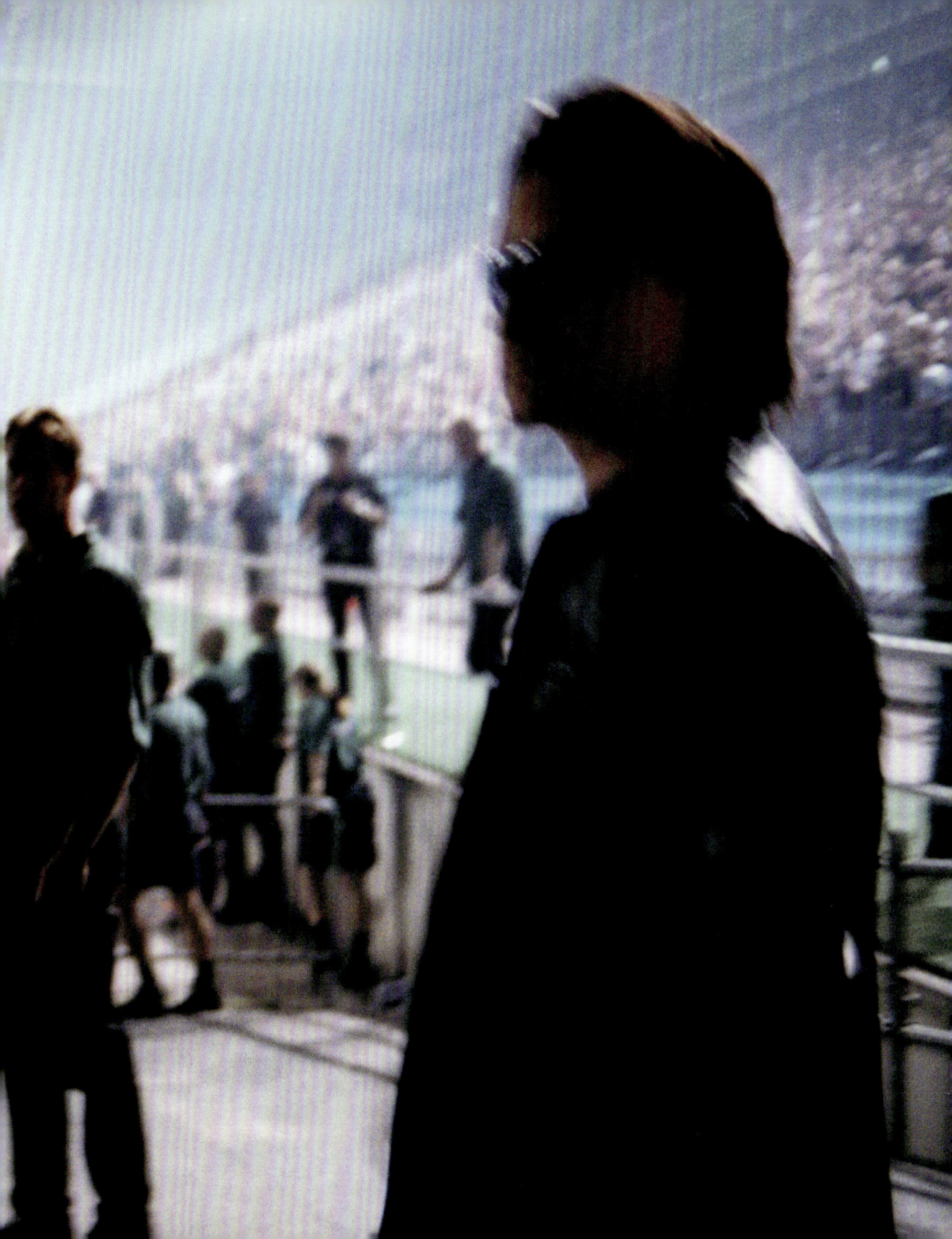

ARNHEM 2001
august

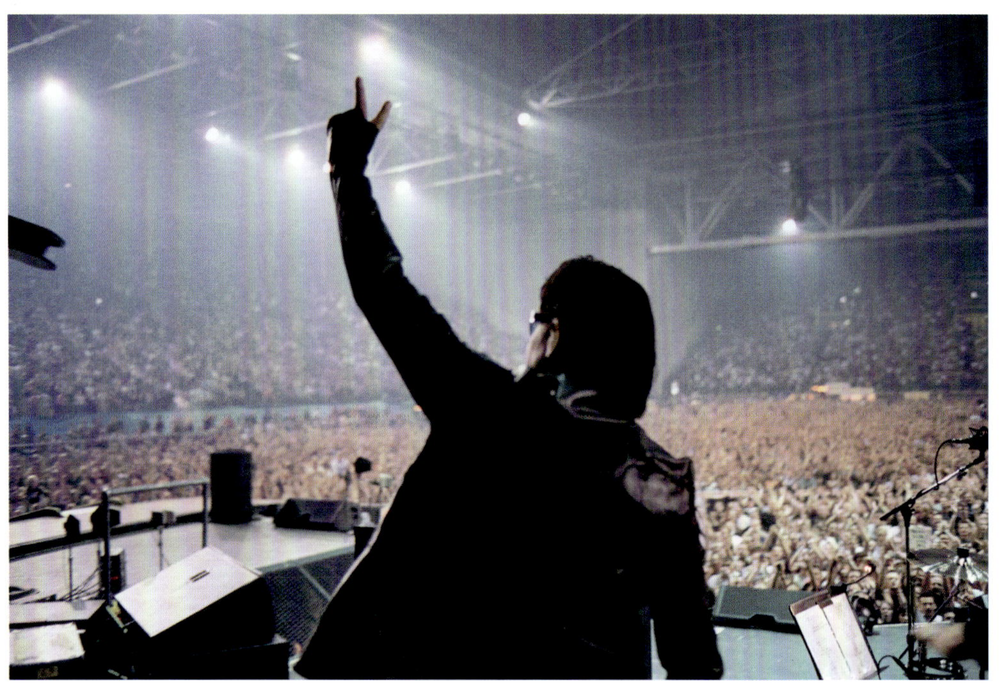

this is cool and scary at the same time. i was just loitering backstage taking a few photos of the band preparing to walk on and decided to follow them to the stage, with the shot on the previous page in mind. as we got to the stairs for the stage, bono told me to follow him onto the stage – i did but with only 6 shots left and no camerabag with me. so on this spread you see 2 out of the 6 photos i took. it was kind of painful as bono was giving me lots of obvious moments for me to shoot and after my six takes, i just had to pretend i was still shooting so as not to look like a total jerk.

the band played holland 3 nights that week, all in the same place and dedicated a song to herman brood every night and played ~~the~~ his version of 'my way' after their last song over the monitors. it went subsequently to number one in holland, knocking U2 off the top spot.

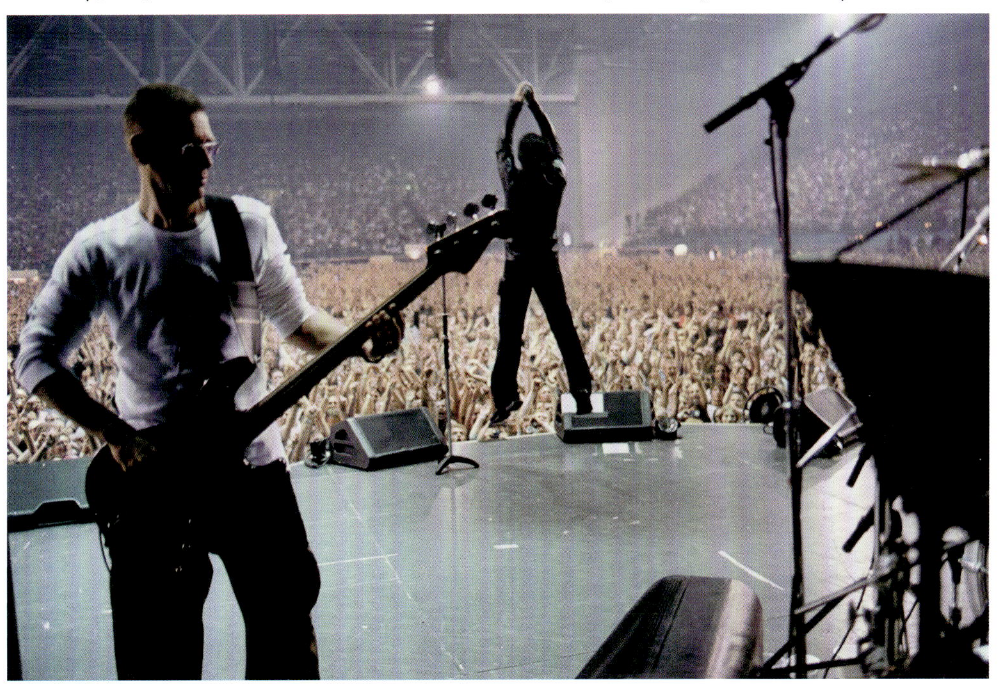

it is kind of unnerving to be in front of so many people with the houselights on, specially when you are out of film. i left after the first song and watched it from the audience side.

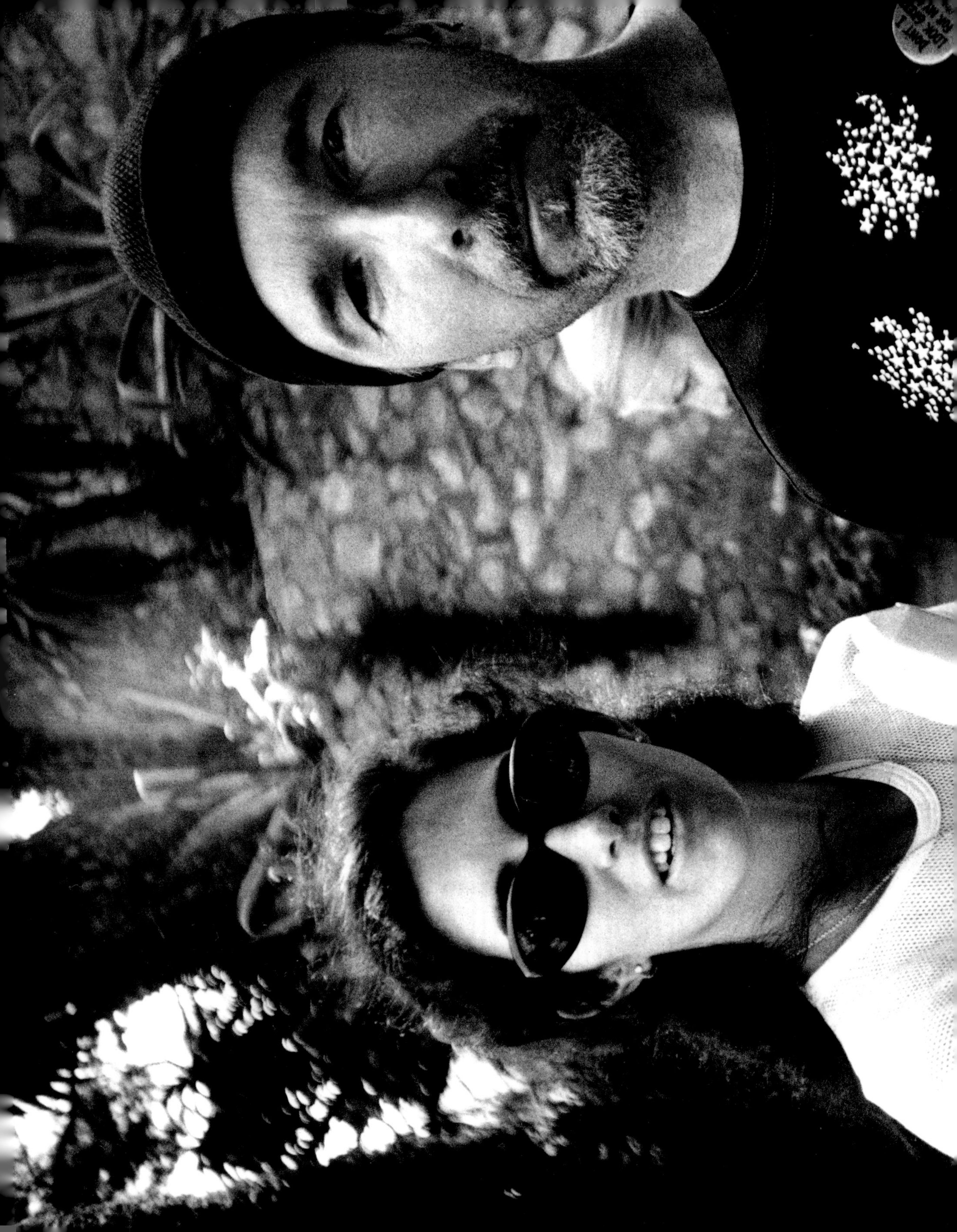

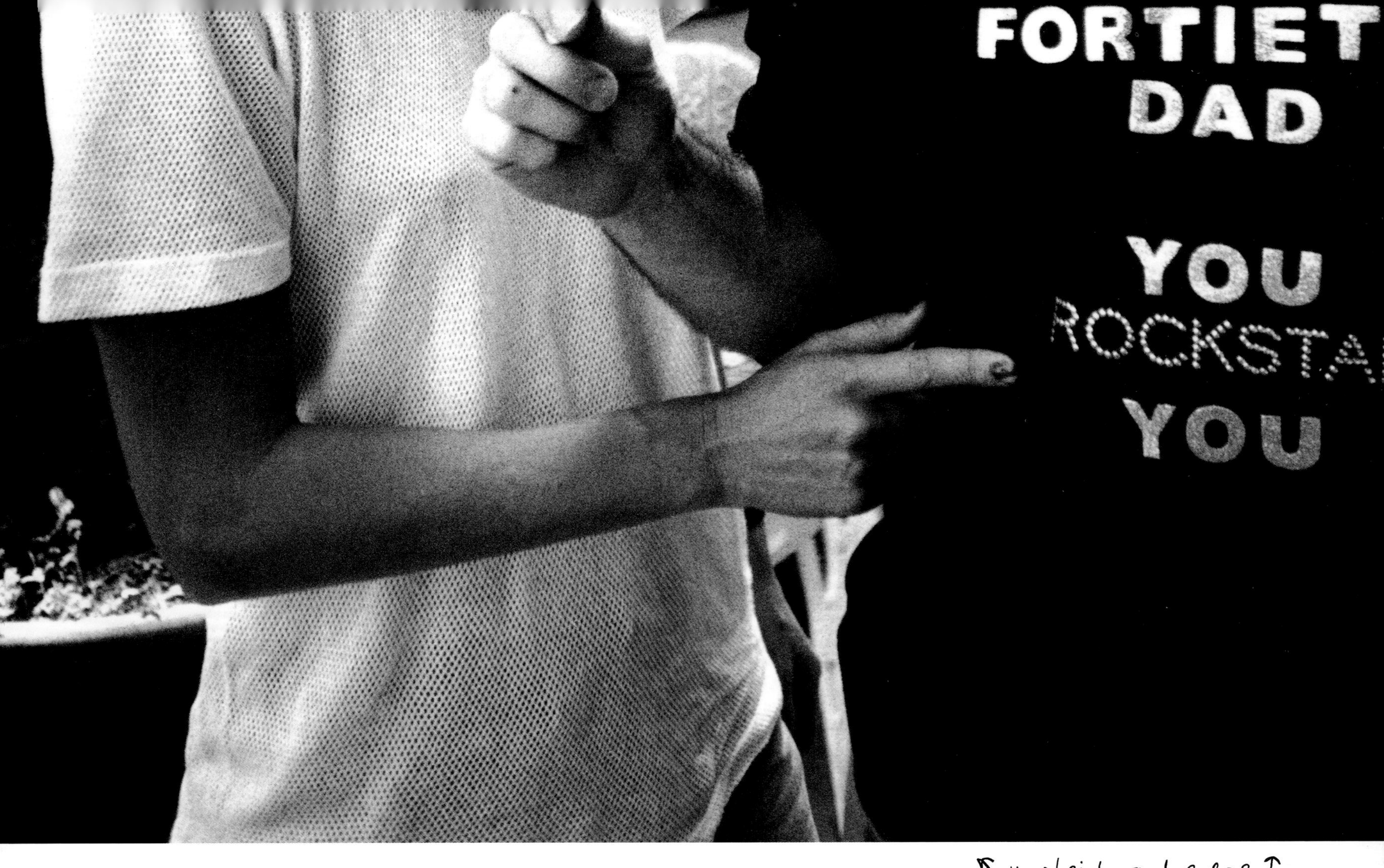

~~FRANCE~~ FRANCE 2002
august

↖ maleigh and edge ↑

edge's birthday party.

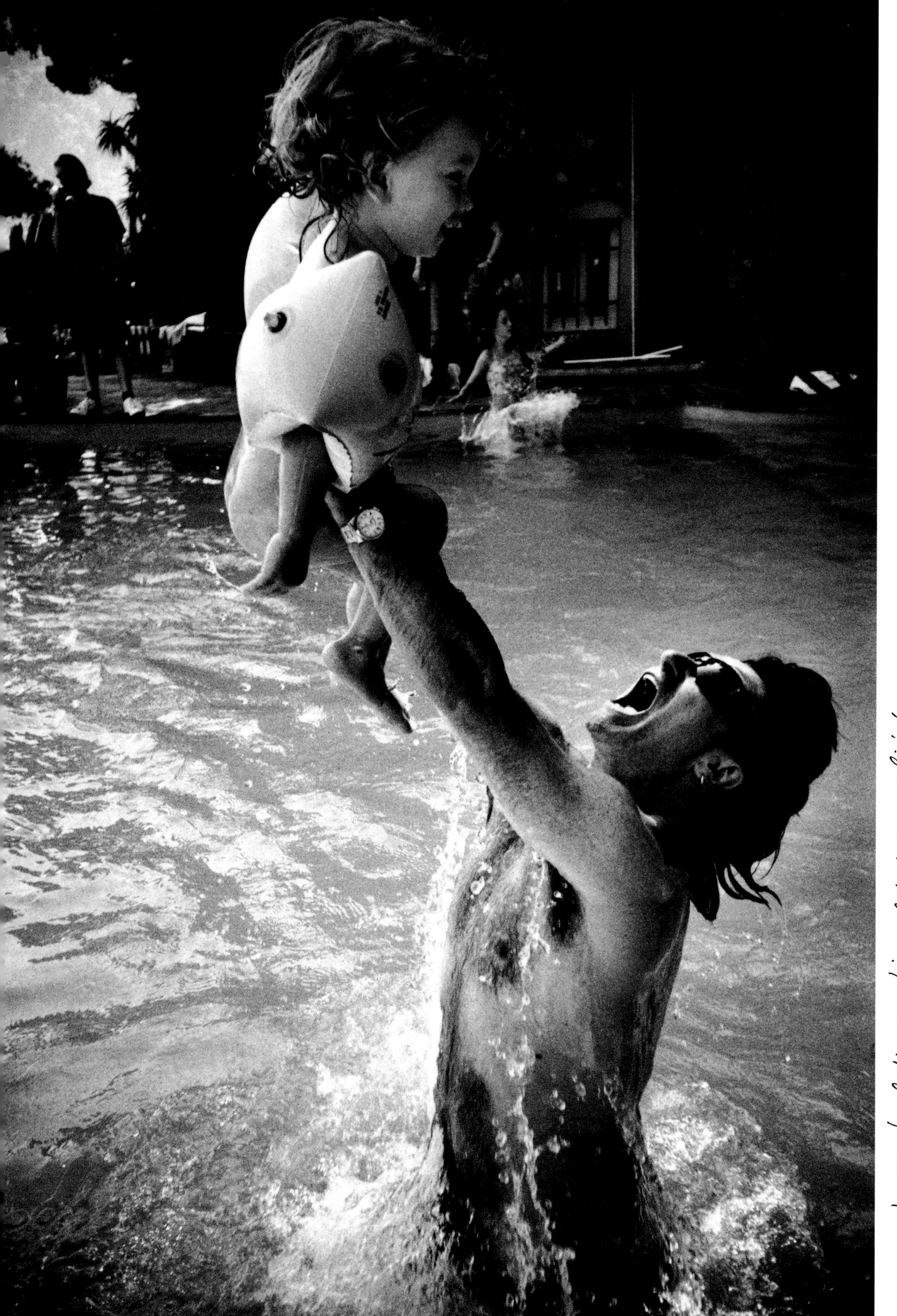

bono holding up his eldest son, elijah.

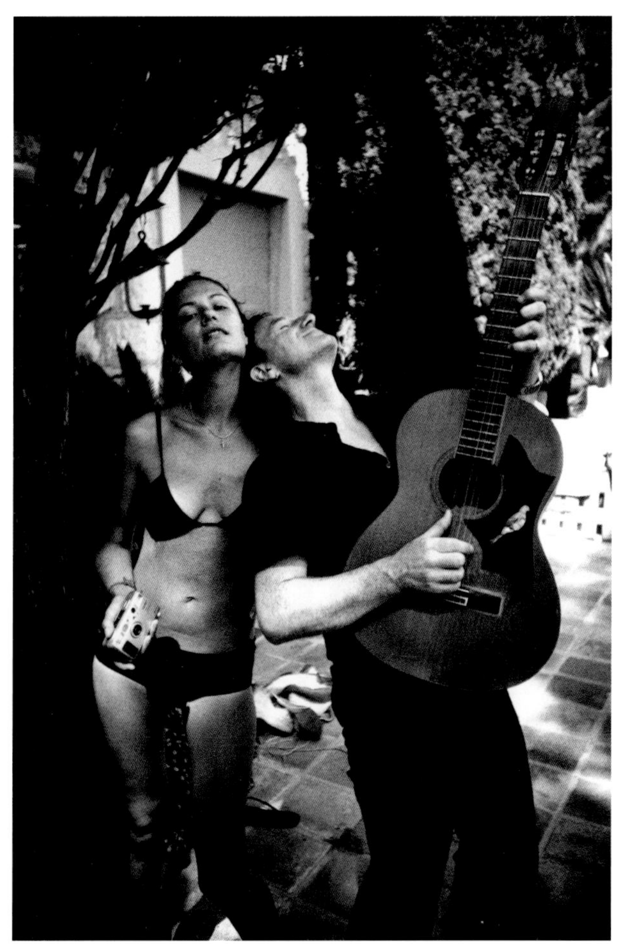

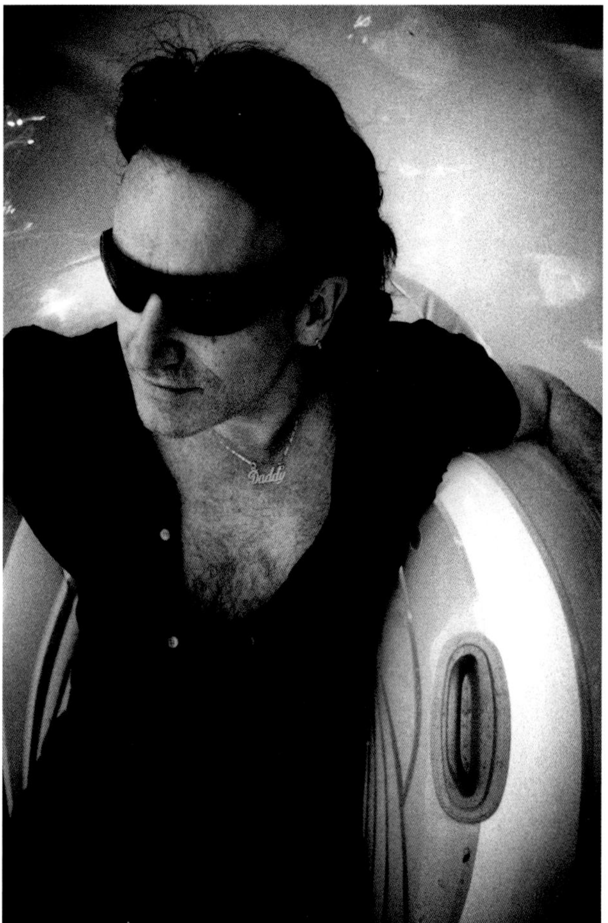

there was a great party for edge's birthday and the main celebration was in the South of france with lots of friends around. bono is serenading artist friend yelena yemchuk on the photo left and floating with his 'daddy' necklace on the right.

FRANCE

2002 august

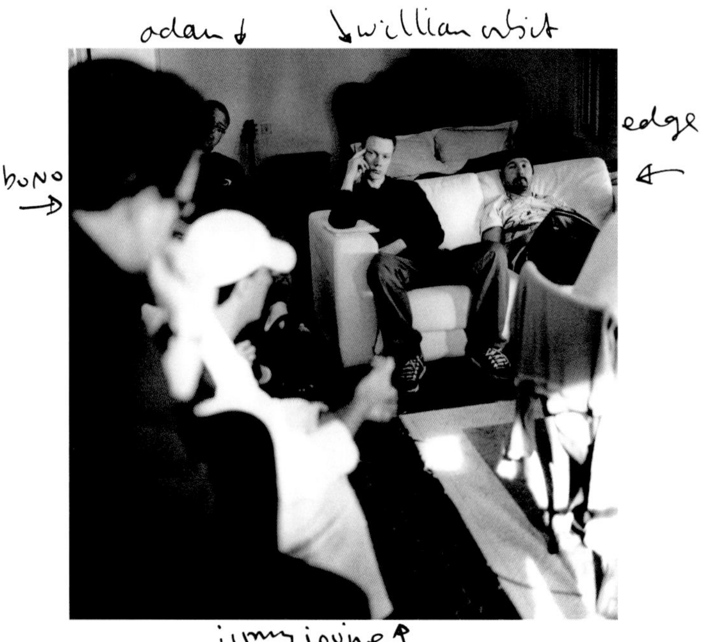

trying to do a photo shoot for Q magazine and some other stuff, we were continuously interrupted by either rain or the need to have meetings about mixes for the 'electrical storm' single. the photo above shows one of these meetings. we ended up with some pretty good portrait shots eventually, taken with the last light of the day and the mountainous coastline in the far back. And i ended up doing the video for 'electrical storm' a few weeks later.

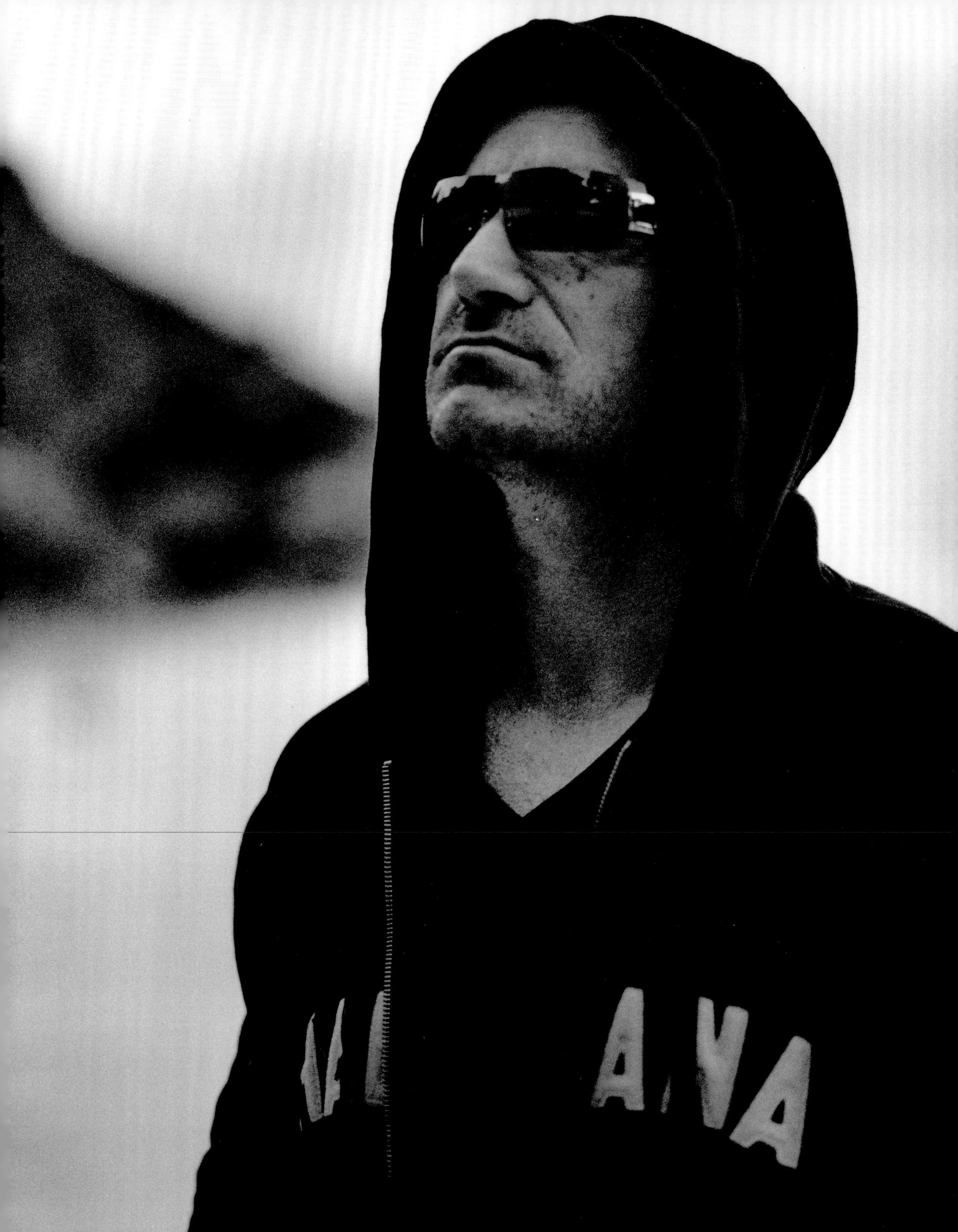

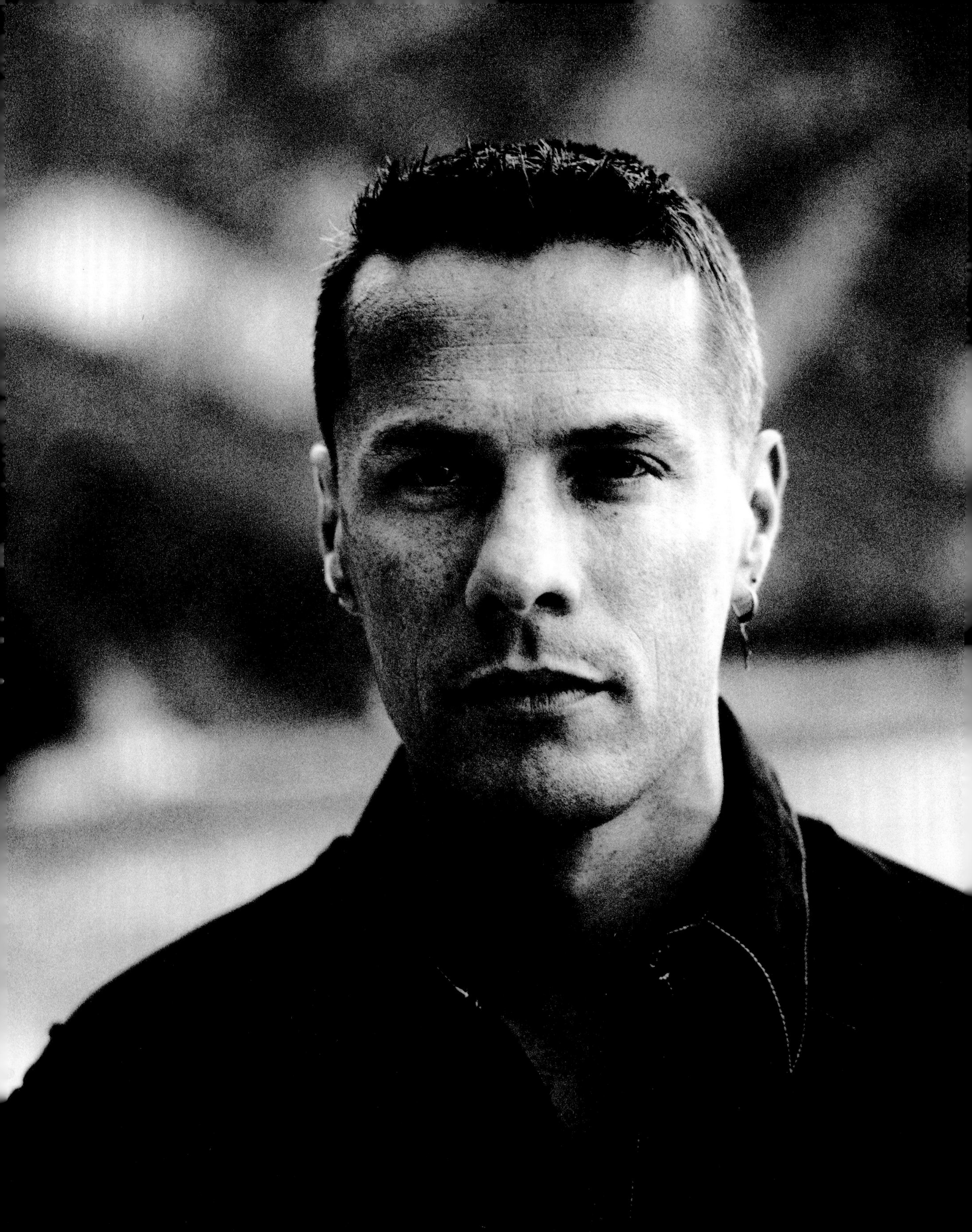

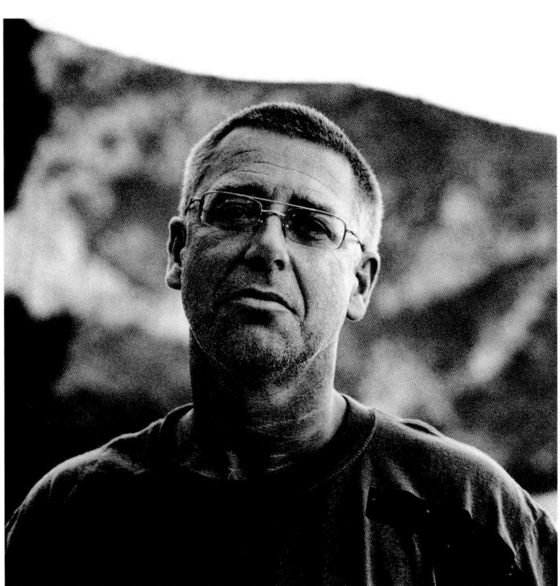

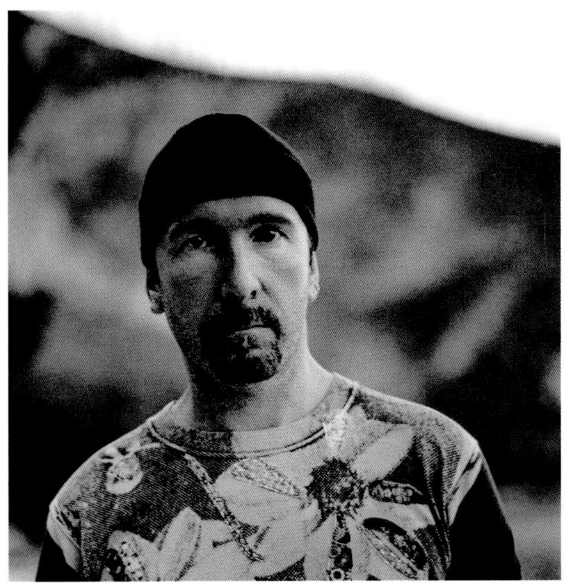

LONDON

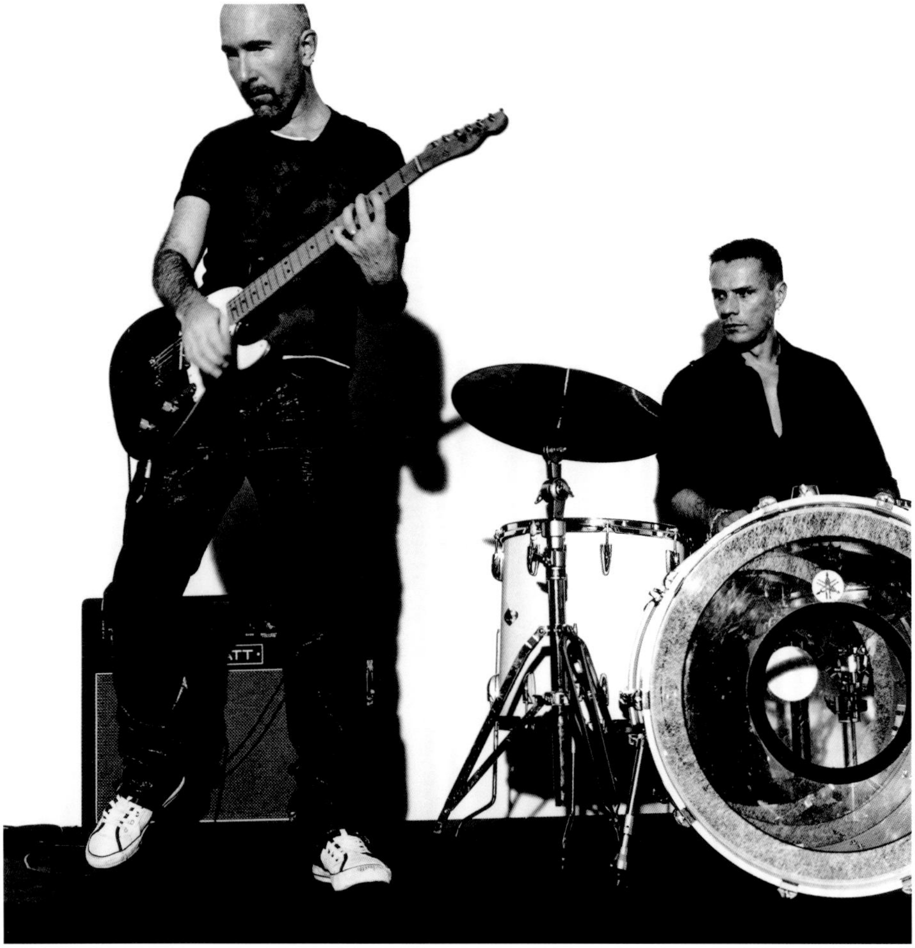

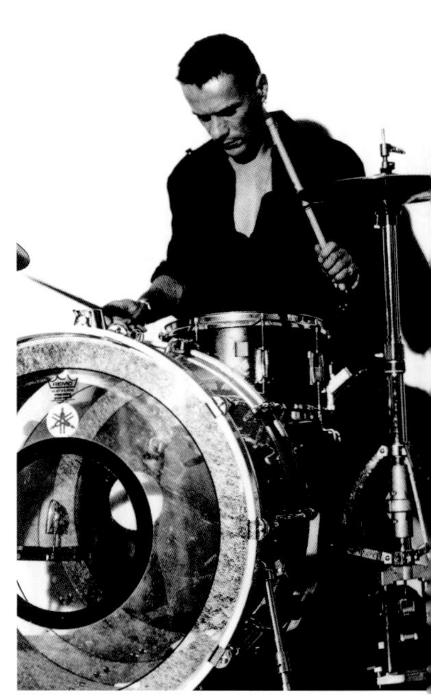

a two day shoot was scheduled for october 2003, trying to get an album cover for the early 2004 release of the new record. fortunately the record was pushed back as this photoshoot was one of the least focussed affairs i have encountered with U2 over the years. their minds were probably with the recording which wasn't going too well i gather, bono had to leave the first day to christie's for his Peter and the Wolf

2003

october

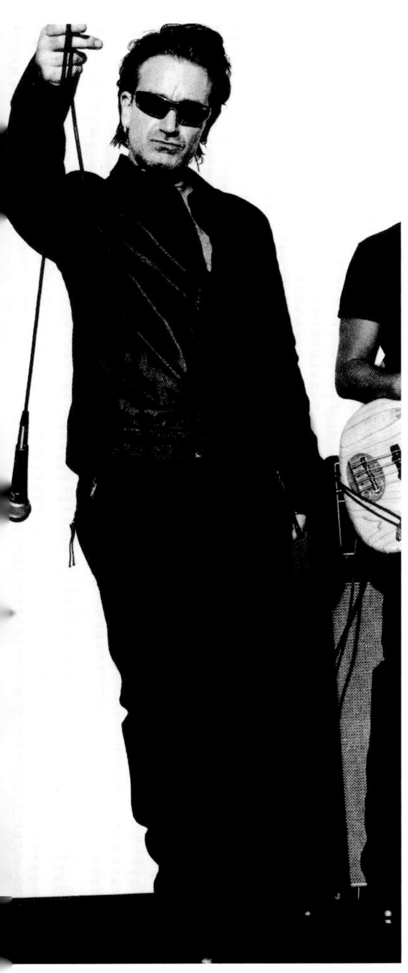

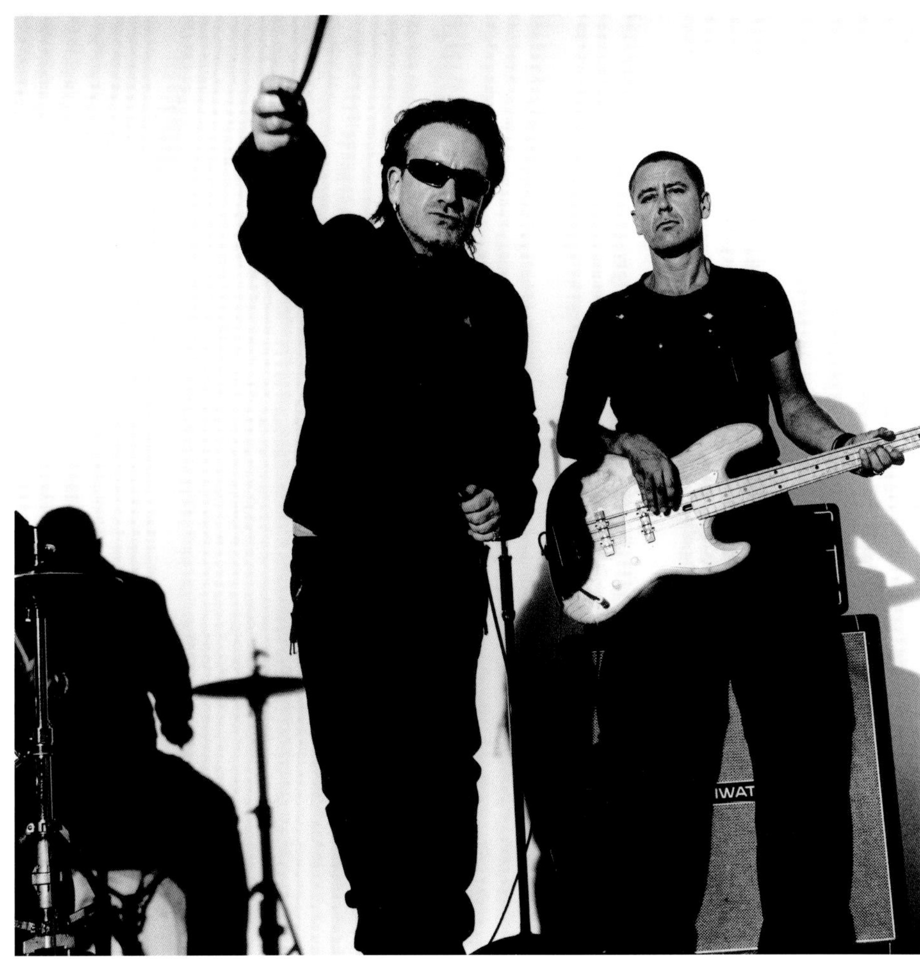

public presentation and so forth. it didn't feel they were all in the same room together and although not planned as such, the above sequence is telling in that sense. in sharp contrast to this was the shoot we did 6 months later in portugal.

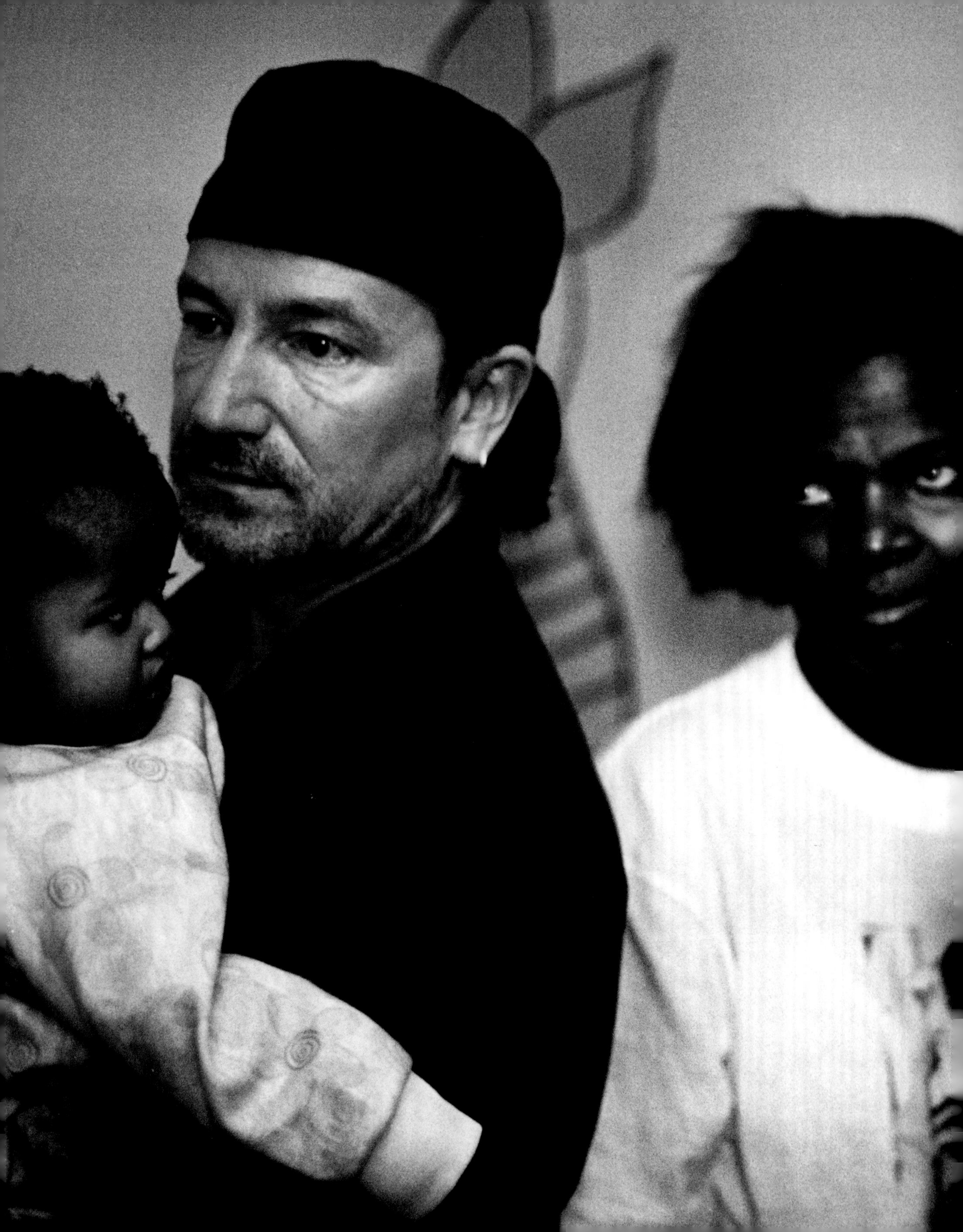

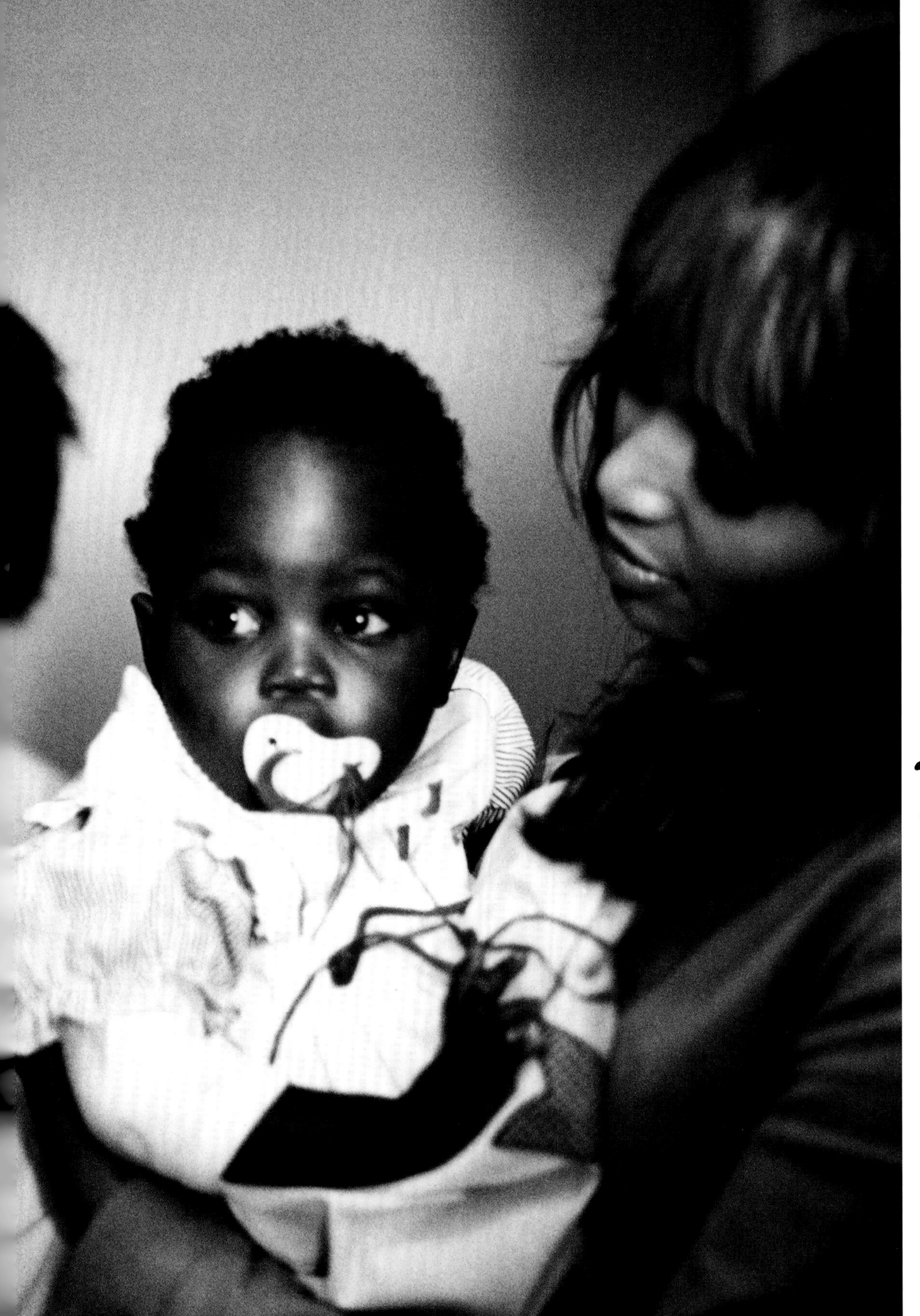

SOUTH AFRICA 2003 november

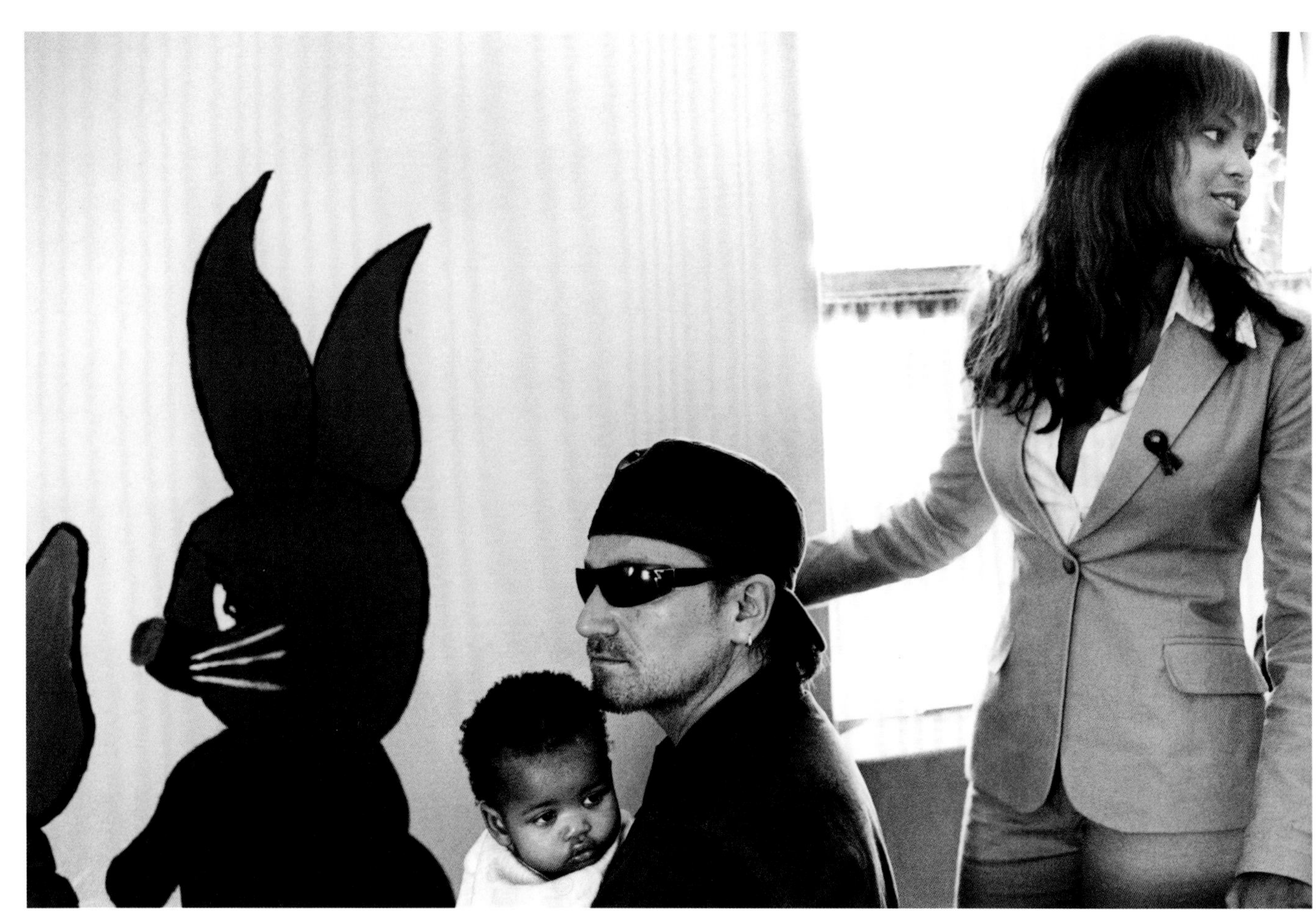

i decided to go to south africa with bono and edge so i could take some photographs that showed more of a social-political side of U2 and Bono in particular. They were in Cape Town as part of a festival to honor Mandela and highlight the AIDS epidemic. one afternoon i went along with Bono and Beyoncé to the township to visit a hospital and a childcare centre amongst other things. above Bono is carrying a dying baby down the stairs - same baby he is holding on the photo on the first spread where he is overcome with emotions as he was just told that this child has not very long to live

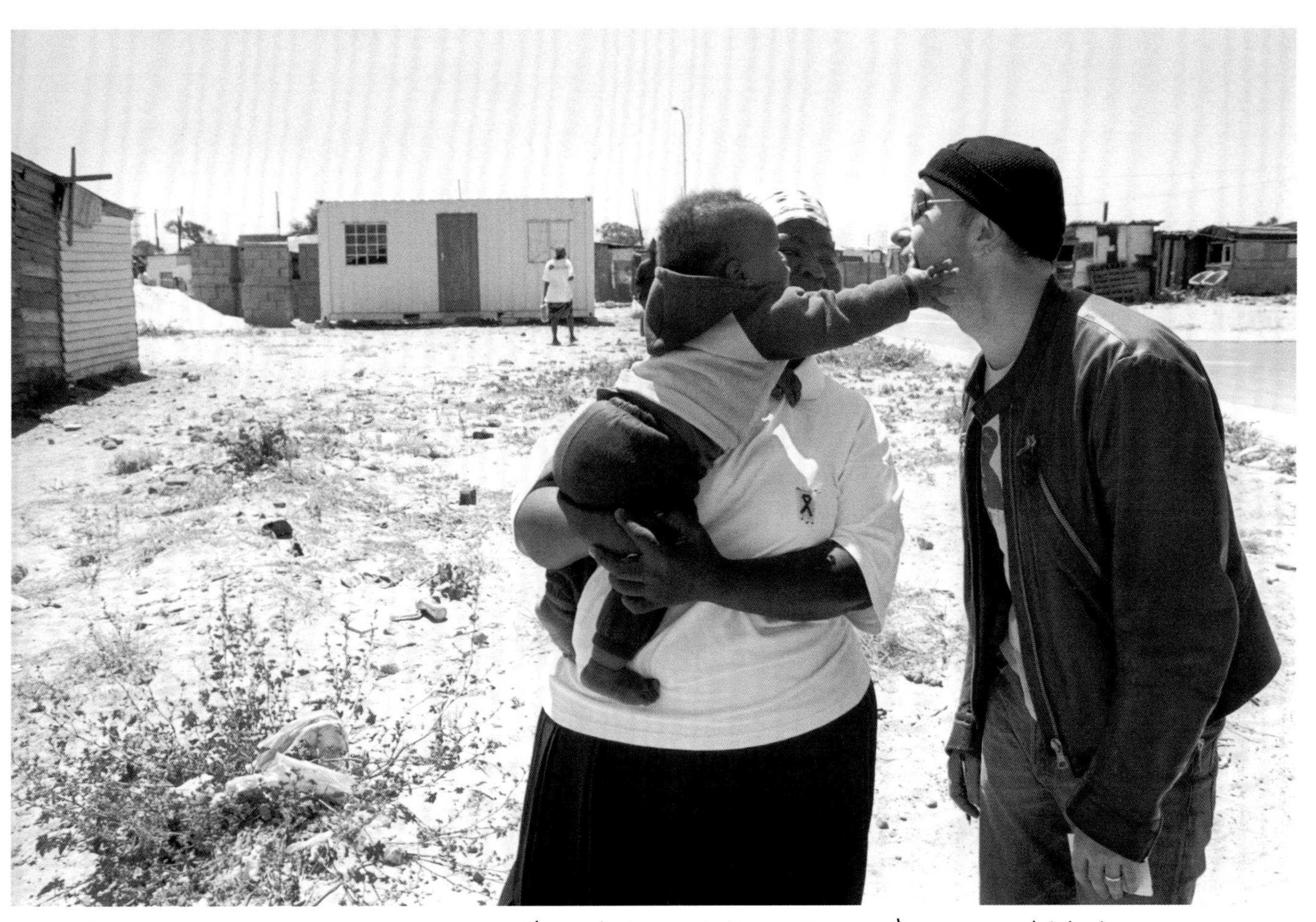

the next day i made a similar trip with edge where we visited a couple of homes of people livin' the townships. the mood of the people seemed in sharp contrast to the squalid conditions in which they lived. it seems to me that they give us more than we give them.

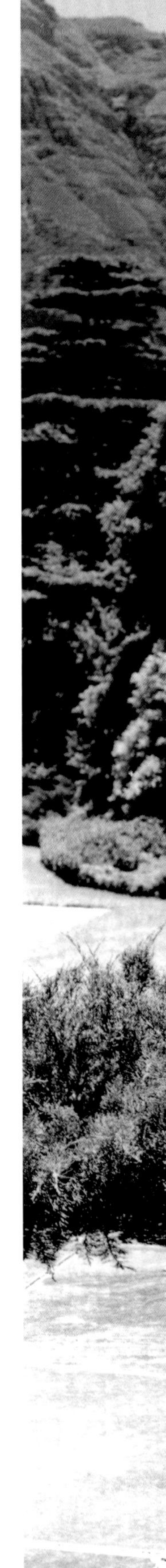

the day after the concert
edge and bono visited the
home of nelson mandela
where this photo of bono
trying to armwrestle mandela
was taken.

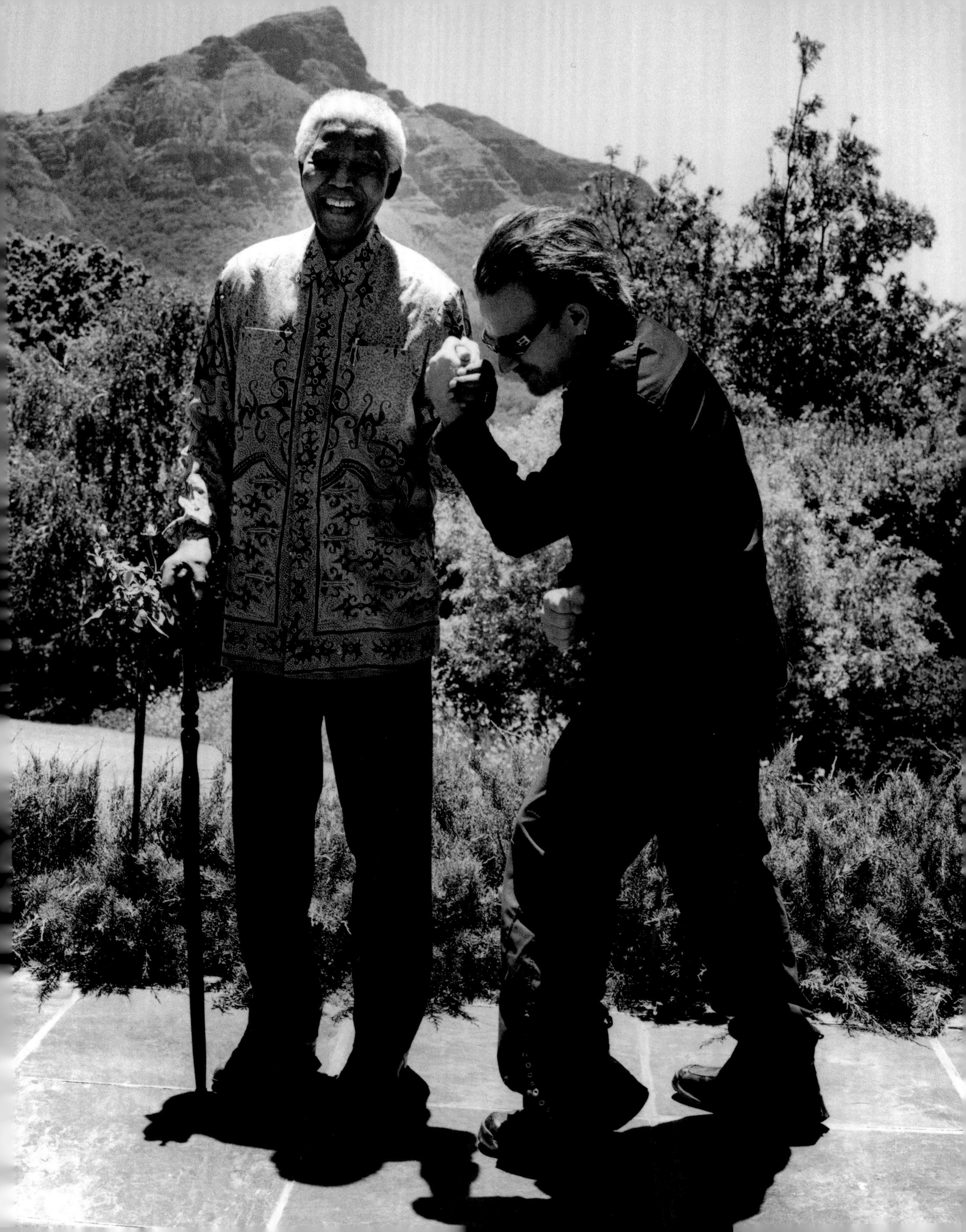

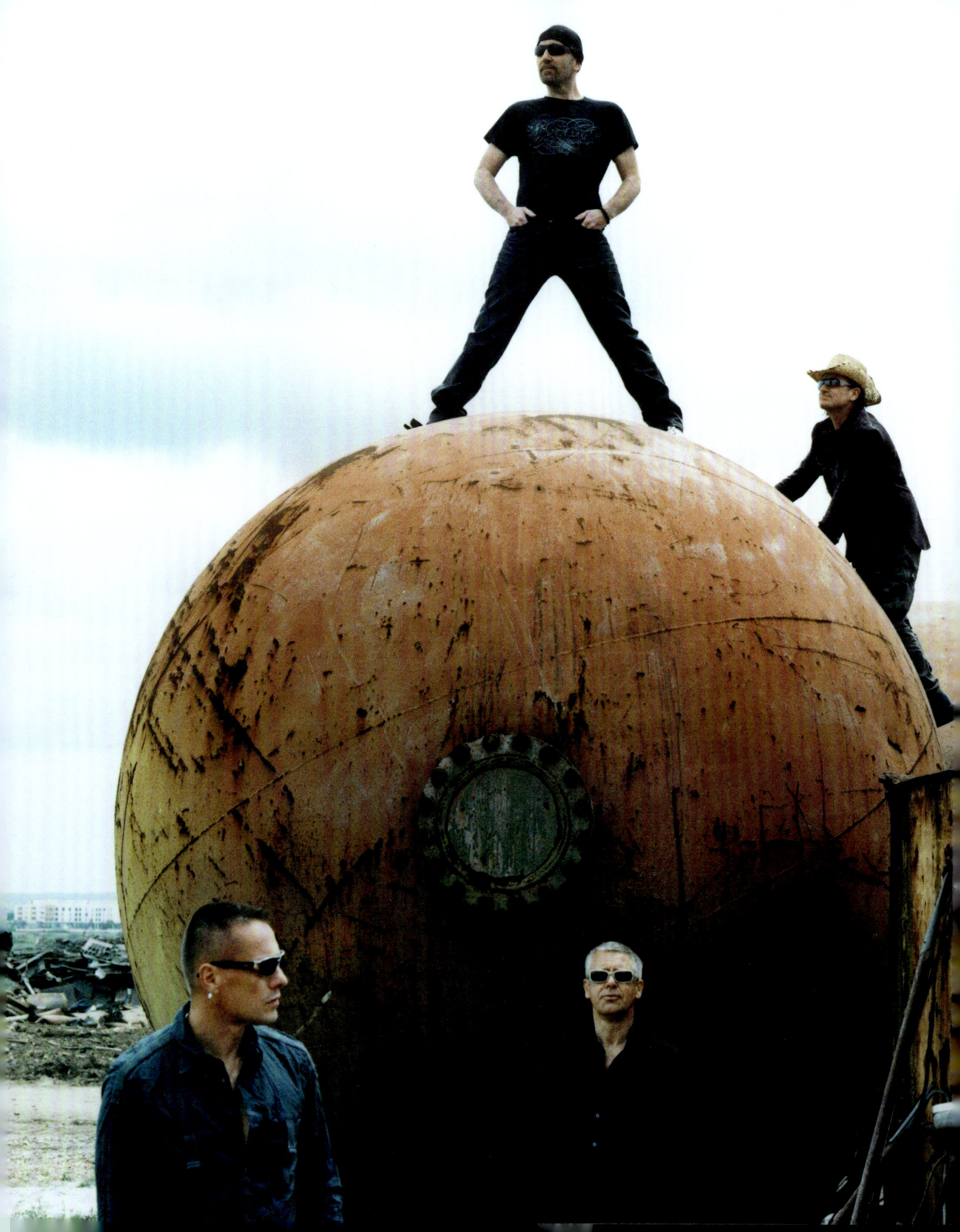

PORTUGAL 2004

april

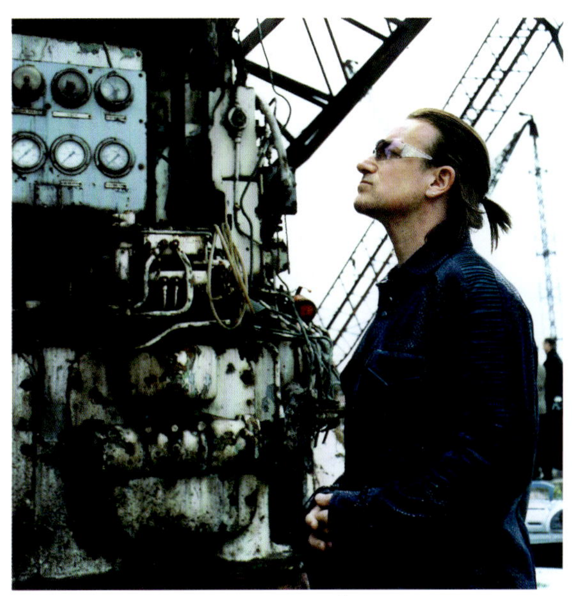

← Bono checking out some old equipment, looking like an eccentric scientist

after the not overly successful shoot in London in 2003, we had to come up with a plan to do another shoot and i suggested to do something in europe but not ireland or england as the band are too familiar with it all and get easily bored and distracted. U2 suggested barcelona but i opted for lisbon and surroundings and they agreed after i went for a 2-day recce and showed them some places via polaroids. it turned out to be a great shoot and the band loved lisbon and all the places near it where we shot. on the left is a hard to find location where ships get dismantled and it felt very fitting for the suggested album title. of course there are always some people who feel the need to climb on round objects.

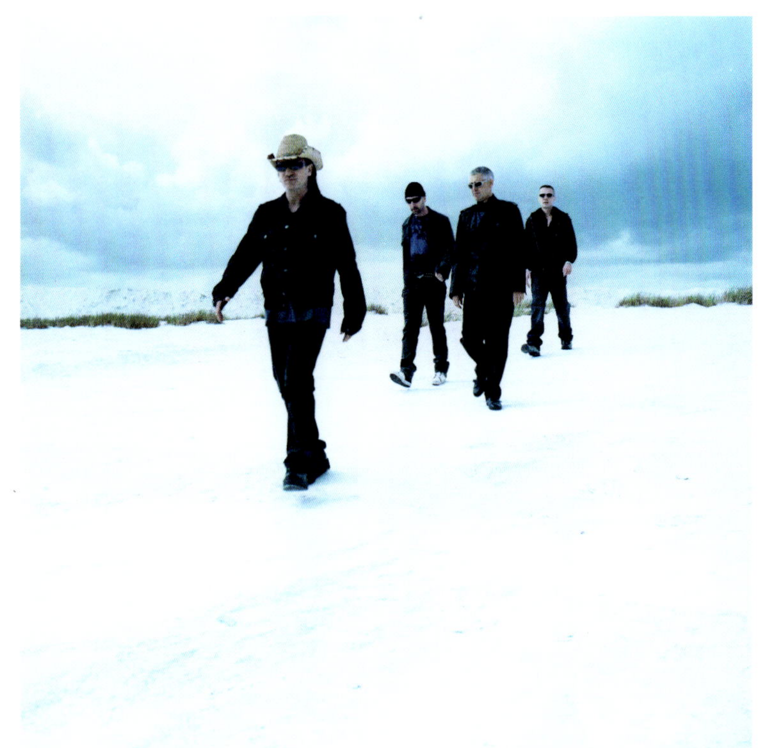

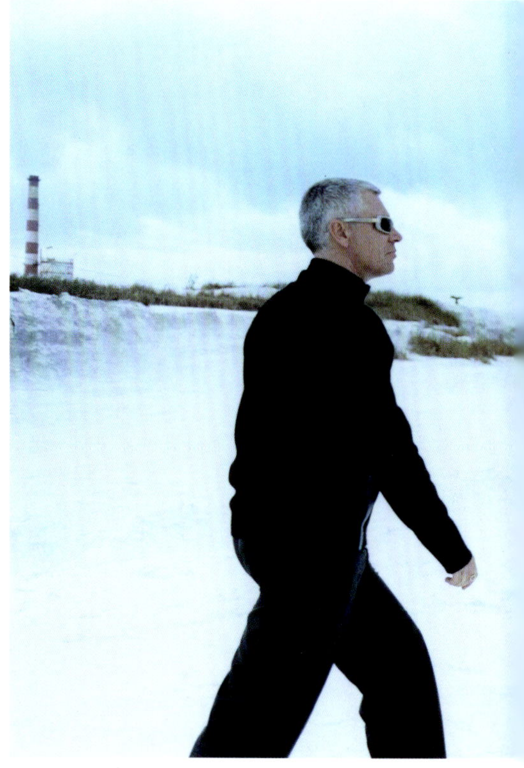

i found an area between a dangerous looking factory complex and the water that is like white dust, fine sand or white ashes. it gave the photos an eerie feel, kind of the aftermath of something pretty awful. like the world had become an arid desert and no-one had informed you about that.

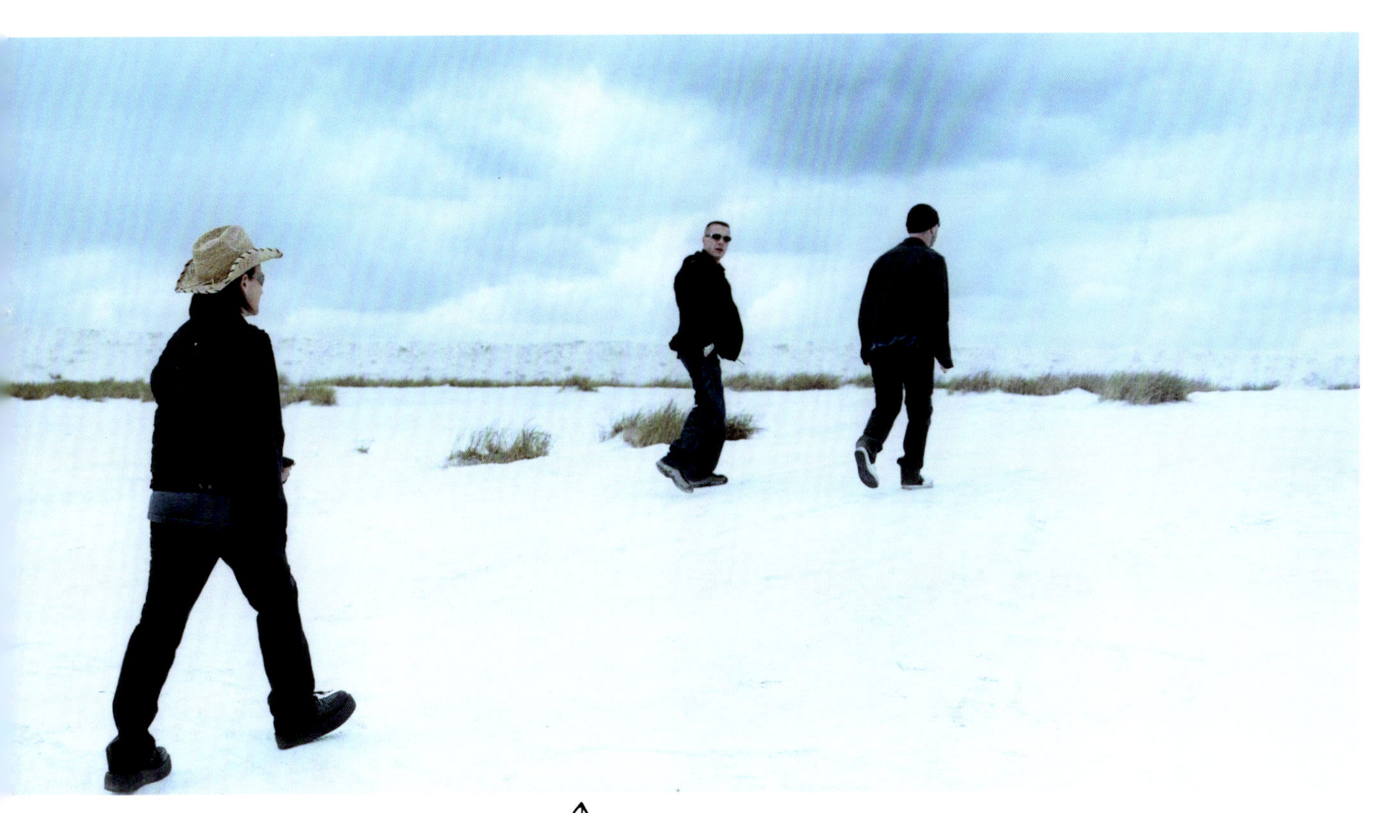

↑
last picture of this book
"and the band & they walked on"

ACKNOWLEDGEMENTS

there are too many people involved in a photobook this size to enable me to remember all and as i wouldn't like to leave anyone out by mistake, i rather say 'thank you' to everyone who was ever involved in the creation of any of the photos in this book. i kind of know who you are!

obviously an exception has to made for Adam, Bono, Edge and Larry. i cannot thank you enough for letting me into your worlds, both private and public ones, for the last 22 years. thank you, THANK YOU, for touching, and retouching, my life. ~~the ride has been wild and fantastic and but i had to throw up at some point and this is it~~.

also major thanks to paul mcguinness, sheila roche, ann louise kelly, candida bottaci, catriona garde, steve matthews, dennis sheehan, monica axelsson, anja grabert, julia haynes, liz lewis, francesca wyllie, herman brood, brian dowling, mike spry, carlo elias, edgar smaling, lothar schirmer, helena christensen, bill clinton, william gibson, paul morley, salman rushdie, michael stipe, wim wenders, steve averill, groninger museum.

this book is made for everyone but specially for my friends including romana bell, fanny and lotta stolberg, splinter chabot, felix grönemeyer and julius engelen.

i love kodak tri-x

i like to salute michael cooper, david gahr, jim marshall, elliott landy, robert frank and lee friedlander.

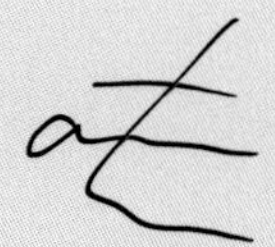

Colophon

DESIGN BY **SMEL**, AMSTERDAM

LITHOGRAPHY BY **EBS**, VERONA

PRINTED BY Sing Cheong Printing Co. Ltd.

COVERPHOTO BY **ANTON CORBIJN**: **U2** DUBLIN 1986

ISBN 978-3-8296-0319-5

A **SCHIRMER/MOSEL** PRODUCTION
WWW.SCHIRMER-MOSEL.COM
WWW.U2-CORBIJN.COM